WINE
ROUTES
OF
AMERICA

WINE ROUTES OF AMERICA

Jan Aaron
assisted by Leslie Jay

E. P. DUTTON
NEW YORK

Published in the United States by E. P. Dutton,
a division of NAL Penguin Inc.,
2 Park Avenue, New York, N.Y. 10016.

Published simultaneously in Canada by Fitzhenry and Whiteside, Limited, Toronto.

Library of Congress Cataloging-in-Publication Data

Aaron, Jan.
  Wine routes of America.

  Bibliography: p.
  Includes index.
  1. Wine and wine making—United States—Guide-books.
  2. United States—Description and travel—1981–   —Guide-books. I. Jay, Leslie (Leslie Anne)
II. Title. TP557.A22 1989   641.2'22'0973   88-31089
ISBN 0-525-48436-1

DESIGN: Stanley S. Drate/Folio Graphics Co. Inc.

10 9 8 7 6 5 4 3 2 1

FIRST EDITION

To my mother and my friends

ACKNOWLEDGMENTS

Special thanks to all the winery owners and wine enthusiasts who so generously took the time and trouble to provide useful information on America's wineries, regional sights and delights, favorite bed and breakfasts, hotels, inns, motels, and restaurants. Without their written materials, interviews, and recommendations, this book would not have been possible. If I have omitted anything, misspelled any name, left something out, they were inadvertent oversights for which I apologize right now. Thanks also to Gene Young, Texpidite, New York City, for his help and to the staff at Lenox Hill Post Office, for keeping track of my mail. Two other people deserve my deepest appreciation. My editor, Sandy Soule, for a huge job well done, and my good friend Lucille Warner for bringing us together and encouraging me along the way.

Contents

4 THE MIDDLE ATLANTIC STATES

5 THE SOUTHERN STATES

6 THE MIDWEST

7 THE SOUTHWEST/WEST

8 CALIFORNIA

9 THE NORTHWEST AND BEYOND

Preface

ᵺ**P**ut your passport away. You don't need to go to Europe for wine touring. Now that wineries in forty states have their welcome mats out, there's high-quality adventure waiting around the next bend on the wine routes of America.

As a travel-and-food writer, I felt America's exciting new wineries deserved this richly detailed guide. This is not a book of wine criticism, but a book to help travelers discover the new wineries and their wines and decide which are most pleasing to their tastes. And since wine is more than wine—it's all the varied pleasures of the good life—I have included everything else the wine lover needs for an enjoyable holiday, whether a day's jaunt near home or a longer stay farther away.

Along the wine routes are restaurants that serve local wines and show considerable culinary dexterity. (Wines are not the only thing changing in America; foods are becoming increasingly sophisticated.) And picnic groves, farm stands, and outdoor markets are here as well to add enjoyment to the wine route. For the end of day I offer country inns, historic hotels, and bed and breakfasts among the many places to stay. And since a wine route must also be entwined with the beauty and romance evoked by images of wine, I found the most scenic routes and breathtaking views along the way.

In my book are a dazzling variety of vineyards and wineries. You will find wineries nestled under great old shade trees spangled with sunlight or in historic settings on verdant country roads with groves just right for an al fresco feast. Some wineries are impressive old structures with formal museums and valuable wine artifacts, and some are are no-frills mom-and-pop affairs out back of the garage; one is on the crumpled side of a volcano.

Hospitality is what they have in common. Simple or elaborate their sites may be, but all welcome visitors. They will invite you in, proudly displaying their wines, explaining how they're made, and offering wine tastings (to buy if you wish). Some offer recipe booklets, cooking demonstrations, or dinner parties in candlelit wine cellars; most will advise on local restaurants serving their wines. Others entice visitors with old-fashioned grape stomping, avant-garde jazz, or ethnic-accented festival days. There are winery owners who will ride you around the fields in haywagons or walk with you through the rows of vines. Others may ask you to help them pick at harvest time.

What makes me sure you're off for an unforgettable experience? The fun I had doing this book, and the people I met, convinced me that if you have the time and an interest in the good life, the place to be is with me on the wine routes of America. Shall we get going now?

Now have fun and don't forget to write: I will be most interested to learn about your experiences and discoveries when using this book. So please drop me a note care of *Wine Routes of America,* E. P. Dutton, 2 Park Avenue, New York, NY 10016. Your suggestions can help make a better second edition, and most useful letters will be rewarded with a free copy of the next wine routes book. Here's to your best trip ever.

JAN AARON

1

Introduction

How to Use This Book

Wineries and Vineyards: Each state starts with information about its wine history, followed by a listing of all the wineries and vineyards you can visit, listed alphabetically by region. Each entry has an at-a-glance section that presents its salient information, followed by a description of the winery's history. The wineries for the most part are listed in alphabetical order, although in some instances grouping by region made more sense. Maps indicate the towns where wineries are located to help you plan the best wine route. If some wineries are described in greater detail than others, it is simply because they may have more of a history. This in no way suggests that the others are not worthy of a visit. A wine discovery comes from the bottle, not from the atmosphere surrounding it. Groups will need to make advance reservations at most wineries.

To See & Do: A tasting of the interesting sights and activities nearby follows each winery or geographic section to provide a break from wine touring. Since doing three or four wineries a day is enough, finding a place to wander in the woods or a key sight-seeing attraction can be a welcome change of pace.

Accommodations: A sampling of places to stay and eat follows each winery or geographic listing; they emphasize the less well-traveled bed and breakfasts, inns and hotels, rather than the conventional motels and hotels, although some of the latter are also included. If you've never stayed in a bed and breakfast, make note—they have all of the comforts of homes, because they are homes, but not all the amenities of hotels, which they are not. This means that you may have to share a bathroom or share the breakfast table with your fellow guests.

Many of the accommodations and restaurant recommendations came from the winery owners themselves. Some descriptions were very detailed, others rather terse. In the case of restaurants, they were usually selected because they serve local food and wines. Eating outdoors in bucolic places is part of the wine experience. So not overlooked in this book are places to buy the best picnic foods—farm stands and farmers' markets—as well as some irresistible places to eat them.

When to Visit: Every season has its charms for visiting wineries, and during each the traveler experiences a different phase of winery life. Yet to most people harvest and wine touring are inexorably entwined. During this time the wineries can be jammed, and likewise accommodations nearby. Be sure to reserve well in advance. Bud-break in spring has a delicacy; summer has beauty, too, and can be crowded with vacationers. Winters in northern climates are times to toast in front of the tasting room fireplace, while in the South there's a different rhythm to life. Visiting for a festival or special event can be fun for visitors who like crowds and hoopla. The festivals and special events at wineries may change at the whim of the winery owners, but many of the larger annual events mentioned in these chapters have been around a while and should be on the calendar when you visit. In truth, you can visit a winery somewhere almost every day of the year—unless they're closed for a holiday or seasonal break. Those dates are listed as well.

Where to Buy Wines: Most wineries sell their wines on-premises; some have tasting shops in locations other than their wineries. Many wineries will send wines UPS within the state. Most accept major credit cards as noted.

About Children: Although most state laws prohibit the sale of wine to minors (anyone under the age of twenty-one), wineries do welcome children and have ample supplies of grape juice for them to sample.

NOTE: Although all information included here is as up-to-date as possible, inevitably some inaccuracies will occur. Restaurants and bed and breakfasts change ownership or close down entirely; wineries are subject to the same situations. We urge you always to call first to confirm the details we have so carefully compiled.

Making Wines

More than soil and climate and quality of the grapes and modern technology, it is still the skill and creativity of the winemaker that make one wine distinct from another or more outstanding than the rest. Major steps in making wine are noted here. Knowing the basics can enhance a winery visit, where details will be given and questions answered.

Before grapes are picked, the winegrower begins to monitor the sugar, pH, and total acidity of the grapes. Samples are taken, and when ready, the fruit is picked as quickly as possible. It is common practice to pick all of one variety in a given location at the same time. Grapes can be picked by machine or by hand.

Warm fruit can have an unfavorable effect on a wine's quality, so grapes are picked before it gets hot or are cooled before they are processed.

Once at the winery, grapes are weighed before they are placed in a crusher-stemmer to separate the fruit from the stems, which are ejected. Then the must (everything but the stems) is pressed to release the juice and pumped to the

Methode Champenoise

Champagne is the name of a province in France renowned for sparkling wine made by *methode champenoise,* and the French feel only they can use this name to identify these wines. America's vintners also use this same painstaking traditional technique to produce wines they label sparkling wines or the generic champagne.

The inventor of *methode champenoise* champagne was a seventeenth-century Benedictine monk named Dom Pérignon. After its first fermentation, a white wine, usually made of either chardonnay or pinot noir grapes, is placed in slender-necked bottles to undergo a second fermentation in the bottle. During this fermentation, a *liqueur de tirage* (shot of sweetened wine) induces yeast cells to begin the formation of the characteristic bubbles.

Champagne bottles are extra strong, and their corks are tightly secured by wire to resist pressure by the gas trapped in the bottle. Once fermented in the bottle, the wine is placed in a *pupitre* (sloping rack) for riddling, a process that involves daily shaking and rotation (*rumuage*) of the bottles for eight to ten weeks, alternately to the right and left, until the bottles are neck downward and sediment is forced to settle in the neck of the bottle. Then the bottles are introduced neck-down into a freezing solution and are chilled below 12 degrees Fahrenheit. After a few minutes in the solution, the sediment in the wine is frozen with a small amount of the wine near the cork. The bottle is then turned upright, the cork is removed, and the gas pressure forces the ice plug to pop out. This is called disgorgement (*dégorgement*). Then a small amount of sugar dissolved in wine—the dosage—is added to the bottle to replace that which has been lost. No dosage is added to champagne labeled "Natural." Finally, the familiar mushroom-shaped cork that crowns champagne is put in place, and the wine is stored for several months before release to the public.

Nowadays, these steps are automated for a number of producers, but there are still those who prefer the old ways. When Dom Pérignon sipped his first glass of champagne, it is said that he exclaimed: "I am drinking stars!" And since then the wine has starred at many festive occasions.

---

fermentation tank—stainless steel, wood, and concrete being among the commonly used receptacles.

The varying amounts of time that the grapes' skins are in contact with the must have the most significant effect, after grape variety, on the type and color of wine made. Most white musts (juice without grape skins) will be pressed right after the crusher-stemmer. Some white varietals are pressed with skins and seeds, which are then discarded. Blush wines also have contact with skins for the desired amount of color. Premium whites come from first pressings only. The clear juice is allowed to settle to remove solids and pulp, and the clarified liquid is then drawn off into a fermentation tank. After one or two weeks at 50 to 70 degrees Fahrenheit, it is ready for aging in small barrels or storage tanks. Whites are ready for bottling within a year; reds take much longer to mature.

Skins are critical to the color, type, and style of red wines. The must is pumped into a tank where it begins fermentation on its own or when special strains of yeast are added. Tremendous amounts of heat are produced in the fermentation stage, so tanks are equipped with cooling devices. Red wines are fermented at higher temperatures than whites, at about 70 to 80 degrees Fahrenheit.

When winemakers decide that fermentation is completed, they draw off the juice and leave the sediment at the bottom of the tank. In red wine, the sediment goes to the presses; in white, the sediment is discarded.

To receive the maximum color and flavor possible during red wine fermentation, the juice is pumped over skins that have risen to the surface or the skins are pushed into the liquid, or both. When this step is completed, the wine is pressed and drawn off into settling tanks, and the sediment is thrown out; the wine is then placed in large oak tanks to undergo a secondary fermentation. The wine can also be bottled after the primary fermentation is completed. After both fermentations red wine is fined (clarified) by adding gelatin or egg white to the tank. During the secondary fermentation, the malic acid found in grapes is transformed into lactic acid and carbon dioxide, enhancing the wine's flavor. Once the secondary fermentation is completed, red wines are blended or put into small oak barrels for aging; some reds are aged in their bottles.

Reading Labels

There's more than a name on a label; small as it is, the knowledge it holds is encyclopedic when it comes to wines. The U.S. Bureau of Alcohol, Tobacco and Firearms requires that labels in all states have the first five points of specific information below; in addition, states may add individual requirements.

1. Brand: Trade name of winery.
2. Wine Type: Varietal, proprietary, or generic. To be a varietal, the wine must contain 75 percent of the grape named on the label; Oregon requires a 90 percent minimum. Labrusca varietal content is 51 percent. In proprietaries and generics the grapes need not be listed on the labels. However, if a domestic generic wine uses certain foreign geographical names to denote origin, style, or class of wine—for instance, Burgundy, Chablis, Rhine, among others—their labels also must declare their true U.S. place of origin. Thus, the label on a New York state or California-produced Chablis has to say Finger Lakes or Napa Valley in addition to Chablis or certain other geographic names. Further limitations on wine labels when it comes to foreign geographic place names may be enacted.

3. Regional Data: A state name can be used if 75 to 100 percent of the grapes come from that state; a county name calls for a 75 percent minimum; the naming of a viticultural area (v.a.) requires that 85 percent of the grapes must have been grown in the v.a. In the case of a varietal, 75 to 95 percent of the grape named must have been grown in the named v.a.

4. Bottler: Name of winery, business address. Further, "made and bottled by," means that the bottler has fermented 10 percent of the grapes in this wine; "produced, grown, and bottled by" means the bottler fermented, aged, and bottled at least 75 percent of the wine. "Grown, produced, and bottled" means, as implied, that the bottler is responsible for everything from vine to finished wine.

5. Alcohol: Read the fine print at the bottom of the label to see that a table wine can range from 7 percent to 13.9 percent alcohol; the label may use "table wine" if the alcohol content is under 14 percent. For sherry, the range may go from 17 to 20 percent; for ports and other dessert wines, 18 to 24 percent. The variance for these wines is 1 percent. Some voluntary information below may also appear on labels.

6. Vineyard Designation: May be used if 95 percent of grapes are from the named site and it is located withing a federally designated v.a.

7. Vintage: Included on label if 95 percent of grapes were grown in year on label.

8. Other: Some winemakers voluntarily note if the wine contains sulfites. The label may also have a wealth of technical data such as the pH, residual sugar, and total acidity, if there are records to support these claims. Such descriptive information as late harvest, reserve, or *naturel* and *brut* for champagnes may also be used but is not mandated.

Tasting Wines

Wine tasting is a chance to experience the wines firsthand. But there is another dimension: part of the adventure is to experience the tasting room. There are those that capture the spirit of a place with a historic setting or decor, others that seem like trips to outer space, and those with no frills at all. Yet, extravagant or rudimentary, the real reason for your visit is to determine which wines best suit your taste. To learn how to taste wine has been made unnecessarily complicated. It's simply a matter of using your senses of sight, smell, and taste, along with a bit of imagination. When tasting wines, try to imagine how they will be used. Some wines are well suited to foods, and others are meant for sipping alone. Here goes:

1. OBSERVE: Look at the wine against the light. Check for a pleasing color and clarity. Whites may range from faintly green-tinted to amber-hued, reds may be crimson to deep maroon. If the red is cloudy and the white has specks

drifting in it, it has failed the sight test. Any wine must please the eye enough to invite a sniff.

2. SMELL: Cup your fingers under the globe of the glass and rotate the wine gently. Then, tip your nose over the edge of the glass and inhale for a few seconds. Look for a winey smell, which is clean and evocative of the particular grape—it may be fruitlike or herbaceous, spicy or floral. Sharp smells, corky smells, and moldy odors are reasons to reject the wine.

3. TASTE: Take a small sip and roll it around your mouth; let it permeate your mouth and taste buds. Most guides to wine tasting make a big point of allowing the palate to experience the wine. This is erroneous advice because the palate is actually insensitive to taste. The wine must be rolled up farther into the nasal cavity, which is sensitive and can detect many nuances about the wine. Then swallow the wine and note the tartness, sweetness, body, and savor the aftertaste, which is what sets a premium wine apart from the ordinary. Before tasting another wine, nibble crackers or bread or take a sip of water offered by the winery to prepare your mouth for the next taste. This also gives the nose a rest so it can go on to detect the next scents.

Another tip is to exercise caution when tasting wines. They are, when all the poetry is removed, alcoholic drinks, and should be handled with care. Each taste is about one ounce, which can add up if you sample several wines. In every tasting room are receptacles for discarding extra wine, and the wineries expect them to be used. (It's not impolite to request a receptacle if there is none.) Another technique is to spit out excess wine into the receptacles—as wine tasters do. Nor will anyone be offended by this gesture. Finally, when traveling these wine routes, it's a good idea to assign driving to someone who does not imbibe the wines but drinks the grape juice offered at many wineries. The chauffeuring can be rotated so all those who wish to taste the wines can have their turn.

Grapes You'll Meet

Four hundred years ago, the first wines of this country were made from muscadine grapes, which grow today as they did then in the southeastern states. Labruscas, grape species native to America, have been bred for wine since the seventeenth century. They long had been the principal grape of the winemaking industry in the eastern part of the country and of the grape-growing industry everywhere in America, with the exception of California. Decreasing quantities of labrusca wines are produced today to meet consumers' demand for less grapey tasting wines. Some winemakers, however, are trying to reinvent labrusca wines in drier versions to fit the times.

Species of native grapes most often encountered are:

WHITE

CATAWBA: Developed early in the nineteenth century and often used today in sparkling wines. Sometimes the wines are pink, but the color has been added by other grapes.

DELAWARE: Pink grape with white juice, less grapey than other native varieties. Named for Delaware, Ohio. Used in sparkling and still wines.

DUTCHESS: One of the old American hybrids, but a wallflower among grapes because it is subject to fungus diseases.

MISSOURI RIESLING: Not a relative of Johannisberg Riesling, it has a Riesling-like taste, and little foxiness.

NIAGARA: Makes a sweet, golden wine with a pronounced grapey aroma and taste connoisseurs call "foxy."

SCUPPERNONG: Southeastern-grown and in the muscadine family, it is not a cluster, but a bunch grape. Makes an intensely flavored, tawny-colored wine. Thomas Jefferson, wine sophisticate though he was, enjoyed more than a sip of Scuppernong in his day.

RED

CONCORD: This dark purple grape is still in the juice-and-jelly hall of fame, but is rapidly disappearing from the list of winemakers' favorites. It is used for some sherries and ports and in sweet kosher wines. This may have been the grape for which they invented the term "foxy."

CYNTHIANA: Found in south-central states, this is an American hybrid that produces a pleasant wine, without foxy aroma.

STEUBEN: Developed at the Geneva Experimental Station in New York, a dark blue grape with almost no foxy taste or smell. Used in making rosés.

Vinifera resulted from crossing French and labrusca varieties and pushed the American wine industry in the new direction of dry wines in the 1970s. They were bred to live through harsh winters and resist fungus. French hybrids have roots deep in American history: one of the earliest American grapes, the Alexander, is said to have been a cross between a French vinifera and a wild labrusca found along the Schuylkill outside Philadelphia. Work is in progress at the Geneva Experimental Station in New York on crossbreeding to produce new varieties of hybrid wine grapes. Listed below are some of the hybrids.

WHITE

AURORA: Hardy, productive grape. Makes a clean, neutral white and is often used for blending. Aged in oak, it has a fuller flavor.

CAYUGA: Developed at the Geneva Experimental Station in New York, this marriage of a Seyval Blanc and another Geneva-developed grape, the Schuyler, produces a delicately flavored, fruity wine.

MELODY: Newly developed white grape being used sparingly at the moment. Makes a light, crisp wine, with fruity to floral bouquet.

RAVAT 51 OR VIGNOLES: Chardonnay parentage. This grape makes a crisp wine, not unlike Chablis (French Chablis is made of Chardonnay). Sweet versions are fruity and delicious.

SEYVAL BLANC: The hands-down winner when it comes to hybrids; makes a dry varietal, late-harvest-style sweet wine as well as a light, sparkling wine. Compares favorably with some of the European wines.

RAYON D'OR: Used in blending to add complexity and occasionally as a varietal.

VERDELET: Light, flowery white wines.

VIDAL BLANC: Soft, semi-dry wine with a fresh, fruity flavor. The late harvest can have a honey flavor in outstanding years.

VILLARD BLANC: Excellent blending wine; also produces a naturally sweet wine.

RED

BACO NOIR: Cabernet Sauvignon parentage; produces dry Bordeaux-style wine. Also can make a rosé and portlike late-harvest wine.

CHAMBOURCIN: Light-bodied red wine; best when oak aged.

CHANCELLOR: Full-bodied, deep red wine.

CHELOIS: Pronounced "chell-wah" (*à la Français*), sometimes "shell-oys"; a dry red wine, improves with oak aging. Often used in proprietary blends.

COLOBEL: Color-intense grape; it is used by winemakers to add color to wine.

DE CHAUNAC: Makes a good dry rosé; also blended with other wines for a medium-bodied red wine.

FOCH OR MARECHAL FOCH: There's Pinot Noir in the ancestry of this grape, which makes a Burgundy-type red wine.

MILLOT OR LEON MILLOT: Similar to Foch.

ROUEGEON: A finicky hybrid and therefore not very popular; makes a dry to semisweet wine.

Vinifera are wine grapes grown principally in Europe, California, Washington, Oregon, and Idaho; grown and used increasingly elsewhere.

WHITE

CHARDONNAY: Burgundy-born; produces a fine, dry, buttery white wine with applelike taste; aged in oak, the flavor becomes even more deep and fruity.

CHENIN BLANC: Loire region grapes; make crisp, dry-to-sweet wine. Grown widely in eastern Washington State and parts of California.

FRENCH COLOMBARD: Crossed from France to California in the 1870s; used in generic and sparkling wines. Now also a varietal with distinct perfume and sweet taste.

GEWÜRZTRAMINER: Clone of Traminer grape, and widely grown in Alsace, makes a medium-bodied, spicy, aromatic wine. Also used for an elegant, sweet dessert wine. Grown in California, the Pacific states, New York, and other locations in the United States.

MULLER-THURGAU: Riesling-Sylvaner cross, it is found in Oregon and makes a mild Riesling-type wine.

MUSCATS—BLANC, CANELLI, EARLY, FRONTIGNAN, OTTONEL: All the same family of grapes; they produce a rich, off-dry to sweet wine with distinctive floral aroma.

PINOT BLANC: Sharper than Chardonnay, but reminiscent of it; makes a white that ages well in oak. Limited acreage in California.

PINOT GRIS: Genetic relative of Pinot Noir; planted mainly in Oregon and could be a strong competitor for Chardonnay's crown if planted more abundantly.

JOHANNISBERG RIESLING, RIESLING, WHITE RIESLING: All three names of the same white grape, which has its origin in the vineyards of the Rhine and Mosel valleys. Makes elegant, stylish, dry, fruity whites and luscious, sweet, late-harvest styles. Incidentally, the name Johannisberg refers to the grape of the old Schloss Johannisberg estate.

SAUVIGNON BLANC: White relative of Cabernet Sauvignon, originating in Bordeaux and Loire; produces a bold, fruity white. Also called Fumé Blanc.

SÉMILLON: Native of Sauterne region, and popular in Washington and California; produces a dry, aromatic wine and a delicious, sweet dessert wine. Blended with Sauvignon Blanc and Muscadelle for depth and complexity.

RED

BARBERA: Made its way to California perhaps with Italian immigrants in the nineteenth century. Makes a soft red wine that improves with oak aging. Commonly used in generic blends.

CABERNET SAUVIGNON: Famous Bordeaux grape; produces California's best red varietal, and Washington's outstanding red as well. Becoming a success in Long Island and the Finger Lakes, and showing some promise in other states. Herbaceous, fragrant, dry wine, with added complexity when aged in oak.

GAMAY: A Beaujolais native; makes a red wine best drunk young.

GAMAY BEAUJOLAIS: Pinot Noir clone; makes a light, fresh wine, best when young.

LEMBERGER (ALSO LIMBERGER): Washington is the place to find this grape, which came to the state in the 1930s from Hungary via British Columbia as a research project at WSU. The grapes are compared to Zinfandel because they can adapt to a number of styles, and, like Zinfandel, have a flavor somewhat like fresh berries.

MERLOT: Grape used in St.-Émilion and Pomerel wines in Bordeaux; makes a smooth red wine bearing similarity to Cabernet Sauvignon.

PETITE SIRAH: A relative of the Rhone-grown Duriff, this species in California produces a red that improves with oak aging. Used in blends with Pinot Noir and found in generics.

PINOT NOIR: Burgundy's great red grape in Oregon's outstanding grape; a considerable accomplishment, since the grape does not prosper well out of its native land. Growers from Oregon to Rhode Island and points in between have also begun to focus on this finicky grape. Pinot Noir grapes can be used for dry, semidry still, and sparkling wines. Wines can be dark red or light red rosés. Smooth textured; subtle suggestion of violets.

SYRAH: Great Rhone variety, just getting started in California. Makes a complex red wine.

ZINFANDEL: This grape makes a red wine with a berrylike aroma and flavor; oak aging makes its berry flavor more pronounced; late-harvest wines are dark and full-bodied, with considerable tannin and alcohol. White Zinfandels are wines made in the same way as a white wine but with red grapes; the finished wine is actually pink in color.

FRUIT WINES

Throughout the country there are wineries producing wines with fruit, from apricots to strawberries—with a difference. The new fruit wines are dry, not sweet, and hold their own as table wines to accompany dinner entrées. Others are served as aperitifs, or are finished like sweet dessert wines. In addition, mead or honey wine is sold at some wineries. Visits to these wineries make fascinating detours along the wine routes of America.

Wine Speak

All the terms below may not be in this book, but they are part of a special language used to describe wines and wine production.

Acid: The acidic taste of tart freshness, caused by the presence of tartaric, citric, malic, and lactic acidity. Balanced acidity in dry table wines ranges from 0.6 to 0.75 percent of volume.

Aftertaste: Lingering, back-of-the-throat taste; it infers complexity.

Aging: Period in which wine matures in barrels or bottles; some premium wines age three years in oak barrels.

Alcohol: Result of fermentation of sugar-containing liquids. Table wines are less than 14 percent alcohol by volume; sherry wines range from 17 to 20 percent; other dessert wines, 15 to 24 percent.

Aroma: The grape smell of a young wine. Disappears with age and is replaced by *bouquet*.

Astringency: Dry, harsh, puckering sensation in mouth after swallowing; caused by excess tannin, especially in young wines; diminishes with age in the bottle.

BATF: Bureau of Alcohol, Tobacco and Firearms, the U.S. Treasury agency that looks after all aspects of winemaking and wine marketing in America.

Balanced: Wine with all elements in harmony.

Barrel Tasting: Sampling wine from the barrel, prior to bottling.

Big: Wine with full body and flavor and color and fruitiness.

Blending: Skill of combining two or more wines to obtain a better, more balanced wine.

Body: The weight and substance of wine in the mouth—actually, the degree of viscosity, dependent on content of sugar and alcohol. Wines can be light, medium, or full-bodied.

Bonded Winery: A winery that has met the federal government's approval through inspection of buildings, equipment, storage, and sincerity of intent for the production of wine. In addition, a state winery license must be issued before production begins.

Botrytis cinerea: "Noble rot," a mold that grows on some white wine grapes in the fall before harvest. Desirable because it dehydrates the fruit, making it sweeter and richer, and results in a silken, elegant dessert wine.

Bouquet: The fragrance of a matured wine when opened; develops further in the glass. *Nose* is the term used to include both aroma and bouquet.

Breathing: Allowing air to reach red wine after drawing the cork. There is disagreement over whether this is really necessary.

Brix: Measurement of weight of sugar content of grapes on maturity.

Brut: Very dry champagne. Little or no dosage (sugar & wine) added.

Character: Positive and distinctive taste giving personality to a wine.

Charmat Process: Bulk process method of making champagne.

Clean: Refers to a well-made wine with no unpleasant taste or smell.

Coarse: Refers to a badly made wine.

Color: Tells a lot about the quality of wine, whether white or red. Clear and bright signal a wine worth tasting. Cloudy and dull? Go on to another wine.

Complexity: Quality of wine reminiscent of flowers and fruits; found in fine wines.

Cooperage: General term for containers of all sizes in which wines are aged; and can be wood or stainless steel.

Crush: Breaking of grape skins that starts the winemaking. *Crush* can also be the term for harvest season itself.

Cuvee: Specific blend of wines used to make champagnes. In the *cuvee* can lie the secret of a great champagne.

Disgorgement: Literally, "throat clearing" in French; in this case, the term for the phase of *methode champenoise* in which sediment is removed from bottles of sparkling wine. The neck of the bottle is frozen, and a plug of ice at the neck, which contains the sediment, is expelled from the bottle once the cork is removed. In French, *dégorgement*.

Dosage: Sugar syrup added to champagnes after *disgorgement* to re-place sugars lost after removal of sediment.

Dry, Semi-dry, Sweet: All three terms describe the amount of residual sugar found in the wine after bottling. Most wines will be fermented dry by the natural consumption of the sugar content by wine yeast. There may be residual sugar after fermentation, but most people cannot taste it. To make a wine semi-dry, some sweetness—sugar or unfermented grape juice ("sweet reserve")—is added before bottling. There are no exact standards for this labeling.

Enology: Science of winemaking; also spelled oenology.

Estate-bottled: Produced and bottled by vineyard owner; in the United States 85 percent of the grapes used must also come from a federally approved viticultural area.

Extra Dry: Misleading term for slightly sweet champagne.

Fermentation: Chemical reaction by which yeasts transform grape sugar into alcohol and carbon dioxide.

Filtering: The process of removing yeasts and other particles from fermented wine.

Fining: Clarifying wine with such agents as gelatin or egg whites to precipitate sediment to the bottom of the tank or barrel.

Finish: Aftertaste of wine.

Fortified Wines: Wines strengthened by the addition of wine spirits, usually brandy, to raise the alcoholic content from under 14 percent to over 18 percent. For example, sherries and ports are fortified wines.

Foxiness: The grapey smell and taste of labruscas (Concord, Catawaba, Delaware, and others).

Generic: Applies to wines named after European producing areas such as Burgundy, Chablis, Rhine, and others. If applied in the United States, the BATF states these wines must be labeled with place of origin, such as "Napa Valley Chablis." The BATF is likely to impose wider restrictions on the use of foreign geographic names on U.S. wines; usage has long angered overseas vintners (especially the French, who object to the name of the Champagne region's being used elsewhere), who claim generic labeling lessens their wines' identity and misleads consumers.

Green: Unripe, harsh wines with unbalanced acidity, unpleasant to taste and smell.

Hard: Excessively tannic. Can mellow in aging.

Harsh: Too hard and astringent. Can soften in aging.

Horizontal Tasting: Tastings of different vintages of the same varietal.

Hybrids: Grape species developed by crossing two or more varieties.

Ice Wine (Eiswein): Wine made from grapes that have been allowed to freeze on the vine and develop a high natural sugar content. The shriveled berries yield small quantities of fragrant, sweet, syrupy juice. Results in an elegant, rich dessert wine. Once made only in Germany, now also made in the United States.

Insipid: Without character, dull. Lacking acidity.

Jeroboam: Double magnum bottle holding the equivalent of four regular bottles, or 104 fluid ounces, or 3.2 liters.

Labrusca: The native North American grape.

Lees: Sediment deposited by fermented wines in casks or tanks.

Long: Lingering flavor in mouth, associated with premium wines.

Magnum: A double-sized bottle.

Malolactic Fermentation: A secondary fermentation, when the malic acid naturally found in grapes is converted to lactic acid and carbon dioxide. If it occurs while wine is still in the barrel, it can enhance flavor.

Mellow: Softened with proper aging.

Methode champenoise: See box on page 3.

Microclimates: Small climates within a larger climate and very important when deciding which types of grapes to grow within the vineyard. A vineyard can have a number of microclimates if the land changes direction or elevation or is near a body of water. The vineyardist must select grape varieties that flourish within the varying microclimates.

Mildew: Disease affecting vines in wet weather.

Must: Grape juice after crushing and during fermentation.

Musty: Stale taste and odor caused by storage in unclean cask.

Oaky: Characteristics of taste and aroma imparted by oak barrels in which wine was aged.

Off-dry: Somewhat, but not extremely, dry.

Oloroso: Sweet, deep-colored, full-bodied sherries.

pH Measurement: The chemical measurement of hydrogen ion concentration that predicts flavor, color, aroma, and other qualities of wine.

Phylloxera: A parasitic vine disease, particularly disastrous to vinifera vines. The phylloxera are plant lice, believed native to vines indigenous to North America. They suck the sap from the roots, which stunts growth and finally kills the vines. In the mid-1800s, phylloxera caused great damage in California, and vines sent from the United States to Europe (probably for experimentation) destroyed many vineyards in various wine regions, particularly in France. The solution was found in grafting *Vitis vinifera* onto native American root stock, which generally are not affected by the root lice.

Premium: U.S. term for high-quality wine.

Proprietary: Term used to describe wine unique to a producing winery. Examples are Richard's Wild Irish Rose, Seaport White, among others.

Residual Sugar: The amount of sugar remaining in fermented wine. It is shown on label as percent of volume. One percent is sweet.

Rosé: Pink wine produced by shortening the time red grapes' skins ferment in the must.

Solera: Spanish system of aging and blending sherries. Wines are stored together in a series of barrels containing wine of various ages. Wine for sale is taken from the oldest barrel, which is always half full. The amount removed is then replaced with the next oldest.

Tannin: Compound in grape skins that provides desirable astringency and flavor and aids the longevity of bottled wines.

Tawny: Descriptive of port and other wines that in maturing have lost their red color and become amberlike.

Tirage: French for "pulling"—the process of drawing wine from barrels into bottles. Also *tirage* (*liqueur de tirage*), the shot of sugar or sweetener dissolved in still wines (with perhaps a yeast starter) to commence secondary fermentation in *methode champenoise* champagne.

Transfer: A step-saving method of making champagne; following the second fermentation, the wine is sent through a filter to remove sediment and is transferred to another bottle, thus saving the removal of sediment by hand known as disgorging.

Varietal: Wine named for the main grape used in its production; to qualify as a varietal such as a Chardonnay or Sauvignon Blanc that wine must be made of 75 percent of the variety named on the label. If labrusca, can be 51 percent of total.

Vats: For fermenting; can be wood, stainless steel, glass, concrete lined with glass, concrete alone.

Vertical Tasting: Sampling a wine in its different stages, from unfermented grape juice to the barrel and bottle.

Vintage: Ninety-five percent of grapes in the bottle must have been harvested in stated year. (They must be marked with the state, county, or viticultural area.)

Viticultural Area (v.a.): The federal government's Bureau of Alcohol, Tobacco and Firearms (BATF), which oversees all wine production in the United States, considers and approves viticultural areas and allows their use on wine labels and advertisements. To qualify, the grape-growing area must have unique characteristics of soil, climate, elevation, or other geographic features that set it apart from neighboring areas. To use on an American label, 85 percent of grapes in the wine must be from the viticultural area. (See the list of v.a.'s in the back of the book.)

Vineyard: Acreage upon which grapes are grown.

Vineyard Designation: Naming a specific vineyard on the label. This can only be done if 95 percent of the grapes came from that vineyard and it falls within an approved v.a.

Vinifera: European grape species to which Chardonnay, Cabernet Sauvignon, Johannisberg Riesling, and Pinot Noir belong. They thrive in California, where the climate is warm and dry, and present a challenge to growers in the colder parts of the United States.

Viticulture: The science of grape growing.

Vitis: The genus of a grapevine; for example, *Vitis vinifera* or *Vitis labrusca.*

Winery: The place where wine is made.

Yeasty: Smells of yeast as in bread; not desirable.

2
New England

North River Winery, Jacksonville, Vermont

When the first European explorers checked out America, they found the Indians made wine from native grapes—a practice adopted by the Pilgrims for their first Thanksgiving meal. But what those early American colonists could not do successfully in New England (or elsewhere in their new land) was grow European grape varieties.

Now European vineferas and French hybrids are flourishing in New England fields and across the land. This is largely due to a combination of new technology and advanced viticultural techniques, and to the passage of farm winery bills. New England winemakers now believe that their rough weather makes better wines and have found some of their microclimates to be remarkably similar to parts of Burgundy, Bordeaux, and—yes, even the hallowed Napa Valley. Judging from their many awards, their beliefs seem founded in fact. Like the early settlers, Americans can now make some interesting discoveries about New England wines.

In 1964, the first of New England's new wineries was founded in Laconia, New Hampshire, followed by a vineyard at Martha's Vineyard—an island named, years ago, for the wild grapes that once covered its shores. The balance of the New England wineries were started after 1975, most of them in Connecticut and Massachusetts. Among the recently named U.S. viticultural areas is the BATF-designated Western Connecticut Highlands, which recognizes the area's unique grape-growing and climatic conditions.

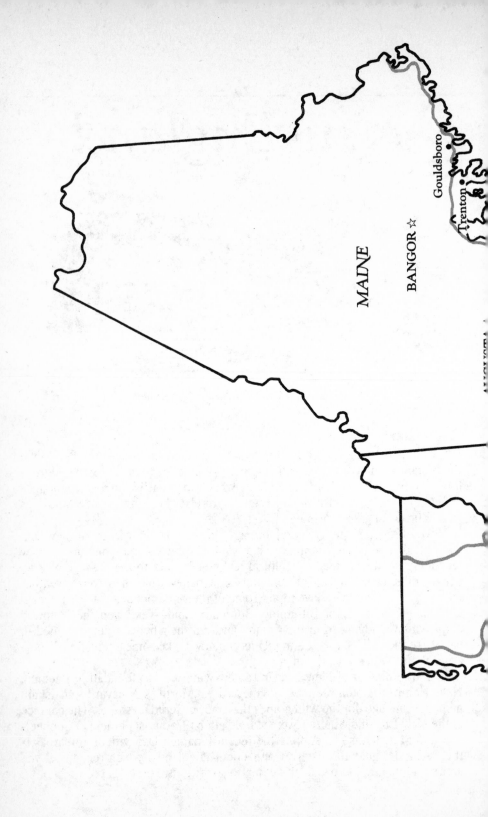

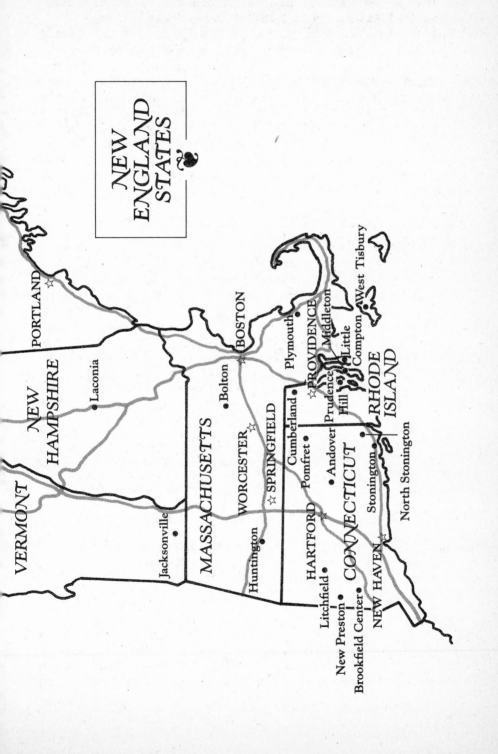

NEW ENGLAND STATES

VERMONT

NEW HAMPSHIRE

PORTLAND

Laconia

MASSACHUSETTS

Jacksonville

Bolton

WORCESTER

Huntington

SPRINGFIELD

HARTFORD

CONNECTICUT

Litchfield

New Preston

Brookfield Center

NEW HAVEN

BOSTON

Plymouth

PROVIDENCE

Cumberland

Pomfret

Andover

Stonington

North Stonington

Prudence
Hill

RHODE ISLAND

Middleton

Little

Compton

West Tisbury

In Colonial days, New England was famous for another intoxicating beverage—rum, the backbone of the area's economy. It was the commoner's drink. Imported Madeira was the preferred toast of the upper crust.

Wines, too, have a valuable tradition in New England's history. In 1632, John Winthrop purchased Governor's Island in Boston Harbor for twenty hogsheads of wine a year to be paid in grape or apple wines. That was fruit wines' fifteen minutes of fame—until now. Today's New England winemakers are reviving the art of fruit winemaking and, at the same time, are changing the image of these wines from sweet and dowdy to elegant and sophisticated. Although store distribution is limited, fruit wines await you on your tour.

Yet another plus beckons the wine tourist in New England. It is the proximity of wineries to historic sites, seaside resorts, and scenic delights. New England wine routes go through the region's prime locations, so why wait? Let's start now.

ࣈ CONNECTICUT

Among the newer American viticultural areas is the BATF-designated Western Connecticut Highlands, which recognizes the area's unique grape-growing and climatic conditions.

Danbury & Litchfield Hills

DiGrazia Vineyards & Winery

131 Tower Road
Brookfield Center, Connecticut 06805
TEL: 203-775-1616
OWNERS: Paul and Barbara DiGrazia
FOUNDED: 1984

AT A GLANCE
Tours & Tastings: Wed.–Sun. 1–6. Guided tours and tastings conducted by one of the DiGrazias are tailored to the individual's interests and can last from fifteen minutes to one hour.
Closed: Mon.–Tues.
Vineyards: A few acres under cultivation in Connecticut are supplemented by larger acreage in Brookfield, NY, near the Connecticut border, for a total of sixty acres in all. Varieties include Seyval, Vidal Blanc, Ravat, Marechal Foch, Leon Millot, and Chancellor.

Wines: Windridge (Seyval Blanc), Meadowbrook (blend of Vidal, Ravat, and Seyval), Candlewood Rosé (blend of Leon Millot and Foch), Fieldstone Reserve (blend of Foch and Chancellor).
Awards: Gold and silver awards to Woodridge, Fieldstone, Meadowbrook in New England competitions; quality awards in International Eastern competitions.
Retail Sales: Wines sold at tasting, tour times.
Credit Cards: None.
Access for Disabled: None.
Foreign Languages: French.
Getting There: Seven miles north of Danbury. Take Federal Road (Rte. 202) to tractor barn, turn onto Rte. 133, and continue to Tower Rd.
Special Wine & Other Events: Release of Newbury Nouveau, sold only at winery.

⅋ Paul DiGrazia has a career in medicine, Barbara is a psychotherapist, and both are authors. They planted their vineyard in 1977 with the help of their children. What started out as a small boutique winery has remained true to its goal of producing quality wines from its own grapes. Production is now around 5,000 gallons.

TO SEE & DO
Winery is located between two New England Lakes—Candlewood and Lake Lillinonan.

ACCOMMODATIONS
Best Western Stony Hill Inn
Route 6, Danbury/Newton Road
Bethel, Connecticut 06801
Tel: 203-743-5533; 800-528-1234
Colonial-style thirty-six-unit motel, with tavernlike dining room on forty-one landscaped acres complete with pond and preening swans, swimming pool and tennis courts. Near Candlewood Lake. Four miles east of Danbury on Route 6.

Danbury Hilton Inn and Conference Center
18 Old Ridgebury Road
Danbury, Connecticut 06810
Tel: 203-794-0600; 800-445-8667
Sleek, modern, Hiltonesque; with health club, indoor swimming pool, and near the Berkshires.

RESTAURANTS
Bella Italia
2 Padanaram Road
Danbury, Connecticut 06811
Tel: 203-743-3828
Italian specialties, as name implies.

⅋ ⅋ ⅋

Hopkins Vineyard

Hopkins Road
New Preston, Connecticut 06777
TEL: 203-868-7954

OWNERS: Judith and William Hopkins
WINEMAKER: William Hopkins
FOUNDED: 1979

AT A GLANCE
Tours & Tastings: May 1–Jan. 1, Mon.–Sun. 11–5; Jan.–Apr., Sat.–Sun. only. Self-guided tours, supplemented with slide show of the dramatic cycles in a vineyard year shown several times a day.
Vineyards: Twenty acres planted to French hybrids in the Western Connecticut Highlands v.a.
Wines: Reds: Leon Millot, Marechal Foch; Whites: Cayuga, Seyval, Ravat, Aurora; also blended wines (Lakeside Whites, Barn Red among these). Yankee Cider, made from locally grown apples.
Awards: A King Midas–size pile of gold and silver awards, won over the years. Frequent winners? White varietals and blends, also cider.
Picnic Area: On the tree-shaded grounds or in the cool and leafy state park at the west end of Lake Waramaug.
Retail Shop: Wines and wine accessories, books, baskets.
Credit Cards: MasterCard, Visa.
Access for Disabled: Limited.
Foreign Languages: None.
Special Wine & Other Events: Winery's Hayloft Gallery showcases the work of local Connecticut artists and artisans.
Getting There: Approximately one hour west of Hartford, one and a half hours north of New York City. From Hartford: Take I-84 to West Farmington (exit 39), turn onto Rte. 4 West, then Rte. 118 to Litchfield and Rte. 202 to New Preston. From New York City: Take Henry Hudson Pkwy. to Sawmill River Pkwy. to I-684 to I-84 East to exit 7. Then take Rte. 7 North to New Milford and pick up Rte. 202 to New Preston. Alternatively, Rte. 7 (often crowded) can be taken out of Danbury (stopping for a visit at DiGrazia Vineyards), then get on Rte. 202 and proceed from there.

❧ Hopkins Vineyard was only founded in 1979, but the Hopkins family has farmed this land for 200 years. The winery is located in an 1850s barn, painted red as in those Grandma Moses paintings, surrounded by lush fields of vineyards, and overlooking Lake Waramaug. Before sipping wine in the attractive Chestnut Bar, visitors can see the winemaking process and fermenting tanks. Wines are stored in the old stone-lined cellars, where temperatures remain constant year-round.

❧ ❧ ❧

Haight Vineyards

Chestnut Hill
Litchfield, Connecticut 06759
TEL: 203-567-4045
OWNER: Sherman Haight, Jr.
FOUNDED: 1975

AT A GLANCE
Tours & Tastings: Mon.–Sat. 10:30–5, Sun. 12–5. Located in hills overlooking Lichfield, the winery is known for sparkling wines made by the traditional *methode champenoise;* and still wines include Chardonnay and Riesling, Seyval Blanc. Picnic area.

TO SEE & DO
Stone-walled fields, red barns, covered bridges, steepled churches—all so quaint and picturesque, visitors might have stumbled onto a set for *It's a Wonderful Life*. To explore the area in depth, contact the Litchfield Hills Travel Council, P.O. Box 1776 (yes, even a colorful box number), New Preston–Marble Dale, CT 06777; tel: 203-888-2214. Ask for both general information and their "Auto Tours" pamphlet.

Auto Tour 1, which goes through the best little towns in Litchfield Hills, is the wine route to and from Hopkins Vineyards. This tour also takes in art galleries, museums, state parks, and Federal-style buildings and towns with fashionable boutiques and restaurants housed in historic settings. For walkers, there's a path up Pinnacle Mountain, near Lake Waramaug, in the Steep Rock Reservation, to get a telescopic view stretching to Massachusetts and New York.

ACCOMMODATIONS
A difficult decision is trying to decide which of the many charming inns to include in this brief section.

Hopkins Inn
Hopkins Road
New Preston, Connecticut 06777
Tel: 203-868-7295
Behind the Federal-style façade beats a friendly, cheerful heart in this inn facing Lake Waramaug. Lodging Apr.–Nov.; restaurant Apr.–Dec., closed Mon. Terrace dining in warm weather. Despite the name, the inn has no connection with the winery. Austrian owner/chef serves Continental foods.

The Inn on Lake Waramaug
North Shore Road
New Preston, Connecticut 06777
Tel: 203-868-0563; 800-525-3644
Early American decor with pine and cherry antiques; copper and silver accessories; American foods and American wines. Snuggle in a canopied bed, with a modern sauna and indoor swimming pool at hand. Game room, canoes, sleigh rides in winter, and more. Open all year.

The Birches Inn
West Shore Road
New Preston, Connecticut 06777
Tel: 203-868-0229
Lake Waramaug has been compared with regions of Austria, so appropriately this inn has an Austrian atmosphere. A cozy place with rooms overlooking the lake. Open all year.

Boulders Inn
New Preston, Connecticut 06777
Tel: 203-868-7918
Built in 1895, the inn and cottages have views of the lake and Litchfield Hills. From dining deck, catch spectacular sunsets. Open all year. Lunch and dinner daily, Memorial Day through Labor Day.

The Mayflower Inn & Restaurant
Route 47
Washington, Connecticut 06795
Tel: 203-868-0515
Thirty acres of historical district are wrapped around this 1894 Colonial inn; the restaurant is noted for Continental cuisine and fine wines.

Covered Bridge Bed & Breakfast
P.O. Box 701A Maple Avenue
Norfolk, Connecticut 06058
Tel: 203-542-5944
This reservation service matches guests with some special old private homes in the northwest corner of Connecticut and the Berkshires.

RESTAURANTS
Hopkins Inn, the Inn on Lake Waramaug, Boulders Inn, and Mayflower Inn (all mentioned above) serve Hopkins Vineyard's wines.

Eastern Coast

Crosswoods Vineyards

75 Chester Maine Road
North Stonington, Connecticut 06359
TEL: 203-535-2205
OWNERS: Susan and Hugh Connell
WINEMAKER: George Sulick, degree in enology from CSU-Fresno
FOUNDED: 1981

AT A GLANCE
Tours & Tastings: Tours by appointment only, Mon.–Fri. 9–4, Sat.–Sun. 12:30–5; show every aspect of this state-of-the-art winery; tastings, by appointment for eight or more, same hours, with or without tour.
Vineyards: Thirty-two acres, all to vinifera varieties—Chardonnay, Johannisberg Riesling, Gewürztraminer, Gamay Noir, and Pinot Noir.
Wines: Varietals from the above and a proprietary blend, Scrimshaw White (Chardonnay and Riesling). The Chardonnay is highly recommended by *The Wine Advocate*.
Picnic Area: Picnic on the grounds, with prior permission.

Retail Shop: Mon.–Fri. Wines sold on site.
Credit Cards: MasterCard, Visa.
Access for Disabled: Production area on one level.
Foreign Languages: French.
Getting There: Crosswoods is five miles northeast of Mystic and two miles north of I-95, exit 92; turn three roads beyond Wyassup Rd.

🍃 Owners Susan and Hugh Connell and their three sons launched Crosswoods in 1981 by planting their first vines after years of planning and soon began earning a name as the place for fine vinifera wines produced by many talented hands. Susan herself had studied enology in Europe and California and apprenticed two years at a wine company in the Hudson Valley; their winemaker, George Sulick, was a winemaker at well-known California wineries. The Connells' consultant, Walter Schug, trained at the renowned Geisenheim Institute and an esteemed California winemaker, has thirty years of winemaking experience.

Plant pathologist Paul Hennen carries out the viticultural program.

The nineteenth-century barn-winery sits in a Norman Rockwell setting on a plateau overlooking the Atlantic Ocean. Inside, it is a model of modern efficiency, with all kinds of the latest equipment needed to produce quality wines. Tours are by appointment because the Connells wish to minimize the disruption of the winemaking process.

ಶಿ ಶಿ ಶಿ

Stonington Vineyards

Taugwonk Road (P.O. Box 463)
Stonington, Connecticut 06378
TEL: 203-535-1222
Owners: Nick and Happy Smith
WINEMAKER: Michael McAndrew
FOUNDED: 1986

AT A GLANCE
Tours & Tastings: Tours Tues.–Sun. 11–5, by appointment only; tastings and sales also 11–5, no appointment necessary. Tours, guided by the Smiths or winemaker McAndrew, take thirty minutes and include every aspect of winemaking, tasting, and a stroll around the vineyards.
Closed: Mon., Thanksgiving, Christmas.
Vineyards: Ten acres planted to vinifera varieties and French hybrids, the largest share to Chardonnay. Additional grapes are purchased from New York's Finger Lakes and Hudson Valley and Massachusetts.
Wines: Chardonnay, Riesling, Pinot Noir, and three blends: white, blush, and red.
Awards: 1987 Seaport White, bronze and Riesling Quality Award in International Eastern wine competition; golds to Blush, Seaport White, and a silver to Chardonnay in Northeastern competition.
Picnic Area: No formal area, but picnicking is permitted.
Retail Shop: Open during winery hours

(listed above) with wines and wine-related merchandise.
Credit Cards: None.
Access for Disabled: None.
Foreign Languages: None.
Getting There: From Mystic, New York, and the west: Take I-95 North to exit 91 (Stonington Borough). Turn left off exit ramp onto Taugwonk Rd., winery is 2.4 miles on the left. From Providence, Boston: Take I-95 South to exit 91; turn right off exit ramp onto Taugwonk Rd. and continue as above, 2.3 miles to winery on left. From Norwich, Hartford: Take Rte. 2 South to Stonington traffic circle; turn right (west) onto Rte. 184 for 2.3 miles. Turn left (south) onto Taugwonk Rd. Vineyard is .6 miles on right.

ಶಿ Nick Smith bought his property in late 1986 from Tom Clarke, who put in the vines in 1979. An investment banker with in-depth knowledge of wines, Smith built a new winery, filled it with stainless steel tanks and the finest imported oak barrels, and installed as winemaker McAndrew, formerly with Haight Vineyards. Storage capacity is now 12,500 cases; production is 3,000 cases annually. The combination has been a winning one: since first releases in 1987, Stonington has been bringing home medals in competitions. Visitors can also find Stonington wines in a number of Connecticut's top restaurants.

TO SEE & DO
Did you know that apple cider was one of America's earliest alcoholic drinks? While in Stonington, visitors can see where it was made long ago at Clyde's Cider Mill (North Stonington Rd.; tel: 203-536-3354), the last steam-powered cider mill in New England, in operation during the fall. Then take a moment to drink in the atmosphere of Stonington Borough, a delightful seaside village within the township of Stonington. Next, attention is turned to nearby Mystic (Rte. 27, 1 mile south of I-95), the old

whaling village where sailors once downed tumblers of rum and shipped off with it as well (Mystic Seaport Museum, open year-round; tel: 203-572-0711, and Mystic Marinelife Aquarium, I-95, exit 90; tel: 203-536-9631). In Groton is the U.S.S. *Nautilus* Memorial, Submarine Force Library, and Museum. Delve more deeply into southeastern Connecticut, and discover that these Mystic sights are part of a microcosm of all New England in this one small area. There is history, art, theater and music, golfing, whale watching, camping, rafting. A bumper crop of fun in one location! For details contact: Southeastern Connecticut Tourism District, 8 Mill Street, New London, Connecticut 06320 (tel: 203-444-2206 or 2357).

ACCOMMODATIONS
Randall's Ordinary
Route 2 (P.O. Box 243)
North Stonington, Connecticut 06359
Tel: 203-599-4540
Long known as a good restaurant located in a National Register of Historic Places landmark dating from 1685, with Colonial-costumed staff and open hearth cooking, Randall's Ordinary is now open also as a charming inn. The inn is located on twenty-seven acres, and innkeepers Cindy and Bill Clark have furnished it with four-poster beds and antiques. Additional rooms in the 1819 Terpenning barn. Modern bathrooms with whirlpool baths; Continental breakfast included in overnight stay. Open hearth breakfast available.

1833 House
33 Greenmanville Avenue
Mystic, Connecticut 06355
Tel: 203-572-0633
The atmosphere is appropriately historic at this B&B near the entrance to the Mystic Seaport Museum. You can see the tall ships from some of the rooms; Continental breakfast is served.

The Inn at Mystic
Junction of Routes 1 & 27
Mystic, Connecticut 06355
Tel: 203-536-9604
Pricey and interesting is this recently restored captain's home from 1904, with period furnishings and old seaport ambience, plus restaurant and seventy-room motel. Some rooms have such modern conveniences as Jacuzzis, and others have terrific views of the harbor—and verandas to enjoy them from.

Red Brook Inn
2800 Gold Star Highway (Box 237)
Old Mystic, Connecticut 06372
Tel: 203-572-0349
Two adjacent Colonial buildings make one cozy, comfortable inn. Authentic period antiques accent the interiors and sometimes "Colonial weekends" treat guests to the old-fashioned ways of open hearth cooking. Two miles from Mystic Seaport.

Taber Motor Inn & Guest House
Routes 1 and 27
Mystic, Connecticut 06355
Tel: 203-536-4904
Small, well-run motel and inn; not the run-of-the-motel variety.

RESTAURANTS
The Floodtide
The Inn at Mystic
Tel: 203-536-9406
Continental cuisine. Fresh lobster, duck; good wine cellar. Sun. brunch; daily buffet breakfast.

Noah's
115 Water Street
Stonington, Connecticut 06378
Tel: 203-535-3925
Casual atmosphere with excellent seafood, homemade pasta, tempting desserts. Connecticut wines.

Randall's Ordinary
Tel: 203-599-4540
(see under accommodations)

Hamlet Hill Vineyards

Route 101
Pomfret, Connecticut 06258
TEL: 203-928-5550
OWNERS: Henry Maubert and John
   Spritzer
WINEMAKER/CONSULTANT: Michel
   Castaing; Bordeaux, France
FOUNDED: 1975

AT A GLANCE
Tours & Tastings: In-depth one-hour
tours, guided or self-guided, start with a
fifteen-minute video covering every
phase of wine production from vineyard
to bottle. Then from a wraparound deck,
visitors see the various steps in winemaking as they occur, followed by a walk
through the adjacent experimental vineyard and a tasting of available wines.
Tours are scheduled when visitors arrive,
any time Mon.–Thurs. 10–5, Nov.–
March; 10–6, March–Nov.; Fri.–Sat. until 5, year-round.
Vineyards: Seventy-three acres, owned
and leased, planted to French hybrids
and viniferas. Expansion program underway with one hundred acres projected by
1993.
Wines: Seyval Blanc, extra dry reserve,
and Seyval Brut, dry Riesling, Chardonnay blush, and other blends are among
the most frequent releases. Production is
now in excess of 12,000 cases annually;
goal is 20,000.
Awards: Auburn Blush and Riesling are
among the gold medal winners.
Picnic Area: In shady groves; bring your
own or call ahead for an al fresco feast.
Retail Shop: Wines and wine-related
items, baskets, books, hampers.
Credit Cards: American Express, MasterCard, Visa.
Access for Disabled: Ramp to tasting
room; winery all on one level.
Foreign Languages: None.

Getting There: Between Mystic and
Sturbridge, Massachusetts. From New
London: Take I-395 North to Rte. 101
(exit 93) and turn left to Hamlet Hill.
Special Wine & Other Events: Springfest
and Harvest Open House.

&❦ Hamlet Hill makes you wonder if
you took the wrong turn and wandered
out of Connecticut and into the twenty-
first century. This sleek, space-age,
dome-topped winery resembles a styl-
ized twelve-sided wine storage tank—a
modern silhouette in the classical countryside. Inside, the latest winemaking
technology includes insulation that as-
sures a perfect temperature for aging
wine. The old is not completely forgotten—the winery offers visitors a walk
through a hundred-year-old oak cask.
New owners Maubert and Spritzer acquired this operation in late summer 1986
and installed French wine consultant
Castaing to oversee harvest and finishing.

❦ ❦ ❦

Nutmeg Vineyards

800 Bunker Hill Road (P.O. Box 146)
Andover, Connecticut 06232
TEL: 203-742-8402
OWNER/WINEMAKER: Anthony "Tony"
   Rosario Maulucci
FOUNDED: 1982

AT A GLANCE
Tours & Tastings: Tours Sat.–Sun. 11–5,
or by appointment or chance; tours are
self-guided at this rustic winery in a
beautiful rural area. Tastings conducted
by owner Maulucci.
Vineyards: Five acres to French hybrids;
berries also grown for wine.
Wines: Baco Noir, Seyval Blanc, Seyval
Sauterne, Antonio, full red blend ("our
best"); blueberry, strawberry, raspberry

wines. Also a Concord wine from the grape of the same name.

Awards: Raspberry, Baco Noir, and Sauterne all have won awards over the years.

Picnic Area: Picnicking permitted on heavily forested, well-maintained farmlands with a pretty pond.

Retail Shop: Sales during the tour and tasting times.

Credit Cards: None.

Access for Disabled: None.

Foreign Languages: None.

Getting There: In Tolland County, two miles off Rte. 6, in Andover, Connecticut, twenty miles northeast of Manchester, Connecticut. From Manchester, go to Bolton Notch, bear right on Rte. 6 toward Willimantic, continue for six miles. Take left on Bunker Hill Rd. after blinking yellow lights on Rte. 6. Two miles up Bunker Hill Rd. on left.

&. Tony Maulucci, a former tool and die maker, quested after something more from life. He got into a whole lot more when he turned 37.8 acres of raw wooded land into a farm winery—boulders, a swamp to turn into a pond, forested land he cleared partially, the balance managed for "the benefit of man and wildlife." From the 5-acre vineyard he planted in 1971, he turns out about 2,000 gallons annually of hand-crafted wines. Presently, new varieties created from experimental plantings show promise.

TO SEE & DO

Wine routes in northeast Connecticut require a full weekend to get the full flavor of this quiet area. For the two wineries and nearby sights allow a full day. Between the modernism of Hamlet Hill and the rustic charms of Nutmeg Vineyards lie a lot of unhurried pleasures. To name a few: the University of Connecticut at Storrs (Tel: 203-486-4520), with William Benton Art Museum (daily except holidays and between exhibitions) and Museum of Natural History (daily); and Nathan Hale Homestead, South Street,

Coventry, built in 1776. Also in Coventry is Caprilands Herb Farm (Silver St., off Rte. 44; seven days a week, 9–5), a huge repository of herbs and spices and a herb data bank, with forums and programs devoted to herb gardening, crafts, and Christmas decorating. Pomfret's Mashamoquet Brook State Park is the site of the Brayton Grist Mill and Marcy Blacksmith Museum (Rte. 44; May–Sept., Thurs. & Sat. 2–4, or by appointment; contact the Pomfret Historical Society, Pomfret Center, Connecticut 06259). Farther north, Woodstock combines a lot of history with an abundance of charm and is a good stop en route to popular Mystic Seaport in the southeast and Old Sturbridge Village, a 200-acre recreation of a nineteenth-century farm town just over the Massachusetts border.

Visit antique and crafts shops and save time to picnic beside a tree-shaded stream, relax in one of five state parks, or stride out on any of several famous hiking trails. For planning help, ask the Northeast Connecticut Visitors District (Box 9, Chase Rd., Thompson, Connecticut 06277; tel: 203-923-2998) for two handy pamphlets: "The Getaway Guide," with three driving tours taking in Hamlet Hill and Nutmeg Vineyards and many other sights, and "Hiking Connecticut's Blue Blazed Trails."

ACCOMMODATIONS

Bed & Breakfasts & Inns
Althhaveigh Inn
Route 195
Storrs, Connecticut 06268
Tel: 203-429-4490
Four rooms and a restaurant in a restored 250-year-old inn.

Cobbscroft
Routes 44 and 104
Pomfret, Connecticut 06258
Tel: 203-928-5560
Antiques and an art gallery in an 1800s home. Full breakfast.

Colonel Angell House
Wright's Crossing Road
R-2, Box 13
Pomfret Center, Connecticut 06259
Tel: 203-928-9257
1772 home and seventy-three acres, full breakfast.

The Inn at Woodstock Hill
Plaine Hill Road and Route 169
Woodstock, Connecticut 06267
Tel: 203-928-7587
Elegant country estate surrounded by acres of lush farmland; Continental breakfast included in rates; restaurant and bar.

Selah Farm
R.R. 1, Box 43
Pomfret Center, Connecticut 06259
Tel: 203-928-7051
Former country estate, extensive grounds and walking paths. Full breakfast. Hamlet Hill nearby.

Wintergreen
Routes 44 and 169 (R.F.D. 87AA)
Pomfret, Connecticut 06259
Tel: 203-928-5741
1800s home in a secluded area overlooking the valley; full breakfast.

Motels
Howard Johnson's
Off I-84
Vernon, Connecticut 06066
Tel: 203-875-0781; 800-654-2000
Sixty-four-unit, full-feature motel.

Quality Inn
Off I-84, 51 Hartford Turnpike
Vernon, Connecticut 06066
Tel: 203-646-5700; 800-228-5151
124-unit, full-feature motel.

RESTAURANTS
These all serve Hamlet Hill wines.

Bald Hill
Route 171
Woodstock, Connecticut 06267
Tel: 203-974-2240
In an old barn, fine country cooking with freshest ingredients is on the menu, which lists salmon and duck with raspberry sauce among the entrées; some pasta dishes. Well known for luscious truffle cake and marjolaine, a rich confection of meringue, chocolate, and other tempting ingredients.

Stables Restaurant
Putnam, Connecticut 06260
Tel: 203-928-0501
This restaurant was once a club house when Putnam Industrial park was a golf course. Old familiars, well prepared, include steak and fettucine Alfredo.

Vernon Stiles Inn
On the Common
Thompson, Connecticut 06277
Tel: 203-923-9571
Innovative menu. Crisp duckling a specialty as well as sole piccata and salmon. Rich desserts.

❧ MASSACHUSETTS

New fruit wines are a nice change of pace, but grape wines await visitors as our wine route sweeps up to Cape Cod and to Plymouth, where Pilgrims once made their wines. The Concord grape was developed near Concord by Ephraim Wates Bull from a wild grape.

Eastern Massachusetts

Chicama Vineyards

Stoney Hill Road
West Tisbury, Massachusetts 02575
TEL: 508-693-0309
OWNERS/WINEMAKERS: George and
Catherine Mathiesen; courses taken
at UC-Davis, Cornell University
FOUNDED: 1971

AT A GLANCE
Tours & Tastings: Apr.–May, Mon.–Sat.
1–5; June–Oct., Mon.–Sat. 11–5 & Sun.
1–5; Nov.–Dec., Mon.–Sat. 1–5; May
26–Sept. 29, Sun. 1–5. Twenty-to-thirty-
minute guided tours about every thirty
minutes by owners and their offspring,
aided in summer by specially trained college students.
Closed: Closed July 4th and Labor Day;
Jan., Feb., March open by appointment
only.
Vineyards: Thirty-five acres in Martha's
Vineyard v.a., planted to vinifera varieties including Chardonnay, Riesling,
Gewürztraminer, Pinot Noir, Cabernet
Sauvignon, Merlot. Zinfandel and Chenin Blanc purchased from California.
Wines: Varietals from the above grapes.
Satinet White (proprietary semi-sweet
Chenin); Sea Mist sparkling wine made
by *methode champenoise.*
Retail Shop: Wines and a selection of
winery-made herb and fruit wine vinegars, berry jams, mustards, and salad
dressings. Vineyard Haven and up-island
towns are dry; stock up here on wines for
restaurant dining.
Credit Cards: MasterCard, Visa.
Access for the Disabled: None.
Foreign Languages: None.
Getting There: From Vineyard Haven,
take state road southwest for 2¼ miles
and take winery turnoff down mile-long
dirt road. You can walk, taxi, rent a
moped, or bike. Cabs in Vineyard Haven

do not have meters; settle fare before you
get in. Be careful: mopeds skid on sand.
Special Wine & Other Events: Christmas
Shop at the winery Nov. 21–Dec. 24 11–
4; gifts for the wine lover and more—
stemware, wine accessories, wreaths,
and festive foods. Almost every day can
be special on the Vineyard with some
pleasant, relaxing activity—a book sale
or bake sale, bird walks or wildflower
walks. The "Martha's Vineyard Guide,"
free and available wherever tourists
are—which is to say everywhere—has
details.

&. George and Catherine Mathiesen
have been wine trailblazers in Massachusetts: in 1971, their vineyard in the
woods of West Tisbury was the first with
European wine grapes in the state since
Colonial days, and the following year it
became the first bonded winery in the
Commonwealth. Their weathered, gray-
shingled winery with fan-shaped window
harmonizes perfectly with the local architecture.
It has always been a family affair, with
the six Mathiesen kids pitching in, full-
time or part-time. Daughter Lynn apprenticed at Domaine Chandon, well-
known California producer of *methode
champenoise* wine, and now draws on
her knowledge to put the sparkles in Chicama's Sparkling Sea Mist. Son Tim, the
winery manager, learned from his parents about growing grapes and making
wine. Today Chicama's annual production is about 17,000 gallons, primarily of
still wines.

TO SEE & DO
People come to the twenty-mile-long island Martha's Vineyard, five miles south
of Woods Hole and eighty miles south of
Boston, to enjoy the glorious beaches. To

help see and feel the history of the area's earlier days, walking tours are the best way to explore the little towns. They are published in the "Martha's Vineyard Guide," mentioned earlier, with easy-to-follow maps to show visitors such landmarks in Vineyard Haven as Seaman's Bethel, Williams Street from the 1800s, and Tisbury Museum (Beach Road, across from fire station, Vineyard Haven, 1–5 P.M.). Walks in the booklet also guide visitors to naturalists' tours, as well as around Oak Bluffs and Edgartown, up-island, the location of Chicama Vineyards. Shopping and browsing in boutiques for island-crafted merchandise is given a high priority among pastimes on the Vineyard.

ACCOMMODATIONS
If you moved all the charming B&Bs and inns on Martha's Vineyard southeast to Rhode Island, they'd probably fill the entire state. Here, then, are a few:

Captain Dexter House
100 Main Street (Box 2457)
Vineyard Haven, Massachusetts 02568
Tel: 508-693-6564
A sea captain's house in 1834, now a delightful inn with period pieces, decked out with fresh flowers in summer and fireplaces for days that are crisp. Homemade breads, preserves, and seasonal fruits are served year-round as breakfast to guests.

Charlotte Inn
S. Summer Street
Edgartown, Massachusetts 02539
Tel: 508-627-4751
Twenty-five charming rooms in five houses, dating from 1802; antique-accented interiors, patios, large verandas, and lavish gardens. L'Etoile Restaurant (see "Restaurants").

Lambert Cove Country Inn
Lambert Cove Road
West Tisbury, Massachusetts 02568
Tel: 508-693-2298
Built in 1790, expanded in the 1920s, and loaded with the comforts of today. Rooms have been individually furnished and are either in the main house or the carriage house. Continental breakfast included in rates. Inn restaurant makes good use of island seafood and garden-fresh produce. Picnic lunches will be packed upon request. Private beach for guests.

RESTAURANTS
In Edgartown, except where indicated:

Brass Bass
162 Circuit Avenue
Oak Bluffs
Tel: 508-693-3300
Lunch, dinner, Sunday brunch. Specializes in seafood. Island's largest selection of wines and beers.

Edgar's
Off Katama Road
Tel: 508-627-8972
The hearty seafood stew *cioppino* is a specality, while the wine list has a number of California selections. Open May–Oct.

L'Etoile
Tel: 508-627-5187
S. Summer Street
Edgartown, Massachusetts 02539
Contemporary French menu in a Victorian setting with lovely garden for outdoor dining. Lamb, lobster, and game specialties. California wines. Open Feb. 15–Dec.

Martha's Restaurant
Main Street
Tel: 508-627-8316
Seafood, steak, and sushi bar. Wines.

Lunch, dinner, Sunday brunch. Major credit cards.

Warriner's
Post Office Square
Tel: 508-627-4488
European country cuisine; snowy white linens, fresh flowers, One hundred and thirty fine wines. Save room for dessert. Elegant and intimate atmosphere. Call for reservations. Major credit cards.

ዄ ዄ ዄ

Nashoba Valley Winery

100 Wattaquadoc Hill Road
Bolton, Massachusetts 01740
TEL: 508-779-5521
PRESIDENT: Jack Partridge
WINEMAKER: Larry Ames
FOUNDED: 1978

AT A GLANCE
Tours & Tastings: Mon.–Thurs. 11–6, self-guided; Sat.–Sun. guided. Winery tours every fifteen to thirty minutes, depending on season, show visitors the steps in fruit winemaking and include tasting of five wines. Self-guided orchard walking tour route is well marked with signs telling how fruits are grown and made into wine.
Orchards: Fifty-acre winery orchard, a veritable Eden with over sixty varieties of antique apple trees, as well as peaches, plums, cherries, strawberries, and raspberries; supplemented by Cape Cod cranberries and Maine blueberries. Wines range from dry to sweet and intensely fruity; several varietal apple wines as well as a *methode champenoise* sparkling apple wine, *brut* finished. Cyser (honey apple) is similar to mead.
Awards: Bumper crop includes gold medals for Dry and Semi-Dry Blueberry and After Dinner Peach; silvers for Cranberry-Apple, Medium-Dry Apple, Strawberry, Sparkling Apple, Pear; bronzes

and honorable mentions for most other wines.
Picnic Area: Tables under the trees.
Retail Shop: Wines, wine accessories, gift items, New England breads and cheeses; "A Partridge in Pear Sauce," winery's own cookbook.
Credit Cards: MasterCard, Visa.
Access for Disabled: Yes.
Foreign Languages: None.
Getting There: Forty-five minutes west of Boston. From I-485: Take Rte. 117 (exit 27) west 1 mile to Bolton Center. Turn left at the blinking light, ½ mile to winery.
Special Wine & Other Events: Sat. in early May: Apple Blossom Festival (orchard and winery tours; Morris dance teams, Bluegrass band, crafts, tug-of-war, and more); Sat. in June and July: "Music in the Orchard" concerts. "Pick Your Own Fruits" available (call for dates); cross-country skiing in orchards during the winter.

ዄ For a change, try Nashoba Valley, the first fruit winery in New England and one of the only orchards anywhere dedicated to growing fruits for wines. Jack Partridge started making fruit wines as a hobby until friends said he should sell them and he took their advice. Since then, he and winemaker Larry Ames have made fruit wine history with exciting new combinations and award-winning wines. The winery, built in 1984, stands in lush fields surrounded by fruit orchards and is equipped with the latest winemaking equipment. Nashoba's aim is to change the image of fruit wines from cloyingly sweet or ciderlike to elegant, serious food wines. Each wine label carries serving suggestions.

TO SEE & DO
Bolton is a pretty country town known for apple orchards, fruit stands, and antique shops. In adjoining Harvard are the Fruitlands Museums, with the eigh-

teenth-century home of Louisa May Alcott, plus separate museums devoted to the Shakers, the American Indian, and nineteenth-century artists (tel: 617-456-3924).

ACCOMMODATIONS

Bed and Breakfasts
Bed and Breakfast Associates—Bay Colony
P.O. Box 166, Babson Park
Boston, Massachusetts 02157
Tel: 617-449-5302
Coordinators will recommend B&Bs in Eastern Massachusetts.

The Carter-Washburn House
47 Seven Bridge Road
Lancaster, Massachusetts 05123
Tel: 508-263-8701
Gracious 150-year-old manor, transformed into a warm and friendly inn. A black cast-iron wood stove shares the same lounge with a TV/VCR and trivia games. Sumptuous breakfast may come with blueberry muffins or baked apples from local farmers' fruits. All this is just off Rte. 2, forty minutes west of Boston.

Sherman-Berry House
163 Dartmouth Street
Lowell, Massachusetts 01851
Tel: 508-459-4760
Victorian home from 1893, filled with antiques and stained glass. In a historic area, near a park designed by Frederick Olmsted. Continental breakfast; sherry served in the afternoon. Twenty minutes west of Boston.

Hotel
Sheraton Boxborough Inn
242 Sheraton Road
Boxborough, Massachusetts 01719
Tel: 508-263-8701; 800-325-3535
143 units, with tennis, indoor and outdoor pools, restaurant.

ᶻᵃ ᶻᵃ ᶻᵃ

Plymouth Colony Winery

Pinewood Road
Plymouth, Massachusetts 02360
TEL: 508-747-3334
OWNER: A. Charles Caranci, Jr.
WINEMAKER: John LeBeck
FOUNDED: 1983

At a Glance
Tours & Tastings: Mon.–Sat. 10–5; Sun. 12–5.
Vineyards: Six acres planted to French-American and American hybrids and vinifera varieties, surrounding ten-acre cranberry bog.
Wines: Cranberry-raspberry blend and Cranberry Grandé; Chardonnay, Riesling, Seyval, Cayuga, and Aurora varietals; white blends under Bog Blanc and Whalewatch White labels. Total production: 3,500 cases per year.
Awards: Best of show for Cranberry-Raspberry and silver for Cranberry Grandé in 1987 New England competition.
Picnic Area: On the grounds, especially attractive in late April when the bogs blossom.
Retail Shop: Sells wines.
Credit Cards: MasterCard, Visa.
Access for Disabled: None.
Foreign Languages: None.
Getting There: From Boston: Take Rte. 3 for a forty-five-minute scenic coastline ride to exit 6. Turn west and follow Rte. 44 to Pinewood Rd. Winery is about three miles south of Plymouth.
Special Wine & Other Events: Cranberry Harvest Festival in Oct.

ᶻᵃ Well-respected winemaker, John LeBeck, with twenty years experience in turning out some of New York State's most praiseworthy wines, now focuses on doing the same in Massachusetts. His cranberry-raspberry wine tastes somewhat like the French liqueur Chambord and is much desired by fanciers of luscious dessert wines. The winery, in a former cranberry screening house dating from 1890, is located in the center of a huge cranberry bog.

TO SEE AND DO

This is Plymouth, Massachusetts—the Rock, the Mayflower, and Plimouth Plantation are to be seen. It's a good stopping-off point en route to the Cape as well.

ACCOMMODATIONS

Be Our Guest Bed & Breakfast
P.O. Box 1333
Plymouth, Massachusetts 02360
Tel: 508-545-6680
Both of these resources will locate B&Bs in Plymouth to suit your taste, historic to traditional.

Western Massachusetts

Huntington Cellars

Route 66
Huntington, Massachusetts 01050
TEL: 413-667-5561
PARTNERS: Marie B. and Chester S. Wilusz, Jr.
WINEMAKER: Chester Wilusz, Jr.
FOUNDED: 1983

AT A GLANCE

Tours & Tastings: Sat.–Sun. 1–6; explanation of winemaking and tasting.
Closed: Jan.–June 1.
Vineyards: French hybrids, viniferas, and American varieties are purchased from California and New York growers.
Wines: Concord, Rougeon, Marechal Foch, Zinfandel.
Retail Shop: Wines sold.
Credit Cards: None.
Access for the Disabled: None.
Foreign Languages: None.
Getting There: Winery is thirty miles northeast of Northampton. Take Rte. 66 west to Huntington Cellars, which is several miles north of Huntington.

❦ This small mom-and-pop winery started as a hobby and grew into a family business; the Wiluszes want it known that their wines are made naturally, without artificial preservatives, and are aged in oak barrels.

TO SEE & DO

At any season, enjoying the grape need not stop at the winery door. Big Y Wines (I-91, Northampton) is a necessary stop on any wine enthusiast's tour. This extraordinary football field–size store is stocked with the wines of the world at wide-ranging prices. The domestics include those rarely seen away from their home bases. Shoppers also flock here from faraway places.

For varied pleasures, the 225 square miles of western Massachusetts's picturesque Hampshire Hills, wine routes enter higher education territory. In Northampton, South Hadley, and Amherst are five colleges and universities, many small towns with fine shops, and cozy places to stay and eat—all within an hour or so of each other. Or head west to the Berkshires, famed home of Tanglewood, Jacob's Pillow, and Norman Rockwell to the south, in the Stockbridge/Lenox area; or, to the north, Sterling Clark Museum and the Williamstown Summer Theater in Williamstown. In both areas, enjoy hiking, skiing, and beautiful vistas around each bend in your wine route whenever you go, especially during colorful fall foliage time.

ACCOMMODATIONS

A variety of bed and breakfast accommodations are available in both Hampshire Hills and the Berkshires. For information on them, contact:

Bed & Breakfast
Box 307
Williamstown, Massachusetts
   01096-0211
Write for pamphlet describing homes and hosts.

Berkshire Bed & Breakfast Homes
Main Street
Williamstown, Massachusetts
   01096-0211
Tel: 413-268-7244
Listings for host homes in western Massachusetts hills and towns and surrounding areas.

Nearest to Huntington Cellars is:
Robert and Barbara Paulson
Allen Coit Road
Huntington, Massachusetts 01050
Tel: 413-667-3208
Guests stay in the solar wing of the Paulsons' home, overlooking the Hampshire Hills. This wing contains a library, a screened porch, a loft room with double and single beds, and another room for sleeping bag travelers. Full American breakfast. Hiking and ice skating at your doorstep, and a good used book shop on premises. The Paulsons are off Rte. 66 near the Westhampton/Huntington line.

Hotel
Hotel Northampton
63 King Street
Northampton, Massachusetts 01060
Tel: 413-584-3100
A revitalized 1927 hotel, tastefully furnished, with larger rooms to the rear. Continental breakfast included in rates.

Wiggins Tavern restaurant on premises. Hotel booked a year in advance for Smith College graduation, parents' weekend.

RESTAURANTS
Beardsley's Cafe
140 Main Street
Northampton, Massachusetts 01060
Tel: 413-586-2699
Appropriately, Aubrey Beardsley's artwork is hung at Beardsley's Cafe, where the decor is Edwardian, the foods French, and the wine list features California and Oregon but no local vintages. Specialties include fresh game birds, grilled salmon, and baked goods made on the premises. Closed major holidays.

Christmas Inn Restaurant
4 Main Street
Williamstown, Massachusetts 01096
Tel: 413-268-7511
Always serves turkey and all the trimmings in perpetually Christmas decor; also fish and ribs. Wine list has California selections. Closed Dec. 24.

Gateways Inn
71 Walker Street
Lenox, Massachusetts 01240
Tel: 413-637-2532
Well-appointed 1920s mansion where owner-chef shows a real flare for shrimp and salmon entrées, delicious pastries. American wine list includes California, Oregon, Idaho, New York, and Massachusetts.

The Colonial Inn at Huntington
Route 122
Tel: 413-667-8737
Early American setting for intimate dining; beef, poultry, and seafood dishes.

ஃ MAINE

Maine's wine routes lead far "Down East" to two Maine farm wineries, both dedicated to showing the world that fruit can make serious, elegant wines. Produced in beautiful rustic settings, they are gaining increasing acceptance among sophisticated consumers.

ஃ ஃ ஃ

Bartlett Maine Estate Winery

Route 1 (R.R. #1, Box 598)
Gouldsboro, Maine 04607
TEL: 207-546-2408
OWNERS: Bob and Kathe Bartlett
WINEMAKER: Bob Bartlett

AT A GLANCE

Tours & Tastings: Open June 1–Oct. 30, Thanksgiving–Christmas; Tues.–Sat. 10–5, Sun. 12–5; by appointment balance of year. Offers tour of winery and description of year-round operation; tasting conducted by Kathe Bartlett.
Orchards: Fruits purchased from Maine growers.
Wines: Dry and semi-sweet fruit wines from freshly harvested wild blueberries, apples, pears, strawberries, raspberries; honey wine. *Methode champenoise* apple-pear wine available at Christmas.
Awards: Bartlett's wines have walked off with multiple medals in both the International Eastern Wine and the New England Wine competitions. Most frequent winner, the Blueberry Semi-Sweet, with Blueberry Dry, Coastal Red, and Apple Semi-Sweet and Dry also cited.
Retail Shop: Wines are sold on site.
Credit Cards: American Express.
Access for the Disabled: "Can be accommodated."
Foreign Languages: None.
Getting There: Twenty-three miles east of Ellsworth on U.S. Rte. 1.
Special Wine & Other Events: Second week in Oct., Winter Harbor Lobster Festival.

ஃ Bob and Kathe Bartlett opened Maine's first commercial winery in 1982, in their handsome modern home built of native stone and wood. Their dream was to plant a vineyard and start a winery. When suitable grapes failed to flourish in this northern clime, they decided to give local fruits a try, and the result has been a history of award-winning fruit wines. During the holiday season, the Bartletts release their Nouveau Blueberry, made in the same way as the French Nouveau Beaujolais, accompanied by the same fanfare as the French wine, to which it has been favorably compared. To meet the increased demand for their wines, they've stepped up production to the point of having to decide whether to move their home away from the winery or vice versa.

TO SEE & DO

A stone's throw away is the less-visited Schoodic Point section of Acadia National Park, as well as the colorful seaside villages of Winter Harbor, Prospect Harbor, and Corea. Head back to Ellsworth, then south on Rte. 3 for the delights of Bar Harbor and Mt. Desert Island and the next winery.

ACCOMMODATIONS

Bed & Breakfast Down East, Ltd.
Box 547, Macomber Mill Road
Eastbrook, Maine 04634
Tel: 207-565-3517
Recommendations for bed and breakfast accommodations throughout Maine.

Sunset House
Route 186
West Gouldsboro, Maine 04607
Tel: 207-963-7156
Dan and Ruth Harper, a warm and hospitable couple, take visitors into their late Victorian three-story home, June to September. Seven spacious bedrooms overlook either ocean or pond. Awaken to a big Maine breakfast with fruit, eggs, fresh-baked goods, and coffee or tea.

🐚 🐚 🐚

Downeast Country Wines

Route 3 (Bar Harbor Road)
Trenton, Maine 04605
TEL: 207-667-6965
CEO: Don Mead
PRESIDENT & WINEMAKER: R. Alison
Wampler
FOUNDED: 1983

AT A GLANCE
Tours & Tastings: Summer, 9:30–6, Mon.–Sat., Sun., 1–5; winter, generally, 10–4 Tues.–Sat., but call beforehand to check. Guided tours all day show steps in winemaking process. "Always something interesting to see here," says Mead.
Orchards: Fruits purchased are Washington County blueberries, Hancock County Apples.
Wines: Semi-sweet Wild Blueberry dessert wine, Dry Wild Blueberry and Sweet Spiced Apple wines, Blue Blush, a blend of blueberry and apple.
Awards: 1988 New England Competition: gold to Spiced Apple, silvers to both blueberry wines; 1988 International Competition: first medal ever given to a blueberry wine—a bronze, went to Downeast's Dry Wild Blueberry.
Retail Shop: Wines and wine accessories.
Access for Disabled: Yes.
Foreign Languages: None.
Getting There: From Ellsworth, take Rte. 3 (Bar Harbor) and enjoy the scenery from Hulls Cove on to the winery located on Rte. 3 and marked with a large sign.
Special Wine & Other Events: Arcady Music Festival sponsor, where Downeast wines are served. Plans to host concerts at winery beginning 1989. In Bar Harbor, Art Exhibit, third weekend in July and Aug., Art Exhibit on Village Green; third weekend in Sept., Marathon Race, Athletic Field.

🐚 Downeast started in Pembroke before moving to its current site, a 100-year-old former blacksmith's shop, redone by Wampler whose background includes the graphic arts. Though the winery now blends old and new, the winemaking is still done the old-fashioned way from traditional recipes going back generations. Recipes have been modified for modern tastes, their original character has been retained by using the old winemaking techniques. Even with current production at 50,000 gallons annually, wines are still made in small lots in barrels holding no more than 60 gallons.

TO SEE & DO
The main town of Mount Desert Island, Bar Harbor, is one of the nation's great holiday resorts and is a good reason to tarry in this area. In season (mid-May through mid-Oct.) Bar Harbor offers a galaxy of attractions, from shops and restaurants, to shows, lectures, and festivals. From Bar Harbor, a grab bag of possibilities includes hopping the Blue Nose Ferry to Nova Scotia or exploring more of vast Acadia National Park, with its spectacular landscapes and seascapes at every turn, whether driving along the shore or standing atop Mt. Cadillac. This huge park has hiking and horseback trails, jogging paths, bicycling, and cross country skiing. Immensely popular (only the Smokies get more visitors), the park is best visited early in June or September when the mass of tourists are not around. (For the Schoodic Point section of

Acadia National Park, see after Bartlett Estate Winery.)

For more information, contact the Chamber of Commerce, 93 College St., P.O. Box 158, Bar Harbor 04609 Tel: 207-288-5103; for Acadia National Park, contact the Superintendent, P.O. Box 177, Bar Harbor 04609, Tel: 207-288-3338.

Indoor-outdoor experiences combine at Stanwood Museum and Birdacre Wildlife Sanctuary (Bar Harbor, Rte. 3, Tel: 207-667-8460), which encompasses 100 acres and includes ornithological exhibits in the former home of early ornithologist-writer-photographer Cordelia Stanwood; the sanctuary includes shelters for injured birds. Sanctuary is open daily from mid-June through mid-Oct. Picnic sites, trails open all year.

Nearby Ellsworth, settled in 1763, destroyed by fire in 1933 and thoughtfully rebuilt to blend the old with the new, offers historic diversions: John Black Mansion, dating from 1820 (W. Main St., Tel: 207-667-8671), a Georgian-style mansion with well-tended gardens and carriage house with carriages and sleighs (June–mid-Oct., Mon.–Sat.), Tisdale House (46 State St. Tel: 207-667-2307), now the city's library, was an early Republic House (Tues.–Sat., closed holidays). Lamoine State Park (Memorial Day–Labor Day, Tel: 207-667-4778) is a popular place for a picnic.

For more information contact the Chamber of Commerce, High St., P.O. Box 267, Ellsworth, Maine 04605, Tel: 207-667-5584.

ACCOMMODATIONS

This major resort area offers a large selection of places to stay and eat that go far beyond the space alloted in this book. A few choices follow that offer visitors something a little out of the ordinary in one way or another. Rates lower in May, June, September, October; lowest in winter. (For Bed & Breakfasts, see after Bartlett Estate Winery.)

Motels

Bay Ledge Motel & Spa
1385 Sand Point Road
Bar Harbor, Maine 04609
Tel: 207-288-4204
Comfortable motel offers each overnight guest a gift bottle of Downeast Wine.

Wonder View
Eden Street
Bar Harbor, Maine 04609
Tel: 207-288-3358; 800-341-1553.
Eighty-two rooms, many with balconies and bay views. Rinehart Dining Pavilion on site; Closed Nov.–mid-May.

Inns

Bay View Inn
111 Eden Street
Bar Harbor, Maine 04609
Tel: 207-288-3173; 800-356-3585
Deluxe resort consisting of a twenty-six-room hotel, six-room inn, and six two- and three-bedroom townhouses. Quiet elegance and a dining room presided over by a talented French chef. Open May–Oct.

Cleftstone Manor
92 Eden Street
Bar Harbor, Maine 04609
Tel: 207-288-4951
Built by the Blair family, best known for Blair House in Washington, D.C., formerly a guest house for heads of state. This late 1800s Victorian has a romantic air. Comfortable rooms with down quilts and some fireplaces. Cheery wicker sunroom. Wine and cheese served after dinner. Picnic places on the grounds. Open mid-May–mid-Oct.

Colonial Motor Lodge
Bar Harbor Road
Ellsworth, Maine 04605
Tel: 207-667-5548
Seventy-eight-room two-story motel, heated pool, and complimentary conti-

nental breakfast. Peak season rates July–Labor Day.

RESTAURANTS
Two among many serving Downeast wines.

Rinehart Dining Pavilion
Eden Street
Bar Harbor, Maine 04609
Tel: 207-288-5663

Former home of mystery writer Mary Roberts Rinehart; serves Italian dishes as well as seafood and ribs. Wine list. Closed Nov.–Apr. (In Wonderview Motel).

Hilltop House
Bar Harbor Road
Ellsworth, Maine 04605
Steak, seafood, pizza. Own baked goods.

❧ NEW HAMPSHIRE

The New Hampshire Winery

Hwy 107 (RFD 6, Box 218)
Laconia, New Hampshire 03246
TEL: 603-524-0174
OWNERS: The Howard Family
FOUNDED: 1986

AT A GLANCE
Tours & Tastings: June 15–Oct. 15, daily, 1–4; Weekends and holidays by appt. only.
Closed: Oct. 15–June 15.
Vineyards: Purchases grapes from local growers.
Wines: Marechal Foch, Blush, Mountain Red, a blend; Apple, Raspberry, and Strawberry dessert wines.
Retail Shop: Wines and gift items.
Credit Cards: None.
Getting There: From Gilmanton Corners, take Hwy. 107 northwest to winery; from Laconia, take Hwy. 107 southeast to winery.

❧ This is New England's as well as New Hampshire's first winery and is now the only winery in the state. Closed for three years, new owners took it over in 1986. In addition to wines, the Howards produce Rock Maple Liqueur, which they say is the original American liqueur of New England, and Switchel, an old-time nonalcoholic drink with an apple cider vinegar base. The liqueur cannot by law be sold at the winery (it is above 60 proof), but is available in package stores.

TO SEE & DO
Laconia is in the center of the Lakes Region. Boat cruises, departing from Wiers Beach and Wolfboro (daily May 21–Oct. 16), moonlight cruises (July–Labor Day) offer pleasant ways to while away the time. Lots of good swimming and boating, too. (For more information, call the Greater Laconia Chamber of Commerce, 9 Veterans Sq., Laconia, New Hampshire 03246, Tel: 603-524-5531.)

ACCOMMODATIONS
Gunstock Inn & Mountain Air Health Club
RFD 4 Box 494
Gilford, New Hampshire 03246
Tel: 603-293-2021; reservations,
    800-654-0180 (New England only)
Intimate 27-room inn open July–October; indoor pool, health club; café.

Margate
76 Lake Street
Laconia, New Hampshire 03246
Tel: 603-524-5210; 800-258-0304 or 0305
  (excluding NH)
146-room motel with a host of amenities;
private beach, rowboats, and boat dock.

RESTAURANTS
Blackstones
76 Lake Street
Laconia, New Hampshire 03246
Tel: 603-524-7060

Garden-surrounded restaurant with peaceful courtyard; fresh seafood among the specialties. Wine list with California selections. Jacket required.

Hickory Stick Farm
2 miles southwest of Laconia
Tel: 603-524-3333
A Colonial farmhouse that is now a charming restaurant and gift shop. Try the duckling. Wine list. Plans to introduce new New Hampshire wines; has California selections.

❧ RHODE ISLAND

Winemakers have settled here because the growing conditions are similar to those in Burgundy and Bordeaux; their goal is to make fine European-style wines from their vineyards. Wine routes can take you to see if they are succeeding and to picturesque communities as well as historic Newport.

❧ ❧ ❧

Diamond Hill Vineyards

3145 Diamond Hill Road
Cumberland, Rhode Island 02864
TEL: 401-333-2751
OWNERS: Peter and Clara E. Berntson
FOUNDED: 1976

AT A GLANCE
Tours & Tastings: By appointment only. A walking tour of the grounds with unusual horticultural plantings, vineyard winery, tasting.
Vineyards: Five acres planted solely to Pinot Noir, some orchard fruits purchased from the Northwest.
Wines: Pinot Noir, Apple, Blueberry, Peach, Raspberry, and Strawberry.
Awards: Gold to Apple.
Retail Shop: Wines sold on-site.
Credit Cards: None.

Access for the Disabled: None.
Foreign Languages: French.
Getting There: Twenty miles north of Providence. From I-295: Take exit 11, go two miles north on Rte. 114, to sign on right.

❧ Clara and Peter Berntson planted their vineyard in 1976 and have pursued one goal ever since: to make a fine Pinot Noir from their own grapes. Their viticultural conditions are the same as those in France for this great but finicky Burgundian grape.

The winery is a new post-and-beam building, built to blend in with the Berntson's eighteenth-altered-in-the-nineteenth-century home. Peter developed a love of fine wine while living in France. While waiting for the Pinot Noir to age, the couple turns out well-regarded fruit wines.

TO SEE & DO

The northeastern corner of Rhode Island is the site of Diamond Hill State Park, Diamond Hill Reservoir, and Ski Valley Skiing Area. Providence, the state capital, is twenty miles south and is well known for Brown University and a number of colleges and universities.

ACCOMMODATIONS

Bed and Breakfast of Rhode Island
P.O. Box 3291
Newport, Rhode Island 02840
Tel: 401-849-1298
Coordinators will try to set you up in a bed and breakfast that fits you to a T—historic, modern, whatever you desire.

Holiday Inns (800-HOLIDAY) are represented in both Providence and N. Attleboro, Massachusetts: Sheraton (tel: 800-325-3535) is in Mansfield; Howard Johnson's Motor Lodges (tel: 800-654-2000) in Pawtucket.

ια ια ια

Sakonnet Vineyards

162 West Main Road (P.O. Box 572)
Little Compton, Rhode Island 02837
TEL: 401-635-4356
OWNERS: Earl and Susan Sampson
WINEMAKER: Jim Amaral
CONSULTANT: John Williams, ex-
    winemaker, Spring Mountain "Falcon
    Crest" Vineyards.
FOUNDED: 1975

AT A GLANCE

Tours & Tastings: Open year round, 7 days a week. Guided tours and self-guided vineyard walk and tastings, Apr. through Oct., 10 to 6; Nov.–Mar., 11–5, tours by appointment.
Vineyard: 25 acres working, planted to vinifera and French Hybrid varieties; 10 acres to be developed.
Wines: Eleven varietal and blended wines, include Chardonnay, Gewurztra-miner, Seyval Blanc and dry Vidal Blanc, among others.
Awards: '89 New England Wine Competition for '87 Dry Vidal Blanc, '87 Gewurztraminer.
Picnic Area: Available in summer, as are chilled wines; shops and fruit stands nearby sell fresh-made, fresh-grown foods.
Retail Shop: About 20 percent of releases sold on site.
Credit Cards: MasterCard, Visa.
Foreign Languages: Some French.
Getting There: Southeastern corner of Rhode Island, approximately 8 miles south of intersection Rtes. 24 & 77. Continuing south on Rte. 77, the entrance is on the left, 2.9 miles past the traffic signal at Tiverton Four Corners.
Special Wine & Other Events: Sakonnet Chefs Program offers three-day classes with accomplished guest chefs; write winery for details.

ια The Sampsons (he's in business in New York, with a California wine background and she's in the theater) bought this winery in 1987 when it was 13 years old and set about making some changes. Among them planting some Cabernet Franc in the vineyard. Their extended growing season, of course, remains the same: it's about two months longer than average, thanks to the moderating influence of the water. The vineyard's fan club, set up earlier, continues as well and those who buy vine rights get a case of wine each year and invitations to special events. Most unusual here is a dry Vidal Blanc. The low sprawling modern winery looks over tree-studded grounds, and current production is 22,000 gallons annually.

Vineland Wine Cellars

909 East Main Road
Middletown, Rhode Island 02840
TEL: 401-848-5161

Jim Amaral, Sakonnet's winemaker, suggests a visit to this new winery which is "right around the corner from his." Call for full details

TO SEE & DO

Little Compton is a restful beach area. From here, it's a breeze to get to the famous resort town of Newport, with its fabled mansions-turned-museums and traditional resort amusements as well—shops, restaurants, water sports, theater, concerts. The Tennis Hall of Fame and America's Cup Races are also Newport attractions. Peak season extends from July through Labor Day. For more information, write: Newport County Chamber of Commerce, P.O. Box 237 MTG, Newport, Rhode Island 02840; tel: 401-847-1600.

ACCOMMODATIONS

The Stone House Club
Little Compton, Rhode Island 02837
Tel: 401-635-2222
Twelve rooms on the ocean; private club welcomes guests introduced by the winery.

Newport offers choices too numerous to list here. Wherever you stay, make reservations early if traveling July to Labor Day, and expect high rates from June through September. Three suggestions are:

The Pilgrim House
123 Spring Street
Newport, Rhode Island 02840
Tel: 401-846-0040
A centrally located Victorian home with attractive period furniture. The third-floor porch is a perfect vantage point for harbor watching.

The Inn at Castle Hill
Ocean Drive
Newport, Rhode Island 02840
Tel: 401-849-3800
One of Newport's most popular inns.

Dates from 1874 and has opulently furnished rooms in the main house, often booked months ahead by regulars, and less elegant rooms in the old servant quarters. Excellent food is another attraction.

The Melville House
39 Clarke Street
Newport, Rhode Island 02840
Tel: 401-847-0640
This eighteenth-century house in a garden is all done up in appropriate Colonial style. A breakfast with homemade muffins and granola is a delicious attraction. Convenient to waterfront and charter boats.

RESTAURANTS

Sakonnet wines are served as specially labeled house wines at the following two restaurants:

Le Bistro
Bowen's Wharf
(off America's Cup Avenue)
Newport, Rhode Island 02840
Tel: 401-849-7778
Fresh seafood and delicious desserts.

Candleworks
New Bedford, Massachusetts 02741
Tel: 617-992-1635
Veal, seafood, poultry; emphasizing fresh New England ingredients.

ð ð ð

Prudence Island Vineyards

Sunset Hill Farm
Prudence Island, Rhode Island 02872
TEL: 401-683-2452
If you have time and a sense of adventure, you might want to visit this winery located on a rather remote island in Narragansett Bay. Chardonnay and Pinot Noir are main vines in the all-vinifera

vineyard, making wines of good reputation. From May 30 to Labor Day, you can drop in for tours and tastings, 10 A.M. to noon; 2 to 5 P.M.; after Labor Day, week-ends 10–3:30. Ferry service from both Bristol and Melville. Call winery for directions and schedules.

❧ VERMONT

This is the place to go to drink in sophisticated fruit wines while enjoying more than a sip of country pleasures.

North River Winery

River Road, Route 112
Jacksonville, Vermont 05342
TEL: 802-368-7557
OWNER/WINEMAKER: Edward Metcalfe, Jr.
FOUNDED: 1985

AT A GLANCE
Tours & Tastings: May–Oct. 31, 11–6 Mon & Wed–Sun.; Nov.–Apr. 30, 11–5 Fri.–Sun. Visitors are informally shown equipment; winemaking and tasting are explained.
Orchards: Apples, peaches, blackberries, raspberries; some additional fruits purchased from Vermont orchards.
Wines: Dry dinner-style fruit wines include Apple, Raspberry-Apple, Apple-Maple, Honey-Apple, Blackberry. Annual production around 5,000 gallons.
Awards: Green Mountain Apple, a blend of four different apples, quality award in International Eastern Wine Competition.
Retail Shop: Wines sold on-site.
Credit Cards: None.
Access for the Disabled: Wheelchair accessible.
Foreign Languages: "Spanish at times."
Getting There: Winery is equidistant from Brattleboro; Bennington; North Adams, Massachusetts; and Greenfield, Massachusetts—all thirty-five minutes (twenty to twenty-five miles) away. From Wilmington, six miles away: Take Rte. 100 South to Jacksonville, Vermont and River Road. From Brattleboro: Take Rte. 9 West to Rte. 100 and turn south. From Bennington: Take Rte. 9 East to Rte. 100 and turn south as above. Hilly but nice biking area. Bike rentals and advice on best routes: Valley Cyclery, Main Street, Wilmington (tel: 803-464-2728); Red Circle's Vermont Gift Center, Brattleboro (tel: 803-254-4933).

❧ Shaded by sugar maples, North River Winery is located in the foothills of Windham County and set along its namesake river—a sight to behold, especially in fall. The farmhouse and winery were built in the 1880s. Metcalfe is dedicated to producing dry fruit wines that compare favorably with top European grape wines.

TO SEE & DO
The wine route is now in Windham County, set between the Connecticut River and the Green Mountains. This is the place to ponder the beauties of nature and be surrounded by the familiar farmland of New England postcard scenes—here a red barn, there a covered bridge, and everywhere a rolling field. In the summer the hills are literally alive with music, with concerts at Marlboro, Brattleboro, and Putney—just three of the delightful towns in addition to Wilmington, West Dover, Newfane, Grafton, and Saxtons River. Throughout the year, there's a bushel of things to do and see: crafts and

antique shops, downhill and cross-country skiing, fall foliage trails, country markets, and more. For details, contact: Brattleboro Chamber of Commerce, 180 Main Street, Brattleboro, Vermont 05301 (tel: 802-254-4565).

ACCOMMODATIONS

The Birchtree Inn
Route 100
Wilmington, Vermont 05363
Tel: 802-464-7707
Bed and breakfast inn; eight guest rooms.

The Hermitage
Coldbrook Road
Wilmington, Vermont 05363
Tel: 802-464-3511
The eighteenth-century feeling is preserved in rooms furnished with antiques; guests have a choice of main house or carriage house accommodations. Game birds are raised here, and game is frequently on the menu—as is trout from the well-stocked stream. 30,000-bottle cellar, Vermont apple wine upon request. Oregon, Washington, California on list.

Brook Bound Lodge
Coldbrook Road
Wilmington, Vermont 05363
Tel: 802-464-5267
Not a romantic getaway, but a place where everyone gets to know everyone—especially at meals at long wooden tables with food passed on platters. Managed by Hermitage.

Misty Mountain Lodge
Stowe Hill Road (P.O. Box 114)
Wilmington, Vermont 05363
Tel: 802-464-3961
A former farm turned into an off-the-beaten-path inn, with friendly atmosphere where everyone mingles. Known for delicious, hearty meals.

Nutmeg Inn
Route 9 (Box 818)
Wilmington, Vermont 05363
Tel: 805-464-3351
A warm and friendly farmhouse with patchwork quilts on the beds and simple charm throughout.

White House of Wilmington
Vermont Hwy. 9 (Box 757)
Tel: 802-464-2135
Intimate twelve-room inn with valley view and continental-style menu in Colonial café. Wine list, with California selections.

RESTAURANTS
The best bets for well-prepared foods and wines are the places to eat in the inns mentioned above. Especially well regarded is The Hermitage.

3
New York State

Bully Hill Vineyards, Hammondsport, New York

New York, one of the first states to produce wines, has long been characterized by labrusca grapes, but the image is peeling away as wineries have changed with the times. Vintners statewide are turning out first-rate classic European-style wines. While still around, most labruscas are headed for coolers and juices-although some still turn up in wines.

With an average crush of 70,000 tons of grapes from over 1,000 growers, New York is in second place when it comes to production of grapes and wines, far behind California, the largest producer. Currently, there are eighty-nine wineries statewide, and as the print appears on this page, there may be more—so often do new entries come into the field. Indeed, seventy-three new wineries have been established since the Farm Winery Act was passed in 1976. According to the New York Wine and Grape Foundation, New York State wineries produce about 30 million gallons of wine, generating gross revenues in excess of $300 million.

New York's main wine territory is upstate, where there are forty-five wineries in two viticultural areas—Finger Lakes District and Cayuga Lake—plus the Lake Erie District with eight wineries and its own v.a. The Hudson River Region v.a. is burgeoning with twenty-one wineries, and Long Island has

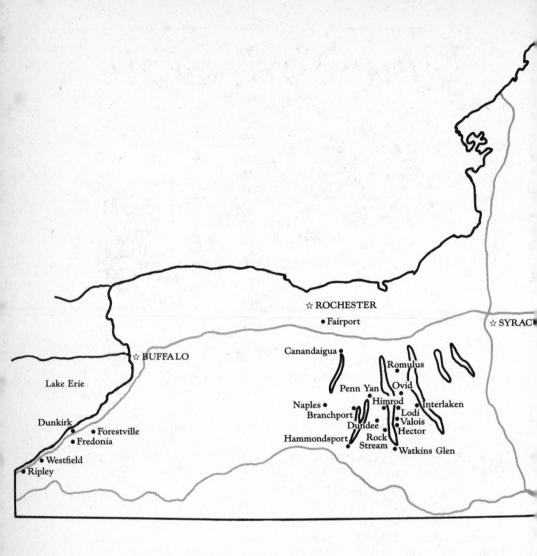

☆ ROCHESTER

● Fairport

Canandaigua ●

☆ SYRAC

☆ BUFFALO

Romulus

Lake Erie

Penn Yan   Ovid

Naples ●   Himrod   Interlaken

Branchport   Lodi

Dunkirk   Dundee   Valois

● Forestville   Hector

● Fredonia   Hammondsport ●   Rock

Stream   Watkins Glen

● Westfield

● Ripley

NEW
YORK
STATE

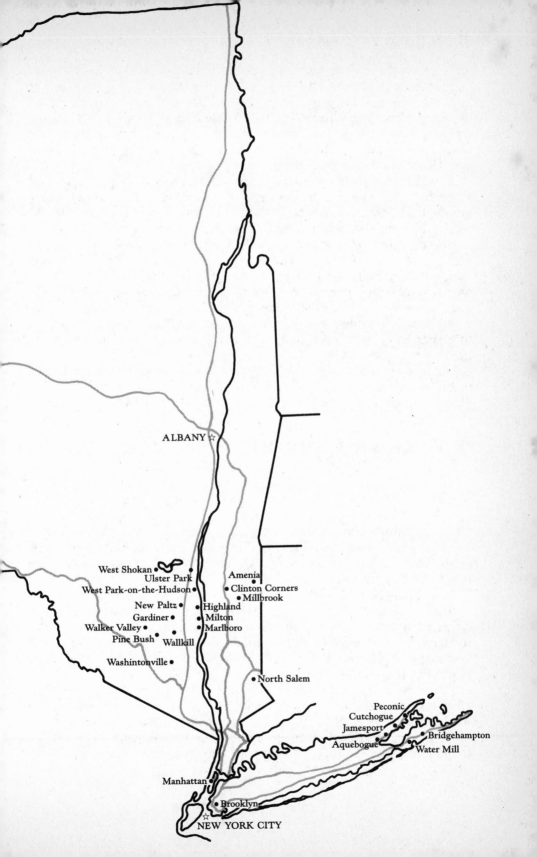

West Shokan •
Ulster Park •
West Park-on-the-Hudson •
New Paltz •
Gardiner •
Walker Valley •
Pine Bush •
Wallkill •
Washintonville •

Amenia •
Clinton Corners •
Millbrook •
Highland •
Milton •
Marlboro •

North Salem •

ALBANY ☆

Peconic •
Cutchogue •
Jamesport •
Aquebogue •
Bridgehampton •
Water Mill •

Manhattan •
Brooklyn •
☆ NEW YORK CITY

fourteen wineries in two v.a.'s, the Hamptons and North Fork and there are three wineries in New York City. As you may know, v.a.'s are federally designated regions characterized by such factors as climate and soil that set them apart from the surrounding area. While each of New York's v.a.'s has unique qualities, they share a common denominator: the influence of bodies of water on their wine production. That also makes New York State vineyards specially scenic for wine travelers.

As added enticements for wine enthusiasts, New York vintners offer foot tours, hayrides, films; slides, concerts, literature on wine and food, picnic groves, talks, tastings, and sales. And the crowds do turn out: over 500,000 tourists visit the state wineries, with a massive turnout at harvest time.

Upstate wine routes stretch through classic country scenes of cows and silos where state parks are prime territories for outdoor activities. Hudson Valley wineries, within easy reach of New York City, take visitors back to the nation's oldest operating winery, established in 1839, while Long Island's routes go way out to land's end. Summer and fall touring in every region invites other stops at appetite-pleasing fruit-and-vegetable stands, where, in addition to berries and peaches, delightful with certain wines, you can buy jams and pies and tomatoes and corn.

For help in planning a New York wine tour, write or phone for festival brochures and other information on New York's wine regions: Wine Country, 350 Elm Street, Penn Yan, New York 14527 (tel: 315-536-7442).

&🍂 LAKE ERIE DISTRICT

Earlier in its history, this region's fame rested solely on grape juice, with acres of land planted to Concords. But times and grapes they are a-changing. Since the 1976 passage of the Farm Winery Act, growers have planted French-American hybrids and European viniferas and several wineries have sprouted up in what has been designated the Lake Erie v.a. Even now, wine grape production is still a drop in the bucket compared with the Concords grown mostly for jelly and juice.

Winemaking here actually dates back to 1824, when Deacon Elijah Fay of Portland planted the first wine grapes—Isabellas and Catawbas—and made wines in his cellar. The deacon's son, Joseph, and his partners, Garrett Ryckman and Rufus Haywood, founded the first commercial winery in 1859 at Brocton; ruins of several others have since been found in the vicinity, where production peaked in 1900 at 2 million gallons.

Concords, introduced in the 1870s—and still the dominant grape—were planted in greatest numbers in the 1880s by grape growers and many others who saw them as a means to prosperity. When their boom went bust, two Prohibitionist dentists, brothers Thomas and Charles Welch, took advantage of the grape glut and set up a plant for their juices and jellies at Westfield, south of Brocton. (Ironically, for a time in the 1950s, the temperance advocates' plant was used to make wines under new owners.) Not surprisingly, Prohibition halted Lake Erie winemaking, but some of the growers survived by providing grapes to juice makers and bootleggers.

While the Chautauqua-Erie area today has relatively few wineries, it has the greatest grape acreage in the state—20,000 acres all told. Indeed, many wineries in New York State purchase their grapes from Lake Erie growers.

Here, meanderers along the wine route will see a distinct climatic region created during the Ice Age. Only the narrow strip extending along the southern shore of Lake Erie for sixty miles and reaching three to sixteen miles inland is conducive to grape and fruit growing. The wineries are strung like beads off Route 20 and are within easy reach of each other. Alternatively, wonderfully scenic Rte. 5 runs along Lake Erie's shores, from Van Buren Point in the south to Mount Vernon in the north, to make all or part of the route a treat for the eyes.

꙰ ꙰ ꙰

Merritt Estate Winery

2264 King Road
Forestville, New York 14062
TEL: 716-965-4800
PRESIDENT/WINEMAKER: William T. Merritt; studied at UC-Davis.
FOUNDED: 1976

AT A GLANCE
Tours & Tastings: Mon.–Sat. 10–5, Sun. 1–5. Family-guided winery tours and tastings, occasionally include vineyard.
Closed: Easter, Thanksgiving, Christmas, New Year's days.
Vineyards: One hundred acres, planted to French-American hybrids and labrusca varieties; orchards for apples, European prunes, peaches.
Wines: Varietals—Seyval Blanc, Aurora, Marechal Foch, Cayuga White, Vidal Blanc, Winemaster's Choice (special cuvee of Foch)—all six vintage dated. Chautauqua White, Red, and Rosé; Chautauqua Niagara; Sangria de Marguerite; Mereo (spiced wine); sparkling Estrolita (spumante style); Seyval Sec; Frizanto Rosso (red).
Awards: Chautauqua Niagara cited in New York State and Eastern Wine competitions; Seyval Blanc, Aurora at New York State Fair.
Picnic Area: Pavilion seats about eighty.
Retail Shop: Wines sold on-site; gifts and baskets.
Credit Cards: MasterCard, Visa.
Access for Disabled: Everything on one floor.
Foreign Languages: None.
Getting There: Merritt is midway between Erie and Buffalo. From Erie, Pennsylvania: Get off I-90 (N.Y.S. Thruway) or scenic Rte. 5 at Dunkirk (exit 59). Turn left on Rte. 60 South to Rte. 20. Go east on Rte. 20 to blinker light at Sheridan Center and follow the signs. From Buffalo: Get off I-90 at exit 58 (Silver Creek); take Rte. 30 West to blinker light at Sheridan Center and follow signs.
Special Wine & Other Events: Shades of Spring—first weekend in March, cross-country skiing, maple sugaring, dog-sleds, and horse-drawn bobsled rides. Sausages, chili, hot Mereo (spiced with cinnamon, cloves, and lemon); Septemberfest, second weekend of Sept., is marked with grape stomping, games, chicken barbecue, carriage rides, petting zoo for the kids.

⊷ When founded in 1976, Merritt Estate Winery became the first farm winery in Chautauqua County under the Farm Winery Law. The homestead itself has been in the family since the 1800s, and many of the vines date back to those days. Proprietor Merritt is winemaker, and his wife, Christi, and the whole family run the winery and vineyard. Production has grown from 16,000 gallons to over 35,000 today. Visitors to the winery drink in views of Lake Erie and acres of undulating vineyard land.

TO SEE & DO
Few wine visitors tour in winter, but those who do can ski the well-maintained cross-country trails through the woods and vineyards at Merritt Estate and sip warm mulled wine in the warming hut. Instruction and ski rentals available.

⊷ ⊷ ⊷

Schloss Doepkin Winery

East Main Road (R.D. #2, Box 114)
Ripley, New York 14775
TEL: 716-326-3636
OWNERS: John S. and Roxann D. Watso
FOUNDED: 1980

AT A GLANCE
Tours & Tastings: May 1–Nov. 1, Mon.–Sun. Noon–5; Nov.–Apr., Thurs.–Sun., for tastings; tours for a fee, by appointment only. The emphasis is on grape growing and winemaking, not entertaining people.
Vineyards: Sixty-two acres planted to labruscas, French-American hybrids, and vinifera varieties.
Wines: Chardonnay, Johannisberg Riesling, Gewürztraminer, Marechal Foch, Landot (Landal); Niagara, Catawba, Seyval Blanc, Concord; Schloss Blanc (dry blend of viniferas); bulk red and white for visitors who bring gallon containers.
Awards: 1981 Chardonnay, Eastern Wine Competition.
Picnic Area: On the grounds.
Retail Shop: Wines, gifts, crafts, art gallery.
Credit Cards: None.
Access for Disabled: None.
Foreign Languages: None.
Getting There: Sixty miles west of Buffalo and thirty miles east of Erie. Get off I-90 at Westfield (exit 60). Left on Rte. 394, right on Rte. 20, left on Old Rte. 20. Follow signs.

⊷ What's in a name? In this case, "Schloss" means "castle" and Doepken (pronounced Depkin) is the maiden name of owner John Watso's wife and partner. Founded in 1980, the vineyard was once property of the old Brocton Wine Company, and the buildings from 1860 are now restored and equipped for winery operations. Two tasting rooms offer visitors a choice of environments—the basement of the 150-year-old barn in the summer; the cozy old farmhouse in winter.

Watso, originally a metallurgist and chemist from Cortland, Ohio, started as a wine hobbyist. When he settled on this location, he pulled out some old Concord vines and replanted new grapes, including viniferas. Buried on the property is the body of a soldier from the War of 1812.

⊷ ⊷ ⊷

Woodbury Vineyards

South Roberts Road
Dunkirk, New York 14048
TEL: 716-679-9463
OWNERS: The Woodbury family and partners
FOUNDED: 1979

AT A GLANCE
Tours & Tastings: Mon.–Sat. 10–5, Sun. 12–5. Thirty-minute guided tours, followed by tasting.
Closed: Easter, Thanksgiving, Christmas, New Year's.
Vineyards: Forty acres planted to vinifera and native American varieties; Seyval Blanc purchased from local growers.
Wines: Estate-bottled, vintage-dated Chardonnay, Johannisberg Riesling, Gewürztraminer, Pinot Noir; vintage-dated Seyval Blanc; Niagara and various blends labeled Glacier Ridge white, rosé; white *methode champenoise* champagnes.
Awards: Over fifty-six medals, including ten gold and nine in international competitions. Most often beribboned: Johannisberg Riesling, Chardonnay, Seyval Blanc, and sparkling wines.
Picnic Area: Tables in the apple orchard.
Shop: Wines sold on-site.
Credit Cards: MasterCard, Visa.
Access for Disabled: Yes.
Foreign Languages: None.
Getting There: 45-miles northeast of Buffalo, 120 miles east of Cleveland. Get off I-90 at Dunkirk (exit 59), turn left on Rte. 60, left on Rte. 20, right on South Roberts Rd.
Special Wine & Other Events: Four festivals a year—May: Apple Blossom and Wine; July: Anniversary; Nov.: Nouveau; Feb.: Glacier Ridge Winter Weekend.

The winery dates back only to 1979, but the Woodbury family has been farming the land since 1910. They were among the earliest, in 1966, to grow viniferas in this traditionally Concord grape belt. Their winery is not architecturally distinguished—a simple, one-story construction—but they could win prizes for friendliness as their wines have for excellence.

Chadwick Bay Wine Co.

10001 Route 60
Fredonia, New York 14063
TEL: 716-672-5000

AT A GLANCE
Tours & Tastings: June 25–Sept. 28; Mon.–Thurs. 9–6; Fri.–Sat. 9–8; Sun. noon–6. Combination winery and country store with crafts, antiques, and cheeses; garden patio. Live entertainment Sat. 1–5, Sun. 1–5:30; summer only. In Fredonia, on Rte. 60, 1½ miles south of I-90, exit 59.

Johnson Estate Winery

West Main Road (Box 52)
Westfield, New York 14787
TEL: 716-326-2191

AT A GLANCE
Tastings and sales, Daily & Sun. 10–6, year-round. Tours Jul.–Aug. Grapes go back over a century on this property, and the winery, founded in 1961, is now the oldest farm winery in New York State. Small lots of wines are made on-site from native and French-American grapes grown near the winery—all carefully supervised by the Johnson family.

TO SEE & DO
In summer, cultural activities and educational activities take center stage at nine-week session of the more than century-old Chautauqua Institution, set on 700 acres along Lake Chautauqua. On-site are hotels and houses of worship, old homes, tennis courts, and a golf course. The area also features summer and winter sports activities and a bumper crop of antique shops in small farm towns.

ACCOMMODATIONS
Finger Lakes Bed & Breakfast Association
P.O. Box 862
Canandaigua, New York 14424
(Write for free directory that covers the Finger Lakes Region.)

The White Inn
52 East Main Street
Fredonia, New York 14063
Tel: 716-672-2103
Elegantly restored Victorian hotel, with restaurant serving local wines.

The William Seward Inn
South Portage Road
Westfield, New York 14787
Tel: 716-326-4151
Built in 1821, the mansion was home first to Secretary of State William H. Seward and later Lieutenant Governor George Patterson, whose family owned it for more than a century. The mansion was moved to its present site in 1963 and purchased by its current owners, the Woods, in 1986. Rooms, some with Lake Erie views, are furnished with antiques; wine, cheese, and appetizers are served each evening, and breakfast is included in the rates.

RESTAURANTS
Fireside Manor
West Lake Road
Dunkirk, New York 14048
Tel: 716-672-4449
Steaks, seafood, and good local wine list.

Vintage Room
(See Quality Inn Vineyard, for address and telephone.) A big fireplace and dark wood seem the right decor for such familiar fare as steak and prime rib as well as an almost forgotten dish, lobster tail. Local wines on list.

Alley Cats Cafe
Just off Water Street at the Village Parking Lot
Fredonia, New York 14063
Tel: 716-673-1277
Little café, open for breakfast, lunch, dinner; famous for Friday night fish fry, deep-fried, panfried, and broiled. Widmer wines.

The White Inn
52 East Main Street
Fredonia, New York 14063
Tel: 716-672-2103
Highly regarded restaurant, where all dishes are fresh, natural, and homemade. Lamb, seafood, veal. In-depth wine list includes Woodbury Widmer, Great Western, Dr. Konstantin Frank, Pindare, and others from N.Y. State. Open breakfast, lunch, dinner, seven days.

❧ FINGER LAKES DISTRICT

Most of the Finger Lakes' forty-five wineries are only a few years old, but the narrow, deep lakes themselves date back to the Glacier Age. The well-drained slopes bordering the dozen eons-old lakes create favorable microclimates for grapes, their waters moderating the frequent harsh winters and forestalling frost in both spring and winter. Similar conditions exist in the wine regions of Germany and France, except that winters in the Finger Lakes are more severe.

The area's 14,000 acres of vineyards are planted mainly along Canandaigua, Keuka, Cayuga, and Seneca lakes. Once the area was mainly known for labruscas, but recent times have seen changes throughout the Finger Lakes. Leading winemakers such as Widmer and Taylor are following the leaders of the "vinifera revolution" such as Willy Frank, Jim Gifford, Hermann Wiemer, Bill Wagner, Peter Johnstone, the Knapps, and the Planes in cultivating varieties such as Johannisberg Riesling and Chardonnay that once were thought impossible to coddle through the cruel winters. Some even harbor hopes for the hard-to-grow Pinot Noir.

Distinct variations in microclimates have created two recognized v.a.'s; the Finger Lakes, and the lower altitude Cayuga Lake. The wineries also vary greatly in many ways, from winemaking styles to architecture and location. To appreciate them properly, allow two or three days.

In more leisurely times, steamers plied the waters, carrying tourists to varied pleasures. Now boats take visitors on pleasure cruises around the lakes and offer peaceful dining decks. Sleek highways border the lakes, but wine routes still go back in time to the oldest bonded winery in the state—then known as Hammondsport and Pleasant Wine Company and now as Great Western, opened in 1860. Visitors also get a taste of miles of classic farmland, dotted with barns, cows, and silos, and quiet little towns. Here is a world-famous vacationland where visitors enjoy all manner of sports, history, and top museums and cultural events.

At harvest (beginning in the last week of August and peaking from mid-September to mid-October) time, the wineries have become increasingly crowded; travel can be heavy on weekends, so make reservations well in advance. Festivals year-round add to the enjoyment of wineries; most of the whoop-de-do, set for summer through the aforementioned crush months.

Canandaigua Lake & North

Canandaigua Wine Company Inc.

116 Buffalo Street (mailing address)
Tasting room address: East Gibson
   Street (Route 21)
Canandaigua, New York 14424
TEL: 716-394-3640 (tasting room:
   716-394-7680)
OWNER: Marvin Sands
FOUNDED: 1945

AT A GLANCE
Tours & Tastings: No individual tours; groups only, by special arrangement; tastings, mid-May to mid-Oct., 11–5 Mon.–Sat., 12–5 Sun.
Closed: Mid-Oct.–mid–May.

Vineyards: Buys grapes from New York State growers.
Wines: J. Roget Champagne; Bisceglia Brothers table wines, ranging from Chablis to Cabernet Sauvignon; Richard's Wild Irish Rose Dessert Wines. Also coolers, fruit wines, brandy.
Retail Shop: Wines for sale.
Restaurant: In Sonnenberg Mansion; lunch and desserts served in Garden Cafe and Peach House.
Credit Cards: None.
Access for Disabled: None.
Foreign Languages: None.
Getting There: Less than ten miles from Thruway exits 44 or 45 in Canandaigua.

Special Wines & Other Events: Sponsors Summerpro, Jul-Labor Day at the Finger Lakes Performing Arts Center, classic concerts, pops and special attractions.

Canandaigua's tasting room in the Sonnenberg Gardens (a major tourist attraction) was formerly the estate's canning cellar, and is known for its stained glass window, "Abundance" created in 1911. The stone walls came from Canandaigua Lake and surrounding area, and the wood accents started out as casks in the wineries. Just outside are nine well-manicured Victorian gardens with fountains, pools and waterfalls and the mansion with 10 well furnished rooms. (Daily mid-May–Mid-Oct., Tel. 716-924-5420, 9:30–5:30; $4.95 adults; $3.95 seniors, $1.25, 6–18, free to those under 6.) Nine well-manicured Victorian gardens with fountains, pools, and waterfalls, plus the mansion with ten well-furnished rooms. (Daily mid-May to mid-Oct., 9:30–5:30; tel: 716-924-5420).

TO SEE & DO

Canandaigua's Main Street is about as well preserved as any you're apt to find in the Finger Lakes area, with many historic homes, churches, and commercial buildings. The Granger Homestead is one of western New York's finest examples of Federal architecture; adjoining is the Carriage Museum (295 North Main Street, Tues.–Sat., May–Oct.; tel: 716-394-1472). Walking tours of downtown available through the historic museum, 55 Main Street (10–5, Tues.–Sat.). The racetrack season is Apr. through Nov., and summer boating regattas are frequent on Canandaigua Lake Inlet.

≈ ≈ ≈

Casa Larga

2287 Turk Hill Road
Fairport, New York 14450

TEL: 716-223-4210
OWNER: Andrew Colaruotolo
FOUNDED: 1974

AT A GLANCE

Tours & Tastings: Year-round tastings, Tues.–Sat. 10–5; Sun. 12–5. Guided tours, May–Dec. 1, Tues.–Sun. 1, 2, 3, and 4 (or by appointment). Highly instructive, with visit to vineyard; crushing, pressing, fermentation room; oak barrel and bottling rooms; conclude with tasting.
Closed: Mon.
Vineyards: Twenty-two acres, primarily planted to vinifera, smattering of French-American hybrids.
Wines: Estate-bottled Chardonnay, Gewürztraminer, Johannisberg Riesling, Cabernet Sauvignon, Pinot Noir, Vidal Blanc, De Chaunac, Delaware. Newest addition is champagne.
Awards: More than two score since first release in 1978; oft-cited: Johannisberg Riesling, Pinot Chardonnay, Gewürztraminer. Recently won a bronze for Brut d'Ottonell in New York Classic.
Picnic Area: On the grounds.
Restaurant: Marble-accented Andrew's Cafe offers a panoramic view of surrounding area, along with cheese, pâté, sandwiches, salads, wines; 11:30–4 Tues.–Sat.
Retail Shop: Wines sold on-site.
Credit Cards: American Express, MasterCard, Visa.
Access for Disabled: Tasting room, café, vineyard.
Foreign Languages: Italian.
Getting There: From N.Y.S. Thruway: Take exit 45 and follow sign to Victor. Turn right onto Rte. 96, then turn right onto Turk Hill Rd.; at second traffic light, proceed 1½ mile to Casa Larga. From downtown Rochester: Take I-490 East, exit at Pittford/Palmyra Rd. (Rte. 31) and head east on Rte. 31. Turn right on Turk Hill Rd. (5th traffic light); proceed 1 mile to Casa Larga.

🍂 Andrew Colaruotolo learned about winemaking in his father's vineyard in Gaeta, Italy. His small family winery sits on land he originally purchased as a site for a housing development. Like some other wineries around the country, Casa Larga selects an artist each year to design a label.

TO SEE & DO
Rochester is just fifteen minutes away. The International Museum of Photography in George Eastman's former home, the Rochester Museum & Science Center, the Memorial Art Gallery at the university, and the Strong Museum (cataloging the cultural and social forces of industrialized America), lead the parade of popular sights. And right in line with these are many historical buildings, including Susan B. Anthony's home. The century-old Lilac Festival, held the third week of each May, attracts visitors from all over the world to a glorious array of 1,200 bushes, including 500 varieties of lilacs and stunning displays of other spring flowers as well—all in Highland Park.

🍂 🍂 🍂

Widmer's Wine Cellars, Inc.

West Avenue
Naples, New York 14512
TEL: 716-374-6311
OWNERS: Canandaigua Wine Company
  (since Oct. 1986)
FOUNDED: 1888

AT A GLANCE
Tours & Tastings: Memorial Day weekend–Oct. 31, Mon.–Sat. 10–4, Sun. 11:30–4:30. One-hour tours take a close look at winemaking from vine to bottle, and at a technique rarely seen—the "cellar on the roof," where several thousand barrels stacked four deep hold aging ports and sherries. They will remain outdoors for four years so they can "breathe" before blending. Other wines mature in cellars indoors. Chalet decor in the tasting room is background to a sit-down lesson in wine appreciation. Tastings can be experienced without tours.
Closed: No tours Oct. 31–May 30.
Vineyards: 225 acres, planted to vinifera, labrusca, and French-American hybrid varieties.
Wines: New focus on vinifera wines, including expanded Johannisberg Riesling production and release of Chardonnay and Cabernet Sauvignon. Well-known for charmat process champagnes and solera-blended sherries. Produces ports, blends, proprietaries, vintage-dated varietals; still and sparkling grape juices.
Awards: Recent awards to Johannisberg Riesling and Seyval Blanc and Lake Niagara Red at New York State Wine Classic.
Picnic Area: Park nearby.
Retail Shop: Wine shop; adjacent gift shop with wine accessories, wine jellies.
Credit Cards: American Express, MasterCard, Visa.
Access for Disabled: None.
Foreign Languages: None.
Getting There: Take N.Y.S. Thruway (I-90) to exit 46 and go south on Rte. 360 to exit 3. Then use Rte. 21 North to Naples. Alternatively, get off Thruway at exit 44 and go south on Rte. 21.

🍂 John Jacob Widmer and his wife, Lisette, were among many Swiss immigrants in the 1880s drawn to this serene valley because it reminded them of their Alpine homeland. With the help of a bank loan, the Widmers put in their first vines on a sunny slope and built their home and the stone-walled wine cellars; the latter still can be seen today. Their son Will attended the Royal Wine School in Geisenheim, from which he imported the old-world wine techniques used with pride at the winery. Will Widmer's innovations included producing vintage-dated wines before others in the area.

Since the early 1960s, Widmer's has changed owners several times and is now part of Canandaigua, New York State's largest winery and the third largest wine company in the United States. Plans are to emphasize more classic European wine production from high-quality vinifera grapes.

TO SEE & DO
Step back in time with a stroll down Naples's Main Street, with its well-preserved historic buildings that have remained largely unchanged since early Widmer's days. New and interesting is the Cumming Center (Gulick Road; tel: 716-374-6160), run by the Rochester Museum and Science Center, a Finger Lakes living museum with themed trails, homestead, multimedia theater, nature shop, and visitors' center.

In summer, there's theater and swimming in a choice of fine lakes; in winter, skiing; and all year round, a terrific view of the surrounding countryside from Gannett Hill, 2,256 feet high, one of the highest points in the area. Modern St. Januarius Church, noted for the Our Lady of the Grapes shrine and grotto is open every day, year-round.

In Geneva, at the north end of Seneca Lake, is the Rose Hill Mansion (Rte. 96A, one mile south of Rtes. 5 and 20), a Greek Revival–style mansion with handsome Empire period furniture (Mon.–Sat. 10–4, Sun. 1–5; May–Oct. 31; tel: 315-789-3848).

Incidentally, Geneva's gracious South Main Street, with old shade trees and gracious homes from bygone days, is said to be "the most beautiful street in America." Continue on this street to Pulney Square and see the attractive campus of Hobart and William Smith colleges. For other activities, see the Canandaigua/Rochester section and the section following Keuka, Seneca, and Cayuga lakes' listings.

ACCOMMODATIONS
Because the area attracts a large number of visitors there are many places to stay in all price ranges.

Bed and Breakfasts, Inns, Small Hotels
Bed & Breakfast Rochester
P.O. Box 444
Fairport, New York 14450
Tel: 716-223-8510
Historic, modern, city, country, lakeside B&Bs in the Rochester area.

Inn a Still Woode
131 East Street
Canandaigua, New York 14424
Tel: 716-394-0504
Historic home, set on four wooded acres, across from Sonnenberg Gardens.

Strawberry Castle Bed & Breakfast
1883 Penfield Road
Penfield, New York 14526
Tel: 716-385-3266
Well preserved, rosy-hued eighteenth-century Italian villa with columns, distinctive moldings and ceilings. Antique interiors and lovely gardens, patio, and pool. Continental breakfast. Eight miles east of Rochester.

Woods-Edge
Near exit 45 (NYS I-90)
P.O. Box 444
Fairport, New York 14450
Tel: 716-223-8510
Surrounded by woods, yet only twenty minutes from downtown Rochester. Contemporary home with antique furniture and barn-beamed ceilings.

Genesee Country Inn
948 George Street
Mumford, New York 14511
Tel: 716-538-2500
Originally a plaster mill, the old building is now a comfortable inn set on six acres with waterfalls and a trout stream on the

grounds. Breakfast is served on the screened porch in fair weather. Seventeen miles southwest of Rochester.

Oliver Loud's Inn
1474 Marsh Road
Pittsford, New York 14534
Tel: 716-248-5200
This old inn once served stagecoach travelers when located in Egypt, New York. Scheduled for demolition in 1985, it was moved by the owners of Richardson's Canal House (see "Restaurants") to provide lodgings for guests. Refurbished in reproductions and historically accurate colors, the inn is a special place to stay, its ambience enhanced by the Erie Canal view and acreage. Continental breakfast with homemade baked goods, cheese, jam, and fruits. Twelve miles southeast of Rochester. Three and a half miles from historic town of Pittsford.

Rose Mansion and Gardens
625 Mount Hope Avenue
Rochester, New York 14620
Tel: 716-546-5426
Historic mansion from 1867 with 4½-acre Victorian gardens, now lovingly preserved by the Landmark Society of Western New York. Appropriately, each guest room is named for a rose and decorated with the flower's colors. There is a conservatory and great hall, dining room, and library.

Strathallan
550 East Avenue
Rochester, New York 14607
Tel: 716-461-5010
Well-appointed 150-room hotel in a quiet neighborhood. Solarium and sauna and hot tub among the amenities; balconies on many rooms. Excellent restaurant. (See "Restaurants.")

Other Lodging

Sheraton Canandaigua Inn
770 South Main Street
Canandaigua, New York 14424
Tel: 716-394-7800
109 rooms, 38 suites, pool, sauna, Jacuzzi, and other accoutrements of large hotel chains. Popular for conventions and meetings.

Yodel Inn Motor Lodge
Route 245
Naples, New York 14512
Tel: 716-374-2458
Reasonable rates. Pool, trout stream, and vineyards nearby. Open year-round, heated and air-conditioned.

RESTAURANTS
Local delicacy in fall is grape pie. Below, a small group of many serving New York wines:

Brandston's
814 S. Clinton Street
Rochester, New York 14620
Tel: 716-461-3736
This former Victorian watering hole has been done up dramatically in black and white. Continental menu features a wide range of well-prepared dishes. Luscious desserts. Wine list includes Dr. Konstantin Frank selections, among others.

Colonial Inn
759 South Main Street
Canandaigua, New York 14424
Tel: 716-394-8323
1830s inn specializing in duck, shrimp, prime rib. Will pack picnics.

The Redwood Junction
Routes 21 & 53
Naples, New York 14512
Tel: 716-374-6360
Swiss chalet–style building. American favorites on menu—steak and seafood. Open 6:30 A.M.–8:30 P.M.; closed Mon.

Bob's and Ruth's

Corner Routes 21 and 245
Naples, New York 14512
Tel: 716-374-5122
Vineyard room, hearty homemade soups, pies, chicken. Open 6 A.M.–8:30 P.M. Wine wall with good New York selections. Closed Nov.–April.

Richardson's Canal House

(See Oliver Loud's Inn for address and telephone.)
Topnotch restaurant on the Erie Canal, with sumptuous food. Duckling a specialty. Good wine list. Patio with view of Erie Canal. Outdoor dining in fair weather. Closed most Sundays, Christmas, and New Year's day.

Spring House

3001 Monroe Avenue
Rochester, New York 14618
Tel: 716-586-2300
Atmospheric former Erie Canal inn with outdoor dining in fair weather. A mélange of continental delicacies on the menu. Extravagant desserts. Wines.

Strathallan

(See "Accommodations" for address and telephone.) Smart, dressy place for well-prepared continental and regional dishes. Fine wine list. Outdoor dining in summer. Jacket required. Serves breakfast, lunch and dinner.

Wild Winds Farm & Village

Clark Street (Corner Route 39)
Naples, New York 14512
Tel: 716-374-5523
More than a place to eat, it's a place to adventure. Specializes in regional foods seasoned with fresh herbs and accented with flowers. Homemade crêpes, quiches, breads, pastries. Wine list. Country store, sugarhouse, nature trail, greenhouses, and gardens. Barbecue pavilion. Open Mon.–Fri. 10–5; May 24–Oct. 26; dinner served Sat. & Sun. Access for disabled. Three miles west of Naples.

Picnic Stop

About 1 mile west of Pittsford, off Rte. 65, is the observation deck at lock 32 of the Erie Canal. Picnic tables are set in a pretty park. After eating, follow the 5½-mile trail that follows the canal east to the quiet town of Fairport.

Roadside Market
Joseph's Wayside Fruit Market
201 South Main Street
Naples, New York 14512
Tel: 716-374-2380
Tempting fruits and vegetables to take along; open daily 8:30–8:30, May–Oct.

Keuka Lake

Wine routes around the Y-shaped, 187-foot-deep lake cover a forty-five-mile corridor of lakeslope vineyards dotted with wineries tucked in hills and valleys.

Keuka Lake can be reached from the south by taking Bath exit 38 off Rte. 17, then Rte. 54 North to Hammondsport, and following the red signs to each winery. From the northeast: Take Geneva exit off I-90 (N.Y.S. Thruway) and Rte. 14 South to Dresden, Rte. 54 south to Penn Yan, and follow red signs to each winery. From the northwest: Take Rochester exit 46 off I-90, then Rte. 390 South to Rte. 17 East, to exit 38 at Bath. From Bath, take Rte. 54 to Hammondsport and keep your eyes on the red signs to each winery.

≈ ≈ ≈

Hunt Country Vineyards

4021 Italy Hill Road
Branchport, New York 14418
TEL: 315-595-2812
OWNERS: Arthur and Joyce Hunt
FOUNDED: 1988

AT A GLANCE
Tours & Tastings: May–Oct., Mon.–Sat. 10–5, Sun. 1–4; other times by appointment. Self-guided walking tours, except Sat., when tours are guided hourly and taken in a haywagon; tastings in retail sales room or outdoors with vineyard view.
Closed: Nov.–Apr.
Vineyards: Seventy-five acres, planted to French-American and American hybrids and vinifera varieties.
Wines: Chardonnay, Seyval, Cayuga, Vidal Ice Wine, Late Harvest Ravat, and Classic Red.
Awards: Silver medal to 1987 Seyval and bronze to 1987 Late Harvest Ravat. Both in 1988 New York Classic.
Picnic Area: Idyllic setting overlooking vineyards. Cheese-and-bread tray available.
Retail Shop: Wines and gifts.
Credit Cards: MasterCard, Visa.
Access for Disabled: None.
Foreign Languages: None.
Getting There: Take N.Y.S. Thruway to exit 42. Go south on Rte. 42 (Newark) to Geneva and take 14A to Penn Yan; turn west on Scenic Rte. 54A to Branchport; winery is one mile up hill on Italy Hill Rd. Winery is one hour north of Corning and one hour south of Rochester.
Special Wine & Other Events: Aug.: Hunt Country Picnic; Oct.: Halloween Weekend.

Although Hunt Country Vineyards formally opened in May 1988, Arthur and Joyce Hunt were involved in winemaking since 1973 at Finger Lakes Wine Cellars. They are the sixth generation of Hunts to farm this land above Keuka's northwest tip since Aaron Hunt bought it in the early 1800s. The Hunts specialize in small lots of vintage varietals—annual total is 4,000 gallons, produced in a rustic old barn filled with the latest winemaking equipment. Visitors are given recipes that harmonize food and wine.

McGregor Vineyard Winery

5503 Dutch Street
R.D. #1 (Box 213)
Dundee, New York 14837
TEL: 607-292-3999
PRESIDENT: Robert H. McGregor
FOUNDED: 1972

AT A GLANCE
Tours & Tastings: Apr.–Nov., Tues.–Sun. 11–5; informal tours and tastings at a lofty height above Keuka Lake with views of vineyards and beyond to Bluff Point. Nov.–Apr. by appointment only.
Closed: Mondays and legal holidays.
Vineyards: Twenty-five acres, planted primarily to viniferas, including some Russian varieties on an experimental basis.
Wines: Estate-bottled Bunch Select Riesling, Johannisberg Riesling; Muscat Ottonel, Pinoit Noir, Gewürztraminer, Chardonnay; Russian varietals—Sereksia, Superavi, Rkatsiteli.
Awards: Gold medals consistently to Muscat Ottonel and Bunch Select Riesling; bronzes to Pinot Noir, among others.
Picnic Area: One table under the trees.
Retail Shop: Wines sold on-site.
Credit Cards: MasterCard, Visa.
Access for Disabled: Yes.
Foreign Languages: None.
Getting There: Take Scenic Rte. 54, along the banks of Keuka Lake, from Hammondsport for about ten miles north or south for twelve miles from Penn Yan to the north corner of Hyatt Hill Road (Country Host Restaurant). Turn up Hyatt Hill Road for about one mile to Dutch Street and turn left for a mile to vineyard and winery.
Special Wine & Other Events: Participant in Keuka Lake Winery Route events.

Bob McGregor, a technological consultant and former project manager at Kodak, chose a picture-perfect site above

Keuka Lake for the winery he tends with his wife, Maggie, and their family. The McGregors founded their vineyard in 1972, and were among the first to coddle finicky viniferas successfully through the cold winters. After eight years of experimenting with grapes and wines, their first releases in 1980 began their prize-winning streak, which continues in international, state, and local competitions. The winery's oak-aged Pinot Noir, one of their earliest and most consistent prizewinners, has been compared by connoisseurs to the best from Burgundy. McGregor's Russian varietals from hardy Eastern European viniferas planted in 1979 have yielded wines promising enough to increase their quantity in the vineyard, and are perfect for toasting the terrific view.

ða ða ða

Bully Hill

Greyton H. Taylor Memorial Drive
Hammondsport, New York 14840
TEL: 607-868-3610
OWNER: Walter S. Taylor
WINEMAKER: Greg Learned
FOUNDED: 1970

AT A GLANCE

Tours & Tastings: May 1–Nov. 30, Mon–Sat. 10–4:30, Sun. 12–4. Every hour, or more frequent, depending on crowd. Tour begins in the vineyard; includes production process, museum, and tasting. Dec. 1–Apr. 30, open for tastings only.
Vineyards: Two hundred acres planted to French-American hybrids.
Wines: Estate-bottled varietals—Cayuga, Seval Blanc, Vidal Blanc, Ravat Noir, Baco Noir; blends; champagnes. 100,000 gallons annually.
Picnic Area: On the grounds.
Restaurant: Champagne Country Cafe on-site (tel: 607-868-3490).

Retail Shop: Wines, winemaking supplies.
Credit Cards: MasterCard and Visa.
Access for Disabled: Yes.
Foreign Languages: Russian, Yugoslavian.
Getting There: Take I-390 to Bath exit; go north on Rte. 54 to 54A and turn left to winery.
Special Wine & Other Events: Winery and museum on-site sponsor many events throughout the year, cooking classes among them.

ða Walter S. Taylor, proprietor of Bully Hill Vineyards, is the grandson of the founder of the Taylor Wine Company (see page 63). Fired from the family company after being openly critical about its use of labruscas, he established Bully Hill in his grandfather's old horse barn to bring out French-American hybrid wines from his own vineyard.

When Taylor Wines was sold to Coca-Cola (the winery was resold to Seagram and is now owned by Vintners International), Walter S. (as he likes to be known) was taken to court and forbidden to use the family name openly on his wines. His responded by staging a widely publicized tasting where he crossed his name off the labels, which resulted in his gaining wide attention for his wines.

A self-taught artist, Walter S. creates his own zany labels. They show goats, a bulldog-chauffeured car, a tuxedo-clad raccoon, self-portraits, and other subjects. Also on the labels are Don't Drink and Drive logos, ingredients and growers, and warnings to pregnant women about drinking. Typical wines bear such names as Love My Goat White, Rosé Wine for Tennis, Old Church Red, and Old Ace No. 45 Rosé. Sold in thirty-four states, they are among the most widely distributed New York wines.

The Greyton Taylor Wine Museum, named for Walter S.'s father and located in the original Taylor Wines winery, displays more than 800 of Walter S.'s works of art, as well as valuable wine artifacts. Any more questions about Bully Hill? Call Walter S. Taylor—his telephone number is on each bottle.

ACCOMMODATIONS
(Bully Hill has its own bed and breakfast; contact the winery for details.)

❧ ❧ ❧

Chateau de Rheims Winery

County Road 88 off Route 54
R.D. 1 (Box 72A)
Hammondsport, New York 14840
TEL: 607-569-2040
OWNER: Philippe Guermonprez
FOUNDED: 1987

AT A GLANCE
Tours & Tastings: Open Mon.–Sat. 9–6, Sun. 12–6; personalized guided tours on demand, followed by tastings; particularly educational for *methode champenoise* champagne and traditional winemaking ways.
Vineyards: Twenty-seven-acre vineyard planted to French-American hybrids, American and vinifera varieties.
Wines: 90 percent *methode champenoise* champagne; Baco Noir, Cayuga, Chablis (blend of Cayuga and Seyval), Delaware, Seyval, Rosé.
Picnic Area: In park behind winery property.
Awards: No competitions as yet.
Retail Shop: Wines sold on-site.
Credit Cards: MasterCard, Visa.
Access for Disabled: By side road.
Foreign Languages: French.
Special Wine & Other Events: Check with winery.
Getting There: One and a quarter hours from Rochester; take I-390 South to Bath exit and Scenic Rte. 54 to winery on County Rd. 88, half a mile south of Hammondsport, near Bully Hill.

❧ Thoroughly schooled in French winemaking, Philippe Guermonprez studied viticulture at Beaune in Burgundy, and enology at the Faculte des Sciences of Dijon. He owns a winery in Rousillon, France, and the Amandaris Vineyards in New Mexico. Guermonprez bought this property, which he runs with his wife and son, from DeMay Wine Cellars in 1987 and has made a lot of changes. While the 27-acre vineyard was being transformed to Guermonprez's tastes, some of the first release wines in 1988 were made from grapes purchased from New York State growers and the *methode champenoise* champagne was produced from the proprietors' own New Mexican–grown Chardonnay.

The champagne is made the old-fashioned way, including hand-riddling and the rest of the painstaking steps. Top-line sparkler, Dom Philip, has a special bottle and label. Red and Rosé champagnes are made from local hybrids.

The winery has a capability to produce 300 bottles of wine a day. The old, rustic atmosphere here is genuine: the stone-and-oak winery, built in 1808, housed Monarch Wines in pre-Prohibition days.

❧ ❧ ❧

Dr. Konstantin Frank (Vinifera Wine Cellars, Inc.)

Middle Road (R.D. 2)
Hammondsport, New York 14840
TEL: 607-868-4884
OWNERS: Frank Family Corporation
WINEMAKER: Eric Fry
FOUNDED: 1960

AT A GLANCE
Tours & Tastings: Mon.–Sat. 9–5; Sun. 1–5; tastings by appointment; tours only if workload permits.
Closed: Legal holidays.
Vineyards: Seventy-six acres planted exclusively to European vinifera grapes.

Wines: Johannisberg Riesling, Chardonnay, Pinot Noir, Cabernet Sauvignon, Gewürztraminer, Muscat Ottonel, Rkatsiteli.
Awards: 1985 Pinot Noir and 1985 Rkatsiteli are among many over twenty-five years.
Retail Shop: Wines sold.
Credit Cards: None.
Access for Disabled: "Always willing to help."
Foreign Languages: German, French, some Russian.
Getting There: On west side of Keuka Lake, 4½ miles north of Heron Hill off Rte. 54A.

&. Pioneer and prophet of New York vinifera wines was Russian émigré Dr. Konstantin Frank, whose inspiration is still felt today. A quarter of a century ago, Frank was the first to prove New York wine traditionalists wrong by showing that vinifera grapes could survive New York's cruel winters. What he did was to graft viniferas to heartier rootstock, as he learned in the Ukraine. First at Gold Seal and then in his own sixty-variety, seventy-six-acre vineyard, he produced prizewinning wines from these vines.

Frank died in 1985 at age eighty-six, but the no-nonsense red-brick winery he launched in 1961 continues under his son Willy's direction. The elder Frank was, in fact, more of a vineyardist than winemaker, and today stylish wines are turned out by Eric Fry, who packed up his favorite barrels and headed east after working for two of California's best wineries, Mondavi and Jordan. Among his award winners have been the above mentioned 1985 Pinot Noir and Rkatsiteli. Samples of the latter, an ancient Russian varietal dating back 5,000 years, were taken as gifts to the Soviet Union by Governor Mario Cuomo.

Trained by Dr. Frank, Willy's brother-in-law Walter Voltz is vineyard manager, assisted by his son, Eric. Seven vinifera varieties best suited to New York State are now cultivated. Willy has improved the equipment and expanded the marketing: Rieslings were shipped to Japan in 1987, a first for any New York winery.

In the Frank trailblazing tradition, Willy will release in 1989 *methode champenoise* sparkling wine under his own Château Frank label, from his stone winery next door to the Frank winery. The wine is from his vineyard planted to the same Pinot Noir, Pinot Blanc, Pinot Meunier, and Chardonnay used in the Champagne region of France—the first vineyard in the country, he says, planted exclusively to these classic varieties for champagne.

&. &. &.

Heron Hill Vineyards, Inc.

Hammondsport, New York 14840
TEL: 607-868-4241
OWNERS: Peter Johnstone and John Ingle, Jr.
PRESIDENT/WINEMAKER: Peter Johnstone
FOUNDED: 1977

AT A GLANCE

Tours & Tastings: May–Nov.; Mon.–Sat. 10–5, Sun. 1–5. Tastings: first wine free, twenty-five cents per taste thereafter. No tours.
Vineyards: Fifty acres, twenty-five each at Keuka Lake and Ingles-owned at Canandaigua Lake; both planted to Chardonnay and Johannisberg Riesling; the latter also has some Seyval and Ravat hybrids. Some non-viniferas bought from growers in Finger Lakes appelation.
Wines: Focus on Johannisberg Riesling, Chardonnay; assorted varietals and blends. Heron Hill labels primarily for German-style wines; Otter Spring labels for wines in the French tradition.
Awards: Johannisberg Riesling is said to be the only wine in America to merit gold

medals in nine consecutive vintages, starting in 1977.
Retail Shop: Wines, assorted accessories, and locally handmade Heron logo pottery, also logo Ts and sweatshirts.
Credit Cards: American Express, MasterCard, Visa.
Access for Disabled: None.
Foreign Languages: None.
Getting There: Five miles north of Hammondsport, south of Dr. Frank's Vinifera Wine Cellars; follow signs on Rte. 54A.

&. Peter Johnstone has one of the best views of Keuka Lake from his striking white, chalet-inspired winery fitted neatly into the side of Bully Hill, and makes crisp white wines that consistently win prizes. Medals are seen in the tasting room. The graceful logo, an in-flight heron, seen on the label, also is carried through on tiles outdoors under the eaves, and on table tops, as well as in photographs, on handmade pottery, and on T-shirts. In the tile-floored tasting room you'll see wrought iron chandeliers, but it's hard to imagine anyone using artificial lights here, so radiantly does natural light stream through the huge windows. At a standup bar or sturdy wood tables visitors savor the view of lake and vineyards while sampling the wines.

Johnstone has come a long way from his early days, when he lived in a trailer on this property. Then, as a newly arrived New York advertising copywriter, he had only experienced wine by the glass—not from the ground up. Furthermore, he did it the hard way: by pulling up the old labrusca vines and planting the third vinifera vineyard on Keuka Lake. He says now that he learned by seeing what went on at the giant Taylor winery nearby. When their tractors rolled by, he also went to work.

Johnstone's idea is to be known for fine Riesling. He attributes his success with Riesling wines to the Finger Lakes' growing conditions, which he says compare favorably with Germany's, where the greatest of these grapes are grown. Annual output is still under 50,000 gallons, and releases sell out quickly.

&. &. &.

Taylor–Great Western–Gold Seal

Route 88
Hammondsport, New York 14804
TEL: 607-569-2111
OWNER: Vintners International
WINEMAKERS: Dr. Andrew C. Rice, Domenic A. Carisetti, Steven Coon, Tim R. Holt, Patricia Jane Herron (one of a few women winemakers), and Jerry A. Koehler
FOUNDED: 1860 (Great Western), 1865 (Gold Seal), 1880 (Taylor).

AT A GLANCE
Tours & Tastings: Take place at Visitor Center for all three wineries: Jan.–Apr., Mon.–Sat. 11–3; May–Oct., Mon.–Sun. 11–4; Nov. & Dec., Mon.–Sat. 11–3. Tours take in the entire history of Finger Lakes winemaking, the process itself, and a tasting—a two-hour experience. Closed: New Year's, Easter, Thanksgiving, and Christmas days.
Vineyards: 1,340 acres planted to native American, French-American hybrids, and vinifera; grapes also purchased from other Finger Lakes and New York state growers.
Wines: Champagnes, varietals, generics, dessert wines, vermouths, proprietaries, and coolers.
Awards: Great Western's 1985 Estate-Bottled Vidal Ice Wine, a rare, rich dessert wine, won both the Governor's Cup (best wine of the show) and a platinum medal (extraordinary wine) at the 1987 New York Wine Classic statewide competition. The 1987 Ice Wine won the Governor's Cup and a gold at the 1988 New York Classic. Bountiful awards for all

three labels go back to 1860s in local, national, and international events; some commemorated at Visitor Center's ceiling-mounted, stained-glass window.

Picnic Area: Park near stream, tables and chairs, barbecue grills, rest rooms.

Retail Shop: Wines, accessories, logo T-shirts, Taylor cookbook, other gifts.

Credit Cards: MasterCard, Visa.

Access for Disabled: Visitor Center only.

Foreign Languages: None.

Getting There: Take Rte. 17 (Southern Tier Expressway) to exit 38 at Bath. From Bath follow Scenic Rte. 54 along the lake for about five miles to Pleasant Valley and turn left. Follow the signs for about half a mile to the Visitor Center.

Special Wine & Other Events: Sponsors Taylor Free Concerts in July and Aug.: Fridays at Taylor Park, Hammondsport; Saturdays at Taughannock Falls State Park, Rte. 89, Trumansburg.

⫘ Three of Hammondsport's oldest wine estates—Taylor, Great Western, and Gold Seal—provide visitors with a complete picture of New York State wines since their beginning the 1800s. Since the spring of 1987, the company has been under the direction of Vintners International, a partnership of former Seagram and Gold Seal executives. The prior owners had been Seagram Company Ltd., which purchased it from Coca-Cola in 1977.

The oldest of the three, Great Western Winery, hummed along as the Hammondsport and Pleasant Hill Wine company, Bonded Winery No. 1, when founded in 1860 by Charles Davenport Champlin and a group of investors who hired French winemakers Jules and Joseph Masson to turn out New York state champagnes. Times have proven this decision still wise. Champagnes remain a Great Western mainstay today, although it also turns out premium wines, vintage varietals, generics, sherries, and ports. Today Great Western's

old wood-and-stone buildings and cellars, listed in the National Register of Historic Places, are still in use.

In 1865, Gold Seal became Bonded Winery No. 2, when founded as the Urbana Wine Company by a group of local investors. Gold Seal became the company's trademark for prizewinning wines, and in 1957 it became the company's name. The rechristening was occasioned by the first bountiful crop of viniferas grown in New York under the direction of winemaker/company president Charles Fournier and Dr. Konstantin Frank (see page 000). Gold Seal still has the largest plantings of viniferas in the East.

Fournier died in 1983, but his name lives on the labels for some of Gold Seal's most prestigious wines. The company also makes estate-bottled table wines, Henri Marchant champagnes, New York State vintage varietals, and premium generic table wines.

Taylor Wine Company began in 1880, founded by a barrelmaker, Walter Taylor, who planted a small vineyard and made wines from Catawba grapes. As the popularity of these wines grew, he took over the former stone winery of Columbia Wine Company to produce wines from native American grapes. An astute decision to switch to juice and sacramental wines helped Taylor to survive Prohibition, which saw the demise of twenty-seven Finger Lakes wineries.

In 1961, the Taylor Wine Company, Inc. acquired Pleasant Valley (Great Western), and by 1964 it began turning out the first Finger Lakes wines made entirely of French-American hybrids. The Taylor firm was family-run until the founder's last son, Clarence, died in 1976. It then became a wholly-owned subsidiary of the Coca-Cola Company, which sold it to Seagram, and it is now owned by Vintners International. The Taylor Wine Company produces premium champagnes, Lake Country and Taylor

New York State premium table wines, Lake Country soft wines, and popular dessert wines.

The various tendrils of these separate stories are brought together in the architecturally uninspired, but otherwise interesting Visitor Center, home to a fascinating museum of wine artifacts; a unique theater, built inside a former gargantuan 35,000-gallon wine tank, where a twenty-minute feature film covering local wine history is presented; and a commodious tasting room with a sixty-six-foot-long redwood-faced bar and a wine shop. The welcome mat extends outside, where tours go by bus to see the various steps in winemaking and view the historic buildings in which this story began.

❧ ❧ ❧

Cana Vineyards

Route 54
Hammondsport, New York
TEL: 607-569-2737
About five miles south
mondsport; Open May–Nov.,
10:30–5, Sun. 12–5. Riesling
wines. Tastings only.

TO SEE & DO
For a scenic and historic adventure,
the Outlet Trail, along Keuka Lake Ou
let between Keuka and Seneca, with
trailheads in Penn Yan and Dresden. In
Penn Yan, the Farmers' Market is held
every Sat., 8–noon, Oct.–May. The
Keuka Maid cruises around the lake;
meals aboard. (For main area sights, see
the end of the Seneca Lake section.)

Seneca Lake

Seneca Lake is thirty-six miles long, plunges 640 feet and is the deepest of the Finger Lakes. Because of its volume, the lake holds the warmth of summer into the fall and winter months. Some experts maintain that this gives the nearby vineyards a wine-growing microclimate that is one of the best for viniferas and all wine grapes.

How indeed viniferas prosper is the subject of increased research at Cornell University's State Agricultural Experimental Station in Geneva, at the northern tip of Seneca Lake. Researcher interest stems in part from the Finger Lakes growers' success with bringing vinifera vines through the harsh upstate winters. Now attention is being turned to other aspects of viticulture such as soil, spacing, pruning, and cloning, which underlie grape quality. Meanwhile, as viniferas hold great promise, hybrids are still a

success among winery visitors and gather top wine prizes in competitions.

Travelers on these wine routes will see that Seneca's wineries do not go back in history. All were founded after the Farm Winery Act of 1976 permitted growers to produce wines from their grapes, although some vineyards go back generations, as do the families working them today. The wineries are within easy driving distance of each other, connected by little towns and lake views.

The region itself can be reached from either I-90 (N.Y.S. Thruway) or Rte. 17 (Southern Tier Expressway). Take I-90 to exit 41 (Seneca Falls) or 42 (Geneva) and continue on Rte. 414 or Rte. 14, respectively. Take Rte 17 to exit 44 in Corning and take Rte. 414 North; or take exit 52 in Elmira and continue on Rte. 14 North toward Watkins Glen.

eries on the West Side of ca Lake

ur Chimneys Farm Winery

lall Road (R.D. #1)
Himrod, New York 14842
TEL: 607-243-7502
PRESIDENT: Walter Pederson
WINEMAKER: Scott Smith
FOUNDED: 1980

AT A GLANCE

Tours & Tastings: May–Oct., Mon.–Sat. 10–6; Sun. 1–6. No tours. Open year-round for sales. Tastings and sales also at New York greenmarkets in Manhattan and Brooklyn, Tues.–Sat. until Christmas. Write or phone winery for schedule.
Closed: Nov.–Apr. 30.
Vineyards: Fifteen acres, primarily planted to Aurora, Delaware; some vinifera and French hybrids.
Wines: Especially known for Late Harvest Delaware; Chardonnay, Cabernet Sauvignon, Vidal Blanc, Seyval Blanc, Eye of the Dove (dry blush), Eye of the Bee (semi-sweet Concord blend), other similarly evocatively named blends.
Awards: Cabernet Sauvignon, Pinot Noir, Late Harvest Delaware.
Picnic Area: Picnic on the spacious grounds on farm-grown, homemade fare you buy on the spot, or bring your own.
Deli: Appetizers, Scandinavian open-face sandwiches, cheese, bread, desserts; coffee and teas.
Retail Shop: Wines, cheeses, fruits, homemade breads; some antiques and gift items.
Credit Cards: MasterCard, Visa.
Access for Disabled: No steps to winery.
Foreign Languages: A United Nations mélange including Danish, Norwegian, Swedish, German, Spanish, French, Portuguese, Korean, and Russian.
Getting There: Take N.Y.S. Thruway to exit 42 and continue on Rte. 14 to Hall Road. The winery is sixteen miles north of Watkins Glen.
Special Wine & Other Events: Last Sat. & Sun. in June: Scandinavian Midsummer Fair; Sat. in Aug. & Sept.: Lake Seneca Chamber Music Series at 7 P.M., with New American cuisine dinner and wine tasting; Organic Renaissance Fair 1st Sat. & Sun. in Aug.

&ea; Four Chimneys is one of a handful of wineries in America that makes no-additives-added wines from organically grown grapes from its own vineyards. Although known for its white wines, Four Chimneys also makes award-winning Cabernet Sauvignon and Pinot Noir.

On the west bank of Seneca Lake, the attractive property has an Italian-style villa with four chimneys, built during the Civil War and now home to the Pederson family, who all help around the winery. The wine shop is in a renovated, nineteenth-century barn, also the setting for the summer concerts.

Walter Pederson, a former Russian life and cultural studies professor at the University of Maryland and an editor at Macmillan, bought the property and started growing grapes in 1976. The first vintage was 1980.

Table grapes have grown on the farm for more than a century. The building now called the Grape House was used to protect picked grapes from ripening in the sun before they could be shipped to the Erie Canal to be sold in New York City and beyond. Winemaker Smith lives there now.

&ea; &ea; &ea;

Lake View Vineyards

Route 14 (R.D. 14)
Himrod, New York 14842
TEL: 607-243-7568
FOUNDED: 1985

Tastings by appointment. Specializing in German-style wines made by a winemaker trained in Geisenheim, Germany. Estate-grown Riesling and Chardonnay.

ï¿¼ ï¿¼ ï¿¼

Giasi Winery

Route 14 (Box 87G)
Rock Stream, New York 14978
TEL: 607-535-7785
OWNER: Vera Giasi

AT A GLANCE
Tours & Tastings: May–Oct., Mon.–Sat. 11–6; Sun. 12–6; tastings and sales. Tours upon request.
Closed: Nov.–Apr.
Vineyards: Eighteen to twenty acres planted primarily to French-American hybrids; additional grapes purchased from local growers. Also cherries, pears.
Wines: Varietals: Cayuga, Seyval Blanc; Blends such as Seneca Gold (Chardonnay, Cayuga, Seyval); Connoisseur (four-year-old red); Convivial (red); Connubial (rosé with sweet finish); Cherry (semi-sweet, from Montmorency cherries).
Retail Shop: Wines sold.
Credit Cards: None.
Access for Disabled: Yes.
Foreign Languages: None.
Getting There: Take N.Y.S. Thruway to exit 42; continue on Rte. 14 to Rock Stream and Giasi Winery.

ï¿¼ Vera Giasi took courses in viticulture and enology at the State University at Stony Brook, Long Island, but winemaking is a family tradition that began in Italy with her husband, Mike's, family. The winery is located in a century-old barn the Giasis converted to serve its new purpose—a former patio is the crushing pad, and what was a basement is now the wine cellar.

ï¿¼ ï¿¼ ï¿¼

Castel Grisch

R.D. 1 (Box 188B)
Watkins Glen, New York 14891
TEL: 607-535-9614
OWNERS: Baggenstoss family
Tiny 2,000-gallon winery in restored barn where visitors can both taste and buy Chardonnay and Riesling and see a "How to Make Wine" display. Plans are for a café with a lake view on what is now the picnic site. Call for details.

ï¿¼ ï¿¼ ï¿¼

Glenora Wine Cellars

Route 14
Glenora-on-Seneca
R.D. 1 (Box 58)
Dundee, New York 14837
TEL: 607-243-5511
OWNER: Ted Griesinger
CELLARMASTER: Tim Miller
FOUNDED: 1976

AT A GLANCE
Tours & Tastings: May–Oct., Mon.–Sat. 10–5, Sun. 12–5; Nov.–Apr., Mon.–Sat. 10–4, ten-minute slide presentation takes you from vine to wine, scored with Vivaldi sound track and narration. No tour. Tastings available.
Closed: Easter, Thanksgiving, Christmas, New Year's Day.
Vineyards: Purchases grapes primarily from Finger Lakes growers; some Long Island. Out-of-state only if the varieties cannot be New York-grown.
Wines: Focuses on whites—Johann Blanc (a Riesling), Johannisberg Riesling, Chardonnay, Gewürztraminer, Late Harvest Ravat, Seyval Blanc, Cayuga white, *methode champenoise* champagne, blanc de blanc.
Awards: Recent winners in 1988 New York Classic competitions: 1987 Chardonnay, and 1987 First Blush.
Picnic Area: Covered patio overlooking

lake, doubles as jazz pavilion during the concert season.

Retail Shop: Wines, gifts.

Credit Cards: MasterCard, Visa.

Access for Disabled: Fully accessible, including lift to cellar.

Foreign Languages: None.

Getting There: Take N.Y.S. Thruway to exit 42; continue on Rte. 4 South for about twenty-four miles to winery on west side of lake.

Special Wine & Other Events: Jazz in the Vineyard Concerts, featuring big names, are a well-known tradition each summer at Glenora; tickets are sold at the winery and through Teletron and Ticketron outlets. Bring your own lawn chair or blanket and plenty of friends.

≈ Glenora Wine Cellars began in 1978 as one of New York's first farm wineries (meaning a maximum production of 50,000 gallons or 21,030 cases annually) and graduated in 1988 to commercial winery status as a result of expansion in its property and production. To add new *methode champenoise* sparkling wines to the menu is a goal. Glenora plans increased vinifera wine production as well, and has been purchasing many more tons of these grapes.

New caves for champagne cellars and top-of-the-line champagne-making equipment are part of the $1.2 million renovation of the winery and visitor center. The winery also has one hundred French oak barrels and plenty of top-of-the-line steel barrels as well. .

On the way to fame Glenora merged with Finger Lakes Wine Cellars and has been much enlarged: patterned after local barns, the expanded Glenora has a spacious red-pine-and-cedar local visitor center and tasting room, with crafts such as handmade grape-patterned quilts for sale alongside the wines. Large windows and a big deck overlook the lake and surrounding fields.

The wooden exterior harmonizes with the area's old barns, yet gives a modern appearance. And as visitors enter there is another link to the past in a realistic painting of the famous local falls that inspired Glenora's label.

Incidentally, the Scottish settled Dundee, as the name implies, and they named Glenora ("Golden Glen").

≈ ≈ ≈

Hermann J. Wiemer Vineyard, Inc.

Route 14 (Box 4)
Dundee, New York 14837
TEL: 607-243-7971; 243-7983
OWNER: Hermann J. Wiemer
WINEMAKER: Dana Keeler
FOUNDED: 1980

AT A GLANCE

Tours & Tastings: May–Nov. 1, Mon.–Sat. 11–4:30, Sun. 12–5; also by appointment.

Closed: Nov.–May 1.

Vineyards: Sixty-five acres, all vinifera, primarily Chardonnay, Riesling, Pinot Noir, Sauvignon Blanc.

Wines: Wiemer primarily explores the themes and variations on Riesling, with a bass note of Pinot Noir, and *arpeggio* from *methode champenoise* champagne.

Awards: Platinum medal, in 1987 New York Wine Classic statewide competition, to 1986 Individual Bunch Select, Late Harvest Johannisberg Riesling (Trockenbeerenauslese), among many awards to Rieslings at various times.

Retail Shop: Sells wines and accessories on-site.

Credit Cards: MasterCard, Visa.

Access for Disabled: One level.

Foreign Languages: German.

Getting There: Fourteen miles north of Watkins Glen on Rte. 14; a few miles north of Glenora Wine Cellars.

✒ Herman Wiemer started his winery after years of producing prizewinning wines from hybrids as winemaker at Bully Hill. Wiemer brought out his own all-vinifera label in 1980 from the vineyard he planted in 1973, with the single idea of producing fabulous European-style wines in the Finger Lakes. Did he succeed?

Today Wiemer's award-winning wines are served in some of Manhattan's classiest restaurants and to first-class passengers on American Airlines flights to Switzerland and Germany. Some of his wines sell out before they are bottled. He has also started a nursery of vinifera clones from which his wine is produced, and ships more than 200,000 cuttings each year to other vineyards across the country.

Wiemer was born in the Moselle Valley into a family of winemakers for over 300 years. Now in the most peaceful of settings, his handsome winery and tasting room are housed in a renovated old Shaker hay barn. Inside, Wiemer has fitted a two-level studio apartment under the high-beamed ceilings, from which he can survey his gleaming steel tanks and French oak barrels.

A field away, across a little footbridge that goes way back in history, is Wiemer's nursery. He is often here, tending the vines or guiding the cloning operation in the grafting room. Next to the winery is a gracious old home Wiemer has restored at great cost with the idea of living in it or renting out to special visitors who wish to stay with a winemaker.

✒ ✒ ✒

The Barrington Champagne Co.

2081 Route 230
Dundee, New York 14837-9425
TEL: 607-243-8844
Tours and tastings by appointment only.

Halfway between Dundee and Wayne. Cool, stone cellars of the 1819 Red Brick Inn are of interest for *methode champenoise* champagne. Ray Spencer, former general manager at Glenora Wine Cellars, makes his bubbly here from Chardonnay and Pinot Noir grapes grown around Seneca Lake and ages it four years before serving and selling it. (See "Accommodations" following Cayuga Lake section for Red Brick Inn.)

✒ ✒ ✒

Squaw Point Winery

Poplar Point Road
Dundee, New York 14837
TEL: 607-243-8602
Open May–Sept., Mon.–Sat. 10–5; Sun. 12–5; call for details. Haywagon tours a specialty.

Wineries on the East Side of Seneca Lake

Hazlitt 1852 Vineyards

Route 414
Hector, New York 14841
TEL: 607-546-5812
OWNER: Jerome Hazlitt
FOUNDED: 1985

AT A GLANCE
Tours & Tastings: Apr.–Nov., Mon.–Sat. 10–6; Sun. 12–6; Dec.–Mar., Fri.–Sat. 10–6, Sun. 12–6. No tours; tastings only.
Closed: Major holidays; call for details.
Vineyards: Forty-seven acres planted to American and French-American hybrids and viniferas.
Wines: Chardonnay, Riesling, Cayuga, Vidal, Baco Noir, Golden Chablis, Red Cat (Catawba).
Awards: Riesling, Vidal Blanc, Baco Noir, Golden Chablis.
Retail Shop: Wines sold on-site.
Credit Cards: MasterCard, Visa.

Access for Disabled: Everything on ground level.
Foreign Languages: None.
Getting There: From Watkins Glen: Take Rte. 414 North for about ten miles. The winery is on the east side of the highway in the village of Hector.

&. This tiny, family-run winery is now operated by the sixth generation of Hazlitts to grow grapes in the hamlet of Hector, on the east side of Seneca Lake. Informality is the order of the day. Visitors are welcome to enjoy wines, popcorn, and a chat, while learning something of local history through the Seneca Indian artifacts and antiques in the tasting room.

&. &. &.

Prejean Winery

2634 Route 14
Penn Yan, New York 14527
TEL: 315-536-7524
FOUNDED: 1985
Tours and tastings May–Nov. 10–6; Dec.–Apr., Sat. & Sun. 10–4; other times by appointment. Modern winery, featuring estate-bottled wines made from vinifera—Chardonnay, Johannisberg Riesling, Gewürztraminer; French and American hybrids—Seyval, Cayuga, Marechal Foch. A fairly new winery making award-winning wines, including a bronze medal for its 1984 Gewürztraminer in the 1988 N.Y. Classic.

&. &. &.

Rolling Vineyards Farm Winery, Inc.

5055 Route 414 (P.O. Box 37)
Hector, New York 14841
TEL: 607-546-9302
OWNERS: Ed and JoAnne Grow
FOUNDED: 1981

AT A GLANCE
Tours & Tastings: May–Oct., Mon–Sat. 10–5, Sun. 12–5; tastings only. Other months by appointment.
Closed: Major holidays; call for details.
Vineyards: Sixty acres planted to vinifera and French-American hybrids.
Wines: Chardonnay, Johannisberg Riesling, Gewürztraminer, Seyval, Vidal, Ravat, Marechal Foch, Chelois, rosé and white blends.
Awards: Seyval tops the list for consistent awards, including the 1985 Governor's Cup; Vidal, Johannisberg Riesling, and Rolling White are among the other repeaters. Recently, a silver for 1987 Vignoles at 1988 New York Classic.
Retail Shop: Wines sold on-site.
Credit Cards: MasterCard, Visa.
Access for Disabled: Yes.
Foreign Languages: None.
Getting There: Seven miles north of Watkins Glen on Rte. 414; east shore of Seneca Lake. South of Hazlitt 1852 Vineyards.

&. This brown-wood barn winery and vineyard has a spectacular view of Seneca Lake, to be savored with their award-winning, estate-bottled wines. Only a fraction of the fruit grown on the site goes into these wines; the rest is sold to other wineries.

&. &. &.

Chateau Lafayette Reneau

Route 414 (Box 87)
Hector, New York 14841
TEL: 607-546-2062
WINEMAKER: Rob Thomas
FOUNDED: 1985
Tours and tastings Mon.–Sat. 10–5, Sun. 12–5. Small, fairly new winery on Seneca Lake's eastern slope, with a fine view and hospitable atmosphere. Next to Rolling Vineyards Farm Winery. Winner of four bronze medals in 1988 New York Classic

for 1986 Seyval, Riesling, Vignoles, and Niagara Mist.

🐌 🐌 🐌

Poplar Ridge

Route 414
Valois, New York 14888
TEL: 607-582-6421
FOUNDED: 1981
Tastings May–Nov., Mon.–Sat. 10–5, Sun. 12–5. Tours by appointment. Twenty-acre vineyards; best known for Cayuga wines and prizewinning 1986 Ravat. Near Gold Seal's vinifera vineyards.

🐌 🐌 🐌

Wagner Vineyards and Ginny Lee Cafe

Route 414
Lodi, New York 14860
TEL: 607-582-6450
OWNER: Stanley (Bill) Wagner
WINEMAKER: John Herbert
FOUNDED: 1978

AT A GLANCE
Tours & Tastings: Mon.–Sat. 10–4, Sun. 10–5. Forty-five-minute tours give good education about winemaking, including a look at a Wilmes press (a low-pressure tank press), fermentation, bottling, and wine cellars with aging wines; includes tasting of seven or eight wines after tour—additional wines fifty cents each or three for $1.25.
Vineyards: 120 acres, planted to vinifera varieties, hybrids, and native American.
Wines: Twenty or more wines include Johannisberg Riesling, Chardonnay, Pinot Noir, Seyval, Ravat, Niagara, proprietaries, and blends.
Awards: Consistently selected by *Wine Spectator*'s panel as one of the top seventy wineries in the world. The Chardon-

nays have won over California wines in competitions; Johannisberg Riesling, Niagara, Delaware, and Seyval Blanc are other high placers. Recently, new Melody won a bronze in 1988 New York Classic.
Picnic Area: Tables under graceful willows and stately pines on extensive lawns.
Café: Ginny Lee Cafe (named for owner Bill Wagner's granddaughter), on spacious striped-tent-covered deck, with white wrought-iron tables and chairs; has spectacular view of Seneca Lake and the vineyards. A cheerful ambience, light meals. Open mid-May–mid-Oct., Mon.–Sat. 11–4, Sun. brunch 10–2, reservations required; Sun. lunch 2–4:30.
Retail Shop: Wines and gifts.
Credit Cards: MasterCard, Visa.
Access for Disabled: Yes.
Foreign Languages: None.
Getting There: N.Y.S. Thruway (I-90) to exit 41, and turn south on Rte. 414 to winery near Lodi.

🐌 Bill Wagner's octagonal winery is a wonderful vantage point for viewing his vineyards, which extend down to Lake Seneca, while tours show visitors the inside story in the pine-and-hemlock-paneled winery. Wagner entered the wine business after spending many years as a grape grower. Even now he supplies grapes to such large wineries as Canandaigua and Taylor.

Vinifera wines are on the increase here, but Wagner Vineyards also continues to innovate with other varieties. In 1988 it was first to commercially produce a new varietal—Melody, which is available only through the winery or its Syracuse shop. This white wine grape was developed and christened by the New York State Agricultural Experiment Station at Geneva. Its clean, crisp, citrus flavor is similar to Cayuga White and Gewürztraminer.

One of Wagner's older wines, Alta B, is on the sweet side and was his late mother's favorite. The name pays tribute to her, as does her picture as a young woman on the label.

TO SEE & DO

In Corning, New York, a gateway to Keuka and Seneca wineries, the fascinating Corning Glass Center is the state's third most popular attraction, after New York City and Niagara Falls. The center houses the world-renowned Glass Museum, with a collection dating back to prehistoric times. One of the exhibits shows wineglasses through the years and traces the history of drinking by the size and shape of the glasses; excellent captions give details. Visitors also get a glimpse of fiber optics of the future, as well as view the Steuben Glass Factory craftsmen at work (open year-round, daily, 9–5; closed Thanksgiving, Dec. 24 and 25, and Jan. 1; Centerway, 607-974-8271). A second major museum in Corning, the Rockwell Museum (corner of Cedar and Denision, Tel. 607-937-5386, open Sept.–June, Mon.–Sat. 9–5, Sun. 12–5; Jul. & Aug., Mon.–Fri. 9–7, Sat. 9–5, Sun. 12–5) has the East's finest collection of art of the American West in striking displays, plus 2,000 pieces of Carder Steuben Glass and turn-of-the-century toys. At 59 West Pulteney Street (not far from the Corning Center) is the restored 1796 Benjamin Patterson Inn (open weekdays, 10–4; tel: 607-937-5281), with log cabin, schoolhouse, gardens.

Virtually every community near the wineries has its restored historic district, but perhaps none compares with Elmira's well-manicured twenty-square-block preserve, listed in the National Register of Historic Places and due to double in size in the next few years. Elmira is Mark Twain territory: he and his family summered at Quarry Farm (Crane Road; tel: 607-732-0993) for twenty years, and Woodlawn Cemetery is his burial site.

Race fans fill Watkins Glen for the Watkins Glen International (Bronson Hill Road; tel: 607-974-7162), an extravaganza of motor sports events (June–Sept.). Famous also is Watkins Glen State Park (lower gorge, entrance off Franklin; tel: 607-535-4511), with its nineteen waterfalls, green and inviting grottos, caverns, amphitheaters. A two-mile trail over bridges offers unforgettable views (Timespell Gift Shop, near lower entrance to park, gives maps, details). Timespell also describes the great park's long history in a sound and light show each night at dusk and again forty-five minutes later.

In Hammondsport, a between-the-wineries stop can be made at the Glenn H. Curtiss Museum (tel: 607-569-2160) for displays devoted to early aviation and other types of transportation such as cars, motorcycles, boats.

Various modes of transportation also await the visitor: board Captain Bill's lake ride at the foot of Franklin Street at Seneca Lake, Watkins Glen (tel: 607-536-4541) for a cruise and a meal. Or enjoy vintage vehicles en route to main attractions: in Corning, a double-decker bus leaves the outlying visitor parking lot (Pulteney and Centerway, every ten minutes, seven days a week, 9–5, May 15–Oct. 15), Elmira's replica turn-of-the-century trolley starts from the Chemung County Chamber of Commerce (215 East Church Street, May 27–Sept. 5, once each hour, Mon.–Fri. 10–4, Sat. & Sun. 12–4); Watkins Glen's turn-of-the-century trolley runs weekends only, 1–7, until June 26. From June 27–Sept. 5, the trolley runs every day from 1 to 7.

Some shopping opportunities include the well-stocked museum stores, the Corning Outlet Store (106 East Third Street, Watkins Glen; tel: 607-535-2139), and the Old Orchard Farm (Rte. 414, five miles north of Watkins Glen in Burdett); for antiques, collectibles, and organically grown produce in season.

FOOD STOPS

Wine Country Provisioner
105 Third Street
Watkins Glen, New York 14891
Tel: 607-243-7301
To pack a picnic for Watkins Glen or a winery visit, stop here for New York and imported cheeses, fresh pâtés, homemade breads, rich desserts, and pastries.

Wixon's Honey Stand
Route 14
Dundee, New York 14837
Tel: 607-243-7301
Glass beehive permits close observation of fascinating hive life while attendant explains its intricacies. Honey, maple syrup, gifts, and beekeeping supplies. Many flavors of ice cream. Open May–Oct. 10 miles north of Watkins Glen; 27 miles south of Geneva.

Cayuga Lake

This wine route follows forty miles of scenic splendor along the west shore of Cayuga Lake. The high lime and pH of the soil, combined with the temperature-tempering 436-foot-deep lake, make this area suitable for growing fragile vinifera and other more hardy grape varieties. Low-lying Cayuga Lake protects grapes from frost in spring and fall, like the other lakes, but also adds additional days to the growing season.

Distinctive soil, climate, history, and geographic features have earned the eighteen vineyards and eight wineries of three counties—Seneca, Tompkins, and Cayuga—the Cayuga Lake v.a. designation by the federal government. The wineries offer views along the lake and stage spirited events on their own or tied to Cayuga Wine Trail themes to delight travelers. A few choice events are mentioned here; for others, contact individual wineries or the Cayuga Wine Trail (P.O. Box 123, Fayette, New York 13065) for an up-to-date listing.

❧ ❧ ❧

Americana Vineyards Winery

East Covert Road
(12 miles north of Ithaca)
Interlaken, New York 14847
TEL: 607-387-6801
FOUNDED: 1981
Open May–Dec., Mon.–Sat. 10–5:30, Sun. 12–5:30; Jan.–Apr., Sat. 10–5:30, Sun. 12–5:30; weekdays call for appointment. Free guided tours offer a chance to cork your own bottle and a tasting. Picnic grounds. French-American and American hybrid wines. Located south of Lucas on East Covert Road, between Rtes. 89 and 96, near Interlaken.

❧ ❧ ❧

Hosmer

Route 89 (Box 264)
Ovid, New York 14521
TEL: 607-869-5585
FOUNDED: 1985
Open May 1–Nov. 30, Mon.–Sat. 10:30–5:30, Sun. 12–6, by appointment. $1.50 for tasting, includes logo glass. Tiny winery with lovely view; 2,500 gallons cellared; Chardonnay, Riesling, Seyval, among the wines available. Half a mile south of Planes Vineyards.

❧ ❧ ❧

Knapp Vineyards

2770 Ernsberger Road (County Road 128)
Romulus, New York 14541
TEL: 607-869-9271
OWNERS: Doug & Suzie Knapp
FOUNDED: 1982

AT A GLANCE
Tours & Tastings: May–Dec. 31, Mon.–Sat. 10–5, Sun. 12–5; Jan.–Apr., weekends only 12–5; tastings (six wines, $1.50) & sales; informal tours on request happily given when not too busy.
Closed: Nov.–Memorial Day.
Vineyards: Sixty-five acres, planted increasingly to vinifera; French-American hybrids, labrusca. An additional 130 acres leased to other wineries.
Wines: Chardonnay, Riesling, Cabernet Sauvignon, Vignoles, Seyval. Dutchman's Breeches (Vignoles & Vidal blend), generic reds and whites; *methode champenoise* Blanc de Blanc and Chardonnay champagnes.
Awards: Consistent medalists: Vignoles and Late Harvest Vignoles, Johannisberg Riesling, Dutchman's Breeches. Recently 1985 Blanc de Blanc received a bronze in the 1988 New York Classic.
Picnic Area: Dotted about property; owners sometimes join visitors for a bite and chat.
Retail Shop: Wines sold on-site.
Credit Cards: MasterCard, Visa.
Access for Disabled: Ramp.
Foreign Languages: None.
Getting There: Take N.Y.S. Thruway to exit 414 onto Rte. 388; continue to Scenic Rte. 89 and turn south along the lake to the winery at 2770 Ernsberger Rd. (County Road 128).
Special Wine & Other Events: June: Anniversary celebration; Nov.: Federweiser, harvest event, and others in conjunction with Cayuga Wine Trail Wineries.

 Although the vineyards were founded in 1971, Doug and Suzie Knapp operated them as absentee owners from the Panama Canal Zone until 1976. There Doug was an electronics engineer and Suzie a teacher and counselor, before they settled upstate.

Initially only grape growers, the Knapps were unhappy selling high-quality, balanced fruit for often mediocre products, so they set up their own winery in 1982 to bring out fruit-worthy wines. Doug indeed believes that the success of a wine is 90 percent in the fruit—"The less tampering with good juice, the more perfect the wine," he says. His theory has paid off, because the self-trained winemaker's wines repeatedly win prizes.

From the Knapps' first vintage of 500 gallons in 1982 to the current 25,000 gallons, steady growth has brought several rewards, among them expansion of the tasting room. There's still an air of comfortable informality about the place. The Knapps conduct the tastings and enjoy wine talk with connoisseurs or teaching novices the fine points of wine tasting; time permitting, they might even carry a good discussion outdoors and join guests for bite of lunch. An expert cook, Suzie teaches well-attended winery cooking classes to show how foods marry with wines.

Lakeshore Winery–Craft Shop

5132 Route 89
Romulus, New York 14541
TEL: 315-549-8461
FOUNDED: 1982
OWNERS: Bill and Doris Brown

AT A GLANCE
Tours & Tastings: Memorial Day–Dec. 31, Mon.–Sat. 11–5, Sun. 12–5.
Closed: Jan.–Memorial Day.
Vineyards: Three owned, two leased; planted primarily to vinifera varieties.
Wines: Chardonnay, Riesling, Cabernet Sauvignon, Gewürztraminer; also Baco Noir and Aunt Clara, a blend.
Retail Shop: Wines; crafts in the loft.
Credit Cards: MasterCard, Visa.
Access for Disabled: Limited access to tasting room and pressing deck area.
Foreign Languages: None.

Getting There: From Swedish Hill Vineyards: Take Ogden Road (County Rd. 124) toward Cayuga Lake and turn south to Lakeshore Winery at 5132 Route 89.

ða Informality prevails here. The wine tasting is laid-back and relaxed. The view is beautiful, and the community craft shop a big drawing card.

ða ða ða

Lucas Vineyards

County Road 150
Interlaken, New York 14847
TEL: 607-532-4825
OWNERS: William and Ruth M. Lucas
FOUNDED: 1980

AT A GLANCE
Tours & Tastings: May 1–Nov. 30, Mon.– Sat. 10:30–5:30, Sun. 12–6; Apr.–Dec., weekends only. Self-guided tours through vineyards, winery; free prepurchase tastings and formal $1.50 tastings with logo glass souvenir, both conducted by Ruth Lucas.
Closed: Major holidays.
Vineyards: Twenty acres planted to vinifera, French-American and American hybrids.
Wines: Vintage-dated Chardonnay, Riesling, Gewürztraminer, Seyval, Cayuga, Ravat, Vignoles, Vidal, Rayon D'Or, De Chaunac; three others: Captain's Belle (blush) and Tug Boat White and Red.
Awards: Medals in a number of regional competitions include double-gold Ravat Vignoles; golds to Cayuga Semi-Dry, Seyval, Vignoles, Captain's Belle; silvers and bronzes to these and others.
Picnic Area: On the grounds.
Retail Shop: Wines sold on-site.
Credit Cards: MasterCard, Visa.
Access for Disabled: None.
Foreign Languages: None.
Getting There: From Hosmer: Take Rte.

89 South to County Rd. 150 and turn west to winery on left before Rte. 96.
Special Wine & Other Events: Aug.: Peach Weekend (features all manner of ripe peach treats).

ða William Lucas is a tugboat pilot in New York Harbor and along the East Coast, which accounts for the nautical theme of some of the labels. In his time off, he works with his wife, Ruth, to bring out award-winning estate wines from their small vineyard and winery in a former cow barn. The Lucas family made a quantum leap from the Bronx to the Finger Lakes in 1974, took Extension courses in viticulture, and consulted with the highly experienced David Bagley of Poplar Ridge before releasing their first wines from their own vines in 1980.

ða ða ða

Planes Cayuga Vineyard

6800 Route 89 at Elm Beach
Ovid, New York 14521
TEL: 607-869-5158
OWNERS: Robert and Mary Plane
WINEMAKER: Robert Plane
FOUNDED: 1980

AT A GLANCE
Tours & Tastings: Late May–Oct., daily 12–5; off-season, weekends 12–4. Twenty-minute winery tours every thirty minutes; vineyard tour during harvest (end of Sept.–Oct. 20); tasting, $1.50, includes glass.
Closed: Major holidays.
Vineyards: Thirty-four acres on a 200-acre plot sloping up from Cayuga's shores, planted to vinifera, French-American, and American hybrids.
Wines: Chardonnay, Johannisberg Riesling, Cayuga White, Chancellor, Serenade series—Solo (100 percent Vignoles), Duet (Cayuga, Ravat, Vignoles blend), Trio (Cayuga, Vignoles, Chancellor).

Awards: Planes Cayuga, White Chancellor, Chardonnay, Johannisberg Riesling, Serenade Solo are often cited.
Picnic Area: Luncheon cart on the deck.
Retail Shop: Wines sold on-site.
Credit Cards: MasterCard, Visa.
Access for Disabled: Limited.
Foreign Languages: None.
Getting There: West side of Cayuga Lake, Hwy. 89, five miles south of Knapp Vineyards.
Special Wine & Other Events: Vertical tastings compare wines from different vintages; wines and food events. Participants in Cayuga Wine Trail events.

ᨘ Bob Plane, retired president of Clarkson University, and his wife, Mary, a former personnel administrator at Cornell University and now vineyard manager, are innovators along the Cayuga Wine Trail. Through their Vignerons program, tiny vineyards are leased to amateur vineyardists and home winemakers, who get lessons from Mary on how to make vines grow. The Planes also give a Cellar Masters course to show amateurs how wines are made at a working winery.

Bob Plane, a director of the Geneva Experimental Station, is backing the increased research on viniferas in New York State and on his own home ground as well. The Planes' 1930s barn winery is on an idyllic site on the west side of Cayuga Lake. The barn's spacious upper level is often the scene of winery events, and has an unforgettable view of the lake, as do the open balcony (used for tastings in fine weather) and a wine sales area. Below in the cellar, full of all the tools of the winemaker's trade, are oak barrels and steel for storing and fermenting wine.

ᨘ ᨘ ᨘ

Swedish Hill Vineyards

4565 Route 414
Romulus, New York 14541

TEL: 315-549-8326
OWNERS: Richard and Cynthia Peterson
FOUNDED: 1986
Open May–Dec., Mon.–Sat., 10–6, Sun. 12–6; Jan.–Apr., weekends 11–5. Tours and tastings. Small estate winery producing prizewinning Late Harvest Vignoles and Vignoles; Chardonnay, Chablis, Chancellor (red); and proprietories. Picnic with a view from deck or grounds. Eight miles south of Seneca Falls.

TO SEE & DO
There is a rich supply of peaceful parks, lake views, and architecture that serve as enduring reminders of local history and blend with Seneca Lake and Keuka Lake attractions.

Life in earlier times is recalled at one of America's most unusual museums, the Waterloo Memorial Day Museum, Main Street, Waterloo (open mid-May–mid-Sept.; Tues., Wed., Thurs., Fri. 1:30–4:30), which commemorates the town's founding of the holiday in May 1866 in displays and artifacts as well as Civil War memorabilia.

Seneca Falls celebrates being the birthplace of women's rights with some of the area's finest sights. Among these are the Women's Rights National Historical Park, where the Visitor Center, 116 Fall Street (open year-round, Mon.–Fri. 9–5; Sat. 10–4; Sun. 12–4; tel: 315-568-2991), has interpretive exhibits on display. The park is home to the white-shutter-trimmed house of suffrage leader Elizabeth Cady Stanton and other women's rights leaders' homes. The recently dedicated Women's Hall of Fame, 76 Fall Street (open year-round, Mon.–Sat. 10–4; summer, Sun. 12–4; tel: 315-568-2936), honors outstanding American women.

At Cayuga, journey through time with the elegant treasures at stately Seward Mansion, a national historic landmark, and the mementoes at the Cayuga Museum of History and Art. The centerpiece of Tompkins County, at the south end of Cayuga Lake, is the town of Ithaca, with many distinctions, the most unusual being that it claims to be the birthplace of the ice-cream sundae. Attend a craft show, festival, or art exhibit on the open Ithaca Commons, or enjoy a cultural event at Cornell University or Ithaca College, which are the heart and soul of this town.

Visit Taughannock Falls, in the state park of the same name, to see one of the highest single, straight-drop waterfalls east of the Rockies; explore the gorges, with other plunging cascades, and head for the hills for a view of the town—especially inspiring at sunset.

ACCOMMODATIONS

It takes about an hour to drive from Seneca/Keuka lakes to Cayuga Lake. That means some of the following places to stay can serve all destinations in the area, as can some of those listed after Canandaigua Lake. When planning, bear in mind any added drive in "Accommodations."

Bed and Breakfast Guide to New York's Finger Lakes
Finger Lakes Association
P.O. Box 862
Canandaigua, New York 14424
Sixty-eight B&B accommodations in the Finger Lakes wine region; send self-addressed envelope for copy of guide.

Dundee
Lakeside Terrace
660 East Waneta Lake Road
R.D. 1, Box 197
Dundee, New York 14837
Tel: 607-292-6606
Comfortable, rustic lakeside home. Swim, fish, sunbathe. Continental breakfast.

The 1819 Red Brick Inn
2081 Route 230
Dundee, New York 14837

Tel: 601-243-8844
Outstanding Federal architecture combined with antique-accented interiors. Four guest rooms, each named for a different wine, two with private bathrooms. The inn also houses the Barrington Champagne Co. (See Seneca Lake wineries listings.)

Willow Cove
77 South Glenora Road
R.D. 1, Box 87
Dundee, New York 14837
Tel: 607-243-8482
200-year-old inn on the west side of Seneca Lake. Big, comfortable living room and spacious porches. Wine and cheese in the evening. Continental breakfast served in dining room.

Ithaca Area
Benn Conger Inn
206 West Cortland Street
Groton, New York 13073
Tel: 607-898-5817
Comfortable, chef-owned country inn about twenty minutes from Ithaca. Spacious acreage for cross-country skiing, hiking. Full breakfast. Renowned wine cellar; see also under "restaurants."

Peregrine House
140 College Avenue
Ithaca, New York 14850
Tel: 607-277-3862
Mansard roof tops a three-story home built in 1874. Marble fireplaces, carved wood ceilings, and Victorian furnishings make this a comfortable, attractive place to stay. Enjoy sherry in the evening. Continental breakfast.

Rose Inn
813 Auburn Road
Route 34 North (P.O. Box 6576)
Ithaca, New York 14850
Tel: 607-533-4202
Built in the 1800s, with a handsome mahogany spiral staircase as focal point.

Valuable antique furnishings and excellent food. Breakfast on German apple pancakes or French toast and homemade preserves; enjoy Continental cuisine for dinner. Set on twenty acres of spacious, well-tended grounds with small apple orchard.

Montour Falls
The Montour House
Montour Falls, New York 14865
Tel: 607-535-2494
Well-restored Greek Revival hotel from 1854, listed in the National Register of Historic Places. The interior features the original white marble fireplaces, curving staircase, and roof skylight. Some rooms have views of gorgeous Chequaga Falls, a block away, just one of thirty waterfalls in the area. The French Quarter restaurant features creole food (see listing under restaurants). Three miles from Watkins Glen, half an hour from Corning.

Seneca Falls
The Gould
108 Fall Street
Seneca Falls, New York 13148
Tel: 315-568-5801
Turn-of-the-century inn with rooms, suites, and a dining room well known for fine wine and food. (See also under restaurants.)

Trumansburg
Sage Cottage
112 East Main Street
Route 96 (P.O. Box 626)
Trumansburg, New York 14886
Tel: 607-387-6449
Restored Gothic Revival home with charming gardens and a cozy ambience. Full breakfasts feature homemade herb breads, jams. Comfortably furnished rooms with many antiques; nice sun porch.

James Russell Webster Mansion Inn
115 East Main Street
(Routes 5 & 20)
Waterloo, New York 13165
Tel: 315-539-3032
Elegant, expensive, antique-filled mansion, with marble bathrooms and canopy beds; fireplaces and air-conditioning; cat figurine museum and real cats as well. Lovely terraced Georgian courtyard. Delicious breakfasts and dinners, the latter only with advance notice.

RESTAURANTS
The following are only a few of the many restaurants in the Finger Lakes now serving locally made wines:

Elmira Heights
Pierce's 1894
228 Oakwood Avenue
Elmira Heights, New York 14903
Tel: 607-734-2022
Four-generation-old family-run restaurant of renown. 35,000-bottle wine cellar, with 60 percent devoted to New York wines. Interpretive American cuisine; rich pastries and desserts served in six turn-of-the-century-style dining rooms.

Hammondsport
Pleasant Valley Inn
Route 54
Bath-Hammondsport Road
Hammondsport, New York 14860
Tel: 607-569-2282
Pretty pink mansion where food has a gentle Mediterranean hint against a Victorian motif. Open year-round for lunch, dinner, Sunday buffet brunch.

Ithaca
Abby's
309 Third Street
Ithaca, New York 14850
Tel: 607-273-1999
New California French cuisine with mesquite-grilled specialties among the offerings. Dinner Mon.–Sun.; Sun. brunch.

Benn Conger Inn
206 West Cortland Street
Groton, New York 13073
Tel: 607-898-5817
French and country Italian cuisine; well-stocked wine cellar. Twenty minutes from Ithaca.

Danny's Place
23 Cinema Drive
Itahca, New York 14850
In Small Mall, behind Sheraton Inn
Tel: 607-257-6656
Light salads, sandwiches; wines and cheeses; full meals.

Greystone Inn
1457 East Shore Drive (Route 34)
King Ferry, New York 13081
Tel: 607-273-4096
Set in a garden-surrounded, nineteenth-century Federalist mansion with elegant furnishings; serves well-prepared Continental foods, individually prepared. Five-hundred-label wine list, 20 percent of it New York State wines. Garden dining in summer.

L'Auberge Du Cochon Rouge
1152 Danby Road (Route 96B)
Ithaca, New York 14850
Tel: 607-273-3464
Award-winning French restaurant, with wines from Hermann J. Weimer, Glenora, and others.

Turback's
Elmira Road (Route 13 South)
Ithaca, New York 14850
Tel: 607-272-6484
Well-known nineteenth-century millionaire's mansion, now features regional dishes and New York wines. In 1988, Turback's also became a winery, producing 200 cases of house white from grapes purchased from Finger Lakes growers.

Seneca Falls
The Gould
108 Fall Street
Seneca Falls, New York 13148
Tel: 315-568-5801
Turn-of-the-century ambience in three atmospheric dining rooms with tasty Continental foods; good wine list. Lunch, Mon.–Fri.; dinner every evening; Sunday buffet brunch.

Montour Falls
French Quarter Restaurant
The Montour House
Montour Falls, New York 14865
Tel: 607-535-2494
French Quarter dining room in elegant, restored Greek Revival hotel from 1854. Classic French, Creole, and Cajun dishes feature locally grown produce and Finger Lakes wines. About three miles from Watkins Glen.

Seneca Lodge
South entrance to Watkins Glen State
  Park
Tel: 607-535-2014
Freshly prepared foods, homemade breads. Popular local lunch and dinner spot. May–Oct. 31.

Markets and Farms
Farmer's Market
Ithaca, New York 14850
Taughannock Boulevard (Sat.), DeWitt Park (downtown) (Wed.), Summers only.

Venture Vineyards
Tel: 607-582-6774
Pick cherries, pears, grapes in season; wines, juices. Off Route 414, south of Lodi, near Seneca Lake.

❧ LONG ISLAND

Long Island wineries are just a decade old and are already gaining quite a reputation for themselves for making premium wines from vinifera grapes. The North Fork's growing season, which averages 200 days, is the same as that in Bordeaux, France. Wineries here draw from 1,000 acres of vineyards planted to vinifera, amounting to more than half the vinifera acreage in the state.

Two distinct microclimates have created two recognized v.a.'s—the Hamptons, characterized by the temperature-moderating effects of the Gulf Stream and the area's sandy-loamy soil, and the North Fork, distinguished by a long growing season and unique microclimate created by its position between Long Island Sound and Great Peconic Bay. To reach the Hamptons, follow Scenic Route 27 all the way to Montauk for spectacular views of the Atlantic. For the North Fork, take Scenic Route 25, which leads past the coves and inlets of Great Peconic Bay and Gardiners Bay on its way to Orient Point.

Wine routes go to one of New York's most fashionable getaway places, the Hamptons, where they now sip local wines with their brie and biscuits, and to the art-and-antiquing territory of the North Fork, dipping briefly into nineteenth-century whaling towns and memorabilia. Here are some of the main Long Island wineries and a list of others to visit while in the area:

North Fork

Twelve of the fourteen Long Island wineries are along the North Fork.

❧ ❧ ❧

Hargrave Vineyard

Alvah's Lane (Route 48)
Cutchogue, New York 11935
TEL: 516-734-5158; Summer,
516-734-5111
OWNERS: Alec and Louisa Hargrave
FOUNDED: 1973

AT A GLANCE
Tours & Tastings: Open daily from Memorial Day to Dec.; call for hours. Guided tours take in vineyard, winemaking, and include comparative tasting.
Closed: Jan. to Memorial Day.
Vineyards: Forty-five acres, all vinifera.
Wines: Cabernet Sauvignon, Chardonnay, Blanc de Noir, Fumé Blanc.

Awards: Gold to 1986 Chardonnay Reserve and bronze to Chardonnay, both in 1987 New York Classic; Bronzes to both wines in 1988 New York Classic.
Retail Shop: Sells wines on-site.
Credit Cards: American Express, MasterCard, Visa.
Access for Disabled: None.
Foreign Languages: None.
Getting There: From Manhattan: Take the Long Island Expressway to exit 70 (Rte. 111 South) to Rte. 25 to the North Fork. Colorful signs mark the way to some of the wineries. Or travel by bus aboard the *Sunrise Express* to the North Fork.

❧ Pioneer Long Island winemakers Alec and Louisa Hargrave first considered California, Washington, and Oregon before settling on the North Fork in the early 1970s. The Hargraves produced their first wines in 1975, and by 1980 were turning out wines with the qualities they desired. They welcome visitors today to a potato barn turned into a winery with one of the most elegant tasting rooms anywhere in the wine world. How many others have stained-glass panels that include a treasured Tiffany original of Millet's *The Sower*? In a nod to European vineyard custom, a rose bush keyed to grape colors marks the end of each row of vines—red roses for red grapes, white for white grapes. Both Hargrave's father and uncle were once directors of the Taylor Wine Company in Hammondsport.

ᐌ ᐌ ᐌ

Lenz Vineyards

Main Road
Peconic, New York 11953
TEL: 516-734-6010
OWNERS: Peter Carroll and John
  Pancoast
WINEMAKER: Dan Kleck
FOUNDED: 1979

AT A GLANCE
Tours & Tastings: Apr.–Nov., daily 11–5; winter weekends, 11–5; guided tours followed by tasting.
Closed: Christmas, New Year's Day.
Vineyards: Total 52 acres, all vinifera, about 30 of them at Carroll's Dorset Farms, 3 miles away, and 21 of these, Chardonnay.
Wines: Chardonnay, Merlot, Lenz Reserve (Cabernet Sauvignon, Merlot, Cabernet Franc blend); Gewürztraminer; *methode champenoise* sparkling wines.
Awards: 1986 Chardonnay and 1987 Chardonnay (Gold Label) and 1986 Gewürztraminer & Merlot, a few among many others.
Retail Shop: Wines sold on-site.
Credit Cards: MasterCard, Visa.
Access for Disabled: None.

Foreign Languages: French, German, Italian.
Getting There: 1½ miles east of Cutchogue, off Rte. 25.

ᐌ Lenz Vineyards, founded in 1979 by Peter and Patricia Lenz, was acquired in September 1988 by Peter Carroll and John Pancoast, both New York management consultants.

The name and everything else hums along as before: Dan Kleck, the Lenzes' winemaker, continues to turn out premium wines, with an emphasis on the Cabernet Merlot blend and Chardonnays. The new partners plan to progressively increase production from 7,000 cases a year to 12,000 by 1990 and seek wider distribution for the wines.

Carroll, the major partner and owner of a 30-acre vineyard nearby, had toyed with the idea of building his own winery but decided instead on the Lenz Vineyards. The property is also as attractive as ever—a series of rose-colored buildings, surrounded by lush gardens, has won a number of architectural awards. Inside are modern stainless-steel tanks and laboratory equipment, as well as French oak barrels.

The Lenzes? They have gone west to a Napa Valley ranch where there is already a vineyard planted to Cabernet Sauvignon.

ᐌ ᐌ ᐌ

Pindar Vineyards

Main Road (Route 25)
Peconic, New York 11958
TEL: 516-734-6200
OWNER: Herodotus Damianos
WINEMAKER: Robert Henn
FOUNDED: 1979

AT A GLANCE
Tours & Tastings: 11–6, Apr.–Dec. 31; tours every half hour cover the entire

winemaking process and end with a tasting.
Closed: Jan.–March.
Vineyards: Two hundred acres planted to seven vinifera varieties.
Wines: Chardonnay, Cabernet Sauvignon, Merlot, Pinot Noir, Johannisberg Riesling, Gewürztraminer, *methode champenoise* champagne.
Awards: More than fifty awards since 1984; most wines cited in New York and international competitions.
Retail Shop: Sells wines on-site.
Credit Cards: MasterCard, Visa.
Access for Disabled: Yes.
Foreign Languages: Greek, Italian.
Getting There: Take the Long Island Expressway to exit 73 (last exit), then head east for fifteen miles.

&. Pindar, housed in a restored hundred-year-old barn, belongs to prominent Long Island physician Herodotus "Dan" Damianos. He started by growing a variety of wine grapes, but has switched to viniferas. This is the largest winery on the North Fork, with 200 acres of vineyards and a total production just short of 40,000 gallons. The winery's award-winning 1984 Chardonnay was the first Long Island wine sold commercially in California.

&. &. &.

Bedell Cellars

Route 25
Cutchogue, New York 11935
TEL: 516-734-7537
Open May–Nov., 11–5 Sat. and Sun. Tiny fifteen-acre vineyard, but expanding. Tours throughout the day with in-

structive lecture; bring lunch and enjoy the picnic tables. Won a bronze in 1988 New York Classic for 1986 Chardonnay.

&. &. &.

Peconic Bay Vineyards

Route 25
Cutchogue, New York 11935
Tel: 516-734-7361
Tours and tastings daily, mid-March to Nov., 11–5; Dec.–March 15 weekends only. Rustic tasting room, wines, wine accessories, herb vinegars, mustards sold.

&. &. &.

Jamesport Vineyards

Route 25
Jamesport, New York 11947
TEL: 516-364-3633
Tours and tastings May–Nov., daily 11–5; Jan.–Apr. weekends only. Guided and self-guided tours and tastings any time.

&. &. &.

Palmer Winery

Sound Avenue
Aquebogue, New York 11931
TEL: 516-722-4080
Self-guided tours, May–Dec., daily 11–5; other times, call ahead. Tours all day on no fixed schedule. Tasting house has a bar from an eighteenth-century English pub. Picnics permitted on deck with vineyard view. Bronze medals in 1988 New York Classic for 1986 Cabernet Sauvignon, Long Island house wine, 1987 Pinot Noir.

South Fork

The Bridgehampton Winery

Sag Harbor Turnpike
Bridgehampton, New York 11968
TEL: 516-537-3155
OWNER: Lyle Greenfield
WINEMAKER: Richard Olsen-Harbich
FOUNDED: 1979

AT A GLANCE
Tours & Tastings: Open May–Nov.,
Mon.–Fri. 11–6; Sun. 12–6; 45-minute
tours, from vine to bottle, include tasting
of two wines. Small fee. Dec.–Apr., Fri.,
Sat., Sun.; tours at 1 and 3.
Vineyards: Thirty acres, planted to vinifera varieties.
Wines: Chardonnay, Johannisberg Ries-
ling, Gewürztraminer, Sauvignon Blanc,
Cabernet Sauvignon, Merlot.
Awards: Recipient of nineteen state and
national awards in 1987 alone. Among
them, platinum to 1986 Riesling, silver to
1986 Chardonnay, both in New York
Wine Classics.
Picnic Area: Formal area in the works;
meanwhile the lawn is the visitors' table.
Retail Shop: Sells wines, jellies, honey;
logo Ts; poster of Gretchen Dow-Simp-
sons's original Bridgehampton label.
Credit Cards: MasterCard, Visa.
Access for Disabled: Limited.
Foreign Languages: German, by appointment.
Special Wine & Other Events: Strawberry
Festival (June), toasts early berries with
Premiere Cuvee Blanc; Bordeaux Fes-
tival (June), tribute to Merlot and
cheeses; Great American Chardonnay
Festival (July 4 weekend); and other sim-
ilarly spirited events, summer to October
harvest.
Getting There: From New York City:
Take the Long Island Expressway to exit
70 (Rte. 111 South) to Rte. 27 East and
continue to Bridgehampton; winery is
about one mile north of the
Bridgehampton monument.

‎ It would be hard to conjure up a
more delightful place for a viewing vineyard than former advertising executive
Lyle Greenfield's Bridgehampton Winery, neatly designed to resemble a typical
Long Island potato barn. The interior is
equally well planned: cellars and winemaking equipment below, the spacious
tasting and retail sales room on the main
level, with sliding glass doors to the deck
and a view of vineyards and beyond. Special events make the winery a popular
local meeting place where people gather
to learn and observe winemaking at close
range.

Winemaker Richard Olsen-Harbich, a
Cornell grad and student of expert
viticulturalist Dr. Robert M. Pool, traces
his heritage back to the Rhine Valley. He
apprenticed under German-born Hermann J. Weimer, whose Finger Lakes
winery vinified Bridgehampton's first
crop in 1982. Bridgehampton's current
production is 9,000 cases a year, and it
often sells out by February of the following year.

The winery's Estate Patron's program
offers members a number of benefits, including a plaque placed on a vineyard
row of twenty-five vines, dedicated to the
patron, plus a case of estate wine and
discounts.

‎ ‎ ‎

Le Reve Winery

162 Montauk Highway
Water Mill, New York 11976
TEL: 516-726-7555
Open daily, Memorial Day to Labor Day,
12–6; closed Dec. 25–March 1; March–

Memorial Day, weekends only. This huge, multimillion-dollar château-inspired structure with copper roof opened in 1987, and is a modern, computerized winery, with vaulted tasting room and terrace with view of Sauvage Vineyards, the winery owner. The first wines are being made from Oregon grapes, until Sauvage vines mature. Winery is a quarter mile east of where Routes 27A and 27 meet. Award-winning white Riesling.

TO SEE & DO

North Fork. Pokes a finger of sand into Long Island Sound, setting it off from Peconic and Gardiners Bay. It's much less crowded and harried than the South Fork and offers many similar advantages—first-class beaches and quiet villages among them.

Visitors will find an interesting history lesson on the Village Green in Cutchogue, at the Old House on Route 25. The house was built in 1649, and is a prime example of English Manor architecture with antique furniture (July–Aug., Sat.–Mon.; tel: 516-734-6532). Nearby are the Wickham Farmhouse (from the early 1700s) and Old Schoolhouse Museum, 1840.

Southold's Village Green Complex (Main Road and Maple Lane, July–Aug. Tues., Thurs., Sun.; tel: 516-765-5500) includes a restored Thomas Moore house (pre-1652) and other exhibits such as a working blacksmith's shop, carriage house, and charming box garden. The Horton's Point Lighthouse is now the Marine Museum on the Sound at Lighthouse Road (July–Aug., Sat. and Sun. only; tel: 516-765-5500). Interesting pottery and other local Indian artifacts are focal points of Southold's Indian Museum (Main Street, Sun.; tel: 516-756-3029).

Another worthwhile stop can be made at the fishing hamlet of Greenport. This nineteenth-century whaling port is now where sleek yachts drop anchor; antique shops and old homes also await. From Greenport, ferries go to Shelter Island; from Orient Point, at the end of Rte. 25, ferries cross to New London, Connecticut.

South Fork. Nautical adventures continue with a stop at Sag Harbor's Whaling and Historical Museum (Garden and Main streets, daily mid-May to mid-Sept.; tel: 516-725-0770). Exhibits show old ships' logs, scrimshaw, and nineteenth-century seafaring artifacts. Nearby, on Garden Street, is the Old Custom House (June–Oct., Tues.–Sun.; tel: 516-941-9444), with a collection of antique furniture.

Art is on display at the Guild Hall Museum in East Hampton (158 Main Street, open daily June–Oct., rest of year closed Mon. and some major holidays, tel: 516-324-0806), and the site is used for poetry readings and lectures. John Drew Theater at Guild Hall is used year-round for plays, films, and musical events (for schedule, tel: 516-324-4050 or 0806).

Also on East Hampton's historic Main Street are the Clinton Academy (151 Main Street, July–Aug., Tues.–Sun. afternoons; May–June, Sept., weekends only; all year by appointment), built as a prep school in 1784 and now a museum of Long Island artifacts, and the Osborn-Jackson House, built about 1725 as a saltbox, later enlarged, and now a museum of decorative arts and period rooms (same hours as the Clinton Academy).

"Home Sweet Home" House and Windmill (14 James Lane; tel: 516-324-0713) is the childhood home of John Howard Payne; it features furniture, English china, other memorabilia, gallery with varying exhibits, twenty-minute guided tour (daily June–Oct., other times by appointment). Mulford House, next door on James Lane (tel: 516-324-6889; same hours as the Clinton Academy), built in 1680, is now an architectural history museum.

Many windmills are located in and

about East Hampton; in addition to the one mentioned above, Hook Mill, from 1808 (38 N. Main Street, on Montauk Hwy; daily from the last Sat. in June to the Sat. after Labor Day), is completely outfitted and offers a twenty-minute guided tour.

Intrepid history lovers will enjoy collections of costumes and other artifacts, as well as a nineteenth-century village street at the Southampton Historical Museum (17 Meeting House Lane, off Main Street; mid-June to mid-Sept., Tues.–Sun.; tel: 516-283-2494). Old Halsey House, built in 1648 (S. Main Street), is the oldest English frame house in New York State, now restored (mid-June to mid-Sept., Tues.–Sun.; tel: 516-283-3527). Parrish Art Museum (25 Jobs Lane, town center; winter daily except Tues. and Wed.; summer also open Wed.; closed holidays; tel: 516-283-2118) is another place you'll want to see.

In Water Mill, the gristmill, dating from 1644, is restored to working order, displays old tools, and is the site of crafts demonstrations (Watermill Rd.; Memorial Day–Labor Day, Mon., Wed., Sun.; before Memorial Day and after Labor Day, weekends and by appointment; tel: 516-726-9685).

Long Island farm stands are another treat for travelers who want to eat fresh foods right away or take them home.

For more information for Greenport and Southold, contact the Chamber of Commerce (tel: 516-477-1383) or visit the tourist information booth on Route 25 between Southold and Greenport; for East Hampton, the Chamber of Commerce (4 Main Street; tel: 516-324-0362); for Southampton, the Chamber of Commerce (76 Main Street; tel: 516-283-0402).

ACCOMMODATIONS

North Fork/Bed and Breakfasts
Goose Creek Guesthouse
1475 Waterview Drive (Box 377)
Southold, New York 11971

Tel: 516-765-3356
Civil War–era home set on six wooded acres; close to beaches and local attractions. Owner is a food writer who dishes up delicious pancakes and other delectables at breakfast.

Mattituck B&B
795 Pike Street
Mattituck, New York 11952
Tel: 516-298-8785
Turn-of-the-century home furnished with antiques and set on landscaped grounds. Wraparound porch.

Other
Sound View Inn
North Road (Box 68)
Greenport, New York 11944
Tel: 516-477-1910
Seventy units, two stories. Kitchens available; heated pool, private beach, sun decks, golf privileges. Café. One and one-half miles northwest on county road, on L.I. Sound.

South Fork/Inns
Maidstone Arms
207 Main Street
East Hampton, New York 11937
Tel: 516-324-5006
In National Historic District. An inn since the 1870s, originally built as a home. Nicely furnished with well-regarded dining room, serving Long Island wines. There's a sitting/breakfast room with glass expanse and a large wood stove.

Mill House Inn
33 Main Street
East Hampton, New York 11937
Tel: 516-324-4300
View of Hook Mill. Full breakfast included in rates.

Sag Harbor Inn
West Water Street
Sag Harbor, New York 11963
Tel: 516-725-2949

New, deluxe inn furnished with eighteenth-century reproductions; private balconies and terraces, near the bay overlooking with harbor. Walking distance from museums and shops. Convenient to beaches. Continental breakfast included in rates.

1770 House
143 Main Street
East Hampton, New York 11937
Tel: 516-324-1770
Seven charming guest rooms and four more at Philip Taylor's down the road, all done up with Early American antiques. Owned and operated by a skilled chef (See "Restaurants"). Two blocks west of Route 27.

Southampton Inn
Hill Street at First Neck Lane
Southampton, New York 11968
Tel: 516-283-6500
Luxury accommodations with pool and poolside service; health club, golf privileges; free transportation to railway station, airports, bus depot. Café. Dancing on Fridays. One block west on Route 27A.

RESTAURANTS
A number of area restaurants now serve local wines; a few follow:

North Fork
Fisherman's Restaurant
Route 25
Cutchogue, New York 11935
Tel: 516-734-5155
Good fresh seafood.

Claudio's
111 Main Street
Greenport, New York 11944
Tel: 516-477-0627
Family-owned since the 1870s; America's Cup memorabilia on the walls, nice view of fishing harbor. Steaks, seafood, own baked goods. Closed mid-Nov. to mid-Apr.

Armando's Seafood Barge
Route 25
(between Southold and Greenport)
Tel: 516-765-3010
World War II vessel, now a restaurant serving delicious seafood. A very unfancy place for excellent, decently priced fresh fish and shellfish. Good selection of local wines. Reservations recommended.

Sound View Inn
(see under "Accommodations" for address, tel.)
Appropriately named, Sound View has a view of the Sound. Fresh seafood is a specialty; fresh-baked goods.

Sept's (roadside stand)
Route 25
East Marion, New York 11939
Seasonal fruits and vegetables.

Cider Mill (roadside stand)
Route 25
Laurel, New York 11948
Breads, fresh-baked pies.

South Fork
The Bowden Square
North Sea Road
Southampton, New York 11968
Tel: 516-283-2800
New American cuisine, with light sauces, herbs, and bright, crisp vegetables. Good wine list. Top choices at any time are the fresh fish dishes; on weekends, ribs are a special. As a tribute to the Hamptons' famous potato fields, chef Dennis Roy makes sure potatoes are always on the menu in novel or classic ways. All desserts are made in-house and include chocolate butterflies, fruit tarts, and cheesecake. Dinner is served on the attractive, awning-covered patio. Lunch is indoors in the atmospheric old tavern. Dinner in the bar off-season. Two blocks south of Route 27.

Lobster Inn
162 Inlet Road (off North Hwy.)
Southampton, New York 11968
Tel: 516-283-1525
Steak and seafood with outdoor eating.
Salad bar.
  Air-conditioning. Closed Thanksgiving
and Christmas.

1770 House
143 Main Street
East Hampton, New York 11937
Tel: 516-324-1770
Owned and operated by classically
trained Cordon Bleu chef Miriam Perle
and her daughter, Wendy Van Deusen.

The setting is intimate, with pine tables
and rose medallion goblets, and fresh
flowers add to its many charms. Nice
wine selection. Starters include Cajun
crabcakes, chilled lobster, or wild mushroom soup. Among the entrées are duck
with lingonberries, rack of lamb, and
fresh fish; fabulous pastries made on-
site. Two sittings, for forty guests at each;
one at 6:30 and the other at 9:15. Two
blocks west on Route 27.

Maidstone Arms
(see under "accommodations" for address, tel., in East Hampton)

ᐱ HUDSON RIVER REGION

Wine routes along the Hudson River stretch from south to north, from the still
splendidly rural town of North Salem to Woodstock, long attractive to those in
the arts. Between these points, a total of twenty-one wineries lie within an
easy drive of New York City, making them good daytrip destinations. A
number of Hudson River wineries are on the west side of the river, from
Woodstock to Washingtonville; others are to the east, from Pine Plains to
North Salem. This is the Hudson River v.a., characterized by the temperature-
moderating flow of the Hudson River and its northward channeling of maritime breezes from the Atlantic Ocean.

  Like those in the Finger Lakes, the Hudson River Valley's wine routes reach
back in time to early winemaking in the 1800s, although most of the wineries
are from the 1970s, when the Farm Winery bill helped the industry to take
root. Rebuilt old barns and other romantic, antique settings make some of
these wineries look as if they've been around quite a while. Long before the
wineries, this area was a magnet for tourists, drawn to a wealth of historic
towns and houses as well as a multitude of warm- and cold-weather sports.
Add the Hudson River for scenery, both majestic and gently bucolic, and this
wine route is hard to beat.

  "From Vine to Wine" tours, conducted by wine expert Steven Epstein,
depart from New York City by deluxe motorcoach to Hudson River wineries.
For eighty dollars per person, each highly instructive tour takes in three
different wineries and every aspect of winemaking, from vineyard exploration
to wine appreciation, topped off with a delicious lunch with glass of wine and
chance to buy wines not yet widely available. For information and schedule,
contact: Hudson River Wine Tours, 163 Third Avenue, Suite 142, New York,
NY 10003 (Tel: 212-228-WINE).

West Side of the River

Adair Vineyards

75 Allhusen Road
New Paltz, New York 12561
TEL: 914-255-1377
OWNERS: Jim and Gloria Adair
FOUNDED: 1984

AT A GLANCE

Tours & Tastings: 12 noon–6 daily, Apr. 1–Nov. 30; self-guided tour of vineyard; guided tour in wine cellar—show how wine is made.
Closed: Dec.–March.
Vineyards: Ten acres—7,000 vines in all—to three whites: Seyval, Chardonnay, Vignoles; two reds: Marechal Foch and Millot; experimental planting of Pinot Noir. Some grapes purchased from other Hudson Valley growers.
Wines: First vintage, February 1988 Seyval Blanc; makes Mountain White, a fruity Seyval wine; Mountain Red (blend of Foch and Leon Millot); Mountain Blush, Baco Noir. Dry Cranberry Cooler.
Picnic Area: Beside brook.
Retail Shop: Wines sold on-site.
Credit Cards: MasterCard.
Access for Disabled: None.
Foreign Languages: Smattering French, German, Spanish.
Getting There: Take N.Y.S. Thruway north to U.S. 44 at Modena; turn north on Rte. 32 for 1 mile to Allhusen Rd. and turn east to winery. From the north: take N.Y.S. Thruway south to exit 18, turn south onto Ohioville Rd. and continue to Allhusen Rd., turn west to winery.
Special Wine & Other Events: Check with winery.

 ❖ Jim and Gloria Adair started their winery after years as wine hobbyists; they invested in a lot of high-tech equipment and plan to produce 10,000 gallons of premium wine a year.

The winery is in a Dutch-style barn about two centuries old and in line for landmark designation. Visitors are welcome to see the winery's first floor until the second floor is renovated for viewing operations.

Adair, a veteran advertising art director in New York City, has used his skills to create a striking label out of Hudson River painter Asher Durand's *The Solitary Oak*; a solitary oak also stands as a sentinel at the head of the vineyard. Adair's well-designed brochure is helpful to understanding the cycles in the grape vine's life as well as wine technology. Plans are to stock a pond with trout and let visitors try their luck. Gloria Adair, formerly a development specialist at a private school in Brooklyn Heights, now works exclusively at the vineyard.

❖ ❖ ❖

Brotherhood Winery

35 North Street
Washingtonville, New York 10992
TEL: 914-496-3661
OWNER: Investor group from Orange
 County, New York
WINEMAKER/EXEC. V.P.: Cesar Baeza
FOUNDED: 1839

AT A GLANCE

Tours & Tastings: Open May–Oct. 11–6 daily; Nov.–Apr., weekends 12–5. $3 adults; children free. Ninety-minute guided tours view the winemaking process and the famous largest-in-the-U.S. aging cellars, housing generations-old handmade casks, and an in-depth tasting.
Closed: Weekdays after the second Friday in November.
Vineyards: Grapes are purchased from New York State growers.
Wines: Historically, best known for sweet

wines and blends. Has been shifting a sizable percentage to drier, more sophisticated European vinifera wines, primarily Chardonnay and Riesling.

Awards: Tons of awards in over a century of production; frequent winners: cream sherries and ports. Recently, a bronze for a Blush Catawba in 1988 New York Classic.

Picnic Area: In tree-shaded groves.

Restaurant: Hors D'Oeuverie; lunch daily; dinner Fri. & Sat.; Sun., champagne brunch showcase for new Blanc de Blancs sparkling wine. Specialties— freshly made fish, beef, veal, poultry entrées; delicious desserts.

Wine Bar: Hors D'Oeuverie has a wine bar offering premium varietals by the glass.

Retail Shop: Wines, gifts.

Cedit Cards: American Express, MasterCard, Visa.

Getting There: Take N.Y.S. Thruway to exit 16 (Harriman); then Rte. 17 West to Monroe and follow Rte. 208 North to Washingtonville and the winery.

Special Wine & Other Events: Frequent festivals, barrel tastings, champagne celebrations and others, but none more delightful than Christmas, marked throughout Dec. with decorations, special drinks, and foods.

⋧ The oldest continuously operating winery in the United States, dating to 1839, is a popular tourist attraction today. Serene on acres of landscaped land, its old fieldstone buildings and cavernous cellars used to stand adjacent to sprawling vineyards, torn up in 1960 to enlarge the parking lot.

The founder, Jean Jaques, arrived here from France in 1810, planted a vineyard, and built a small winery he called Blooming Grove. His first wines were sold to the church for sacramental purposes and later to nearby residents as medicine.

Commercial sales began when Jaques's sons sold the wines to New York wine merchants Jesse and Edward R. Emerson. They in turn bought wines from the Brotherhood religious community near Amenia, blended them with what they bought from Jaques, and sold them under the Brotherhood label. Ultimately, the Emersons purchased Jaques's property, rechristened it Brotherhood, and constructed the buildings and cellars seen today.

Long known for sweet wines, Brotherhood's recent shift to drier, European-style releases is in response to consumers' moves to more sophisticated wines and is part of an overall modernization plan.

TO SEE & DO
Goshen Historic Track (Park Place), dating from 1838, is harness racing's oldest track, with races from late May to mid-July (tel: 914-294-5333). Walking tours, crafts and antiques sales, musical performances during the summer. Visitors should also see the Trotting Horse Museum (240 Main; tel: 914-294-6330; open daily, closed Thanksgiving and Christmas), site of the Trotters Hall of Fame. Exhibits many Currier & Ives trotting prints and other memorabilia; library and gift shop.

Historic sites to be seen at Newburgh include Hasbrouck House, built in 1750, which served as George Washington's headquarters for some months (84 Liberty St., open May–Dec., Wed.–Sun.; winter schedule on request; tel: 914-561-2585) with eighteenth-century military exhibits; Crawford House, built around 1829, with wood-carved interiors and period furniture (open year-round, Sat. & Sun.; tel: 914-561-2585); New Windsor Cantonment, from 1782 (Temple Hill Rd., 5 miles west of Washington's Headquarters; open mid-Apr. to Oct., Wed.–Sun.; tel: 914-561-1755), last encampment of the Continental Army, devoted to eighteenth-century military life; and Knox's Headquarters, from 1754

(Forge Hill Rd., off intersection of Rtes. 94 & 32, open Apr.–Dec. Wed.–Sun.; tel: 914-561-5498), a former Georgian-style home of an eighteenth-century merchant that was used by Knox during the Revolutionary War. Seen now are period furnishings, crafts, and herb gardens; frequent crafts demonstrations and concerts and events.

Newburgh boasts the largest historic district in New York State, with prime examples from the eighteenth and nineteenth centuries; to wrap up the sites concisely, there are guided Architectural Gems Tours (contact the Visitors Center, 87 Liberty St., opposite Washington's Headquarters; tel: 914-565-6880), which operate May–Oct., Sat. and Sun.; at other times by appointment.

At Mountainville (6 miles south via Rte. 32), the century is contemporary at the Storm King Art Center (Old Pleasantville Rd.), a 400-acre outdoor sculpture park (open Apr.–Nov., daily except Tues.) and indoor museum (open mid-May to Oct., daily except Tues.). For both, tel: 914-534-4115.

For more information, contact the Eastern Orange County Chamber of Commerce, 47 Grand Street, Newburgh, New York 12550; tel: 914-562-5100.

Head farther south to see Boscobel Restoration (Rte. 9D; tel: 914-265-3638), a mansion-showcase for artists of the Hudson River School set in a garden with a fountain encircled by magnificent tulip and rose gardens (open Apr.–Oct., daily except Tues., 9:30–5; Nov., Dec., March, 9:30–4; last admission half an hour before closing). Nearby are West Point and the West Point Museum, with an in-depth general military collection (open daily, year-round, 10:30–4:15; tel: 914-938-2638 or 3507).

ACCOMMODATIONS
Holiday Inn
Route 90 (Old Route 17K)
Newburgh, New York 12550

Tel: 914-564-9020
Better than average motel with 121 rooms; pool, café, bar, entertainment.

(For restaurants, see other sections of the Hudson River Region.)

ð ð ð

Baldwin Vineyards
1766 Hardenburgh Estate
Pine Bush, New York 12566
TEL: 914-744-2226
OWNERS: Jack and Pat Baldwin
FOUNDED: 1982

AT A GLANCE
Tours & Tastings: Open Apr.–Dec. 10–6 daily; winter weekends, 10–5; and by appt.
Vineyards: Thirty-seven acres vinifera and hybrid varieties. Fruits grown also.
Wines: Chardonnay, Johannisberg Riesling, Seyval, Landot, Vignoles, Vidal, Chancellor; Strawberry, Apple, Cherry.
Awards: 1986 Late Harvest Vidal in two New York Classics; Seyval, Vidal, Riesling, Landot, Rosé, Vignoles, and others at varying times.
Picnic Area: Near the Shawangunk River.
Café/Wine Bar: Smoked trout, salmon, quiche, cheese, and other light fare, and wines by bottle or glass. Hours: Fri., Sat., Sun. 11:30–5. Open May–Oct.
Retail Shop: Sells wines on-site.
Credit Cards: MasterCard, Visa.
Access for Disabled: Yes.
Foreign Languages: None.
Getting There: From New Jersey, New York City, and Westchester: Take the N.Y.S. Thruway North to exit 16 and take Rte. 17 West. Continue twenty miles to exit 119 (Rte. 302 North). Go ten miles to Pine Bush. From Connecticut, Putnam County, southern Dutchess County: Cross the Newburgh-Beacon Bridge on I-84 West. Take exit 8 to Rte. 52 West.

Continue sixteen miles through Walden to Pine Bush. From upstate: Take exit 17 off N.Y.S. Thruway South. Continue on Union Ave., ½ mile past I-84 and turn left at second traffic light to Rte. 52 West. Travelers going north or south can enjoy the slower, more scenic Rte. 9W, which follows along the Hudson at least part of the way. In Pine Bush, from the light at the intersection of Rtes. 52 and 302, follow signs north 1 mile to Baldwin Vineyards; the winery is just across the Shawangunk River.

Special Wine & Other Events: Strawberry, Raspberry festivals; Nouveau Release, and other festivities.

&‌ Though Jack and Pat Baldwin's winery dates only from 1982, the Hardenburgh Estate goes back to 1786. The historic remodeled barn winery houses a state-of-the-art, computer-operated press and oak barrels and steel tanks for fermentation and aging wines.

This small family winery grew out of a love affair with wine that began in 1974 on a trip to Europe and included Pat's gift to Jack one Christmas of a 500-bottle wine cellar. Their wine odyssey took them to the Napa Valley and the Finger Lakes, to seminars and conventions about wine, and to experimentation with a home winemaking kit for their first wines. All this time, they toyed with the idea of going into winemaking to earn their livelihood.

Residents of New Jersey, the Baldwins moved to Pine Bush in 1981 and, with the help of daughter Wendy, planted their ten-acre vineyard on land carefully chosen for its similarity to some great wine regions of France and Germany. The Baldwins went into the winemaking business full-time when Jack's company had a cutback in staff. He took a buyout and changed his career. They now make more than a dozen wines—one of them a Landot Noir that *Wine Spectator* said

was "as good as a top Volnay or premium California Pinot Noir, wines more than twice as expensive."

&‌ &‌ &‌

Brimstone Hill Vineyard

Brimstone Hill Road (R.D. 3, Box 36)
Pine Bush, New York 12566
TEL: 914-744-2231
OWNERS: Richard and Valerie Eldridge
FOUNDED: 1979

AT A GLANCE
Tours & Tastings: June–Aug., Thurs.–Mon. 11–6; at other times by appointment. This tiny four-acre vineyard winery produces primarily French-American hybrid wines, in the French style, in tribute to Valerie Eldridge's family in the Loire Valley, who counsel the couple on winemaking techniques. Brimstone White, a blend, won a gold medal at a New York State Fair, just one of the winery's awards.

TO SEE & DO
Newburgh and New Paltz are approximately fifteen miles from the Pine Bush wineries. They are also fifteen miles east of Ellenville and its nearby national landmark, Ice Caves Mountain, with self-guided tours of caves and rugged rock formations; canyons, five-state lookout, picnic site (open daily April–Nov.; tel: 914-647-7989).

ACCOMMODATIONS
The Nevele
Nevele Road
Ellenville, New York 12428
Tel: 914-244-0800; 800-647-6000
1,000-acre resort estate, with 450 rooms in main building and annexes; all manner of sports and a sports director to get you to private lake, golf, pool, ice skating rink, ski lift, and many more.

&‌ &‌ &‌

Benmarl Wine Company, Ltd.

Highland Avenue
Marlboro, New York 12542
TEL: 914-236-4265
OWNER: Mark Miller
WINE CONSULTANT: Jacques Recht (see
  Ingleside Plantation, Oak Grove,
  Virginia, page 000).
FOUNDED: 1971 (vineyard 1788)

AT A GLANCE
Tours & Tastings: May 1–Dec. 20, Tues.–
Sun. 11–4. Owner- or staff-guided tours
blend area's history with all aspects of
vineyard and winery operation; include
visit to art museum and tasting. Fee in-
cludes Benmarl glass.
Closed: Major legal holidays.
Vineyards: Seventy-two acres owned and
one hundred leased, all planted to
French-American hybrids, some vi-
nifera.
Wines: Focus is on hybrid blends; Char-
donnay, Chancellor varietals; apple wine.
Produces 10,000 gallons annually.
Awards: A bumper crop since first re-
lease, including a silver medal for 1982
Chardonnay.
Picnic Area: With beautiful river view.
Restaurant: Bistro specialty is light
French cuisine, prepared by chefs trained
at Culinary Institute in Hyde Park; week-
ends only, 11–5.
Retail Shop: Wines sold on-site.
Credit Cards: MasterCard, Visa.
Access for Disabled: None.
Foreign Languages: French.
Getting There: Approaching on scenic
9W from south: Look carefully for Con-
way Road (on left) about ¼ mile after K-
Jax Motel on right. Benmarl is exactly 1
mile farther on right. Drivers approach-
ing on 9W from north: Pass the village of
Marlboro and look for Conway Road, 2
miles past village on the right.
Special Wine & Other Events: Concerts
in the vineyards; the Fete de Muguet,
which heralds the arrival of the *muguet*

(lily of the valley) with an elegant dinner;
other events vary from year to year.

&. Benmarl is one of the most attractive and interesting wineries in New
York—for its beautiful location above the
Hudson, its historic vineyard and vignerons program, and its quiet atmosphere of a European country home
filled with works of art.

Miller bought his vineyard used—150
years ago by A. J. Caywood, who developed the Dutchess grape—and says
that it is presumed to be the oldest con-
tinually operating vineyard in the United
States. He and his family replanted the
early labruscas with French hybrids and
Vitis vinifera.

An illustrator, Miller came to winemaking after years of living in France.
His experiences are well documented in
his book *Wine—a Gentlemen's Game:
The Adventures of an Amateur Winemaker Turned Professional.* Dene, his
late wife, an architect, redesigned the
crumbling old farm buildings into a rustic
estate clustered around a fountain.

From Burgundy, the Millers brought
back the notion of the Societe des Vignerons. This is a cooperative association that offers members vine rights to
two vines each and permission to help
with harvest, the right to a case of personally labeled wine each year, as well as
banquet and other benefits.

Miller's son Eric and his wife, Lee,
now own and operate the enchanting
Chaddsford Winery in Chadds Ford,
Pennsylvania (see page 000).

Benmarl, by the way, is Gaelic for
"slate hill."

&. &. &.

Cagnasso Winery

Route 9W
Marlboro, New York 12542
TEL: 914-236-4630

OWNER: Joe Cagnasso
FOUNDED: 1977
Cagnasso spent twenty-five years working for other wineries, such as Gallo and Brotherhood, before he and his assistant, June Ramey, planted their ten-acre vineyard to French-American hybrids. Their handmade wines are sold only from their picturesque barn/tasting room, which looks out over rows of grape vines and orchards. Tastings in summer and fall, 10–4:30 daily.

ã ã ã

Windsor Vineyards and Great River Winery

104 Western Avenue
Marlboro, New York 12542
TEL: 914-236-4440
Makes California and New York State wines and champagnes. Tastings daily, 10–5; closed New Year's Day, Easter, Thanksgiving, Christmas. Wine shop.

TO SEE & DO
Fifteen minutes away in the Shawangunk Mountains, you can climb, bike, and hike in dazzling scenery. For city sights, head to Poughkeepsie, site of Vassar College, founded in 1891. On the sprawling campus, the art gallery has visiting hours daily throughout the academic year and at other times by appointment (tel: 914-452-7000, ext. 2645). Clinton House State Historic Site, built in the 1700s (Main & N. White sts.; Mon.–Fri., closed major holidays; tel: 914-471-1630), the museum of The Dutchess County Historical Society, also has its welcome mat out to visitors. Two miles south of the Mid-Hudson Bridge, at 370 South Rd. (U.S. 9), the 150-acre Locust Grove was home to Samuel Morse, artist and inventor of the telegraph, and was rebuilt by Morse in the mid-1800s to resemble a Tuscan villa. Both Morse and subsequent owner Martha Innis Young collected what is now interesting memorabilia, dolls, books, souvenirs, paintings, and more— now on display. Wildlife park and hiking trails. Guided tours. (Memorial Day weekend to Sept., Wed.–Sun.; tel: 914-454-4500.)

For more information, contact the Chamber of Commerce, 80 Washington Street, Poughkeepsie, New York 12601; tel: 914-454-1700.

ACCOMMODATIONS

Bed and Breakfasts & Inns
One Market Street
Cold Spring, New York 10516
Tel: 914-265-3912
The view from this Federal-style building takes in the mountains and lush valley. There is one suite only, with its own kitchenette well stocked with provisions to make a delicious Continental breakfast.

The Mill Farm
66 Cricket Hill Road
Dover Plains, New York 12522
Tel: 914-832-9198
This comfortable Colonial in the midst of fields and horse farms has a big porch and a mountain view. Cozy, antique-filled bedrooms, a swimming pool when it's hot, and a roaring fire inside when it's not. Hearty breakfast.

Hotel Wyndham Poughkeepsie
40 Civic Center Plaza
Poughkeepsie, New York 12601
Tel: 914-485-5300
Plush new hotel in downtown Poughkeepsie, with guest rooms overlooking the Hudson; American regional cuisine in Tudor Room, with wine list including Hudson River Valley wines. Lobby bar, nightclub. Adjacent Mid-Hudson Civic Center. Complimentary transportation to airport.

RESTAURANTS
A few restaurants that serve local wines.

Pleasant View Hotel's Raccoon Saloon
146 Main Street (Route 9W)
Marlboro, New York 12542
Tel: 914-236-7872
A hotel in 1834, now Don and Rita Truesdell's easygoing, informal restaurant with spectacular Hudson River view. The Truesdells' son, Ed Goodwin, is the chef. He is a Culinary Institute graduate whose specialties include fresh-from-scratch soups, quiche, chicken breasts, and fish entrées, as well as Chocolate Midnight and other desserts. A place other guidebooks ignore, but almost a club to locals.

Treasure Chest
588 South Road
Junction IBM Road and U.S. 9
Tel: 914-462-4545
Fresh seafood and steaks; served indoors in one of the area's oldest houses, with handsome eighteenth-century interior; and outdoors in fair weather. Wine list includes West Park wines. Three miles south of the Mid-Hudson Bridge.

(Also see under "Accommodations" the Tudor Room in the Hotel Wyndham.)

🐾 🐾 🐾

El Paso Winery

Route 9W, Box 170
Ulster Park, New York 12487
TEL: 914-331-8642
OWNER/WINEMAKER: Felipe Beltra
FOUNDED: 1977

AT A GLANCE
Tours & Tastings: Apr.–Dec. 31, noon–6 Mon.–Fri., Sat. & Sun. 10–6; tastings, no tours.
Closed: Jan.–March; Easter Sunday, July 4, Thanksgiving & Christmas days.
Vineyards: Grapes purchased in Finger Lakes District.

Wines: Seyval Blanc and Niagara varietals and blends, dry to sweet.
Retail Shop: Wines sold on-site.
Credit Cards: None.
Access for Disabled: Yes.
Foreign Languages: Spanish
Getting There: Take Scenic Route 9W, ten miles north of the Mid-Hudson Bridge or four miles south of Kingston.

🐾 Felipe Beltra learned to make Spanish-style wines at his father's winery in Uruguay, which serves as inspiration today at his winery, housed in a rebuilt barn.

🐾 🐾 🐾

Regent Champagne Cellars

(formerly Hudson Valley Wine Co.)
200 Blue Point Road
Highland, New York 12528
TEL: 914-691-7296
OWNER: Herbert Feinberg
WINEMAKER: Edward Gogel
FOUNDED: 1907

AT A GLANCE
Tours & Tastings: Daily, Apr. 2–Nov. 2, 9–5; Mar.–Dec., weekends; weekend fee includes bread sticks, cheese, wineglass. Guided, one-hour tour views the winemaking process (vine to bottle), museum, includes tasting of six wines. Hayride tours, weather permitting. Tour hours vary seasonally.
Closed: Easter Sunday, Thanksgiving, Christmas, New Year's days.
Vineyards: Fifty acres planted primarily to Catawba; others Concord, Delaware, Iona, some Baco Noir and Chelois. California grapes purchased.
Wines: Old-time winery now pursuing champagnes; continuing with its traditional line of estate-bottled labrusca blends; Chelois varietal; also apple and sparkling grape juices, apple cider.
Picnic Area: On lavish estate grounds.

Retail Shop: Wines sold on-site.
Credit Cards: American Express, MasterCard, Visa.
Access for Disabled: Limited.
Foreign Languages: None.
Getting There: Take N.Y.S. Thruway to exit 18 (New Paltz), then go east 5 miles on Rte. 299 to 9W and turn south for 3½ miles to the Regent Champagne Cellars (Hudson Valley Wine Co.).
Special Wine & Other Events: Special events and festivals every weekend, March 15–Dec.; contact winery for schedule.

From 1907 to 1970, the Hudson River Wine Company, recently renamed Regent Champagne Cellars, kept its considerable charms a secret. The founders, investment broker Aldolpho Bolognesi and family, permitted no visitors.

When the new owner, Herbert Feinberg, a former owner of Monsieur Henri wines, took over in 1972, the public was cordially invited in to explore a perfect replica of a Tuscan estate with stone buildings for the winery and workers' homes, and a clock tower, all clustered around a courtyard, with an impressive fourteen-room manor house as focal point. This grand mansion, with gleaming hardwood floors and glowing stained-glass windows, is now open only for special buffet luncheons. With these attractions—as well as vineyards and miles of trails through grounds punctuated with orchards, picnic groves, and pools—the handsome 310-acre property high above the Hudson now plays host to thousands of visitors each year.

Like a page from the past, Feinberg continues to bring out the old labrusca wines. Since the summer of 1988, there has been a new winemaker, Edward Gogel, and a new emphasis on champagnes. The champagnes of the winery's early years were reputedly some of the best in America. Gogel, who has made a wide variety of wines in Illinois, California, New York, North Carolina, and Florida, plans to make his newest champagnes by the *methode champenoise,* transfer, and charmat methods.

Rivendell Wines/Chateau Georges Winery

714 Albany Post Road
Gardiner, New York 12525
TEL: 914-255-0892
OWNERS: The Ransom family
WINEMAKER: James Moss
FOUNDED: 1982

AT A GLANCE

Tours & Tastings: Mon.–Sat., 11–5; Sun., 12–6. "Open every day, rain or shine."
Vineyards: Over twenty acres, planted mainly to French hybrids; additional grapes purchased from the Finger Lakes District.
Wines: New owners focusing on vinifera wines; list to include increased Chardonnay, Johannisberg Riesling, Cabernet Sauvignon; continued production of Vidal, Seyval Blanc, and Ravat, among others.
Awards: 1985 Chardonnay and 1986 Seyval Blanc in 1987 New York Classic, among many others; 3 bronzes in 1988 New York Classic to 1987 Vidal Blanc, Bonheur, and 1985 Late Harvest Ravat.
Picnic Area: On grounds, and indoors.
Deli: Rivendeli serves light lunches, pâté, cheeses, and wine, to eat in or on the deck.
Retail Shop: Wines sold on-site.
Credit Cards: All major cards.
Access for Disabled: Ramp to winery.
Foreign Languages: None.
Getting There: From New York City: Take N.Y.S. Thruway to exit 18 (New Paltz) and go west on Rte. 292; take left fork onto Libertyville Road; vineyard is four miles on right.

🍂 Rivendell Wines/ Chateau Georges Winery is the new name for the Gardiner Vineyard and Farms. The winery was re-christened when the Ransom family took it over with plans to increase production of classic European-style wines to suit more sophisticated tastes. The new wines have met with critical acclaim.

The winery occupies what was a summer camp for children with counselors' quarters, infirmary, and Olympic-size pool. The former arts-and-crafts building, with a floor-to-ceiling stone chimney, is now the tasting hall and wine shop, which the Ransoms are enlarging; the cellar is underneath.

🍂 🍂 🍂

Magnanini Farm Winery

501 Strawbridge Road
Wallkill, New York 12589
TEL: 914-895-2767
Tours and tastings by appointment. Hybrid wines; restaurant, with hand-painted murals, open Thurs. and Fri. evenings, Sat. and Sun. afternoons and evenings. Northern Italian cuisine served Fri. and Sat. at 7, Sun. at 1. By reservations only.

🍂 🍂 🍂

Royal Kedem Winery

Dock Road
Milton, New York 12547
TEL: 914-795-2240
PRESIDENT: Herman Herzog
WINEMAKER: Ernest Herzog
FOUNDED: 1948

AT A GLANCE

Tours & Tastings: May 1–Dec. 31, Sun.–Fri. 10–5; Sundays only Jan. 1–Apr. 30; tourgoers see a film, *The Art of Winemaking,* and get a thorough explanation of winemaking from beginning to end as they walk through the plant; tasting of many wines.

Closed: Sat., all Jewish holidays; Mon.–Fri., Jan. 1–Apr. 30.

Vineyards: 170 acres planted to vinifera, labrusca, French hybrids; some additional grapes purchased.

Wines: Varietals, Sauvignon Blanc, Zinfandel, De Chaunac, Seyval, Aurora Blanc, champagne, blends and fortified wines to total forty-eight in all. Sparkling and still grape juice under three labels: Kedem, Matuk, Baron Jacquab de Herzog; imports kosher wines from France, Italy, Israel, California.

Awards: Bumper crop since 1848, with medals in Vienna, Budapest, and Paris, and now in the United States. Golds have gone to New York State Champagne and Honey Wine and Plum Royale, the latter in the 1986 New York Wine Classic.

Picnic Area: Tables with Hudson view.

Retail Shop: Wines and gifts.

Credit Cards: American Express, MasterCard, Visa.

Access for Disabled: None.

Foreign Languages: Hebrew, Spanish.

Getting There: Take N.Y.S. Thruway to exit 17 (Newburgh), then take Scenic Rte. 9W to Milton. At the blinking light, turn east toward the river and follow the signs.

Special Wine & Other Events: First three Sundays in Nov., Harvest Festival, bands and entertainment.

🍂 When Kedem Winery says its wines are made the old-fashioned way—it means it. Eight generations of Herzogs have been producing Kedem wines since 1848. The family makes kosher wines by traditional methods from recipes handed down through the generations. The Herzogs not only make sweet wines that people often associate with kosher products, but dry ones as well. With a total production of 1.2 million gallons a year, Kedem accommodates twenty-eight varieties of wines.

The first long chapter of the Herzogs' story began in a Czechoslovakian village generations ago and came to an end during the German occupation, when the family emigrated to America. Highly regarded in Eastern Europe as winemakers, they first set up shop on New York's Lower East Side before establishing a major winery in the Hudson Valley.

Kedem entertains thousands of tourists every year. The tasting room is a mere upstart when compared to the family's long heritage—it's in a refurbished 120-year-old former New York Central Railroad station on the west bank of the Hudson. In 1985, a new winery was built—it's high-tech modern.

TO SEE & DO

Nearby New Paltz was founded by a small group of Huguenots in 1678, and their calling cards still can be seen in the town's six stone houses, on Huguenot Street, which are full of valuable heirlooms and are open to visitors. The area has other historic buildings, including the charming Locust Lawn estate (four miles south on Route 32), home to the Federal-style Hasbrouck Mansion, a farmers' museum, the Terwilliger Homestead and bird sanctuary, and the nineteenth-century Synder Estate, on Route 213 in Rosendale, with a delightful carriage and sleigh museum. (All are open Memorial Day weekend to Sept., Wed.–Sun.; tel: 914-255-1660.) Families should head to Widmark Farms, in Gardiner, with performing bears, beekeeping demonstrations, and friendly animals to pet (performances, mid-May to mid-Oct., Sat., Sun., holidays; tel: 914-255-6400). Back in New Paltz, at the SUNY college campus, there are always cultural events and campus tours (tel: 914-257-2414). The big August event each year is the Ulster County Fair; fairgrounds is two miles southwest on Libertyville Road.

For more information, contact the Chamber of Commerce, 4 Terwilliger Lane, New Paltz, New York 12561; tel: 914-255-0243.

ACCOMMODATIONS

(see also Newburgh, Poughkeepsie)

Captain Schoonmaker's B&B
County Route 213 West
High Falls, New York 12440
Tel: 914-687-7946
Three historic landmark buildings here add up to one terrific B&B, with Early American furniture, plants, books, and family memorabilia. Breakfast might include a soufflé, baked apples, homemade bread, and fresh pastries. Wine and cheese are offered before dinner on Saturdays. Bonuses are the garden, patio, and solarium.

Mohonk Mountain House
Mohonk Lake
New Paltz, New York 12561
Tel: 914-255-1000; 212-233-2244
This venerable castle on the mountain has managed to maintain excellence since 1869, and is still run by descendants of the founding family. Rooms are furnished with Victorian pieces. Meals are homespun and nicely served. Hudson Valley and Finger Lakes wines are available. A wealth of activities: swimming, boating, hiking, cross-country skiing, gardens, on-site museum, greenhouses, picnic area, tennis, golf, and more on this 2,000-acre preserve.

RESTAURANTS

Beekman Arms
Beekman Square
Rhinebeck, New York 12572
Tel: 914-876-7077
This restaurant is in an historic inn built in 1786 and is appropriately antique, with a cheery fire in winter months. Specialties include blackened redfish, veal, prime ribs. Fresh baked goods are served. Local wines. Cozy fireplace. Delightful place to stay, also.

Dominick's
30 North Chestnut Street
New Paltz, New York 12561
Tel: 914-255-0120
Wine barrel table and Mediterranean decor set the stage for Italian and Continental specialties, Taylor, California wines. Chef-owned. Closed Mondays, Thanksgiving, Dec. 24 and 25, two weeks in January.

Chez Marcel
Route 9G
Rhinebeck, New York 12572
Tel: 914-876-8189
French foods; wine list. Does own baking. Closed Mondays, Jan. 1, Dec. 25. Quarter mile north of Route 9.

ə̀ ə̀ ə̀

Walker Valley Vineyards

Route 52
Walker Valley, New York 12588
TEL: 914-744-3449
OWNER: Gary Dross
FOUNDED: 1978

AT A GLANCE
Tours & Tastings: Open daily, June 20–Oct. 20, 10–5:30; Oct. 21–June 19, weekends, 10–5. Tourgoers see photographic display on grape growing, are guided through winemaking, and conclude with tasting.
Closed: Oct. 21–June 19, weekdays.
Vineyards: 9 acres of hybrids and viniferas.
Wines: Chardonnay, Pinot Noir, Johannisberg Riesling; Cayuga White, Seyval, Marechal Foch, Blush, Rayon d'Or, Ravat; Catskill cooler, other wine coolers.
Awards: Gold 1986 Seyval, aged in Yugoslavian oak; silver 1986 Seyval; bronze 1986 Ravat in 1987 New York Classic; many others in competitions involving 1,300 wines from thirty states.
Retail Shop: Sells wines on-site.

Credit Cards: None.
Access for Disabled: None.
Foreign Languages: None.
Getting There: From Ellenville: Take Rte. 52 East for 7 miles. From Pine Bush: Take Rte. 52 West for 4 miles.

ə̀ Gary Dross, a former college instructor, bought an old farm, cleared the land, dug the pond, restored the house, planted his vineyards, and made the wine for the winery he built on the old stone foundation of a burned-down cow barn. He also did well enough to expand his winery, add new equipment, and enlarge his cellar and tasting room with a porch overlooking his pond. He plans a café, perhaps open by now, where visitors can sip wine and drink in the peaceful view of vineyards, pond, meadows, and shade trees.

Dross's dedication is enviable, but not unusual, among the new breed of winemakers in the Hudson Valley or around the country. Unlike some others, this winemaker would like to remain small enough to handle everything himself. When time permits Dross likes to show visitors what he does, and personally presides over the tastings of acclaimed wines rarely found outside the winery or a few local shops.

(For accommodations and restaurants, see the section after Baldwin Vineyards and other Western Hudson Valley wineries.)

ə̀ ə̀ ə̀

West Park Wine Cellars

Route 9W
West Park-on-Hudson, New York 12493
TEL: 914-384-6709
OWNER AND WINEMAKER: Louis J.
  Fiore
WINE CONSULTANT: John Williams
  (Napa–Finger Lakes background).
FOUNDED: 1980

Tours & Tastings: Fri.–Sun. 11–6. Self-guided tours illustrated with video show, including tastings.
Closed: Jan.–May; Mon.–Thurs. May–Nov.
Vineyards: Ten acres planted only to Chardonnay; plans to expand to twenty-five.
Wines: Chardonnay.
Awards: In New York State Fair and other competitions.
Picnic Area: Peaceful setting overlooking vineyards and Hudson River.
Café: Tables inside winery. Innovative menu created by students of New York Culinary Institute. Light dishes might include smoked trout, fruit, cheese, French bread, pâté, pastas to eat in or take out on the grounds in fair weather. Open May 27–Dec. 31, Fri., lunch and dinner, noon–11. Live jazz bands on Fri. nights. Sat–Sun. lunch, noon–4. For information and reservations, call 914-384-6709.
Retail Shop: Wines, gifts.
Credit Cards: MasterCard, Visa.
Access for Disabled: None.
Foreign Languages: None.
Getting There: Take N.Y.S. Thruway to exit 18 (New Paltz); turn right (east) on Rte. 299 to Rte. 9W; turn left (north) on Rte. 9W and continue approximately 2.8 miles to winery.
Special Wine & Other Events: Art shows featuring area artists.

❤ West Park is the only vineyard in the Hudson Valley focusing on a single variety of vinifera. Although uncommon in America, in Europe, one species often is cultivated—the fine wines of Burgundy are made this way. Now proprietor Lou Fiore wants to show that Burgundian techniques and the greatest Burgundian grape, Chardonnay, can be translated into a Burgundian-style wine here in the Hudson Valley. He decided on this single-minded approach because Chardonnay is his favorite wine.

Fiore's quest for the perfect Chardonnay is aided by John Williams, proprietor/winemaker of the esteemed Frog's Leap Vineyards of St. Helena, California, who drops in from time to time at critical winemaking stages, and part-time winemaker Nelda Bennett, who studied at Geisenheim, Germany. Since his first Chardonnays were released in 1984, they have won praise from wine connoisseurs.

Louis J. Fiore, a former New York computer consultant, purchased his 800-acre property from Christian Brothers, a religious order. Ninety-seven acres now serve the winery and vineyards and were a former dairy farm. The property is both a state-of-the-art production operation and a showcase for West Park wines. The renovated buildings, on tree-shaded, trail-laced grounds, have stained-glass windows depicting wine scenes, a handsome party room with a barrel-rounded roof, and marble and tile accents.

(For accommodations and restaurants, see previous entries at New Paltz and entries following Woodstock Winery.)

❤ ❤ ❤

Woodstock Winery

62-1 Brodhead Road
West Shokan, New York 12494
TEL: 914-657-2018
OWNERS: Judy and George Boston
FOUNDED: 1983

AT A GLANCE
Tours & Tastings: Weekends, 11–4, by appointment. Leave message.
Closed: Some July & Aug. weekends; call ahead.
Vineyards: Purchases all grapes from New York growers.
Wines: Seyval Blanc, Chardonnay, Ravat, sparkling wines. Dry Hudson Valley apple wine.
Awards: 1983 Seyval Blanc (first vintage silver, Eastern Wine Competition); 1985

Late Harvest Ravat, 1986 New York Wine Classic; among others.
Retail Shop: Sells wine on-site.
Credit Cards: None.
Access for Disabled: None.
Foreign Languages: None.
Special Wine & Other Events: In Kingston, twenty-five miles away, evening cruises on the Hudson River feature wine and cheese and Mozart (Great Hudson Sailing Center, Rondout Landing; tel.: 914-338-7313 or 338-0071).
Getting There: Take N.Y.S. Thruway to exit 19 (Kingston); take Rte. 28W to Olivebridge and cross the Ashokan Reservoir. Take Rte. 28A North to Sandy's Ceramics; turn left onto Brodhead Road, continuing about 1.3 miles to winery.

꙳ George and Judy Boston's all-white winery could serve as an inspiration to all wine hobbyists who dream of going into the wine business and making a go of it. George, an ex-computer consultant, experimented first with a home winemaking kit and worked during the crush at Mark Miller's Benmarl before striking out on his own in 1983.

He now produces wines in the even-temperatured cellar of the couple's passive solar home near Woodstock. Judy, in sales at a New York radio station, serves as everything but winemaker.

The Bostons once dreamed of vineyards, but their site is not suitable for growing grapes. This is why they buy their grapes from New York growers. The winery's location is one of the most attractive in the area—at the bottom of High Point Mountain and near the sparkling Ashokan Reservoir, which supplies water to New York City.

Woodstock wines are also sold Saturdays at the Union Square Greenmarket in New York City.

TO SEE & DO
A main stop off the wine route for most visitors is Woodstock, fifteen miles from its namesake winery, a prominent artists' colony since the early 1900s. Ambling around the village's center and stopping in its little shops for local arts and crafts is a favorite activity, as is stopping at the Woodstock Artists Association Gallery (28 Tinker Street, Village Green Center, Wed.–Sun.; tel: 914-679-2436), to see works by local and nationally known artists. From June to Labor Day, Maverick Summer Concerts (Maverick Road), attract prominent musicians as they have since 1912, when they were established (Box 102, Woodstock, New York 12498; tel: 914-679-8746). For more information, contact the Chamber of Commerce, P.O. Box 36, Woodstock, New York 12498; tel: 914-679-6234.

Some twenty miles away, Kingston, the first capital of New York, is a nice place to while away the hours before boarding the wine-and-cheese-and-Mozart cruise offered locally. Among Kingston's numerous historic sites is the Senate House, built in 1676 (312 Fair Street, Stockade District). The meeting place of the first Senate has Dutch-style decor, a museum, and Colonial boxwood gardens (Wed.–Sun., tours every half hour; Jan.–March Sun. only; tel: 914-338-2786); the Old Dutch Church (Main and Wall streets) dates from the nineteenth century (Mon.–Fri.; tel: 914-338-6759). Another interesting place, Rondout Landing, buzzes with maritime activities. The place to book and board the Sailing Center's aforementioned wine, cheese, and Mozart cruise (tel: 914-338-7313 or 338-0071), it is also the site of the Hudson River Maritime Center/Museum (tel: 914-338-0071), a living museum, as well as a treasury of maritime artifacts. From Rondout Landing, the *Rip Van Winkle* takes passengers for a scenic cruise to West Point (tel: 914-255-6515).

A big draw for visitors each year is Stone House Day, on the second Saturday in July, at the nearby village of Hurley. Costumed guides lead tours into several privately owned Colonial stone houses, and there are antiques, a re-created Revolutionary War encampment, foods, and a fair (tel: 914-331-4121). While in Hurley, be sure to see the Hurley Patenee Manor (Old Rte. 209; tel: 914-331-5414), combining a seventeenth-century Dutch cottage with an eighteenth-century English country manor; fascinating lighting scenes.

For more information about Kingston, contact the Chamber of Commerce of Ulster County, 7 Albany Avenue, Kingston, New York 12401; tel: 914-338-5100.

ACCOMMODATIONS

Bed and Breakfasts
Cold Brook Inn
Coldbrook Road and Nissen Lane
Boiceville, New York 12412
Tel: 914-657-6619
Get a welcome glass of wine at this century-old farmhouse, and enjoy antique furnishings in the bedrooms. Big breakfast with fresh-ground coffee, homemade baked goods, eggs, country sausage, and bacon. Diverse outdoor activities include hiking, cross-country skiing, fishing. Arts-and-crafts browsing for less sports-minded travelers. Twenty miles west of Kingston.

House on the Hill
Old Route 213, Box 86
High Falls, New York 12440
Tel: 914-687-9627
Handmade quilts are cozy touches at this Colonial home, where visitors also find flowers and fruit in their rooms. Complimentary wine and cheese are served. Mornings start with a full breakfast. There are sports activities galore nearby, as well as woods for a hike, spacious lawns, and a glassed-in porch overlooking the placid pond. Ten miles south of Kingston.

Other
Howard Johnson's Motor Lodge
Route 28
Kingston, New York 12401
Tel: 914-338-4200; 800-654-2000
118-room motel with two pools, one outdoors, lifeguard; sauna, café, bar, room service; patios. Within sight of exit 19, N.Y.S. Thruway.

Ramada Inn
Route 28
Kingston, New York 12401
Tel: 914-339-3900; 800-2-RAMADA
Better-than-average 150-room motel; indoor poor, lifeguard; coffee in rooms, café, bar, room service. Health club. Just north of exit 19, N.Y.S. Thruway.

RESTAURANT
Hillside Manor
240 Boulevard
Route 32S
Kingston, New York 12401
Tel: 914-331-4386
Country inn decor and view are setting for Northern Italian dishes. Makes own pasta. Wagner Wines. Chef-owned.

East Side of the River

Cascade Mountain Winery

Flint Hill Road
Amenia, New York 12501
TEL: 914-373-9021
OWNER: William Wetmore
FOUNDED: 1977

AT A GLANCE

Tours & Tastings: Year-round, Mon.–Sun. 10–6.
Vineyards: Fourteen acres planted to French and American hybrids.
Wines: Estate-bottled Seyval Blanc,

most bemedaled Chancellor, Vignoles, Baco Noir, Leon Millot, Aurora; blends include New Harvest Red, Little White, Rosé, and others; sweet strawberry wine.
Awards: Claims more awards in recent years than any other Hudson Valley winery; bringing home the gold; Seyval Blanc, Vignoles, and Spring Fever.
Picnic Area: Delicious picnic lunch served outdoors in bucolic setting.
Restaurant: Talented Culinary Institute grad Melissa Bernard oversees inventive menu featuring foods of the Hudson River region to go with Cascade Vineyards' wines. Pâtés, smoked trout, pastas, soups, fruit desserts, and other delicacies. Lunch daily 12–3. Dinners from 7, second and fourth Sat. each month. By reservation.
Retail Shop: Wines and gifts sold on-site in tasting room.
Credit Cards: MasterCard, Visa.
Access for Disabled: None.
Foreign Languages: Spanish.
Getting There: From Amenia, north three miles to Webutuck School. At winery sign, turn left three miles on Haight Rd. to T; left at T and continue one mile to winery.
Special Wine & Other Events: July & Aug. concert series.

ɘ William Wetmore, novelist and free-lance writer, planted his vineyard in 1972 and became one of the first wineries in Dutchess County since Thomas Lake's Brotherhood made wines at Amenia in the 1960s. Wetmore and his wife, Margaret, and son, Charles, share the winery chores. Father and son built the wood winery themselves in 1977 as part of a school project for Charles, then a senior in high school. They finished in time for the first fall crush of 2,500 gallons. Current production is 15,000 gallons. The property is properly described by Wetmore as "rural splendor." The winery is set amidst seventy acres of woods,

ponds, fields, and, last but not least, vineyards.

ɘ ɘ ɘ

Clinton Vineyards

Schultzville Road
Clinton Corners, New York 12514
TEL: 914-266-5372
PRESIDENT: Ben Feder
FOUNDED: 1977

AT A GLANCE
Tours & Tastings: Sat. & Sun., 9–5.; a call ahead is advised.
Closed: Weekdays.
Vineyards: Seyval Blanc, Johannisberg Riesling.
Wines: Seyval Blanc, Johannisberg Riesling; *methode champenoise* Seyval Naturel; semi-dry apple wine.
Awards: Oft-awarded Seyval Blanc.
Picnic Area: "Munch in the fields."
Retail Shop: Wines sold on-site.
Credit Cards: American Express, MasterCard, Visa.
Access for Disabled: None.
Foreign Languages: None.
Getting There: From the south: Take the Taconic State Pkwy. north to the Salt Point Tpke. exit. Turn right and go through Clinton Corners. Make a sharp left onto Schultzville Rd. You will go under the Taconic. The vineyard sign will be at the first lefthand turn west of the parkway. From the north: Take the Salt Point Tpke. exit off the Taconic and turn left, following the instructions above from there.

ɘ Ben Feder, formerly a well-known graphic designer in publishing, has planted his vineyard primarily to Seyval Blanc, and he makes wines from an old barn. He also grows a little Johannisberg Riesling, for a limited-edition botrytised wine. But mainly he pursues the perfect Seyval Blanc in its two guises, still and sparkling. Like many European vintners, Feder wants to be well known for his vintages, not for his wide variety of wines. So far, he seems to be succeeding. Noted critics have raved about his Seyval Blanc, judges have given them gold medals, and renowned New York City restaurants such as the Four Seasons, Oyster Bar, and Windows on the World have had Clinton Vineyards wines on their lists.

Like other small wineries, Clinton is run with the owner's wife's, Kathy's, help. Here also Clinton Vineyards' fans help pick grapes at the harvest and are rewarded with a grand meal. Interested? To find how out this works, call the vineyard.

🐚 🐚 🐚

Millbrook Vineyards

Wing and Shunpike Roads
Millbrook, New York 12545
TEL: 914-677-8383
OWNER: John S. Dyson
WINEMAKER: John Graziano
FOUNDED: 1979

AT A GLANCE

Tours & Tastings: Daily 11–6, May–Oct. Guided tours followed by tasting of six or seven wines. At other times by appointment.

Vineyards: Forty-eight acres, all vinifera; forty acres planted to well-known French varieties; eight acres experimental plantings of lesser-known North Italian and French Alps species.

Wines: Vintage-dated, estate-bottled Chardonnay, Claret (blends Merlot, Cabernet Sauvignon, Cabernet Franc); Pinot Noir, Riesling. Hunt Country blends: White (Riesling, Gewürztraminer, Pinot Meunier), Rosé (Pinot Noir and Pinot Meunier), Red (Cabernet Franc and Pinot Noir).

Awards: Bronzes to 1986 Chardonnay and 1987 Riesling in 1988 New York Classic.

Picnic Area: In pastoral splendor.

Retail Shop: Wines sold on-site.

Credit Cards: American Express, MasterCard, Visa.

Access for Disabled: Limited.

Foreign Languages: French.

Getting There: From the south: Take Taconic State Pkwy. to Rte. 44 (Millbrook exit) and continue east on Scenic Rte. 44 to Rte. 82 North. Continue 3½ miles to Shunpike Rd. (Rte. 57). Turn right and drive 3 miles to Wing Rd. Take a left on Wing Rd. to Millbrook sign on the right. From Albany: Take I-90 South to the Taconic State Pkwy. and continue south to Rte. 44; proceed as above.

🐚 Going into winemaking after having other successful careers is not unusual. But it never figured into the plans of former New York Commissioner of Agriculture John S. Dyson, although he played a principal role in the creation of the Farm Winery Act that streamlined New York's wine industry. The bill made it more attractive to own small wineries by lowering license fees and allowing vintners to sell to the public. Dyson decided on grapes as an income-producing crop later, when he bought an old dairy farm off the auction block. Dairy prices were down, but fruit was a viable crop.

As commissioner, Dyson became friendly with the late Dr. Konstantin Frank, the extraordinary viticulturalist who was first to grow vinifera vines successfully in New York State. Frank has been Dyson's inspiration in his current venture. And, like Frank, Dyson has his own lofty goals.

He wants to make wines to rival Burgundy's in the Hudson River Valley, where indeed growing conditions and soil are comparable to those of the Côte de Beaune. (Another all-vinifera winery, West Park Wine Cellars, on the west side of the Hudson, has similar aims; see page 98).

Dyson's winemaker, Graziano, is sent periodically to France to fine-tune his techniques; grapes here are hand-picked, a tradition at fine châteaus, and wines are aged in the finest French oak.

The winery, a converted old hip-roofed Dutch barn, also has Continental charm. Graceful Tuscan arches set off the temperature-controlled aging room; a graceful floor-to-ceiling Palladian window in the spacious tasting room offers a view of vineyards and acres of beautiful country beyond.

Dyson, who helped create the "I Love New York" campaign, now has another theme. He sees the Hudson Valley as "Wine Country—A Place to Relax and Dream" and a magnet to New Yorkers in the same way Napa Valley draws thousands of San Franciscans.

a a a

North Salem Vineyard

Hardscrabble Road (R.R. #2)
North Salem, New York 10560
TEL: 914-669-5518
OWNER: Dr. George W. Naumburg, Jr.
FOUNDED: 1965

AT A GLANCE
Tours & Tastings: Sat. & Sun., 1–5, year-round; tours are informal and guided over walkways that permit good views of a working winery and go on to the balcony for vineyard view; questions are encouraged and fully answered. Tastings, with or without tour, in sleek, spacious tasting room.
Closed: Weekdays.
Vineyards: Eighteen acres, planted to Seyval, Marechal Foch, Chancellor, De Chaunac.
Wines: Seyval Blanc and a variety of red blends.
Picnic Area: Outdoors on the grounds, or tables indoors in the pleasant tasting room; a basket lunch of bread, cheese, fruit, and a glass of wine is offered for a modest sum.
Retail Shop: Sells wines and gifts on-site.
Credit Cards: None.
Access for Disabled: Limited.
Foreign Languages: French.
Getting There: From the south: Take I-684 to exit 8 (Hardscrabble Rd.) and continue to winery, not far from Connecticut border.

a Dr. George W. Naumburg, Jr., a retired psychiatrist, and his wife, Michelle, got under way in 1965 with a vineyard planted to the first of thirty-six varieties as an experiment to see which would flourish in their soil. This first juice was sold to home winemakers. Four species remain, including the Seyval, source of vintage after vintage since 1981.

With no winemaking experience, Naumburg learned by consulting the skilled winemaker Philip Wagner, founder of Boordy Vineyard in Maryland, and attended courses at Geneva in upstate New York. Now a serious winemaker, he sells his wine to visitors to the winery.

Naumburg's winery is in a rebuilt cow barn with cathedral ceilings. In dramatic contrast is the high-tech tasting room, with glass ceiling, tiled floor, and tiled tasting bar.

Naumburg grew up on a farm in Westchester in a family where wine was appreciated with meals. And as any psychiatrist knows, early influences shape our later lives.

TO SEE AND DO
In Millbrook, visit the Innisfree Garden (Tyrrel Rd., near South Millbrook; tel: 914-677-8000), dedicated to Eastern and Western civilizations and their influence on gardens (open May–Oct., Wed.–Sun., Mon. holidays).

A must-see when meandering in the Hudson River Valley is Hyde Park, known principally for the Roosevelt-Vanderbilt National Historic Site (tel: 914-229-9115 or 229-9116), with the home of Franklin D. Roosevelt (his birthplace; earliest part of the house predates Roosevelt days; Roosevelt's grave and that of his wife, Anna Eleanor Roosevelt, in the rose garden). (Apr.–Oct., daily; Nov.–March, Thurs.–Mon.; closed Jan. 1, Thanksgiving Day, Dec. 25); the Franklin D. Roosevelt Library and Museum (interesting exhibits cover the president and first lady's lives) (tel: 914-229-8114; open daily; closed Jan. 1, Thanksgiving Day, Dec. 25); the Vanderbilt Mansion, a superb Beaux-Arts mansion designed for Frederick W. Vanderbilt by McKim, Mead, and White, prominent architects, with handsome period interiors (Apr.–Oct., daily; Nov.–March, Thurs.–Mon.; closed Jan. 1, Thanksgiving Day, Dec. 25); and the Eleanor Roosevelt National Historic Site, two miles east of the Roosevelt home (shuttle bus transportation is available), her country home and a fine reflection of her life.

Mills-Morris State Park (three miles east on U.S. 9 in Staatsburg) is the place to relax and enjoy sports, picnics, and to inspect Mills Mansion, a sixty-five-room, nineteenth-century mansion filled with elegant furnishings and elaborate Flemish tapestries. Formerly the home of Ogden Mills, it was designed by the highly respected McKim, Mead, and White.

See also the Edwin A. Ulrich Museum (Wave Crest-on-the-Hudson) on Albany Post Road for a collection of Waugh family drawings covering the years 1814–1973 (tel: 914-229-7107; May–Sept., Fri.–Mon.; other days by appointment).

For further information contact the Columbia County Development Department, 414 Union Street, Hudson, NY 12535, tel: 800-777-9247.

Ambling around Fishkill can also be rewarding for its ties to Colonial America: the Madame Brett Homestead, from 1709, visited by such luminaries as Washington and Lafayette, with authentic old furnishings and garden (May–Oct., Fri.–Sun. afternoons; tel: 914-831-6533), the Van Wyck Homestead Museum, circa 1732, once a supply depot for the Continental Army (Memorial Day–Labor Day, Sat. & Sun. afternoons; tel: 914-896-9560), and Mount Guilan Historic Site, around 1730 to 1740, in Rombout Village, Beacon, headquarters of Baron von Steuben during the American Revolution (May–Dec., Wed. & Sun. afternoons, by appointment; tel: 914-831-8172).

For more information, contact the Greater Southern Dutchess Chamber of Commerce, NY9 Plaza (R.R. 1, Box 52, Fishkill, New York, 12524; tel: 914-897-2067).

ACCOMMODATIONS
(See other Hudson River Valley entries also.)

Troutbeck Inn
Leedsville Road (P.O. Box 26)
Amenia, New York 12501
Tel: 914-373-9681
A lovely inn on weekends only; during the week it's a conference center and executive retreat. The Tudor-style manor was built in 1918, and there are rooms in a farmhouse built much earlier, with a modern addition that blends right in. The inn is noted for excellent food, which can be enjoyed by casual visitors as well as overnight guests. A typical five-course meal might feature game, a seafood bisque, roast lamb entrée, salad, and a rich dessert. Cascade Mountain Wines are served. Surrounded by 442 acres, with hiking trails and cross-country skiing; jogging, two pools—one of them heated—two tennis courts, and a lake for fishing.

RESTAURANTS

Two highly rated restaurants with well-planned wine lists can be found high above the Hudson at the Culinary Institute of America in Hyde Park (North Road, 1½ miles south on U.S. 9; 1½ miles north of the Mid-Hudson Bridge). Reservations and jacket are required at both. American Bounty (Tel: 914-471-6608) specializes in American regional cuisine in a setting high above the Hudson. Closed Sun., Mon., major holidays, three weeks in July, two weeks at Christmas. The Escoffier Room has continental and French specialties (Tel: 914-471-6608). (Holidays and days open are same as for American Bounty).

Auberge Maxime
Ridgefield Road
North Salem, New York 10560
Tel: 914-669-5450
French cuisine with classics such as duck à l'orange and airy dessert soufflés. North Salem wines on list. Outdoor dining in fair weather. Jacket required.

Emily Shaw's Inn
On N.Y. 137 near Pound Ridge
Tel: 914-764-5779
Atmospheric Colonial house decked out with antiques; serves American specialties, with trout and deep-dish pie on the most-wanted list. Well-stocked wine cellar with North Salem wines among the selections. Closed Wednesdays. Jacket required.

Harralds
Stormville, New York 12582
Tel: 914-878-6595
Chef-owned restaurant with classic Continental dishes, carefully prepared. Choices include truite au bleu from restaurant's own tank, breast of duckling, luscious desserts. Wine list includes Millbrook and Benmarl selections. Cozy fireplace. Open 6–midnight; closed Sun.-Tues., Dec. 24–25, Jan. Reservations required.

Le Chambord
Hopewell Junction, New York 12533
Tel: 914-221-1941
French chef, Georgian Colonial setting, and delicious foods such as swordfish scallopine with lobster and shrimp mousse or classical entrées such as rack of lamb; desserts such as raspberries in ground almond shells, and a wine list including Millbrook, West Park, Clinton Vineyards, and others. Reservations.

Plumbush
Route 9D
Cold Spring, New York 10516
Tel: 914-265-3904
Well-prepared Continental foods, with trout from restaurant tank a specialty; veal and duck; elegant fritters for dessert. Cozy ambience in Oak Room; local artworks on display. Wine list scanty on New York vintages; many California selections.

Troutbeck Inn
(See under "Accommodations.")

❧ BROOKLYN AND MANHATTAN

Of the handful of wineries located in metropolitan cities, there are two in New York. Wine routes to them lead through fascinating areas where immigrants and entrepreneurs found new opportunities and still do.

So why are these wines different from all other wines? They are kosher, which means they are made by Orthodox or Hasidic Jews under supervision of an Orthodox rabbi; they can contain no glycerines, gelatins, or corn products. Nor can filtering agents be used, and fermentation is not aided by yeast. But there is nothing in the Good Book that says kosher wines have to be sweet; they can be dry indeed.

Briefly, here is the story of how kosher wines became sweet: in the beginning, Leo Star, a winemaker on Wooster Street, created a sweet red Concord grape wine for retailers to sell at Passover. Then it came to to pass that these wines were also sold to non-Jews who liked their sweet taste.

Star took this as a sign that his wines were well liked because they were kosher, and he contacted Manischewitz about using the famous kosher food manufacturer's label on them. Permission was granted and the sweet Concord kosher wine was soon on its way to becoming the tradition it is today. Even now, most Passover wines are sweet Concord and many still bear the Manischewitz label. But times and wines they are a changin'.

🍂 🍂 🍂

Crown Regal Wine Cellars

657 Montgomery Street
Brooklyn, New York 11225
TEL: 718-604-1430
OWNER/WINEMAKER: Joseph Zakon
FOUNDED: 1981

AT A GLANCE
Tours & Tastings: By appointment only.
Vineyards: Purchases French and American hybrids and vinifera varieties from Finger Lakes and Long Island growers.
Wines: Kesser Concord; Joseph Zakon Winery De Chaunac, Chardonnay, Riesling, Niagara Blanc, Seyval, 770 blend.
Awards: Bronzes for Blush Spumante and 1986 Riesling in 1988 New York Classic.
Retail Shop: Wines for sale on-site, by appointment.
Credit Cards: None.
Access for Disabled: None.
Getting There: Call 718-330-1234 for the most convenient public transportation from a specific New York starting point.

🍂 As a boy, Joe Zakon, an Orthodox Jew, learned that the great kings of Israel enjoyed wine. Yet, when he was old enough to participate in the blessing of wines during the Sabbath and other ceremonies, he couldn't imagine such awful stuff gracing a king's table. In fact, he was right; they never did, sweet kosher wine being strictly an American invention.

After studying kosher wine production and poring over books on winemaking at the library, Zakon decided that he knew what was wrong: kosher methods overpressed Concord grapes, which gave the wine its syrupy taste and smell—*foxy* is the wine connoisseur's word for the grapey aroma.

This led Zakon to experiment with grapes to produce wines that really once might have graced King Solomon's table; his De Chaunac is in fact in the wine cellar at the governor's mansion in Albany.

Zakon's mainstay is still a sweet Concord; his other wines include a dry-finish Concord, Chardonnay, and Seyval, among others, depending on the harvests each year. They ferment in plastic barrels; French oak will come later when he fulfills his dream of having a full-fledged winery under the Brooklyn Bridge.

Zakon's wines have crossed the bridge and are found in Florida, California, and Wisconsin.

TO SEE & DO

The winery is in the Crown Heights section of Brooklyn, a working-class neighborhood, home to many Orthodox Jews. Brooklyn itself has enough sightseeing to fill a book of its own. Highlights are the celebrated Brooklyn Academy of Music, America's oldest performing arts center, with a reputation for exciting New Wave presentations (30 Lafayette Ave.; tel: 718-636-4100); the Brooklyn Botanic Garden (Eastern Pkwy., opp. Prospect Park; daily except Mon.; tel: 718-622-4433), fifty-two acres with conservatory, braille garden, Japanese garden (Apr.–Oct), rose garden (June–Oct.), shop and plant sales; directly across is Prospect Park, planned by Olmsted and Vaux, designers of Central Park, whose 526 acres include Grand Army Plaza to the north and Lefferts Homestead, an eighteenth-century Dutch Colonial farmhouse, as well as ball fields, a skating rink, and more. The Brooklyn Museum (200 Eastern Pkwy.; tel: 718-638-5000) has an extensive Egyptology collection as well as others from the world over; lectures, film, gallery, shop (daily except Tues.; closed Jan. 1, Thanksgiving Day, Dec. 25).

RESTAURANTS

You probably won't find Zakon's wines in the following two Brooklyn restaurants, among many in New York City serving New York State wines:

Gage & Tollner
372 Fulton Street
Brooklyn, New York 11201
Tel: 718-875-5181
Old Brooklyn ambience in restaurant established in 1879. Lovely old gaslight fixtures. Excellent New York wine selection. Some traditional dishes, such as lamb chops, and some interesting fish specialties. Braille menu.

The River Cafe
1 Water Street
Brooklyn, New York 11201
Tel: 718-522-5200
In the East River, at the foot of the Brooklyn Bridge on a river barge, with memorable view. Serves new American cuisine; specialty is red snapper baked in saffron oil, sautéed quail. Wine list includes Hermann Weimer, Hargrave, and Wagner, and, at times, others. Piano music.

ও ও ও

Schapiro's Wine Company, Ltd.

126 Rivington Street
New York, New York 10002
TEL: 212-674-4404
OWNERS: The Schapiro family
FOUNDED: 1899

AT A GLANCE

Tours & Tastings: Sun. 11–4, cellar tour with history of the winery and tasting.
Closed: Sat. and Jewish holidays.
Vineyards: Grapes purchased from Finger Lakes growers. Also New York blackberries, cherries, honey.
Wines: Concord, Chablis, Blanc de Blanc, Rosé, Burgundy; blackberry, cherry, pina cocatina (wine version of pina colada), Mead (honey); Rhine, sangria.
Retail Shop: Wines sold on-site.
Credit Cards: None.
Access for Disabled: Wide doors.
Foreign Languages: Yiddish.
Getting There: Call 718-330-1234 for transportation information.

ও This winery was founded in 1899 by Samuel Schapiro, from Glitzia, Austria, and is still run by his descendants. Schapiro first started a restaurant, which he turned into the winery operating today in a building more than a century old.

TO SEE & DO

This is the Lower East Side, once home to many Jewish immigrants, and traces of their past remain today. Early arrivals were peddlers, and from there became small retailers or pushcart owners. Their stores remain, mainly on Delancey and Orchard streets; many now owned by today's immigrants, some still owned by Jewish merchants who speak Spanish to their clients as well as Yiddish and English. Bargain hunting is the main activity (Jewish-owned shops close on Saturdays and Jewish holidays). There are also architectural reminders of the early days, perhaps the most famous is the Williamsburg Bridge (east end of Delancey St.), built in 1903 and boasting some of the earliest steel towers used on a bridge. The Henry Street Settlement at 466 Grand Street and the Forsyth Street Synagogue (now the Seventh-Day Adventist Church) at Forsyth and Delancey are other architectural landmarks, as is the striking Eldridge Street Synagogue (Congregation Khal Adas Jeshrun-Anshe Lubz), an amalgam of Romanesque, Gothic, and Moorish style, which, alas, has seen much better days (14 Eldridge Street, between Canal and Forsyth sts.).

ACCOMMODATIONS

Because Manhattan has a wealth of hotels, there is not room to list them here. Contact the New York City Convention and Visitors Bureau for a full list: 2 Columbus Circle, New York, New York 10018 (tel: 212-397-8222).

RESTAURANTS

The following is a mere tasting of New York restaurants with New York wines on their lists. Reservations are essential.

American Harvest Restaurant
Vista International Hotel
3 World Trade Center
New York, New York 10048
Tel: 212-938-9100

Regional American dishes with American wines to go with them; from New York State: Wagner and Hermann J. Weimer, others at times. In the same hotel is the Greenhouse Restaurant & Wine Bar. More regional American cuisine, casual.

Keen's
72 West 36th Street
New York, New York 10018
Tel: 212-947-3636
Turn-of-the century atmosphere with clay pipes from the 1800s a focal point of the decor; old photos and other memorabilia. American and Continental cuisine; mutton and lamb specialties. Good selection of New York wines.

Oyster Bar & Restaurant
Grand Central Terminal
New York, New York 10017
Tel: 212-490-6650
Famous old restaurant with tiled floors and brass accents; known for abundant selection of fresh-caught fish and seafood and, of course, an oyster bar. Dr. Konstantin Frank's Vinifera Wine Cellars, Clinton Vineyards, Woodbury Vineyards, on wine list.

The Four Seasons
99 East 52nd Street
New York, New York 10022
Tel: 212-754-9494
Stunning Philip Johnson–designed pool and grill rooms with Picasso tapestry and renowned cuisine and wine cellar. Lenz, Bridgehampton, Hermann J. Weimer, among the American wines. Inventive American dishes. Elegant desserts and attentive service.

Barclay Restaurant
Inter-Continental Hotel
111 East 48 Street
New York, New York 10017
Tel: 212-755-5900

Two rooms with panoramic view. French cuisine. Wine list includes New York State selections. Closed Sun., Mon., Jan. 1, Dec. 25, last two weeks in July, first and second weeks in Aug. Classical harpist during evenings.

Windows on the World
1 World Trade Center
107th Floor
New York, New York 10048
Tel: 212-938-1111
Graciously designed in tiers with sweeping view of New York Harbor. American regional cuisine; excellent cellar. Nonmembership fee charged at lunch. Also Cellar in the Sky, a wine cellar setting.

4

The Middle Atlantic States

❦

Alba Vineyard, Finesville, New Jersey

❧ MARYLAND

❧*L*ike many early settlers in America, those in Maryland made apple, berry, and dandelion wines. State winemakers today, like their counterparts around the country, are committed mainly to French hybrids and vinifera varieties of grapes. But old traditions continue: visitors also find some old-fashioned fruit wines and ciders on the wine routes winding through miles of rolling hills and into historic places.

Maryland's wine production now exceeds 300,000 bottles annually, totaling more than $1.5 million in sales. There are eleven wineries in Maryland, mainly in Baltimore, Frederick, and Carroll counties, plus a Farm Museum that stages an annual Wine Festival. More about that later. . . . First, the vineyards and wineries:

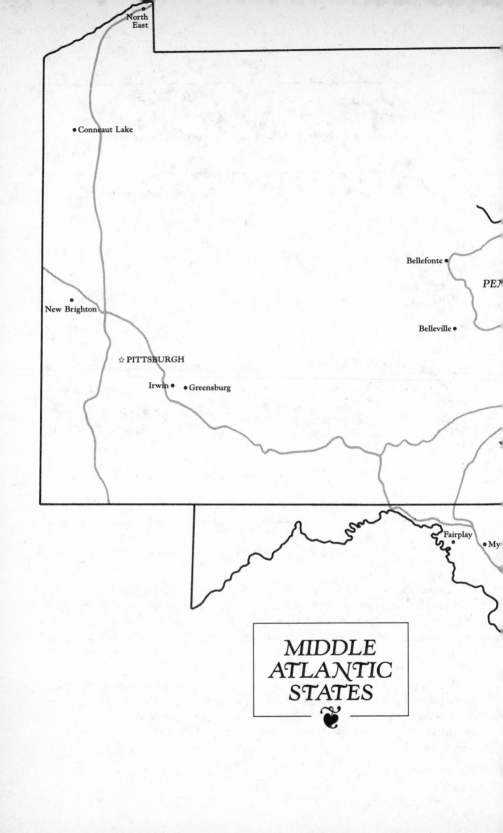

North
East

• Conneaut Lake

Bellefonte •

PE

Belleville •

•
New Brighton

☆ PITTSBURGH

Irwin • • Greensburg

Fairplay
• • My

MIDDLE
ATLANTIC
STATES

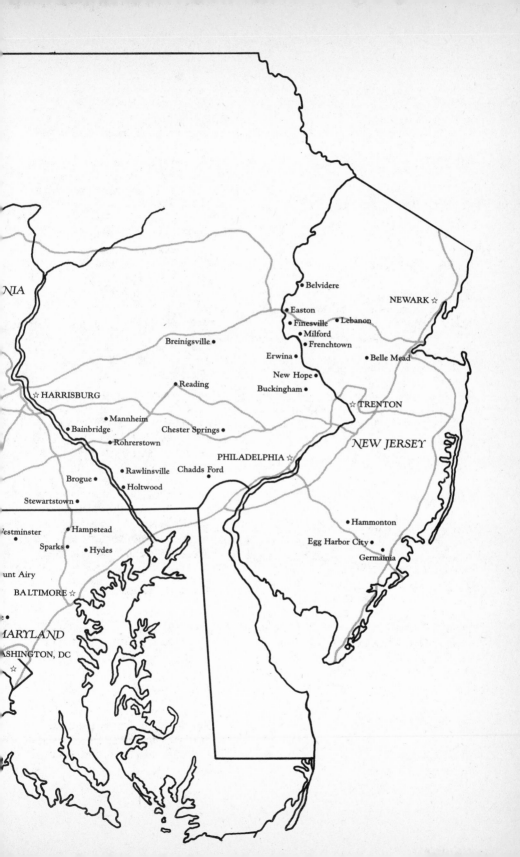

Baltimore County

Boordy Vineyards

12820 Long Green Pike
Hydes, Maryland 21082
TEL: 301-592-5015
PRESIDENT/WINEMAKER: Robert Deford
  III, enology courses at UC-Davis

AT A GLANCE

Tours & Tastings: Mon.–Sat. 10–5, Sun.
1–4; teach how wine is processed, aged,
and bottled; followed by a tasting and
vineyard stroll. Reservations needed for
groups of ten or more.
Closed: Christmas, New Year's, Easter,
Thanksgiving.
Vineyards: Fourteen acres planted to
French hybrids and vinifera.
Wines: Seyval Blanc and Vidal Blanc,
Vin Gris (a blush), Chardonnay, and
Cabernet Sauvignon. Generics include a
very popular nouveau red, bottled every
year in November. Boordy also makes
Wassail, a spiced wine traditional at
Christmas.
Awards: Nouveau and Seyval Blanc.
Picnic Area: On the spacious grounds.
Retail Shop: Sells wines, books, gift
items related to wine.
Credit Cards: MasterCard, Visa.
Access for Disabled: Ramp for wheel-
chairs.
Foreign Languages: None.
Getting There: Take Baltimore Beltway
to exit 29 (Cromwell Bridge Rd.) and go
north 2.9 miles to end. Go left onto Glen
Arm Rd., 3.2 miles to the intersection
with Long Green Pike. Take a left and go
2 miles to winery's entrance on left.
Boordy sign is to the right, opposite the
entrance.
Special Wine & Other Events: Nouveau
and Wassail parties are held Sundays,
Nov.–Dec.

&a Boordy is usually the name on
everyone's lips when they speak of Maryland wines. The oldest and largest winery
in the state, it was founded at Riderwood
in 1945 by Philip Wagner, fine wine de-
votee, editor at the *Baltimore-American
Sun*, and his wife, Jocelyn. Wagner pre-
dicted that one day vineyards would
flourish throughout the United States
with the introduction of French hybrids.
How right he was! Indeed, he was instru-
mental in widening their use by providing
hybrid rootstocks to a number of eastern
U.S. vineyards. His book *American
Wines and How to Make Them* no doubt
inspired others to explore this field.

Under Wagner's guidance, Boordy
Vineyards produced some highly praised
wines. In 1980, the Defords, family
friends and former suppliers of some
Boordy grapes, took over. They re-estab-
lished the winery near their own vineyard, and are today carrying on the
Boordy name and Wagner's goal of producing praiseworthy wines. Production is
now around 90,000 bottles or 18,000 gallons annually.

While they are only twenty minutes
from Baltimore, the vineyards seem a
world away in a pastoral setting amid
rolling hills. The picturesque winery is a
renovated nineteenth-century barn, with
thick stone walls and hand-hewn beams.

&a &a &a

Woodhall Vineyards and Wine Cellars Inc.

15115 Wheeler Lane
Sparks, Maryland 21152
TEL: 301-771-4664
OWNERS/WINEMAKERS: Albert and
  Diane Copp, Herbert and Rufus
  Davis, Michael and Helene
  DeSimone, Kent and Carolyn Muhly
FOUNDED: 1982

AT A GLANCE

Tours & Tastings: Sat.–Sun. 1–5 or by appointment. Conducted tours are tailored to participants' interests: "They can be understood by the novice or made highly technical for the expert," say the owners.

Closed: Jan. and Feb.

Vineyards: Eight acres planted to Seyval Blanc, Vidal, Johannisberg Riesling, Chardonnay, Cabernet Sauvignon, Marechal Foch, Chambourcin.

Wines: Whites—Seyval, Vidal, Johannisberg Riesling; Reds—Garnet, a nouveau-style wine, Chambourcin, Cabernet.

Retail Shop: Wines sold on-site.

Credit Cards: None, but will accept checks.

Access for Disabled: Entire operation at ground level.

Foreign Languages: Danish.

Getting There: Take I-83 North to exit 24 (Belfast Rd.); go west 1 mile to Wheeler Lane; left (south) ½ mile to Woodhall entrance on left. Approximately twenty miles from Baltimore city center.

&❧ Originally amateur winemakers, the Woodhall group turned pro in 1982 and has since been turning out small quantities of high-quality wines barrel-aged in small oak casks. Woodhall's farm, built circa 1790, in the hills of Western Run Valley, is located in a National Register historic district. A converted dairy barn from the 1930s houses the winery.

ACCOMMODATIONS

(See also Carroll County section and Frederick County and To See & Do for Washingthon County.)

For bed and breakfast recommendations statewide, contact:

The Traveller in Maryland
P.O. Box 2277
Annapolis, Maryland 21404
Tel: 301-286-6232

Inns

Spring Bank Farm
Harmony Grove, 7945 Worman's Mill
  Road
Frederick, Maryland 21701
Tel: 301-694-0440
This 1880s mansion, on the National Register of Historic Places, has high ceilings, plaster ceiling medallions and moldings, and marble fireplaces. Extensive, well-tended grounds.

The Strawberry Inn
17 Main Street
New Market, Maryland 21774
Tel: 301-865-3318
Five double rooms (one barrier-free) furnished with antiques; Continental breakfast delivered to your room.

Winchester Country Inn
430 South Bishop Street
Westminster, Maryland 21157
Tel: 301-876-7373
One of Maryland's oldest inns, Winchester Country Inn dates from the 1760s and is under a mile from the Carroll County Farm Museum, site of the annual Maryland Wine Festival. Antiques fill the interiors; full breakfast and afternoon sherry are included in the room rates.

The Turning Point Inn
3406 Urbana Place
Urbana, Maryland 21701
Tel: 301-874-2421
A turn-of-the-century mansion with four antique-filled guest rooms and a delightful restaurant for breakfast, lunch, and dinner.

Marriott's Hunt Valley Inn
Shawan Road
Hunt Valley, Maryland 21030
Tel: 301-785-7000; 800-228-9290
Typical Marriott accommodations, with indoor and outdoor pools, restaurant.

RESTAURANTS

Peerce's Plantation
Dulaney Valley Road
Phoenix, Maryland 21131
Tel. 301-252-3100
Reservoir view outside, Old South interiors, and a Continental menu, starring veal dishes and California vintages. Jacket required.

Country Fare Inn
100 Painters Mill Road
Owings Mills, Maryland 21117
Tel: 301-363-3131
Continental cuisine. Boordy wines.

Turning Point Inn
(See under "Accommodations." Serves American-style cuisine.)

Hampton National Historic Site
535 Hampton Lane
Towson, Maryland 21204
Tel: 301-823-7054
Lunch or tea by reservation only, in tea room or patio; late Georgian mansion with period furnishings. Off Dulaney Valley Road.

Carroll County

Montbray Wine Cellars, Ltd.

818 Silver Run Valley Road
Westminster, Maryland 21157
TEL: 301-346-7878
PRESIDENT/WINEMAKER: Dr. G. Hamilton Mowbray, founder American Wine Society, wine appreciation teacher, adviser to vineyardists and winemakers, conducts guest lectures and tastings throughout the eastern United States.
FOUNDED: 1966

AT A GLANCE
Tours & Tastings: Mon.–Fri. 10–6, Sun. 1–6; include vineyards and cellars; tasting often conducted by Dr. Mowbray. Weekend visitors should call in advance.
Closed: Christmas Day.
Vineyards: Nineteen acres owned and eleven leased, planted to vinifera varieties.
Wines: Cabernet Sauvignon, Chardonnay, Johannisberg Riesling, Seyve-Villard, and Garnet (a blend).
Awards: Does not enter competitions.
Picnic Area: In shady grove near winery.
Retail Shop: Sells wines and related items.

Credit Cards: None.
Access for Disabled: No.
Foreign Languages: French.
Getting There: From Westminster: Take Rte. 97 North (toward Gettysburg) seven miles to Silver Run Valley Rd., turn right; winery is two miles on left. From Gettysburg: Take Rte. 97 South sixteen miles to Silver Run Valley Rd., turn left; Montbray is two miles on left.
Special Wine & Other Events: Hosts American Wine Society Regional Conference third weekend in May.

🍷 Mowbray deserves to be toasted as a trailblazer in U.S. wines for being the first to produce a varietally labeled wine from the French hybrid Seyve Villard, also known as Seyval Blanc (1966); for initiating Maryland's commercial Chardonnays and Rieslings (both 1969), and Cabernet Sauvignons (1976); for creating America's first "ice-wines" (1974), made from Rieslings frozen on the vines; and for nurturing the world's first "clone vineyard" of vines propagated from a single cell of French hybrid Seyve Villard, 5-276 (1977). The French government awarded him the Croix de Chevalier du

Merite Agricole for his endeavors in winemaking and education, and he holds the American Wine Society's Award of Merit. Mowbray's wife, Phyllis, has played a key role in Montbray's success. She is cellarmaster today at Montbray in the undulating hills of Silver Run Valley.

Also in Carroll County:

ᖋᖋ ᖋᖋ ᖋᖋ

Whitemarsh Cellars

2810 Hoffman Mill Road
Hampstead, Maryland 21074
TEL: 301-848-4488
FOUNDED: 1981
From Rte. 40 in Westminster: Turn at McDonald's; go east on Gorsuch Rd., right on Coon Club Rd., left on Hoffman Mill Rd. to 2810.

Tours, tastings, sales by appointment, daily 10–6; nominal tour fee deducted from purchases. Varietals such as Chardonnay and Riesling, made in small oak barrels; also champagne. Picnicking and trout fishing nearby.

Wine Festival: The last weekend in September is the Maryland Wine Festival at the Carroll County Farm Museum. For a modest admission price (call 301-848-7775 for all details), visitors get an attractive engraved wineglass and eleven one-ounce samplings of Maryland's wines from each participating winery. Included also is entry to the museum, itself a fascinating glimpse of late nineteenth-century farm life through live crafts exhibits and historical memorabilia.

ACCOMMODATIONS

(See also Baltimore-Frederick county listings, and Baltimore at end of section.)

Quality Inn
Route 140 at Rtes. 31 & 32
Westminster, Maryland 21157
Tel: 301-857-1900; 800-228-5151
102 rooms. Pool, café. Better-than-average motel.

Frederick County

Berrywine Plantations, Linganore Wine Cellars

13601 Glisans Mill Road
Mount Airy, Maryland 21771-8599
TEL: 301-662-8687
PRESIDENT: John P. Aellen, Jr.
WINEMAKER: Anthony Aellen (studied at UC-Davis)
FOUNDED: 1981

AT A GLANCE

Tours & Tastings: Mon.–Sat. 10–6, Sun. 12–6; $2 per adult. Aellen family members themselves guide guests over every step of the winemaking process—crushing, fermenting, bottling. A highlight is the aging cellar in a converted turn-of-the-century dairy barn and the tasting room with original Colonial pillars. Tasting features a selection of twenty-five grape and fruit wines.
Closed: Major holidays.
Vineyards: Forty acres in Maryland's first designated viticultural area, Linganore, planted with French hybrids and supplemented with hybrids and vinifera varieties from other area vineyards. Fruits and berries are also grown for wines.
Wines: Vidal Blanc, Chancellor, Marechal Foch; Harvest Moon, a hybrid blend; red and white sangria; fruit wines. Medieval Mead, a specialty, was served to Prince Charles and Lady Diana when they visited Washington. New edition is

Melody, a New Finger Lakes–bred hybrid. Three labels are used: the Linganore label is for wines made of grapes from the Linganore v.a. They are estate-labeled if made only from Berrywine's vineyards; most are also vintage-dated. The Plantation label is used on wines made of grapes grown outside the Linganore viticultural area and on May and sangria wines. Berrywine is the label for ten lightly sweetened specialty wines, such as Dandylion and Mead.

Awards: Does not enter competitions.

Picnic Area: On the spacious grounds of this 230-acre farm.

Retail Shop: Wines, books on cooking with wine and winemaking, cork pullers and other gift items, insignia T-shirts.

Credit Cards: Choice, MasterCard, Visa.

Access for Disabled: Some ramps.

Foreign Languages: None.

Getting There: Berrywine is 39 miles from both D.C. and Baltimore beltways. From Baltimore: Take I-70 West to exit 60 (New Market), and go north on MD Rte. 75 for 4.5 miles. Turn right just before concrete bridge onto Glisams Mill Rd. and go 3.7 miles to winery. From D.C.: Take I-270 North to Hyattstown exit (Rte. 109); go left on 109, then left again on Rte. 355 and right on Rte. 75 for 13 miles. Then turn right just before concrete bridge onto Glisans Mill Rd. and proceed 3.7 miles to winery.

Special Wine & Other Events: Great Strawberry Wine Festival, first weekend in June; Razz, Jazz, Cajun Festival, third weekend in July; New Festival, third weekend in Aug.; Maryland Wine Festival, last weekend in Sept.; Wine & Foliage Festival, third weekend in Oct. Typical events feature craftsmen and artisans at work, music and other entertainment, foods, and wines.

&. In 1971, the Aellens moved with their six kids to their 230-acre dairy farm. Visitors find it memorable to be guided by members of this hospitable family, who are truly knowledgeable about their wines and enjoy showing off their turn-of-the-century two-story barn-winery built the old way—with pegs, not nails.

&. &. &.

Elk Run Vineyard, Inc.

15113 Liberty Road
Mount Airy, Maryland 21771
TEL: 301-775-2513
OWNERS/WINEMAKERS: Fred and Carol
    Wilson (courses in enology and
    viticulture at University of Virginia)
FOUNDED: 1983

AT A GLANCE

Tours & Tastings: Tours of vineyard and winery; tastings every weekend, Sat.–Sun. 1–5 P.M., and weekdays by appointment.

Closed: Weekdays.

Vineyards: Four acres planted to viniferas and supplemented by Maryland and New York fruits: Cabernet Franc, Merlot, Chardonnay, Cabernet Sauvignon, Riesling, and Seyval Blanc are grapes used.

Wines: Chardonnay, Cabernet Sauvignon, Riesling, Seyval Blanc, Sweet Cabernet and Chablis-blush, under two labels: Elk Run Vineyards and Liberty Tavern.

Awards: Chardonnay, Cabernet Sauvignon, Riesling, Sweet Katherine (a sweet, "sensual" Cabernet Sauvignon), Seyval Blanc, and Annapolis Sunset (a Chablis blush).

Retail Shop: Wines sold on-site.

Credit Cards: MasterCard, Visa.

Access for Disabled: Ramps for wheelchairs.

Foreign Languages: Some French and German.

Getting There: Twenty miles (forty-five minutes) from D.C. and twenty-six miles from Baltimore. From Washington: Take I-270 to Rte. 27, then to Rte. 26, and proceed to Elk Run. From Baltimore: Take Rte. 26 direct to Elk Run. Train station, bike rentals near Elk Run.

Special Wine & Other Events: First Sat. each month, 7 P.M., wine analysis and educational tastings with complimentary foods; last Sat. in June, Annual Festival.

€ Elk Run was first a vineyard and nursery selling grafted vinifera vines. It's no wonder that the winery's Chardonnay and Rieslings are frequent prizewinners when you know the Wilsons studied with Dr. Konstantin Frank, an important force in eastern U.S. winemaking, renowned for these same two wines. The Wilsons also toured wineries in France, Germany, and California before turning to commercial winemaking. Their wine tasting and sales room is in the former summer kitchen of a 1750s house.

€ € €

Byrd Vineyard and Winery

Church Hill Road
Myersville, Maryland 21773
TEL: 301-293-1110
FOUNDED: 1976
Eleven miles west of Frederick; exit 42 off I-70, Main St. north to Church Hill Rd., and right one mile to winery. Tours, tastings, and sales Sat.–Sun. 1–5; closed Jan. First wines produced in the Catoctin v.a., thus originating the Catoctin Appellation. Estate-bottled Cabernet Sauvignon, Chardonnay, and others. Wine Harvest Festival first weekend in Oct.

Montgomery County

Catoctin Vineyards

805 Greenbridge Road
Brookville, Maryland 20833
TEL: 301-774-2310
OWNERS: Robert Lyon; Shahin Bagheri; Ann, Jerry, and Molly Milne
WINEMAKER: Robert Lyon (graduate in enology, UC-Davis)
FOUNDED: 1983

AT A GLANCE
Tours & Tastings: Sat–Sun. 12–5, otherwise by appointment. Guided winery tour covers winemaking process, followed by a tasting conducted by winemaker Lyon. Vineyard is in Frederick County, forty miles away.
Closed: Jan. and Feb.
Vineyards: Thirty-two acres planted to French-American hybrids and viniferas.
Wines: Oak-fermented Chardonnay is most widely known, but also produced is Chardonnay fermented in stainless steel tanks, Cabernet Sauvignon, Johan-
nisberg Riesling, Seyval, Vidal, and Eye of the Oriole (a blended wine). Annual crush is 75 tons or 12,000 gallons.
Awards: Chardonnays and Johannisberg Riesling have been cited often among more than twenty-five awards since 1984.
Picnic Area: On the grounds.
Retail Shop: Wine sales daily 12–5; wine accessories also sold.
Credit Cards: MasterCard, Visa.
Access for Disabled: No.
Foreign Languages: Farsi, limited Spanish.
Getting There: Equidistant from Baltimore, Frederick, and D.C. From Frederick: Take I-70 to Rte. 97, turn off at Rte. 650 (New Hampshire Ave. extended), go north to winery. From Baltimore: I-695, take I-70 to Rte. 29 and continue south through Ellicott City to Rte. 108. Turn west on 108 to Rte. 650 and continue north four miles to winery. From D.C.: Take I-495 (Capital Beltway) on New Hampshire Ave., onto Rte. 650 at

Ashton and continue to winery. The winery is adjacent to hiking and biking routes around the Tridelphia Reservoir. **Special Wine & Other Events:** Open House weekends in Oct.–Nov., 12–5.

☙ While you're not supposed to put new wine in old bottles, there's nothing against putting a new winery in an old one. This is what Catoctin's owners did— they established their winery in what was the Swiss chalet–style building formerly housing La Provenza Vineyards. Winemaker Lyon also had former affiliations—with Chateau Montelena in the Napa Valley and Byrd Vineyards in Virginia. He concentrates on classic wines, working from a winery equipped with both oak barrels and the latest technology.

ACCOMMODATIONS AND RESTAURANTS
(See the Frederick and Baltimore County listings.)

Washington County

Ziem Vineyards

Route 1, Box 161
Fairplay, Maryland 21733
TEL: 301-223-8352
OWNERS: Robert and Ruth Ziem
FOUNDED: 1977

AT A GLANCE
Tours & Tastings: Thurs.–Fri. 1–6, Sat. 11–6; tours of winery in a converted barn are followed by tastings alongside stream and 200-year-old springhouse, weather permitting.
Closed: Sun.; Thanksgiving, Christmas, New Year's days.
Vineyards: Seven acres planted to French hybrids and native American Dutchess grapes.
Wines: All fifteen are varietals, such as Chancellor, Marechal Foch, Chambourcin, Chelois, Seyval, Vidal, Dutchess, and Aurora. Some limited-quantity wines available only at winery.
Retail Shop: Wines sold on-site.
Credit Cards: None.
Access for Disabled: No.
Foreign Languages: None.
Getting There: 75 miles from D.C. and Baltimore. From Baltimore: Take I-70 (or from D.C. take I-270/70) to Rte. 65. Go ½ mile south to Rench Rd., right for 2 miles to Rte. 632. South for 4 miles to Rte. 63 at Downsville, then left to Rte. 63 for ¼ mile to Ziem Vineyards.

☙ At this tiny family winery in a converted barn, all wines are aged in small oak barrels. The red wines are unfiltered and unrefined. The goal here is to produce eastern U.S. wines that do not imitate European or California styles. Ziem Vineyards dates from 1972, but the Ziems' old stone house and the springhouse out back of it are circa 1740.

TO SEE & DO
Most Maryland wineries are in the central part of the state, at any time of the year a harvest of sights, ripe and ready for the picking. Baltimore, Frederick, and Carroll counties all played important roles in U.S. history during the Colonial, Revolutionary, and Civil War eras. To be savored today are streets that have become architectural museums of that past; the downtowns of Mount Airy, Frederick, and New Market are among Maryland's many sites listed in the National Register of Historic Places. The Historical Society of Carroll County proudly boasts of a ghost in its well-furnished Shellman House (open Tues.–Fri. 9–4 year-round; Sat. 10–4, Sun. 12–4,

June–Sept.; tel: 301-848-6494). The history of the central Maryland counties is also colorfully retold in unusual museums—with farm (May–Oct. weekends 12–5; July–Aug. daily, except Mon., 12–5; tel: 301-848-7775) and railway museums (May–Oct. Sun. 1–4; tel: 301-868-5849), both in Carroll County, and a fire museum (May–Oct. Sun. 1–4; tel: 301-321-7500) in Baltimore County among them. A four-hour cruise takes visitors from Havre de Grace across upper Chesapeake Bay to the Sassafras River on weekends (tel: 301-939-9385).

This is pleasant, rural countryside where Thoroughbred horses are raised and can be seen grazing in lush pastures. Here you can spread out a picnic near a covered bridge or lookout point or enjoy thousands of acres of rich parklands that offer visitors outstanding recreational activities. Fall foliage is dramatic during the Catoctin colorfest; the Ladew Topiary Gardens and Manor House (in nearby Hartford County) are among the great gardens of the world (mid-Apr. to Oct., Tues.–Fri. 10–4; Sat.–Sun. 12–5; house, Wed., Sat., and Sun. during garden hours; tel: 301-557-9466). Nor are shoppers overlooked: New Market (on U.S. 144; more than fifty shops open weekends; some during the week; closed Mon.) is the antiques capital of Maryland. Westminster is the site of the Farmer's Market (Agricultural Center, Sat. 8–1, late June to early Sept. 8:30–3), where you can pick up delectable baked goods and fresh produce for picnics plus local arts and crafts.

Wineries can also be visited from Baltimore, which, as a phoenix of U.S. cities, has risen from urban blight to become a prime example of urban renewal. Here the Inner Harbor offers sights from art museums to the city zoo. A variety of cruises offer a refreshing way to explore the Inner Harbor—some on sleek ships with lunch or dinner; others aboard historic schooners.

For a gastronomical adventure, Baltimore's seven historic markets offer a way to experience a diversity of flavors of a wide variety of foods, in these locations:

Belair (1818), Gay and Forest, Oldtown Mall.

Broadway (1784), Broadway & Fleet streets.

Cross Street (1842), Light and Cross streets, Union Square.

Hollins (1835), Hollins and Carrollton streets, Union Square.

Lafayette (1869), Penn and Eutaw streets.

Lexington (1782), Lexington and Eutaw streets.

Northeast (1878), Monument and Chester streets.

The westernmost winery in Maryland, Ziem, is a short drive from Shepherdstown, West Virginia, with many interesting sights, such as the Civil War Battlefield at Antietam (between winery at Fairplay and Shepherdstown on Rte. 65, Sharpsburg, Maryland; Visitor Center open daily; closed Jan. 1, Thanksgiving, Christmas; field open daily until dark, tel: 301-432-5124). Shepherdstown, the oldest town in West Virginia, has an historic district well worth seeing. Nearby also in Washington County, Maryland, are Barron's C & O Canal Museum (Sat.–Sun. 9–5; tel: 301-432-8726) and the C & O Canal National Historical Park (sunrise to sunset; tel: 301-739-4200), a 184.5-mile towpath along the Potomac River from Georgetown to Cumberland.

Fairs and special events abound in Maryland year-round. Some annual events are the Preakness Festival in Baltimore in mid-May and the Maryland State Fair at Timonium in late August.

The brief space allotted here for sightseeing allows only for sips of information. To drink more deeply, here's where you can get packets of pamphlets for planning your visit:

Carroll County Office of Public Information and Tourism
225 North Center Street
Westminster, Maryland 21157
Tel: 301-848-4500

Visitors Information Center
Frederick County
19 East Church Street
Frederick, Maryland 21701
Tel: 301-663-8687

Baltimore Office of Promotion and Tourism
34 Market Place, Suite 310
Baltimore, Maryland 21202
Tel: 301-752-8632; 301-837-INFO (24 hr. information)

Washington County Tourism Division
Court House Annex
Hagerstown, Maryland 21740
Tel: 301-791-3130; 301-797-8800 (24-hour information)

ACCOMMODATIONS
Bavarian Inn and Lodge
Route 1, Box 30
Shepherdstown, West Virginia 25443
Tel: 304-876-2551
Stone Colonial house from the 1930s and four Swiss chalets from 1981. Innkeeper/owner Edward Asam, formerly from Munich, dishes up German specialties in a delightful restaurant. Rooms have four-posters and antiques. Crafts and antique shops nearby.

The Thomas Shepherd Inn
Corner of German and Duke Streets
  (P.O. Box 1162)
Shepherdstown, West Virginia 25443
Tel: 304-876-3715
Victorian charm and gracious hospitality of innkeepers/owners Ed and Carol Ringoot; clean, comfortable; delicious breakfast. Outdoor sports such as white-water rafting, canoeing, hiking nearby.

A major city, Baltimore has accommodations of every type, with all major chains represented. Some of the more unusual places to stay are:

Admiral Fell Inn
888 South Broadway
Baltimore, Maryland 21231
Tel: 301-522-7377; 800-BXB-INNS
On the historic waterfront, part of the restored structure dates back to the 1800s. Furnished with antiques and reproductions, with canopied beds and color TVs. Restaurant on-premises, with more nearby in Little Italy.

Peabody Court
612 Cathedral Street (at Mt. Vernon
  Place)
Baltimore, Maryland 21231
Tel: 301-727-7101; 800-732-5301
Everything is tasteful at this small luxury hotel—attractive rooms furnished in good reproductions of French Directoire furniture; a Baccarat chandelier illuminates the lobby. One restaurant for light meals and breakfast, another, atop the hotel, with a view and expensive French food.

The Shirley House
205 West Madison Street
Baltimore, Maryland 21201
Tel: 301-728-6550
Century-old restored hotel with Victorian and Edwardian antiques, stained-glass windows, mirrored fireplaces, and oak staircase. Cozy living room with fireplace and library. In historic Mt. Vernon; walking distance from downtown and Inner Harbor.

Society Hill Hotel
58 West Biddle Street
Baltimore, Maryland 21201
Tel: 301-837-3630
Turn-of-the-century home, now a small hotel with individually decorated rooms; brass bedsteads, hardwood furniture,

and fresh bouquets to brighten all. Opposite Myerhoff Symphony Hall; van service to harbor and business center.

RESTAURANTS
Baltimore has many restaurants for all tastes and pocketbooks; among those serving Maryland wines are:

Louie's Bookstore Cafe
518 North Charles Street
Baltimore, Maryland 21201
Tel: 301-962-1224
This interesting restaurant is tucked behind a bookstore and well known for fresh seafood and rich pastries. Listen to chamber music and admire original works of art while sipping Boordy wines. Closed major holidays.

Pimlico
1777 Reisterstown Road
Pikesville, Maryland 21208
Tel: 301-486-6776
The chef offers Maryland seafood among other entrées and memorable desserts. Wine list with Boordy and Catoctin selections.

Thompson's Sea Girt House
5919 York Road
Northern Parkway
Baltimore, Maryland 21212
Tel: 301-435-1800
Since 1885, a place for famous Maryland crabcakes and lobster. Wine list. Nautical setting.

❧ NEW JERSEY

New Jersey wine routes lead from the southern shore, with its sun-kissed beaches, to the wine-sharp air of the lakes and rivers and mountains of the Skylands Region. New Jersey's fifteen wineries are small family affairs where you can taste wines that generally don't make it out-of-state or indeed much farther than the winery door. The wineries are located near premium sights to keep tourists very busy investigating the past and, in some cases, enjoying the present at Atlantic City pleasure domes. In season, stops at farms and markets with luscious produce add interest, and throughout the year quality restaurants and ethnic fare make this route a satisfying culinary experience.

Southern New Jersey

The history of New Jersey wine began in Atlantic County in 1864, at the Renault Winery, now the largest in the state, producing some 46,000 cases annually. The next oldest winery, Tomasello, founded in 1933, is also in this region. Southern wine routes can take in great contrasts—from the razzle-dazzle of Atlantic City's casinos, to the 20,000-acre solitude of Brigantine Wildlife Refuge, home to many migrating birds, to the Victorian splendor of Cape May.

❧ ❧ ❧

Renault Winery

72 North Bremen Avenue
Egg Harbor City, New Jersey 08215
TEL: 609-965-2111
PRESIDENT/OWNER: Joseph Milza
WINEMAKER: W. Bacon
FOUNDED: 1864

AT A GLANCE
Tours & Tastings: Mon.–Sat. 10–5, Sun.

12–5; forty-five-minute tours ($1 per person) journey through more than a century of history, then glimpse winemaking today, and conclude with a tasting.

Closed: Easter, Thanksgiving, Christmas, New Year's.

Vineyards: 100 acres planted on a 1,000-acre farm, to French hybrids, vinifera, and native American varieties. Noah grape planted here is found only in New Jersey.

Wines: Varietals include Chardonnay, Cabernet Sauvignon, and French Colombard, and such generics as Chablis, Burgundy, Rosé, Sauterne, white champagne, blueberry champagne, sparkling Burgundy.

Awards: White champagne, from Louis Renault's original recipe, has garnered a number of medals, and a more recent creation (blueberry champagne) was cited in Austria as "Best in Class" for specialty wines.

Picnic Area: Tables on the grounds.

Restaurants: The casual Garden Cafe (open Mon.–Sat. 12–4) has brass and stained glass reminiscent of a French brasserie; the classy Restaurant Atop-the-Winery (open Fri.–Sat. from 5, Sun. from 3) has booths made from barrel staves or French antique furnished rooms; the monasterylike setting of the Wine Cellar is candlelit for weekend buffets and catered affairs.

Retail Shop: Wines, champagnes, and wine-related items.

Credit Cards: MasterCard, Visa.

Access for Disabled: Entrance ramp.

Foreign Languages: None.

Getting There: 16 miles west of Atlantic City off Rte. 30. From Garden State Pkwy.: South exit 44 (North exit 36) to Rte. 563; follow Egg Harbor City signs. From Philadelphia: Atlantic City Expressway to exit 17, north on Rte. 50 to Moss Mill Rd. From Atlantic City: Rte. 30 West to Bremen Ave. From Cape May and other South Shore points: Take the Garden State Pkwy. North to exit 36; go north on Rte. 563 and turn right onto Bremen Ave.; follow Bremen Ave., 2¼ miles to winery.

Special Wine & Other Events: Festivals are part of the tradition at this winery— not only at the traditional harvest time but throughout the year with all manner of events.

🍃 The oldest bonded winery in New Jersey and the third oldest in the United States (first is Cucamonga in California; second, Brotherhood of New York) was founded in 1864 by Louis Nicholas Renault. He came to America in 1855 on behalf of the ancient champagne house of the Duke of Montebello at Rheims, France, to establish a vineyard free of phylloxera (an aphid ravaging the grape vines of Western Europe). When his first vines planted in California were destroyed by this same pest, Renault headed east to plant a vineyard of the native labrusca, with a tough pest-and-disease-resistant root system.

The winery prospered—indeed, Egg Harbor was called the "Wine City"—and became the nation's largest distributor of champagne. When Renault died at age 91 in 1913, son Felix took over for six years before selling the operation to John D'Agostino and family. They continued to operate even during the fourteen Prohibition years, when the enterprising owners got a government permit to market Renault Wine Tonic, with an alcoholic content of 22 percent, through the nation's drugstores. So popular was this elixir that the winery worked day and night to fill orders.

The picturesque winery that crowds come to see today is largely the handiwork of D'Agostino's sister Maria. She created the château-style hospitality house as a place to tell the history of Renault as well as the museum to display her priceless collection of wineglasses. Visitors also see old winemaking apparatus, the modern winery, vast cellars, and then taste wines popular through the years, which are now produced by current owner Joseph P. Milza, former newspaper owner and publisher.

≈ ≈ ≈

Tomasello Winery

225 North White Horse Pike
Hammonton, New Jersey 08037
TEL: 609-561-0567
PRESIDENT: Charles S. Tomasello
FOUNDED: 1933

AT A GLANCE

Tours & Tastings: Tastings at Hammonton, Mon.–Fri. 9–8, Sat.–Sun. 9–6; tours, by appointment, cover all operations of the farm and winery and include a tasting; tastings also at winery outlet in historic Smithville (tel: 609-561-0567).
Closed: Christmas, New Year's, and Easter days.
Vineyards: 100 acres planted to French hybrids, native American and vinifera varieties.
Wines: Chardonnay, Villard, Chenin Blanc, Sauvignon Blanc, French Colombard, Labrusca; rosé, Burgundy, Chianti, and others; *methode champenoise* sparkling wines.
Retail Sales: At both winery and outlet shop in Smithville; the latter has museum of old winemaking equipment and display explaining how it is done today.
Credit Cards: MasterCard, Visa.
Access for Disabled: None.
Foreign Languages: None.
Getting There: To Hammonton from Atlantic City: Take Rte. 30W ½ mile after mile marker 29; or Atlantic City Expressway to exit 28, Hammonton, then take 54N to 30W; left on 30W for ½ mile. To Smithville from Atlantic City: Take Indiana Ave. to Absecon Blvd. (Rte. 30) to Rte. 9 North. To Hammonton from Cape May: Go north on Garden State Pkwy. to exit 38A, Atlantic City Expressway and follow directions above. To Smithville from Cape May: Go north on Garden State Pkwy. to exit 50, cross over to southbound lane and continue to exit 48 (Smithville) to Rte. 9 South.
Special Wine & Other Events: In Smithville.

≈ Frank Tomasello, a farmer, made a little wine for his friends in pre-Prohibition days. After Prohibition was repealed, he founded the winery in 1933 and made wine the old-fashioned way—without scientific controls. Since then his sons and grandsons have joined the business to add sophistication to the winemaking and multiply output significantly from the original 5,000 gallons a year. The winery now makes and bottles twenty-five wines, one-third of them sweet. Tomasello wines are also sold on a limited basis in Washington, Maryland, and Pennsylvania.

≈ ≈ ≈

Sylvin Farms

24 Vienna Avenue
Germainia, New Jersey 08215
TEL: 609-778-1494
OWNERS: Franklin and Sylvia Saleck
FOUNDED: 1985
Five acres planted to twenty-five vinifera varieties; new and promising. Tours by appointment.

TO SEE & DO
Visitors make a beeline for Atlantic City and try to break the bank at one of the casinos. Or perhaps a preferred pastime is times past, only forty-five miles away in Cape May. This beach resort community is a National Historic Landmark town, where hundreds of gingerbread-style buildings survive; tour them on a walking tour sponsored by the Mid-Atlantic Center for the Arts, which also sponsors the summer theater and Victorian programs.

Other Cape May diversions are bird-watching, hiking, biking, swimming, tennis, and strolling the old boardwalk. For more information, contact the Chamber of Commerce, Cape May Court House, Cape May, New Jersey 08201 (tel: 609-465-7181).

ACCOMMODATIONS

Atlantic City offers everything from lavish casino hotels to modest budget hotels. For a full range of options, contact the Atlantic City Convention and Visitors Bureau, 2304 Pacific Avenue, Atlantic City, New Jersey 08401; tel: 609-348-7100.

Mainstay
635 Columbia Avenue
Cape May, New Jersey 08204
Tel: 609-884-8690
Well restored and furnished by preservationists Tom and Sue Carroll, the house was built in 1872 by wealthy gamblers and expanded in 1890. Victorian furnishings extend to the bathrooms, with wood-framed copper tubs now banked by ferns. Breakfasts on the veranda or in the high-ceilinged dining room with red sway-tied draperies. Make summer reservations before March.

Abbey
Columbia Avenue and Gurney Street
Cape May, New Jersey 08204
Tel: 609-884-4506

Fine Gothic Revival building from 1869, with gaslit guest rooms appointed with marble-topped vanities, walnut high-headboard beds, and other period pieces. Bathrooms have stained-glass windows and brass chandeliers.

Barnard-Good House
238 Perry Street
Cape May, New Jersey 08204
Tel: 609-884-5381
Second Empire Victorian, built in 1869, has many antique accents. The delicious breakfast features homemade breads and unusual preserves.

Brass Bed Inn
719 Columbia Avenue
Cape May, New Jersey 08204
Tel: 609-884-8075
This Gothic Revival, circa 1872, has been restored with many original furnishings, and lots of guess-what-kind-of beds.

Chalfonte Hotel
301 Howard Street
Cape May, New Jersey 08204
Tel: 609-884-8934
The Chalfonte is Cape May's oldest hotel, dating from 1872. Period furnishings are not on view here—just basic essentials for a beach holiday. The first-rate food is served in an old-fashioned dining room.

Skylands Region

Wine routes become scenic as Route 29 hugs the Delaware River after Trenton to Lambertville, and into the hilly wine territory of Hunterdon County in northwest New Jersey. The routes meander through miles of picturesque countryside, passing beside streams and lakes set against mountain backdrops, take in some gastronomic delights at farms and markets, and offer a taste of history.

In all, seven wineries—an eighth is in Somerset county—and thirteen vineyards have been started in the area since 1981, when the legislature passed the Farm Wineries Act. Winegrowers here call themselves "the new pioneers" and tell about how tomato-and-corn farmers laughed when they decided to put in wine grapes. They are not laughing now. The fledgling wine industry seems well on its way. In this new wine territory some wineries are open during the week, others on weekends only. Be sure to phone before you set off.

Take note that on a weekend in mid- to late August, the Hunterdon Wine Growers Association hosts a big festival for most of the state's wineries, with tasting, music, food, and other merriment. For time, date, and place, check with any of the wineries in this book.

≥ ≥ ≥

Alba Vineyards

Route 627
Finesville, New Jersey 08848
TEL: 201-995-7800
PRESIDENT/WINEMAKER: Rudolf C. Marchesi
FOUNDED: 1982

AT A GLANCE

Tours & Tastings: Tues.–Fri. 11–5, Sat. 11–5, Sun. 12–5; twenty-minute guided tours zoom in on barrel-aging room, crushing deck, storage, bottling rooms. Longer harvest tours allow time to observe equipment in use. All tours begin and end in tasting/sales room.

Closed: Mondays; Thanksgiving, Christmas, New Year's days.

Vineyards: Thirty-five acres planted to well-known French hybrids and vinifera varieties as well as the lesser-known Geneva White III, supplemented with Seyval Blanc purchased in Warren County.

Wines: Limited quantities of varietals and blends are produced each year, depending on the harvest. Whites usually include Chardonnay, Seyval Blanc, and Rieslings, as well as blended styles; reds: Cabernet Sauvignon, Harvest Nouveau,

and blends; specialty wines; apple and raspberry. Current production is around 6,500 cases per day.

Awards: Governor's Cup in 1987 for 1985 Warren County Cabernet Sauvignon; also awarded state's best in New Jersey winegrowers competition. High honors also include a gold medal to Red Raspberry in New Jersey Winegrowers 1986 and 1985 International Eastern Competition. Other winners over the years: Riesling, proprietor's red and white reserves, and apple wine.

Picnic Area: Sites scattered around the hillside vineyards.

Retail Shop: Sells wines and wine accessories. Alba also has a retail shop on Rte. 17 in Paramus. Wines distributed in New York and Florida.

Credit Cards: American Express, MasterCard, Visa.

Access for Disabled: Ramp to winery.

Foreign Languages: French, some Italian and Spanish.

Getting There: 6 miles south of Easton, 75 miles west of New York City, and 60 miles north of Philadelphia. From New York City: Take Rte. 178 West to exit 7 (Bloomsbury); right on Rte. 173 West for 1.3 miles, left on Rte. 639 West (to Warren Glen) for 2.8 miles to stop sign at junction on Rtes. 519 and 627 South. Stay on Rte. 627 South for 2.4 miles to winery on right. From Philadelphia area: Take Rte. 195 North to NJ Rte. 29. Take Rte. 29 North to Milford, then follow Rte. 519 North to Warren Glen (first stop sign) and turn left at stop sign on 627 South. Winery is 2.2 miles on right.

Special Wine & Other Events: Nov. 15: Alba Annual Harvest Nouveau Release; third weekend in April: celebration of spring; June 21: summer solstice; mid-March: prerelease. Winemaking course held at Alba for six weeks each fall. For events schedule ask to be put on quarterly newsletter mailing list. Alba also notes that Balloonsbury takes place in nearby Bloomsbury the first weekend in August.

🦋 A bass player, guitarist, and pianist, Rudolf Marchesi tried winegrowing in California before returning to his native New Jersey to set up Alba in 1981. His thirty-five-acre vineyard is the largest in the region and is planted to vinifera and French-American hybrids. The century-old limestone barn was remodeled to create a winery and tasting room. On the hillsides are picnic tables, perfect for enjoying wines and admiring the rolling hills and Delaware River views. The grape arbor is a lovely place to sit on a sunny day, sip wine, and contemplate the scenery.

🦋 🦋 🦋

DelVista Vineyards

Everittstown Road
R.D. 1, Box 84
Frenchtown, New Jersey 08825
TEL: 201-996-2849
CO-OWNERS: James and Jonetta Williams
WINEMAKER: James Williams (courses in enology at Allentown College)
FOUNDED: 1982 (vineyard 1978)

AT A GLANCE
Tours & Tastings: Tastings Wed.–Sun. 11–5, Memorial Day to Labor Day; Wed.–Fri. 2–4, Sat.–Sun. 1–5 thereafter. Tours on Sat. and Sun. or by appointment.
Vineyards: Ten acres planted to vinifera and French hybrids.
Wines: Whites: Aurore, Chardonnay, Seyval Blanc, White Riesling, Sylvaner-Riesling, Vidal Blanc, Villard Blanc; reds: Cabernet Sauvigon, Claret, De Chaunac Nouveau (DelVista label); blended whites, reds, and May wine (DeerHaven Cellars label). Capacity is 5,000 gallons.
Awards: DeerHaven Cellars's Vin Rosé

and Vin Rouge; DelVista's White Riesling.
Picnic Area: On the grounds with Delaware River view.
Retail Sales: Wines sold.
Credit Cards: American Express.
Access for Disabled: No steps.
Foreign Languages: None.
Getting There: One mile north of Frenchtown on Rte. 513, at mile marker 1, west side.

🦋 Psychologist James Williams and his artist wife, Jonetta, wine buffs for twenty-five years, grow and make wines in the Delaware Valley v.a., where conditions are similar to those in the wine regions of Germany. This is wine-grape history territory as well: in the 1800s, French revolutionary refugee Paul Prevost experimented here with vinifera varieties that he cross-pollinated with native grapes to produce the American Delaware species, considered one of the best of the labrusca-vinifera hybrids.

Truly wine pioneers in northwest New Jersey—theirs was the first winery to be licensed in recent times—the Williamses planted more than twenty varieties of grapes to discover which would do best in their soil and climatic conditions. James Williams tends the vines and wines and Jonetta designs their striking labels. The couple tests their wines with foods so they can recommend combinations to customers.

🦋 🦋 🦋

Four Sisters Winery

Route 519, R.D. 1, Box 258
Belvidere, New Jersey 07823
Tel: 201-475-3671
PROPRIETORS: Matty and Laurie Matarazzo
WINEMAKER: Laurie Matarazzo
FOUNDED: 1984

AT A GLANCE
Tours & Tastings: Tours Sat.–Sun. 11–6. They typically include one of the vineyards, the crushing floor, the wine cellar, the bottling room, and a tasting. Sales/tastings only, March–Dec. 11–6, seven days a week; Jan.–Feb., Wed.–Sun. 11–6. **Closed:** Mon. and Tues., Jan.–Feb.
Vineyards: Seventeen acres planted primarily to French hybrids. Some viniferas and a few labruscas.
Wines: Focus on whites—Vidal, Seyval, Riesling, Cayuga, White Niagara, and a blend; two reds—Chancellor and Papa's Red, a blend; Rosé. Four fruit wines—apple, raspberry, strawberry, and peach.
Awards: Vidal Blanc has been most frequently awarded, with Chancellor and Rosé also garnering prizes.
Picnic Area: Deck adjoining winery with view of scenic valley.
Retail Shop: Wines and gift baskets.
Credit Cards: MasterCard, Visa.
Access for Disabled: Ramp to tasting and sales room and deck.
Foreign Languages: None.
Getting There: From Phillipsburg: Take Rte. 519 North to Belvidere; if coming from Tewksbury Wine Cellars, take Rte. 513 South to I-78 West to Phillipsburg, then go north on Rte. 519.
Special Wine & Other Events: June: Strawberry Festival; Aug.: Peach Festival; Oct.: Harvest Festival and crushing parties, where you might be asked to help with the crushing; Dec.: Santa's Wine Shop. Also midnight hayrides; Apr.–Dec. wine-and-cheese tastings, and others. Modest fee or free, depending on event.

🍂 Four Sisters started as a 1-acre experiment on 390 acres of softly rolling Warren County farmland and grew into 17 acres of grapes, mostly French hybrids. Before long a cedar-sided winery was built, christened Four Sisters after the Matarazzos' four daughters, and a new product for the farm—wine—was on its way into the world. Each daughter is also honored with a fruit wine named for her. The warm-natured proprietors are happy to give personal attention to visitors so that each visitor gets an enjoyable education at the winery.

🍂 🍂 🍂

King's Road Vineyard

Route 579, Box 352B
Milford, New Jersey 08848
TEL: 201-479-6611
OWNERS: John and Marie Alplanalp
WINEMAKER: Klaus Schreiber
FOUNDED: 1984

AT A GLANCE
Tours & Tastings: Sat.–Sun. 12–5; also 12–5 on weekends of Columbus Day, Memorial Day, Labor Day, July 4; other times by appointment.
Closed: Weekdays, Thanksgiving, Christmas, and New Year's.
Vineyards: Eleven acres in Central Delaware Valley v.a.; planted primarily to viniferas and French hybrids, focusing on whites—Aurora, Seyval Blanc, Niagara, Villard Blanc, Chardonnay.
Wines: Varietals from the above varieties; 1,000-case output.
Awards: Aurora, in both state and international competitions; Seyval Blanc in state competition.
Picnic Area: Tables on spacious lawns and woodlands.
Retail Sales: Wines and gifts.
Credit Cards: None.
Access for Disabled: One step up from parking to winery area; wide doors and ramps in winery.
Foreign Languages: German and French when the winemaker is on-hand.
Getting There: Take I-78 to Pattenburg, exit 11. Follow Rte. 614 South to junction to Rtes. 614 and 579 (approximately three miles). Then go west on 579 for two miles to winery on your left.

🍂 The winery started operating in 1984, but the fieldstone dairy barn with wood-paneled interior housing it goes back more than one hundred years. To add to its charms, the tasting room is done up like an eighteenth-century tavern.

Vinifera whites thrive on eleven acres of this hundred-acre property on a southern slope of the Musconetcong Ridge. Winemaker-manager Schreiber, a mechanical engineer who has taken winemaking courses, says the first vines in 1981 were Chardonnay.

King's Road derives its name from an actual road that cut through the property during the Revolutionary War days. Originally an Indian path, it was later used to transport pig iron from the furnace at Bloomsbury to the forge at Pittstown.

🍂 🍂 🍂

LaFollette Vineyard and Winery

64 Harlingen Road
Belle Mead, New Jersey 08502
TEL: 201-359-5018
OWNERS: John and Miriam Summerskill
FOUNDED: 1979

AT A GLANCE
Tours & Tastings: By appointment.
Vineyards: 10,000 Seyval Blanc vines.
Wines: Estate-bottled Seyval Blanc.
Getting There: From Princeton: Take Rte. 206 for seven miles north and turn right at Gulf station onto Harlingen Rd.

🍂 Huguenots from the Loire Valley, the LaFollettes first settled in New Jersey in 1750 before moving west. A descendant, Miriam LaFollette Summerskill, returned with her husband to established LaFollette Vineyards. Their aim is to produce the finest Seyval Blanc to rival top French wines.

🍂 🍂 🍂

Tewksbury Wine Cellars

Burrell Rd., R.D. 2
Lebanon, New Jersey 08833
TEL: 201-832-2400
OWNER: Dr. Daniel F. Vernon
FOUNDED: 1979

AT A GLANCE
Tours & Tastings: Sat. 11–5, Sun. 1–5, for tours, tastings, and sales; wines are also sold Wed. 3–5. Trained guides conduct tours of vineyard and winery, and cover entire vinification process if tourgoers are interested. $2-per-person tasting charge refundable if two bottles are purchased.
Closed: Labor Day, Christmas, New Year's.
Vineyards: Twenty acres, with more than 18,000 vines; largest planting of viniferas in New Jersey. Also French-American hybrids. If necessary, additional grapes are purchased to make wines.
Wines: Whites (most widely praised)— Chardonnay, Gewürztraminer, oak-aged Seyval Blanc, Dry Chenin Blanc. Reds— Harvest Nouveau and Chambourcin; Oldwick Apple, cranberry-apple, and peach (Tewksbury Wine Cellars label); white table wine, Sangria under Hunterdon Hills Winery label. Seasonal and special limited-quantity wines include a private reserve Chambourcin, aged in oak three years; also apple, cranberry-apple, peach, and pear wines.
Awards: Gold and best-of-class designations for 1983 Chardonnay in the International Eastern wine competition. Apple wine merited a gold medal; peach was cited for quality.
Picnic Area: Picnic tables on the lawn or near the pond, with ducks to share spare crumbs.
Retail Shop: Wines, gifts.
Credit Cards: None.
Access for Disabled: Limited. No stairs.
Foreign Languages: None.
Getting There: From I-78: Take exit 24

and travel north of Oldwick for 3½ miles. Turn left on Sawmill Rd., go ½ mile and bear right at fork onto Burrell Rd. The winery is 6 miles up the road on right.
Special Wine & Other Events: Tewksbury's many festivals include a Blossom Festival in June, Spring Festival on Father's Day weekend, and Harvest Festival on the third weekend in Sept. Wines, foods, crafts, music, tours, and more.

❧ Dr. Vernon, a practicing veterinarian, has located his winery in a converted horse hospital near Oldwick. The former operating room holds fermentation tanks, and the recovery stalls are used for case storage. The property also has an eighteenth-century farmhouse and barns, and visitors to the grounds are welcome to pet the horses and cows.

TO SEE & DO

Beyond the wineries, there's a good deal to attract visitors to northwest New Jersey, with historic towns, shopping, and outdoor sports offering lively diversity. Tree-filled forests and mammoth parks make the area justly famous for hiking, biking, cross-country skiing, and horseback riding. The Delaware Water Gap National Recreation Area and the Poconos are just two of the pretty places to enjoy these and other active diversions.

For indoor fun, Lambertville, at the southern end of this region, is renowned for antiques, good food, and the handsomely renovated Inn at Lambertville Station. Famous for shopping opportunities are Flemington's outlet stores for brand-name merchandise, from basic household appliances to luxurious furs. For an arts break, head to the Hunterdon Arts Center in Clinton (tel: 201-735-8415), housed in a nineteenth-century stone gristmill, for exhibitions, films, theater, crafts, music, and history.

Unusual museums include the Franklin Mineral Museum (Evans St. in Franklin, off Rtes. 23 and 517; open Wed.–Sat. 10–4, Sun. 12:30–4:30; tel: 201-827-3481) and the USGA's Golf Museum (Liberty Corner Rd., Rte. 512, Far Hills; tel: 201-234-2300), for displays of golf memorabilia.

There's also history—at the eighteenth-century Waterloo Village (Byram/Stanhope, exit 25 off Rte. 180 or north on Rte. 206; tel: 201-347-0900); at the Morristown National Historic Park, where Washington and his men spent winters; at Washington's headquarters and troop huts (exit 32 off Rte. 287); and at nearby old farms and homes at Speedwell Village (Rte. 187 to Rte. 24, then 202N to Speedwell Ave., Morristown; tel: 201-540-0211).

ACCOMMODATIONS

Choose between northwest New Jersey or the Bucks County area around New Hope, Pennsylvania, and see the wineries in both locales during your stay.

Chestnut Hill on-the-Delaware
63 Church Street
Milford, New Jersey 08848
Tel: 201-995-9761
An 1860 Neo-Italianate structure with five well-furnished rooms and a veranda overlooking the Delaware. A full breakfast is served.

Colligan's Stockton Inn
Route 29
Stockton, New Jersey 08559
Tel: 609-397-1250; 800-368-7272
Built in 1710 and used as an inn since 1830, when it served stagecoach passengers, Colligan's Stockton is restored with antiques and period reproductions. Meals are served in several dining rooms, and the attraction for you will be an extensive wine list—California wines are prominent among the selections, but

oddly enough, there are none from the area.

Old Hunterdon House
12 Bridge Street
Frenchtown, New Jersey 08825
Tel: 201-996-3632
Stately 1865 mansion, renovated and well run, with fireplaces, garden, and patio. Sherry nightcap at bedside, afternoon tea with biscuits, and Continental breakfast with home-baked goods delivered in baskets to each room. Frenchtown has a quaint charm, good places to eat and walk. Near DelVista Vinyards.

Inn at Lambertville Station
11 Bridge Street
Lambertville, New Jersey 08530
Tel: 609-397-4400; 800-524-1091
Forty-five-room inn combining country atmosphere with all amenities. Restaurant in old train station.

The Whistling Swan
Main Street, Box 791
Stanhope, New Jersey 07874
Tel: 201-347-6369
This delightful Victorian mansion has all manner of gables and turrets, and a stoned-pillared veranda from which to contemplate Lake Musconetcong, where you can rent a boat. Rooms are themed— Oriental, Art Deco, and such—to make each an individual experience, and each has a private bathroom, some with claw-foot tubs. Breakfast is hearty Continental. Fifteen minutes from Four Sisters Winery.

RESTAURANTS AND PICNIC FIXINGS
For the crusty breads and delicious foods befitting a picnic with wine, see the first two recommendations, courtesy of Alba Vineyards, both in Milford. Few restaurants presently serve the wines.

The Baker
60 Bridge Street
Tel: 201-994-4040
Excellent wheat rolls, scones, breads— healthful as well.

The Little Shop near the Bridge
In the Old Railway Station
Tel: 201-955-2550
Delicious foods to carry out include quiches, soups, pâtés, cookies; also French cheeses and other delicacies. Eat surrounded by historic railway station or on the deck.

Black Forest Inn
249 U.S. 206N
Stanhope, New Jersey 07874
Tel: 201-347-3344
German, Continental cuisine in a 1900s setting.

Colligan's Stockton Inn
(See "Accommodations" for address, tel.)

₰ PENNSYLVANIA

In the early days, William Penn compared this area to France; he planted a vineyard in 1684, which was unfortunately unsuccessful. In 1793, someone got the bright idea to try grape growing using native American species, which continues even now. More recently, promising newcomers combined with growing conditions distinctive enough to earn the area three viticultural areas (v.a.'s)—Lake Erie, Lancaster Valley, and Cumberland Valley—make touring Pennsylvania's wineries a satisfying experience.

Southeastern Pennsylvania

The southeastern Pennsylvania wine routes include some terrific contrasts, from the rural beauty of Bucks County to the sophistication of Philadelphia, from the elegance of Longwood Gardens to the old-world ways of the Amish, as well as historic York. A leisurely tour might begin thirty-five miles north of Philadelphia in New Hope and wind through back roads, taking in the scenery, sights, and wineries along the way, ending up in York.

& & &

Buckingham Valley Vineyards and Winery

Route 413
Buckingham, Pennsylvania 18912
TEL: 215-794-7188
OWNERS: Jerry and Kathy Forest
FOUNDED: 1966

AT A GLANCE
Tours & Tastings: Tues.–Fri. 12–6, Sat. 10–6, Sun. 12–4; self-guided tours with explanations on a script keyed to wine-making sights, concluded with a tasting.
Closed: Mondays and holidays.
Vineyards: Twenty acres planted primarily to French-American hybrids, also American hybrids, Cayuga, and Niagara.
Wines: Mainly varietals, vintage and estate-bottled. Dry reds: Baco Noir, De Chaunac, Chelois; red blend. Whites: Vidal Blanc, Seyval Blanc, Cayuga White, Niagara. Rosés: Rosette, Rosé Concordia, Red Sangria. Apple and strawberry wines.
Awards: Does not enter competitions.
Retail Sales: Wines.

Credit Cards: No credit cards; checks accepted.
Access for Disabled: Only to tasting room.
Foreign Languages: None.
Getting There: Two miles south of the village of Buckingham on Rte. 413.

& The Forests have traveled to forty countries to study and observe grape growing and winemaking. They started as amateur winemakers thirty-six years ago, before establishing one of Pennsylvania's first farm wineries in 1966. Today, it is one of the few wineries in the state producing estate-bottled, vintage varietals. The winery is located in the middle of the vineyards and combines the old methods with new technology: small oak barrels hold thousands of gallons of wine for patient aging, and up-to-the-second stainless steel equipment is used for sterile processing and bottling.

TO SEE & DO
Space permits only a snifter-size listing of Bucks County's many attractions. In general, the area is at its best off the beaten path in side street shops, walks along the towpath, and historic Washington Crossing Park. Should these activities seem too tame for your taste, there are raft and inner tube trips down the Delaware, plus canoeing and fishing. The arts are well served with the Bucks County Playhouse, one of the most famous summer stock theaters in the country—and also one of the oldest. This eighteenth-century gristmill was converted into a theater in 1939. To get all the details, contact the Bucks County Tourist Commission, 152 Swamp Road,

Doylestown, Pennsylvania 18901 (tel: 215-345-2552).

❧ ❧ ❧

Bucks County Vineyards and Winery

Route 202, R.D. 1
New Hope, Pennsylvania 18938
TEL: 215-794-7449
OWNER: Arthur Gerold
FOUNDED: 1973

AT A GLANCE
Tours & Tastings: Mon.–Fri. 10–5, Sun. and holidays until 6 P.M. $1 charge Sat., Sun., holidays, for tour, tasting, and museum visit (children always free). Guided tour takes visitors from cellar to bottling and aging, to museum (more later about this), and includes tasting of wines.
Closed: Thanksgiving, New Year's, and Christmas.
Vineyards: Two acres owned and sixty-five leased—all in Pennsylvania. Grape varieties are French hybrids and native American.
Wines: Sweet naturals: Pink Catawba, Niagara, Concord, Sangria. Generics: Country White, Red, and Pink; Labrusca. Varietals: Aurora, Chelois, Dutchess, Seyval Blanc, and Vidal Blanc. Also produced: an award-winning Blanc de Blanc *methode champenoise* champagne, Dutch Apple wine.
Awards: Gold awards to both champagne and Concord; bronze to Vidal Blanc.
Retail Shops: In addition to wines, Grape Vine Boutique features gifts to enhance the enjoyment of wines. Bread and Cheese Shop sells homemade French breads and croissants and cheese made from Amish farm milk. Also runs wine-and-cheese shops at VF Complex Reading China and Glass Outlet, Wyomissing; Reading Outlet Center, 8th and Windsor sts., Reading; Hess's Dept. Store, Allentown.
Credit Cards: None.

Access for the Disabled: Ramps to cellar and main winery.
Foreign Languages: "Un peu de Francais."
Getting There: Three miles south of New Hope (itself thirty-five miles north of Philadelphia) on Rte. 202.
Special Wine & Other Events: Festivals salute Italian music and wine, July 17–18; art, Aug. 16–17; harvest, Sept. 20–21; Octoberfest, Oct. 3–4; Nouveau, Nov. 16–17.

❧ Arthur Gerold, former owner of Brooks-Van Horn Costume Co., America's largest theatrical costumers, and a one-time theatrical producer, rang up the curtain on Bucks Country Vineyards in 1973. Now his red-barn winery provides several good reasons for paying a visit. Its hayloft houses a fascinating Fashion and Wine Museum displaying costumes worn by famous stars (Rosalind Russell's Auntie Mame, Mary Martin's Peter Pan, and many more), as well as a collection of seventeenth- and eighteenth-century wineglasses, wine artifacts, and artworks. The property was granted to Jacob Holcomb in 1717 by William Penn and now houses Pennsylvania's largest farm winery, bottling 850 cases per day.

TO SEE & DO
In addition to the Bucks County activities mentioned earlier, antiquers and art lovers should stop at Peddler's Village between New Hope and Lahaksa, near the winery. There's an outdoor flea market and an artists' cooperative called Upstairs Gallery (tel: 215-794-8486) in town that is also the headquarters of the Arts Alliance of Bucks County (tel: 215-794-8405) and its gallery.

❧ ❧ ❧

Sand Castle Winery

River Road (Rte. 32)
P.O. Box 177
Erwinna, Pennsylvania 18920

TEL: 215-294-9181
OWNERS: Joseph & Paul Maxian
FOUNDED: 1986

AT A GLANCE
Tours & Tastings: Mon.–Fri. 9–4; Sat. 10–6; Sun. 12–6 tastings and sales; tours by appointment.
Vineyards: 38 acres planted to vinifera varieties.
Wines: Johannisberg Reisling, Chardonnay, Cabernet Sauvignon, and Pinot Noir.
Awards: No competitions entered as yet.
Picnic Area: Planned.
Retail Shop: Wines sold on-site.
Credit Cards: American Express, Visa.
Access for Disabled: When new winery is completed in 1992.
Foreign Languages: Czech, Slovak.
Getting There: 12 miles north of New Hope, off River Road (Rte. 32.)

 The name that is often mentioned when Pennsylvanians speak of promising new wineries is Sand Castle. This is the ambitious undertaking of the Maxian brothers, who emigrated in 1969 from Bratislava, Czechoslavakia, a region renowed for wines even before the arrival of ancient Celtic tribes. Each year, they bring a master winemaker from their homeland to make wines from estate-grown grapes. From a production of 2,500 cases in 1987, Sand Castle turned out 8,000 cases in 1988. The Maxians are building a replica of a splendid tenth-century Bratislavan castle to house their winery that should be ready to receive visitors in the early 1990s. Among the local restaurants serving Sand Castle wines is the Golden Pheasant, well-known for its inventive cuisine. (See "Restaurants".)

ACCOMMODATIONS
This area is paved with charming inns, so a few only:

Black Bass Hotel
Route 32
Lumberville, Pennsylvania 18933
Tel: 215-297-5770
Possibly the area's most famous hotel, seven miles north of New Hope and situated on the canal. This has been a haven for travelers since the 1700s. Rooms are furnished with authentic eighteenth- and nineteenth-century antiques. Delightful place to dine. (See "Restaurants.")

Barley Sheaf Farm
Route 202
Holicong, Pennsylvania 18928
Tel: 215-794-5104
Ten-room 1740 stone farmhouse, on a thirty-acre farm; furnished with antiques. Swimming pool, shade trees, in a peaceful setting.

Pineapple Hill
1324 River Road
New Hope, Pennsylvania 18938
Tel: 215-862-9608
Five rooms in an eighteenth-century farmhouse with every modern convenience, family heirloom furnishings; Continental breakfast and delightful afternoon tea.

The Whitehall Inn
Pineville Road
(R.D. 2, Box 250)
New Hope, Pennsylvania 18938
Tel: 215-598-7945
An elegant and gracious 1794 manor house set on twelve country acres. Delicious breakfast with fresh juice, blueberry pancakes, sourdough rolls, berries; plus afternoon tea, sherry. Chocolates on pillows and a complimentary bottle of local wine. Antique-accented rooms with fireplaces; tennis court and swimming pool.

RESTAURANTS
Black Bass Hotel
  (See "Accommodations" for address, telephone.)

Enjoy a Delaware River view from this veranda dining room as well as such American dishes as New England lobster pie, crisp duckling, or fresh trout. Some Pennsylvania wines. Reservations necessary.

Golden Pheasant Inn
River Road
Erwinna, Pennsylvania 18920
Tel: 215-294-9595

Velvet settees shaded by Tiffany lamps or a bright and cheery solarium are settings for diners in this restored 1800s inn where the chef-owner has a French culinary flare. Known for bouillabaisse with crusty bread or steak au poivre and desserts worth saving room for. Some Pennsylvania wines. Closed Mon. Six guest rooms available.

Chester County/Brandywine Valley

Chaddsford Winery

Route 1, P.O. Box 229
Chadds Ford, Pennsylvania 19317
TEL: 215-388-6221
OWNERS: Eric and Lee Miller
FOUNDED: 1982

AT A GLANCE
Tours & Tastings: Tastings and sales are Tues.–Sat. 10–5:30, Sun. 12–5; tours Sat. and Sun. and by appointment. Covered are production, fermentation, barrel-aging and bottling cellars, followed by tasting.
Closed: Mondays.
Vineyards: Grapes are purchased from Pennsylvania growers, primarily in the southeastern part of the state.
Wines: Chardonnay, Cabernet Sauvignon, Johannisberg Riesling, Chambourcin, and Seyval Blanc; Chaddsford Red and White, and Niagara; also produces sparkling and apple wines.
Awards: Does not enter competitions.
Picnic Area: On the winery's back deck, lawn, or near small estate vineyard.
Retail Shop: Wine and wine-related items. Also in Philadelphia at two locations: the Spruce Street Wine Cellar, 16th and Spruce (tel: 215-735-5164); the Market at New Market, 2nd and Lombard (tel: 215-925-8015); and in the Reading Terminal Market (tel: 215-238-0978).

Credit Cards: American Express, MasterCard, Visa.
Access for Disabled: Limited to ramp entrance to building.
Foreign Languages: French.
Getting There: On Rte. 1, five miles south of Rte. 202 intersection. From Philadelphia: Take I-95S to Rte. 322W, left on Rte. 1 for six miles. From Wilmington: Take Rte. 52 to Rte. 1 and then go one mile north to winery.
Special Wine & Other Events: Festivals, celebrated throughout the year, are capped by a Candlelight Christmas. The winery is host to outdoor concerts and other activities; events, themes vary.

&. Eric Miller knew he wanted to be in the wine business all of his life; as a child he spent time near some famous European vineyards and went on to help his folks for seventeen years at Benmarl Vineyards in New York's Hudson Valley. His wife, Lee, formerly wrote about wine, including a book on East Coast wineries and grape varieties.

The Millers searched widely for premium wine-growing lands before relocating to southeastern Pennsylvania and settling their family into the 200-year-old house on their current property. Their goal is to make a variety of the world's classic wines, from light and fresh to rich, earthier styles, with nuances that complement local foods. The Millers' roadside winery is in a Norman Rockwell–looking 100-year-old barn equipped with the latest technology, French oak barrels, and decorated with antiques. Chaddsford's first harvest of 7,000 gallons in 1983 sold out immediately. Today, production approaches 50,000 gallons of wine, and the brand's acclaim is mounting steadily as well.

TO SEE & DO
From Chaddsford Winery, a short stroll down the renovated Road to Nottingham leads to Barns-Brinton, a 1700s tavern, authentically restored by the local historical society. Next door to the winery is the Antique Mall. An artists' community, Chadds Ford itself is filled with well-preserved historic homes. Two miles away are the 350-acre Longwood Gardens and the Brandywine River Museum with its famed Wyeth collection. Brandywine Battlefield Park is another area attraction. Thirty minutes away in Delaware is Winterthur Museum with its extensive American furniture and arts collection.

≈ ≈ ≈

Fox Meadow Farm

Clover Mill Road
R.D. 2, Box 59
Chester Springs, Pennsylvania 19425
TEL: 215-827-9731
OWNERS: Harry and Alice Mandell
FOUNDED: 1983

AT A GLANCE
Tours & Tastings: Sat. 10–5, Sun. 1–5, or by appointment; guided tour takes about forty-five minutes to see the winery in action and sample wines in the tasting room.
Closed: All except above times.
Vineyards: Five acres planted to ten varieties of French hybrids.

Wines: Chancellor, Vidal, Seyval, and hybrid blends.
Retail Shop: Wines sold on-site; you might also find some homemade blueberry, strawberry, and currant jams and jellies.
Credit Cards: None.
Access for Disabled: None.
Foreign Languages: None.
Getting There: From Chadds Ford: Take Rte. 202 to Westchester; pick up Rte. 113 and go through Chester Springs and make a right on Clover Mill Rd. to the winery. From Phoenixville: Take Rte. 113 South and turn on Clover Mill Rd. to the winery.

≈ The Mandells toast history with their farm and barn winery. During the Revolutionary War, the property's original owners sheltered wounded and retreating soldiers following the Battle of Brandywine (now commemorated with a memorial park). When the Mandells moved here in 1980, they found the soil ideal for wine grapes, and so began a new chapter in the farm's history: the vineyards, planted in 1982, produced their first wines in 1984.

ACCOMMODATIONS

Bed and Breakfasts
Le Clos Normand
773 Marlboro Spring Road
Kennett Square, Pennsylvania 19348
Tel: 215-347-2123
A two-story, red house with Norman French ambience, reflecting the owner's background. Gracious blend of antiques and contemporary furnishings, with works of art and fresh flowers. Croissant French toast at breakfast; wine, tea, coffee, always on hand for guests.

Meadow Spring Farm
201 East Street Road
Kennett Square, Pennsylvania 19348
Tel: 215-444-3903

A welcome with wine awaits at this country B&B. There's a hot tub and screened-in porch, and a hearty breakfast as well.

Inns

Mendenhall Inn
Route 52, P.O. Box 208
Mendenhall, Pennsylvania 19357
Tel: 215-388-1181
Early settlers from England started this place as a lumber mill in the 1700s. Has a renowned restaurant on-site.

Duling-Kurtz House and Country Inn
146 South Whitford Road
Exton, Pennsylvania 19341
Tel: 215-524-1830
Rooms are in a restored turn-of-the-century barn, with period reproductions. Original 1830's house is now a restaurant featuring French foods and trout from a pond on the property.

RESTAURANTS

Dilworth Inn
Briton's Bridge & Old Wilmington Pike
West Chester, Pennsylvania 19380
Tel: 215-399-1390
Continental and French specialties with a few surprises on the menu. Extensive wine list includes Chadds Ford wines. Jacket required.

Marshalltown Inn
1300 Strausburg Road
West Chester, Pennsylvania 19380
Tel: 215-692-4367
In this eighteenth-century inn, the menu is country French, with fresh seafood on the most wanted list. Luscious pastries. Wine list changes frequently and sometimes includes local offerings.

South-Central Pennsylvania

The routes to wineries here are within easy reach of Lancaster City, with its many shops and amusements. They also offer ample opportunities to get out of town and explore the Amish way of life, which has remained relatively unchanged over the years. For diverting excursions through the beautiful countryside, take a horse-and-buggy tour (near Bird-in-Hand) or board the Strasburg Railroad, which chugs the territory today as it did in its turn-of-the-century glory days. Hershey is also nearby, with Chocolate World and other sights. Berks County is renowned as the factory outlet center of the world. So come see, sip, and shop in the area.

Lancaster County/Hershey

Lancaster County Winery, Ltd.

Rawlinsville, Pennsylvania 17584
TEL: 717-464-3555

OWNER/PRESIDENT: Suzanne W. Dickel
FOUNDED: 1979

AT A GLANCE
Tours & Tastings: Tours take in the winery only at 11, 12, 1, 2, and 3 daily. No Sunday tours. Tastings/sales Mon.–Sat. 10–4, Sun. 1–4.
Closed: Thanksgiving, Christmas, month of Jan., Wed. and Sun. Feb.–March.
Vineyards: Twelve acres planted to French hybrids.
Wines: Estate-bottled Vidal and Seyval blancs, Rayon D'Or, Marechal Foch, Chancellor; red and white generics and Chablis. Spiced apple wine is another specialty.
Retail Sales: Wines sold on-site.
Credit Cards: MasterCard, Visa.
Access for the Disabled: Except for bathrooms.
Foreign Languages: None.
Getting There: From Lancaster: Take Rte. 222, then Rte. 272 South; turn right

on Baumgardner Rd. for one mile, then left on Rawlinsville Rd. for two miles.
Special Wine & Other Events: Third Sat. in Oct.: Octoberfest; Columbus Day Weekend: Civil War battle reenacted by Civil War units from seven states; Nov. 28–29: Country Food Sampler in the Dickels' 1821 kitchen; first weekend in Dec.: candlelight tours and tastings, holiday treats.

&. This atmospheric winery is situated on a plantation in continuous operation since 1718, while the Dickel farmhouse dates from the 1820s. On special occasions visitors are invited inside to see the restored kitchen and may tour the estate on a hayride. At Christmas the farm winery, lit by tiny lights, is indeed a fetching sight.

TO SEE & DO

There are bushels of activities and amusements to keep you busy in Lancaster County—the Amish and Mennonite communities, shops, amusement parks, museums, foods to try, and things to buy. The first order of business is to write or call the Pennsylvania Dutch Visitors Bureau (501 Greenfield Road, Lancaster, Pennsylvania 17601; tel: 717-299-8901) for brochures on what you wish most to see and do. Once in Lancaster, take a guided tour to get an overview and after that pick and choose the places you wish to savor. Flea markets for incurable collectors can be found at Rawlinsville (two miles west on Rte. 272) in Griest's old red barn, and in Buck (Rte. 272 south of Lancaster) at the Jocky Lot. Both are open seven days a week. When hunger strikes, Cherry Hill Orchards Outlet, Lancaster, offers greater abundance than its name implies—it's a year-round farmer's market and cornucopia of produce. Forty-four Turkey Hill Minit Markets have cheeses and other picnic foods.

&. &. &.

Mount Hope Estate Winery

Route 72
Manheim, Pennsylvania 17546
(Mailing address: Box 685, Cornwall, PA 17016)
TEL: 717-665-7021
PRESIDENT: Charles J. Romito
WINEMAKER: Frank Mazza (studied in Germany)
FOUNDED: 1980

AT A GLANCE

Tours & Tastings: Winery tours by appointment only; tastings Mon.–Sat. 10–6, Sun. 12–6, year-round; tours of Victorian Mount Hope Mansion conclude with formal wine tasting/appreciation in billiards room. Admission to grounds: $3.50 adult, $1.50 ages 6–11.
Closed: Christmas, New Year's, Thanksgiving.
Vineyards: Ten acres tucked into the sprawling fifty-acre estate grounds are planted to Riesling and Vidal Blanc; other acreage under contract in Adams and Lancaster counties supplies additional varieties.
Wines: Riesling, Chardonnay, Vidal and Seyval blancs, Chambourcin. Also Concord, strawberry, cherry, pear, and blackberry wines; spiced holiday and spiced apple drinks.
Awards: Numerous in Pennsylvania competitions.
Picnic Area: In formal garden.
Retail Shops: Vintage Wine Shop and Mansion Gift Shop; other retail outlets on Rte. 340 between Bird-in-Hand and Intercourse; Park City Shopping Center, West Mall, Lancaster. Tastings, sales, baked goods at the latter.
Credit Cards: MasterCard, Visa.
Access for Disabled: No.
Foreign Languages: None.
Getting There: The mansion is located north of Manheim on Rte. 72, half a mile from exit 20 of the Pennsylvania Turnpike, sixteen miles from Lancaster and

fourteen miles from Hershey. Beautiful bike trails in the area.

Special Wine & Other Events: The biggest celebration is the Pennsylvania Renaissance Faire, extending from Labor Day to Columbus Day. A huge spectacle each weekend features jesters and knights, maidens and monsters, and much frolicking on the grounds. In December, the Victorian Charles Dickens Christmas; other events, such as jazz and classical music concerts, take place during the summer. Check with winery.

☙ Winemaking started here in the 1980s, but the mansion's history is much longer. Built of sandstone in 1800 in the Federalist style by Bates Grubb, a wealthy industrialist, its simple façade was flamboyantly embellished with Victoriana by five succeeding generations of Grubbs. Enclosed in castle walls, the staggering interior decor of the thirty-two-room mansion has a circular walnut staircase, a ballroom, a solarium, a greenhouse, and overstuffed, tufted sofas and other furnishings—all painstakingly restored in 1980 by lawyer/entrepreneur Romito; his partner, Mazza; and local investors.

Tour guides in costumes from the Victorian 80s through the Roaring 20s, the periods spanned by the Grubb family, take visitors through the mansion and provide a tasting of wines from the estate's vineyards. Stroll on your own along the boxwood-bordered garden paths beside luxuriant cypress and candelabra pines and sassafras trees.

TO SEE & DO

In addition to the Lancaster area sights and attractions listed after the Lancaster County Winery, Manheim is fourteen miles from Hershey—a name that evokes visions of chocolate as quickly as it takes to pucker up for a kiss. Key attractions in Hershey include Chocolate World, a simulated chocolate factory tour and delicious experience, created when the real factory could no longer handle the number of tourists; Hersheypark (tel: 717-534-3900), a theme park with rides and amusements for kids of all ages; Hershey Museum of American Life (tel: 717-534-3439); Hershey Gardens, with twenty-three acres of beautiful plantings (tel: 717-534-3492); plus nineteenth-century houses Hershey built for employees (For information on Hershey attractions, call Hershey Visitor Center. tel: 717-534-3005); Indian-Echo Caverns (three miles west of city); and Dan-D Village (also three miles west), with antique dolls and an orchard for apple pickers.

ACCOMMODATIONS

Hershey
(See also Lancaster County listings.)

Hotel Hershey
Off Routes 322 and 422, P.O. Box BB
Hershey, Pennsylvania 17033
Tel: 717-533-2171; 800-533-3131

Hershey Lodge and Convention Center
Chocolate Avenue at University Drive
Hershey, Pennsylvania 17033
Tel: 717-533-3311; 800-533-3131
The Depression-era Hotel Hershey's exterior is that of a fantasy castle on a hill, with stained-glass windows in the dining room overlooking gazebo-accented gardens; rooms are modernized and devoid of special character. The motel-like Hershey Lodge, devoid of personality, has a swimming pool, tennis courts, and a movie theater. For more about what to do in Hershey, contact the Harrisburg and Hershey Tourist Promotion Agency, 114 Walnut Street (P.O. Box 969), Harrisburg, Pennsylvania 17108 (tel: 717-232-4121). To get there; take Rte. 72 North to Rte. 322 and go west to Hershey.

RESTAURANTS
Hotel Hershey
(See under "Accommodations" above for location and telephone numbers.)

Gracious circular dining room with stained-glass windows and garden views. Whether staying at hotel or lodge, make reservations at check-in if you wish to eat here. Selection of Pennsylvania wines, and Continental menu.

Alfred's Victorian Restaurant
38 North Union Street
Middletown, Pennsylvania 17057
Tel: 717-944-5373
Twenty-room Victorian mansion listed on the National Register of Historic Places; specialties include tortellini Alfredo with heapings of cheese and cream. Six miles from town.

🐚 🐚 🐚

Nissley Vineyard and Winery Estate

R.D. 1, Box 92-B
Bainbridge, Pennsylvania 17502
TEL: 717-426-3514
OWNER: the J. Richard Nissley family
FOUNDED: 1977

AT A GLANCE
Tours & Tastings: Mon.–Sat. 12–5; Sun. 1–4, Apr.–Dec. Guided tours through well-equipped modern winery, include tasting. $2 for adults, children under 12 free. Schedule varies on festival days.
Closed: Easter, Thanksgiving, Christmas, New Year's days; Sundays Jan.–March.
Vineyards: Forty-eight acres planted to French hybrids, native/hybrid American.
Wines: Primarily vintage-dated, Seyval and Vidal blancs, Aurora, Ravat 51, De Chaunac, Chancellor, Niagara, Concord. Proprietary whites and reds; apple wine; berry cooler.
Awards: Total over sixty. Gold medalists: 1986 Holiday Red (in International Eastern Wine Competition) and Apple (in Pennsylvania Wine Competition); frequently cited over the years: Bainbridge White and Red; Seyval Blanc, Niagara, De Chaunac.
Picnic Area: Lawns and groves, brookside nooks on the 300-acre estate.
Retail Shop: Wines, related accessories. Nissley has wine shops in Harrisburg's Colonial Park Mall (Lancaster, across from Central Market) and in the Ardmore Farmers' Market.
Credit Cards: MasterCard, Visa.
Access for Disabled: None.
Foreign Languages: None.
Getting There: From Hershey: Take Rte. 745S to Elizabethtown, and Rte. 241S through Elizabethtown. Continue about 4 miles, then make a left onto Rte. 441, and travel 2½ miles to Nissley sign at Wickersham Rd. Turn left and follow signs. From Lancaster or York: At Columbia, take Rte. 441N off Rte. 30. Continue on Rte. 441N for 8 miles to Wickersham Rd. Turn right on Wickersham and follow signs to winery.
Special Wine & Other Events: July 4– Labor Day: Sat. evening lawn concerts; early Sept.: Harvest Festival.

🐚 Behind the fieldstone façade echoing the style of the eighteenth century beats the heart of a thoroughly modern winery. The winery was patterned after both the centuries-old stone arch bridge and the mill on the property. The entire package now sits attractively wrapped in 300 acres of rolling Pennsylvania farmland and woodlands. Hiking is permitted.

🐚 🐚 🐚

Tucquan Vineyard

Drytown Road, Box 1830
Holtwood, Pennsylvania 17532
TEL: 717-284-2221
FOUNDED: 1968
OWNERS/WINEMAKERS: Thomas and
Lucinda Hampton

AT A GLANCE

Tours & Tastings: Tastings Mon.–Sat. 11–5; tours by appointment (made one day in advance) permits owners to give personal attention to visitors. Thirty-minute tour covers all the salient points of making wine, with deck stop to view the vineyard, crush pad, and press.

Closed: Sundays; last full week in June.

Vineyards: Ten acres, primarily French hybrid and labrusca.

Wines: Marechal Foch, Seyval, Chancellor, Steuben, Catawba, Niagara, and Concord; peach wine, apple wine, and cider are also produced.

Awards: Bushels of honors have been awarded to these wines; recent gold medalists: Tucquan's Chancellor and peach wines.

Picnic Area: Scenic deck overlooks vineyard and Susquehanna River for a smashing thirty-mile view.

Retail Shop: Wines and gift items.

Credit Cards: MasterCard, Visa.

Access for Disabled: Yes.

Foreign Languages: None.

Getting There: From Lancaster: Take Rte. 222, then Rte. 272 South to the Buck (a crossroads with a few bldgs.); turn right on Rte. 372 for about four miles. Then take a right on Hilldale Rd. (the second right after the entrance to Muddy Pond Park) and a left on Drytown Rd.

๘ With the Hamptons' 1968 plantings, Pennsylvania had its first commercial vineyards since the 1880s, when the vines were destroyed by disease and excessive cold. At first the Hamptons catered to amateur winemakers and homemakers making jellies and jams. They launched their winemaking career in 1977 in the barn-winery they built behind their 1890s farmhouse. The Hamptons don't aggressively court visitors through ads or publicity: "The secret of our success is good service and good products," they say. Their strategy works. They get repeat customers—who bring their friends.

TO SEE & DO

Lavish array of Lancaster sights; forty minutes away is York, fifty to Baltimore.

๘ ๘ ๘

Victorian Wine Cellars

2225 Marietta Avenue (Box 6146)
Rohrerstown, Pennsylvania 17603
TEL: 717-397-0851
OWNER: Richard J. Tobias
FOUNDED: 1982

AT A GLANCE

Tours & Tastings: Tues.–Sat. 12–7 (open holiday Mons.); ten-minute guided tour of winery followed by a fifteen-minute tasting.

Closed: Sun. and Mon.

Vineyards: All fruits—grapes as well as berries and apples—are purchased from Lancaster and York County growers.

Wines: Seyval, Vidal, Marechal Foch, Cayuga; blueberry, strawberry, elderberry, and apple dessert wines.

Awards: Much-heralded strawberry, blueberry, and apple wines.

Retail Sales: In winery during tour hours.

Credit Cards: MasterCard, Visa.

Access for Disabled: Limited; there are steps to basement sales area.

Foreign Languages: None.

Getting There: From Lancaster: Take Rte. 23 two miles west to winery in Rohrerstown.

๘ Victorian Cellars, one of the smallest federally bonded wineries in the state of Pennsylvania, is located in a home built in 1870. The high ceilings and thick stone walls provide an ideal environment for making wines. The thirty-foot hand-dug well helps maintain the right temperature for aging wine. Fruit wines get top billing here.

ACCOMMODATIONS (see also Hershey)

Some 5 million tourists visit the Pennsylvania Dutch area each year, and all kinds of accommodations await them—and you. A few selections only are listed below.

Bed and Breakfasts & Inns
Bed & Breakfast of Lancaster County
P.O. Box 19
Mountville, Pennsylvania 17554
Tel: 717-285-7200
Reservations for Lancaster, Hershey, Harrisburg, Gettysburg, Reading, York.

Groff Farm—"Abend-Ruhe"
2324 Leaman Road
Lancaster, Pennsylvania 17602
Tel: 717-687-0221
Century-old farmhouse with warmth and charm; handicrafts on display are by hostess. Continental breakfast features homemade sweet breads and fresh fruits.

Witmer's Tavern
2014 Old Philadelphia Pike
Lancaster, Pennsylvania 17602
Tel: 717-299-5305
A national historic landmark, this is a pre-Revolutionary War inn with authentic antique furnishings and working fireplaces. Continental breakfast.

Motels & Lodges
Red Caboose Motel
Strasburg, Pennsylvania 17579
Tel: 717-687-6646
Old railroad cabooses turned into snug motel, Victorian dining car restaurant with appropriate red plush, globe lamp decor.

Soudersberg Motel
U.S. 30, Box 1
Soudersberg, Pennsylvania 17577
Tel: 717-687-7607
Heated pool, color TV, and bus or privately guided tours; convenient to Strasburg Railroad and Dutch Wonderland. Eight miles east of Lancaster.

Timberline Lodges & Hearthroom Restaurant
44 Summit Drive
Strasburg, Pennsylvania 17597
Tel: 717-687-7472
Offers either rustic, private lodges with kitchens or a room in the main wing that also has a well-decorated restaurant. Three miles south of Strasburg, off Rte. 896.

RESTAURANTS
Old Greenfield Inn
1858 Hempstead Road
Lancaster, Pennsylvania 17602
Tel: 717-393-0668

The Lemon Tree
1766 Columbia Avenue (Route 462)
Lancaster, Pennsylvania 17602
Tel: 717-394-0441
A ten-minute drive west of downtown Lancaster takes you to this converted 1800s farmhouse. Both the above restaurants serve Continental foods, which are more compatible with wines than typical Pennsylvania Dutch dishes.

York & Adams Counties

Allegro Vineyards

Sechrist Road (R.D. 2, Box 64)
Brogue, Pennsylvania 17309
TEL: 717-927-9148
OWNERS: John H. and Timothy R. Crouch
FOUNDED: 1980

AT A GLANCE
Tours & Tastings: Year-round, Wed.–Fri. 2–7, Sat.–Sun. 12–5; informal tours.
Closed: Major holidays.
Vineyards: Fourteen acres planted to such varieties as Cabernet Sauvignon, Chardonnay, Seyval and Vidal blancs.

Wines: Cabernet Sauvignon, Seyval, Vidal, Vin Blanc, Vin Rouge, and Vin Rosé; strawberry wine and Celeste (grape-and-peach blend).

Awards: Over thirty awards since opening in 1981 in state, national, and international competitions.

Retail Sales: Wines sold on-site.

Credit Cards: None.

Access for Disabled: None.

Foreign Languages: None.

Getting There: From Lancaster: Take I-30 West to York, turn south on I-83 to Rte. 74 for fifteen miles southeast to Brogue, then turn on Sechrist Rd. to winery.

๖ This tiny winery was established in 1978, had its first commercial release in 1980, and has been making award winners since its earliest days.

๖ ๖ ๖

Naylor Wine Cellars Inc.

Ebaugh Road (R.D. 3, Box 24)
Stewartstown, Pennsylvania 17363
TEL: 717-993-2431
PRESIDENT: Richard H. Naylor
FOUNDED: 1978

AT A GLANCE

Tours & Tastings: Mon.–Sat. 11–6, Sun. 12–5, and during festival times.

Closed: Christmas, Thanksgiving, Easter.

Vineyards: Thirty-five acres, planted to eastern labrusca, French hybrid, and vinifera varieties. They yield 90 percent of the grapes needed; the remainder is purchased from area growers to produce in excess of 8,750 cases annually.

Wines: Twenty varietals and generics from the above, and five fruit wines; labels are Naylor, Ruby Grenadier, Golden Grenadier.

Awards: From first wines to present, wines have been awarded medals; international awards have gone to Chambourcin and Nouveau.

Retail Shop: Wines and related items. Also Naylor Wine Shoppe (North) in North Mall Factory Outlet, York (tastings, sales, gourmet foods, gifts).

Credit Cards: MasterCard, Visa.

Access for Disabled: Yes.

Foreign Languages: None.

Getting There: South on I-83 to exit 1; turn east on Rte. 851 for four miles to Stewartstown, to Rte. 24. Go north on Rte. 24 for two miles, turn left to winery.

Special Wine & Other Events: Festivals first weekend in June and Oct. have live music, free tours, tastings; also food-and-wine-tasting seminars for nominal charges.

๖ When Richard Naylor set up his winery in a old potato cellar in 1978, he rang in the rebirth of winemaking in York County, which had been the site of America's second commercial winery in 1807. Naylor's main goal is to produce wines that pay tribute to both the early wine heritage in this part of the country and his German ancestry. He focuses on big, flavored wines and strong fruit flavors.

Naylor's winery, in a new building, is 1,000 feet up on a historic plateau known in Revolutionary War days as "The Barrens." The name came about because Indian tribes burned the trees and bushes to create flatlands for grass in order to lure game they hunted. Scotch, Irish, and German immigrants later settled into farming here.

๖ ๖ ๖

Stephen Bahn Winery

Goram Road (R.D. 1, Box 758)
Brogue, Pennsylvania 17309
TEL: 717-927-9051
OWNERS: Anne and Stephen Bahn
WINEMAKER: Stephen Bahn (degree in enology and viticulture, UC-Fresno)
FOUNDED: 1981

AT A GLANCE
Tours & Tastings: Tours are not a main event, but tastings, conducted by the owners themselves, are held regularly Sat. 12–5, Sun. 1–5; other times by appointment.
Closed: Major holidays.
Vineyards: Six acres planted to French hybrids, American and vinifera varieties.
Wines: Johannisberg Riesling, Cabernet Sauvignon, Vidal and Seyval blancs, Chardonnay, Gewürztraminer, Pinot Noir; fruit wines include cherry, peach; a spiced red wine is made Oct.–Dec. 25.
Awards: Winners have been Gewürztraminer, Nouveau, Riesling, Seyval.
Retail Sales: Wines, gifts, gourmet foods.
Credit Cards: MasterCard, Visa.
Access for Disabled: Limited.
Foreign Languages: French.
Getting There: Follow Rte. 74 South from Red Lion eleven miles through Brogue and turn left at winery sign. Go three miles on right.

❧ There is warm and friendly ambience at this small, family-owned winery, where you will find award-winning wines. From the lawn or patio, see the rolling Susquehanna River. Nearby is the John Wright Factory Store for crafts, cast-iron reproduction Vermont wood stoves and decorative items. Hours: Mon.–Sat. 11–5, Sun. noon–5.

TO SEE & DO
For nine days during 1777, York was the first capital of the United States. A number of buildings and monuments around town depict this brief moment in U.S. history. Furthermore, York is sixteen miles north of Gettysburg, with its renowned Gettysburg National Military Park, which offers films, tours, museums, and activities devoted to this bloody battle. To see also is an original draft of Lincoln's Gettysburg Address at the site where he delivered it. For lighter amusement, visit the markets, orchards, and antique shops with merchandise ripe and ready for picking. For information to help you plan ahead, contact the Gettysburg Travel Council, Carlisle Street, Gettysburg, Pennsylvania 17325 (tel: 717-334-6274).

❧ ❧ ❧

York Springs Vineyard & Winery

420 Latimore Road
York Springs, Pennsylvania 17372
TEL: 717-528-8490
PRESIDENT: Andrew C. Campbell
FOUNDED: 1978

AT A GLANCE
Tours & Tastings: Thurs.–Sat. 12–5.
Closed: Jan.–March.
Vineyards: Vinifera varieties, Pinot Noir, Chardonnay, Cabernet Sauvignon.
Wines: Varietals from the above and a blended red.
Awards: Chardonnay 1984 won a gold medal, and Cabernet Sauvignon 1985 a silver.
Retail Sales: On-site. Also in Camp Hill Shopping Mall, Camp Hill, Pennsylvania.
Credit Cards: MasterCard, Visa.
Access for Disabled: None.
Foreign Languages: None.
Getting There: From York Springs: Two miles north on Rte. 94, then right on Lattimore Rd. to winery.

ACCOMMODATIONS
Cameron Estate Inn
R.D. 1, Box 305
Donegal Springs Road
Mount Joy, Pennsylvania 17552
Tel: 717-563-1773
Between Lancaster and York, this historic fourteen-room mansion, restored as a comfortable inn, is surrounded by a thirteen-acre garden and has its own trout stream. Home in the past to Simon Cameron, Lincoln's first Secretary of War, it is now run by Abe and Betty Groff, who are also well known for their

excellent Groff's Farm Restaurant, three miles from the inn. The rooms are tastefully appointed in antique reproductions, Oriental carpets, and beds topped with examples of the famous locally made quilts. Naylor wines are served here.

Spring House
Muddy Creeks Forks
Airville, Pennsylvania 17302
Tel: 717-927-6906
Eighteen miles south of York, a restored eighteenth-century stone house in a quaint valley village of clapboard buildings. The house is decorated with antiques, handmade quilts, and pottery. Full breakfast features wild fruit preserves, meats, breads. Trout fishing, canoeing, and swimming at your doorstep.

RESTAURANTS
Accommac Inn
Accomac Road
Wrightsville, Pennsylvania 17368
Tel: 717-252-1521
This atmospheric restaurant's eighteenth-century decor is enchanced by a river view, and the French country menu is a welcome sight with such seasonal dishes as pheasant with truffles and crisp roast duckling. Excellent wine list.

Meadowbrook Inn
2819 Whiteford Road
York, Pennsylvania 17402
Tel: 717-757-3500
Veal and seafood are especially well prepared at this restaurant in a handsome old mansion surrounded by lawns and flowers.

ða ða ða

Calvaresi Winery

832 Thorn Street
Reading, Pennsylvania 19601
TEL: 215-373-7821

OWNER/WINEMAKER: Tom Calvaresi (courses in enology, Penn State)
FOUNDED: 1981

AT A GLANCE
Tours & Tastings: Tues.–Fri. 7–9, Sat.–Sun. 1–5; otherwise by appointment.
Closed: Thanksgiving, Christmas, Easter.
Vineyards: French hybrid and American varieties are purchased from Clover Hill Farm (next listing on this wine route).
Wines: Not all fourteen wines are available at the same time, but they include such American varietals as Cayuga, Concord, Niagara, and Catawba, and French hybrids Seyval, Chelois, Rayon D'Or, and Chambourcin Rosé.
Awards: Among Pennsylvania's most awarded wines.
Retail Shop: On-site.
Credit Cards: None.
Access for Disabled: None.
Foreign Languages: None.
Getting There: From Reading: Go north on Rte. 61, two miles to Windsor St. Go left on Windsor, then take first left onto Thorn St. to winery on right.
A small in-home winery, producing 3,000 gallons a year.

TO SEE & DO
Shopping is the main activity of most visitors to this area, known as the outlet capital of the world, but Reading's heritage goes back to Colonial days and William Penn. You can see the restored homesteads of Daniel Boone and Conrad Weiser, and the historic iron-making village, home of one of America's earliest industries. For information on these attractions and the fairs, festivals, crafts, and more, contact the Berks County Pennsylvania Dutch Travel Association, Sheraton Berkshire Inn, Route 422, Paper Mill Road, Wyomissing, Pennsylvania 19610 (tel: 215-375-4085).

ACCOMMODATIONS

Bed & Breakfasts

Amy Nawa Enterprises
Pennsylvania Hosts Bed and Breakfast
819 Madison Avenue
Reading, Pennsylvania 19601
Tel: 215-372-3346

Bed & Breakfast of S.E. Pennsylvania
R.D. 1, Box 278
Barto, Pennsylvania 19504
Tel: 215-845-3526

EL Shaddai
229 Madison Avenue, Hyde Villa
Reading, Pennsylvania 19605
Tel: 215-929-1341
Century-old stone farmhouse comfortably appointed with a sitting room and inside hearth as well as an outdoor porch; full breakfast with homemade jams.

Hotels/Motels

Sheraton Berkshire
Route 422 at Paper Mill Road exit
Reading (Wyomissing), Pennsylvania
  19610
Tel: 215-376-3811; 800-325-3535
257 typical Sheraton rooms; indoor pool, sauna, exercise room, and more.

Dutch Colony Inn
14635 Perkiomen Avenue
Reading, Pennsylvania 19606
Tel: 215-779-2345
Refurbished rooms on landscaped grounds with all motel amenities at reasonable rates. At East Junction Reading Bypass and Route 422.

RESTAURANTS

Widow Finney's
4th and Cherry streets
Reading, Pennsylvania 19605
Tel: 215-378-1776
Restored historic complex with eighteenth-century log house and nineteenth-century market house; a list of Pennsylvania wines.

Cafe Restaurant
Reading Outlet Center
8th and Windsor streets
Reading, Pennsylvania 19604
Tel: 215-393-5495
Features Bucks County wines.

❧ ❧ ❧

Clover Hill Vineyards & Winery

Old Route 222 (R.D.2)
Breinigsville, Pennsylvania 18031
TEL: 215-395-2468
OWNERS: John and Pat Skrip
FOUNDED: 1985

AT A GLANCE

Tours & Tastings: Tours of vineyard and winery by appointment; tastings Wed.–Sat. 11–5, Sun. 12–5.
Closed: Thanksgiving, Christmas, New Year's, Easter, July 4, Labor Day, Memorial Day.
Vineyards: Twenty acres planted 85 percent French-American hybrid; 15 percent American.
Wines: Varietals from above grapes.
Awards: Golds in 1987 to Clover Hill White (Vidal), Seyval Blanc, and Alden, and bronzes to Catawba and Cayuga White; 1988 silvers to Rayon D'Or, Ravat; bronzes to Clover Hill White, Cayuga White, Vidal Blanc, and Chambourcin—all in Pennsylvania competitions.
Retail Sales: All available wines sold on-site.
Credit Cards: None.
Access for Disabled: Yes.
Foreign Languages: None.
Getting There: From Allentown: Take I-78 (Rte. 22) to Rte. 100 South. At second traffic light, make a right onto Schantz Rd. Continue 2.7 miles on Old Rte. 222. Turn left onto Old Rte. 222.

Vineyard and winery are located 500 feet on right from intersection.

Special Wine & Other Events: Early Sept.: Harvest Feast at the vineyard/winery.

🐌 One of Pennsylvania's newest wineries, located in rural Lehigh Valley, where you'll enjoy the view along with your wine.

TO SEE & DO

Nearby Allentown has a history dating back to Colonial times. Stop by Zion's Reformed Church to see where the Liberty Bell was safely hidden when the British captured Philadelphia in 1777 (622 Hamilton at Church St.; tel: 215-435-4232), and if time permits, visit Allentown's many historic homes, now restored and open to the public. The town also boasts two very unusual museums—one devoted to the iron-and-steel industry, housed in a reconstructed iron furnace; the other is dedicated to the cement industry. For a change of pace, stroll through the flower gardens in Trexler Memorial Park or ride the waves or roller coasters at Dorney Park Wildwater Kingdom. For full details, contact the Lehigh Valley Convention and Visitors Bureau, P.O. Box 2605, Lehigh Valley, Pennsylvania 18001; tel: 215-266-0560.

ACCOMMODATIONS

Bed and Breakfasts & Inns
Blair Creek Inn
RD 2
Mertztown, Pennsylvania 19539
Tel: 215-682-6700
This former Quaker meetinghouse is now an elegant inn set on spacious grounds. Known primarily for its well-appointed restaurant (see "Restaurant"), its luxury suites deserve as much acclaim. Convenient for visiting Calvaresi Winery in Reading as well as Clover Hill.

Longswamp Bed and Breakfast
R.D. 2, Box 26
Mertztown, Pennsylvania 19539
Tel: 215-682-6197
Ten miles southwest of Allentown and a bit beyond Clover Hill; you could also make this tour headquarters for visiting Calvaresi Winery. It's a historic old house—comfortable, with high ceilings, big fireplaces, antiques, and well-stocked bookcases. The big breakfast features home-dried fruits, quiche, homemade breads.

Glasbern
R.D. 1, Box 250
Fogelsville, Pennsylvania 18051
Tel: 215-285-4723
Cathedral-ceilinged barn converted into a comfortable inn with mammoth glass windows ("Glasbern") and majestic pines beyond. A country feeling—wood-burning stove in lounge, dried floral arrangements, baskets, candles. A hot tub; jogging, walking, and bicycling on sixteen-acre grounds.

Hotel
Hilton Hotel
904 Hamilton Mall
Allentown, Pennsylvania 18102
Tel. 212-433-2221; 800-445-8667
All the amenities of a Hilton and a 23-room executive level with deluxe suites. Centrally located downtown.

RESTAURANT
Blair Creek Inn
(See "accommodations" for address, telephone number.)
An elegant chef-owned restaurant known for unhackneyed Continental dishes. The well-stocked wine cellar yields an occasional bottle of Pennsylvania wine among a wide variety of other selections.

North-Central Pennsylvania

Brookmere Farm Vineyard Inc.

Route 655 (R.D. 1, Box 53)
Belleville, Pennsylvania 17004
TEL: 717-935-5380
PRESIDENT: Donald Chapman
FOUNDED: 1984

AT A GLANCE
Tours & Tastings: Tastings Mon.–Sat.
10–5, Sun. 1–4. Winter hours subject to
change. Tours by appointment only.
Closed: Major holidays.
Vineyards: Five acres planted to vinifera,
French hybrids; supplemented with
grapes purchased in Carlisle and York.
Wines: Varietals and blends from the
above grapes; fruit wines are also pro-
duced.
Awards: Strawberry and blended wine
have received awards.
Picnic Area: On the grounds.
Retail Shop: Wines sold on-site and at the
Wine Cellar, Governor Snyder Mansion,
Selinsgrove.
Credit Cards: MasterCard, Visa.
Access for Disabled: None.
Foreign Languages: None.
Getting There: Belleville is thirty miles
south of State College; take Rte. 150 to
Rte. 29 through McAlevy's Fort to Rte.
305 to Belleville, and turn onto Rte. 655
to winery. From Huntingdon: Take Hwy.
22 to Mill Creek and turn onto Rte. 655 to
winery.
Special Wine & Other Events: Biggest at-
traction is the huge farmers' market
every Wed., three miles from winery.

‌ Don and Susan Chapman are transplanted New Englanders who began
making wine after years working in Pennsylvania's steel industry. They began
growing grapes in 1982 on lands surrounding the stately nineteenth-century
Brookmere mansion, seen on their label.

Their winery's sales began in 1984 with
their first vintage of 8,000 gallons.

TO SEE & DO
Nearby Huntingdon offers the Swigart
Museum, a changing collection devoted
to the American automobile (Rte. 22; tel:
814-643-0885). Also on Rte. 22 are two
caves of interest—the Lincoln Caverns
(tel: 814-643-0268) and the Indian Caverns (tel: 814-632-7578).

ACCOMMODATIONS
Contact the Chapmans about bed and
breakfast at the winery.

Raystown Country Inn
Fourth Street at U.S. 22 (R.D. 1, Box
353)
Huntingdon, Pennsylvania 16652
Tel: 814-643-3934
High-caliber motel with very tasty cui-
sine, prepared to order from fresh
ingredients. Seventy-six double rooms.
Swimming pool, cross-country skiing.

‌ ‌ ‌

Kollin Vineyards & Winery

R.D. 1, Box 439
Bellefonte, Pennsylvania 16823
TEL: 814-355-4666
OWNERS: John and Martha Kollen
FOUNDED: 1979

AT A GLANCE
Tours & Tastings: May 1–Oct. 1; Tues.–
Fri. 1–6, Sat. 10–6, Sun. 1–4; Oct.–Apr.:
Wed.–Fri. 1–6, Sat. 10–6. Guided tour
includes slide film and tasting.
Closed: Thanksgiving, Christmas, month
of Jan.
Vineyards: Six acres planted to French
hybrids and American varieties.
Wines: All but one wine are blends,
either dry or semi-sweet. The exception
is crisp, dry Seyval Blanc, bottled as a
varietal; blended white combines Aurora

with Delaware; rosé is a blend of Steuben and Rosette, with small amount of De Chaunac; reds blend De Chaunac and Foch and are barrel-aged for two years and bottle-aged for a year. Two labels are used: Kollen Vineyards, and Happy Valley for sparkling wine.

Awards: Many awards make Kollen wines beribboned as war heroes; among the most celebrated is the Seyval, which has scored high at Eastern International competitions and state events.

Picnic Area: Clusters of tables near the vineyards, stream, and the hillside shelter.

Retail Shop: Sales room is only retail outlet; some restaurants feature Kollen wines.

Credit Cards: MasterCard, Visa.

Access for Disabled: Ramp to building.

Foreign Languages: None.

Getting There: From State College: The 5-mile trip begins by taking Hwy. 322 West (North Atherton St.) to Stevenson Rd. (about 4 miles from State College). Take a right through Waddle to Hwy. 550, then another right 1½ miles to winery. Beautiful hiking trails and scenic biking routes (rentals available at Bike Shop, W. College Avenue, State College; tel: 814-238-0020).

Special Wine & Other Events: State College, site of Penn State, is abuzz with educational and cultural activities. Football in the fall and Central Pennsylvania's Festival of the Arts, during the second week in July, are but two enjoyable events.

⤷ At John and Martha Kollen's winery, you drink in the scenery of the Alleghenies as you sip and savor award-winning wines.

ACCOMMODATIONS
(See also listings after Brookmere.)
Prices are higher, and reservations very hard to get on football weekends; two-day minimum stays are often required.

Bed and Breakfasts
Rest & Repast Bed & Breakfast Service
P.O. Box 126
Pine Grove Mills, Pennsylvania 16868
Tel: 814-238-1484
Recommendations for bed and breakfast accommodations in Bellefonte and nearby areas.

Inn/Motor Hotel
In State College:

Sheraton Motor Inn
240 South Pugh Street
State College, Pennsylvania 16801
Tel: 814-238-8454/800-325-3535
One-hundred-eighty-two-room Sheraton with such deluxe features as steam baths in some of the top rooms. Indoor pool and sauna.

Nittany Lion
North Atherton Street (Business Rte. 322)
State College, Pennsylvania 16803
Tel: 814-231-7500
On Penn State campus, a comfortable 140-room inn. Drop in Mon.–Sun. and enjoy chamber music in the lobby.

RESTAURANTS
Tavern Restaurant
220 East College Avenue (P.A. 26S)
State College, Pennsylvania 16803
Tel: 814-238-6116
Well-prepared veal and seafood dishes served in an Early American setting, with historic prints on the walls. Extensive wine list.

Victorian Manor
901 Pike Street
Lemont, Pennsylvania 16851
Tel: 814-238-5534
The building dates from the 1800s and the interior is, appropriately, Victorian. The chef-owner serves a delicious array of Continental entrées and luscious desserts. Wine list. Reservations advised.

Southwestern Pennsylvania

Lapic Winery Ltd.

682 Tulip Drive
New Brighton, Pennsylvania 15066
TEL: 412-846-2031
PRESIDENT: Paul Lapic
FOUNDED: 1977

AT A GLANCE

Tours & Tastings: Mon.–Sat. 10–8; Sun.
1–5; slide show, tour of winery, tasting.
Closed: Christmas, Easter, and Election
days.
Vineyards: Two acres planted to French
hybrids; additional grapes from other
Pennsylvania growers.
Wines: Primarily whites: Seyval and
Vidal blanc; Cayuga White, Delaware,
Dutchess, Catawba, and Concord.
Awards: Gold medals have gone to
Seyval and Vidal blancs.
Retail Shop: Wines sold at winery and
Lapic Wine Shop.
Credit Cards: American Express, Mas-
terCard, Visa.
Access for Disabled: None.
Foreign Languages: None.
Getting There: From Pittsburgh: Take
Rte. 65 North to Rochester (approx. 25
miles). From Rochester: Take Rte. 68
West for 4 miles onto Tulip Dr. Winery is
½ mile on the left.

Special Wine & Other Events: How
about the World Championship Snow
Shovel Riding Contest? It's here in
Beaver County, along with the Maple
Syrup Festival, the River Regatta, a host
of arts, crafts, and food festivals, an air
show, Candlelight Christmas, and more.

Lapic was the first winery in southwest
Pennsylvania; a family operation, it welcomes families on Sundays, and the
Lapics remind visitors to wear comfortable shoes for the vineyard stroll.

TO SEE & DO

The Beaver County Promotion Agency,
14th and Church streets, Ambridge,
Pennsylvania 15002, is your best source
for area information. Attractions include
the extensive gardens at both Community College and Old Economy Village, a restored nineteenth-century
Harmonists' community; Merrick Gallery's works from the American Hudson
River School and European Romantic
period; and Royce Theatre, a scale model
composite of the great movie palaces of
the 1930s. Fall foliage is particularly
beautiful in these parts, but summer
shines as well with a host of outdoor
activities at Brodhead Cultural Center,
on Penn State's Beaver Campus at
Monaca, Pennsylvania 15061 (tel: 412-
775-8830). And nearly all year long,
markets burst with farm-fresh products
to savor on the spot or take along for
later on.

ACCOMMODATIONS

Bed and Breakfasts
Pittsburgh Bed and Breakfast
2190 Ben Franklin Drive
Pittsburgh, Pennsylvania 15237
Tel: 412-367-8080
Recommendations for Pittsburgh and
western Pennsylvania.

Motels/Motor Hotel
Best Western Conley's Motor Inn
Big Beaver Boulevard
Beaver Falls, Pennsylvania 15010
Tel: 412-843-9300/800-5528-1234

Holiday Inn
P.A. 18 North at P.A. Turnpike exit 2
Beaver Falls, Pennsylvania 15010
Tel: 412-846-3700/800-HOLIDAY
One-hundred-fifty-eight rooms with in-
door pool and expected amenities.

RESTAURANTS

Didios Restaurant and Lounge
416 Delaware Avenue
Rochester, Pennsylvania 15074
Tel: 412-774-3100
Italian specialties, seafood, prime ribs, and steaks. Casual.

Wooden Angel
Sharon Road and Leopard Lane
Bridgewater, Pennsylvania 15009
Tel: 412-774-7880
Americana setting for rack of lamb, fish, shellfish, and extensive American wine list. Wine cellar room.

❧ ❧ ❧

Shuster Cellars

2900 Turkey Farm Road
Irwin, Pennsylvania 15642
TEL: 412-351-0979
PRESIDENT: Anthony J. Shuster
WINEMAKER: Steve Shephard
FOUNDED: 1984

AT A GLANCE

Tours & Tastings: Tour and tasting dates are scheduled several weeks in advance by the winery. Groups preferred. A $2 charge per person includes a sit-down tasting of a variety of wines, while winemaker gives details on appropriate wine-food combinations. Cheeses are served. Tour of wine cellar, sales room visit, and a gift goblet winds up the tour/tasting.
Closed: Official holidays.
Vineyards: 2½ acres planted to Seyval; additional grapes are purchased from Erie and northwest Pennsylvania growers.
Wines: Volkswine in Chablis, rosé, and Burgundy styles; Diamond (a semi-sweet blend); Chelois, Concord, Foch, and Seyval; Vidal and Seyval Reserve; production exceeds 90,000 bottles annually.
Awards: Garnering top awards are Diamond and Foch in state and International Eastern Wine Competitions; awards also to Chelois, Vidal, rosé wines
Retail Sales: All wines sold on-site.
Credit Cards: None.
Access for Disabled: None.
Foreign Languages: Slovenian.
Getting There: From Turnpike exit 7: Take Rte. 30W toward Pittsburgh to first traffic light; turn right onto Barnes Lake Rd., go approximately 1 mile to stop sign. Turn left and go approximately 1 mile until you see Carradam Golf Course on left. Turn right onto Turkey Farm Rd. Continue on the road for ¾ mile until you see yellow house on left. Turn right onto winery road to top of hill. Go down right side of winery; parking is just beyond winery door. "Please do not block doorway," asks Shuster.

❧ Shuster, formerly a builder and still in the building components business, made wines as a hobby for twenty years before turning pro. He strives for a homemade taste today but with the barest hint of characteristic sediment and a more pleasant finish. The Mission-style winery he designed is set among the pine trees. "We used oak, cherry, and walnut woods right from the area," he says, describing the rich walls and ceilings, which are further accented with stained glass and a view of the wooded area. Inside, visitors are surprised to find that most of the winery is underground and has an overhead walk to give visitors a two-story look down to the entire winemaking process. "This winery was built to suit the surroundings," Shuster says. His wines are local favorites, served at several area restaurants, and are gathering wider fame.

ACCOMMODATIONS

The best choices are in Pittsburgh, 23 miles northeast of Irwin.

For information, contact the Greater Pittsburgh Convention and Visitors Bureau, 4 Gateway Center, Pittsburgh, Pennsylvania 15222, tel: 412-281-7711.

ða ða ða

Hillcrest Winery

Humphrey Road
R.D. 2, Box 301
Greensburg, Pennsylvania 15601
TEL: 412-832-5720
French hybrid and vinifera wines; tours and tastings by appointment only. Ask for directions when you call.

Northwestern Pennsylvania

The wine route now turns scenic along the shores of Lake Erie, through some of the state's richest and oldest grape-growing territory, in a region often referred to locally as "North East."

Special note: North East is also the name of a city and the site of an annual wine festival in the last weekend each September, when the town turns into a celebration of music, special foods, arts, crafts, and other merriment.

ða ða ða

Conneaut Cellars

Route 322, P.O. Box 5975
Conneaut Lake, Pennsylvania 16316
TEL: 814-382-3999
WINEMAKER: Dr. Alan Wolf
FOUNDED: 1982

AT A GLANCE
Tours & Tastings: Mon.–Sat. 10–6, Sun. 12–6; tours begin on the hour.
Closed: Mon., Jan.–March.
Vineyards: Grape varieties, purchased from Erie area growers, include vinifera, French hybrids, and native American.
Wines: White blends, Seyval and Vidal blancs, Riesling, and Chardonnay; red blends and De Chaunac and Cabernet Sauvignon; also rosé wines.
Awards: Gold medals to Chardonnay and De Chaunac.
Retail Shop: Wines and gift items.
Credit Cards: MasterCard, Visa.
Access for Disabled: All on one floor with wide doors.
Foreign Languages: German.
Getting There: Take exit 36B from I-79 and proceed approximately six miles west on Rte. 322 to Conneaut Lake. Walking distance from town.
Special Wine & Other Events: Second weekend in Sept.: Conneaut's Wine Harvest Festival, features grape stomping, good food, amateur winemakers' contest and judging, music, crafts, and more. In this resort area, there are all kinds of events every week, from June to Oct.

ða Alan Wolf, a former professor, likes to name many of his wines after local landmarks and historical figures. Thus the literature describing them can be quite educational: one semi-sweet wine, Princess Snowater, uses the Indian word for Conneaut; a medium-bodied red, Colonel Crawford, honors a Crawford County frontier hero. To make his wines, Wolf draws on thirty years of experience in pleasing a broad spectrum of tastes.

TO SEE & DO

A family resort area with hiking, boating, and various other outdoor diversions in and about Pennsylvania's largest natural lake. Nearby Meadville, named for David Mead, revolutionary war ensign, has several historic sights and the 7,994-acre Erie National Wildlife Refuge. Edinboro, a resort city, is also the site of Edinboro State College.

ACCOMMODATIONS

Holiday Inn/Edinboro Castle
U.S. 6N (W), 3 miles east of I-79, exit 38
Edinboro, Pennsylvania 16412
Tel: 814-734-5650/800-238-8000
One-hundred-five-room motel with all the comforts; 18-hole golf course among the diversions.

David Mead Inn
455 Chestnut Street (U.S. 19)
Meadville, Pennsylvania 16335
Tel: 814-336-1692
Sixty-seven rooms and a heated pool.

RESTAURANT

Charlie's Restaurant & Pub
1340 Conneaut Lake Road
Meadville, Pennsylvania 16335
Tel: 814-724-8300
Prime rib and delicious pies are the winning combination here; local wines.

🌿 🌿 🌿

Heritage Wine Cellars, Inc.

12162 East Main Road (Route 20)
North East, Pennsylvania 16428
TEL: 814-725-8015
OWNERS: the Bostwick family
WINEMAKER: Robert C. Bostwick
FOUNDED: 1978

AT A GLANCE

Tours & Tastings: Seven days a week, 9–8 (summer), 9–6 (winter), for tours that show pressing operation, fermentation area, bottling line, tasting room, and retail shop.

Vineyards: Over 400 acres on Bostwick family farms amply supply the needs of the winery with vinifera, French hybrids, and American varieties, including the rare Gladwin 113.

Wines: Chardonnay, Sauvignon Blanc, Seyval and Vidal Blancs, Riesling; also Concord, Niagara, Delaware, Dutchess, Gladwin 113. Also produced are fruit wines and sparkling wines with Baskin-Robbins–style names—Plum Crazy, Very Beary Blackberry, and others; also Plum Splash Cooler and Sangria.

Awards: Sangria, Sweet Rosé, Plum Crazy.

Retail Shop: Wines, homemade jellies, handcrafted items—toys, Colonial dolls, Amish quilts. Also tastings and sales at Heritage Wine Cellars, Giant Eagle and Unity Plaza, Latrobe; 1715 Route 286 South, Indiana; and Route 66 between Apollo and Vandergrift, North Vandergrift.

Credit Cards: MasterCard, Visa.

Access for Disabled: Rear entrance to tasting room.

Getting There: Approximately ten miles east of Erie, just off the intersection of Rte. 20 and I-90 (exit 12).

Special Wine & Other Events: Aug. 23–24: Heritage Wine Cellars holds its annual Winefest; nominal entry fee, entertainment, foods, and wine tasting. Participant, last weekend Sept.: Wine Country U.S.A., the toast to the area's wineries.

🌿 Several generations of Bostwicks are involved in Heritage Winery, which draws from the family's 400-acre vineyard, planted on several farms, to make a broad range of wines. It is said to be the only winery producing wine from the hard-to-cultivate Gladwin 113; only ¾ acre is planted to this species in the vast vineyards. The property is in the Lake Erie viticultural area, which stretches

100 miles along the coast and only 5 miles inland.

The winery proper is in a restored eighteenth-century barn. With eight-foot-long black walnut beams (held with wooden pegs) and Colonial decor, it looks nearly as rustic now as it did in its old Dutch-German days.

For accommodations and restaurants, see the end of this section.

ᨦ ᨦ ᨦ

Mazza Vineyards

11815 East Lake Road
North East, Pennsylvania 16428
TEL: 814-725-8695
PRESIDENT/OWNER: Robert Mazza
WINEMAKER: Gary Mosier (courses in
   Geneva, Switzerland)
FOUNDED: 1972

AT A GLANCE
Tours & Tastings: Mon.–Sat. 9–5, Sun. 12–4:30; half hour guided tours supplemented by slide show.
Closed: Christmas, Thanksgiving, and New Year's.
Vineyards: Mazza's grapes and fruits are purchased from local growers.
Wines: Seyval Blanc and Vidal Blanc, Riesling, Cayuga, Catawba, Concord, Niagara, Vidal Ice Wine, Champagne. Also citrus and berry coolers, spiced apple, strawberry wines; bubbling white and rosé, and special holiday wine.
Awards: Ice Wine has merited highest award, while Riesling and Vidal have been close behind.
Retail Shop: On-site and at Mazza Wine Shop, Millcreek Mall, Erie.
Credit Cards: MasterCard, Visa.
Access for Disabled: None.
Foreign Languages: Italian.
Getting There: Fifteen miles east of Erie and six miles from exit 11 off I-90.

Special Wine & Other Events: Labor Day Weekend; Harvest Festival, with grape stomping, hayrides, tasting.

ᨦ Mazza's Mediterranean-style winery toasts both his Italian heritage and the blending of the ancient art of winemaking with modern techniques and equipment. An interesting label on the winery's award-winning ice wine depicts *Winter in Wine Country* by Erie-born artist James E. Sabol, and shows Vidal grapes at harvest and the winery in the background.

TO SEE & DO
An offbeat attraction is Mums by Paschke (12266 East Main Road, North East; tel: 814-725-9860), which all began with a few blossoms in the Paschke family's front yard fifty years ago. Now browsers and buyers come from far and wide to admire acre after acre of 150 varieties of fluffy, colorful mums, the indoor display of 1,200 plants, fresh local fruits, pumpkins, gourds, and Indian corn—all for sale. Horse-and-buggy rides and special attractions on Sundays.

For other local sight-seeing, check with the Niagara Falls Welcome Center, I-90, exit 12, 7 A.M. to 7 P.M., 814-725-5769 seven days a week.

ᨦ ᨦ ᨦ

Penn Shore Vineyards and Winery

10225 East Lake Road
North East, Pennsylvania 16428
TEL: 814-725-8688
OWNERS: George F. Luke, Philip B.
   McCord, George Sceiford
FOUNDED: 1969

AT A GLANCE

Tours & Tastings: Daily June–Oct., Mon.–Sat. 12–6; Nov.–May, Mon.–Sat. 9–5. Sun. 12–6 year-round. Fifteen-minute guided tours; Oct.–May self-guided tours. Photographic display supplements experience. Tastings follow tours, year-round.

Closed: New Year's and Easter.

Vineyards: Buys all grapes from nearby growers.

Wines: Concords; Ravat Blanc, Seyval, and Vidal and other hybrid varietal wines.

Retail Shop: Wines and gifts sold on site.

Access for Disabled: Limited.

Special Wine & Other Events: Participant in wine festival last weekend in September.

Getting There: From North East, go north on Rte. 89 to Rte. 5 and turn left to winery about 1½ miles farther on your left.

🌶 The 175,000 gallon Penn Shore winery is one of state's largest and oldest, having been started shortly after the passage of the Limited Winery Law, which permits wine sales by farm wineries. While the winery's early reputation was built on sweet Concord wines, its newer Signature Vintage label covers premium wines for drier tastes.

🌶 🌶 🌶

Presque Isle Wine Cellars

9440 Buffalo Road
North East, Pennsylvania 16428
TEL: 814-725-1314
OWNERS: Marlene B. & Douglas P. Moorhead
FOUNDED: 1964

AT A GLANCE

Tours & Tastings: Tues.–Sat. 8–5, guided winery tours and tastings. Appointments necessary for vineyard walk.

Closed: Sun. and Mon.

Vineyards: Twenty acres planted to vinifera and hybrid varieties.

Wines: Cabernet Sauvignon, Cabernet Franc, Gewürztraminer, Chardonnay, Seyval, Vidal Blanc, and others.

Picnic Areas: Tables near winery or lawn bordering creek.

Retail Shop: Wines, cheese, winemaking supplies sold on site.

Access for Disabled: None.

Special Wine & Other Events: Participant in wine festival end of September.

Getting There: On Rte. 20, between Harbor Crest and Down East.

🌶 The oldest winery in Pennsylvania and known for excellent vinifera and hybrid varietals, especially Cabernet Sauvignon.

ACCOMMODATIONS

Brown's Village Inn
51 East Main Street
North East, Pennsylvania 16428
Tel: 814-925-5522
A delightful country inn and restaurant, dating back to 1820.

In Westfield, New York (sixty miles east of North East, Pennsylvania)
The William Seward Inn
South Portage Road
Westfield, New York 14787
Tel: 716-326-4151
The residence in 1820 of William Seward, secretary of state under both Lincoln and Andrew Jackson, the house was purchased in 1859 by George Patterson, lieutenant governor of New York. In the

Patterson family for one hundred years, it was moved from town to its present site about twenty-five years ago, renovated, and opened in 1983 as an inn by Barbara and Bruce Johnson. Antiques, some original to the home, have been used to give a period flavor, and there are beautiful Lake Erie views, plus good food and hosts.

RESTAURANT
Dry Dock
3122 Westlake Road
Erie, Pennsylvania 16505
Tel: 814-853-6145
Seafood, mesquite-grilled foods, and fresh pasta in a nautical setting.

5
The Southern States

❧

Biltmore Estate, Asheville, North Carolina

❧**A**labama, Arkansas, Florida, Georgia, Louisiana, Mississippi, North Carolina, Tennessee, Virginia, West Virginia? Will any of these ten states ever challenge the Napa Valley when it comes to winemaking? Probably not. Yet southern winemakers have not been dozing in the sun—they are producing premium wines. Much of the output is minuscule compared to California's output—a few hundred cases rather than many thousands. Distribution may go no farther than the county in which they are made—or even the winery itself.

That does not mean everything produced here is unknown. During the last decade, a number of southern wines have captured wide attention among the world's wine connoisseurs. This acclaim is hardly new: winemaking stretches back to the New World's first settlers, as you'll see as we take a state-by-state look at the area's vineyards and wineries.

❧ ALABAMA

Alabama's fledgling wine industry did not get its start until 1979, when The Native Farm Wine Act was passed by the state legislature. That act allows a winery owner to bottle a maximum of 100,000 gallons of wine a year, providing 75 percent of the fruit used is the farmer's own and alcohol content is not more than 14 percent. Before that, winemaking in Alabama was a hobby, with the product made and consumed at home.

The routes to these wineries abound with both urban and bucolic sights in and about Birmingham.

SOUTHERN
STATES

❧ ❧ ❧

Braswell's Winery

7556 Bankhead Highway
Dora, Alabama 35062
TEL: 205-648-8335
OWNER/WINEMAKER: Loy Wayne
  Braswell
FOUNDED: 1984

AT A GLANCE

Tours & Tastings: Tues.–Sat. 11–7;
"tour" is a videotaped presentation on
winemaking.
Closed: Sun. and Mon.
Vineyards: 207 acres owned, planted to
native American grapes, Muscadine,
Scuppernong, Niagara, Concord; also
berries, fruits.
Wines: Table wines from above grapes;
berry and fruit wines.
Awards: Scuppernong, plum and straw-
berry wines have won silver and bronze
medals respectively in southeast compe-
titions.
Retail Shop: All wines are sold on-site.
Credit Cards: None.
Access for Disabled: None.
Foreign Languages: None.
Getting There: Winery is twenty-five
miles west of Birmingham on Bankhead
Hwy., three miles south of Sumiton, in
Jefferson County.
Special Wine & Other Events: In Bir-
mingham: Festival of Arts, mid-April;
Summerfest, July & Aug.; Baseball (Bar-
ons) in season.

❧ As a boy, Wayne Braswell learned
to make blackberry wine from his part-
Cherokee grandmother. A wine hobbyist
for forty years, he went commercial in
1984. His winery is housed in what had
been the private nightclub he and his
wife, Ruth, ran for eighteen years.

TO SEE & DO

Birmingham is sight-seeing territory and
the site of one of the country's most unusual attractions—the Sloss Furnace (beside First Avenue North viaduct,
entrance at 32nd Street North; tel:
205-324-1911; open Tues.–Fri. 10–4, Sat.
10–4, Sun 12–4), which marks the town's
rich industrial heritage and is listed on
the National Register of Historic Places
as the only example of early twentieth-
century iron-making preserved today.
The idea is to explore an industrial plant
and see how it works. At Vulcan Park,
atop Red Mountain (open daily 8–10:30
P.M.; tel: 205-328-6198), iron ore is on
display—and so is a spectacular view of
the surrounding area. A leading local
landmark is the beautiful Arlington
Antebellum Home and Gardens, circa
1850, Victorian furnished (331 Cotton
Avenue, Southwest; Tues.–Sat. 9–4:30,
Sat. 1–4:30, open year-round; tel:
205-780-5656). In and about the area, big
is in: the Botanical Gardens (2612 Park
Lane Road; open daily, sunrise to sunset;
tel: 205-879-1227) claims the biggest conservatory in the Southeast, and Riverchase Galleria (south of Birmingham, in
Hoover, intersection I-459 & U.S. 31
South) boasts of the world's biggest enclosed atrium and longest skylight (it
stretches nearly one-quarter of a mile)
covering 188 shops and stores, cafés, and
court. So large is the fountain near the
entrance that when drained it can be
used as an amphitheater. Big, too, is
the Birmingham Museum of Art (2000
8th Avenue North; open Tues.–Sat.
10–5; Thurs. 10–9, Sun. 12–6; tel:
205-254-2565). The Southeast's largest
municipal art center, it houses the Kress
collection of Renaissance art as well as
some excellent Remington bronzes. Racing fans should note that the Turf Club
(East Birmingham, U.S. 11 and I-20, near
I-459), features races 180 days a year,
Tues.–Sat., on a relatively new $64.5-mil-
lion-dollar track. For details, contact
Greater Birmingham Convention and
Visitors Bureau, 2027 First Avenue
North; tel: 205-252-9825.

ACCOMMODATIONS
Birmingham Bed & Breakfast
P.O. Box 31328
Birmingham, Alabama 35222
Tel: 205-591-6406
Bed and breakfast homes in and around
Birmingham.

The Mountain Brook Inn
2800 U.S. Highway 280 South
Birmingham, Alabama 35223
Tel: 205-870-3100; 800-523-7771
A well-equipped hotel with special weekend packages. One hundred sixty-two
rooms; moderate rates.

The Tutwiler Hotel
Park Place and 21 Street North
Birmingham, Alabama 35203
Tel: 205-322-2100; 800-228-0808
Handsomely restored historic hotel.

**The Wynfrey Hotel at Riverchase
   Galleria**
1000 Riverchase Galleria
Birmingham, Alabama 35244
Tel: 205-987-1600; 800-522-5282
New seventeen-story luxury hotel with
all amenities set amid 188 shops and gal-
leries.

ADD ARKANSAS

As far back as the early 1800s, Swiss and German immigrants found Arkansas
soil conditions compatible with grape growing for winemaking. The wineries
described below are run by descendants of some of those early wine pioneers.
Visiting them is just one reason you'll enjoy yourself on this wine route along
the Arkansas River. Beyond their pleasures is the chance to lose yourself for a
time in the beautiful Ozark Mountains.

ADD ADD ADD

Cowie Wine Cellars Inc.

Route 2, Box 799
Paris, Arkansas 72855
TEL: 501-963-3990
PRESIDENT/WINEMAKER: Robert G.
   Cowie
FOUNDED: 1967

AT A GLANCE
Tours & Tastings: Mon.–Sat. 9 to dusk;
show and explain Cowie's methods of
winemaking.
Closed: Sun.
Vineyards: Two acres leased and planted
to native American species; the remain-
ing grapes and fruits are purchased in
Arkansas.
Wines: Cynthiana, Dry Niagara, Bur-

gundy, Muscadine, Catawba; also straw-
berry, wild plum, and Mead.
Awards: Cynthiana and Dry Niagara
have won medals.
Retail Shop: Wines, winemaking and
beermaking supplies.
Credit Cards: None.
Access for Disabled: None.
Foreign Languages: None.
Getting There: Winery is three miles west
of Paris on Hwy. 22.
Special Wine & Other Events: In Aug.:
Arkansas Championship Grape Stomp, a
crowd-pleaser with arts and crafts, rides
for kids, bluegrass band. Also Annual
Grape Stomp on steps of Capitol in Little
Rock. In spring: local winemakers' wines
are judged at the Arkansas Amateur
Wine Competition. The town of Paris
hosts Mount Magazine Frontier Days
each Oct.

◆ This story starts in the 1800s, when the Cowies' great-great-uncle Joseph Bachman moved from Switzerland to Altus and dedicated himself to propagating new varieties of grapes from native American species. Bachman's early wine creations included a silver prize and citation winner at the Louisiana Purchase Exposition in 1904.

Today, the Cowies' family-run cellars at Paris continue to produce notable wines from native grapes. Their attractive stone-and-cedar winery is nestled in a pine grove. Inside, the handsome stained-glass window, created by a Benedictine monk, is just one of the attractions awaiting visitors. They also come to see the unusual "Gallery of Barrels," depicting the family's history hand-painted on barrel heads. Among the eleven Cowie wines are limited editions, with labels designed by local artist Susan Morrison.

TO SEE & DO
Survey the surroundings from Mount Magazine; at 2,753 feet it's the highest mountain in Arkansas in the Ozark National Forest. And take time for a serenity break with a visit to the Subiaco Benedictine Abbey in Subiaco, built with Roman-style arches by early Swiss settlers.

ACCOMMODATIONS
For more information, contact the Chamber of Commerce, 613 Garrison Avenue, Fort Smith, Arkansas 72901 Tel: 501-763-6118.

The People's Motel
Paris, Arkansas 72855
Tel: 501-963-2161
In Clarksville, sixteen miles east of Paris. Basic motel.

Bed & Breakfast of Arkansas Ozarks
Route 1 (Box 38)
Calico Rock, Arkansas 72519
Tel: 501-297-8764

Bed and breakfast recommendations for the Ozarks area, including Fort Smith, with easy access to wineries.

◆ ◆ ◆

Post Familie Vineyard & Winery

Route 1, Box I
Highway 186
Altus, Arkansas 72821
TEL: 501-468-2741
PRESIDENT: Mathew Post, Sr.
FOUNDED: 1880

AT A GLANCE
Tours & Tastings: Mon.–Sat. 8–7; tastings, sales. Tours Mon.–Sat. 10–4, upon request, start in fermenting and production area and go through storage and bottling, end up in tasting room.
Closed: Sun., Christmas, Election Day.
Vineyards: 150 acres planted in Altus v.a. on St. Mary's Mount, to Chardonnay, Seyval, Aurora, Delaware, Villard Catawba, Ives, Niagara, Carlos, and Noble.
Wines: Over twenty varieties from native American and French-American hybrid grapes. Included are estate-bottled, vintage-dated Seyval Blanc, Ives Noir, and Cynthiana; Burgundy, Catawba. Also sherry, port, and champagne; non-alcoholic Muscadine juice.
Awards: Silver to reds Cynthiana and Ives Noir; bronzes to Aurora Blanc, Pink Catawba, and Niagara.
Retail Shop: Wines and juices sold on-site.
Credit Cards: None.
Access for Disabled: Yes, tours and tastings and bathroom.
Foreign Languages: None.
Getting There: Forty miles east of Fort Smith. The winery is one block north of Hwy. 64 in Altus, on Hwy. 168. From Texarkana in the south or Fayetteville in the north: Hwy. 23, one of the most spectacularly scenic roads in the country, runs through the Ozark National Forest

into Hwy. 64 at the Ozark turnoff to the winery. It's also one hundred miles west of Little Rock via I-40.

Special Wine & Other Events: First Sat. in Aug.: Annual Grape Festival; First Sat. in May: Altus Springtime Gala; third Sat. in Aug.: Ole' Fashun Square Gathering; mid-Sept. to Nov. 5: fall foliage tours into Ozark Mountains.

&❧ Five generations of Posts continue a family tradition of harvesting grapes and making wine, begun in 1880 by Jacob Post, a German immigrant and founder of Altus viticulture. He sold the first Altus wines from his cellar to passengers on the Iron Mountain Railroad when the trains halted near his farm for fuel and water. The estate-bottled wines are now grown in vineyards atop St. Mary's Mount in the Altus v.a., and the latest technology is combined with old-fashioned methodology to produce them.

(For To See & Do and Accommodations, see after Cowie Cellars.)

❧ ❧ ❧

Wiederkehr Wine Cellars

Champagne Drive
Route 1, Box 14
Altus, Arkansas 72821
TEL: 501-468-2611
OWNERS: The Wiederkehr family
FOUNDED: 1880

AT A GLANCE
Tours & Tastings: 9–4:30 Mon.–Sat. Thirty-minute tour; covers modern winery and old cellar, production methods, and ends in the tasting room with film on historic highlights. Vineyard tour is self-guided and offers superb views of the Arkansas River Valley.
Closed: Sun.
Vineyards: 350 acres planted to native American and French-American hybrids and vinifera varieties.

Wines: Of the approximate 2 million gallons produced, 75 percent are still table wines, about 15 percent sparkling, and 10 percent are fortified and fruit wines. Among the best-known wines from Wiederkehr are vintage-dated Johannisberg Riesling, Gewürztraminer; proprietary Muscato di Tanta Maria, and Hans Wiederkehr Extra Dry Champagne.

Restaurant: Weinkeller, Swiss-American menu; Mon.–Sat., lunch, 11–3, dinner, 5–10. Die Trauben Stube, cocktail lounge; 5–1 A.M., entertainment Wed., Sat.
Retail Shop: Wines, gift shop.
Credit Cards: None.
Access for Disabled: Yes.
Getting There: From Fort Smith: Take I-40 East to exit 41; then follow signs on Hwy. 186 to Wiederkehr.
Special Wine & Other Events: Weinfest is first two weekends in October; Christmas tree lighting and New Year's Eve celebrated. Call for details.

❧ The oldest and largest winery in the South, Wiederkehr Wine Cellars' chalets on the southern slopes of the Ozarks might look at home in the Swiss Alps. Wiederkehr is now in the hands of the third generation of its Swiss founders, Johann Andreas Wiederkehr. In 1880, he excavated the original wine cellar, today listed in the National Register of Historic Places, and built what is now the winery restaurant.

TO SEE & DO
In Ozark wine country along the Arkansas River, flowery meadows and fertile pastures give way to vineyards in an area widely known for its scenic beauty. With an abundance of lakes and streams, outdoor recreational activities include fishing on Ozark Lake and white-water

rafting on Mulberry River. I-23 goes through the immense Ozark National Forest, a favorite for hiking and other outdoor activities.

ACCOMMODATIONS
Fort Smith offers many selections, or choose a bed and breakfast. See "Ac-commodations" following Cowie Wine Cellars for helpful addresses.

RESTAURANTS
See Wiederkehr Wine Cellars.

❧ FLORIDA

The first wines in America were produced in 1562 in north Florida by early French Huguenot settlers from the native southern Scuppernong grapes. Later, in the 1830s, a handful of French colonists followed the Marquis de Lafayette to a small parcel of land deeded to him by the fifth U.S. president, James Monroe, where they planted the grape vines now entwined in Florida's history.

By the 1880s experimentation with native American grapes by a French-born vintner, Emile DuBois of Tallahassee's San Luis Vineyards, put Florida wines in the spotlight. Today considered one of the outstanding early innovators of the American wine industry, DuBois planted over 150 varieties of grapes for still wines, sparkling wines, brandies, and cordials. By 1889, at the peak of his 4,000-gallon production, his wines rivaled the best in France and indeed received numerous medals at the 1892 Paris Exposition. DuBois's fame lasted until 1904, when a local ordinance prohibiting the sale of alcohol in the county shut him down. He then moved to New Jersey and eventually returned to France. Florida boasts also of having been home in the 1800s to one of the few early women vineyardists, M. Martin of Hermitage.

❧ ❧ ❧

Lafayette Vineyards and Winery, Ltd.

6505 Mahan Drive
Tallahassee, Florida 32308
TEL: 904-878-9041
PRESIDENT: C. Cary Cox, general partner
WINEMAKER: Jeanne Burgess
FOUNDED: 1982

AT A GLANCE
Tours & Tastings: March–Aug., Mon.–Sat. 10–6; Sept.–Feb., Tues.–Sat. 10–6; year-round, Sun. 12–6. Self-guided tours include slide presentation and look at winemaking from a wide walkway about twenty feet above the winery. Tastings with or without a tour. Vineyards can be seen from balcony. Tastings follow tour. **Closed:** Mon., Sept.–Feb.; Christmas, Thanksgiving.
Vineyards: Thirty-eight-acre vineyard planted to native American, French hybrids. Experimental acreage to Chenin Blanc and Cabernet Sauvignon. Additional grapes purchased from Florida growers.
Wines: Varietals—Stover, Suwannee, Blanc du Bois, white and red Muscadine; also, Nouveau Muscadine Nobel, Plantation white (a Muscadine blend) and

Blanc de Fleur (nonvintage sparkling wine made from Muscadine Magnolia and Florida-hybrid Stover).

Awards: Oft-awarded in international, Florida, and other-states-sponsored competitions: White Muscadine, sweet and semi-sweet; Stover Special Reserves; Blanc de Fleur; and Plantation White.

Picnic Area: On the grounds.

Retail Shop: Wines, gifts.

Credit Cards: MasterCard, Visa.

Access for Disabled: Ground-level retail shop for tasting and slide presentation.

Foreign Languages: None.

Special Wine & Other Events: In March, at winery: Good Life Celebration; Apr., in town: Springtime in Tallahassee; Nov., at fair grounds; Market Days.

Getting There: About one mile west of exit 31A off I-10. Can be reached by taxi from town. Miccosukee Rd., a designated bicycle trail, goes to the winery. Bikes can be rented at Rainbow Bikes (631 W. Tennessee, tel: 904-222-1021), Great Bicycle Shops (210 W. College Ave., tel: 904-224-9090; 1910 Thomasville Rd., tel: 904-224-7461; and 916 Lake Bradford Rd., tel: 904-575-7217).

&♣ This winery sits in the rolling hills and mossy oaks north of Tallahassee. Its eastern edge adjoins the original Lafayette land grant, thus the name. The winery's charming French Provincial architecture honors its Gallic roots, while crushed coquina shells and coral fragments embedded in the stucco finish pay tribute to Florida. Winemaker Jeanne Burgess, trained in enology at Mississippi State, disarmingly assigns her wines such personalities as "vivacious and flamboyant."

TO SEE & DO

Tying right in to wine history is the San Luis Mission, formerly the site of wine pioneer Dubois's winery and vineyards (open Mon.–Fri. 10–5, Sun. 12–4; closed Sat.; tel: 904-488-1484). A bumper crop of other historic sights include the Museum of Florida History, which incorporates a slice of town including the old state Capitol, old Union Bank, and more. At each site, visitors learn something about the building's past and its relationship to Florida history. For a brochure and map, stop at the museum in the Gray Building (tel: 904-488-1484). Restored homes on East Park Avenue and Calhoun Street and Pebble Hill Plantation (Thomasville) should also be on the agenda.

ACCOMMODATIONS

Governor's Inn
209 South Adams
Tallahassee, Florida 32301
Tel: 904-681-6855
Forty-one luxurious rooms, some with antiques, four-poster beds, fireplaces.

Wakulla Springs and Lodge
Wakulla Springs, Florida 32305
Tel: 904-224-5950
The hospitality of an old southern hotel in a scenic jungle location with glass-bottom boat cruises over Wakulla Falls. Eleven miles south of Tallahassee.

Susina Plantation
Route 3, Box 1010
Meridian Road (S.R. 155)
Thomasville, Georgia 31792
Tel: 912-377-9644
Eight suites, in old plantation house on 115 acres. Tennis courts, swimming pool, fishing, jogging, horseback riding. Rates include breakfast and dinner with wine. Twenty-two miles north of Tallahassee.

RESTAURANTS
All in Tallahassee.

Andrew's 2nd Act
Adams Street Cafe
Andrew's Upstairs
228 South Adams
Tallahassee, Florida 32301

Tel: 904-222-3446
These three restaurants share a building, while offering different dining experiences. Upstairs' new American menu features pizzas and southwestern dishes and an extensive all-American wine list. 2nd Act's Continental menu offers sauce-topped entrées, flambéd desserts, and a wine list from local to imported vintages; Cafe, open at lunch, serves sandwiches and light meals.

Anthony's
1950-G Thomasville Road
Tel: 904-224-1447
Italian foods.

Chez Pierre
115 North Adams Street
Tel: 904-222-0936
French cuisine. Delicious soups and luscious desserts. Gourmet shop on same site with wines, cheeses, other delicacies.

Cross Creek Restaurant
6737 Mahan Drive
Tel: 904-877-4130
Southern homestyle cooking; cobblers, pies.

San Carlos Winery

112 South 3rd Street
Fernandina Beach, Florida 32034
TEL: 904-277-3236
OWNERS: James R. and Karen A.
  Gildenston
WINEMAKER: James R. Gildenston
FOUNDED: 1985

AT A GLANCE
Tours & Tastings: 10–5 Mon.–Sat. Includes a look at a streamlined winemaking operation, followed by tasting. Evenings by appointment.
Closed: Sun., Christmas, New Year's, and Thanksgiving.

Vineyards: Native American Muscadines purchased from Florida growers.
Wines: Welder (Bronze Muscadine) for whites; Noble (Black Muscadine) for reds.
Awards: Silver to dry red and bronze to semi-dry reds.
Retail Shop: Wines sold on-site.
Credit Cards: MasterCard, Visa.
Access for Disabled: None.
Foreign Languages: None.
Getting There: Fernandina Beach is approximately thirty-five miles north of Jacksonville. By boat, it is the first stop in Florida on the Intracoastal Waterway, going south; winery is within walking distance of the marina. By car: Take I-95 to Fernandina Beach/Callahan/Amelia Island exit on A1A to Fernandina Beach. For walkers, the winery is a little over a block from Centre St. in Fernandina Beach.
Special Wine & Other Events: On Amelia Island: in Apr., women's tennis tournament; Sept., DuPont All-American Tennis Tournament; first weekend in May, at Fernandina Beach, Shrimp Festival, art show, seafood, crafts.

The Gildenstons arrived in 1976 aboard their ketch and decided to drop anchor for good at Fernandina Beach. They took up professional winemaking in 1985 after some years of experimentation, and now have a winery capacity of 4,000 gallons. The winery's name is derived from historic Fort San Carlos, built by the Spanish in 1816 on a bluff overlooking Amelia Bay. The wood fort and tall ships appear on the San Carlos label.

TO SEE & DO
Fernandina Beach, settled in 1686, has a thirty-block downtown area listed on the National Register of Historic Places; the Palace Saloon is Florida's oldest saloon. The Florida Museum of Transportation and History, South 3rd Street, has tours Monday through Friday at 11 and 2.

ACCOMMODATIONS
The Bailey House
28 South 7th Street
Fernandina Beach, Florida 32034
Tel: 904-261-5390
An 1895 Queen Anne Victorian, ornamented with turrets and stained glass, and decorated with period antiques.

1735 House
584 South Fletcher
Amelia Island, Florida 32034
Tel: 904-261-5878
Charming country inn with cheerful rattan and wicker furniture, antiques. Continental breakfast.

The Seaside Inn
1998 South Fletcher
Amelia Island, Florida 32034
Tel: 904-261-9084
A moderately priced B&B.

Amelia Island Plantation
800 Amelia Parkway South
Amelia Island, Florida 32034
Tel: 904-261-6161; 800-874-6878
A 1,300-acre luxury resort with 500 villas, 17 swimming pools, 24 tennis courts, 27 holes golf.

❧ GEORGIA

The wine industry in this state, important in the early 1900s, was born again in 1983. To visit Chickamauga, in the northwest corner of Georgia, the road passes ancient rock formations standing as sentinels above the flower-filled valleys, perfect views of the Appalachians; heading for Baldwin, in northeast Georgia, you'll find a treasury for handicrafts and a Bavarian-style village.

❧ ❧ ❧

Georgia Wines Inc.

Route 3 (P.O. Box 98-P)
Chickamauga, Georgia 30707
TEL: 404-931-2851
PRESIDENT/WINEMAKER: Dr. Maurice S. Rawlings
FOUNDED: 1983

AT A GLANCE
Tours & Tastings: Fri. 4–7, Sat. 12–5. Tasting Center (on I-75) at the KOA campground on Georgia 2A (Battlefield Pkwy.) open daily Mon.–Sat. 11–6.
Closed: Sun., holidays.
Vineyards: Fifty-four acres, planted to five varieties of Muscadines and two French hybrids. Some grapes purchased from vineyards in Tennessee, New York, California.

Wines: Over 10,000 gallons are produced, each wine incorporating vineyard-grown grapes with others from more distant points. Included are Muscadines, Rieslings, Niagaras, Catawba, Chenin Blanc, Zinfandel, Concord, Alwood, and Cabernet Sauvignon. Unusual are two champagnes made, respectively, of blended Rieslings and Muscadines. Some peach wines are also produced.
Awards: Every wine has won an award at one time or another. Highest placer is White Muscadine, which brought home the gold at the Atlanta International Wine Festival when a panel of seventy-two judges evaluated it against 1,000 white varietals. Zinfandel, made from California grapes, has been judged superior to California's when entered in an Atlanta International Wine Festival.
Retail Shop: Wines sold at winery and

tasting center in KOA campground. Home winemaking supplies at winery.
Credit Cards: None.
Access for Disabled: Yes.
Foreign Languages: German, French.
Getting There: Twelve miles south of Chattanooga and Rock City on Chattanooga Valley Rd., Hwy. 193. From Lafayette: take Hwy. 136 West to Hwy 193 and turn north; three miles to winery. To get to KOA campground tasting center: Take Hwy. 193 from winery to Battlefield Pkwy. (Georgia 2A), turn east to exit 141 and you'll see the tasting center on I-75. Accessible by taxis and bus.
Special Wine & Other Events: Octoberfest, Springfest (Apr.); seminars at various times.

✺ Dr. Maurice S. Rawlings, specialist in cardiovascular diseases, assistant clinical professor at the University of Tennessee, and author of a number of medical and philosophical books, has apparently come up with the right prescription for wines made primarily from native American grapes. He began in 1983 by producing 1,000 gallons of wine in his mountainside winery, and now he produces over 11,000 gallons. All wines are hand bottled, hand corked, and made with water from the subterranean depths of Lookout Mountain. The winery, a southern farm cabin made of railway ties, is on the lower slopes of this mountain.

TO SEE & DO
Chug on over to Chattanooga to visit the Tennessee Valley Railroad Museum (4119 Cromwell Rd.; tel: 615-894-8028), the site of the Fall Color Cruise through the Grand Canyon of the Tennessee River in October. Before heading off, however, lace up your hiking boots and head over to the Chickamauga National Park (U.S. 27, year-round, closed Christmas), where fifty miles of hiking trails await. This, the nation's oldest and largest military park, recalls the Civil War battle that left 35,000 casualties in 1863. In downtown Chickamauga there's more Civil War memorabilia in the Gordon-Lee Mansion, a makeshift hospital during the worst days of the war, and in many other buildings listed on the National Register of Historic Places. Now marching ahead as did Sherman to Atlanta, make a stop at Rock City (daily, except Christmas, 8:30–sundown), atop Lookout Mountain astride the Georgia-Tennessee border (in sight of I-24, I-59, I-75), for a sweeping view of the Appalachians and rock formations. Lookout Mountain's Flight Park for hang gliding (off Scenic Hwy. 189) welcomes spectators (tel: 404-398-3549 for driving instructions).

ACCOMMODATIONS
Johnson's Scenic Court
Scenic Highway
Lookout Mountain, Tennessee 37350
Tel: 404-820-2000
Two miles from Rock City, with seven-state view. Complimentary breakfast. Pool and tennis courts.

For more accommodations in the Northwest Georgia Mountains, contact Northwest Georgia Mountains Travel Association, P.O. Box 169, Mt. Berry, Georgia 30139, Tel: 414-291-1883, or choose sophisticated surroundings in Chattanooga. For more information, contact the Chattanooga Convention & Visitors Bureau, 1001 Market Street, Chattanooga, Tennessee 37402, Tel: 615-756-8887.

✺ ✺ ✺

Habersham Vineyards and Winery

P.O. Box 426
Highway 365
Baldwin, Georgia 30511
TEL: 404-778-5845
PRESIDENT: Tom Slick
FOUNDED: 1983

Tours & Tastings: Usually 10–4 Mon.–Sat., but you are advised to phone in advance.
Closed: Sun., some holidays and election days.
Vineyards: Thirty acres owned, eight acres leased; planted to vinifera and French-American hybrids; some fruits and juices purchased from other growers in and out of Georgia.
Wines: Chardonnay, Riesling, Sauvignon Blanc, Seyval, Vidal, white Muscadine, blush, Pinot Noir, Cabernet Sauvignon, all under the Habersham label; Etowah Ridges label on generics.
Awards: Whites are generally front-runners here, especially the white Muscadine, which has consistently brought home the gold from the Atlanta International Wine Festival; another high placer has been Vidal; in the reds, Cabernet Sauvignon has been a silver medalist.
Retail Shop: Wines sold on-site.
Credit Cards: MasterCard, Visa.
Access for Disabled: None.
Foreign Languages: None.
Getting There: Winery is four miles south of Cornelia, twenty miles north of Gainesville on Hwy. 365 (I-985); forty-one miles from I-85. From Atlanta: Take I-985; north of Gainesville it becomes Hwy. 385. From Athens, or Commerce, take U.S. 441 North. From Clayton or Tallulah Falls: Take U.S. 441 south. U.S. 441 has access to Hwy. 365 in either direction.
Special Wine & Other Events: Georgia Mountain Fair at Hiwasee, northwest of Habersham Winery, offers a colorful experience (take U.S. 141 to U.S. 76 and turn west; tel: 404-896-4191). At Helen (take Hwy. 365 to Rte. 17 West), a winter carnival, hot-air balloon races, and Oktoberfest are main attractions.

ख In the Blue Ridge Mountains, Habersham makes a dozen or so wines patterned along European styles but with a regional flavor.
Another northeastern winery:

ख ख ख

Chateau Elan, Ltd.

Route 1, Box 563-1
Hoschton, Georgia 30548
TEL: 404-867-8200; 800-233-WINE
FOUNDED: 1984
Extensive vineyards planted to vinifera and French hybrids. Best known for whites, especially Chardonnay. Open Mon.–Sat. 10–4.

TO SEE & DO
Outdoor activities abound in this northeast mountain region. Hike along the rugged Appalachian Trail, raft the turbulent white water, or explore undeveloped wilderness areas. For the less adventuresome, the town of Helen (Hwy. 365 to Hwys. 105 and 17) re-creates a corner of Bavaria in Georgia with alpine-style architecture, *biergartens,* and typical crafts. (See above for special events in Helen.) The Quinlan Arts Center (U.S. 129 and Hwy. 80), near Gainesville, houses traveling exhibits of local, regional, and national art (Mon.–Fri. 10–12, 1–4; Sun. 2–4). Fall's artistry paints the leaves spectacularly, especially along the Richard Russell Scenic Highway (runs south of Blairsville, via U.S. 19 and U.S. 129 on Hwy. 180 to designated Hwy. 348; 14.1 miles), elevations 2,040 to 3,644 feet.

ACCOMMODATIONS
The Dunlap House
635 Green Street
Gainesville, Georgia 30501
Tel: 404-236-0200
Historic luxury B&B inn, with fine restaurant across street; see Rudolph's under "Restaurants."

Hilltop Haus
P.O. Box 154
Chattahoochee Street
Helen, Georgia 30545
Tel: 404-878-2388
Contemporary home with scenic location, fireplaces, and wood-paneled walls. Homemade preserves with hot biscuits accompany hearty breakfast.

Helendorf River Inn
P.O. Box 305
Main Street, right before the bridge
Helen, Georgia 30545
Tel: 404-878-2271
Bavarian-accented interiors with Chattahoochee views.

Tanglewood Resort Cabins
Chimney Mountain Road
P.O. Box 435
Helen, Georgia 30545
Tel: 404-878-3286
Fully furnished, secluded cabins in mountain forest setting with deck and picnic tables.

RESTAURANT
Rudolph's on Green Street
700 Green Street
Gainesville, Georgia 30503
Tel: 404-534-2666
Restored historic home, with creative American cuisine. Lunch, dinner, or Sunday brunch. Same ownership as the Dunlap House (see "Accommodations").

❧ LOUISIANA

Les Orangers Louisiana Ltd.

Highway 23 North
Port Sulphur, Louisiana 70083
TEL: 501-564-2929
OWNER/PRESIDENT: Hazel Solis
FOUNDED: 1981

AT A GLANCE
Tours & Tastings: Includes the log cabin winery, beautiful orange grove, and a walk on the levee to see ocean ships go by, plus a tasting; 10–5, Oct.–Jan. Call in advance is advised.
Closed: Feb.–Sept.
Grove: Fifteen acres growing world-famous Louisiana Navel Oranges.
Wines: Orange wine, fermented with added sugar.
Retail Shop: The Antiques Cabin; sells wine and gifts.
Credit Cards: Discover, MasterCard, Visa
Access for Disabled: None.
Foreign Languages: French.
Getting There: About forty-five miles south of New Orleans. From New Orleans: take the ferry at Canal Street or Jackson Avenue, or cross the Mississippi on the Greater New Orleans Bridge. Head south on Hwy. 23 through the towns of Algiers, Gretha, Belle Chase, Myrtle Grove, City Prive, and Happy Jack.
Special Wine & Other Events: First weekend in Dec.: Plaquemines Parish Orange Festival & Fair in historic old Fort Jackson, on the Mississippi River, about fifteen miles south of Les Orangers; attracts 25,000 visitors each year.

❧ Originally part of a 2,700-acre land-grant given in 1790 by the king of Spain to Juan Ronquillo, the present orange grove dates back to 1902, when it was planted by Ovide Marcel Solis, a farmer and the great-great-grandson of Manuel Solis, one of Louisiana's first riverboat pilots. Keeping traditional orange wine-making thriving today is owner Hazel Solis, one of Ovide's four daughters. The tiny winery is located in an old log cabin.

ACCOMMODATIONS

It seems doubtful that visitors would seek accommodation in Port Sulphur when New Orleans is but forty-five miles away. However, should there be overnight plans in mind, try:

Palm Terrace Hotel
Highway 23
Port Sulphur, Louisiana 70083
Tel: 504-564-2567
Twenty-five-room motel.

RESTAURANTS

Sig's Antique Restaurant
Port Sulphur, Louisiana 70083
Excellent steaks.

Buddy's Seafood Restaurant
Port Sulphur, Louisiana 70083
Good food, good value; plenty of local color. Two miles south of winery.

❧ MISSISSIPPI

The wine industry was reborn here in 1977 and flourishes now. Routes to the vineyards offer views of the fertile, moss-hung marshlands of the Mississippi Delta country and the historic city of Natchez, with 500 well-preserved antebellum mansions.

❧ ❧ ❧

Claiborne Vineyards

302 North Highway 49W (P.O. Box 350)
Indianola, Mississippi 38751
TEL: 601-887-2327
OWNER: Claiborne Barnwell
FOUNDED: 1984

AT A GLANCE

Tours & Tastings: Tastings most Sats. and at other times by appointment. Personalized tours of this small vineyard give visitors a true feeling of what goes into making wines by traditional European methods.
Vineyards: Five acres planted to French hybrids and vinifera varieties.
Wines: Seyval Blanc, Baco Noir, Cabernet Sauvignon, Chardonnay, Sauvignon Blanc.
Retail Shop: Wines sold on-premises.
Credit Cards: American Express, MasterCard, Visa.
Access for Disabled: None.
Foreign Languages: None.

Getting There: One-half mile north of intersection of Hwy. 49 and Hwy. 82.
Special Wine & Other Events: Spring Crawfish Festival at Moorhead. Early Apr. Catfish Festival at Balzoni.

❧ Claiborne Barnwell's tiny winery is located in an old southern plantation commissary; he is a nephew of Craig Claiborne, former *New York Times* food editor and well-known cookbook author.

❧ ❧ ❧

Old South Winery

508 Concord Street
Natchez, Mississippi 39120
TEL: 601-445-9924
OWNER: Dr. Scott O. Galbreath, Jr.
FOUNDED: 1979

AT A GLANCE

Tours & Tastings: Short tour of winery 10–6 daily, followed by tastings with complimentary wine and cheese. Groups by appointment only; $3 per person.

Vineyards: Thirteen acres planted to Muscadine hybrids Carlos (white) and nobel (red) in acreage near winery as well as thirty miles east.

Wines: Twelve different wines, including dry and sweet varietals and generics, all under the Old South label.

Awards: Often awarded: Miss Carlos Dry; others have been Miss Scarlet (sweet wine), Carlos (semi-dry), Southern Belle (sweet white), and Sweet Magnolia (a sweet white blend).

Retail Shop: All wines sold on-premises.

Credit Cards: Cash or check only.

Access for Disabled: Winery is on one level.

Foreign Languages: None.

Getting There: Winery is right in Natchez; just go north on Concord Street.

Special Wine & Other Events: The "Pilgrimage" or "open house" is an old Mississippi rite of spring in early March to early Apr. In Natchez, the Pilgrimage is also held during the first two weeks of Oct. and is coordinated with other activities showing local cultural and artistic attractions.

&. Galbreath ancestors brought Muscadine vines from South Carolina to Mississippi in the 1800s. The century-old tradition of winemaking now includes three of the Galbreath children, who studied enology at Mississippi State University. The winery is a major Natchez tourist attraction, and the wines are attracting attention in national competitions (but are available only locally).

TO SEE & DO

More than 500 antebellum homes survive in Natchez because the city, being of no military importance, was barely touched by the Civil War. Some grand mansions, such as Stanton, are open year-round; others welcome visitors only during the twice-a-year Pilgrimages. Beyond Natchez to the north, from Fayette to Washington, is the most scenic stretch of the memorable pine-and-oak-lined Natchez Trace Parkway. At one time an Indian trail that connected Natchez with Choctaw and Chickasaw villages, the parkway now offers sightings of Indian mounds from bygone days.

ACCOMMODATIONS

If you plan a Pilgrimage visit, contact Natchez Pilgrimage Tours, Canal Street Depot, Natchez, Tennessee 39120 (tel: 601-466-6631; 800-647-6743), which represents seven antebellum bed and breakfasts and offers a tour of four antebellum homes, full breakfast, and lunch at Carnegie House Restaurant for a package price.

The Burn
712 North Union Street
Natchez, Mississippi 39120
Tel: 601-442-1344
A Greek Revival mansion, dating from 1832, with handsomely restored spacious rooms, and such gracious touches as lovely china and gleaming silver at meals. On three acres, with pool, patio, and camellia garden.

Natchez Eola Hotel
110 North Pearl Street
Natchez, Mississippi 39120
Tel: 601-445-6000
Built in 1927 and recently renovated with appropriate old southern ambience. Located in the center of town; a luxury accommodation. Good food and a grand view from the rooftop bar/lounge.

Monmouth Plantation
P.O. Box 1736
36 Melrose Avenue
Natchez, Mississippi 39120
Tel: 601-442-4852
Dates from 1818; combines authentic period decor and furniture with all the modern comforts, such as air-conditioning. Big breakfast and complimen-

tary wine and snacks in the afternoon. Old slave quarters are now a museum.

፨ ፨ ፨

The Winery Rushing

Post Office Drawer F
Old Orient Road
Merigold, Mississippi 38759
TEL: 601-748-2731
OWNER/WINEMAKER: Sam Rushing
FOUNDED: 1977

AT A GLANCE

Tours & Tastings: Twenty-minute guided tours wind up with tastings; 10–5 Tues.–Sat.
Closed: Mon., Sun., holidays.
Vineyards: Twenty-five acres in Mississippi Delta v.a. They are across the bayou from the winery, planted to native Muscadines, Carlos, Magnolia, and Noble. Fruits and berries also grown.
Wines: Estate-bottled Muscadine varietals; generics—Sweet Red, Rosé, White, and Sweet White.
Awards: Carlos, red, and Noble won national awards 1977–78; no longer enters competitions.
Restaurant: Top of the Cellar Tea Room, owned and operated by Diana Rushing; open 11:30–1 (see under "Restaurants" below).
Retail Shop: Wines, Muscadine juice, preserves and syrup, blackberry jelly, huckleberry preserves, and boysenberry syrup. The shop also sells supplies for amateur winemakers (including vines), and a number of gifts such as cork pullers, T-shirts, Delta recipes cookbook, and stone-ground cornmeal. Diana Rushing's wine muffin mix is among the most popular items.
Credit Cards: None. Will accept personal checks.
Access for Disabled: Wheelchair access difficult.
Foreign Languages: German.

Getting There: Winery Rushing is three miles east of Merigold, ninety miles south of Memphis, Tenn., and ninety miles north of Vicksburg, Miss. From Memphis: Take Hwy. 61 and turn east at Old Drew Rd. for three miles to winery.
Special Wine & Other Events: Annual Wine Fest, with grape stomping, amateur wine contests, and other merriment. For the date, call anytime after Jan. 1.

፨ Sam and Diana Rushing bring to their native American winemaking an enjoyment of European wines acquired when they lived abroad. Granted "Bonded Winery Permit No. 1," they founded in 1977 the first winery in Mississippi since Prohibition. Then, in 1984, the U.S. government designated the Mississippi Delta the Southeast's first viticultural area, making their wines Mississippi's first estate-bottled wines. The winery sits near cotton and soybean fields, crops that Sam Rushing's family farmed for six generations until he switched to grapes. After the September harvest, Rushing vines are made into wreaths to be sold at the winery shop.

TO SEE & DO

The Rushing Gristmill, located near the site of a century-old mill, is powered by an antique John Deere "A" model tractor. Stone-ground cornmeal is freshly prepared only as needed and is also for sale in the winery shop.

ACCOMMODATIONS

Holiday Inn
U.S. 61
Cleveland, Mississippi 38732
Tel: 601-846-1411; 800-HOLIDAY
119 rooms, with pool, wading pool, bar, café, and room service. One mile south of Cleveland; ten minutes south of Merigold.

RESTAURANTS

Top of the Cellar Tea Room
(See "Restaurant" section of the Winery

Rushing listing for address and telephone)
Adjacent to the Winery Rushing. Filled with family antiques and handmade Mississippi furnishings, the restaurant also has a deck overlooking the Sunflower River where guests can sip a complimentary glass of wine with a selection of appetizers. Two daily entrées are attractively presented on locally made pottery, and a choice of rich desserts polishes off the meal. Open 11:30–1 Tues.–Sat. Reservations necessary.

❧ NORTH CAROLINA

Beating this guide to the punch by some 465 years, Italian explorer Giovanni da Verrazano was first to write, in 1524, that many vines grew naturally here and "without doubt, they would yield fine excellent wines." Settlers apparently found it so: in 1565, when English officer Sir John Hawkins relieved the French at Fort Caroline, what do you think he discovered? Some twenty hogsheads of Muscadine wine.

In 1584, Sir Walter Raleigh's explorers in the New World wrote home rapturously of the abundance of grapes on the Carolina coast; in fact, some sources say that Raleigh himself found the Scuppernong grape on Roanoke Island and went on to introduce it elsewhere. Some historians say that in the seventeenth century North Carolinians used wines as currency.

Commercial winemaking was under way by the 1870s at Castle Hayne Vineyard Company, and soon other wineries thrived around the state. The industry's leader in North Carolina was the Bear family, one of the largest Muscadine users in the United States; their winery at Wilmington produced 200,000 gallons a year. In 1902, the Bears had several drummers on the road and an agent in New York to handle their far-flung sales. The industry was shut down by Prohibition, declared state-wide in 1909.

From the early 1960s onward, there has been renewed interest throughout the South in Muscadines, and with it, North Carolina's wine industry is thriving again.

❧ ❧ ❧

The Biltmore Estate Wine Company

1 Biltmore Plaza
Asheville, North Carolina 28803
TEL: 704-255-1776
OWNER: William A. N. Cecil
WINEMAKER: Philippe Jourdan (native of Provence, France)
FOUNDED: 1970

AT A GLANCE

Tours & Tastings: Estate open every day, 9–5; winery tours and tastings Mon.–Sat. 11–7, Sun. 1–7. Tours and tastings here are as good a look as you will ever get at winemaking. The story is vividly told through video, exhibits, artifacts, and views of actual winemaking from various vantage points. Winery and estate tour is $17.50 per adult; students 12–17, $13; young children free with parent. The winery tour takes about thirty minutes, but allow half a day for the whole experience, from living room to tasting room.

Closed: Thanksgiving, Christmas, New Year's days.

Vineyards: 107 acres planted primarily to viniferas, including reds (Cabernet Sauvignon, Cabernet Franc, Pinot Noir, Gamay, Merlot), whites (Chardonnay, Gewürztraminer, Sauvignon Blanc, White Riesling), and hybrids (Villard Blanc, Vidal Blanc, and Seyval).

Wines: Production is 35,000 cases per year of red, white, rosé, and *methode champenoise* champagne. The Chateau Biltmore label denotes fine-quality varietals; the Biltmore Estate label, both premium blends and varietals.

Awards: Award winners include Blanc de Blanc Dry Sparkling and Pinot Noir, Biltmore Estate Cardinal's Crest, Blanc de Blanc Brut Sparkling, Chardonnay Sur Lies, Johannisberg Riesling, and Chenin Blanc.

Restaurants: The Stable Cafe, in a restored stable, offers counter service for sandwiches and snacks year-round. Deerpark, in what was a dairy barn, offers table service with a courtyard view and a selection of European and American dishes and Biltmore wines.

Retail Shop: Sells wines, wine books, coolers, glasses, and other wine accessories.

Credit Cards: American Express, MasterCard, Visa.

Access for Disabled: Elevators in buildings; wheelchairs on-premises.

Foreign Languages: None.

Getting There: In Asheville, three blocks north of exit 50 or exit 50B on I-40.

Special Wine & Other Events: Christmas is marked with great fanfare at the estate: beautiful decorations, holiday music, tastings, tours; Nov. 28–Dec. 30. The Festival of Flowers in Apr. celebrates the spring displays in the gorgeous gardens, and an October event heralds the fall colors.

The 107-acre vineyard and 90,000-square-foot winery take up but a tasting-size portion of the vast 8,000 acres (there were originally 125,000, but some were deeded to the United States) of well-manicured grounds housing the 255-room Biltmore Estate and Gardens. Formerly home to George W. Vanderbilt, railroad and steamship magnate, the mansion—America's largest private residence—was completed in 1895, opened to the public in the 1930s, and is listed in the National Register of Historic Places.

The lavish estate gardens and grounds were designed by landscape architect Frederick Law Olmsted. The vineyards, planted only in 1970, are across the river from the house and overlook a thirty-five-acre lake created to irrigate them. Bonded in 1977, the winery produced its first wines in 1979. Tours take in the well-appointed rooms and the gorgeous gardens, as well as the vineyards and winery, which opened to the public in 1985.

Biltmore's venture into winemaking was started by William A. V. Cecil, president and owner of the property and grandson of Vanderbilt, who had always wished to keep the estate working in the European tradition. The winery was originally built as a dairy barn by Richard Morris Hunt, also architect of the mansion. In addition to top-of-the-line winemaking equipment, the winery has six striking stained-glass windows designed by John LaFarge, mentor to Louis Comfort Tiffany. A clock tower tops the winery in the tradition of European wine estates.

TO SEE & DO

Asheville's most well known attraction is the Biltmore Estate, but very interesting as well is the Thomas Wolfe Memorial, the famous author's wood-frame boyhood home. (48 Spruce Street; tel: 704-253-8304; Mon.–Sat. 9–5, Sun. 1–5). On the Blue Ridge Parkway east of

Asheville, the Folk Art Center (tel: 704-298-7928, daily 9–5), a shared endeavor of the Southern Handicraft Guild, has a lot to offer handicraft fanciers. A gateway to areas of great natural splendor, Asheville adjoins the Great Smokies and forests renowned for exquisite waterfalls.

ACCOMMODATIONS
Albermarle Inn
86 Edgemont Road
Asheville, North Carolina 28801
Tel: 704-255-0027
Eight charming Victorian rooms, each with a private bathroom, in a home listed on the National Register of Historic Places. Breakfast includes fresh-baked pastries and breads. Open Apr. 1–Dec. 1.

Cedar Crest Victorian Inn
674 Biltmore Avenue
Asheville, North Carolina 28803
Tel: 704-252-1389
Circa 1891, this Queen Anne Victorian has rich wood paneling and gleaming beveled and stained-glass interiors. The bedrooms are well furnished with antiques and fine linens. A delicious Continental breakfast features fruits and a variety of breads.

Flint Street Inns
116 Flint Street
Asheville, North Carolina 28801
Tel: 704-253-6723
Restored to their Victorian heyday with stained-glass windows and period decor, these neighboring houses are listed on the National Register of Historic Places. Fresh biscuits accompany the full southern breakfast.

The Ray House
83 Hillside Street
Asheville, North Carolina 28801
Tel: 704-252-0106
Restored 1891 home with big porch where you can eat a Continental breakfast of homemade foods.

Red Rocker Inn
136 North Dougherty Street
Black Mountain, North Carolina 28711
Tel: 704-669-5991
Named for the variety of red rockers on the wraparound porch, this comfortable old house is decorated with handmade quilts and coverlets and perky curtains. The red-and-white decor in the dining room sets the scene for sumptuous southern meals with wickedly rich desserts. In the garden, the red-and-white impatiens and geraniums carry through the color scheme. Located seventeen miles east of Asheville, off I-40.

🍂 🍂 🍂

Duplin Wine Cellars

Highway 117
Rose Hill, North Carolina 28458
TEL: 919-289-3888
PRESIDENT: David Fussell
WINEMAKER: Jeff Randall
FOUNDED: 1975

AT A GLANCE
Tours & Tastings: Any time, 9–5 Mon.–Sat. The tour includes a ten-minute film on southern winemaking, a plant visit, and tasting of half a dozen wines. Groups of twelve or more must telephone for reservations.
Closed: Christmas, Sun.
Vineyards: 500 acres planted to Muscadine varieties most famous in the South: Scuppernong and later descendants, Carlos and Magnolia.
Wines: Still reds, rosés, whites; dessert sherry, brandy. Muscadine champagne and sparkling Scuppernong. Also nonalcoholic sparkling Scuppernong juice.
Awards: Gold medals have gone to Duplin's Magnolia and to sparkling Scuppernong competing in Madrid, Spain;

International Eastern Wine Competition awards to champagne, Scuppernong, Magnolia, and Carlos wines.
Picnic Area: Adjacent to the winery.
Retail Shop: All wines except brandy for sale; also gift items, homemade wine jellies, juices. Recipe handouts.
Credit Cards: MasterCard, Visa.
Access for Disabled: No stairs.
Foreign Languages: None.
Getting There: Rose Hill, in Duplin County, is located on Hwy. 117, midway between Goldsboro and Wilmington in eastern North Carolina. The winery, in town, is accessible by foot, taxi, bus, or car.
Special Wine & Other Events: September Wine Festival.

ĕ Duplin, in a former warehouse, is in the middle of North Carolina grape-growing territory. Wines are made only from Muscadines. When visiting here stop to see the small museum of antique wine-making artifacts.

TO SEE & DO
Twelve miles north of Rose Hill, at Kenansville, over twenty-five homes are more than a century old; see Liberty Hall as a prime example of Greek Revival architecture and attend "The Liberty Cart: A Duplin Story" outdoors in summer. Or head south one hour from Rose Hill to the coast, where the U.S.S. *North Carolina* Battleship Memorial stands at Wilmington—sound and light performances in summer dramatize the vessel's great importance during World War II. For a most agreeable history lesson, take a walking tour (Tues.–Sat. 10–5; tel: 919-763-9328) through Wilmington's well-preserved historic district and visit the New Hanover Museum, which documents Cape Fear's history during the Civil War. A few miles up the coast, at Greenfield Gardens (tel: 919-763-9871), spectacular azalea and camellia displays peak in Apr., while Poplar Grove Planta-

tion (Mon.–Sat. 9–5; Sun. 12–6; tel: 919-686-9989) near Wilmington is a year-round attraction.

ACCOMMODATIONS
Squire's Vintage Inn
Highway 24 East
Warsaw, North Carolina 28349
Tel: 919-289-1831

Rose Hill Motel
Highway 117 North
Rose Hill, North Carolina 28458
Tel: 919-289-3136

Wallace Liberty Inn
Highway 117 North
Wallace, North Carolina 28466
Tel: 919-285-7586

RESTAURANTS
Country Squire
Highway 24 East
Warsaw, North Carolina 28349
Tel: 919-296-1727

Special Food Note: Buy a bottle of Duplin wine and head along the coast to the village of Calabash at Tubbs Inlet near the South Carolina border. Here, twenty-two little restaurants serve fresh-caught seafood along with the local favorite, hush puppies.

ĕ ĕ ĕ

Southland Estate Winery

Interstate 95, exit 98
Selma, North Carolina 27576
TEL: 919-965-3645
PRESIDENT: David Fussell
FOUNDED: 1986

AT A GLANCE
Tours & Tastings: Mon.–Sat. 9–6. Tours take in winery, museum, bottling area, underground cellar, an audio-visual presentation, and a tasting.

Closed: Sun., Thanksgiving, Christmas, New Year's.
Vineyards: Five acres planted to native Muscadines
Wines: Similar to Duplin's, also headed by Fussell.
Cafe: Cellar Cafe serves sandwiches and other entrées and Southland wines.
Retail Shop: Wine and gifts.
Credit Cards: American Express, MasterCard, Visa.
Access for Disabled: Bathrooms and tour.
Foreign Languages: None.
Getting There: Southland Estate Winery is one mile east of Selma and five miles northeast of Smithfield; thirty miles from Raleigh, off I-95 at exit 98. Winery is 700 yards from I-95. Billboards direct you to the winery; two Welcome Centers on I-95, operated by the state, have brochures. You can reach the winery by bus and taxi from town.

🍷 Southland Winery, a new venture for Duplin's David Fussell, is located in a two-story red-roofed, southern colonial-style structure, set on the 23.4-acre site bordered by woods and overlooking a lake. Plans call for a 5,000-square-foot wine-production facility, including a wine cellar and bottling and labeling opera-

tions. The goal is to turn out world-class wines from southern Muscadines and to provide visitors with a glimpse of a premium winery through tours, tastings, and ambience.

ACCOMMODATIONS
Selma offers a wide range of accommodations, as does Smithfield.

Holiday Inn
Box 529, Junction U.S. 70A at I-95
Smithfield, North Carolina 27577
Tel: 919-965-3771/800-HOLIDAY
One hundred and nineteen rooms, pool, café.

Another North Carolina winery to visit:

🍷 🍷 🍷

La Rocca

408 Buie Court
Fayetteville, North Carolina 28304
TEL: 919-484-8865
By appointment only; Muscadine wines—Carlos, Magnolia, others. In Fayetteville city limits, three blocks from Cape Fear Valley Hospital.

🍷 SOUTH CAROLINA

Wine routes here travel through flat tobacco and soy fields so unlike the undulating valleys of Napa and Burgundy that it may come as a surprise that wines are being made here—French-accented wines at that!

🍷 🍷 🍷

Truluck Vineyards

Route 3, P.O. Drawer 1265
Lake City, South Carolina 29560
TEL: 803-389-3400
OWNERS: Dr. James P. Truluck, Jr., and Jay Truluck

WINEMAKER: Jay Truluck (UC-Davis, Mississippi State)
FOUNDED: 1976

AT A GLANCE
Tours & Tastings: Mon.–Sat. 10–8:30; fifteen-minute guided tours of production process and constant-sixty-degree underground cellars, followed by tasting.

Closed: Thanksgiving, Christmas, New Year's, July 4.

Vineyards: Fifty-three acres planted with 120 varieties, including 35 varieties of Munsons from Texas; New York hybrids, Cayugas, and French hybrids, viniferas.

Wines: The Chambourcin grapes have produced prizewinning whites and rosés. Other varietals are Cayuga White, Ravat Blanc (similar to a Chardonnay), Golden Muscat, Cabernet Sauvignon, Verdalet, and Munson Red (a blend).

Awards: Chambourcin has been highly decorated with gold and silver at Atlanta International Competition; many bronzes to Carlos (a medium-sweet dessert wine).

Picnic Area: Bucolic setting near duck pond.

Retail Shop: Wines, cooking wines, wine vinegar, goblets, wine accessories, and books.

Credit Cards: MasterCard, Visa.

Access for Disabled: The winery is all on one level, the cellar below.

Foreign Languages: None.

Getting There: From Lake City in northeastern South Carolina: Take Hwy. 378 North to Godwin Welsh store and turn right on Rte. 3 two miles to winery and vineyard.

Special Wine & Other Events: Three annual events: spring, late June, and Oct. The last is usually a jazz festival; the others take shape as they are planned. At all, Truluck's crawfish are served, cooked fresh from their pond. Check winery for exact dates, admission price (or lack thereof). In Florence, twenty miles north on Rte. 52, the October Fall Festival coincides by a day or two with the winery's event. Call the Florence Museum for details (tel: 803-662-3351).

ᴥ James Truluck had never sipped wine until he did a two-year tour of duty for the Army Dental Corps in the Loire Valley of France. There he toured the vineyards and noted the soil was similar to that on his farm in the low country of South Carolina. "Why couldn't grapes grow back there?" he wondered.

At home he began experimenting with a few vines in his backyard, pressing his first wines on an 1865 cider press. Today Truluck still practices dentistry, but winemaking is far more than a hobby. His vineyards, sprouting hybrids of French ancestry, now cover fifty-three acres of what had been tobacco land, and his wines have become an international success.

There's a strong French accent at the winery: the low white buildings are new, but are designed to resemble the old wineries he admired in France. And, as is often the case with the French, Truluck's entire family gets into the winemaking act. What do you get to eat at festival times? *Mai oui!* It's French, too. The delicacy *ecrevisse* (crawfish)—from the local pond—is served to visitors who come to revel here. Miles of nature trails also await travelers.

TO SEE & DO

Florence, about twenty miles north via U.S. 52, founded in the 1850s, is now home base to the minor league Florence Blue Jays, affiliated with the Toronto Blue Jays. Diversions include the Florence Air & Missile Museum (at the airport on U.S. 301, open daily; tel: 803-665-5118); a park and monument to Timrod, poet laureate of the Confederacy, in the old schoolhouse next to the Florence Museum (558 Spruce Street, open Tues.–Sun.; tel: 803-662-3351). Between Florence and Lake City, on U.S. 52, is Lynches River State Park (tel: 803-389-2785), delightful for picnicking and featuring an Olympic-size swimming pool as another refreshment. For more information, contact Pee Dee Tourism Commission, Lunn House, Sheraton Road, P.O. Box 3093, Florence, South Carolina 29502 (tel: 803-669-0950).

ACCOMMODATIONS

Nearest places to stay are in Lake City itself or in Florence, twenty-three miles to the north; available are local and chain motels, including:

Ramada Inn
I-95 E U.S. 52
Florence, South Carolina 29503
Tel: 803-669-4241
One hundred and seventy-nine rooms, pool, health club, and other motel amenities.

Quality Inn–Downtown
Dargan and Palmetto streets
Florence, South Carolina 29501
Tel: 803-662-6341; 800-228-5151

Eighty-one rooms, pool, café, bar, room service.

Quality Inn I-95
Box 1512
Florence, South Carolina 29503
Tel: 803-669-1715; 800-228-5151
Ninety-one rooms, pool, tennis, putting green. Five miles northeast at I-95, exit 169.

Special Food Note: For delicious picnic supplies, head for the Farmers' Market in Florence, at the intersection of U.S. 52 and I-95 (Mon.–Sat. 7–7). You'll find fresh local fruits and vegetables, local delicacies, plus bedding, baskets, and plants, too.

↝ TENNESSEE

In his autobiography, Mark Twain describes the legacy from his father as "a fine estate in the region of Jamestown where wild grapes of a promising sort grew." Though neither Twain nor his father ever cultivated the grape, some early German and English settlers did so with some very good results. Now, a century after Twain, wine routes take visitors to the region on the lush Cumberland Plateau that Twain mentioned and to a winery in the woods that he might well have enjoyed himself.

↝ ↝ ↝

Highland Manor Winery

Highway 127 South (P.O. Box 203)
Jamestown, Tennessee 38556
TEL: 615-879-9519
PRESIDENT: Fay Wheeler
WINEMAKER: O. Irving Martin
(Tennessee's first university-trained enologist)
FOUNDED: 1979 (first Tennessee winery licensed in the twentieth century)

AT A GLANCE

Tours & Tastings: Mon.–Sat. 10–6. Instructive guided tours, about every half hour, show how wines and *methode*

champenoise champagne are made, and include testing. Winery closes if sold out, so it's best to call in advance.
Closed: Sun.; at dusk, Nov.–end Apr.; legal holidays.
Vineyards: Eight acres planted to native American, French hybrids; grapes grown for winery by other Tennessee growers.
Wines: Alwood, Catawba, Concord, Cayuga, Cabernet Sauvignon, white Rieslings, Gewürztraminer; generic reds and whites; Muscadine champagne. Best known for yearly "limited reserve" fine Muscadine wine.
Awards: Gold medal for quality awarded to Muscadine in Madrid, Spain, 1983 and 1984. Chardonnay, rosé, Muscadine

champagne also international gold medalists for quality.

Retail Shop: Wines sold on-site.

Credit Cards: None.

Access for Disabled: Nothing special, but "all are welcome."

Foreign Languages: German.

Getting There: Located in central Tennessee on U.S. Hwy. 127, thirty-three miles north of I-40 at Crossville, approximately four miles south of Jamestown, ninety miles west of Knoxville.

Special Wine & Other Events: Victorian Rugby, Spring Festival, and Fall Pilgrimage (house tours).

ᴥ History repeats itself: A nearby vineyard in the English-settled town of Rugby flourished in the 1800s and won several gold medals in the Cincinnati competitions back in those days. Years later, wines from Highland Manor are reaping medals in Madrid and more—in 1981, one bottle of Highland Manor Cabernet Sauvignon sold at auction for $425, outpricing a 1961 Chateau Latour and a 1970 Mouton Rothschild. The winery building has an English feel to it—Tudor style with dark beams, half-hidden in the woods.

Proprietor Fay Wheeler, who grew up in the area, remembers his family making homemade jams and juice from wild Tennessee grapes. Some of this stuff used to end up surreptitiously as wine in the hands of Wheeler and his brothers. Later in the Air Force, he toured the wine regions of Europe; when he returned home, Wheeler and his Edinburgh-born wife, Kathy, started Highland Manor.

TO SEE & DO
Wine routes lead through wooded glens ("hollers" hereabouts) and small meadows fragrant with wild roses to spectacularly scenic Pickett State Park, off Route 154, north of Jamestown. The Big South Fork National River and Recreation Area—where wine routes can become white-water routes through deep, fern-decked sandstone gorges—are natural attractions for the adventuresome.

Routed back in time, there's Rugby, once a utopian Victorian English settlement (open March–Dec.), where you can spend a peaceful night in Newbury House, an old inn with a notable restaurant. From the less distant past in the lush Wolf River Valley to be seen is the former home of Sgt. Alvin C. York, World War I's most decorated hero. While there, see also the antebellum York Gristmill.

ACCOMMODATIONS
Capri Terrace Motel
714 Main Street (P.O. Box 127)
Crossville, Tennessee 38555
Tel: 615-484-7561
Two-story, 145 rooms, some with kitchens. Pool and café. A quarter-mile north on U.S. 127; two and a half miles south of I-40.

Newbury House and Pioneer Cottage
Rugby, Tennessee 37733
Tel: 615-628-2441
Old inn in historic setting.

ᴥ ᴥ ᴥ

Smoky Mountain Winery

Brookside Village
Highway 321 North
Route 2, Box 989
Gatlinburg, Tennessee 37738
TEL: 615-436-7551
PROPRIETORS: Everett and Miriam
 Brock
WINEMAKER: Patrice Fischer-Johnson
 (enology degree, UC-Fresno)
FOUNDED: 1981

AT A GLANCE
Tours & Tastings: Daily 10–5, March–Dec.; Sat. & Sun. only, 10–5, Jan.–Feb. An intimate look at a small winery, with time to browse through the cellar and see

the oak barrels, casks, tanks, other wine-making equipment, followed by tasting.
Closed: Mon.–Fri., Jan. & Feb.
Vineyards: All grapes purchased from local growers.
Wines: Chardonnay, Riesling, French hybrid varietals, native American varieties.
Awards: In local, Florida, and Indiana competitions, several wines took gold and silver medals; also first and second prizes in the International Eastern Wine Competition.
Retail Shop: Located next to tasting bar; wines, wine accessories, winemaking supplies, and locally made crafts.
Credit Cards: MasterCard, Visa.
Access for Disabled: Yes.
Getting There: Gatlinburg is thirty-five miles southeast of Knoxville. The winery is on Rte. 321 in Brookside Village complex, approximately three miles from traffic light 3. Reachable from town by bus, taxi, bike, or on foot.
Special Wine & Other Events: Twelve days of Christmas specially celebrated in Gatlinburg.

🐌 Small winery with an inviting hospitality room where visitors can sample wines in a relaxing setting.

TO SEE & DO
Gatlinburg is the overly touristy staging ground for the glorious Great Smoky Mountains National Park; Ober Gatlinburg Ski Area will appeal in winter to winter sports enthusiasts.

ACCOMMODATIONS
Brookside Resort
Roaring Fork Road, P.O. Box 47
Gatlinburg, Tennessee 37738
Tel: 615-846-5611
250 motel and cabin units, with pool, spacious grounds.

Buckhorn Inn
Tudor Mount Road
Route 3, Box 393
Gatlinburg, Tennessee 37738
Tel: 615-436-4668
White-pillared structure with antique appointments in public rooms. The seven double bedrooms are cozy, with spindle beds and some antiques; in the four cottages, a fire crackling in your fireplace takes the nip out of the air in winter, and a screened-in porch offers a cool place to sit in warm months. Meals include hearty breakfasts and dinners with home-baked breads.

LeConte Lodge
P.O. Box 350
Gatlinburg, Tennessee 37738
Tel: 615-436-4473
For the adventurous, cabins with no modern conveniences—no electricity or indoor plumbing—accessible by footpaths from five to nearly nine miles long. However, clean linens and fresh food, and, of course, fabulous views await hikers. Open Apr. through Oct. Write far in advance for reservations. Atop Mount LeConte in the Great Smoky Mountains National Park.

🐌 🐌 🐌

Laurel Hill Vineyard

1370 Madison Avenue
Memphis, Tennessee 38104
TEL: 901-725-9128
OWNER/WINEMAKER: Raymond Skinner, Jr.
FOUNDED: 1984

AT A GLANCE
Tours & Tastings: Generally Mon.–Fri. 10–12:30, 1:30–5; other times by appointment. "Because the vineyards are one hundred seventy-five miles east of Memphis and require special attention

during the growing season—April through August—the winery's hours may be slightly altered. Please call us before you visit." Because the vineyards are not at the winery, photographs show tours how they grow.

Closed: Lunch 12:30–1:30, and for vineyard work and harvest.

Vineyards: The 7½-acre vineyard is up in the hills, 175 miles east of Memphis. Planted to French-American hybrids, vinifera, and native American species.

Wines: Varietals include Vidal Blanc, Chardonnay, Riesling; two red blends.

Awards: First releases were in 1985; both Central Gardens Red and Vidal Blanc won awards in Tennessee Farm Wine Growers Association competition.

Retail Shop: Wines sold at winery.

Credit Cards: None. Will accept checks.

Access for Disabled: Ramps and bathroom.

Foreign Languages: "Y'all," says Mr. Skinner.

Getting There: Laurel Hill Winery is in Memphis on Madison Ave., two stoplights east of the Madison Interchange of I-240, halfway between the Medical Center and Overton Square. The winery is accessible by bus and taxi, and is on a popular bike route.

Special Wine & Other Events: May–early June: Memphis in May, annual cultural festival featuring a different country each year.

❧ Laurel Hill's winery is in an original Sears Roebuck catalog home, circa 1918, remodeled by its new occupant. Owner/winemaker Skinner takes growing and making wines seriously, having taken courses at various universities and being in a leadership role in Tennessee's winegrowing and winemaking associations. Skinner teaches a wine appreciation course through Memphis State University's Continuing Education Department.

TO SEE & DO
Memphis's many well-known attractions include the Mississippi River, Mud Island, Beale Street, Victorian Village, Brooks Memorial Art Gallery, and Overton Park and Zoo. For more information, contact the Convention and Visitors Bureau, 203 Beale Street, Suite 305, Memphis, Tennessee 38103; Tel: 901-526-4880.

ACCOMMODATIONS
Bed & Breakfast Host Homes of Tennessee
P.O. Box 110227
Nashville, Tennessee 37222
Tel: 615-331-5244
Will make recommendations in Memphis and elsewhere in Tennessee.

Lowenstein-Long House
217 North Waldran Boulevard
Memphis, Tennessee 38105
Tel: 901-527-7174
Turn-of-the-century Victorian stick-style architecture with cozy and cheerful interiors. In the center of town, with patio and large yard. Near Overton Square and Laurel Hill's winery. French spoken here.

Peabody
149 Union Avenue
Memphis, Tennessee 38103
Tel: 901-529-4000
A Memphis classic, famous for its daily duck march, and recently restored to its original glory.

RESTAURANTS
Overton Square, not far from Laurel Hill's winery, is a complex of restaurants and shops. At this writing, none of these or others in Memphis were serving Laurel Hill wines, but this may have changed by now.

❧ ❧ ❧

Monteagle Wine Cellars

Highway 64/41A (P.O. Box 638)
Monteagle, Tennessee 37356
TEL: 615-924-2120
FOUNDED: 1986
PRESIDENT: Joe E. Marlow, Sr.
WINEMAKER: Robert M. Burgin (B.S.,
enology and viticulture, MSU)

AT A GLANCE
Tours & Tastings: Mon.–Sat., 9–6 in winter, 9–8 in summer. Tour gives an in-depth view of winemaking, the cellar and bottling areas, and concludes with tasting.
Closed: Christmas, Thanksgiving.
Vineyards: French hybrid and native American grapes, purchased from Tennessee and out-of-state growers.
Wines: Sauvignon Blanc, Riesling, Marechal Foch, Niagara, Concord, white Muscadines. Annual production 18,000 gallons.
Awards: Twenty-two prizes in international and regional meets since first releases in 1987; repeated winners—white Riesling and Muscadine.
Picnic Area: With a view of the surrounding area.
Retail Shop: Wines, wine accessories, logo-imprinted gift items. Grapevine Shop sells arts and crafts.
Credit Cards: American Express, MasterCard, Visa.
Access for Disabled: Ramps and toilets.
Getting There: Monteagle is forty-five miles west of Chattanooga on I-24 and eighty miles southeast of Nashville on I-24. To get to winery: Take Monteagle/Sewanee exit (#134) off I-24, turn left on Hwy. 64/41A. Winery is 400 yards on the right.
Special Wine & Other Events: Fall and spring wine festivals are planned; call for details.

🐬 ". . . ain't much to look at," as the song goes. True, the architecture isn't notable at this ranch-style redwood-and-native-stone winery, but the unforgettable Cumberland Valley views make up for any plainness. The rewards of making the trip also include a chance to taste the critically acclaimed white Muscadine and Riesling and the other wines that can be found nowhere else—distribution stops at the winery door.

TO SEE & DO
Atop the Cumberland Plateau, at 2,100 feet, history and beauty meet. Near the winery is the Sunday School Assembly, a more-than-102-year-old Chatauqua retreat. Six miles away in Sewanee is the campus of the University of the South, founded in 1867. Within easy reach is the South Cumberland Recreation Area State Park, with a wealth of natural attractions, including the Lost Cove Caves, Sewanee Natural Bridge, Foster Falls, Savage Gulf and Falls, and the Great Stone Door, an unusual rock formation.

ACCOMMODATIONS
Edgeworth Inn
Monteagle Assembly
Monteagle, Tennessee 37356
Tel: 615-924-2669
Historic bed and breakfast inn.

Jim Oliver's Smoke House
Highway 64/41A
Monteagle, Tennessee 37356
Tel: 615-924-2268; 800-241-1740 (in-state)
Eighty-four moderately priced rooms and cabins; swimming pool and tennis. Restaurant specializes in fried chicken and, of course, country ham. Campground also available.

Holiday Inn
Highway 41A at I-24
Monteagle, Tennessee 37356
Tel: 615-924-2221; 800-HOLIDAY
One hundred twenty rooms, pool, café.

❧ VIRGINIA

Thomas Jefferson would have been happy indeed to discover that Virginia has become one of the top ten wine-producing states in the country. The third president of the United States, and arguably the founder of the American wine industry, tried but failed to produce fine wines from vinifera vines at Monticello over 200 years ago. He always believed it could be done.

In 1610, Lord De La Warr, the first governor of Virginia, also tried unsuccessfully to produce wine from imported vines shipped to him from London. De La Warr's early attempt at fine winemaking went largely unnoticed except by wine historians, as did George Washington's similar attempts at Mount Vernon.

Indeed, Jefferson did a jeroboam-size job to encourage wine development in his state. A grape grower, wine collector, and wine consultant to five presidents (including himself) Jefferson wrote widely of his belief in the suitability of Virginia's climate and soil for making superior wine. But he didn't always practice what he preached. Well known was his fondness for North Carolina's Scuppernong wine, made from a common Muscadine old De La Warr would have shunned. Jefferson, however, thought Scuppernong wine could hold its own on the best tables of Europe.

Virginia's wine industry got a real boost in 1835, when viticulturalist Dr. D. N. Norton of Richmond developed the first "nonfoxy" American wine grape. From this fruit came a claret toasted world-wide by connoisseurs, and the impetus for many Virginians to plant vineyards. Development concentrated in Albemarle Valley, still a major wine-producing center today, and Charlottesville became known as the wine capital of the country. The Rivanna River was claimed to be America's Rhine—a claim later made by early settlers of the Missouri River Valley.

Virginia's vineyards now extend from the Allegheny Mountains to Chesapeake Bay. The state has five viticultural areas: Monticello, Shenandoah Valley, Rocky Knob, North Fork at Roanoke, and Northern Neck/George Washington Birthplace.

Before taking off on this route, make a note of a statewide wine event that has been around for a few years and seems destined for many more. It's the annual Spring Wine Weekend at the Homestead, Hot Springs, Virginia (tel: 703-839-5500), to which many winemakers bring their recent releases for tasting. Be sure to reserve well in advance. How much Jefferson, the bon vivant, would have enjoyed all this wine hullabaloo!

According to him, wine was like fine friendship: raw when new and ripened with old age. So let's start getting acquainted with Virginia's wineries. To make it easy, many of them display the state highway sign with grape bunch logo, starting ten miles before the winery. The signs do not appear on interstates or limited-access roads.

Central Virginia

This area is still the heart of Virginia wine territory. The route goes through quiet, colorful country to wineries dotted one after another. A bonus here is traveling on Scenic Route 4—the Constitution Route, so named because Thomas Jefferson and many of the framers of the Constitution traveled on this peaceful, dogwood-bordered road. Unless otherwise indicated, the central Virginia wineries and vineyards listed are in the Monticello viticultural area. While tour-and-tasting times are given, you should call ahead to verify supplies in the case of small producers. For accommodations, restaurants, and what to see and do in the area, see the end of this section.

ᘒ ᘒ ᘒ

Barboursville Vineyards

R.F.D. 1, Box 136
Barboursville, Virginia 22923
TEL: 703-832-3824
PRESIDENT: Gianni Zonin
WINEMAKER: Adriano Rossi (degrees in
  enology and viticulture from School
  of Enology in Alba, Italy)
FOUNDED: 1975

AT A GLANCE
Tours & Tastings: Self-guided one-hour tours, about every hour, Sat. 10–4; conclude with a tasting. Tours take in the entire winery—crushing, pressing, fermentation, and bottling, plus the historic landmark surroundings. Tastings, without tours, are available daily from 10–4.
Closed: Sun., New Year's Day, Thanksgiving Day.
Vineyards: Forty-three acres, planted to *Vitis vinifera*: ten each Cabernet Sauvignon and Chardonnay, five each Riesling and Sauvignon Blanc, four each Gewürztraminer and Merlot, three acres to Pinot Noir, and one to Cabernet

Franc; minor plantings of Semillon and Malvasia. Also, nursery where high-quality viniferas are grafted for new plantings and sold to other growers.
Wines: Current production about 20,000 gallons. Included are Krystal Pinot Noir Blanc, Chardonnay, Riesling, Gewürztraminer, Merlot, Cabernet Sauvignon, Cabernet Sauvignon Blanc (a blush), and Rosé Barboursville (made with red and white grapes).
Awards: Most awarded: the Riesling, medium-dry wine; has taken a gold at an International Expo in Milan, high awards elsewhere.
Retail Shop: Wines sold on-site.
Credit Cards: None.
Access for Disabled: Everything is on the same level.
Foreign Languages: French, Italian.
Getting There: Barboursville is seventeen miles northeast of Charlottesville, in Orange County. At Rte. 20 & Rte. 33, take 20 South for 200 yards, turn left on Rte. 678 for half a mile, then right on Rte. 777 for 500 yards, and another right at first driveway and sign.
Special Wine & Other Events: Twice-a-year wine festivals, end of Nov. and mid-May.

ᘒ Barboursville is on the 830-acre former plantation of James Barbour, governor from 1812 to 1814. The site, a registered historic landmark, includes the impressive remains of Barbour's neoclassical-style mansion, designed by Thomas Jefferson, and gutted during a Christmas Day fire in 1814. The Zonin family, involved in viticulture in Italy since 1821, owned the first Virginia winery to successfully grow vinifera vines in 1976, making Jefferson's predictions come true.

ᘒ ᘒ ᘒ

Burnley Vineyards & Winery

Route 641 (mailing address: Route 1,
  Box 122)
Barboursville, Virginia 22923
TEL: 703-832-3874
PRESIDENT: C. J. Reeder
WINEMAKER: Lee Reeder
FOUNDED: Vineyard, 1976; winery, 1984

AT A GLANCE
Tours & Tastings: Fri., Sat., & Sun., Apr.
1–Dec. 31, 10–5. Tour guides keep
everything going at a comfortable pace
so there is never a wait for the experience, which takes forty-five minutes from
first step to last sip. Other times by appointment.
Closed: Jan., Feb., and March. Open by
appointment during these months.
Vineyards: Ten acres, some of the earliest cultivated in this area; planted to
viniferas and French hybrids.
Wines: Chardonnay, Cabernet Sauvignon, Riesling, Vidal Blanc, Rivanna Red
(French hybrid mixture).
Awards: Frequent gold medalist Chardonnay is the much-decorated hero;
other medal winners have been Cabernet
Sauvignon and Riesling.
Picnic Area: On the grounds.
Credit Cards: None.
Access for Disabled: Easy to tour the
winery, but the tasting room is upstairs.
Foreign Languages: Russian.
Getting there: From Charlottesville: Go
north fifteen miles on Rte. 20 and take a
left on Rte. 641 for three tenths of a mile;
entrance is to your left.
Special Wine & Other Events: See end of
Central Virginia section.

🍂 Burnley is a small operation where
you're bound to meet a member of the
Reeder family as a guide or in the tasting
room or at some other point during your
visit. A real beauty is the newly built
cathedral ceilinged tasting room with
thirty-foot balcony offering a spectacular
view of the Virginia countryside. Burn-

ley's reputation became widely known
beyond the state line after an article in
Connoisseur magazine.

🍂 🍂 🍂

Chermont Vineyard and Winery

Route 1, Box 59
Esmont, Virginia 22937
TEL: 804-286-2211
PRESIDENT/WINEMAKER: John O.
  Sherman, Jr.
FOUNDED: Vineyard, 1978; winery, 1981

AT A GLANCE
Tours & Tastings: Tues.–Sat. or by appt.
anytime.
Vineyards: Ten acres planted to Chardon-
nay, Riesling, Cabernet Sauvignon.
Wines: Varietals from above varieties.
Awards: 1981, 1982, 1983 Cabernet Sau-
vignon lead with three silvers and four
bronzes; runner-up is Chardonay, with
bronzes for 1981, 1982, 1983 releases.
Retail Shop: Wines sold on-site.
Credit Cards: None.
Access for Disabled: Ramp entry and
toilet facilities.
Foreign Languages: None.
Getting There: From intersection of Rtes.
6 & 626: Go toward Howardsville, 5.6
miles on Rte. 626 to vineyard and winery.

🍂 At this two-level structure, the
lower level cellar is ten feet underground,
and the accent is on the wine, not the
atmospheric details.

🍂 🍂 🍂

Mountain Cove Vineyards
La Abra Farm & Winery, Inc.

Route 718 (R.F.D. 1, Box 139)
Lovington, Virginia 22949
TEL: 804-263-5392
PRESIDENT/WINEMAKER: A. G. Weed II
FOUNDED: 1978

AT A GLANCE

Tours & Tastings: Free tours seven days a week, daily, 1–5. Groups must call in advance. Half-hour tours take participants through the entire process, from vine to wine, and are keyed to visitors' level of knowledge. Tastings follow tours.

Closed: Mon. & Tues., Jan.–Mar. Christmas, New Year's, and Thanksgiving.

Vineyards: Thirteen acres planted to six varieties of hybrid wine grapes.

Wines: Baco Noir, Villard Blanc, Chelois, Skyline Red and White (under the Mountain Cove Label); also La Abra Peach and La Abra Apple. Total annual output is approximately 4,000 cases.

Awards: Skyline Red (a blend) and peach and apple wines have won bronze awards.

Picnic Area: Yes; beautiful outdoor setting.

Retail Shop: All wines sold, as are wine accessories.

Credit Cards: None.

Access for Disabled: The winery is all on one level; ramp to sales room; bathrooms are marginal.

Foreign Languages: Spanish, Portuguese, Chinese, and some French "if pressed."

Getting There: From Rte. 29, just north of Lovington: Go west on Rte. 718 and follow signs for 3½ miles to winery.

Special Wine & Other Events: Annual Fiesta de Primavera—Sat. and Sun. of Memorial Day weekend: live music, food, and crafts.

🍂 Weed, a Vietnam veteran and formerly with the World Bank, says his fieldstone winery is located in the prettiest valley in Virginia.

🍂 🍂 🍂

Misty Mountain Vineyards

Star Route 2, Box 458
Madison City, Virginia 22727
TEL: 703-923-4738

OWNER: Dr. J. M. Cerceo
WINEMAKER: Eric Brevart
FOUNDED: 1983

AT A GLANCE

Tours & Tastings: By appt.

Closed: Thanksgiving, Christmas, Easter, July 4.

Vineyards: 110 acres owned and 35 acres leased, planted primarily to vinifera varieties—Riesling, Chardonnay, Cabernet, Merlot, Pinot Noir, Seyval Blanc.

Wines: First crush was 1986 and white Riesling, Chardonnay, Cabernet, and Merlot were produced.

Awards: Silvers to Chardonnay and Chablis (Seyval blend) at 1988 Grand National Competition, Silver for Reisling at Atlanta International event; Gold and Best of Show to Chardonnay at Vinifera Wine Growers Association of Virginia competition.

Picnic Areas: Nothing formal, but visitors can bring picnics and settle somewhere on the 425 well-tended acres.

Retail Sales: Yes.

Credit Cards: None.

Access for Disabled: Yes.

Foreign Languages: French, Italian.

Getting There: Misty Mountain is seven miles northwest of Madison township, between Charlottesville and Culpeper. From Charlottesville: 90 north on Rte. 29 through town of Madison, then north to Rte. 231 toward Sperryville, then turn left on Rte. 651 right on Rte. 652, left on Rte. 698, which ends at winery. It's a twelve-minute drive from Rte. 29.

🍂 Appropriately, Misty Mountain is located on a mountain farm with a historic house dating from 1813, a stone's throw from Shenandoah National Park. Winery and manor house are built in the architectural style typical of this Virginia area during the late 1800s. The property borders Monticello v.a.

🍂 🍂 🍂

Montdomaine Cellars, Inc.

Route 720 (Route 6, Box 168-A)
Charlottesville, Virginia 22901
TEL: 804-971-8947
CHIEF OPERATING OFFICER: Layne
  Witherell
WINEMAKER: Shep Rouse (UC-Davis,
  master's in winemaking)
FOUNDED: 1977

AT A GLANCE
Tours & Tastings: Guided one-hour tours, 10–4 weekdays; weekends Apr.–Nov. 10–5. Guides take individual levels of sophistication into consideration as they show visitors around the underground winery. Tours followed by tastings of at least five wines.
Closed: Christmas, New Year's Day.
Vineyards: On seventy-five acres are six vineyards located a few miles from the winery, planted exclusively to *Vitis vinifera* varieties including Chardonnay, Cabernet Sauvignon, Merlot, Riesling, Pinot Noir, Cabernet Franc, and Sauvignon Blanc. The vines lead properly protected lives: they enjoy lazy summer days on a cozy southeast slope, shaded from the afternoon sun and shielded from winter winds by trees to the north.
Wines: Montdomaine produces only vinifera varietals.
Awards: Gold medals to Merlot and Riesling, silvers to Chardonnay and Cabernet Sauvignon, and bronze to Cabernet Blanc (first blush wine produced in Virginia entirely from Cabernet Sauvignon grapes).
Picnic Areas: Tables set in wooded areas near the winery.
Retail Shop: Wines sold on-site.
Credit Cards: MasterCard, Visa.
Access for Disabled: None.
Foreign Languages: None.
Getting There: Montdomaine is about thirteen miles south of Charlottesville. From exit 24 on I-64 (Monticello, Michie Tavern exit): Follow Rte. 20 south for approximately thirteen miles. Turn right on Rte. 720 and proceed for about half a mile; then turn right into the vineyard and proceed to winery.

❧ Montdomaine is known for its state-of-the-art, modern 20,000-gallon underground winery, tunneled into a hillside. Below are over one hundred French oak barrels at a temperature maintained near 60 degrees to help develop the wines' bouquets. Modernity aside, Montdomaine has an old-fashioned informal side, best experienced during harvest, when visitors may be asked to lend a hand.

❧ ❧ ❧

Oakencroft Vineyard & Winery

Route 5
Charlottesville, Virginia 22901
TEL: 804-296-4188
OWNER: Mrs. John B. Rogan
WINEMAKER: Deborah Welsh (student of Belgian enologist Jacques Recht, Ingleside Winery)
FOUNDED: 1983

AT A GLANCE
Tours & Tastings: Apr.–Dec., Mon.–Fri., 9–4; Sat.–Sun., 11–5. Tour guides show you around the winery and vineyards located on Mrs. Rogan's husband John's registered polled Hereford farm. There's a $1-per-person charge for groups of ten or more.
Closed: Major holidays.
Vineyards: Seventeen acres planted to Chardonnay, Seyval Blanc, Cabernet Sauvignon, and Merlot.
Wines: Estate-bottled and vintage-dated varietals.
Awards: Seyval Blanc started out by winning a bronze medal when first released in 1983 and has picked up some silvers in the ensuing years; since 1985, Chardonnay has also won awards.
Retail Shop: Wines sold on-site and in shops around town.

Credit Cards: None.
Access for Disabled: None.
Foreign Languages: None.
Getting There: From Rte. 654 at Barracks Rd. light in Charlottesville: go 3½ miles west on Barracks Rd. to Oakencroft sign on split rail fence on left and continue on winding road to the winery.
Special Wine & Other Events: See end of Virginia section for Monticello Wine Festival.

&. Oakencroft is as pleasing to the eye as a pastoral painting. The remodeled red-barn winery looks out on a lake that's a popular stopover for Canadian geese, and the vineyards and Blue Ridge Mountains can be seen behind the barn.

Owner Felicia Warburg Rogan started with fifty plants on an acre of land and made a few bottles of wine in her garage. She now harvests seventeen acres producing 7,000 gallons of wine, a selection of which can be tasted in the tile-floored tasting room with red barnboard walls and antique wine accessories.

The following four Central Virginia vineyards are outside the Monticello viticultural area. Prince Michel Vineyards, Rapidan River Vineyards, and the aforementioned Misty Mountain Vineyards are in a group that has applied for the Montpelier viticultural area designation, which may be given in 1989.

&. &. &.

Prince Michel Vineyards

Route 29 (Star Route 4, Box 77)
Leon, Virginia 22725
TEL: 703-547-3707
GENERAL MANAGER: Joachim Hollerith
WINEMAKERS: Joachim Hollerith
  (degree in viticulture and enology,
  University of Geisenheim, Germany)
  and Alan Kinne
FOUNDED: 1983

AT A GLANCE

Tours & Tastings: Tours, guided or self-guided, 10–5 daily, permit visitors to view winemaking step-by-step in the 150,000-gallon winery. There's also a wine museum, a film on the history of wine and viticulture, a gift shop, and a tasting room.
Closed: Thanksgiving, Christmas, and New Year's days.
Vineyards: 110 acres make this the largest vinifera vineyard in Virginia. Varieties planted here are Chardonnay, Pinot Noir, Cabernet Sauvignon, Riesling, Merlot, and Gewürztraminer.
Wines: Blush de Michel, White Burgundy, Chardonnay, Cabernet Sauvignon, Pinot Noir, White Riesling; Gewürztraminer, champagne planned.
Awards: Prince Michel's whites, Chardonnay (aged in French oak casks), and Riesling (a German-style semi-sweet wine), have all won awards. Another awarded white is Vavin Nouveau—a blend of Chardonnay and Riesling wines.
Retail Shop: Prince Michel wines, and many items related to storage, service, and enjoyment of fine wines, such as fine linens and crystal; Appalachian ceramics and Virginia crafts.
Credit Cards: MasterCard, Visa.
Access for Disabled: Yes.
Foreign Languages: German.
Getting There: Winery is located on the west side of Rte. 29, ten miles south of Culpeper and eight miles north of Madison.
Special Wine & Other Events: Oktoberfest, modeled after those in Germany, is held with all the oompah associated with this tradition.

&. The French Provincial-style winery is an area landmark, with its extensive vineyards sprawling over fields and into the foothills of the Blue Ridge Mountains. It boasts of a visitors center with wine museum, gift shop, and tasting room. From these vineyards come 80,000 cases of premium wines, sold throughout Virginia and the Midatlantic region.

&. &. &.

Rose Bower Vineyard & Winery

Route 686 (P.O. Box 126)
Hampden-Sydney, Virginia 23943
TEL: 804-223-8209
OWNERS: Tom and Bronwyn O'Grady
WINEMAKER: Tom O'Grady (vinologist for fifteen years)

AT A GLANCE
Tours & Tastings: The vineyard and winery are open to visitors for sales, Mar. 15–Dec. 15, Tues.–Sun. Tours by appt. Call for hours. Tom O'Grady himself takes visitors on tours, which start with a walk around the vineyard with its graceful gazebo, include the winery with its underground, candlelit cellar, and conclude with a tasting.
Closed: Jan., Feb., Sept., Oct.
Vineyards: Eleven acres planted to French hybrid and vinifera grapes.
Wines: Limited bottlings of oak-fermented Chardonnay, Johannisberg Riesling, Seyval Blanc, claret, rosé, dessert wines. Each variety is vintage-dated and released at the season when it would be most enjoyed.
Awards: Gold medal awarded Chardonnay 1985. Riesling, Seyval Blanc, Rosé O'Grady have also received awards.
Picnic Area: Yes.
Retail Shop: Wines sold on-site.
Credit Cards: MasterCard, Visa.
Access for Disabled: None.
Foreign Languages: Some French.
Getting There: From Farmville: Take Rte. 15 to Worsham, right on Rte. 665, 2 miles to second fork & bear left on Rte. 604, 3 miles & right on Rte. 686, 1½ mile to red entrance sign on right.
Special Wine & Other Events: Festivals in Nov. (Festival Nouveau), March (St. Pat-

rick's), May (budbreak), July, and Aug. (harvest); Oct. (autumn color).

&. A poet-in-residence at Hampden-Sydney College, Tom O'Grady makes wines by classic eighteenth-century techniques: they are aged in lightly toasted oak barrels, clarified with natural ingredients, siphoned rather than pumped when possible, and only lightly filtered. Originally the wines were offered only from the 225-year-old Rose Bower Cottage, in the manner of a small Burgundian chateau, but now also the wines can be purchased in shops, restaurants, and by mail and phone orders as well.

&. &. &.

Stonewall Vineyards

Route 1, Box 107A
Concord, Virginia 24538
TEL: 804-993-2185
OWNERS: Howard and Betty Bryan
WINE CONSULTANTS: Luci Morton and Jacques Recht
FOUNDED: 1983

AT A GLANCE
Tours & Tastings: Apr.–Dec., Tues.–Sat. 1–6, Sat. year round. Other times by appt. Tours include vineyard and small but well-equipped winery, where wines are made in small lots with great attention to quality.
Closed: Major holidays.
Vineyards: Seven acres owned, five leased, all planted to French hybrids, native American, and vinifera varieties: Cabernet Sauvignon, Cayuga White, Chardonnay, Chambourcin, Verdelet, Vidal Blanc.
Wines: Most are varietals, though one or two blends are made, as is spiced mead in fall. Output is small and supplies are limited.
Awards: Award winners are Verdelet, Cayuga, claret.

Retail Sales: Wines sold on-site.
Credit Cards: None.
Access for Disabled: Everything is on one level.
Foreign Languages: Spanish, French, German ("but not too well").
Getting There: Fifteen miles east of Lynchburg and twelve miles west of Appomattox. From Rte. 460 in Concord: Go north six miles on Rte. 608, take a left on Rte. 721; winery is on the left.
Special Wine & Other Events: The second weekend in Oct. is Railroad Day, celebrated at historic Appomattox. Appomattox Historical Park is open daily.

🍂 Stonewall is a small, well-equipped, family-owned-and-operated winery, where wines are made in small batches with great attention to quality.

TO SEE & DO
Wine routes entwine with history in a treasure trove of early Americana. To be seen in the area are the illustrious homes of Jefferson at Monticello, James Monroe at Ash Lawn, and James Madison at Montpelier, as well as Castle Hill and Swannanoa mansions. Central Virginia is one of the most abundantly beautiful wine routes, with easy access to the Blue Ridge Parkway, the Appalachian Trail, and Shenandoah National Park. Charlottesville, a popular base for wine touring, is the site of the University of Virginia; renowned for horses, the area also offers steeplechase events. Be sure to stop by Virginia's wine museum at Michie Tavern in Charlottesville (daily 9–5; tel: 804-977-1234); instructive exhibits trace Virginia's wine history from Jamestown to the present. For more information, contact the Thomas Jefferson Visitors Bureau, P.O. Box 161, Charlottesville, Virginia 22902; tel: 804-295-3131.

ACCOMMODATIONS
Central Virginia, and Charlottesville in particular, has its share of major national

hotel chains and a fine supply of charming inns and B&Bs; we've room for just a tasting below. Wherever you stay, be sure to book far in advance on big University of Virginia weekends.

Guesthouses Reservation Service
P.O. Box 5737
Charlottesville, Virginia 22905
Tel: 804-979-7264
Offers a choice of budget, moderate, or deluxe accommodations in bed and breakfasts in and about the Charlottesville area.

Fountain Hall
609 South East Street
Culpeper, Virginia 22701-3222
Tel: 703-825-6708
Furnished with antiques; has a cozy, old-fashioned feeling. Continental breakfast.

Mayhurst
Route 15 South (P.O. Box 707)
Orange, Virginia 22960
Tel: 703-672-5597
Zany architecture is but one enjoyable feature of this early Victorian with a rooftop gazebo and a National Historic Register listing. The spacious rooms have floor-to-ceiling windows of the original handblown glass and fireplaces. Full breakfast with Virginia ham and homemade muffins; port at tea time—tea, too.

Inns, Resorts, Motels
Boar's Head Inn
P.O. Box 5185 (Ednam Forest)
Charlottesville, Virginia 22905
Tel: 804-296-2181
Owned by John B. Rogan, husband of Felicia Warburg Rogan, head of Oakencroft Winery. A combination country estate and forty-five-acre sports resort with two swimming pools, tennis and squash courts, fishing, golf, a jogging trail—and an excellent reputation. American cuisine and Oakencroft wines.

Silver Thatch Inn
3001 Hollymead Drive
Charlottesville, Virginia 22901
Tel: 804-286-4686
Tim and Shelley Dwight run a cozy,
antique-filled inn, dating from 1780, set
on a three-acre estate with swimming
pool and tennis courts. A number of
winery owners recommend it as a place
to have Virginia wines with meals or as
an aperitif in the intimate little bar.

High Meadows
Route 4, Box 6
Scottsville, Virginia 24590
Tel: 804-286-2218
Innkeepers Peter Sushka and his wife,
Mary Jane Abbitt, run a twenty-two-acre
estate where you stay in a seventeen-
room home from the 1800s. The well-
restored interiors are highlighted with
antiques, fireplaces, original woodwork.
Stroll the old footpaths bordered by dog-
woods, creeks, ponds, and Pinot Noir–
planted vineyards.

Traveler's Inn
7 West Confederate Boulevard (U.S.
  460)
Appomattox, Virginia 24522
Tel: 804-352-7451
Sixteen rooms, a pool. Not long on
charm, but convenient for visiting Stonewall Vineyards as well as Appomattox.

RESTAURANTS
Many Virginia wine country restaurants
serve locally made wines and menus

well-matched with them, but space permits listing only a few throughout this
section. Those below are in Charlottesville, except where noted.

Boar's Head Inn
(See also under "Accommodations.")
Tel: 804-296-2181
Well-prepared American favorites such
as prime rib and veal served in a reno-
vated old grist mill; Oakencroft wines.

C & O
515 East Water Street
Tel: 804-971-7044
Fresh and sprightly new American cuisine with a slight French accent.

Heritage House
R.R. 6, P.O. Box 100X
Farmington, Virginia 23901
Tel: 804-392-6221
Prime rib, seafood, and other American
classics.

Michie Tavern
Route 6, P.O. Box 7A
Tel: 804-977-1234
Meals served in a converted slave house
that is over 200 years old, called "The
Ordinary." Features special dishes of the
Colonial period.

Silver Thatch Inn
(See also under "Accommodations.")
Tel: 804-978-4686

Eastern Virginia

Accommack Vineyards

Route 607 (P.O. Box 38)
Painter, Virginia 23420
TEL: 804-442-2110
OWNERS: Jim and Gerry Keyes
First farm winery on eastern shore. Nine

acres planted to vinifera varieties. Wines
include Cabernet Sauvignon, Chardonnay, and Riesling. Tours 12–4 Tues.–Sun.
Picnic area. From Painter: Drive one mile
south on U.S. 13 to Rte. 607, left half a
mile to winery on right.

ᵧ₳ ᵧ₳ ᵧ₳

Ingleside Plantation Vineyards

Route 638 (P.O. Box 1038)
Oak Grove, Virginia 22443
TEL: 804-224-8687
OWNER: the Flemer family
WINEMAKER: Jacques Recht (professor
   of enology and fermentation,
   University of Brussels)
FOUNDED: 1980

AT A GLANCE

Tours & Tastings: Fifteen-minute tours,
10–5 Mon.–Sat., Sun. noon–5. Take in
the winery, followed by a tasting of a
number of Ingleside wines. Visitors can
wander on their own through the vineyards and well-tended grounds of the
2,000-acre plantation, which has been in
the Flemer family for nearly 200 years.
Closed: Thanksgiving Day, Christmas
Day, and New Year's Day.
Vineyards: Fifty acres, planted to several
dozen varieties of American, vinifera,
and French-American hybrids.
Wines: Champagne accounts for 5 percent of the annual production; still wines
include Cabernet Sauvignon, Chardonnay, Johannisberg Riesling; Chesapeake
Blanc, Chesapeake Claret, and Ingleside
White are blends.
Awards: A galaxy of sixty different
awards in state, national, and interna-
tional competitions. Frequent winner:
vintage-dated Cabernet Sauvignon (both
1981 and 1982) and Chardonnay 1983
(cited in London and San Francisco competitions).
Picnic Area: Near the vineyards, with tables; large enough for parties.
Retail Shop: Wines, gift items.
Credit Cards: None.
Access for Disabled: Limited.
Foreign Languages: French, German.
Getting There: From Fredericksburg: Ingleside is a 30-mile drive east on Rte. 3 to
Oak Grove. Then turn right on Rte. 638

South and proceed 2½ miles to winery
entrance. This historic wine route takes
in a taste of Westmoreland County, birthplace of both George Washington and
General Robert E. Lee.
Special Wine & Other Events: Ingleside
Plantation Wine Festival is held in the
spring, featuring tours, tastings, regional
foods, music, and arts and crafts.

ᵧ₳ Making plants flourish seems to
come naturally to the Flemers: For over
thirty years, half of their massive estate
has been devoted to a famous nursery,
one of the largest suppliers of landscape
plants on the eastern seaboard. Now,
from their multiacre vineyard, come acclaimed wine grapes.
   In 1960, Carl Flemer started with an
experimental vineyard of French-American hybrids, and from this he and son
Doug turned to commercial winemaking
in 1980. Coincidentally, he met French-
trained winemaker Jacques Recht from
Brussels, who was in America on a boating holiday. Recht came aboard as a consultant and stayed on as resident
winemaker. He turns out Ingleside's
prizewinning wines in a former dairy
barn, following methods used by small
European chateau wineries.

TO SEE & DO

Stratford Hall Plantation (eight miles
from Oak Grove; Rte. 214, off Rte. 3),
was home to four generations of the Lee
family, including two signers of the Dec-
laration of Independence and General
Robert E. Lee. This is a 1,600-acre working plantation, with gardens, stable,
gristmill, and restored home (open daily,
9–4:30; tel: 804-493-8038). Washington's
Birthplace National Monument (five
miles from Oak Grove; Rte. 204 off Rte.
3) is a reconstructed house in the style of
the original farmhouse that was the first
president's childhood home. Live demonstrations show eighteenth-century
plantation life (open daily, 9–5; tel:

804-224-1732). For a leg-stretcher, there's Westmoreland State Park on the Potomac (seven miles from Oak Grove; Rte. 347 off Rte. 3), with swimming, boating, fishing, hiking, nature walks, picnic sites, playground, cabins and campsites.

ACCOMMODATIONS
The Inn at Montross
Courthouse Square
Montross, Virginia 22520
Tel: 804-493-9097
Run by Ellen and Michael Longman, more-than-a-century-old inn furnished with antiques and period reproductions. Comfortable bedrooms and serene surroundings. Rates include breakfast of muffins, croissants, fresh fruit. Other meals served with Ingleside wines.

RESTAURANTS
The Inn at Montross
(See under "Accommodations" above for address, telephone, description.)

ta ta ta

Williamsburg Winery

2638 Lake Powell Road
Williamsburg, Virginia 23185
TEL: 804-229-0999
OWNERS: Pat & Peggy Duffeler
WINEMAKER: Steven R. Warner, formerly with Montdomaine, UC-Fresno trained.
FOUNDED: 1984

AT A GLANCE
Tours & Tastings: Jan.–Feb., Wed.–Sun.; Mar.–Dec., Tues.–Sun., 10–5; small fee for tasting.
Closed: Mon.–Tues., Jan.–Feb.; Mon., Mar.–Dec.
Vineyards: 25 acres adjacent to winery; 22 at Somerset. Vineyards (Monticello v.a.) near Charlottesville, planted primarily to Chardonnay, followed by Riesling, Cabernet Sauvignon; Seyval Blanc, Cabernet Franc, Merlot; two experimental acres planted to Italian grapes and Semillon. Some additional grapes purchased from Tydeswall Vineyards.
Wines: White blends, blush, Chardonnay, Cabernet Sauvignon; some stocks not yet producing.
Awards: Gold to first release, Governor's White (Riesling and Vidal blend) produced at Burnley Vineyards, in Norfolk Yacht and Country Club's Virginia Wine Competition.
Retail Shop: Wines sold on site.
Credit Cards: MasterCard, Visa.
Access for Disabled: "Perhaps when construction is complete."
Foreign Languages: French, Italian, German, some Portuguese.
Getting There: Take I-64 to exit 57A onto Rte. 199W; from 199 turn onto Brookwood Lane, take left onto Lake Powell Road and go 9/10 of a mile to winery entrance on left.

ta The Duffelers spent fifteen years in Europe, where they acquired a taste for fine wines they feel can be duplicated with the help of Virginia's microclimates, modern technology, and a sense of tradition and values. The grand plans for their 300-acre property bordering the James River and College Creek include the winery inspired by eighteenth-century architecture of the Bland plantation, its occupant 200 years ago, and a 68-room country inn modeled after the wine châteaus in France. Historic Williamsburg itself is only two miles away.

TO SEE & DO
Williamsburg, once the second capital of Virginia, now, as a multi-million-dollar restoration, is a magnet for tourists. Travelers should first stop at the Visitors Center, Colonial Pkwy. and V.A. 132, for pamphlets, tickets, and an orientation film. Continue on from there or contact for information in advance The Williamsburg Foundation, P.O. Box C, Williamsburg, Virginia 23187, tel.

804-229-1000. Houses, shops, and exhibits peopled by a Colonial-costumed populace; William & Mary College and other attractions await visitors' inspection.

ACCOMMODATIONS

Until the inn is finished at the winery, head to Williamsburg. More than a million visitors step back into history at Williamsburg each year, and there are all manner of accommodations to fit every pocketbook. The most desired places to stay are in the historic area, owned and operated by the Williamsburg Foundation (tel: 800-HISTORY for information or write the address above).

Bed and Breakfasts
The Travel Tree
P.O. Box 838
Williamsburg, Virginia 23187
Tel: 804-253-1572
Recommendations for bed and breakfasts in Williamstown, Jamestown, and Yorktown.

OTHER
Colonial Houses
Francis Street
Williamsburg, Virginia 23187
Tel: 804-229-1000; 800-HISTORY
Restored Colonial homes furnished in early American style. Enjoy dining, swimming, and other sports at Williamsburg Inn.

Williamsburg Motor House
Box B (Opposite Visitors Center)
Tel: 804-229-1000; 800-447-2679
Better-than-average motel with 219 rooms with pool and other sports activities and café.

Williamsburg Inn
Francis Street
Williamsburg, Virginia 23185
Tel: 804-229-1000; 800-HISTORY
Refined, elegant, and handsomely furnished in the Regency style. 102 rooms.

Pool, tennis, lawn games, golf. Excellent food (see Regency Dining Room under "Restaurants").

Williamsburg Lodge
South England Street
Williamsburg, Virginia 23185
Tel: 804-229-1000; 800-447-8976
Well-furnished rooms in lodge adjacent to restored area. Pool, tennis, lawn games, golf. Good restaurant.

RESTAURANTS
Regency Dining Room Williamsburg
(See Williamsburg Inn under
  "Accommodations.")
Tel: 804-229-2141
Quiet and refined dining; start with smoked trout followed by snapper, braised quail, rack of lamb entrées. Background music; wine list. Outdoor dining in fair weather. Dancing on weekends after nine. Tie and jacket required.

Williamsburg Lodge
(See under "Accommodations")
Tel: 804-229-1000
Popular for Sunday brunch; less formal than the Inn. Continental dishes with an Italian accent. Chesapeake Bay Fish dinner on Fri.–Sat. Wine list. Cocktails outdoors in fair weather.

Cascades
(See Williamsburg Motor House under
  "Accommodations.")
Tel: 804-229-1000
Seafood specialties; buffet meals. Outdoor dining in fair weather.

Chowning's Tavern
Duke of Gloucester Street
Tel: 804-229-2141
Eighteenth-century ale house with Colonial fare, table games, and strolling minstrels. Wine served, although in these surroundings punch or grog might be more fitting. Pretty garden.

King's Arms Tavern
Duke of Gloucester Street
Tel: 804-229-2141
Sit under a scuppernong grape arbor
when it's fair, or inside in a restored
eighteenth-century tavern, and dine on

Colonial dishes such as game pie, ven-
ison stew, or oyster pie with Virginia ham
and fresh-baked rolls. Apple cider is the
preferred partner with foods, although
some heartier wines would do. Bal-
ladeers at dinner.

Northern Virginia

Farfelu Vineyard

Highway 647
Flint Hill, Virginia 22627
TEL: 703-364-2930
OWNER/WINEMAKER: Charles J. Raney
FOUNDED: 1967

AT A GLANCE
Tours & Tastings: By appointment only
Vineyards: Six acres planted to Chardon-
nay, Cabernet Sauvignon, Merlot, Chan-
cellor, De Chaunac, Cayuga.
Wines: Limited quantities of Cabernet
Sauvignon, Chardonnay, and other vari-
etals from grape varieties above, and pro-
prietary whites and reds.
Retail Shop: Wines sold on-site.
Credit Cards: None.
Access for Disabled: None.
Foreign Languages: None.
Getting There: Approximately sixty-five
miles west of Washington, D.C., on the
doorstep of the Shenandoah National
Park and Skyline Drive. Four miles east
of Flint Hill, thirteen miles west of Mar-
shall on Rte. 647. Skyline Drive hikers
might ankle right on in.

• A pioneer among Virginia's vineyardists, Charles Ramey started one of
the state's first farm wineries, in 1966, by
planting a few vines alongside the old
apple orchards. So began a decade of
experimentation on several varieties he
now uses to produce wine in his 130-
year-old converted barn, set in the rolling
hills overlooking the Rappahannock
River.

TO SEE & DO
Adjacent to Farfelu, the Skyline Drive
skims along the crest of the Blue Ridge
Mountains, turning your wine route into
more than one hundred miles of spectacularly scenic vistas. The drive runs
through Shenandoah National Park,
where you can enjoy miles of delightful
hikes, breathtaking views, and old mountain homesteads, plus Luray Caverns,
craft and antique shops, picnic groves,
and horseback trails. Near the park exits
are fresh produce stands and orchards
where you can buy your favorites or pick
your own. Late summer berries are quite
a treat with some of the Virginia wines.
(See also suggestions following Oasis,
Piedmont, and Shenandoah vineyards.)

ACCOMMODATIONS
Along the drive itself are lodges and cab-
ins. For information on them, contact
ARA Virginia Sky-Line Company, Inc.,
P.O. Box 727, Luray, Virginia 22835 (tel:
703-743-5108). Among the inns and
B&Bs in the area are:

Caldonia Farm
Route 1, Box 2080
Flint Hill, Virginia 22627
Tel: 703-675-3693
Stone home from 1812, adjacent to Shen-
andoah National Park. Full breakfast and
welcoming drink.

Conyers House
Slate Mills Road
Sperryville, Virginia 22740
Tel: 703-987-8025

Two centuries old, attractive rooms, foothills location. Located south of Sperryville, off Route 231.

≈ ≈ ≈

Meredyth Vineyards

Route 628 (P.O. Box 347)
Middleburg, Virginia 22117
TEL: 703-687-6277
OWNERS: Dody and Archie Smith, Jr.
WINEMAKER: Archie Smith 3rd
FOUNDED: 1972

AT A GLANCE

Tours & Tastings: 10–4 daily, including Sat. & Sun., and by appointment. Guided one-hour tour of the winery and cellars with explanation of winemaking and tasting.
Closed: Christmas, New Year's, Thanksgiving, and festival days.
Vineyards: Sixty acres planted to French-American hybrids and vinifera varieties, with a small patch of labrusca, makes this among the largest of Virginia's wineries. Some fruits purchased from Burnley Vineyards in central Virginia.
Wines: Vintage-dated, estate-bottled wines. Known especially for Seyval Blanc and Chardonnay; other whites are Villard Blanc, Sauvignon Blanc. Reds include Cabernet Sauvignon, De Chaunac, Villard Noir, Marechal Foch, and Harvest Red (a blend); also produced are Harvest Blush, Aurora Blanc, Rougeon Rosé. Aurora and Riesling are exceptionally fruity, the result of botrytis (the "noble rot").
Awards: Some eighty awards have been given to Meredyth wines since 1979, from earliest to recent crushes; most frequently cited have been Chardonnay, Seyval Blanc, and Cabernet Sauvignon. A Meredyth Seyval Blanc has been served in the White House.
Picnic Area: In the vineyard.

Retail Shop: Wines, homemade Meredyth wine jelly, wine accessories, and gifts.
Credit Cards: MasterCard, Visa.
Access for Disabled: Difficult, but possible, except for downstairs cellar.
Foreign Languages: A little French and Spanish.
Getting There: About an hour's drive from Washington, D.C., just outside Middleburg. At the Middleburg blinker on Rte. 50, turn south, stay on paved road for 2½ miles to Rte. 628. Turn right on 628 to entrance.
Special Wine & Other Events: Monthly events—a lobster dinner, crab fests; poetry readings, theatricals, winemaking classes.

≈ Set in the silt-loam foothills of the Bull Run Mountains, Meredyth is a Smith family affair—in addition to Archie Jr. and his wife, Dody, who acts as bookkeeper, there's winemaker Archie 3rd, a former Oxford philosophy professor, and daughter Susan, a vice president of the firm. Another son, Robert, an architect in Washington, helped design the winery, a stable converted from the days when Smiths were cattle and corn farmers. Archie Jr. has been in the forefront of the Virginia wine industry: a founder and president of the Virginia Wineries Association, he lobbied for the 1980 law that gave tax breaks to farm wineries. The Smiths cultivated a taste for fine wine while traveling abroad, and they use European methods to make their wines today. The wines are distributed more widely than most farm wineries—in eleven other states.

TO SEE & DO

For once, the word *charming* is apt when applied to historic Middleburg, a town with antique shops, good restaurants, and atmospheric inns and bed and breakfasts.

ACCOMMODATIONS
The Red Fox Inn & Tavern
2 East Washington Street
Middleberg, Virginia 22117
Tel: 703-687-6301; 800-223-1728
Part of this inn and tavern dates back to 1728. Today, five suites and seventeen doubles, cozy and comfortable, with private attached bathrooms, await visitors. The pine bar in the tavern was a Civil War operating table. Good food and local wine. Truffles and fruit on bedside tables.

RESTAURANTS
In addition to the Red Fox Tavern, try:

Windsor House
22 West Washington Street
Middleburg, Virginia 22117
Tel: 703-687-6800; 478-1300 (D.C. area)
An old English setting adds to the enjoyment of well-prepared seafood and pasta. Outdoor dining in fair weather.

ðŸ¥‚ ðŸ¥‚ ðŸ¥‚

Oasis Vineyard

Highway 635
Hume, Virginia 22639
TEL: 703-635-7627
OWNER/WINEMAKER: Dirgham Salahi
FOUNDED: 1980

AT A GLANCE
Tours & Tastings: Tours 10–4 daily. See the vineyard, winery, and 10,000-foot underground cellar; two films (winemaking and wine appreciation) available on request. Following are tastings conducted by either Salahi himself or his wife, Corrine. There is a $2.50-per-glass charge for champagne tasting. The Salahis suggest several unhurried visits to savor special times at the vineyard and to sample seasonal releases.
Closed: New Year's, Christmas, and Thanksgiving days.
Vineyards: Forty acres devoted mainly to viniferas, but there are some French hybrids and American varieties.
Wines: A *methode champenoise* champagne, made of Chardonnay and Pinot Noir blend; reds such as Merlot, Cabernet Sauvignon, Chelois; whites include Riesling, Gewürztraminer, Sauvignon Blanc, and Seyval Blanc.
Awards: Wines have gotten recognition in competitions since first releases, each cited at least once. First Virginia winery to win a gold medal in an international wine competition for its French-style champagne.
Picnic Area: An oasis within Oasis is the large picnic area outdoors and tables indoors in tasting room; banquet facilities handle large parties.
Retail Shop: Wines and gift items.
Credit Cards: MasterCard, Visa.
Access for Disabled: Yes.
Foreign Languages: French, Italian.
Getting There: From Washington, D.C.: Go west on I-66 to Marshall (2nd exit), Rte. 647 from Marshall, right on Rte. 635 for ten miles to winery. From Front Royal or Skyline Drive: Take Rte. 522 South toward Flint Hill for seven miles, left on Rte. 635 for one mile. Easily accessible to hikers on Skyline Drive.
Special Wine & Other Events: Spring Festival in May; dinners and tastings year-round.

ðŸ¥‚ Since 1980, Oasis has grown into one of the largest wineries in Virginia, bottling 400 cases per day. Newly designed in the French Provincial style, the winery at Oasis Vineyards has a handsome tasting room with a stone fireplace and a great view of the forty-acre vineyard and the Blue Ridge Mountains. A winemaker with thirty years of experience, Jerusalem-born Salahi says that making a bottle of wine is like trying to help a child mature. The Salahis enjoy talking to visitors about wine and teaching them about it in easy-to-understand ways.

TO SEE & DO

The major beauty spot and attraction is the 100-mile Skyline Drive. Also in this area are some interesting historic towns, such as Washington, Virginia (Rte. 211, thirteen miles east of Skyline Drive), laid out more than 200 years ago by George Washington, with quaint shops, arts and crafts. For a change of pace from historic to prehistoric, see the Skyline Caverns (Front Royal, one mile from northern entrance to drive; tel: 703-635-4545), with formations millions of years old, and the Thunderbird Museum & Archeological Park (Rte. 737, six miles south of Front Royal off Rte. 340; tel: 703-635-7337), tracing 11,000 years of history—to name only a few attractions.

ACCOMMODATIONS

(See also recommendations for Middleburg.)

Constant Spring Inn

413 South Royal Avenue, Route 340
Fort Royal, Virginia 22630
Tel: 703-635-7010
Family-run 1920s home, with big front porch. Virginia hams and pan-fried perch, biscuits and fruit cobbler among the homestyle dishes in the dining room.

The Foster-Harris House

P.O. Box 333
Washington, Virginia 22747
Tel: 703-675-3757
Renovated Victorian B&B filled with charm and antiques. Coffee and bagels or croissants at breakfast, and wine and cheese in the afternoon.

The Inn at Little Washington

Middle & Main Streets (P.O. Box 300)
Washington, Virginia 22747
Tel: 703-675-3800
Luxurious country-style inn with an English look, at the foot of the Blue Ridge Mountains; excellent restaurant. Garden terrace, fountains.

Shenandoah Countryside

Route 2 (Box 377)
Luray, Virginia 22835
Tel: 703-743-6434
New brick farmhouse with old-fashioned hospitality and a classic view of the picturesque countryside. You get comfortably furnished rooms, a big breakfast with pancakes, homemade breads, and eggs; wines, cookies, and Virginia peanuts later in the day.

RESTAURANTS

The Inn at Little Washington, mentioned above, has a restaurant highly praised by guests and critics alike.

ᘖ ᘖ ᘖ

Piedmont Vineyards & Winery

Route 626 (P.O. Box 286)
Middleburg, Virginia 22117
TEL: 703-687-5528
OWNER: Mrs. William E. Worrall
WINEMAKER: Curtis Sherrer, graduate,
 UC-Davis
FOUNDED: 1973

AT A GLANCE

Tours & Tastings: Seven days a week, 10–5, Apr.–Dec.; Jan.–March, Wed.–Sun. 10–4. Tours are notable for their history of the site as well as a thorough look at every step in winemaking; concluded with tasting.
Closed: Thanksgiving, Christmas, and New Year's days.
Vineyards: Virginia's first commercial vinifera vineyard has 30 acres, 16.5 planted to Chardonnay, 7.6 to Sémillon, and 5.1 to the French hybrid Seyval Blanc.
Wines: Vintage-dated varietals and blends from the above varieties, plus Hunt Country White and Little River White.

Awards: Silver medals have been twice awarded the Sémillon, one in London competition. Silver medal to Chardonnay in a New York competition.
Picnic Area: Lovely setting under the trees.
Retail Shop: Wines, gifts.
Credit Cards: MasterCard, Visa.
Access for Disabled: Yes. If special assistance is needed, call in advance with specifics.
Foreign Languages: German.
Getting There: Three miles south of Middleburg on Rte. 626; take a left at the winery sign, follow signs to winery.
Special Wine & Other Events: Middleburg Wine Festival at Piedmont, second Saturday every August. Dinners are also held; call for details.

᪥ Way back when Thomas Jefferson was trying to coax vinifera vines to grow at Monticello, there already was the 500-acre Waverly Farm, with its handsome colonial mansion—now Piedmont Vineyards & Winery. Where Jefferson failed and modern scientists had grave doubts, Mrs. Thomas Furness succeeded. In 1973, at age seventy-five, she founded Virginia's first commercial vinifera vineyard. Furness's family continues her work, and daughter Mrs. William E. Worrall now guides Piedmont's operations.

Today, the vineyard is proud to be one of a handful of domestic vintners successfully producing the delicate Sémillon. Bottles of this special wine come with a work of art that won't strain the pocketbook—the label is created by an American artist selected each year by Piedmont.

For accommodations and restaurants, see the listings following Meredyth Vineyards, Oasis and Willowcraft.

᪥ ᪥ ᪥

Willowcroft Farm Vineyards

Route 2, Box 174-A
Leesburg, Virginia 22075
TEL: 703-777-8161
OWNERS: Lew and Cindy Parker
WINEMAKER: Lew Parker
FOUNDED: 1979

AT A GLANCE
Tours & Tastings: By appointment only. "Call first. You're always welcome, but we're not always home," advise the Parkers.
Vineyards: Two acres owned, two acres leased; planted to vinifera and French hybrids.
Wines: Chardonnay, Riesling, Cabernet Sauvignon, Seyval Blanc.
Awards: Gold to Riesling, silver for the Seyval Blanc, both at Governor's Cup 1986 competition; bronze for Chardonnay from Vinifera Growers Association.
Retail Sales: Local restaurants.
Access for Disabled: No.
Foreign Languages: French.
Getting There: Thirty miles west of D.C. South from Leesburg on Rte. 15, right on Rte. 704, immediate left on Rte. 797 (dirt road), 3.1 miles to sign; the farm will be on your right. Thirty-five minutes from D.C. Beltway on Rte. 7.

᪥ Willowcroft, Virginia's northernmost winery, offers panoramic views of the entire Loudon Valley and the Blue Ridge Mountains from its location on top of Mount Gilead. The rustic farm dates from the 1800s, and the small family winery is in the old barn, where the cellar provides even, cool temperatures for limited quantities of wine. Shading the springhouse today is the old namesake willow tree. On the banks of the Potomac, Leesburg is the site of Chesapeake and Ohio National Historic Park; to the southwest is Manassas National Battlefield Park.

ACCOMMODATIONS

Inns
Colonial Inn
19-21 South King Street
Leesburg, Virginia 22075
Tel: 703-777-5000
Ten guest rooms with eighteenth-century decor, four-poster beds; complimentary Continental breakfast.

Little River Inn
Route 50 (P.O. Box 116)
Aldie, Virginia 22001
Tel: 703-327-6742
The rooms are in cottages appointed with antiques and set on five acres with a swimming pool and resident sheep and donkey. Full breakfast has its charms also—fresh Dutch apple babies are one of them, plus sausages, muffins, fruit, and hot or cold cereals.

Other
Westpark
Leesburg, Virginia 22075
Tel: 703-777-1910
Modern 132-room hotel with period reproduction furnishings and a championship golf course with a twenty-four-tee driving range.

RESTAURANTS
Also enjoy Colonial Inn, above and Windsor House (see after Farfelu).

The Green Tree
15 South King Street
Leesburg, Virginia 22075
Tel. 703-777-7246
Authentic eighteenth-century cuisine, coupled with a delightful setting and good Virginia wine list.

Shenandoah Valley

Wine routes lead through the glorious 200-mile Shenandoah Valley, extending between the Shenandoah and Blue Ridge mountains. Long known for its agricultural abundance, the area has been gaining a reputation for premium wine production. (For accommodations and Restaurants, see the end of this section.)

❦ ❦ ❦

Guilford Ridge Vineyard

Route 2, Box 117
Luray, Virginia 22835
TEL: 703-778-3853
PROPRIETORS: John Gerba, Jr., and Harland L. Baker
CELLARMASTER: Harland Baker (UC-Davis)
FOUNDED: 1983

AT A GLANCE
Tours & Tastings: Open throughout the year. Call for an appointment for tastings/tours/sales. Special tastings ($4 per person) for small groups include regional and seasonal foods.
Vineyards: Four acres planted to vinifera and vinifera-hybrids.
Wines: Guilford Ridge's goal is to produce distinctive regional premium wines through the traditional European technique of assembling (blending) the finest varietals of each vintage. Page Valley White and Red and vinifera-hybrid varietals currently available.
Awards: Does not enter competitions.
Retail Shop: Wines are sold on-site and at a nearby restaurant/wine shop.
Credit Cards: None. Personal checks accepted.
Access for Disabled: "None, other than the willingness to accommodate."

Foreign Languages: None.
Getting There: From traffic light intersection in Luray at U.S. 211 (business) & U.S. 340: Go four miles south on Rte. 340, west for one mile on Rte. 632 to vineyard entrance.
Special Wine & Other Events: Around Labor Day each year the Page Valley Fete celebrates the vintage-in-the-making. Other events blend the performing and visual arts with wine tastings.

🌿 Vineyards flourished in Page Valley before Prohibition and again in the 1940s. In 1971, Guilford Farm, as it was then known, began more than a decade of experimentation to determine that their rocky clay-loam soil and climatic conditions at 1,100 feet were conducive to premium wine production. Spectacular valley-long mountain vistas at sunset and moonrise inspired the winery's label. Sunset "winedowns" (wines by the glass, with picnic and entertainment) in summer sometimes mark this magical time of day.

🌿 🌿 🌿

Shenandoah Vineyards

Route 3, Box 323
Edinburg, Virginia 22824
TEL: 708-984-8699
OWNER: Mrs. Emma F. Randel
WINEMAKER: Jack Foster
FOUNDED: 1976

AT A GLANCE
Tours & Tastings: Self-guided tours 10–6. Visitors take clearly written scripts in hand and go at their own pace through each phase of winemaking, starting in the vineyard and ending in the tasting room.
Closed: Thanksgiving, Christmas, New Year's, and Easter days.
Vineyards: Four vineyards totaling forty-eight acres, owned and leased, planted to six minor Ravat varieties as well as Cabernet Sauvignon, Chambourcin, Riesling, Seyval and Vidal blanc, Chardonnay, Pinot Noir. Vineyards were planted in 1976, 1981, 1982, 1983.
Wines: Varietals from the above listed grapes as well as blends of Shenandoah Blanc, Shenandoah Ruby, and Blushing Belle.
Awards: Of a galaxy of over thirty award winners, the brightest stars have been Chambourcin and Cabernet Sauvignon, with Pinot Noir and Seyval Blanc shimmering nearby.
Picnic Area: Under the trees near the vineyard.
Retail Shop: Wines, vineyard logo T-shirts, hats, cork pullers, and glasses.
Credit Cards: MasterCard, Visa.
Access for Disabled: Back entrance with ramp.
Foreign Languages: French.
Getting There: From Edinburg: Exit off I-81, west on Rte. 675 heading away from Edinburg; take right on first road (Rte. 686). Winery, 1½ miles farther, is marked with winery barrel sign on left.
Special Wine & Other Events: Annual Harvest Festival is always held the Sun. after Labor Day. Grape stomping, music, food, tastings; $2. Many other events during the year. Information sent upon request.

🌿 Starting modestly in 1976 with one vineyard, Emma Randel and her late husband, James, then residents of New Jersey, decided to "go all out" and turn an old red barn in Edinburg into the high-beamed winery visitors enjoy now. From one small vineyard grew the current forty-plus acreage, and a winery bottling 400 cases a day. A native of the Shenandoah Valley, Randel now lives in the home next to the winery.

TO SEE & DO
Edinburg is home to the Heritage Toy Museum (tel: 703-984-9577; Tues.–Sun. 10–4, Apr. 1–Oct. 31), with trains, 40,000

toy soldiers, miniatures, and dolls. South of Edinburg, at New Market (I-81, exit 67), is the New Market Battlefield and Hall of Valor, tracing the entire history of the Civil War. Four miles north of New Market are the Shenandoah Caverns, with colorful formations, the state's only caverns with an elevator to and from the sights (exit 68 off I-81; tel: 703-477-3115; open all year at 9 a.m.; closing times vary; tours every twenty minutes). Shenandoah Vineyards is only a thirty-five-minute drive from postcard pretty Skyline Drive, with vistas and viewpoints and the lush and lovely Shenandoah National Park. En route to Skyline Drive are the famous Luray Caverns. The largest in Virginia, they house the world's only stalacpipe organ, and icicle-like formations (stalactites on ceiling; stalagmites on floor) going back 7 million years and up as high as sixty feet (tours every twenty minutes, starting at 9; closing times vary; tel: 703-743-6551).

ACCOMMODATIONS
Mary's Country Inn
218 South Main Street
Edinburg, Virginia 22824
Tel: 703-984-8286
A miller's house built in 1840, then enlarged and "Victorianized" in 1890 and 1910. Cozy and charming; homemade muffins served with your big country breakfast. Lovely garden and lawn croquet.

The Inn at Narrow Passage
U.S. 11 South (P.O. Box 83)
Woodstock, Virginia 22664
Tel. 703-459-8000
This historic log inn was built in the 1740s as a haven for settlers against the Indians, later a stagecoach stop, and in 1862 Stonewall Jackson's headquarters during the Valley Campaign. The restored inn boasts of antiques, fireplaces, porches, and hiking and fishing right out the door.

The Candlewick Inn
127 North Church Street
Woodstock, Virginia 22664
Tel: 703-459-8008
Charming country-style rooms; breakfast of home-baked breads, rolls, jam, fruit, cheese, coffee or tea; served in your room or on the sun porch.

RESTAURANTS
Edinburg Mill Restaurant
Main Street
Edinburg, Virginia 22824
Tel: 703-934-8355
A working mill for 150 years. Next door to Mary's Country Inn.

Spring House
325 South Main Street
Woodstock, Virginia 22664
Tel: 703-459-4755
A log cabin filled with Early American antiques is the setting for American specialties.

The Willson Walker House Restaurant
30 North Main Street
Lexington, Virginia 24450
Tel: 703-463-3020
Built as a private home in 1820 in the classical revival style, Walker House was converted to a meat market and grocery store in 1911. In the historic district, decorated with antiques, and featuring regional dishes made from fresh local ingredients and local wines. Open for lunch and dinner, Tues.–Sat.

Southwest Virginia

Chateau Morrisette Winery, Inc.

Blue Ridge Parkway (near milepost 172)
(Route 1, Box 659)
Meadows of Dan, Virginia 24120
TEL: 703-593-2865
PRESIDENT: David Welch Morrisette
HEAD WINEMAKER: Steve Warner
(master's in enology, UC-Fresno)
FOUNDED: 1983

AT A GLANCE
Tours & Tastings: Seven days a week, 10–5; tours take in entire winemaking process, include tasting; hosted by Brenda Warner.
Vineyards: Thirty-five acres owned and twenty-five additional leased, planted to vinifera and French hybrids, in Rocky Knob viticultural area.
Wines: Chardonnay, Riesling, Merlot, Cabernet Sauvignon, Cabernet Blanc, Seyval and Vidal blanc; Sweet Mt. Laurel and red and white table wines.
Awards: Recently to Chardonnay, Seyval Blanc, and Riesling, and "too many others to list," says Morrisette.
Picnic Area: Tables on deck and on grounds under the trees.
Deli: Buy picnic fare at winery's Weathervane Deli.
Retail Shop: Wines sold on-site.
Credit Cards: None.
Access for Disabled: Wheelchair and ramp.

Foreign Languages: French.
Getting There: Near milepost 172 on Blue Ridge Pkwy., 4½ miles north of Mabry Mill; follow signs.
Special Wine & Other Events: Sept. 27: Cabbage Harvest Festival; Oct. 11, Annual Fall Foliage Festival.

ها This beautiful native-stone-and-wood winery with stained-glass windows and wooden floors started out as a family hobby. Morrisette and his father first planted grapes in 1978 to make wine for their own use. The small winery is now a commercial success, producing 25,000 gallons annually.

Blue Ridge Parkway, one of the great scenic drives of America, is almost at the winery's door.

ACCOMMODATIONS
Brookfield Inn
P.O. Box 341
Floyd, Virginia 24091
Tel: 703-763-3363
Perched atop a mountain in the Blue Ridge range, this comfortable country home is surrounded by wooded acreage with a pond and nature trails. Comfortably furnished bedrooms and relaxing living area. Full breakfast features Virginia ham, eggs, and biscuits.

ها WINE FESTIVALS & EVENTS

Noted throughout this section have been events at vineyards; here are a few annuals that unite many of the wineries; for dates/details/admission fees contact source given or Wine Marketing Program, VA Dept. of Agriculture & Consumer Services, Division of Markets, P.O. Box 1163, Richmond, Virginia 23209; Tel: 804-786-0481.

February—Annual The Best of Virginia Wine Competition and tasting hosted by Norfolk Yacht and Country Club; Tel: 804-423-4500.

March—Virginia Wine & Food Weekend at the Homestead; Tel: 804-839-5500.

May—Montpelier Festival—Tours of mansion grounds; hot air balloons, cart rides, wine tastings and more. Tel: 703-832-5555.

June—Virginia Wineries Association Wine Festival at; the 4-H Center, Front Royal, VA. Virginia's largest wine event. Tastings, foods, crafts, pony rides, prizes and grape stomping. Write for details to: WVA P.O. Box 96, Barboursville, Virginia 22923.

August—Annual Wine Festival, the oldest in the state; 18 wineries participate. Contact for details: WVGA, Box P, The Plains, Virginia 22171; Tel: 703-754-8564.

October—Bacchanalian Feast at Boar's Head Inn Charlottesville, 7-course meal with wines and entertainment; Tel: 804-296-4188.

October—Monticello Wine & Food Festival at Boar's Head Inn wine themed exhibits, tastings from several wineries, tours. Tel: 804-296-4188.

October: Town Point/Wine Festival in Norfolk; Tel: 804-627-7809.

❧ WEST VIRGINIA

Three West Virginia vineyards and wineries are producing small lots of quality wines that are beginning to be cited with awards and noticed by serious wine drinkers. These may be tender young wine routes, but they go through some of the country's most historic territory as well as its most scenic. Small wine events and many local festivals add old-fashioned fun to West Virginia visits.

❧ ❧ ❧

Fisher Ridge Wine Co.

Fisher Ridge Road
Liberty, West Virginia 25124
TEL: 304-342-8702
PRESIDENT/OWNER/WINEMAKER: Dr.
   William E. Ward
FOUNDED: 1977

AT A GLANCE
Tours & Tastings: By appointment. Tours, customized to fit tourgoers' interests, include tastings.
Vineyards: Total seven acres (three bearing) in Kanawha Valley; Rayon D'Or, Seyval, Chardonnay, Riesling, Cabernet Sauvignon, Vidal, Sigfried, Megnieu, Vignoles, White Rogue, and Aurora. Four acres under cultivation divided between Seyval and Vidal. Additional grapes purchased from vineyards outside West Virginia.
Wines: Small lots of predominantly white, dry, and intensely fruity wines from above grapes, plus Zinfandel, Cabernet, and Vignoles.
Credit Cards: MasterCard, Visa.
Access for Disabled: Limited.
Foreign Languages: None.
Getting There: From Charleston: Go north on I-77 to Kenna. Take Rte. 34 Southwest for 8 miles, then turn right onto Fisher Ridge Rd. and go three miles to winery.

Special Wine & Other Events: Invitational fine arts show at winery. Sternwheel Regatta turns Charleston's Kanawha River levee into a ten-day festival every Aug., climaxed by the East's fastest sternwheelers and tugs.

🍷 Fisher Ridge, the only winery in the Kanawha Valley viticultural area, is operated by Ward and his wife, Louise Pearson, vineyard manager. Some Fisher Ridge proprietaries have striking modern art labels created by West Virginia artists.

TO SEE & DO
In Charleston, tour the gold-domed state capitol, overlooking the Kanawha River (E. Kanawha Blvd.; tel: 304-348-3809), then head over to Coonskin Park for a full range of outdoor recreational facilities (off Rte. 114; tel: 304-345-8000), or to the Kanawha State Forest for more of the same, plus camping and hiking (tel: 304-345-5654).

ACCOMMODATIONS

Bed & Breakfast
Benedict Haid Farm
16 Dutch Ridge Road
(Mailing address: 8 Hale Street)
Charleston, West Virginia 25301
Tel: 304-346-1054

Hotel Chains/Charleston
Charleston Marriott Town Center
200 Lee Street
East Charleston, West Virginia 25301
Tel: 304-345-6500; 800-228-9290
354 units, pool, tennis, health club and all the usual amenities.

Motels/St. Albans
El Rancho
2843 MacCorkle Avenue
St. Albans, West Virginia 25177
Tel: 304-727-2201
Café on the premises, modest. Ten miles west on U.S. 60, exit I-65.

Smiley's
6210 MacCorkle Avenue Southwest
St. Albans, West Virginia 25177
Tel: 304-766-6231
Pool, racquetball court, entertainment at night, café. Six miles west on Hwy. 60.

RESTAURANTS
Chilton House
2 6th Avenue
St. Albans, West Virginia 25177
Tel: 304-722-2918
Elegant dining in restored 1849 home on riverbank.
Continental menu. Wine list.

🍷 🍷 🍷

Robert F. Pliska & Company Winery

101 Piterra Place
Purgitsville, West Virginia 26852
TEL: 304-289-3493
PRESIDENT: R. Elizabeth Haley-Pliska
WINEMAKER: Robert F. Pliska (master's in enology, enology education services)
FOUNDED: 1975

AT A GLANCE
Tours & Tastings: Tues.–Sat. 1–4, Apr. 16–Oct. 15; by appointment other times (see "Special Wine & Other Events").
Closed: Sun., Mon.
Vineyards: Fourteen acres planted to vinifera and hybrids such as Chancellor and Aurora.
Wines: Varietals and blends labeled 101 Piterra Place or Assumptive; Mountain Mama Apple Wine.
Awards: Both 101 Piterra Place and Assumptive labels have won awards.
Retail Shop: Wines are on sale at winery; part of the proceeds from each sale go to provide homes, work, and recreational activities for mentally retarded adults in rural West Virginia areas.
Credit Cards: None.

Access for Disabled: Wheelchair access to winery and tasting room.
Foreign Languages: French.
Getting There: Hampshire County is 120 miles west of D.C. From Washington: Take U.S. 50 through Winchester, Virginia, to Junction, West Virginia. Turn south on U.S. 220 for 4½ miles to winery at Purgitsville. From Cumberland, Maryland: Take U.S. 220 40 miles south to winery.
Special Wine & Other Events: Singalong Wine Tastings at various times. Taste of the East benefit in Aug. aids mentally retarded with ten or more eastern wineries participating; Wine Heritage of West Virginia and Hardy County in Sept.; Foreign Wine Independence Day on July 4; Christmas Open House; and more.

&a Pliska, a professor of management philosophy, and his wife, Elizabeth, world traveler, wine scholar, and expert in the care of the mentally retarded, have a classic Mediterranean-style winery. Their production combines traditional winemaking techniques with the latest scientific developments. "Each wine, like each person, is unique in personality and character," they say about understanding and enjoying wine.

TO SEE & DO
Of historic interest nearby is the Nancy Hanks Memorial. (For accommodations and restaurants, see the end of West-Whitehall Winery Ltd.)

&a &a &a

West-Whitehall Winery Ltd.

Fried Meat Ridge Road
Route 1, Box 247-A
Keyser, West Virginia 26726
PRESIDENT/GENERAL MANAGER:
  Stephen D. West

VICE PRESIDENT/WINEMAKER: Charles
  Whitehall
FOUNDED: 1981

AT A GLANCE
Tours & Tastings: Apr.–Christmas, Sun. 2–5; otherwise by appointment. Visitors see short slide show on grape growing and winemaking; tour of the winery and vineyard includes tasting.
Vineyards: Six acres, planted to French-American hybrids and Chardonnay, some trial Riesling; other grapes are purchased from growers in eastern West Virginia.
Wines: Whites—Aurora, Chardonnay, Seyval Blanc; blends—Highland Red and Highland Rosé.
Awards: Seyval Blanc is a frequent gold and bronze winner; other winners are Aurora and Highland Red.
Retail Shop: Wines sold on-site.
Credit Cards: None.
Access for Disabled: Level entry into winery.
Foreign Languages: None.
Getting There: West-Whitehill is in Mineral County, 20 miles south of Cumberland, Maryland. From D.C., winery is about 115 miles northwest. Take U.S. 220 to Keyser turnoff onto Rte. 46 and follow it to Fried Meat Ridge Rd. and winery.
Special Wine & Other Events: This is festival country, and here's a sampling of some of them: in July, the Outdoor Civil War Drama, McNeils Rangers, Larenim Park, Burlington; second weekend in Sept., Hampshire Heritage days; last weekend in Sept., Heritage Weekend, Moorehead; third weekend in Sept., Treasure Mountain Festival, Franklin; first weekend in Oct., Old-Fashioned Apple Festival, Burlington; first weekend in Oct., Mountain State Forest Festival, Elkins; second weekend in Oct., Autumn Glory Festival, Oakland.

&a Attorney Stephen D. West and college professor Charles D. Whitehall both tend the vineyard at their namesake property; winemaker Whitehall has taken enology courses in Virginia. Their winery in rural West Virginia offers a beautiful view of the surrounding mountain ranges.

TO SEE & DO

Outdoor enthusiasts head for such attractions as Blackwater Falls State Park, named for the spectacular five-story falls from the Blackwater River, and a multitude of recreational activities (32 miles west of Davis off Rte. 32; tel: 304-259-5216); Deep Creek Lake Summer and Ski resorts; Spruce Knob and Dolly Sods Wilderness areas—to name only some opportunities for hikers, white-water canoers and rafters, and spelunkers. Seneca Rocks await climbers. Visitors can go down in the ground to see Smoke Hole Caverns, and up in the hills on the old-timey Cass Scenic Railroad for the best view of the mountains. South a ways is some of the nation's most spectacular country in Monongahela National Forest in the Allegheny Range, with great scenery and grand adventures for outdoors enthusiasts.

Wine routes continue into Maryland from Keyser; travel up Rte. 202 to Cumberland, then swing over to Scenic Hwy. 40, leading to Maryland's delightful wineries, starting with Frederick County locations. The route works vice versa, needless to say, from Maryland to West Virginia. (See page 000 for more on Maryland wine routes.)

ACCOMMODATIONS

McMechen House Inn
109 North Main Street
Moorefield, West Virginia 26836
Tel: 304-538-2417
A combination Federal and Greek Revival–style building from 1855, the inn was alternately staff headquarters for both Confederate and Union troops. Now accented with Victorian furnishings and run by Art and Evelyn Valetto, rates include Continental breakfast with homemade rolls and muffins.

Among the motels near Keyser are:

Potomac Motel
U.S. 220 (P.O. Box 421)
Keyser, West Virginia 26726
Tel: 304-788-1671
Fifty-six units, swimming pool, lounge, restaurant; one mile south of Keyser.

Among the motels in Cumberland, Maryland (ten miles north of Keyser) are:

Diplomat
Route 220
Cumberland, Maryland 21502
Tel: 301-729-2311
Fifteen rooms, view of hills, café nearby.

Maryland
Route 3, Bedford Road
Cumberland, Maryland 21502
Tel: 301-729-2836
Fifteen units, some with kitchens; café opposite. Three miles north on U.S. 220.

RESTAURANTS

Au Petit Paris
86 East Main Street
Frostburg, Maryland 21532
Tel: 301-689-8946
French menu. Wine list.

Bistro
37 North Centre
Cumberland, Maryland 21502
Tel: 309-777-8462
Continental foods. Wine list. Luscious desserts.

6

The Midwest

Hermannhof Winery, Hermann, Missouri

*F*ine wine from Minnesota?

A tall tale? Not anymore! Now increasing numbers of wine lovers are beginning to realize that from Paul Bunyan territory to Mark Twain country, quality wines are rising like bubbles in champagne. Some of these vineyards and wineries in Ohio and Missouri were around for many years before Prohibition; others are new, in such unexpected climates as Wisconsin and Minnesota. Historic Illinois towns, Indiana farm country, and Iowa back roads are other stops on today's wine routes.

ILLINOIS

Wine routes in Illinois trace the state from south to north, east to west, but their roots do not go very deep. While there have been wineries in Illinois since the 1800s to serve the railroads, those now welcoming visitors are much younger, dating primarily from the late 1970s. With the exception of Galena Cellars, the winemakers of Illinois are just that—winemakers. Their bottles do not begin in their own vineyards. Instead, they graft their skills on to carefully selected grapes trucked in from out of state. The fruit is then cleaned, crushed, pressed, fermented, bottled, and sold on each of the premises.

There is an old saying that a great winemaker can make a great wine with fine grapes, while an indifferent winemaker can make a good wine with the same grapes. Now you can judge what the following winemakers do with top-quality grapes (and fruits) cultivated in diverse vineyards.

THE
MIDWEST

Lake
Leelanau • Omena
Suttons Bay •
Sturgeon
Bay

• Traverse City

MICHIGAN

☆ GRAND
RAPIDS
• Fennville
• Kalamazoo
Paw Paw
• Buchanan

• Fenton
DETROIT ☆

Middle
Bass
Island Kelley's
Put-in-Bay • Island
Port Clinton
Sandusky

Madison • Conneaut
• Geneva
☆ CLEVELAND
Avon Lake
☆ AKRON
Morton • Manchester

INDIANA

OHIO

Dover •

Waldo •

Troy • ☆ COLUMBUS
INDIANAPOLIS • Springfield
☆ Lebanon
• Morrow
• Unionville ☆ Silverton
Bloomington CINCINNATI
• Manchester

Borden •

Chateau Ra-Ha

2324 North 57th Street
Washington Park, Illinois 62204
TEL: 618-271-9290
OWNERS/WINEMAKERS: Harry and Rita
  Hussmann
FOUNDED: 1985

AT A GLANCE

Tours & Tastings: Seven days a week, 10–6; tastings in winery.
Vineyards: Grapes and fruits are purchased from growers around the country. They focus on American hybrids such as Catawba and Cynthiana, vinifera varieties such as Chenin Blanc and Zinfandel.
Wines: More than twenty current releases include varietals and blends from the above grapes, and fruit wines.
Awards: Many as amateur winemakers before founding winery.
Retail Shop: Wines sold on-site.
Credit Cards: None.
Access for Disabled: Ground-level doorways.
Foreign Languages: None.
Getting There: Washington Park, Illinois, is six miles east of St. Louis, Missouri, in southwestern Illinois. Take I-70 to Hwy. 111, exit 6; go south and turn left onto Hill Ave. to N. 57th; winery is in the rear of 2324.
Special Wine & Other Events: Last week of July: St. Louis—Strassenfest; Oct.: Collinsville, Illinois—Italifest.

🐚 A tiny winery tucked away in an Illinois home where pride is taken in producing small lots of a variety of handcrafted wines.

TO SEE & DO

Washington Park is minutes away from St. Louis, Missouri, and riverfront attractions. Also on the famous St. Louis list are Gateway Arch, Museum of Transportation, and, as a switch from winemaking, the Anheuser-Busch Brewery.

Kids of all ages will head to Six Flags Amusement Park.

ACCOMMODATIONS

Bed and Breakfasts
Bed & Breakfast St. Louis
4418 West Pine
St. Louis, Missouri 63108
Tel: 314-533-9299
For recommendations throughout St. Louis.

Lafayette House
1825 Lafayette Avenue
St. Louis, Missouri 63104
Tel: 314-772-4429
Victorian town house near downtown; valuable antiques among the furnishings; deck with view of the arch. Full breakfast; wine, cheese and crackers in the late afternoon.

Inns & Hotels

St. Louis is home to all the chain hotels and motels, from Red Roof to Howard Johnson's, from Holiday Inn to Sheraton.

Seven Gables Inn
26 Meramec
Clayton, Missouri 63105
Tel: 314-863-8400
The architect had Nathaniel Hawthorne's *House of Seven Gables* in mind when this apartment building was designed in the early 1900s. Now it's a quiet hotel with comfortable rooms and two well-regarded restaurants (see under "Restaurants" below). There is a garden courtyard and a park nearby for jogging, swimming, tennis, and ice skating.

RESTAURANTS

Bernard's and Chez Louis
Seven Gables Inn (see under
  "Accommodations" above)
Bernard's serves light meals, while Chez Louis serves elegant French cuisine. Both share a well-stocked wine cellar.

🐚 🐚 🐚

Galena Cellars Winery

515 South Main Street
Galena, Illinois 61036
TEL: 815-777-3330
OWNERS: the Lawlor family
WINEMAKER: Christina Lawlor (degree
in enology, UC-Fresno)

AT A GLANCE
Tours & Tastings: Summer, 10–5 Mon.–
Sun.; Jan.–March, Fri.–Sun. 10–5. Tours
take in historic winery site and include
tasting; check for tour timing.
Vineyards: Own vineyards near Galena
and in Prairie du Chien, Wisconsin,
planted to Marechal Foch, Seyval and
Vidal Blanc; additional grapes/fruits pur-
chased from various Upper Midwest
growers.
Wines: Varietals from the above as well
as Niagara and Catawba; blends such as
Oktoberfest, port; specialty is fruit
wines—cranberry-apple, peach, cherry.
Awards: Too numerous to list; include
"Best of Show" in midwestern competi-
tions.
Restaurant: Galena Cellars' third-floor
and open-air café.
Retail Shop: Wines, wine accessories,
gourmet foods.
Credit Cards: American Express, Mas-
terCard, Visa.
Access for Disabled: Yes.
Foreign Languages: None.
Getting There: Galena Cellars is in down-
town Galena, Illinois, 150 miles west of
Chicago in northwestern Illinois. Take
I-90, which feeds into Rte. 20, to Galena.
Fifteen miles southeast of Dubuque,
Iowa, take Rte. 20 South to Galena.
Special Wine & Other Events: A profes-
sionally staged one-man play, *Galena
Rose,* attracts numerous summer visi-
tors. For a listing of the interesting events
filling the Galena calendar throughout
the year, write to Galena/Jo Davies
Chamber of Commerce, 101 Bouthillier
Street, Galena, Illinois 61036; or call, 10–
4 daily, 815-777-0203; 800-892-9299 (in Il-
linois); or 800-874-9377 (nearby states).

🐌 Take a historic town, add the latest
winemaking equipment, blend in a
skilled winemaker—in this case, Christina Lawlor—to turn out wines, from dry
to sweet, to satisfy a wide variety of
tastes. This in short is the success formula at the Lawlor family wineries, all
set along the upper Mississippi. (For two
other Lawlor wineries, see entries for
Wisconsin, Iowa.)

For Galena Cellars, the Lawlors'
largest property, an 1840s granary building has been transformed into a winery,
restaurant, and outdoor café, with outstanding results. The four-story, suspended, brass-trimmed oak staircase
leading to the third-floor restaurant was
made from huge beams, removed from
the second and third floors to create a
lofty two-story space. For the second-
floor tavern, layers of paint and plaster
were stripped away to reveal warm red
brick, further enhanced with redwood
panels, banded to resemble huge barrels.
The tasting room bar was made from oak
casks, and they too are banded to have a
barrel look. From the outdoor deck,
there's a splendid view of the Civil War–
era buildings along Main Street.

TO SEE & DO
Galena is one of the best preserved
Victorian-era cities in the nation, with
nearly 85 percent of its buildings listed
on the National Register of Historic
Places. Ulysses S. Grant was a Galena
resident, and he is remembered today
with Grant Park and tours of his home.
Galena was a nineteenth-century lead
mining center, and important to Mississippi River trade; today, canoes can be
rented for paddling on the Galena River.

To best see the treasury of historic architecture, take a stroll with the easy-to-
follow pamphlet/map available at the Information and Visitors Center at the Illi-

nois Central Depot (tel: 815-777-0203). From May through October, a number of homes are open to provide a glimpse of Galena's glorious past. A wide variety of sports can be enjoyed year-round, as well as the peaceful charm of the surrounding countryside, with three splendid state parks, ranging in size from 297 to 2,500 acres.

ACCOMMODATIONS

Bed and Breakfasts
Aldrich Guest House
900 Third Street
Galena, Illinois 61036
Tel: 815-777-3323
Historic home where Grant himself partied; his troops drilled nearby. Victorian decor, antiques, and a central location near all main sights. Full breakfast.

Avery Guest House
606 South Prospect Street
Galena, Illinois 61036
Tel: 815-777-3883
Century-old home, a two-block stroll from downtown. The owners are musically inclined and serve a Continental breakfast of homemade baked goods, cheeses, and jams.

Belle Aire Mansion
11410 Route 20 West
Galena, Illinois 61036
Tel: 815-777-0893
Surrounded by spacious lawns and trees, this is a Federalist-period house filled with antiques. Wine and fruit at the end of day; Continental breakfast.

Stillman Manor Inn
513 Bouthillier
Galena, Illinois 61036
Tel: 815-777-0557
Closer still to Grant's home, another treasure trove of antiques and old-fashioned comforts. Continental breakfast. Lunch and dinner served; steaks, shrimp specialties.

Hotels
Desoto House
230 South Main Street
Galena, Illinois 61036
Tel: 815-777-0090
When opened for business in 1855, Desoto House was known as the best hotel west of New York City, enjoyed in its heyday by such notables as Ulysses S. Grant and Abraham Lincoln. An $8 million renovation completed in 1986 has restored its stylish Victorian-period charms. Two atmospheric restaurants include the Grand Court, in a greenery-decked courtyard, for breakfast, lunch, and Sunday buffet brunch; and Truffles, a dressier dinner restaurant in the grand style of the 1880s and specializing in American foods.

Farmers' Home Hotel
334 Spring Street
Galena, Illinois 61036
Tel: 815-777-3456; 800-255-2525
Originally a nineteenth-century bakery and boardinghouse, this was the place farmers stayed and socialized when they came to market. Restored with antique furnishings, it is an excellent example of Galena's old commercial architecture. Complimentary full breakfast. The hotel's pub serves Galena Cellars wines. Bikes for rent at the hotel.

Eagle Ridge Inn and Resort
U.S. Route 20, Box 777
Galena, Illinois 61036
Tel: 815-777-2444; 800-323-8421 (out of state); 800-892-2269 (in state)
Lodge and resort homes on wooded acreage perched on a bluff above a lake. Two eighteen-hole golf courses among the main attractions. Or just relax in a shady nook; fish, ride, sail, or hike; cross-country ski over vast lands in winter. The dining room with wood ceiling and wide windows offers a grand view of Lake Galena.

RESTAURANTS
(See under winery listing; also Desoto House, Farmers' Home Hotel, Eagle Ridge Inn & Resort and Stillman Manor.)

Kingston Inn
300 North Main at Franklin
Galena, Illinois 61036
Tel: 815-777-0451
Seafood, salad bar, and wine cellar in a former Victorian ice cream parlor. Guitar player at dinner. Outdoor garden.

🍇 🍇 🍇

Lynfred Winery

15 South Roselle Road
Roselle, Illinois 60172
TEL: 312-529-WINE
OWNER/WINEMAKER: Fred E. Koehler
FOUNDED: 1977

AT A GLANCE
Tours & Tastings: Daily 11–7; conducted by daughter Diane Koehler.
Closed: Christmas, New Year's days.
Vineyards: Most grapes come from California, some from Washington and Oregon and Alto Pass, Illinois. Fruits mainly from Michigan.
Wines: More than thirty wines in all, about twelve of them fruit; total over 4,000 cases annually. Typical are Chardonnay, Vidal and Seyval Blanc, Cabernet Sauvignon, two Johannisberg Rieslings—one from Napa and the other from Washington grapes—and Gewürztraminer, among others. Fruit wines include such familiars as apple and raspberry as well as rhubarb, elderberry, and currant.
Awards: Top honors have gone to Chardonnay, Cabernet Sauvignon, Seyval and Vidal Blanc (all Illinois grapes), Zinfandel. Fruit wines: plum, peach, apple, rhubarb.
Retail Shop: Products sold on-site; can

be shipped throughout the state of Illinois.
Credit Cards: MasterCard, Visa.
Access for Disabled: None.
Foreign Languages: None.
Getting There: Northeastern Illinois: six miles west of O'Hare Airport on Roselle Rd., just south of Irving Park Rd., the second driveway off the railroad.
Special Wine & Other Events: Lynfred Wine Extravaganza, first weekend in August: grape stomping contests for kids and adults, bed races, barrel races, music, food, wine raffles, and wine prizes.

🍇 Koehler and his late wife, Lynn, started the winery in a historic 1912 home they painstakingly restored in every detail to its original Victorian style. The winery has burgundy velvet walls, a wood-burning fireplace, leaded stained-glass windows with grape designs, highly polished oak floors, and an 1800s Brunswick bar as centerpiece of the tasting room. The basement, now the wine cellar, has eighteen-inch-thick walls to provide proper temperature for wines. Koehler wines are tested by a taste panel during the bottling. Their competition? Gold-medal California wines. Wine experts consider Koehler one of the gurus of the fruit wine category. His plans are to expand behind his original building so production can include fine champagne.

ACCOMMODATIONS
Hyatt Regency Woodfield
1800 East Golf Road
Schaumburg, Illinois 60194
Tel: 312-885-1234; 800-228-9000
Nice small Hyatt with pretty plants and a friendly, homelike feeling. Across from the celebrated Woodfield Shopping Mall.

RESTAURANTS
All locations below are within easy reach of Chicago's downtown and serve Lynfred's wines.

Allgauer's
2855 North Milwaukee Avenue
Northbrook, Illinois 60062
Tel: 312-541-6000
Continental specialties. Popular for Sunday champagne brunch. Adjoins forest preserve and namesake hotel located on the North Shore.

Geja's Cafe
340 West Armitage
Chicago, Illinois 60614
Tel: 312-281-9101
Well-known gathering place for wine lovers who come to sample a large selection of wines by the glass accompanied by cheeses, seafood, and a classical guitarist.

Port Edward
20 West Chicago
Algonquin, Illinois 60102
Tel: 312-658-5441
Seafood is served in a nautical setting enhanced by a view of the Fox River. Wine cellar. Art gallery and gift shop on site.

The Cottage
525 Torrence Avenue
Calumet City, Illinois 60409
Tel: 312-891-3900
A stone fireplace and walls hung with copperware and fresh plants form the cozy background for a Continental-style menu. Wine list. About nineteen miles south of downtown Chicago.

ও INDIANA

This state is no upstart when it comes to status wines. As far back as 1802, wine was produced here by Swiss immigrant followers of John James Dufour, who settled in the area now known as Switzerland County and founded the city of Vevay. Well into the 1820s Indiana was America's leading wine-growing region. In 1845, the decline set in when phylloxera (a parasitic plant disease) destroyed the vines.

The state now produces red and white wines of distinctive style from French-American grapes. Prime wine routes wind mainly through three areas—near the sandy dunes of Lake Michigan, in the highlands of south-central Indiana, and along the Ohio River. Two wineries in Indianapolis offer tastings from grapes grown as far away as California.

Central Indiana

Chateau Thomas Winery

501 Madison Avenue
Indianapolis, Indiana 46225
TEL: 817-634-9463
PRESIDENT: Charles R. Thomas
CELLARMASTER/WINEMAKER: Steven
    Thomas (courses at UC-Davis/Napa
    Valley School of Cellaring)
FOUNDED: 1974

AT A GLANCE
Tours & Tastings: Noon–5 Mon.–Thurs., Fri. & Sat. 11–6, Sun. 12–5. See cellars, try the wines.
Closed: Christmas and Easter.
Vineyards: All vinifera varieties from California.
Wines: Chardonnay, still and sparkling; Sauvignon Blanc; Riesling; Cabernet Sauvignon; Merlot; Pinot Noir; port.

Awards: Indiana State Fair gold medals for all but Pinot Noir and sparkling Chardonnay; bronzes and special mentions to them in Eastern International Competition. Governor's Trophy at 1988 state fair for "Best Overall Performance."
Retail Shop: Wines sold on-site.
Credit Cards: None.
Access for Disabled: None.
Foreign Languages: Spanish.
Getting There: Near the center of Indianapolis, half a mile from I-65. Taxi and bus service from town.

⋟ Thomas, a doctor and wine hobbyist, turned pro when he took courses in California and opened his winery.

⋟ ⋟ ⋟

Easley's Winery

205 North College Avenue
Indianapolis, Indiana 46202
TEL: 317-636-4516
PRESIDENT: John J. Easley
FOUNDED: 1974

AT A GLANCE
Tours & Tastings: Tours for groups of twelve or more, modest fee; tastings free to walk-in visitors.
Closed: Sun., Christmas, Election days.
Vineyards: 120 acres at Cape Sandy, on the southern slopes of the Ohio River, planted to French hybrids.
Wines: Seyval Blanc, Marechal Foch, Chelois, Baco Noir, Aurora, Seibel 13053, De Chaunac, and mulled May wine.
Awards: Does not enter competitions.

Retail Shop: Wines sold on-site.
Credit Cards: None. Checks accepted.
Access for Disabled: None.
Foreign Languages: None.
Getting There: In downtown Indianapolis.

TO SEE & DO
The name Indianapolis is synonymous with the Indy 500, held Memorial Day weekend; throughout the year, you can see the top speedsters at the Indianapolis Motor Speedway's Hall of Fame. Museums of art and Indian heritage are among cultural attractions.

ACCOMMODATIONS
All major chains are represented in and about Indianapolis.

Hollingsworth House Inn
6054 Hollingsworth Road
Indianapolis, Indiana 46254
Tel: 317-299-6700
A mid-1800s Greek Revival-style farmhouse with a National Register listing. Luxury linens, antiques, and little comforts like thick towels make this a first-class place. Sunny breakfast nook is the cheerful setting for a delicious, hearty, full breakfast.

The Canterbury Hotel
123 South Illinois Street
Indianapolis, Indiana 46225
Tel: 317-634-3000; 800-538-8186
Small, luxury hotel with Chippendale and Queen Anne furniture. Continental breakfast served in quiet parlor. Food some of the best in town; good wine list—California, French, German selections.

South-Central Indiana

Bloomington Winery

1022 North College Avenue
Bloomington, Indiana 47401
TEL: 812-339-7233

PRESIDENT/WINEMAKER: James ("Jim") Butler
FOUNDED: 1983

AT A GLANCE
Tours & Tastings: Weekdays, except

Tues., 12–7; Sun. 1–7 for tastings. Informal tours given when people drop in and staff is not too busy to show visitors around. "Just ask, we love to tell people what we're doing," says Butler.

Closed: Tues.; also Christmas, New Year's, Election days.

Vineyards: Grapes purchased in southern Indiana.

Wines: Seyval Blanc, Aurora, De Chaunac, Marechal Foch, *methode champenoise* champagne.

Awards: Oft-awarded Aurora in Indiana and eastern competitions.

Retail Shop: Wines, locally made delicacies such as cheeses, smoked meats, apple butter and popcorn, honey, syrup, persimmon pulp, sorghum, and more.

Credit Cards: MasterCard, Visa.

Access for Disabled: None.

Foreign Languages: None.

Getting There: The winery is ten blocks north of the downtown square; many regular customers just walk in.

&. Small, friendly winery located in a seventy-year-old, two-story house; winemaker had ten years of experience in eastern wine industry before starting this venture.

&. &. &.

Oliver Winery

8024 North Highway 37
Bloomington, Indiana 47401
TEL: 812-876-5800
PRESIDENT: William A. Oliver
FOUNDED: 1972

AT A GLANCE

Tours & Tastings: Mon.–Sat. 11–6, Sun. 12–5, tastings and sales; tours of the cellar, Sat. at 12:30, 2, 4. Tour takes in winemaking process in nearby building and ends with tasting of wine with crackers in another stone building nearby.

Closed: Thanksgiving, Christmas, New Year's, and Election days.

Vineyards: Fifteen acres planted to French hybrids; balance of grapes purchased from Michigan, New York, California growers.

Wines: Varietals include Seyval Blanc, Vidal Blanc, Vidal Suisse Reserve (German-style wine), Marechal Foch; soft whites, red, whites (blends of Aurora, Concord, Catawba); Mead (honey-based wine), and Beanblossom Apple (made from local crops).

Awards: Several awards at Indiana State Fair and International Eastern Competition; soft wines most heralded.

Picnic Area: Tables with valley view.

Retail Shop: Wines, wine accessories, logo-imprinted souvenirs, cheeses, wild honey, and other locally made delicacies.

Credit Cards: MasterCard, Visa.

Access for Disabled: None.

Foreign Languages: None.

Getting There: Forty miles south of Indianapolis. From Bloomington: go eight miles north on Hwy. 37.

Special Wine & Other Events: First weekend in June: Wine Festival; last weekend in Sept.: 4th Street Art Festival; early Oct.: Hill Hundred-Mile Bicycle Race (draws 4,000–5,000 participants); last weekend in Apr.: Little 500 at Indiana University.

&. Bill Oliver, professor of law at nearby Indiana University, helped get the Small Winery Act passed in his state and then, with his wife, Mary, set up the state's first post-legislation winery—now its largest. Oliver's wood-walled tasting room is a nice environment for sampling wines—comfortable oak furniture and a big stone fireplace to toast by on winter days. The winery's logo-imprinted hot-air balloon can sometimes be seen overhead around town. While few small wineries ship wines beyond the state line, Oliver's Mead (honey-based wine) goes to eight states, and overseas to Hong Kong and Singapore, with Japan waiting in the wings. Nearer to home, Oliver has a tasting room at the restored Union Station in downtown Indianapolis.

TO SEE & DO

In this quiet university town, you might want to stop at the Visitors Center to find out about Indiana University's tours and special events and museums. Lake Monroe awaits seven miles southeast of town for all water sports (Rte. 446; tel: 812-837-9546); McCormick's Creek State Park has hiking trails through its lime-stone canyons, also camping facilities (twelve miles northwest on Rte. 46; tel: 812-829-7233).

ACCOMMODATIONS

(Also see Brown County listings.)

In Bloomington, Best Western Fireside Inn (800-528-1234); Howard Johnson's Motor Lodge (800-654-2000); Holiday Inns (800-238-8000); Ramada Inns (800-228-2828), and TraveLodge (800-255-3050).

Brown County

Possum Trot Vineyards

8310 North Possum Trot Road
Unionville, Indiana 47468
TEL: 812-988-2684
OWNERS: Ben and Lee Sparks
FOUNDED: 1978

AT A GLANCE

Tours & Tastings: March–Dec., weekdays 10–6 (or sunset, whichever comes later), Sun. 12–6; Jan.–March, call for appointment. Brief "show-and-tell" tour by one of the Sparkses gives the essentials of winemaking, followed by tasting. $1 per person.

Vineyards: French hybrid vineyard destroyed by frost, so grapes are purchased from southern Indiana growers, primarily from Ohio River Valley viticultural area.

Wines: Varietals include Vignoles, Vidal and Seyval Blanc, Marechal Foch; blends include Festival White and Zaragueya Sangria; mulled wine and Sparkling Niagara.

Awards: Zaragueya Sangria and mulled wine.

Picnic Area: Tables in lush wooded setting.

Retail Shop: Wines; also souvenirs such as T-shirts, wine accessories.

Credit Cards: MasterCard, Visa.

Access for Disabled: Yes.

Foreign Languages: None.

Getting There: From Bloomington: S.R. 45 to Trevlac, turn west on North Shore Dr. for 2.1 miles to Possum Trot Rd. Turn right to winery on right.

Special Wine & Other Events: Early Oct.: Craft Balloon Festival at Possum Trot Vineyards. Visitors to nearby Nashville are entertained from the first daffodil of spring to the last snowflake in winter with log cabin tours, quilt shows, bluegrass music, church fairs, parades, and old-fashioned Christmas festivities among the scheduled activities.

    🍇 The Sparkses, self-taught winemakers, make their wines in a rustic, sloped-roof building half hidden by huge trees, flame-colored in fall. Red table wine made from Marechal Foch is aged in American white oak—*Quercus alba*, crafted from the owners' Possum Trot forest.

TO SEE & DO

Wine routes now cross one of the regions renowned for natural beauty, where huge state parks and forests surround you with mammoth trees and sparkling lakes and opportunities for an array of recreational activities and breathtaking fall foliage. In Nashville, the county seat, are museums, including what must be one of the most unusual in the United States—a museum saluting the life and times of Depression-era bank robber John Dillinger. The Country Museum is housed in a log cabin (tel: 812-988-2526). This is also the site of the Little Nashville Opry, the Brown County Playhouse, and 250 shops—crafts, handmade jewelry, and antiques are among the wide variety of merchandise. Other shopping opportunities can be found in many of the surrounding little country towns. For more information, contact the Brown County Chamber of Commerce, P.O. Box 164, Van Buren Street, Nashville, Indiana 47448; tel: 812-988-7303.

ACCOMMODATIONS

Bed and Breakfasts
Allison House
99 South Jefferson Street
Nashville, Indiana 47448
Tel: 812-988-6664
Restored Victorian home full of local arts and crafts that may well whet your appetite for the shops nearby. Continental breakfast of homemade baked goods.

Sunset House
Rural Route 3 (P.O. Box 127)
Nashville, Indiana 47448
Tel: 812-988-6118

Contemporary house with deck and patio and nicely furnished guest rooms with private entrances. Continental breakfast.

Other Accommodations
Abe Martin Lodge
P.O. Box 25
Nashville, Indiana 47448
Tel: 812-988-4418
In Brown County State Park. Sixteen lodge rooms, fifty-eight motel cabins, and twenty housekeeping cabins. Hiking trails, picnic areas, two lakes, tennis courts, naturalist services. Dining room.

Brown County Inn
Routes 135 & 46 (P.O. Box 128)
Nashville, Indiana 47448
Tel: 812-988-2291
Rustic motel/inn near downtown Nashville; year-round swimming, tennis, miniature golf, and other sports.

Seasons Lodge
560 State Highway 46 East (P.O. Box 187)
Nashville, Indiana 47448
Tel: 812-988-2284
Rustic but modern facility. Some suites with fireplaces; caters to conferences. Year-round swimming; horseback riding, golf, tennis, skiing nearby.

Southern Indiana

Huber Orchard Winery

Route 1 (P.O. Box 202)
Borden, Indiana 47106
TEL: 812-923-WINE
OWNERS: the Huber family
WINEMAKER: Gerald Huber (courses at Ohio State University)
FOUNDED: 1978

AT A GLANCE
Tours & Tastings: Daily 10–5, self-guided tours and tastings; guided tours by appointment. Inquire about Sat. & Sun. tours that take in the farm and show the vegetables, fruits, and pines in various cycles of development.
Closed: Major holidays.
Vineyards: Fifteen acres planted to American, American hybrids, and French-American hybrids such as Concord, Niagara, Catawba; Aurora, Seyval and Vidal Blanc, Chancellor, De Chaunac. Also, apples, strawberries, peaches, and other fruits.
Wines: Seventeen grape wines, including varietals and blends; six fruit wines.
Awards: Over fifty awards since 1979 in competitions pitting their wines against

eastern, national, and international contenders. Holder of the Governor's Trophy for "Best of Show" at the Indiana State Fair.

Picnic Area: Tables about the grounds and near the duck pond.

Restaurant: Eat in the comfortable dining area with exposed brick walls, high-ladderback chairs, and big windows to let the light in and let you see out to the farmlands. Cheese trays, ready-made sandwiches, plus cheeses, sausages, fruits, vegetables, breads.

Retail Shop: Wines, cheeses, sausages, jams; crafts, glassware, home wine-makers kits.

Credit Cards: American Express, MasterCard, Visa.

Access for Disabled: None.

Foreign Languages: None.

Getting There: Huber Orchard Winery is fourteen miles northwest of Louisville, Kentucky. From Louisville: Take I-64 to Greenville exit (119), follow Huber Winery signs. Then go west on U.S. 150, four miles to Navilleton Rd. (across from bank), turn right, and follow the orchard/winery signs for six miles.

Special Wine & Other Events: Labor Day weekend: Wine Festival; "Good Pickin's" newsletter offers periodic updates on events and innovations.

❧ "Hoosier Homestead Farm" is the recognition given Indiana farms like the Hubers' that have been in the same family more than one hundred years—this one since 1843. Today this handsome farm is worked by brothers Gerald and Carl, their wives, Mary Jeanne and Linda, and their children, and is a friendly place for families to visit at any time during the year. Visitors can pick fruits and berries, cut down a Christmas tree, buy gifts in the converted hayloft with gleaming red oak floors or in the farm market and winery shop.

The winery is located in a renovated 1930s barn. Operations started in 1978

and production now is about 17,000 gallons annually. All wines at hand come only from grapes and fruits grown on the farm.

TO SEE & DO

Louisville, fourteen miles away, is the best base for your visit to Huber Orchard Vineyard. Known as the site of the Kentucky Derby on the first Saturday in May each year and all the festivities surrounding it, the city is also home to the Kentucky Center for the Arts. The Humana Festival of New American Plays at the Actors Theater each March attracts international acclaim. The J. P. Speed Art Museum is the largest and oldest in the state. *The Belle of Louisville*, a stern-wheeler, offers trips on the river; Locust Grove and Farmington are historic homes. For a complete calendar of events and activities, write to the Department of Travel Development, Capital Plaza Tower, Frankfort, Kentucky 40601; tel: 502-564-4930.

ACCOMMODATIONS

Bed and Breakfasts
Kentucky Homes Bed & Breakfast, Inc.
1431 St. James Court
Louisville, Kentucky 40208
Tel: 502-583-7341
Coordinators will locate accommodations to suit your tastes.

Hotels/Motels
Most major chains are represented in Louisville. Here is one.

The Brown, a Hilton Hotel
335 West Broadway
Louisville, Kentucky 40202
Tel: 502-234-1234; Reservations: 800-HILTONS
Well-restored 296-room 1923 hotel with manor house furnishings and artwork. Grand lobby with bronze, marble, and richly ornamental plaster is a sight to see.

Seelbach Hotel
500 Fourth Avenue
Louisville, Kentucky 40202
Tel: 502-585-3200
An elegant 322-room hotel from the 1900s, painstakingly restored with murals by Arthur Thomas. Pioneer and Indian murals focal points in the lobby. Oak Room restaurant. (See "Restaurants.")

RESTAURANTS
Joe Huber Restaurant
This is a Huber family restaurant in Borden; ask directions at the Huber Orchard Winery.

Casa Gristani
1000 Liberty Street
Louisville, Kentucky 40204
Tel: 502-584-4377
Well-prepared Italian dishes in modern surroundings. Wine list; outdoor dining in fair weather. Art exhibits.

Oak Room
(See under Seelbach Hotel.)
Stylish, refined dining on favorite American dishes.

❧ IOWA

Iowa had a thriving wine industry as far back as the 1800s but little to show for it after Prohibition. Some wines produced today seem to hark back to earlier days as wine routes entwine with the historic Amana Colonies. Wine routes also travel to two newer wineries, where history is being made by winemakers introducing new wines—one in a fascinating old setting.

Amana Colonies

Seven historic villages make up the Amana Colonies (twenty miles northwest of Iowa City and eighteen miles southwest of Cedar Rapids), founded in 1854. The Amana colonists came to America from Germany in 1842 to live near Buffalo, New York. Finding it too urbanized, they pressed west and purchased the land that makes up the colonies today. Originally they were a religious-communal society—all property was owned by the group, and both church and secular decisions were made by the same leaders. In 1932, the people voted to separate "church and state" and since then the Amana Colonies have operated as part of the world of private enterprise.

In the wine department the focus is on sweet fruit wines. One of the Amana wineries produces a small quantity of wine from French hybrid grapes—perhaps a sign of the future for all.

❧ ❧ ❧

Ackerman Winery

Box 108
South Amana, Iowa 52334
TEL: 319-622-3379
OWNERS: Les and Linda Ackerman
FOUNDED: 1956

AT A GLANCE
Tours & Tastings: No tours; tastings Mon.–Sat. 10–5, Sun. 12–5.
Vineyards/Orchards: French hybrids and fruits and berries purchased from Midwest growers.
Wines: Seventeen fruit and berry wines, including cranberry, wild elderberry,

mulberry, rhubarb, peach, plum, apple; flowers also—dandelion, red clover, and others. Varietals: Vidal Blanc and Marechal Foch.

Awards: Vidal Blanc, blueberry and cranberry wines—mid-American competitions.

Retail Shop: Wines and cheeses; handicrafts, German glass and steins.

Credit Cards: MasterCard, Visa.

Access for Disabled: None.

Foreign Languages: German.

Getting There: Twenty miles northwest of Iowa City; take State Hwy. 6 to South Amana and turn right to Ackerman Winery.

Special Wine & Other Events: See the end of the Amana Colonies section.

🐛 Three generations of Ackermans have made fruit and berry wines in the Amana Colonies.

🐛 🐛 🐛

Ehrle Bros. Winery

Main Street (P.O. Box 10)
Homestead, Iowa 52236
TEL: 319-622-3241
PRESIDENT: Linda C. Ackerman
FOUNDED: 1945

AT A GLANCE

Tours & Tastings: Daily 9–5 for sales, tastings, and self-guided tour of aging rooms.

Closed: Major holidays.

Vineyards/Orchards: Iowa and out-of-state fruit used.

Wines: Assorted fruit wines.

Awards: Gold medals for both Raspberry Sweet and Raspberry Extra Sweet in Midwest Wine Competition.

Retail Shop: Sells wines on the premises.

Credit Cards: MasterCard, Visa.

Access for Disabled: None.

Foreign Languages: German.

Getting There: From Iowa City: Take Hwy. 6 Northwest; Homestead is before turnoff to Amana.

🐛 🐛 🐛

Sandstone Winery Inc.

304 Second Street
Amana, Iowa 52203
TEL: 319-622-3081
PRESIDENT: Elsie Mattes
FOUNDED: 1960

AT A GLANCE

Tours & Tastings: No tours, except on Amana Festival Days (see end of Amana Colonies section); tastings Mon.–Sat. 9–8, Sun. 10–5.

Closed: Thanksgiving, Christmas, New Year's days.

Vineyards: All fruits are purchased from Michigan, Wisconsin, and Oregon growers.

Wines: Rhubarb, cherry, strawberry, plum, blackberry, and more.

Retail Shop: Wines and selected gifts.

Credit Cards: American Express, MasterCard, Visa.

Access for Disabled: All on one level.

Foreign Languages: German.

Getting There: Twenty miles northwest of Iowa City, on U.S. 6 and State 151. Sandstone is on the main street of village in center of town.

Special Wine & Other Events: See the end of the Amana Colonies section.

🐛 The Sandstone Winery is located in one of the first houses built in the Amana Colonies, now a national historic landmark.

🐛 🐛 🐛

Village Winery

Main Street
Amana, Iowa 52203
TEL: 319-622-3448
PRESIDENT: Eunice Krauss
FOUNDED: 1973

AT A GLANCE
Tours & Tastings: Mon.–Sat. 9–5, Sun. 12–4; view winemaking through window, tastings, and sales.
Closed: Thanksgiving, Christmas, New Year's days.
Vineyards/Orchards: Fruits purchased from Michigan, Missouri, Illinois.
Wines: Assorted fruit wines.
Retail Shop: Wines and large selection of Hummels and Anri woodcarvings; other collectibles.
Credit Cards: American Express, MasterCard, Visa.
Access for Disabled: None.
Foreign Languages: German.
Getting There: Twenty miles northwest of Iowa City on U.S. 6 and State 151.

Special Wine & Other Events: Early Dec.: prelude to Christmas, involves wineries and many others. In May: Maifest; June: VIP Golf tournament; early Aug.: Arts Fest; mid-Aug.: Holzfest (wood crafts); Sept.: Oktoberfest. For details and dates, contact Amana Colonies Travel Council, Amana, Iowa 52203; tel: 319-399-3838.

TO SEE & DO
See the seven small villages clustered in the fertile Iowa River Valley, with old architecture and tidy gardens. In July and August, Lily Lake, located between Middle Amana and Amana, wears a coverlet of lotus blossoms. Shop in some of the colonies' seventy stores. Look for Amana woolens (Little Amana Woolen Mill Display Room and Store), handmade calico quilts, and local crafts. Three museums and ten major restaurants are additional attractions.

ACCOMMODATIONS
Die Heimat Country Inn
Homestead, Iowa 52236
Tel: 319-622-3937
Restored B&B built in 1858. Furnished in handcrafted cherry and walnut furniture and antiques. Continental breakfast with home-baked rolls.

Guest House Motel
Amana, Iowa 52203
Tel: 319-622-3599
Renovated sandstone guest house more than a century old and new motel provide thirty-eight units with a country look.

The Rettig House Bed & Breakfast
Middle Amana, Iowa 52203
Tel: 319-622-3386
Homey old-world Amana atmosphere; breakfast in the old kitchen house.

Amana Holiday Inn
Little Amana, Iowa 52203
Tel: 319-668-1175; 800-HOLIDAY

RESTAURANTS
Colony Market Place Restaurant and Shops
South Amana, Iowa 52334
Tel: 319-622-3235
Food served family style. Historic town well.

Central Iowa

Private Stock Winery

706 Allen Street
Boone, Iowa 50036
TEL: 515-432-8348
OWNERS: Tom and Rose Larson
WINEMAKER: Tom Larson (M.A., UC-Davis)
FOUNDED: 1977

AT A GLANCE
Tours & Tastings: Mon.–Fri. 10–8, Sat. 10–7; see production process and taste wines.
Closed: Christmas and New Year's days.
Vineyards/Orchards: Ten acres planted to American and French hybrids; additional grapes from growers around the country.

Wines: Ruby Cabernet, Marechal Foch, and blended sweet and dry white wines are among fourteen wines produced; fruit wines include apple, strawberry, pear, blueberry, and cranberry.
Awards: Bronze to sweet white and strawberry.
Retail Shop: All products sold at winery.
Credit Cards: MasterCard, Visa.
Access for Disabled: Level entry.
Foreign Languages: None.
Getting There: Forty-two miles north of Des Moines and fifteen miles west of Ames. Winery is in downtown Boone off Hwy. 30, north of I-80. From Des Moines: Take I-35 to Ames, then Hwy. 30 to Boone.
Special Wine & Other Events: Second weekend following Labor Day: Pufferbilly Days, with famous steam locomotive No. 1385; other sights and sounds recall historic railroad days.

ఆ Tom Larson began by buying all his fruit, and since 1981 has been growing grapes to supplement purchased crops. Current production plans call for 9,000 gallons a year. The emphasis is on sweet wines for local tastes; a few are dry. The winery is easily one of Boone's most colorful buildings, featuring a bold mural of winemaker Larson with glass raised in a toast. The modest tasting bar is studded with barrels.

TO SEE & DO
The wooded hills and fertile valleys of Boone and the early days of railroading are closely entwined, and are remembered not only with the aforementioned Pufferbilly Days but in many ways, including the Iowa Railway Museum, the Scenic Valley Railroad (offering rides in vintage cars), and the longest and highest double-track bridge in the world, now on the National Register of Historic Places. Boone is also the birthplace of Mamie Dowd Eisenhower (Nov. 14, 1896), and her restored Victorian home is open from April through December with memorabilia of her early years as well as her days as first lady during the 34th presidency. For more information, contact the Boone Area Chamber of Commerce Convention and Visitors Bureau, P.O. Box 306, Boone, Iowa 50036; tel: 515-432-3342.

ACCOMMODATIONS
Bed & Breakfast in Iowa Ltd.
P.O. Box 430
Preston, Iowa 52069
Tel: 319-689-4222
Statewide recommendations for B&Bs.

B & B On Ash
517 Ash Avenue
Ames, Iowa 50010
Tel: 515-292-9382
A 1913 frame-and-stucco home with cheerful atmosphere, nice fireplace to warm by in winter, and deck to cool off on in summer. Full breakfast with fresh-ground coffee.

Imperial Inn
1215 South Story Street
Boone, Iowa 50036
Tel: 515-432-4322
Indoor swimming pool on premises, sauna; Chinese-American restaurant.

Christina Winery

123 A Street
McGregor, Iowa 52157
Tel: 319-873-3321
OWNERS: The Lawlor Family (For other Lawlor wineries, see Galena, Illinois, and La Crosse, Wisconsin, and their tasting room in Dubuque, Iowa.)
FOUNDED: 1972

AT A GLANCE
Tours & Tastings: Daily, summer Mon.–Sun. 10–5; Jan.–Mar., by appointment.

ఆ The first of the Lawlor family's wineries is housed in a handsome Romanesque building that was built during the nineteenth century and was the office of the Diamond Jo steamboat lines, one of the most important riverboat lines and with close ties to Galena, Illinois, site of another Lawlor winery. Their Iowa winery, like the others, features wines made by its namesake Christina Lawlor—French hybrids, vinifera, and fruit wines running from sweet to dry. Across from the McGregor winery is attractive Triangle Park.

TO SEE & DO
This once-busy river port is now a small quiet town (pop. 800) attractive to artists and weekenders from larger cities. Big weekend art festivals take place on Memorial Day and the first weekend in October.

ACCOMMODATION
Holiday Shores
Box 297
McGregor, Iowa 52157
Tel: 319-873-3449
Pleasant 33-room motel overlooking Mississippi.

Port of Dubuque—Wine Tasting
Second Street & Harbor
Dubuque, Iowa 52001
Tel: 319-583-6204
This is a tasting room run by the Lawlor family (see above) at the historic Ice

House Harbor. The wines—French hybrids, fruit and vinifera varieties—are those featured at other Lawlor wineries. (See Illinois and Wisconsin.) Open daily, Memorial Day–Oct.; Nov.–Dec., weekends 10–6.

TO SEE & DO
In the Ice Harbor area Roberts River Rides offers sightseeing or dinner cruises (Tel: 319-583-1761); The Woodward Riverboat Museum is the showcase for the sidewheeler *Wm. M. Black* and the National Rivers Hall of Fame. (Tel: 319-557-9545) Many shops at the Ice Harbor are also of interest to visitors.

ACCOMMODATIONS
Best Western Midway Motor Lodge
3100 Dodge Street
Dubuque, Iowa 52001
Tel: 319-557-8000; Reservations:
  800-528-1234
One-hundred-sixty-one-room motor hotel, with indoor pool, restaurant.

Redstone Inn
504 Bluff
Dubuque, Iowa 52001
Tel: 319-582-1894
Fifteen rooms and suite in an atmospheric refurbished three-story 1800s inn furnished in period pieces. Café, bar.

⬥ MICHIGAN

Early in their history, Michigan wineries clustered in the southwest to be near growers of Concords and other native American grapes. Approximately 600 farms in this region, totaling 16,000 acres of vineyards, still produce Concords in massive quantities, primarily for juice, jellies, and jams.

Some southwestern winemakers use Concords today, but more frequently rely on French-American hybrids for their wines. Newer winemakers in northwest Michigan have catered since their outset to more sophisticated tastes and have planted their fields with French-American hybrids and European varieties. The state boasts four viticultural areas—Lake Michigan Shore, Fennville, Lake Leelanau, and Old Mission Peninsula.

Only four of Michigan's sixteen wineries predate the 1970s. Much of this growth, as elsewhere in the United States, has taken place in the last two decades due to the passage of liberalized farm winery laws.

For all concerned, the harsh winters would be inhospitable to fine grapes if it were not for the Great Lakes. They moderate the harsh winters and hot summers, making Michigan a prime winemaking state; the lakes keep spring temperatures cooler to retard budding and warmer in the fall to shield grapes from frost.

On a tour of Michigan wineries your wine routes will go through two main areas along the shores of Lake Michigan—the southwest and northwest. Delicious diversions for travelers on these choice wine routes are silver white beaches, fields of wildflowers, and quiet little villages filled with history.

Southwest Michigan

Fenn Valley Vineyard

6130 122 Avenue
Fennville, Michigan 49408
TEL: 616-561-2396
PRESIDENT: William Welsch
WINEMAKER: Doug Welsch
FOUNDED: 1973

AT A GLANCE

Tours & Tastings: Mon.–Sat. 10–5, Sun. 1–5. Visitors take in the entire winemaking operation from the observation deck, assisted by explanations posted on signs and continuous showings of an eight-minute slide presentation. Tastings offer wines of visitors' choice.
Closed: Thanksgiving, Christmas, New Year's, Easter days.
Vineyards: Fifty-two acres planted to vinifera and French-American hybrids in Fennville, Michigan's first viticultural area. Peaches also grown.
Wines: Estate-bottled Chardonnay, Johannisberg Riesling, Gewürztraminer, Seyval and Vidal Blanc, Chancellor, Vignoles, Marechal Foch. Also peach, blueberry, and raspberry wines.
Awards: Over 130 since 1976.
Picnic Area: Tables on the grounds.
Retail Shop: Wines, food delicacies; stemware, wine accessories, wine vinegars, winemaking supplies.
Credit Cards: MasterCard, Visa.
Access for Disabled: None.
Foreign Languages: None.
Getting There: Take I-196 to exit 34 (Fennville); go east on M-89, 3½ miles; turn south on 62nd St. for one mile to 122nd; proceed ¼ mile to winery on the right. Winery is 40 miles southwest of Grand Rapids; I-96 skirts Lake Michigan south of Holland for a scenic drive.

🐦 William Welsch searched the eastern seaboard before he selected this site for his vineyard on the same latitude as the classic winegrowing regions of northern Europe. He reasoned rightly that he could turn out vinifera varietals here. Since then, he has added winter-hardy French-American hybrids. His old-world wines are produced with a modern flourish—computerized vineyard management programs ensure proper growth and size of fruit. Hand-picked fruit is vinified with a combination of the traditional and high-tech methods. New vintage releases are introduced with artists' labels.

🐦 🐦 🐦

Peterson & Sons Winery

9375 East P Avenue
Kalamazoo, Michigan 49001
TEL: 616-626-9755
OWNER/WINEMAKER: Duane Peterson
FOUNDED: 1983

AT A GLANCE

Tours & Tastings: By appointment. Tiny winery, in home basement and garage.
Closed: Major holidays.
Vineyards: All fruits purchased from Michigan growers.
Wines: Native American; vinifera varieties—Chardonnay and Riesling; French-American hybrids—Seyval and Vidal Blanc, Marechal Foch. Also fruit wines.
Awards: Gold medal to rhubarb-raspberry, quality/bronze awards to Chancellor Noir and black and red raspberry—all in International Eastern Wine Competition.
Retail Shop: Wines sold.
Credit Cards: None.
Access for Disabled: None.
Foreign Languages: None.
Getting There: Winery is between Battle Creek and Kalamazoo. From I-94: Take exit 85 (Galesburg); go south to blinker light; right at light. Then south 2½ miles to P Avenue, turn west (only way you can turn), and winery sign is on tree.

&. A wine hobbyist before he made winemaking his career, Duane Peterson turns out wines under the Naturally Old-Fashioned Wines label to let everyone know he uses no chemicals of any kind in his wines. Visitors to his tiny winery get more than tastings—they get recipes for using his wines and reprints of articles that explain the benefits of natural wine. Peterson recycles his own wine bottles and offers a quarter refund to customers who return them.

&. &. &.

St. Julian Wine Company, Inc.

716 South Kalamazoo Street
P.O. Box 127
Paw Paw, Michigan 49079
TEL: 616-657-5568
PRESIDENT: David R. Braganini
WINEMAKER: Chas Catherman
FOUNDED: 1921

AT A GLANCE

Tours & Tastings: Mon.–Sat. 9–5, Sun. 12–5; tours continuous all day, start from hospitality room and last about an hour (with tasting). Trained tour guides put an average of 250,000 visitors annually through a thorough lesson in winemaking, concluded with a tasting.
Closed: Thanksgiving, Christmas, New Year's, Easter.
Vineyards: Private growers provide grapes from the Lake Michigan Shore viticultural area.
Wines: Still wines include Vidal and Seyval Blanc, Vignoles, Niagara, Chancellor; sparkling wines are *methode champenoise* sparkling wines. Sparkling nonalcoholic wines and cider are other products. Famous among the wines are Solera Cream Sherry and Chancellor Noir, the first red wine to win a Best of Show at a Michigan State Fair.
Awards: Enough awards for an epic novel.
Picnic Area: Two tables out front.
Retail Shop: Wine, cheese, gift items.
Credit Cards: American Express, MasterCard, Visa.
Access for Disabled: Ramp into hospitality room and barrier-free bathroom.
Foreign Languages: None.
Getting There: Take I-94 to exit 60 (Paw Paw) and continue two blocks north to winery.

&. St. Julian started in 1921 as the Italian Wine Company in Windsor, Ontario. Founder Mariano Meconi moved the business after the repeal of Prohibition in 1933, first to Detroit and then to Paw Paw to be nearer the vineyards. The winery is run today by a member of the original family.

The winery visitors now see was built in 1971 after a fire destroyed the earlier building. While the first structure was not built with tours in mind, the new winery comfortably holds 250 visitors at a time.

St. Julian more or less mirrors what has happened to Michigan's, and to some extent America's, wineries, outside California and the Northwest. Throughout the 1930s this winery's success depended on sweet wines from Concord grapes. Since the 1970s, to satisfy more sophisticated tastes, it has started producing drier table wines.

St. Julian, after buying a trickle in the 1970s, now claims to be Michigan's largest single buyer of premium French-American hybrid wine grape varieties. Currently, they make up 88 percent of the winery's grape consumption. Wine production is in excess of 1,200 cases a day. The company operates a second winery at Frankenmuth and tasting centers throughout Michigan.

ॐ ॐ ॐ

Tabor Hill Vineyard & Winecellar

185 Mount Tabor Road
Buchanan, Michigan 49107
TEL: 616-422-1161
OWNER: David P. Upton
WINEMAKER: Richard Moersch (Napa Valley–trained)
FOUNDED: 1967

AT A GLANCE
Tours & Tastings: Thirty-minute guided tours, from vineyard to cellar, with hand-carved 330-gallon oak barrels; include tasting; Apr.–Dec.; Mon.–Fri. 11–5. Tastings and sales, Jan.–March, Fri.–Sat. 11–5, Sun. 11–5, year-round. Nomi-nal tasting fee applied to purchase of wines.
Closed: Christmas, New Year's days.
Vineyards: Thirty acres planted to vinifera varieties and French hybrids.
Wines: Seventeen wines, primarily whites, including Johannisberg and white (Mosel-style) Rieslings; Chardonnay, both estate-bottled and barrel-fermented; proprietary whites; cream sherry; reds and rosés include Cabernet Sauvignon, Noir Nouveau, Sangria, Rosé, Red Bud Trail blends; Pink Delaware; *methode champenoise* champagne, sparkling nonalcoholic white champagne, and raspberry wine.
Awards: Silver medals to Chardonnay (Moersch Vineyard), Berrien Ridge, red blend; gold to Hartford Cream Sherry.
Restaurant: Nicely decorated, with cozy fireplace aglow in winter; screened-in outdoor terrace dining. Features country grilled specialties. Open all year, lunch or dinner; reservations recommended.
Retail Shop: Wines sold on-site.
Credit Cards: MasterCard, Visa.
Access for Disabled: Ramps, bathroom.
Foreign Languages: None.
Getting There: Take I-94 to exit 16 (Bridgman), and follow signs for six miles to winery.
Special Wine & Other Events: July 23–24: Jazz Festival, combines music, wine, and picnics at the restaurant. Sept. 10–11: Harvest Festival, kicks off grape harvest with Lake Michigan's largest competitive grape stomp. Fine foods, music, wines.

ॐ In 1968, Carl Bainholzen and Len Olson began experimenting with twenty-six varieties of vinifera and French hybrids at what became Tabor Hill's thirty-acre vineyard. Only eight of these vines remain today to pay tribute to the two pioneers of European-style wine-making in Middle America. Recycled boards from a nineteenth-century barn have been used to make the winery, with a spacious tasting bar from which you can see Lake Michigan's famous sugar-fine sand dunes. This area is laced with cross-country ski trails for winter visitors' enjoyment.

ʝ̀ ʝ̀ ʝ̀

Warner Vineyards

706 South Kalamazoo Street
Paw Paw, Michigan 49079
TEL: 616-657-3165
PRESIDENT: James J. Warner
WINEMAKER: Nathan G. Stackhouse
  (graduate, UC-Davis)
FOUNDED: 1939

AT A GLANCE

Tours & Tastings: Summer, Mon.–Sat. 9–6, Sun. 12–6; winter, Mon.–Sat. 10–5, Sun. 12–5. Comprehensive guided tours give visitors an in-depth look at how wines are made, and include a tasting.
Closed: Thanksgiving, Christmas, New Year's, Easter.
Vineyards: 250 acres in the Lake Michigan Shore v.a. First French hybrids put in during the mid-1960s, to which vinifera varieties have been added. Other grapes purchased from selected southwestern Michigan growers. Experimental nursery for grape vines not currently grown in the state.
Wines: Full line of fifty table wines—dry to sweet, fruit and berry, *methode champenoise* champagne and other sparkling wines—for three brands: Cask, Warner (premium wines), and Great Lakes Coolers. There is also a line of juices.
Awards: A constellation of awards is displayed at the winery. Much honored have been Warner Brut Champagne, made by the *methode champenoise*, and Solera sherries and ports—using the traditional Spanish and Portuguese technique of blending each new vintage with those of the past.
Retail Shop: Wines, gift items, stemware.

Restaurant: Wine Garden Restaurant, on the riverbank, serves simple foods with Warner wines. Open 11–3, July–Sept.
Credit Cards: American Express, Carte Blanche, Diner's Club, Discover, Master-Card, Visa.
Access for Disabled: Limited to tasting room.
Foreign Languages: None.
Getting There: Next door to St. Julian. Take I-94 to exit 60 (Paw Paw) and continue two blocks north to winery.

ʝ̀ One of the oldest wineries in Michigan, Warner is the Midwest's largest. With 3 million gallons of storage capacity and a production of 8,000 cases a day, it also ranks in the upper third of the country's top hundred wineries.

The firm was founded by grape grower and banker John Turner, grandfather of James J., the current president, who is proud to point out that Warner Brut Champagne is still hand riddled, a time-consuming process, often automated these days.

Tourgoers can taste this champagne and other wines in the Wine Haus, Paw Paw's former waterworks, now a registered state historic sight. There is also a slide presentation to view in a 1912 railway car and, of course, the tour itself.

Special Wine & Other Events: In early Sept.: Michigan Wine & Harvest Festival. Participants are southeast wineries. Three-day celebration in Kalamazoo and Paw Paw with great outpouring of activities from bed racing to wine and food tasting. For details, contact the Michigan Wine & Harvest Festival, 128 North Kalamazoo Mall, Kalamazoo, Michigan 49007; tel: 616-381-4003

TO SEE & DO

Two lovely lakeside area resorts are: South Haven, which may have been Lake Michigan's oldest resort; and Saugatuck, with boating and fishing, art galleries, and summer theater. The town of Holland is a sight to see in the spring, with miles of tulips (be sure to reserve well in advance); Windmill State Park and the Dutch village recall the community's heritage.

ACCOMMODATIONS

Motels & Hotels—both modest, but acceptable and on wineries' doorstep.
Green Acres Motel
38254 Red Arrow Highway West
Paw Paw, Michigan 49079
Tel: 616-657-4037

Lakeside Hotel
202 West Michigan Avenue
Paw Paw, Michigan 49079
Tel: 616-657-9946

Bed and Breakfasts & Inns
Dutch Country Bed and Breakfast
399 East 16th Street
Holland, Michigan 49423
Tel: 616-396-3344

Hidden Pond Farm
5975 128th Avenue
Fennville, Michigan 49408
Tel: 616-561-2491
Twenty-eight wooded acres are the setting for this separate guest quarters containing bedrooms, baths, living room, den, plus patio and deck.

The Last Resort
86 North Shore Drive
South Haven, Michigan 49090
Tel: 616-637-8943
Renovated 1883 house, now with snug rooms named for the nineteenth-century sailing ships assembled in this city. Watching the setting sun from the veranda is a pleasant activity at the close of the day.

Kenah Guest House
633 Pleasant Street
Saugatuck, Michigan 49453
Tel: 616-857-2919
Set on a hill, this house was built in the 1800s, with stained-glass windows, wood-carved landscapes, and beamed ceilings added in the 1920s. The solarium was built by H. E. Tallmadge, follower of Frank Lloyd Wright.

The Park House
888 Holland Avenue
Saugatuck, Michigan 49453
Tel: 616-857-4535
In this, the oldest house in Saugatuck, listed on the National Register of Historic Places, visitors find comfortable queen-size beds and a cozy ambience. A wraparound porch and parlor are fine places for relaxing.

Wickwood Inn
510 Butler Street
Saugatuck, Michigan 49453
Tel: 616-857-1097
In a garden setting, with individually decorated comfortable rooms; library and garden room bar where guests congregate.

RESTAURANTS
Sayfee's East
3555 Lake Eastbrook Boulevard
Grand Rapids, Michigan 49506
Tel: 616-949-5750
Continental menu.

Paw Paw

Little River Cafe
South Kalamazoo Street
Tel: 616-657-6035
Across from St. Julian Wine Company
and Warner Vineyards.

Northwest Michigan

Except for Chateau Traverse in the Old Mission Peninsula v.a., the following vineyards are located in the Lake Leelanau viticultural area.

えぁ えぁ えぁ

Boskydel Vineyard

Route 1 (P.O. Box 522)
Lake Leelanau, Michigan 49653
TEL: 616-256-7272
OWNER/WINEMAKER: Bernard Rink
FOUNDED: 1975

AT A GLANCE
Tours & Tastings: Seven days a week, 1–6; tastings and tours on demand, except at harvest time.
Closed: Thanksgiving, Christmas, New Year's, and Easter days.
Vineyards: Twenty-five acres planted to French-Amerian hybrids including the varieties below and Marechal Foch and Cascade Noir.
Wines: Top wines are Vignoles, Seyval Blanc, Aurora Blanc De Chaunac.
Awards: Vignoles have received a first in class.
Retail Shop: Wines sold.
Credit Cards: None.
Access for Disabled: Yes.
Foreign Languages: None.
Getting There: From Traverse City: Take Rte. 633 North to Rte. 644 and continue to Boskydel.

えぁ This is a story about Bernie Rink, a retired librarian, who named his winery after a series of never-published children's books: "The Elves of Bosky Dingle." Much of the reason that grape growing has a happy ending in this seemingly hostile northern climate is based on Rink's early research, for which he has been widely honored in the state. Rink first learned winemaking as an Ohio farm boy from his grandfather and father, who did a little wine bootlegging during Prohibition. Then, twenty years ago, Rink figured out how proper orientation to the water could help grapes grow. Now Rink's five sons pitch in around the place. Andrew, for one, conducts tastings in the winery, where visitors also are greeted by literary quotations.

えぁ えぁ えぁ

Chateau Grand Traverse

12239 Center Road
Old Mission Peninsula
Traverse City, Michigan 49684
TEL: 616-223-7325
OWNER: Edward O'Keefe
WINEMAKER: Mark Johnson
  (Geisenheim-trained)
FOUNDED: 1974

AT A GLANCE
Tours & Tastings: Mon.–Sat. 11–6, Sun. 12–6. Guided tours except in winter; vineyard, winemaking, tasting included.
Vineyards: Michigan's only all-vinifera vineyard, one hundred acres in Old Mission Peninsula v.a.; cherries.
Wines: A pronounced German accent in Riesling wines, also Chardonnay, Merlot, Gamay Beaujolais, Pinot Noir. Ice Wine, Trockenbeerenauslese, cherry-based spiced wine.
Awards: King Midas hoard of gold and silver in state, national, and international competitions. Consistently cited: Late Harvest and Botrytis Berry Select Rieslings and Chardonnays.
Picnic Area: On the grounds.
Retail Shop: Wines and gifts.
Credit Cards: MasterCard, Visa.
Access for Disabled: Yes.
Foreign Languages: None.
Getting There: From Traverse City: Take U.S. 31 West to M-37, then head north on M-37 for seven miles.

&. What makes this place so interesting is that founder Edward O'Keefe, despite all warnings that vinifera varieties could never make it through Michigan's subzero winters, got his vines to not only survive but thrive and produce award-winning wines. O'Keefe, a wine importer, had a hunch that the moderating influence of Grand Traverse Bay could create an ideal microclimate. With a team of experts from Geisenheim Viticultural and Enological Institute in West Germany, he put in his vines after moving one million cubic yards of earth to turn the rolling hills into a sun-facing slope to supply maximum warmth. The winery was fitted with the latest state-of-the-art winemaking technology, and the rest, as they say, is history, one that wine connoisseurs take seriously. Tasters today experience the wines, guided by winemaker Johnson or Edward O'Keefe 3rd.

&. &. &.

Good Harbor Vineyards

Route 1, Box 888
Lake Leelanau, Michigan 49653
TEL: 616-256-7165
PRESIDENT/WINEMAKER: D. Bruce
   Simpson (courses at UC-Davis)
FOUNDED: 1980

AT A GLANCE
Tours & Tastings: May.–Nov., Mon.–Sat. 11–6, Sun. 12–6; Nov.–Apr., occasional Sats., call ahead; self-guided tours of winery with tastings conducted by staff.
Closed: All times but those above.
Vineyards/Orchards: Twenty acres focusing on whites, Riesling, Seyval, Vignoles, and Chardonnay; occasionally additional grapes of these same varieties are purchased, as are De Chaunac and Marechal Foch for red wines. Apples, pears, cherries.
Wines: Varietals: Seyval, Vignoles, and Riesling; blends: Trillium, sparkling Trilliom; wines from fruits.

Awards: Gold, silver, and bronze at Michigan State Fair, Midwest Wine Competition, Eastern International Competition, Indiana State Fair, and National Restaurant Classic.
Retail Shop: Wines sold on-site.
Credit Cards: MasterCard, Visa.
Access for Disabled: Yes.
Foreign Languages: None.
Getting There: Three miles south of Leland on scenic highway M-22. The winery is behind Manitou Farm Market and Bakery, one of Michigan's finest farm markets, a must stop for picnic foods or food fanciers.

&. Long-time Leelanau Peninsula fruit growers, the Simpson family turned their attention to winemaking in 1980. The central idea here is to start with the best grapes and fruits and to treat them as gently as possible to produce high-quality table wines. Apparently, the theory has paid off: since its founding in 1980, Good Harbor has won more than forty awards against stiff competition.

&. &. &.

Leelanau Wine Cellars Ltd.

P.O. Box 68
Omena, Michigan 49674
TEL: 616-386-5201
PRESIDENT: Michael Jacobson
FOUNDED: 1975

AT A GLANCE
Tours & Tastings: Apr. 15–Dec., Mon.–Sat. 11–5; Sun. 12–5. Twenty-minute guided tour includes winery and vineyard.
Closed: Jan.–Apr. 15.
Vineyards/Orchards: Thirty-five acres planted to vinifera varieties and French hybrids. Apples, peaches, pears, Montmorency and Morello cherries. Some additional grapes and fruits purchased in Leelanau County.

Wines: Chardonnay, Cabernet Sauvignon, Seyval Blanc, Aurora, De Chaunac, Merlot, Vignoles, Baco Noir; *methode champenoise* champagne. Fruit wines from varieties above. Spiced cherry wine.
Awards: Consistently awarded gold, silver, and bronze in state and regional competitions.
Retail Shop: Wines sold on-site.
Credit Cards: American Express, MasterCard, Visa.
Access for Disabled: Yes.
Foreign Languages: None.
Getting There: Twenty-five miles north of Traverse City, on Cty Rd. 626.

⊷ Omena is headquarters for Leelanau Limited, which has sales and tasting rooms at Traverse City and Frankenmuth. The winery believes that the long north-south hills in the area called "drumlins" and the many large bodies of water hereabouts are the best possible growing conditions for fine wine grapes. It's good territory for bicycling, hiking, and cross-country skiing, too.

⊷ ⊷ ⊷

L. Mawby Vineyards

4519 Elm Valley Road (P.O. Box 237)
Suttons Bay, Michigan 49682
TEL: 616-271-3522
OWNER/WINEMAKER: Lawrence Mawby
FOUNDED: 1977

AT A GLANCE
Tours & Tastings: May 1–Oct. 31,Thurs.–Sat., 1–6 tastings; tours by appointment.
Closed: Except as above.
Vineyards: Six acres (leased) to vinifera and French hybrids.
Wines: Focus is on whites: Vignoles, Marechal Foch, Seyval, Pinot Noir, Pinot Gris, Chardonnay, proprietary white, Sandpiper, Sparkling Brut, barrel-fermented red and white.

Awards: Vignoles and Vignoles Reserve.
Retail Shop: Wines sold on-site.
Credit Cards: MasterCard, Visa.
Access for Disabled: None.
Foreign Languages: None.
Getting There: Mawby is south of Suttons Bay, off M-22 on Elm Valley Rd., between Hilltop Rd. and Fort Rd. Bicycles can be rented in Traverse City, three miles to the south of Suttons Bay, for a truly nice ride out.

⊷ Lawrence Mawby offers estate-grown-and-bottled wines that are rarely clarified and filtered. With proper cellaring, they will mature in the bottle after purchase. Supplies are limited—total annual production is only 12,000 cases—and wines are rarely available beyond the winery's doors.

Special Wine Events: Most northwest wineries participate in one or both of two major Leelanau events: the Leland Food and Wine Festival in June, with cooking demonstrations, winery tours and tastings, symposiums, amateur winemaking competition, and shoreline cruises; and on Labor Day weekend, the Leelanau Peninsula Wine Fest. Mushroom connoisseurs should note that May is morel picking time.

TO SEE & DO
Michigan's much-loved Leelanau Peninsula is renowned for outdoor recreation, but is also marked with years of history. Nature is responsible for the abundance of lakes and sugar-white beaches bordering the bays, the gargantuan trees in forest tracts, and the undulating dunes of Sleeping Bear Dunes National Lakeshore. But human hands produced the quaint little villages with historic sights. A must for food-and-wine lovers is the aforementioned Manitou Market & Bakery, adjacent to Good Harbor Vineyards (on M-22, three miles south of Leland;

8–6 May–Oct.), for fine fruits, vegetables, fresh-baked goods. Shopping opportunities include antique nautical pieces, handcrafted stoneware, handstitched quilts, and leather wear. For pamphlets and a map, contact the Leelanau County Chamber of Commerce, Route 2, Box 466, Suttons Bay, Michigan 49682; tel: 616-271-3542.

ACCOMMODATIONS

A major resort area offers diverse accommodations from rustic cabins by the week to historic inns, as shown in the few mentioned below:

Grand Traverse Resort Village
6300 U.S. Route 31 North (P.O. Box 404)
Traverse City, Michigan 49684
Tel: 616-938-2100; 800-632-4310 (in
    state); 800-253-7350 (outside state)
Over 700 luxurious hotel rooms and condo units, plus all conceivable activities.

Leelanau Country Inn
149 East Harbor Highway (M-22)
Maple City, Michigan 49664
Tel: 616-228-5060
A pleasant ten-room inn, with year-round restaurant specializing in fresh seafood flown in daily from Boston, homemade pasta, and country specialties.

The Leland Lodge
585 Pearl Street (P.O. Box 344)
Leland, Michigan 49654
Tel: 616-256-9848
Well-known local inn with antique furnishings. Turn-of-the-century area photos turn the bar's walls into an interesting history lesson. Restaurant serves locally produced foods and homemade desserts; well known for Sunday brunch.

The Homestead
Woodridge Road
Glen Arbor, Michigan 49636

Tel: 616-334-3041
Grand, stately inn is surrounded by the Sleeping Bear Dunes National Lakeshore, covering 1½ miles on Lake Michigan's beach. Sixty rooms in lodge, plus two hundred condos; full resort amenities and activities, elegant or informal dining; bar, dancing.

Riverside Inn & Gallery
302 River Street
Leland, Michigan 49554
Tel: 616-256-9971
Restored 1902 antique-accented country inn. Six guest rooms; breakfast with homemade breads.

RESTAURANTS

See also Grand Traverse Resort Village, Leelanau Country Inn, Leland Lodge, and Homestead, listed above.

The Bluebird Restaurant and Bar
102 East River Street
Leland, Michigan 49654
Tel: 616-256-9081
Popular since 1927 for local specialty, fresh whitefish; other seafood dishes and steaks, rich desserts, salad bar. East of the M-22 bridge.

La Becasse
4385 County 616
Burdickville
Glen Lake, Michigan 49664
Tel: 616-334-3944
Well reviewed by leading major restaurant critics for well-prepared French foods. At the junction of Routes 675 and 616.

The Epicure
Suttons Bay, Michigan 49682
Tel: 616-271-3025
Imaginative food accenting regional dishes. Will make box lunches.

The Beech Tree
Northport, Michigan 49670
Tel: 616-386-5892
Tea room setting; makes box lunches.

Sweitzer's Family Restaurant
Gerilickville, Michigan 49684
Tel: 616-947-0493
Moderately priced. View of the bay from every table. Just north of M-72 on M-22.

Southeast Michigan

Seven Lakes Vineyard

1111 Tinsman Road
Fenton, Michigan 48430
TEL: 313-629-5686
CO-PARTNERS: Christian and Harry
  Guest
WINEMAKER: Christian Guest
FOUNDED: 1978

AT A GLANCE

Tours & Tastings: Mon.–Sat. 10–5, Sun. 12–5. Call in advance in winter. In-depth guided tour gives thorough view of winemaking from vine to bottle, includes tasting.
Closed: Thanksgiving, Christmas, New Year's days.
Vineyards/Orchards: Twenty-five acres planted to French-American hybrids; fifteen acres of eight apple varieties on dwarf trees.
Wines: Estate-bottled Vignoles, Aurora, White Cascade, De Chaunac, Rosé De Chaunac, Seyval and Vidal Blancs. Also six blended wines including Michigan nouveau, traditional Bordeaux style; Sangria, spiced wine, and apple wine.
Awards: Golds to Vignoles and White Cascade, and silver to De Chaunac.
Picnic Area: Along the trails in the surrounding woods and on winery lawn. Visitors can get maps showing trails and picnic areas when buying bottles of wine, then map out their own adventures.
Retail Shop: Wines and gift items.
Credit Cards: None.
Access for Disabled: yes.
Foreign Languages: Spanish.
Getting There: Take I-75 fifteen miles south from Flint or thirty-five miles north from Detroit; winery is near historic Holly, Michigan.
Special Wine & Other Events: Spring and fall wine festivals. In Holly, Carry Nation Festival, weekend after Labor Day; Dickens Christmas, late Nov.–mid-Dec.

⛟ Harry Guest and his son Christian could not have found a more dramatic place for their home, vineyard, and winery—one hundred acres of gently rolling farmland, including thirty-five wooded acres carpeted with wildflowers and populated with birds, deer, possum, and rabbit, playing hide-and-seek between the 200-year-old oak, maple, and hickory trees. Visitors can use the hiking and cross-country skiing trails that cut through the woods.

The handsome winery has plenty of windows, so tasters can savor wine with a view. In fall, cider joins the list of offerings for sale, as do apples (picked or those you pick yourself); a bonus is the brilliant display of fall foliage.

TO SEE & DO
Holly, a stone's throw from Fenton, was in its heyday a great railway junction where many VIPs got off to change trains, and some stayed off. For instance, Barnum of Barnum and Bailey Circus fame had a great showy home in Holly on College Street. (Its replica is in New York state.) So you can step right up and see it and other old mansions as you stroll through the streets today. Stroll down restored Battle Alley, a nineteenth-century street featuring working craftsmen, and many antique and specialty shops.

ACCOMMODATIONS
Hyatt Regency
1 Riverfront Center West at Saginaw
   Street
Flint, Michigan 48502
Tel: 313-239-1234; 800-228-9000
Deluxe 428-room hotel with indoor pool,
café, bar. Free airport transportation.

Sheraton Inn
G-4300 West Pierson Road
Flint, Michigan 48504
Tel: 313-732-0400; 800-325-7170
Motel with 190 rooms, health club,
lighted tennis courts, indoor pool. Free
railroad, bus station, and airport trans-
portation.

RESTAURANT
Holly Hotel
110 Battle Alley
Holly, Michigan 48442
Tel: 313-634-5208

At the site of Michigan's first railway
junction, the Holly Hotel, built in 1891,
having survived two fires, has been
painstakingly restored to its ornate Victorian and Queen Anne splendor. A landmark for gourmands, the hotel has a wine
list of 150 wines, champagnes, and liqueurs. Special events at the Holly include the Fresh Morel Mushroom
Festival in late May, special wine tastings
and wild game dinners in fall, and a Victorian feast at Christmas. On the whim-
sical side, the day in 1908 that pro-
Temperance leader Carry Nation visited
Holly is toasted each September on the
weekend following Labor Day. Holly's
chef will pack you a "Perfect Picnic"
basket—a three-course meal with wine
in a wooden basket to go.

₰ MINNESOTA

Wine is new to Minnesota, but the locations of these two wineries take you
back in history.

₰ ₰ ₰

Alexis Bailly Vineyard

18200 Kirby Avenue
Hastings, Minnesota 55033
TEL: 612-437-1413
PRESIDENT: David A. Bailly
FOUNDED: 1977

AT A GLANCE
Tours & Tastings: Fri.–Sun. 12–5; tours
are continuous through vineyard and
winery, and include tastings.
Closed: Nov.–May.
Vineyards: Twelve acres planted mainly
to French-American hybrids, some vinifera and native American. Some grapes
purchased from other Minnesota vineyards.

Wines: Wines are Leon Millot, Marechal
Foch, and Seyval Blanc. Also Hastings
Reserve (made from Riparia, a Min-
nesota wild grape), port dessert wine,
plus Country White and Country Red
wines.
Awards: In Wineries Unlimited as many
as twelve awards, including several
"Best of Class" when up against 600
other wines. Wines well critiqued in Eu-
rope as well as United States.
Picnic Area: Tables on the grounds.
Retail Shop: Wines sold on-site.
Credit Cards: None.
Access for Disabled: Ramp.
Foreign Languages: French.
Getting There: Thirty-five minutes from
Minneapolis and St. Paul. From St. Paul:
Take U.S. 61 South through Hastings to
180th Street; go west one mile to winery.

David Bailly removes his vines from trellises and then coddles them through the harsh winter by covering them with straw mulch or dirt. Doing so successfully, he became the first to make wine from 100 percent Minnesota grapes. In 1973, he also became the first to construct a building in Minnesota just to make wines. It is built of native stone and pine; inside the fermentation tanks are redwood, and the aging barrels are oak. Bailly's wines travel widely and are on restaurant wine lists in New York, Phoenix, and Los Angeles, as well as those of the Twin Cities. Alexis Bailly, the vineyard's namesake, was Bailly's great-great-great-grandfather. A pioneer in these parts, Bailly's ancestor also traveled: he was sent packing for selling whiskey to the Indians, but he came back and founded the town of Hastings.

TO SEE & DO
Set on the Mississippi River, Hastings has interesting old houses, beautiful views from the bluffs, and a number of good trails into the woods. Good shopping, too. The Twin Cities, nineteen miles way, have many cultural attractions, including the Guthrie Theater, Walker Art Center, Art Institute, Omni Theater, and Science Center, that are worthy of your attention.

ACCOMMODATIONS
There are many large hotels and motels in and about the Twin Cities, and motels nearby. Here's an interesting alternative near the winery:

Thorwood
649 West Third Street
Hastings, Minnesota 55033
Tel: 612-437-3297
A gracious 1880 French Second Empire–style house, with lavish ceilings and marble fireplaces. A full breakfast is served, and wine and snacks are placed in your room.

RESTAURANT
Mississippi Belle
101 East Second Street
Hastings, Minnesota 55033
Tel: 612-437-5694
Steak, lobster, and Bailly and other wines served in an old riverboat atmosphere.

Scenic Valley Winery

101 Coffee Street
Lanesboro, Minnesota 55949
TEL: 507-467-2958
FOUNDED: 1984

AT A GLANCE
Tours & Tastings: May 1–Dec. 31; show and tell involving seeing the equipment and telling how it works followed by tasting.
Closed: Jan.–Apr. 30, except by appointment
Vineyards/Orchards: All fruits are purchased from local growers.
Wines: Rhubarb, strawberry, raspberry, apple, elderberry, and wild plum fruit wines.
Retail Shop: Wines sold on-site.
Credit Cards: None.
Access for Disabled: Limited.
Foreign Languages: None.
Getting There: Get a beauty bonus by taking Scenic Rte. 61 from Hastings along the muddy Mississippi to Hwy. 16 West (south of La Crescent), following the bluff-lined Root River to winery in the center of town.

Tiny fruit winery in a building that in the 1930s housed a creamery.

TO SEE & DO
This historic town on the Root River has many buildings from the 1800s. It is surrounded by wooded bluffs and has splendid places to hike, bike, canoe, and ski cross-country; all equipment can be rented.

ACCOMMODATIONS

Mrs. B's Historic Lanesboro Inn
101 Parkway
Lanesboro, Minnesota 55949
Tel: 507-467-2154
An old furniture store is now a handsome, well-furnished inn with a good restaurant featuring American cuisine with occasional Scandinavian dishes.

Carrolton Country Inn & Cottage
Route 2, Box 139
Lanesboro, Minnesota 55949
Tel: 507-467-2257
Cozy country farmhouse from 1882 with old potbelly stove and many other antiques. Convenient to the winery, as well as to antique and craft shops.

❧ MISSOURI

Missouri has over thirty wineries, sharing space with scenic river valleys and rolling wooded hills. The state has two viticultural areas, at Hermann and Augusta, the latter being America's first designated v.a. in 1980. Missouri wineries now make wine from French-American hybrid varieties, while continuing to use native American grapes as they did when wine production was at its peak in 1866. Back then, the state was the second largest producer of wine in the country, and American wine research and study was centered in St. Louis.

In 1843 early German settlers found the rolling, wooded hills along the Missouri River Valley in Hermann reminiscent of their native Rhine River homeland. In a sip of time, the area became known as the Rhineland on the Missouri (a similar claim is made for Virginia's Rivanna River).

A bit later Italian immigrants discovered that the lush Ozark Highlands resembled northern Italy's wine regions, and planted thousands of acres of vines. Today both areas are wine centers, although most of Missouri's grapes are grown in the Ozarks.

Numerous festivals offered by wineries act as magnets to tourists, with events saluting the harvest and the spring. Also celebrated are dozens of other things, from the Fourth of July to the release of America's only sparkling mead. Sometimes an entire town kicks up its heels when the wineries celebrate.

For travelers ready for a two-wheel adventure, bike tours of Missouri wineries are organized by the St. Louis Touring Society. (Contact the Touring Cyclist; tel: 314-739-5780). Whatever your mode of travel, Missouri's wine routes lead through a rich tapestry of sights to peaceful towns with rows of pleasant homes on quiet streets populated with friendly people.

Missouri River Wineries

Wineries are located on Rte. 94, the scenic Lewis and Clark Trail, and Rte. 100, the scenic river road—two of America's notable wine routes.

❧ ❧ ❧

Bias Vineyards and Winery

Highway 100
(Route 1, Box 93)
Berger, Missouri 63014
TEL: 314-834-5475
PRESIDENT: James H. Bias, Jr.
FOUNDED: 1980

AT A GLANCE
Tours & Tastings: Mon.–Sat. 10–6, Sun. 12–6. Golf carts provided to ride around the vineyards; includes tour of winery and tastings.
Closed: Thanksgiving, Christmas, New Year's days.
Vineyards: Seven acres planted to Catawba, Seyval and Vidal Blancs, Marechal Foch, and De Chaunac in the Hermann viticultural area.
Wines: Varietals from the above varieties; proprietary blends; mead (honey wine); blackberry wine.
Awards: Several silvers, single gold and bronze—all at the Missouri State Fair.
Picnic Area: Wine garden picnic area.
Retail Shop: Wines sold on-site
Credit Cards: None.
Access for Disabled: Limited.
Foreign Languages: None.
Getting There: Seven miles east of Hermann on Hwy. 100. Left on Rte. B through Berger.
Special Wine & Other Events: Labor Day weekend: preharvest festival with grape tasting, music, craft demonstrations, hors d'oeuvres. First weekend in May: Festival of New Wines. Weekends in Oct.: Oktoberfest tours, hors d'oeuvres,

and merriment. Many other food-wine events March–Dec.

❧ Bias is a small family business where the accent is on premium wines and personal attention. The Bias vineyards date from 1980, and are 600 feet from the winery building. Nearby are vineyards dating from 1843.

❧ ❧ ❧

Eckert's Sunny Slopes Winery

Sunny Slope Highway
Route 2 (P.O. Box 817)
Washington, Missouri 63090
TEL: 314-968-2151
OWNERS: Roxanna and John Eckert
FOUNDED: 1981

AT A GLANCE
Tours & Tastings: Weekends, Apr.–Dec., Sat. & Sun. 12–6; conducted by the owners.
Closed: Jan.–March.
Vineyards: Ten acres planted to French hybrids.
Wines: Varietals—Vidal and Seyval Blanc, Chancellor, Chambourcin; some aged in American oak.
Picnic Area: On the grounds.
Retail Shop: Wines sold on-site.
Credit Cards: MasterCard.
Access for Disabled: None.
Foreign Languages: None.
Getting There: On Sunny Slope Hwy off Rte. KK, 4½ miles southwest of Hwy. 100.
Special Wine & Other Events: Participant in Maifest; Oktoberfest on weekends throughout months of May and October.

❧ The Eckerts both have careers in the airline industry—he's a pilot; she's a hostess—and they have set their sights high—the production of distinguished varietal wines. Their winery is operated from an antique-filled two-story log house dating from the late 1700s and set on a working farm with dogs, cats, and ducks. The lush vineyards, planted in 1981, surround a handsome brick eighteenth-century Federal-style house. The Eckerts let you explore the historic buildings, walking trails, and vineyards on your own, and then show you around the winery.

ಶಾ ಶಾ ಶಾ

Hermannhof

330 East First Street
Hermann, Missouri 65041
TEL: 314-486-5959
PRESIDENT: James Dierberg (since 1978)
FOUNDED: 1852/1978

AT A GLANCE
Tours & Tastings: Mon.–Sat. 9:30–5:30, Sun. 12–5:30; hourly tours are as good a look at winemaking as are offered anywhere, with the added bonus of the ten handsome stone cellars and the "smokehaus," where sausages and cheeses are made. Tasting of ten wines indoors or outside in fair weather; small charge for premium wines at tasting.
Closed: Thanksgiving, Christmas, New Year's, Easter days.
Vineyards/Orchards: Total forty-two acres of vineyards on this site and ten miles away, planted to French-American hybrids and native American varieties; some acreage from 1837 remaining planted in 1979; additional grapes purchased. Cherries also grown.
Wines: Norton, Seyval and Vidal Blanc, Villard Blanc, blends; *methode champenoise* sparkling wines, cherry wine.
Awards: All have won gold, silver, and bronze medals.
Picnic Area: In the courtyard or dining

room; bring your own or buy from the selection of Hermannhof cheeses and sausages and other foods from deli on premises.
Restaurant: Weinstube, with German decor and menu. Lunch only.
Retail Shop: Wines and gifts. Cooperage craft shop next door to winery.
Credit Cards: MasterCard, Visa.
Access for Disabled: Limited.
Foreign Languages: German.
Getting There: Take I-70 to Hwy. 19 South to Hermann, then east on Hwy. 100 one block to winery. Hermannhof is an easy walk from Hermann, or is accessible by boat.
Special Wine & Other Events: Mid-March: Wurstfest; first three weeks in May: Maifest; Oct. weekends: Oktoberfest. All with German food, music, dancing.

Hermannhof's current owners took over in 1978, but the winery itself, a national historic site, dates back to the early days of Missouri winemaking. The property fell into decline from Prohibition until its recent restoration. Today, Hermannhof is a place to step into the past for a few relaxing hours. Unless it's festival time: then you kick up your heels with the others.

The following Augusta wineries are in the Augusta viticultural area, the first federal wine district in the United States.

ಶಾ ಶಾ ಶಾ

Montelle Vineyards at Osage Ridge

Highway 94, Box 147
Augusta, Missouri 63332
TEL: 314-228-4464
PARTNERS: Bill and Joanne Fitch, Buzz and Nancy Peek, Bob and Judy Silfer.
WINEMAKER: Bob Silfer
FOUNDED: 1987

AT A GLANCE

Tours & Tastings: Mon.–Sat. 10–5:30, Sun. 12–5:30. Informal tours, take in vineyard, processing area, and cellar (upon request), and include tasting.

Vineyards: Five acres owned, planted mainly to French-American hybrids; some native American purchased; twenty-five additional acres planted to French hybrids managed by winery group.

Wines: Seyval and Vidal Blanc, Aurora, Leon Millot, Cynthiana, Marechal Foch, Baco Noir, De Chaunac; Concord, Catawba, and blends. Fruit wines—apricot, blackberry, gooseberry, cherry, apple.

Awards: Numerous for varietals and blends.

Picnic Area: Tables overlook Missouri River Valley.

Retail Shop: Wines, cheeses, sausages.

Credit Cards: MasterCard, Visa.

Access for Disabled: Yes.

Foreign Languages: None.

Getting There: The winery is 2½ miles east of Augusta, off and 15 miles southwest of U.S. 40, on Hwy. 94. Or a scenic 2½ mile hike from Augusta.

Special Wine & Other Events: Scheduled throughout the year; phone for details, dates.

❥ Montelle at Osage Ridge was founded in 1987 by blending two wineries—Montelle Vineyards, founded by the late Clayton Byers in 1970, and Osage Ridge Winery, founded by the current partners in 1984. Wines are turned out by the same winemaker as before the merger.

The winery's location on a ridge looming 400 feet above the Missouri River makes it a splendid place to sip wine while watching the river roll by and view the vineyard-dotted hilltops of the Augusta v.a. and the village below.

❥ ❥ ❥

Mt. Pleasant Wine Co.

101 Webster Street
Augusta, Missouri 63332
TEL: 314-228-4419
OWNERS: Lucian and Eva Dressel
FOUNDED: 1881/1966

AT A GLANCE

Tours & Tastings: Mon.–Sat. 10–5:30, Sun. 12–6. Twenty-minute guided tours every hour show all phases of winemaking, underground stone cellars from 1881, followed by a tasting of entire line.

Closed: Christmas, New Year's, Easter days.

Vineyards: Seventy acres planted primarily to French-American hybrids, some vinifera and native American.

Wines: America's only sparkling mead (honey wine), Rayon D'Or Nouveau White. Also Seyvals and Vidal Blanc, champagne, white and red blends, after-dinner wines.

Awards: Tradition of winners going back to gold medals in Columbian Exposition of 1893 and World's Fair of 1904 continues today. Recent awards include Best of Class to port and silver to Sauvignon Blanc in International Eastern Wine Competition as well as five of eleven gold medals for various wines at Missouri State Fair.

Picnic Area: On terrace in garden near winery.

Retail Shop: Wines. Shop across the way has cheeses and sausages for picnickers.

Credit Cards: MasterCard, Visa.

Access for Disabled: None.

Foreign Languages: French, German.

Getting There: From St. Louis: Take Hwy. 40 west to Hwy. 94. Take Scenic Hwy. 94 (Louis and Clark Trail) southwest for eighteen miles to Augusta.

Special Wine & Other Events: A most event-full winery. In May: Strawberry Festival: ripe berries picked at sunrise for sale at winery, sparkling wines, strawberry dishes in restaurants. In June: New

Champagne Festival; July: Days of Bees and Druids Sparkling Mead Festival, dishes with Missouri honey; Aug.: State Fair Awards, gold medal cheeses and wines; Sept.: White and Red Grape Harvest Days; Nov.: Fall Art Show, works by professional artists and potters on sale.

⏃ Mt. Pleasant's label was appearing on wines in the 1880s, when Missouri ranked second as a wine-producing state. Founded by Frederich Münch, German immigrant, wine book author, state senator, and noted winemaker, the winery was one of the eleven established in Augusta by early German setlers, all of which closed during Prohibition. Accountant and wine enthusiast Lucian Dressel and his wife are now reestablishing the winery's reputation for quality wines. They are made in the old high-ceilinged single-story brick winery and aged underground in the old stone cellars in casks holding 50,000 gallons of wine. The property, at the edge of town on a high bluff, offers a scenic view of the valley.

⏃ ⏃ ⏃

Stone Hill Wine Company

Highway 19
(Route 1, Box 26)
Hermann, Missouri 65041
TEL: 314-486-2221
OWNERS: L. James and Betty A. Held
FOUNDED: 1847/1965

AT A GLANCE
Tours & Tastings: Summer, Mon.–Sat. 8:30–7:30; winter, Mon.–Sat., 8:30–5; Sun., 12–6 all year. $1.50 adults, 50 cents children, for guided tour; free tasting, with or without tour.
Closed: Thanksgiving and Christmas.
Vineyards: Sixty acres planted to native American varieties and French-American hybrids; some additional grapes are purchased.

Wines: Varietals from the above; sparkling wines. Famous for Norton, made from grapes cultivated from vine cuttings remaining from the original estate. Missouri Riesling and Harvest Peach wines are also well known.
Awards: Won international gold medals in the 1800s, and the tradition continues today in state and other competitions.
Picnic Area: On the patio.
Restaurant: Vintage 1847 Restaurant in the old carriage house and barn next to the winery; German and other specialties. Sample wines before making selection for meal. Hours: 11–10.
Retail Shop: Wines, cheeses, other foods, gifts.
Credit Cards: MasterCard, Visa.
Access for Disabled: None.
Foreign Languages: None.
Getting There: From Saint Louis: Take I-70 to Rte. 19 and go south fifteen miles to Hermann, to winery at south end of town. Stone Hill sits on hilltop overlooking Hermann.
Special Wine & Other Events: March: Wurstfest—tours, tastings, and demos on how wurst is best made. Aug.: Great Stone Hill Grape Stomp.

⏃ Stone Hill is a good place to pause for a splendid valley view from the tower atop the main building and a painless history lesson in its artifact-filled attic museum. Built in 1847 by German immigrant Michael Poeschel, this winery was a huge success story. By 1900 it was the third largest in the world, producing over 1 million gallons a year and winning a glittering array of international gold medals. When Prohibition ended its prosperity, the limestone wine cellars—said to be the largest series of vaulted cellars in America—were used for forty years to grow mushrooms. Today the cellars once again house wines. The new tasting room in the old winery is particularly romantic, lit by an early American chandelier. This current revival is the patient work of

Betty Ann and James Held, local grape growers who bought the historic property and began restoring it in 1965.

A second Stone Hill Wine Company at New Florence (off I-70 and Hwy. 19, one hour west of St. Louis) produces champagne; tourgoers see champagne making and tasters sample sparklers and other Stone Hill wines. There's a gift shop with stemware, cheeses, and other items. Open daily.

All Missouri Wine Event: The Annual Art Fair & Winefest in May at the Rennick Riverfront Park in Washington (tel: 314-239-2715) is the largest all-Missouri wine-tasting event in the state, offering unlimited tasting of over sixty-five wines from twelve regional wineries. On display are local and midwestern artists' works. Admission $5 to wine pavilion; art exhibits are free.

TO SEE & DO

The 130-mile stretch of the lower Missouri River Valley between St. Louis and Jefferson City is a patchwork quilt of charm stitched together by rolling wooded hills and peaceful towns. Between winery visits you can spend time poking around the old houses and shops in Augusta, Washington, and Hermann, where twenty-two well-preserved city blocks are listed on the National Register of Historic Places. Augusta is especially dramatic by candlelight during the Annual Christmas Walk, when the wineries, shops, restaurants, and bakeries participate in preholiday festivities. Another colorful event is Augusta Country Days in early May, featuring antiques, crafts, music, foods, wine tastings (Tel: 314-228-4406).

Usually, the loudest sounds heard hereabouts are tug whistles on the rivers, with two exceptions. On all weekends in May and again in October, thousands of people flock to the area for festivals that transform the peaceful enclave into a boisterous scene of oompah merriment. The wineries get into the act with tastings and their brand of fun. For more information, contact the Augusta Visitors Association, Augusta, Missouri 63332 (tel: 314-228-4381); the Washington Chamber of Commerce, 323 West Main Street, Washington, Missouri 63090 (tel: 314-239-2715); or the Hermann Chamber of Commerce, 115 East 3rd Street, Hermann, Missouri 65041 (tel: 314-486-2313; in Missouri 1-800-HERMANN).

ACCOMMODATIONS

During the May and October festivals, be sure to book rooms well in advance.

River Country Bed & Breakfast
1 Grandview Heights
St. Louis, Missouri 63131
Tel: 314-965-4328
Contact for lodgings in historic houses and hotels.

The Schwegmann B&B Inn
438 West Front Street
Washington, Missouri 63090
Tel: 314-230-5025
Listed on the National Register of Historic Places, overlooking the Missouri River, this Georgian brick house dates from 1861. Antiques and handmade quilts; continental breakfast of fresh-ground coffee, imported cheeses, homemade breads, and grape juice from nearby vineyards.

Zachariah Foss Guest House
4 Lafayette Street
Washington, Missouri 63090
Tel: 314-239-6499
This is the oldest frame building in Washington, built in 1846 by cabinetmaker Zachariah Foss. Two big claw-foot bathtubs occupy the bathroom and there are quilts to warm up the nights and air-conditioning for cooling down. A bottle of wine and flowers is a welcome gift. Full breakfast.

RESTAURANTS

You'll find Missouri River Valley wines on a number of wine lists in restaurants in the St. Louis metropolitan area. Nearer home base, try:

Washington
Atwaters Ltd.
216 Front Street
Tel: 314-239-0272

Elijah McLean's Restaurant
600 West Front Street
Tel: 314-239-4404

Asinger's in the Park
1898 Highway 100 East
Tel: 314-239-7735

Hermann
Hermannhof Weinstube
At the Hermannhof Vineyards. Open for lunch only.

Vintage 1847
At the Stone Hill winery. Open 11–10 daily.

Ozark Highlands Wineries

Scenic rivers and parks extend your wine routes pleasurably, from Onondaga Cave in the east to Montauk in the south, with Maramec Spring in the center. If you're starting out from St. Louis or other distant point, and the weather looks doubtful, don't cancel your plans—call one of the wineries to check conditions. It's often clear in the Ozark Highlands when it's rainy elsewhere. Reminder: bike tours of these wineries, like those in the Missouri River Valley, are available (tel: 314-739-5780).

ᘒ ᘒ ᘒ

Carver Wine Cellars

P.O. Box 1316
Rolla, Missouri 65401
TEL: 314-364-4335
OWNERS: Mary M. and Lawrence Carver
FOUNDED: 1979

AT A GLANCE

Tours & Tastings: Mon.–Sun. 12–6; self-guided tours; tastings conducted by owners.
Closed: Christmas, New Year's.
Vineyards: Seven acres planted to vi-

nifera and French-American hybrids; some American varieties.
Wines: White Riesling, Chardonnay, Cabernet Sauvignon, Vidal and Seyval Blancs, Chancellor, Baco Noir, and Blanc de Noir (white wine made with black grapes); Catawba and Cayuga white.
Awards: Gold, Blanc de Noir; silver, Vidal and Chancellor; bronze, Seyval.
Picnic Area: Park-like picnic area, patio winery.
Retail Shop: Wines sold on-site.
Credit Cards: MasterCard, Visa.
Access for Disabled: None.
Foreign Languages: None.
Getting There: From I-44 in Rolla, take Hwy. 63 South 8 miles to Vida. Turn right on Rte. W, ¼ mile to Hill Rd., then right ½ mile to fork in road. Take the left fork to winery. Tasting and sales room and red wine production on Hwy. 63 about 300 ft. north of Rt. W.
Special Wine & Other Events: Monthly buffets.

ᘒ Small winery, offers a selection of French-American hybrid wines, but is proudest of producing vinifera wines from Missouri-grown grapes.

ᘒ ᘒ ᘒ

Ferrigno Winery

Highway B
(Route 2, P.O. Box 227)
St. James, Missouri 65559
TEL: 314-265-7742
OWNERS: Susan and Richard Ferrigno
FOUNDED: 1981

AT A GLANCE
Tours & Tastings: Mon.–Sat. 10–6, Sun. 12–6. Tours by appointment.
Closed: Major holidays.
Vineyards: Sixteen acres close to winery. Planted to native American and French-American hybrids.
Wines: Vidal and Seyval Blanc; Chelois, De Chaunac, Baco Noir, Concord. Vino di Famiglia semi-sweet red blend.
Awards: Vino di Famiglia, Chelois.
Picnic Area: In shady garden overlooking vineyards.
Retail Shop: Wines, Missouri cheeses, sausages, and gift items.
Credit Cards: Cash or personal checks only.
Access for Disabled: Garden only.
Foreign Languages: None.
Getting There: Take I-44 to St. James turn-off and take Rte. B north to winery, 3½ miles beyond St. James Winery.
Special Wine & Other Events: May–Sept.: Fri. eve. buffet served in wine garden. Known for music events from baroque to bluegrass.

ᴥ A renovated 1930s dairy barn, loaded with rustic charm, houses the winery on the main floor and the tasting room in the loft. The vineyards date back to the 1920s, when they were put in by Italian settlers. The Ferrignos added French hybrids when they took over in 1976. The vineyards are nearby, rare in this part of Missouri, another reason people like to look around the site. The Ferrignos were in fact grape growers for five years prior to starting their winery.

ᴥ ᴥ ᴥ

Heinrichshaus Vineyards & Winery

Route 2 (P.O. Box 139)
St. James, Missouri 65559
TEL: 314-265-5000
OWNERS: Heinrich and Lois Grohe
FOUNDED: 1979

AT A GLANCE
Tours & Tastings: Mon.–Sat. 9–6, Sun. 12–6; tasting and sales.
Closed: Thanksgiving, Christmas, New Year's.
Vineyards: Ten acres planted to classic American and French-American hybrids.
Wines: Seyval and Vidal Blancs, Baco Noir, Chancellor, Cynthiana, De Chaunac, Catawba.
Picnic Area: Tree-shaded tables near winery.
Retail Shop: Wines, Missouri cheeses, sausages, paintings; handmade pottery, wine racks, and other wine accessories.
Credit Cards: MasterCard, Visa.
Access for Disabled: None.
Foreign Languages: German.
Getting There: Winery is off the St. James exit on I-44; follow the south outer road to Rte. KK East to the Rte. U bridge, then go north to winery.

ᴥ Born and raised in Germany's Rhine Valley, Heinrich Grohe blends wines the European way, and specializes in dry wines.

ᴥ ᴥ ᴥ

Rosati Winery Inc.

Route 1, Box 55
St. James, Missouri 65559
TEL: 314-265-8629
PRESIDENT: Robert H. Ashby
FOUNDED: 1934

AT A GLANCE
Tours & Tastings: Mon.–Sat. 8–6, Sun. 12–6. Self-guided tours assisted by educational signage and pictures on area his-

tory and winemaking Rosati-style, followed by tasting of the seventeen Rosati wines.

Closed: Thanksgiving, Christmas, Easter.

Vineyards: Fourteen northeast of winery planted to Cynthiana, Riesling (labrusca); Concord and Vidal Blanc; remainder of grapes purchased from area growers.

Wines: Varietals, Vino di Tavola (full-bodied dry blend); fruit and berry wines, sangria, and spice wine. Well known for a variety of sparkling wines.

Awards: Elvira and Chancellor were recent winners.

Picnic Area: Picnic patio outside winery.

Restaurant: Leo Cardetti's Ristorante features pasta and other Italian foods. Fri.–Sun. 11–9.

Retail Shop: Wines, cheeses, fruit juices, and gifts.

Credit Cards: MasterCard, Visa.

Access for Disabled: Limited to first floor, rest rooms, sampling, and sales.

Foreign Languages: None.

Getting There: Located between St. James and Cuba off I-44. Westbound exits F and ZZ, cross overpass, and continue west. Eastbound, exit St. James, drive south on Rte. 68, then east on KK to winery.

Special Wine & Other Events: During June: Wine Expo—Rosati offers new wines and a tour of the old settlement in classic automobiles. Sept.: Vintage Celebration brings special foods from Leo Cardetti's, music, and the classic automobiles roll again.

&. Established in 1934, this small family winery keeps changing with the times while continuing to toast its classic Italian roots. The old brick winery and the restaurant next door are accented with farm implements from the early Rosati days. Among the pleasures outdoors are the wine garden, pond, and gently rolling hills reminiscent of northern Italy.

&. &. &.

St. James Winery, Inc.

540 Sidney Street
St. James, Missouri 65559
TEL: 314-265-7912
OWNERS: James R. Hofherr and Patricia A. Hofherr
WINEMAKER: James R. Hofherr
FOUNDED: 1970

AT A GLANCE

Tours & Tastings: Winter, Mon.–Sat. 8–6; Summer, Mon.–Sat. 8–7; Sun. 12–6 all year. Self-guided tour with instructive signs takes you through all the steps of winemaking; tasting follows.

Closed: Christmas, Thanksgiving.

Vineyards: Seventy acres planted to American and French-American hybrids, located two miles east of winery.

Wines: Rougeon, Ravat (Vignoles), Villard Noir, join the expected Vidal and Seyval Blancs. American varieties include Isabella, one of the earliest known native grapes. Fruit wines.

Awards: Prizewinners include Velvet Red (Concord wine), Delaware, strawberry.

Retail Shop: Wines, cheeses, home winemaking supplies, glassware.

Credit Cards: MasterCard, Visa.

Access for Disabled: Everything on one floor.

Foreign Languages: None.

Getting There: Take I-44 to St. James exit, and the north access road (Hwy. B) east.

Special Wine & Other Events: Participant in area events.

&. The cedar-shingled, gabled tasting room blends in with the rustic surroundings, but inside the winery beats a 21st-century heart, as seen in the latest modern winemaking equipment. Grapes are machine picked in the nearby vineyard. St. James is one of the Ozark Highlands' biggest wine producers, bottling about 600 cases per day.

The winery's land was associated with another avant-garde adventure years ago when its owner was St. James Aircraft Co. Inc.: on June 26, 1926, Charles A. Lindbergh landed here and took the local folks up for rides costing $3 to $5—not a cheap thrill for those days!

SPECIAL WINE EVENTS

Two main events each year involve Ozark Highlands wineries in a flurry of free attractions: Wine Expo, during the second week of June, is the occasion to release new vintages, a parade of foods, and such eye-catching activities as crafts demonstrations, art shows, and music. The Vintage Harvest Festival, held the third weekend after Labor Day, is marked concurrently with the town of St. James's Grape and Fall Festival. Festival activities include touring wineries, gospel and bluegrass concerts, a baked goods auction, parades, and culminates in the big Harvest Dinner, with country foods, music, and wine.

TO SEE & DO

A small town with 3,000 people and one taxi, St. James is best seen by strolling around the historic area, with buildings dating back to the 1870s, when it was an important iron industrial town. Nearby is Meramec Spring Park, where the namesake spring gushes forth with 90,000,000 gallons a day, a refreshing sight to 400,000 people annually (seven miles southeast of St. James on Hwy. 8; tel: 314-265-7387). Meramec Caverns are another famous sight, as is Onondaga Cave in the state park of the same name.

Seventeen miles southeast of St. James, Rolla offers one of the country's most unusual sightseeing experiences—an award-winning copy of Stonehenge, England's ancient megalith. For more information, contact the Rolla Area Chamber of Commerce, 901 Elm Street, Rolla, Missouri 65401; Tel: 314-364-3577.

ACCOMMODATIONS

Rolla is the site of locally and nationally known accommodations including Holiday Inn and Howard Johnson's. During special events times, rates go up.

Ferrigno Winery
(See winery listing for address, telephone.)
Bed and breakfast; guest house.

Howard Johnson's
127 Howard Johnson's Drive
Rolla, Missouri 65401
Tel: 314-374-7111; 800-654-2000
Eighty-room, full-service motor hotel with pool, bellhops, the works. At the junction of I-44 and Business Loop 44.

East of Kansas City

Bristle Ridge Vineyard & Winery

P.O. Box 95
Knob Noster, Missouri 65336
TEL: 816-229-0961
OWNER/WINEMAKER: Edward L. Smith
FOUNDED: 1979

AT A GLANCE

Tours & Tastings: Sat. 10–6, Sun. 12–6; tours cover everything from vineyard to bottling and tasting.
Vineyards: Five acres planted to French-American hybrids.
Wines: Ten wines, ranging from dry to sweet, include Seyval and Vidal Blancs, rosé, and Burgundy styles. Also, strawberry wine and hard cider.
Picnic Area: Panoramic twenty-five-mile view.
Retail Shop: Wines, cheeses, breads.
Credit Cards: None.
Access for Disabled: None.
Foreign Languages: None.
Getting There: 50 miles east of Kansas City, between Warrensburg and Knob Noster, ½ mile south of Hwy. 50 in Montserrat.

Special Wine & Other Events: Festivals third weekend in May and second and third weekends in October. New wines (grape juice for the kids), food, and music.

🍇 This winery is in an old water tower on a ridge. The highest point around here, it was used as a lookout during the Civil War. From here you can see forever while sipping wines in the comfortable tasting room.

🍇 🍇 🍇

Midi Vineyards

Route 1
Lone Jack, Missouri 64070
TEL: 816-566-2119
This tiny winery in the countryside east of Kansas City offers American Catawba and Concord wines, dry to sweet, as well as Lone Jack, a blend of grapes and ap-ples. Part of the fun here comes from ferrying yourself out to an island in the nearby lake, where tables and benches await picnickers. Tours and tastings year-round. Located 1½ miles north of Hwy. 50.

TO SEE & DO
Off Hwy. 50 near Lone Jack is the James A. Reed Memorial Wildlife Sanctuary.

ACCOMMODATIONS
Kansas City is home to dozens of top-notch hotels; for a B&B try:

The Fountains
12610 Blue Ridge
Grandview, Missouri 64030
Tel: 816-763-6260
Guest quarters with private entrance and patio, barbecue and gazebo. Near Kansas City's famous plaza, the Truman Library and Home, Nelson-Atkins Art Gallery.

Southeastern Missouri

Moore-Dupont

Interstate 55 (P.O. Box 211)
Benton, Missouri 63736
TEL: 314-545-4141
This is one of the newer wineries. It draws its grapes from the vast Moore-Dupont vineyards, the largest in the state. Located in new wine-growing territory along the Mississippi River, it primarily uses French hybrids. Still wines, but some *methode champenoise* champagne is produced at Springfield. Tours, tastings; deli and gift shop. Picnic area adjoins winery. Take I-55 South from St. Louis to Benton. Easy to see from the highway, with a red sloping roof.

TO SEE & DO
Cape Girardeau, 125 miles south of St. Louis, perched above the Mississippi, was a thriving antebellum river city. Architectural souvenirs of those days are the Court of Common Pleas Building (Spanish and Themis streets), where Civil War prisoners were held, and the Glenn House (325 South Spanish Street; tours, Apr.–Dec., Wed.–Sat., closed Thanksgiving and Christmas, tel: 314-334-1177) filled with antiques and memorabilia. Ten miles north, the Trail of Tears Park recalls the forced march of the Cherokee Indians from their homeland to Oklahoma and is a popular recreational site.

A prime time to visit Cape Girardeau is the second week in May, which is Rose Week, when more than 1,000 roses are at their blooming best in Capaha Park. (Perry Avenue and Parkview Drive, May–Sept. Blooming seasonal park open year-round. Tel: 314-335-3170. For more information contact Convention/Tourism Bureau, 601 North Kingshighway, P.O. Box 98, Cape Girardeau, Missouri 63901. Tel: 314-335-3312.)

ACCOMMODATION
Howard Johnson
Cape Girardeau, Missouri 63901
Tel: 314-334-0501; 800-654-2000
Eighty-three rooms, two pools, twenty-four-hour café. Two miles west of town at junction of County Rd. at I-55.

RESTAURANTS
Royal N'Orleans
300 Broadway at Lorimar
Cape Girardeau, Missouri
Tel: 314-335-8191
French-Creole dishes, some flambéd at tableside. Rich desserts. Wine list.

❧ OHIO

"But Catawba wine/Has a taste more divine/More dulcet, delicious, and dreamy."

Thus swooned poet Henry Wadsworth Longfellow in comparing Ohio's famous Catawba with the other locally made wines, when the state led the nation in wine production in the 1860s. Will today's Ohio wines bring out the poet in you? Perhaps.

With forty-four wineries, and more opening like buds on the vine in spring, Ohio is again making some praiseworthy wines. Longfellow's beloved Catawba, like the poet, is not forgotten, but no longer is it the favorite crop. As do others elsewhere, Ohio winemakers vinify European-style grapes. Currently a total of more than 2,000 vineyard acres are planted, 60 percent for juice and jelly, 35 percent for wine, and 5 percent for table use. Ohio has the distinction of having sufficiently varied climate and historical conditions to earn the state five federally recognized viticultural areas—Lake Erie, Isle St. George, Grand River Valley, Ohio River Valley, and Loramie Creek.

A rich diversity of wines are to be met along Ohio's wine routes, but they cannot be introduced for free. You must by law pay a modest amount for tastings—a fee deducted from your purchases at a number of wineries. Sunday sales are permitted by local option. A number of Ohio restaurants serve local wines by the glass to introduce diners to their fine qualities. Quite a few wineries are located near Lake Erie's shores, and blend well with a wealth of resort pleasures, historic riches, and covered bridges. (Ohio's 175 covered bridges is the second largest total in the country.)

Visitors will want to see both the picturesque coastal town wineries and ferry to those on scenic islands off the mainland before moving on. Central and southwest wine routes meander through quiet country lanes; this is great antiquing country. Meanwhile, further adventures await travelers along the rich Ohio River Valley and beside sleepier tributaries, where wine cellars are greatly rewarding and archaeological sites dip back into prehistoric times.

Three main wine events (make hotel plans early and ask about special rates) should be considered when planning visits to the state: The Columbus Wine and Arts Festival, during the second weekend in March at the Ohio State

Fairgrounds, features fifteen to twenty wineries, crafts displays and demonstrations, and live entertainment. Ohio Wine Month, held in June, features nearly every winery in the state in one or more special events (mentioned throughout this chapter). The Geneva Grape Jamboree, during the third weekend in September, was recently named one of the top ten festivals in the United States. It features two parades, grape stomping, bus tours of wineries, and many special events.

Additionally, wineries also get celebratory when the mood strikes. So enough of these explanatory aperitifs. Let's be off for robust adventures in Ohio.

Northeast Ohio

Breitenbach Wine Cellars, Inc.

Route 1
Dover, Ohio 44622
TEL: 216-343-3603
OWNERS: Cynthia and Dalton Bixler
WINEMAKERS: Dalton, Anita, and
    Jennifer Bixler
FOUNDED: 1979

AT A GLANCE
Tours & Tastings: No tours. Tastings Mon.–Sat. 9–6. Der Marktplatz shop also open Sun. 11–6.
Closed: Sun., Thanksgiving, Christmas, and New Year's.
Vineyards/Orchards: All grapes purchased from Ohio growers; fruits grown include blackberries, raspberries, peaches, and apples.
Wines: Chancellor, Seyval and Vidal Blanc, Baco Noir, Catawba, Niagara, Concord; peach, blackberry, raspberry, strawberry, and other fruit wines.
Awards: First Crush (Catawba): gold; Frost Fire (Niagara): silver; Dusty Miller (Delaware): bronze; Peach: silver.
Retail Shop: Wines, Ohio cheeses, smoked meats, Amish crafts; old and new quilts, dolls. No wine sales Sun., but store is open for sales of other items.
Credit Cards: American Express, MasterCard, Visa.
Access for Disabled: Ground-floor access.

Foreign Languages: None.
Getting There: Located on Rte. 39 (designated a scenic highway and a popular bike tour route), 2½ miles west of I-77.
Special Wine & Other Events: In and about the area: Ohio Swiss Festival—onsite; Four Season's Arts & Crafts Fair; Christmas in the Barn.

&. This is the only winery located in Ohio's "Little Switzerland." It is in Ohio Amish country as well, and there's more: it's also a country store and a horse farm. Visitors can shop six days a week, but never on Sundays as far as wine sales go.

TO SEE & DO
The wine routes enter a nearby nineteenth-century preservation zone where you can explore three historic communities: Roscoe (381 Hill Street, Coshocton, all-year, tel: 614-622-9310), a restored 1830s Ohio and Erie canal town, visitor participation; Schoenbrunn Village (New Philadelphia; Missionary Village) (May–Oct., closed Mon.–Tues; tel: 216-874-3636), log structures circa 1877, including Ohio's first schoolhouse, guided tours; Zoar Village (May–Oct., closed Mon.–Tues; tel: 216-874-3011), built by a German religious group, 1817–1898, with costumed guides. To the west of Dover on Scenic Rte. 30 is Sugarcreek,

where you will find the Alpine Hills Historical Museum (108 Main Street, June–Oct., daily; tel: 216-852-4113), showcase for Amish and Swiss heritage.

ACCOMMODATIONS

Cider Mill Bed & Breakfast
Second Street (P.O. Box 441)
Zoar, Ohio 44697
Tel: 216-874-3133
Housed in an 1863 cider mill in historic Zoar village; antique furnishings.

Atwood Lake Resort
S.R. 542 (P.O. Box 96)
Dellroy, Ohio 44620
Tel: 216-735-2211; 800-362-6406 (in Ohio)
Resort hotel in Atwood Lake Park with indoor and outdoor pools, fishing, boating, bicycling, tennis, eighteen-hole golf course, and restaurant. Stages Ohio Winter Winefest in February, a formal dinner with wines and fondues with sherries and ports; tastings and seminars.

RESTAURANTS

Atwood Lake Resort
(See under "Accommodations" above)

Inn on the River
County Road 111 and 82
Zoar, Ohio 44697
Tel: 216-874-4717
This historic restaurant, housed in an 1829 inn, is worthy of a visit.

&⁊ &⁊ &⁊

Buccia Vineyard

518 Gore Road
Conneaut, Ohio 44030
TEL: 216-593-5976
OWNERS: Fred and Joann Buccia
FOUNDED: 1978

AT A GLANCE

Tours & Tastings: Mon.–Sat. 1–6; tours upon request. During Sept. & Oct., visitors are invited to tour the vineyards and help with the chores. Also to be visited are cellars, tasting room.
Closed: Sun.
Vineyards: Four acres, planted to French-American hybrids and American varieties.
Wines: Baco Noir, Aurora, Steuben, Vignoles.
Awards: Oft-awarded: Maidens Blush (Steuben).
Retail Shop: Wines, gift items, insignia T-shirts.
Credit Cards: None.
Access for Disabled: Tasting room easily accessible.
Foreign Languages: None.
Getting There: From Cleveland: Go east on Rte. 90 to Rte. 7; exit at Conneaut. North on Rte. 7 to Rte. 20; Rte. 20 West to Gore Rd.; west on Gore Rd. to 518, Buccia Vineyard. Good bicycle roads and cross-country skiing trails.
Special Wine & Other Events: First weekend in Oct.: Conneaut's Octoberfest, on Main St. Covered Bridge Festival also in Oct.

&⁊ Fred Buccia wears several hats: he's the local tax assessor and real estate appraiser for Ashtabula County and a city councilman. He and his wife, Joann, made home wine for years before turning commercial. Now all hands help out— the four children (ages four to fourteen) and visitors too—if you drop by at harvest time, grape picking may await. Then relax in the tasting room, reminiscent of a *trattoria*, with lattice-divided booths and tables with checked cloths.

TO SEE & DO

Conneaut is so far to the northeast in Ashtabula County that it nudges against Pennsylvania. Many covered bridges are here. Conneaut Township beach is noted for beauty and its proximity to this and the Markko Vineyard (see page 260). When not splashing in the surf, stop at the Conneaut Memorial Railway Museum to see railway memorabilia displayed in an old New York Central passenger depot. Open Memorial Day to Labor Day.

For more information, contact the Ashtabula Chamber of Commerce, 4423 Main Avenue, P.O. Box 96, Ashtabula, Ohio 44004, tel. 216-998-6998.

ACCOMMODATIONS
Travelodge
I-90 & Ohio 45
Austinburg, Ohio 44010
Tel: 216-275-2011
Above-average 48-room motel, complimentary Continental breakfast. Restaurant, putting green, heated pool.

RESTAURANTS
No local restaurant serves Buccia wines, but they can be found at Atwood Lake Resort (see listing following Breitenbach Wine Cellars).

&ъ. &ъ. &ъ.

Chalet Debonné Vineyards

7743 Doty Road
Madison, Ohio 44057
TEL: 216-466-3485
OWNERS: the Debevc family
WINEMAKER: Anthony Carlucci
(enology degree, Michigan State University)
FOUNDED: 1972

AT A GLANCE
Tours & Tastings: Tues.–Sat. 1–8; hourly tours of the winery. During harvest, tours are given between pressing operations. Tasting trays offer a sampling of ten wines arranged in appropriate tasting order—$3 for premium wines; $2.50 for others.
Closed: Sun., Mon., month of Jan., except by appointment.
Vineyards: Fifty acres planted to French-American hybrids and vinifera varieties, primarily whites. Red and white labruscas.
Wines: Nineteen different wines under two labels: Chalet DeBonné (quality wines at reasonable prices) and Debevc Vineyards (premium wines, made of the finest vinifera and French-American hybrids grown each season).
Awards: Gold awards to Delaware and Johannisberg Riesling; silver to Cabernet.
Retail Shop: Wines, logo-imprinted glassware, and gift items.
Credit Cards: MasterCard, Visa.
Access for Disabled: Limited.
Foreign Languages: Slovenian.
Getting There: Fifty miles east of Cleveland. Take I-90 to Madison exit; south on Rte. 528 (cross Grand River) to Griswold Rd. (first left). There will be signs to the winery at this point. Take Griswold east to Emerson. North on Emerson to Doty, and stay east on Doty to the winery.
Special Wine & Other Events: Participant, last weekend in Apr.: Columbus Wine and Arts Festival—jazz, quartet singing, dance performances, crafts; June: Ohio Wine Month—celebrated with Annual Hare & Hound Hot Air Balloon Race, live music Fri. night and Sat. afternoon; last Weekend in Sept.: Geneva Grape Jamboree (in downtown Geneva)—parades, grape stomping, foods, wines, juices.

&ъ. Anthony Debevc, like his Yugoslavian immigrant father, was a grape grower in Madison and a wine hobbyist all of his life. His son, Tony, Jr., graduated with a pomology degree (fruit culture) from Ohio State University. Now with winemaker Carlucci, the younger men blend their formal knowledge with the elder Debevc's practical know-how to make some memorable wines.

From the outside, Chalet Debonné looks like an old-world Alpine chalet, but the sophisticated equipment in the cellar definitely is of the modern age. Upstairs, an antique wine press in the hospitality room is a reminder of former days. Here too are weathered barn siding walls and an oversized fireplace. From the adjacent glass-walled, plant-hung greenhouse there's a view of the vineyards, not far from where the family first started grape growing in pre-Prohibition days.

TO SEE & DO

In nearby West Geneva: Shandy Hall (6333 South Ridge, open May–Oct., Tues.–Sat. 10–5; Sun. & hols. 1–5; 216-466-3680), built in 1815, depicts Western Reserve living, complete with the furnishings of the Harper family, whose descendants lived in this house for 120 years. Along Lake Erie, Geneva State Park offers recreational activities summer and winter (OH Rte. 534; tel: 216-466-8600). Nearby are Thunder Hill and Hemlock Springs golf courses, Fairport Harbor Lighthouse, Holden Arboretum.

ACCOMMODATIONS

Quail Hollow Inn
I-90 and Route 44
11080 Concord-Hampden Road
Painesville, Ohio 44077
Tel: 216-352-6201; 800-792-2791
Resort on 700 acres, with eighteen-hole golf course, indoor/outdoor pools, restaurants, cross-country skiing.

RESTAURANTS

The Old Tavern
Unionville, Ohio 44088
Tel: 216-428-2091
Cozy fireplace is focal point of this restaurant that is well known for duck and desserts. Wine list.

≈ ≈ ≈

Ferrante Wine Farm Winery

5585 Route 307
Geneva, Ohio 44041
TEL: 216-466-6046
OWNERS: the Ferrante family
WINEMAKER: Nicholas Ferrante
FOUNDED: 1937

AT A GLANCE

Tours & Tastings: Tours Sat. & Sun. afternoons. "Grape to glass" is the tour theme; family members take visitors around and explain how wine is made, rounded out in season with vineyard hayrides to view growing, harvesting. Tastings Mon. 11–5, Tues.–Thurs. 11–8, Fri. & Sat. 11–midnight, Sun. 11–7.

Vineyards: Forty-five acres planted to native American and French-American hybrids.

Wines: The varietals and blends derived from blancs Seyval, Vidal, and Villard; Cayuga, De Chaunac, Aurora, Catawba, Niagara, Delaware, Concord.

Awards: Most of the eleven wines have won awards in state and international competitons.

Café: Outdoors on plant-decked patio overlooking the vineyards or indoors at tables looking out on vineyards through barrel-round windows. On order are homemade pizza and other light Italian delicacies.

Retail Shop: Wines sold on-site.

Credit Cards: MasterCard, Visa.

Access for Disabled: None.

Foreign Languages: None.

Getting There: From Cleveland: Take I-90 to Rte. 528, turn south for five miles to Rte. 307 and Ferrante Wine Farm.

Special Wine & Other Events: Sat. 3–7, Fri. & Sun. 8–11:30; Italian accordion music, singing, singalongs, and dancing. During June Wine Month, special foods on weekends.

≈ Small family winery in the Ferrante family since 1937, with a zest for entertaining visitors. Strictly homespun foods and entertainment can make a nice change of pace during a wine tour. (For accommodations and restaurants, see preceding entry, Chalet Debonné.)

☙ ☙ ☙

Klingshirn Winery
33050 Webber Road
Avon Lake, Ohio 44012
TEL: 216-933-6666
PRESIDENT: Allan A. Klingshirn
FOUNDED: 1935

AT A GLANCE
Tours & Tastings: Mon.–Sat. 10–6. Informal tours given when time permits by family members; special welcome mat is out during annual pressing, when grape juice is sold fresh from the press for drinking, jelly/winemaking, or freezing.
Closed: Sun., holidays.
Vineyards: Eighteen acres owned, planted to labrusca and French-American hybrids, some additional from Vermilion and Geneva area growers.
Wines: Emphasis is on labrusca varietals and blends; two French hybrids, Chancellor and Vidal Blanc. Varietals include Chancellor and Vidal Blanc.
Awards: Nearly every wine in line glitters with bronze or silver from Ohio state competitions; Chancellor earned an award for excellence in International Eastern Wine Competition.
Retail Shop: Wines sold on-site.
Credit Cards: MasterCard, Visa.
Access for Disabled: Yes.
Foreign Languages: Limited German.
Getting There: From Cleveland: Take I-90 to exit Rte. 83 (Avon Lake, No. Ridgeville). Proceed north on Rte. 83 for 1.6 miles to Webber Rd. (Central Telephone Exchange Bldg. on corner), turn left on Webber Rd., continue 0.6 mile to Klingshirn Winery.

Special Wine & Other Events: In May: Avon Festival of Flowers and Homespun Festival; June: Ohio Wine Month—Klingshirn sponsors photo contest with local photo club; Oct.: Avon Lake Homecoming Festival—parades, bus tours take in wineries and other attractions. For a calendar and a colorful Lorain County map, contact the Lorain County Visitors Bureau, Inc., P.O. Box 567, Lorain, Ohio 44052 (tel: 216-245-5282).

☙ Klingshirn vineyards go back in the family more than seventy-five years, while the winery started in 1935. That was the year a bumper grape crop inspired Albert Klingshirn to roll some barrels into his cellar and start making wine commercially. Now, three generations and lots of modern equipment later, son Allan and his family continue to make wine. The original cellar, still in use, is topped by a new building where the only antiques are for display.

TO SEE & DO
Klingshirn is just one of many intriguing places in Lorain County. Another is the French Creek District (Rtes. 254 & 611, Avon, Ohio 44011; tel: 216-934-6119; open year-round, daily), consisting of ten antique shops and boutiques housed in restored 1830s buildings. There are also a fair share of historic homes and cultural institutions, including the Firelands Association for Visual Arts, at Oberlin, a showcase for artists and craftspeople of the area, plus flea markets, antique fairs, campgrounds. Golf courses are abundant within this county's boundaries, with two of them in Avon—Avondale and Bob-O-Link.

ACCOMMODATIONS
Nearby Westlake offers a Holiday Inn on Clemens Road, and a Red Roof on the same road.

Williams House
249 Vinewood
Avon Lake, Ohio 44012
Tel: 216-593-5089
Comfortable B&B home in a quiet residential neighborhood a few blocks from the public beach. Full breakfast and arrival snacks make visitors feel welcome.

Ramada Aqua Marine Resort
216 Miller Road
Avon Lake, Ohio 44012
Tel: 216-933-2000; 800-362-2570
All kinds of recreational facilities—golf, tennis, jogging track, and much more. 241 rooms, three restaurants, lounges, walking distance to Lake Erie.

Saddle Inn
33481 Lake Hill Road
Avon Lake, Ohio 44012
Tel: 216-933-6102
Twenty-six rooms. Just Friends Restaurant, adjoining the inn, is a popular meeting place. Nicely furnished and pleasant place.

Scottish Inns
2800 West Erie Avenue
Lorain, Ohio 44052
Tel: 216-244-5251
50-room inn; swimming pool.

RESTAURANTS
Castle on the Lake
2532 West Erie Avenue
Lorain, Ohio 44052
Tel: 216-244-1488
Good wine list. Steak and seafood specialties.

Stella's Italian Restaurant
446 Avon Belden Road
Avon Lake, Ohio 44012
Tel: 216-933-3801
Italian foods, pizza.

Grassie's Wayside Inn
447 Oberlin Road
Elyria, Ohio 44035
Tel: 216-322-0690
Italian specialties.

Roman Room Restaurant
2001 Broadway
Lorain, Ohio 44052
Tel: 216-244-4919
Homemade pasta; walnut crust cream pies.

ટા ટા ટા

Markko Vineyard

South Ridge Road (R.D. 2)
Conneaut, Ohio 44030
TEL: 216-593-3197
OWNERS: Arnulf Esterer and Thomas H. Hubbard
WINEMAKER: Ali Nuernberg (diploma in enology, Dijon, France)
FOUNDED: 1968

AT A GLANCE
Tours & Tastings: Mon.–Sat. 11–6. Guided tours on demand; tastings are by appointment only. Fifty-cents-per-wine-tasting charge refunded if case of wine is bought.
Closed: Sun.
Vineyards: Fourteen acres planted only to vinifera varieties, Reisling, Chardonnay, Cabernet Sauvignon, Pinot Noir. Some Chambourcin.
Wines: Markko vintage-dated varietals from above vinifera grapes; Chambourcin; Covered Bridge red and white non-vintage table wines.
Awards: Chardonnay and Johannisberg Riesling consistent gold, silver, and bronze award winners through the years.
Picnic Area: On wooded grounds.
Retail Shop: Wines sold on-site.
Credit Cards: MasterCard, Visa.
Access for Disabled: Limited.
Foreign Languages: French, German, Japanese, Russian, Arabic.
Getting There: Sixty-five miles east of Cleveland. Take I-90 to Kingsville exit. Then go north and west on South Ridge Rd. to winery.
Special Wine & Other Events: End May–June: Ohio Wine Month—blessing of the

vines, hailed with dinner and classical music concert; third Sat. in Sept.: Odds and Ends Auction Sale.

* Arnulf Esterer walked away from a job as an industrial engineer to take up winemaking in Conneaut; his wife, Kate, and three sons and a daughter pitching in beside him. He was well prepared for his new challenge, having studied for two years with pioneer vinifera planter in up-state New York Dr. Konstantin Frank, and put his knowledge to good use. Es-terer is justly proud of being one of the first Ohio winemakers to cultivate vin-ifera grapes on Lake Erie's shores. Today his vintage-dated varietals earn highest praise from wine experts. This small, classical winery is in a peaceful wooded setting.

(For activities, accommodations, and restaurants, see the earlier section fol-lowing Buccia Vineyard.)

* * *

The Winery at Wolf Creek

2637 Cleveland-Massillon Road
Morton, Ohio 44203
TEL: 216-666-9285
OWNER/WINEMAKER: Andrew M.
   Wineberg

AT A GLANCE

Tours & Tastings: Tues.–Thurs. 12–8, Fri.–Sat. 12–12. Wineberg takes visitors through winemaking from grape to glass. Tasting includes all wines.
Closed: Sun., Mon.
Vineyards: Fourteen acres planted pri-marily to seven types of French-Amer-ican hybrids.
Wines: Seyval, Vidal, De Chaunac, Vi-gnoles; Cayuga White, Delaware. Cold fermented from hand-picked grapes.
Awards: Vignoles, gold; Cayuga White, silver.
Retail Shop: Wines sold on-site.
Credit Cards: None.

Access for Disabled: Ramp access to winery.
Getting There: From Akron, seven miles to the west: Take I-77 to I-76; continue to exit 14. The winery is two miles to the north.

* This is one of Ohio's newest win-eries and is set a bit apart from the other northeasterners. Founder Wineberg's educational background was in literary and dramatic criticism. He has worked in widely diverse fields, from management to restoration carpenter. His winery is unusual architecturally—in an Art Nouveau barn, it sits on a hill overlook-ing the vineyards, a large lake, and the city.

TO SEE & DO

Akron area sight: Stan Hywet Hall and Gardens (714 North Portage Path, Akron, Ohio 44303; tel: 216-836-5533; Tues.–Sat. 10–4, Sun. 1–4), former home of Frank A. Seiberling, founder of Good-year & Seiberling Rubber, and a foremost example of Tudor Revival architecture in America. Among the museums: Akron Art Museum (70 East Market Street; tel: 216-376-9185; closed Mon.) and Railways of America Museum (120 East Mill Street; daily 11–11; tel: 216-253-5858), with 1,100 cars and railway memorabilia dating back to 1830. To the north is fa-mous Blossom Music Center (1145 Steels Corners Road, Cuyahoga Falls, Ohio 44223; tel: 216-566-9330; open June–Sept.); Cuyahoga Valley Recrea-tional Area extends from Akron to Cleveland, offering 250 historical struc-tures and archaeological sites and nature programs (for information, call 216-650-4636). The Cuyahoga Valley Steam Train (Peninsula, Ohio 44264; tel: 216-468-0797), a 1918 steam engine with vintage cars, will take you there and back to Akron. For further information, contact Akron/Summit Convention and Visitors Bureau, 1 Cascade Plaza, sublevel, Akron, Ohio 44308, tel: 216-376-4254.

ACCOMMODATIONS

Akron offers too many hotels and restaurants to list here. A few suggestions below:

Bed & Breakfasts

Portage House
601 Copley Road
State Route 162
Akron, Ohio 44320
Tel: 216-535-9236
Welcoming Tudor-style 1912 home surrounded by spacious lawns and near a wall that was once the western boundary of the United States.

Inn/Hotel

Hilton Quaker Square
135 South Broadway
Akron, Ohio 44308
Tel: 216-253-5970
Hilton in a structure that is in the national register of historic places. A renovated 1880s Quaker Oats mill and silo, it is now a hotel, shopping, and restaurant complex.

Salt Fork Lodge
P.O. Box 7
Cambridge, Ohio 43725
Tel: 800-AT-A-PARK

Ninety minutes south of Akron off I-77. Relaxing country setting, accommodations in lodge or cabins. Site in January of Ohio Wines Weekend. Features wine tasting, culinary events, workshops, and discussions with winemakers; also gourmet bazaar, cooking demonstrations, nature walks and indoor recreational activities—pool, game room. There's also fifteen miles of hiking trails, winter sports.

RESTAURANTS

The Pub
5416 Darrow Road
Hudson, Ohio 44236
Tel: 216-650-1994
Fresh seafood and other entrées with a Continental touch. Wine list.

Silver Pheasant
3085 Graham Road, Graham Road Plaza
Stow, Ohio 44224
Tel: 216-678-2116
Pheasant, flambéd dishes. Wine list.

Ohio River Valley Region

Colonial Vineyards

6222 North State Route 48
Lebanon, Ohio 45036
TEL: 513-932-3842
OWNERS: Marion and Norman Greene
FOUNDED: 1978

AT A GLANCE

Tours & Tastings: Mon.–Sat. 11–8; tours of vineyards and winemaking process, tastings.
Closed: Sun.
Vineyards: Twenty acres planted to French-American hybrids and American varieties.

Wines: De Chaunac, Villard Blanc, Aurora, Seyval Blanc, Marechal Foch, Catawba, Niagara.
Awards: Niagara and Villard Blanc, bronze medals.
Retail Shop: Wines; cheeses available for wine tasting.
Credit Cards: None.
Access for Disabled: Ramp to tasting room.
Foreign Languages: None.
Getting There: From Cincinnati: Take I-71 to Lebanon, then State Rte. 48 North to first farm south of Ridgeville.

This tiny farm winery is located in a barn, built in 1857, that provides a rustic setting for tasting wines. When owner Norman Greene is away tending to his computer systems job, his wife, Marion, manages the vineyard and runs the tasting room. Both Greenes have taken extensive wine courses at Ohio State University.

TO SEE & DO

Lebanon Raceway (665 North Broadway, P.O. Box 58, Lebanon, Ohio 45036; tel: 513-932-4936; Jan.–May, Sept.–Dec.), a harness horse racetrack. Prefer to ride them yourself? Try Sugarcreek Stables (7735 Wilmington-Dayton Road, Centerville, Ohio 45459; tel: 513-443-0052) for trail rides on 600 acres of forest reserve. Good antique hunting—Waynesville is the antique capital of the Midwest—at Ye Olde Village Trader (61 South Main Street, Waynesville, Ohio 45068; tel: 513-897-4946), a sixteen-dealer mall. For the daring, gliders and sky divers are in the area.

ACCOMMODATIONS

Golden Lamb
27 South Broadway
Lebanon, Ohio 45036
Tel: 513-621-8373
Ohio's oldest inn, built in 1803; period furnishings, Shaker museum, dining accommodation, and tours.

Three B's Bed 'n Breakfast
103 Race Street
Spring Valley, Ohio 45370
Tel: 512-862-4241
Old farmhouse with comfortable rooms appointed with family heirlooms. Full breakfast. Retired air force officer in command.

RESTAURANTS

(See listing for Golden Lamb in "Accommodations" above.)

Meier's Wine Cellars, Inc.

6955 Plainfield Pike
Silverton, Ohio 45236
TEL: 513-891-2900
OWNER: Paramount Distillers Inc.
FOUNDED: 1856

AT A GLANCE

Tours & Tastings: Open Mon.–Sat. 9–5. Tours Memorial Day–Oct. 31, on the hour, 10–3; at other times by appointment. In-depth guided tour gives thorough education on winemaking, tasting; film and display of wine memorabilia included.
Closed: Sun., Thanksgiving, Christmas, New Year's.
Vineyards: Three-hundred-acre vineyard on Isle St. George, planted to vinifera, French-American hybrids, labruscas.
Wines: Varietals from varieties most often grown in Ohio, and blends.
Awards: A glittering galaxy over the years.
Snack Bar: Wine and cheese available in landscaped garden.
Retail Shop: Wines and gift items.
Credit Cards: American Express, MasterCard, Visa.
Access for Disabled: Limited.
Getting There: From Cincinnati: Take I-71 to exit 12 (Montgomery Rd.). West on Montgomery Rd. to Plainfield Pike. Go north on Plainfield Pike to winery on left.

Ohio's oldest and biggest winery. Currently stores 2,850,00 gallons; bottles 3,000 cases a day. Part of Firelands Cooperative.

TO SEE & DO

Cincinnati's bumper crop of cultural attractions and strong regard for history can keep you pleasantly occupied. Acclaimed attractions include the art museum, opera (the second oldest in the country), symphony, ballet, and theater. History speaks, not only through restored homes but at a community at Sharon Woods Village (Sharon Woods Park; tel: 513-897-2692; open year-round), an 1880s period setting with farmhouses, depot, and doctor's office. To sightsee the old-fashioned way, there are Horsedrawn Tours (46 Fifth Avenue; tel: 606-431-6600), with narration during your horse-and-carriage ride. Beechflats Mall (3224-3226 Harrison Avenue; tel: 513-481-4030; open year-round) offers shopping in six restored vintage buildings.

ACCOMMODATIONS

For hotels, motels, restaurants, consult the Cincinnati Convention and Visitors Bureau, 300 West Sixth Street, Cincinnati, Ohio 45202, tel: 513-621-2142.

Ohio Valley Bed & Breakfast
6876 Taylor Mill Road
Independence, Kentucky 41051
Tel: 606-356-7865
Bed and breakfasts, from modern to rustic cabins, in the Cincinnati area, northern Kentucky, southeastern Indiana.

RESTAURANTS

Heritage Restaurant
7664 Wooster Pike
Cincinnati, Ohio 45227
Tel: 513-561-9300
Of historic interest; former 1827 gristmill on the Miami-Erie Canal. Hickory roasted beef, seafood. Wine list. Herbs and vegetables from the garden.

る る る

Moyer Vineyards

3859 U.S. Highway 52
Manchester, Ohio 45144
TEL: 513-549-2957
OWNERS: Ken and Mary Moyer
WINEMAKER: Ken Moyer
FOUNDED: 1973

AT A GLANCE

Tours & Tastings: Open for tastings and sales, Mon.–Sat. 11–9; winery tours 11:30–4. See an international assortment of modern equipment at work—Italian crushers, French pressers, good old-fashioned American know-how.
Closed: Sun., month of Jan.
Vineyards: Ten acres planted to French hybrids.
Wines: Natural red, white, and rosé; River Valley red, white, and rosé; varietals Villard Blanc, Blanc de Noir, Vidal Blanc, Chambourcin, and *methode champenoise* champagne (from Moyer Texas Champagne Co.; see listing on page 310, in chapter 7).
Restaurant: A delicious combination—intimate 100-person setting with gorgeous view of the Ohio River, and dishes prepared under Mary Moyer's watchful eye—poached scallops, crabmeat, steaks, Mary's secret pie. Moyer wines, of course. Hours: Mon.–Thurs. 11:30–9, Fri.–Sat. 11:30–10.
Retail Shop: Wines sold on-site.
Credit Cards: MasterCard, Visa.
Access for Disabled: Limited.
Foreign Languages: None.
Getting There: From Cincinnati, take scenic U.S. 52 along the Ohio River for seventy miles to Manchester. Or go by boat (your own or check to see if any Cincinnati boat tours go upriver) and drop anchor at the winery.
Special Wine & Other Events: Second Thurs. in June (confirm with winery): Ohio Wine Week—celebrated with hot-air balloon, band. First weekend in Aug.: Manchester HOPE Festival.

る Ken and Mary Moyer's is a thoroughly modern winery—architecturally and technologically, and offers a well-rounded experience, combining wines with well-prepared foods. The Moyers will be happy to advise you on particular dishes that partner well with their wines.

TO SEE & DO

Scenic are the wine routes along U.S. 52—and educational, too, with stops at General U. S. Grant's birthplace, a restored cottage at Point Pleasant (May–Sept., weekends; tel: 513-831-9071), and Rankin House at Ripley (May–Sept., Wed.–Sun.; tel: 513-392-1627), an important underground railway stop. Travel back in time by driving up Scenic Rte. 41 North from Manchester to Peebles to see Serpent Mound State Memorial (off Rte. 41 at 3850 SR 73), the largest serpent-shaped mound in the United States, with a museum of pottery and other artifacts; and the Davis Memorial (Twp. Rd. 126-129), an eighty-acre nature preserve with impressive geological fault, dolomite cliff faces, diverse flora.

ACCOMMODATIONS

Bed and Breakfasts
The Bayberry Inn Bed & Breakfast
25675 State Route 41N
Peebles, Ohio 45660
Tel: 513-587-2221
Open May 15 to Oct. 15. Warm, welcoming Victorian home located near Serpent Mound. Big front porch and hearty breakfast.

RESTAURANTS
(See page 264 for information about the restaurant at Moyer Vineyards.)

ૐ ૐ ૐ

Valley Vineyards

2041 East U.S. Highway 22-3
Morrow, Ohio 45152
TEL: 513-899-2485
OWNERS: Ken and James Schuchter
FOUNDED: 1970

AT A GLANCE
Tours & Tastings: Mon.–Thurs. 11–8, Fri. & Sat. 11–11; for both tastings and tours.

Closed: Sun., Thanksgiving, and Christmas.

Vineyards: Forty acres planted to French-American hybrids; native American varieties and a sprinkling of vinifera.

Wines: Fourteen wines. Unusual among them is Blue Eye, a light-colored red made from a new American hybrid grape; more familiar are Baco Noir, De Chaunac, Vidal Blanc, and other varietals from Concord, Catawba; proprietary red, rosé, sangria, and Honey (mead).

Awards: Vidal Blanc, gold; Baco and Honey (mead), both silver.

Picnic Area: Yes.

Retail Shop: Wines sold on-site.

Credit Cards: MasterCard, Visa.

Access for Disabled: Ramps to winery.

Foreign Languages: German.

Getting There: From Cincinnati: Take I-71 or I-75 north to I-275 (Circle Freeway) east. Drive east on I-275 to U.S. 22 and Rte. 3. Use exit 50 (Montgomery Rd.) and turn right on U.S. 22 and Rte. 3 and continue on for 11½ miles to winery.

Special Wine & Other Events: Last weekend in Sept.: Valley Wine Festival (50,000 people); June 15–Sept. 15: outdoor steak dinners.

ૐ Brothers Ken and Jim Schuchter couldn't have chosen a more delightful spot than the rolling hills along the Little Miami River for their chalet-inspired brick, wood, and stucco winery, surrounded by neatly landscaped grounds. The Schuchters, who are truck farmers as well as vintners, are among the few to vinify the relatively new Blue Eye grape, which was developed in Missouri and which has made its way into Ohio. They consider their dry, light red Blue Eye varietal one of their outstanding wines. You can savor the flavor and bouquet of this wine, and others, in the wood-paneled, barrel-accented tasting room.

TO SEE & DO

Fort Ancient State Memorial (6123 Rte. 350, Oregonia, Ohio 45054; Tel: 513-932-2360) is a nearby archaeological site and museum featuring two ancient prehistoric Indian cultures, Hopewell and Fort Ancient. To canoe, kayak, or tube on the meandering Little Miami, contact Morgan Canoe Livery (Rte. 350 at Fort Ancient Park, 2247 Moor-Saur Rd., Morrow, Ohio 45152; tel: 513-932-7658). A bargain paradise is the Factory Outlet Mall (5300 Kings Mill Dr., Kings Island, Ohio 45034; tel: 513-421-5532), housing diverse factory outlets and discount stores. Lebanon is not far, so check out the sights mentioned after Colonial Vineyards.

ACCOMMODATIONS

Bed and Breakfast
Locust Hill
1659 East U.S. 223
Morrow, Ohio 45152
Tel: 513-899-2749
Victorian farmhouse, cozy with antiques and handicrafts. Bikes and a sailboat are on hand for your use; full breakfast.

Resort
Near Kings Island, 1,600-acre family entertainment complex, with six theme areas.

Kings Island Inn
5961 Kings Island Drive
Kings Island, Ohio 45036
Tel: 513-241-5800; 800-582-3050
Resort hotel adjacent to Kings Island; indoor and outdoor pools, tennis courts.

Central Ohio

Hafle Vineyards Winery

2369 Upper Valley Pike
Springfield, Ohio 45502
TEL: 513-399-2334
OWNER/WINEMAKER: Daniel D. Hafle
FOUNDED: 1974

AT A GLANCE
Tours & Tastings: Mon.–Thurs. 11–8, Fri.–Sat. 11–10, for tastings, sales. Tours upon request.
Closed: Sun., Jan., Feb.
Vineyards: Five acres, west of the Mad River, planted to Seyval and Niagara; additional grapes purchased from Ohio growers.
Wines: Niagara, Chancellor, Catawba, Concord, Delaware, Seyval.
Awards: Seyval in Ohio Wine Competition.
Retail Shop: Tasting room/shop.
Credit Cards: MasterCard, Visa.
Access for Disabled: Parking lot and winery on same level.

Foreign Languages: None.
Getting There: Northwest of Springfield on the Upper Valley Pike. From I-70: Take Rte. 68 North five miles to Rte. 41 exit, turn left (west) on Rte. 41 and follow for one mile to the first intersection (Upper Valley Pike). Turn right (north) and winery is one mile on left.
Special Wine & Other Events: Weekend events—Memorial Day weekend, Spring Wine Festival, July 4 Jubilee, Labor Day Festival. Dinner served Fri. and Sat. in summer; lunch, summer weekdays. Corn roasts, live music, and many other events, including cross-country skiing on the grounds in winter.

  Dan Hafle, Sr., brought out the Carry Nation syndrome when in 1979 he started his winery in what had previously been a dry area. Local antialcohol lawmakers charged he was violating zoning laws, claiming winemaking was a manufacturing business. Undaunted, Hafle took his case to the Ohio Legislature and lobbied successfully for legislation that protects all farm winemakers from a reoccurrence of this problem: the law states that winemaking is not manufacturing but a way to preserve and sell grapes.

Since Hafle's death in 1983 the winery has been run by his eldest son, Daniel D., assistant to his father since the winery's founding and frequent participant in winemaking seminars at Ohio State. Visitors to the winery will find themselves in a remodeled 1910 Amish stable, where the horse stalls are now fitted out as booths in the tasting room.

TO SEE & DO
Main area attractions are Antioch College and Wittenburg University. Of interest in Springfield are: Hertzler House (George Rogers Clark Park, Rtes. 4 and 369; tel: 513-324-7316; Apr.–Oct.), a restored 1854 home noted for a multiplicity of porches and rooms; and Pennsylvania House (1311 West Main Street; tel: 513-322-2704), a restored 1820s stagecoach inn. The Clark County Fairgrounds (exit 59 off I-70) periodically houses antique and flea markets. From Springfield, the adventurous can take Mad River canoe trips of three to sixteen miles (Morgan's Mad River Outpost, 5605 Lower Valley Pike; tel: 513-882-6925; open Apr.–Oct, daily).

ACCOMMODATIONS
Holiday Inn South
383 East Leffel Lane
Springfield, Ohio 45505
Tel: 513-323-8631; 800-HOLIDAY
One hundred fifty rooms with the usual motel amenities. "Holidome."

≈ ≈ ≈

Wyandotte Wine Cellars Inc.

4640 Wyandotte Drive
Columbus, Ohio 43230

TEL: 614-476-3624
OWNERS: Bill and Jane Butler
FOUNDED: 1976

AT A GLANCE
Tours & Tastings: Mon.–Sat. 10–6; tours and tastings.
Closed: Sun.
Vineyards: All fruits purchased from Ohio, Michigan, and New England growers—except rhubarb, which is homegrown.
Wines: Seyval and Vidal blanc demi-sec; Baco Noir, Delaware, Niagara, Concord, Pink Catawba. Rhubarb, red raspberry, currant, strawberry, dandelion fruit wines.
Awards: A treasury of gold, silver, and bronze awards in state and international competitions. Most often cited: red raspberry, Niagara; Seyval and Vidal Blancs are close behind.
Retail Shop: Wines, Amish cheese and gift items.
Credit Cards: None. Personal checks accepted.
Access for Disabled: Limited.
Foreign Languages: None.
Getting There: Ten miles northeast of downtown Columbus. Take I-270 to Rte. 161 East, continue for one mile, turn south (right) and onto Cherry Bottom. Continue one mile, turn right (west) on Wyandotte Dr.

≈ The only winery in Columbus. Built of brick, wood, and stone, with spacious lawns and shade trees.

TO SEE & DO
In Columbus, see the Ohio Village (1985 Velma Avenue; tel: 614-466-1500), a reconstructed nineteenth-century community, with working craftspeople, restored inn, and restaurant. For unusual shopping experiences, visit the Greater Columbus Antiques Mall (1045 South High Street; open daily, year-round; tel: 614-443-7858), eighty-five antiques dealers in a Victorian home; or the Con-

tinent/the French Market (6075 Busch Boulevard; tel: 614-846-0418), seventy shops emphasizing food and gourmet cookware, seven restaurants, and a host of cafés in an old-world setting.

North of the winery are the Hanby House (160 Main Street, Westerville, Ohio 43081; tel: 614-891-6980; Sat.–Sun. May–Sept.), a stop on the underground railway; and Olentangy Indian Caverns (1779 Home Road, Delaware, Ohio 43015; tel: 614-548-7917; Apr.–Oct. daily), a tri-level cavern and cave-house museum.

ACCOMMODATIONS

Columbus, of course, has its fair share of nationally known hotel and motel chains. For a change of pace try:

The Worthington Inn
649 High Street (Route 23)
Worthington, Ohio 43085
Tel: 614-885-2600
Beautifully restored inn, built in 1831 as a stagecoach stop. Guest rooms combine Victorian or Colonial decor with all modern amenities. Restaurant serves French and Continental cuisine in elegant surroundings. Fifteen miles north of Columbus.

Columbus Bed & Breakfast
763 South Third Street
German Village
Columbus, Ohio 43206
Tel: 614-443-3680
B&B recommendations in Columbus, including historic restored German Village.

෨ ෨ ෨

Shamrock Vineyard

Rengert Road
Waldo, Ohio 43356
TEL: 614-726-2883
OWNERS/WINEMAKERS: Tom and Mary Quilter
FOUNDED: 1984

AT A GLANCE

Tours & Tastings: Wed.–Sat. 1–6, Mon.–Tues. by appointment. Call Jan.–Feb.
Closed: Sun.
Vineyards: Four acres; French-American hybrids, native American varieties.
Wines: Aurora, Vidal and Seyval Blancs; Chancellor Noir and rosé; Windfall White (a Seyval and Niagara blend); and Nouveau Foch.
Awards: De Chaunac, bronze; Windfall White; Chancellor Rosé.
Retail Shop: Wines sold on-site.
Credit Cards: None. Checks accepted.
Access for Disabled: Yes.
Foreign Languages: French and Italian understood.
Getting There: 35 miles north of Columbus. Take U.S. 23 North and turn east on Waldo-Fulton Rd. for 1.4 miles; then north on Gearhiser Rd. for 1.1 miles to Rengert Rd., east on Rengert across the Marion-Morrow County line, and turn into first lane to Shamrock Vineyard.

෨ When Dr. Tom Quilter, a retired surgeon, and his wife, Mary, began their operation in 1971, they introduced commercial grape planting to north-central Ohio. Quilter has studied at UC-Davis; both he and his wife annually attend the grape-and-wine course at Ohio State to keep abreast of the latest in their field.

TO SEE & DO

Nearby, President Harding's restored home, museum, and tomb (380 Mount Vernon Avenue, Marion, Ohio 43302; tel: 614-387-9630; May–Oct., closed Mon.–Tues.). In Delaware, Ohio Wesleyan University, Olentangy Indian Caverns (1779 Home Road; tel: 614-548-7917), natural limestone caves, re-creation of pioneer/Indian villages; and the Delaware County Historical Society Museum (tel: 614-369-3861) and Perkins Observatory (tel: 614-363-1257)—the latter three all conveniently located on or near U.S. 23.

ACCOMMODATIONS
Holiday Inn
351 South Sandusky Street
Delaware, Ohio 43015
Tel: 614-363-1262; 800-HOLIDAY
One hundred rooms with indoor pool, hot tub, sauna.

Gathering Inn
259 South Sandusky Street (at Route 42)
Delaware, Ohio 43015
Tel: 614-363-1143
Motel with sixty-six rooms, swimming pool. Restaurant specializes in prime rib.

Harding Motor Lodge
1065 Delaware Avenue
Marion, Ohio 43302
Tel: 614-383-6771; 800-258-1980 (in Ohio)
Large motel with all facilities.

ða ða ða

Stillwater Winery Inc.

2311 West Street (Route 55)
Troy, Ohio 45373
TEL: 513-339-8346
OWNER: Harry A. Jones III
FOUNDED: 1981

AT A GLANCE
Tours & Tastings: Tours Fri.–Sat. 8 P.M.; tastings Jan.–Nov., Tues.–Fri. 4:30–11, Sat. 1–11, Dec., Mon.–Sat. 1–11.
Closed: Sun.
Vineyards: Twenty acres to French hybrid and labrusca varieties; some grapes from other Ohio growers.
Wines: Sixteen wines, the majority still. Among these Seyval and Vidal Blanc, Aurora, Villard Noir, Concord, Catawba, De Chaunac, Chelois; blended red and white. Also *methode champenoise* sparkling Catawba; red and black raspberry, strawberry wines.
Awards: Cayuga, Catawba, strawberry wines.

Picnic Area: On roof of innovative winery. Snacks, pizza sold, or bring your own.
Retail Shop: Wines sold on-site. Local art and handicrafts for sale.
Credit Cards: None.
Access for Disabled: Winery on one level.
Foreign Languages: None.
Getting There: From Cincinnati: Go north on I-75 to Rte. 55 and turn west for half a mile to winery.
Special Wine & Other Events: First Sat. after Labor Day: Annual Grape Stomp and Goat Races.

ða Want to go "down under" for wine—without visiting Australia? In the case of Stillwater Winery, that is just what visitors get—a trip down under. Once past the big glass expanse in front, everything is underground—processing, storage, the sales area, and the tasting room—all crowned by at least three feet of landscaped earth. This innovative design ensures optimum wine storage temperatures and requires a minimum use of energy. Winter visitors toast by two big fireplaces in the tasting room—the only heat ever needed to keep everything warm and cheery.

Owner Jones was a newcomer to winemaking when he opened to the public in 1982, but had been a grape grower for many years. The winery takes its name from the Stillwater River, four miles away, and location of the vineyards.

TO SEE & DO
America's oldest and largest military museum is nearby at Wright Patterson Air Force Base (Route 44, ten miles northeast of Dayton; tel: 513-255-3254; open daily); half an hour's drive south is the Neil Armstrong Museum (I-75 at Bellefontaine Street, Box 1978, Wapakoneta, Ohio 45895; tel: 419-738-8811; open daily March–Nov.), an air-and-space museum in the hometown of the first man on the

moon. Brukner Nature Center (5995 Horseshoe Bend Road, Troy, Ohio 45373; tel: 513-698-6493, open daily year-round) is 150 acres of woods and hiking trails; an interpretive building houses exhibits, library, and live animals—good leg stretcher territory.

ACCOMMODATIONS
Holiday Inn
I-75 and Route 55
Troy, Ohio 45373
Tel: 513-335-0021; 800-HOLIDAY
One-hundred-room motel, heated pool, restaurant.

Northwest Ohio

Engels and Krudwig Winery Museum and Historic Tavern

220 East Water Street
Sandusky, Ohio 44870
TEL: 419-627-9622
MANAGED BY: Zettler family
FOUNDED: 1863

AT A GLANCE
Tours & Tastings: Open for tours Mon.–Sat. at 1, 3, and 5 in season (Memorial Day to Labor Day); off-season by appointment. Included are museum and historic cellars; fee of $2 (adults) or $1 (under twelve or over sixty-five) is refundable on purchase of wine by bottle.
Closed: Hours vary off-season.
Vineyards: Twelve acres planted with eight varieties, primarily Johannisberg Riesling and Chardonnay.
Wines: Johannisberg Riesling, Chardonnay varietals; oak-aged Vignoles; blended reds and whites, dry to sweet.
Lounge: The Island Connection, in historic cellar, features wines and light foods.
Retail Shop: Grape Gift Shoppe has wines, related gifts, and souvenirs.
Credit Cards: None.
Access for Disabled: Limited.
Foreign Languages: None.
Getting There: If coming from the east (Avon Lake area): Take Rte. 6 to Sandusky, through vineyard territory along Lake Erie, stopping at Vermilion to see Great Lakes Historical Society Museum. Rts. 6, 101, 4, and 250 converge in Sandusky at the City Square (Washington Street and Columbus Avenue). From there the winery is 2 blocks north and 1½ blocks east. Travelers using Rte. 250 can stop off in Milan, southeast of Sandusky, and visit Thomas Edison's birthplace (tel: 419-499-2135), seven rooms filled with history. If coming by ferry, E & K is 2 blocks east and 2 blocks south of the Cedar Pt. ferry dock.

🍇 This old winery has been run by the Zettler family, owners of Kelley Island Wine Co., since 1986. E & K's story, however, began in 1860, when Jacob Engels planted a ten-acre vineyard and later built a winery nearby of locally quarried blue limestone. By 1878 R. P. Krudwig had joined Engels, and together they built E & K to a leadership position, shipping their wines throughout the United States. E & K survived Prohibition by making sacramental wines, and expanded greatly in the 1930s. Competition from Californian and European wines and the ensuing lack of interest in native American grape wines eventually forced E & K's closure in 1959 by heirs of the owners. The winery was renovated and reopened in the 1970s by the Feick family, until the Zettlers stepped in. The on-site museum is a good place to learn the winery's history and that of the area's wine industry.

TO SEE & DO
The winery is in the downtown historic district, near shops and museums and four miles from Cedar Point Amusement Park (May–Sept.; tel: 419-626-0830) with fifty-seven rides, animals, a hotel, camping, swimming, boating, and other attractions. (See also after Firelands Winery for more information.)

ॐ ॐ ॐ

Firelands Winery (formerly Mantey Vineyards)

917 Bardshar Road
Sandusky, Ohio 44870
TEL: 419-625-5474
OWNER: Paramount Distillers
WINEMAKER: Claudio Salvador
    (Institute for Viticulture and Enology, Conegiano, Venice, Italy)
FOUNDED: 1880

AT A GLANCE
Tours & Tastings: June–Sept. 1, Mon.–Sat. 10–3. Tours on the hour, take about one hour, and include winery (15 minutes), tasting and sales room (thirty minutes). Sept. 2–May 31, tours by appointment only. Tastings Sept. 2–May 31, Mon.–Fri. 9–5, Sat. 10–3.
Closed: Sun.
Vineyards: Thirty acres planted to Seyval, Baco Noir, Rosette, Catawba, Concord. Grapes purchased from Isle St. George and Lake Erie v.a. growers.
Wines: Chardonnay, Johannisberg Riesling; Seyval, Vidal, Baco Noir, Gewürztraminer, among others. Recently added estate-bottled wines. Two labels are used—Firelands for premium varietals from French-American and vinifera

grapes; Mantey for others. Grape juice also produced.
Awards: Seyval and Vidal Blancs frequently awarded medals in national and state competitions.
Picnic Area: In garden near gazebo.
Retail Shop: Wines, wine-related items; home winemaking center.
Credit Cards: American Express, MasterCard, Visa.
Access for Disabled: Limited.
Foreign Languages: Italian.
Getting There: In the heart of the Lake Erie vacation area, Firelands is located west of Sandusky, off Rte. 2 at the Rte. 6 exit.
Special Wine & Other Events: At Firelands: concerts, hayrides, five-mile run, and other attractions. In the area: Erie County Vineyard Days, last weekend in Sept. and first weekend in Oct., includes Boeckling's Festival of Grapes (Sandusky), Dick Goddard's Woolly Bear Festival (Vermilion), Kelley's Island Harvest Festival, Country Harvest of Crafts and Antiques (Birmingham). For the rest of the year, there are enough festivals in this five-county area to fill a county four times its size.

ॐ Firelands was founded a few years ago as a wine cooperative, but Mantey Vineyards, as it was formerly known, began more than a century ago as a small fruit farm in Venice, Ohio, now part of Sandusky. The Edward Mantey farmhouse, built in the 1800s, and the original wine cellars today form the centerpiece of a new winery bearing some resemblance to a French country château next to the thirty-acre vineyards. Stacks of barrels mark the entrance to the winery.
As a cooperative, Firelands presses and processes grapes for Lonz and Mon Ami, two other area wineries, and also presses, centrifuges, and stores juice for processing for Meier's Wine Cellars in

Cincinnati. The parent company for all these wineries is Paramount Distillers.

Firelands is a major producer of wines made from local grapes. It is the second largest winery in Ohio, with a 600,000 gallon storage capacity and the ability to bottle over 1,000 cases per day. An estimated 6,000 tons of fourteen different varieties of grapes are crushed annually at Firelands.

TO SEE & DO
This five-county area, known as the Firelands, got its name from an act of Congress following the Revolutionary War: settlers were given parcels of land in the territory as recompense for the burning of their homes by British soldiers. This region today is a prime family vacation destination, where there are island explorations, outdoor sports, and museums. Take the *Good Time II* cruise ship out of Sandusky for a leisurely sightseeing trip; visit Cedar Point, with fifty-seven rides, theaters, and animals; or simply relax and enjoy some wonderful scenery. For information, contact the Lake Erie Firelands Tourist Council, P.O. Box 321, Castalia, Ohio 44824.

ACCOMMODATIONS
Pipe Creek
2719 Columbus Avenue
Sandusky, Ohio 44870
Tel: 419-626-2067
Comfortable Queen Anne Victorian is set on an acre of land with a creek and shady trees. Big rooms furnished with antiques are a treat for the weary, and a full breakfast is made fresh when you awake. Wine is offered to guests on the patio.

Sheraton
1119 Sandusky Mall Boulevard
Sandusky, Ohio 44870
Tel: 419-625-6280; 800-325-3535
Just off Route 250, behind the Sandusky Mall.

One hundred forty-two rooms, with pool and expected Sheraton amenities.

Sawmill Creek
2401 Cleveland Road West
Huron, Ohio 44839
Tel: 419-433-3800
240-unit resort with indoor-outdoor pool, extensive water sports; fishing charters. Late May–early Sept. is peak season; lower rates remainder of year.

RESTAURANTS
In Sandusky
Bay Harbor Inn
Causeway Drive
Tel: 419-625-6373
View of bay and marina and fresh seafood are starring attractions, along with pastas and lamb and prime rib. Wine list. Open 5–10, closed Sun. in winter and major holidays. Located outside of Cedar Point.

Stone House
1338 Perkins Avenue E
Tel: 419-625-4141
Nineteenth-century stone house; chef's specialties are seafood, steaks, and chops. Baked goods made on-site. Wine list with local wines.

Tony Jay's
Tel: 419-625-6280
Italian cuisine. Wine list. Breakfast, lunch, dinner served. Open 7 A.M.–10 P.M. Located in the Sheraton, see under "Accommodations" for address.

≈ ≈ ≈

Heineman Winery

Catawba Street
Put-in-Bay, Ohio 43456
TEL: 418-285-2811
OWNER: Louis V. Heineman

WINEMAKER: Edward P. Heineman
(enology degree, Ohio State)
FOUNDED: 1888

AT A GLANCE
Tours & Tastings: May 15–Sept. 15, 11–5, continuous tours of winery and Crystal Cave ($2 adults, $1 children 6–12); includes complimentary glass of wine or grape juice. Tastings without tour May 1–Oct. 15. Open for sales year-round.
Closed: No tours Sept. 16–May 14.
Vineyards: Thirty-five acres planted mainly to labruscas; some French hybrids.
Wines: Sixteen varieties of Catawba, including Sweet Belle (unchanged since Prohibition), and newer French-American hybrids produced only in the last few years.
Awards: Full constellation over the years.
Picnic Area: In wine garden; cheese plate available.
Retail Shop: Wines sold on-site.
Credit Cards: MasterCard, Visa.
Access for Disabled: None.
Foreign Languages: None.
Getting There: If coming from the east (Lorain County wineries) at Huron: pick up Rte. 2 to exit 6 (Rte. 53), north to Catawba Point. From other points: Take Ohio Turnpike to exit 6 (Rte. 53), north to Catawba Point. Take Miller Boat Line to Put-in-Bay. Bike rentals at the ferry dock.

&. During excavations for a well in 1897 on the property of the winery, founded ten years earlier by Gustave Heineman, workmen broke open a hollow rock lined with glittering blue-white crystals. This brilliant discovery is believed to have been the world's largest geode—known now as the Crystal Cave—with some shimmering celestite crystals as large as three feet long by eighteen inches in diameter. Said to be the only one of its type in the United States, this cave is a major tourist attraction. Some handsome Crystal Cave celestite specimens can also be seen in the Smithsonian Natural History Museum in Washington, D.C.

Winery tours include the cave as well as a wine tasting in the wood-paneled tasting room or the flower-filled wine garden. The winery is now run by Gustave's grandson, Louis, and his son, Edward, and bottles 200 cases per day. If the cave is unique, so today is the Heineman Winery—the only remaining winery on Put-in-Bay, once home to many. Vineyards still flourish here in great abundance, though.

TO SEE & DO
Peaceful South Bass Island, also known as Put-in-Bay, is a resort with swimming and boating as major activities. Sights to see are Perry's Victory and International Peace Memorial (Apr.–Oct.; tel: 419-285-2184), a 352-foot Doric column offering a commanding view of the surroundings; Perry's Cave (May–Sept.; tel: 419-285-3491), fifty-two feet below ground; and the Viking Longhouse (May–Sept. tel: 285-7553). Put-in-Bay Bikes & Train Tours (tel: 419-285-4855) helps visitors explore the island's sights and scenery.

ACCOMMODATIONS
The Vineyard
P.O. Box 283
Put-in-Bay, Ohio 43456
Tel: 419-285-6181
Stay with the Barnhills, wine grape growers, in their 130-year-old frame house on twenty acres of vineyard land. Wine and cheese upon arrival. Newly renovated rooms with antique furnishings. Private beach; full breakfast.

The Landings
Toledo Avenue (P.O. Box 94)
Put-in-Bay, Ohio 43456
Tel: 419-285-3931
Newly rebuilt resort located on Lake Erie; swimming, boating.

Park Hotel
Put-in-Bay, Ohio 43456
Tel: 419-285-3581
Turn-of-the-century hotel facing De Rivera Park, overlooking the harbor.

᠔ ᠔ ᠔

Lonz Winery

1 Fox Road
Middle Bass Island, Ohio 43446
TEL: 419-285-6411
OWNER: Paramount Distillers
WINEMAKER: Claudio Salvador
(Institute for Viticulture and Enology, Conegiano, Venice, Italy) (shared with others in Firelands Cooperative)
FOUNDED: 1865

AT A GLANCE

Tours & Tastings: May–Sept. 30. Forty-five-minute guided tours start on the half hour beginning at 12:30 daily; last tour, 4:30; $1.25 per adult, 50 cents per child. Includes twelve-minute slide presentation on history of winery and founding Lonz family, walk through 100-year-old limestone cellars; explanation of how to drink and appreciate wine at wine tasting bar (grape juice is also on hand).
Closed: Oct.–Apr.
Vineyards: Ten acres planted to Catawba; other varieties purchased from Isle St. George (North Bass Island) and Lake Erie Appellation growers.
Wines: Twenty-five still and sparkling wines, including famous Isle de Fleurs *methode champenoise* champagnes, aged sherry, vinifera varietals; also coolers, sparkling juices, and cider.
Picnic Area: Tables, fire rings, water, rest rooms.
Snacks: Sandwiches, snacks, pizza.
Retail Shop: Wines, wine accessories, nautical gifts. Shop hours Mon.–Thurs. to 8, Fri. to 10, Sat. to midnight, Sun. 1–6.

Credit Cards: American Express, MasterCard, Visa.
Access for Disabled: Except cellar.
Foreign Languages: None.
Getting There: Miller ferry (Catawba Port), Parker Ferry (Port Clinton), or Put-in-Bay Water Taxi. Or Island Airlines, Port Clinton. Bikes and cars can be brought by ferry. Dockage for 150 boats available at Lonz Marina.
Special Wine & Other Events: Every weekend during summer: music, five-mile run, and more. Sept.: Annual Grape Festival.

᠔ Lonz Winery was opened during the Civil War by Andrew Wehrle, a German stonecutter who carved the limestone cellars, now listed on the National Register of Historic Places. By 1875 Wehrle's Golden Eagle Winery was one of the largest producers of wine in the United States, with a storage capacity of 500,000 gallons.

During the 1800s the winery was the toast of the townfolk, who used to come out in steamboats from Erie, Detroit, and Buffalo to sip wines, dance in the ballroom Wehrle built above his cellars, and spend the night in the sixty-room hotel adjoining the winery. Fire brought an end to the glamour in 1924 by destroying the dance pavillion and hotel, which were never rebuilt. The Lonz family, wine producers on Middle Bass since 1884, purchased the property after the disaster.

Under George Lonz, the winery prospered during Prohibition by switching to grape juice in a big way. His calling card is seen today in the form of his winery design—a fanciful-looking castle. By the 1930s and 1940s, Lonz Winery was widely known for Isle de Fleurs Champagne—made then and now by the *methode champenoise*.

The terrace of the winery offers a perfect place to sip some bubbly or still wine and contemplate the lake. Wine is just one of the reasons to visit Lonz—it's a pleasant day's outing, with swimming, picnicking, biking, and boating. You can poke around Port Clinton, where there's an African Lion Safari, drive through a wild animal park, see beautiful Sandusky Bay, and water taxi over to Put-in-Bay.

❧ ❧ ❧

Mon Ami Winery

3845 East Wine Cellar Road
Port Clinton, Ohio 43452
TEL: 419-797-4445
OWNER: Paramount Distillers (Firelands Cooperative)
FOUNDED: 1870/1934

AT A GLANCE

Tours & Tastings: May–Oct., daily 2–4; Winter, weekends only, by request. Tours $1; tours with wine tasting with cheese and crackers $1.50. Tasting offered without tour. Old, still-in-use wine cellars are covered on tour, along with fermenting room.
Vineyards: Mon Ami buys all of its grapes.
Wines: *Methode champenoise* sparkling wines, native American blends, fortified wines.
Picnic Area: In woodsy outdoor picnic site.
Restaurants: Choose between Chalet's informal light meals and Mon Ami's extensive menu. Eat outdoors in the garden when it's nice; inside by the fireplace when it's not.
Retail Shop: Wines and gift items.
Credit Cards: American Express, MasterCard, Visa.
Access for Disabled: Yes.
Getting There: Take the Ohio Tpke. to Rte. 53 (exit 6), continue north on Rte. 53 to Port Clinton area and Rte. 2. East on Rte. 2 to Mon Ami. If coming from east (Lorain County area wineries), you can pick up Rte. 2 at Huron and go on to Port Clinton.

❧ Nestled in woods, Mon Ami has stood the test of time; for more than one hundred years, wines have been produced in this old stone building. It's interesting even now to see the cellars where *methode champenoise* sparkling wine is still made along with other wines.

Another winery to visit:

❧ ❧ ❧

Kelley's Island Wine Company

P.O. Box 747
Woodford Road
Kelley's Island, Ohio 43478
TEL: 419-746-2537
The Zettler family's other winery (see Engels and Krudwig Winery), in a nineteenth-century stone house, producing European-style French hybrid and vinifera wines. Picnic on a covered patio or tables set in the acre-large wine garden shaded by large sugar maples and bordered by grape vines and flowers and herbs. Gift shop. Take the ferry from Marblehead. Easy walk from downtown, or rent a bike. Open Memorial Day to Labor Day, Mon.–Sat. 10–7, Sun. 12–5; at other times by appointment. Closed Nov.–Apr.

TO SEE & DO

Lush and green, Kelley's is aptly nicknamed the Emerald Isle. The island also has importance as the site of 30,000-year-old glacial grooves and a limestone slab marked with prehistoric Indian pictographs. Many stately mansions, a 600-acre state park, and many special events are other visitor attractions. The local Chamber of Commerce has details (tel: 419-746-2360). For other area activities, accommodations, and restaurants, see after Firelands and Lonz Wineries.

❧ WISCONSIN

The wine routes of Wisconsin make their way through three great resort areas; they dip briefly into a community near Lake Michigan whose roots lie in the 1800s and go west to historic La Crosse along the Mississippi River.

Winemaking is very old in this region, going back to the 1800s and Agoston Haraszthy. Best known for his success in California, Haraszthy first tried and failed to make European-style wines in Wisconsin. The present crop of vintners lean toward fruit wines, but there are also enough first-rate grape wines for a full-flavored experience.

Though Wisconsin's wines are just beginning to make a name for themselves, the local cheeses have long been known as worthy partners for wines, and they make visits even more delicious.

Lake Wisconsin Area (South-Central Wisconsin)

Bountiful Harvest Winery

Interstate 90 and Highway 60 (R.R. 3)
Lodi, Wisconsin 53555
TEL: 608-592-5254
OWNERS: Glen and Mary Spurgeon
FOUNDED: 1983

AT A GLANCE
Tours & Tastings: Mon.–Sun. 9–5, tastings.
Closed: Thanksgiving, Christmas, New Year's, Easter.
Vineyards/Orchards: Fruits from Wisconsin and Michigan growers.
Wines: Fruit wines only—specialty is honey wine (mead). Seasonal—strawberry, peach, cranberry-apple.
Awards: Peach—gold and bronze—in Indiana State Fair and Eastern International Wine Competitions.
Retail Shop: Wines and made-in-Wisconsin items—cheeses, sausages, spices, herbs, jellies; winemaking supplies; locally made pottery and crafts.
Credit Cards: MasterCard, Visa.
Access for Disabled: None.
Foreign Languages: None.

Getting There: From Milwaukee: Take I-90/94 West to Hwy. 60 near Lodi. From Prairie Du Sac (Wollersheim Winery below): Take Hwy. 60 to I-90/94, near Lodi.

❧ When Glen and Mary Spurgeon ran out of room at their Uplands winery, they relocated their fruit wine cellars here.

❧ ❧ ❧

The Wollersheim Winery

Highway 188 (P.O. Box 87)
Prairie Du Sac, Wisconsin 53578
TEL: 608-643-6515
OWNERS: JoAnne and Robert Wollersheim
WINEMAKER: Philippe Coquard (professional degree in enology, Macon & Paris, France)
FOUNDED: 1857

AT A GLANCE
Tours & Tastings: Year-round, Mon.–Sun. 10–5. Forty-five-minute tour, every hour in peak season ($2 per adult) and at

11 and 2 in winter; slide show on grape growing and winemaking, history of winery.

Closed: Thanksgiving, Christmas, New Year's, Easter.

Vineyards: Twenty-five acres, all planted to French-American hybrids, except two acres of vinifera. Additional grapes purchased from midwestern and New York growers.

Wines: Best known are estate-bottled, vintage-dated Domaine Reserve (Burgundian-style), Ruby Nouveau (released Nov. 15); varietal-bottled Johannisberg Riesling and Sugarloaf White (Mersault-style). Other vintage-dated varietals include Chardonnay, Seyval Blanc, Pinot Noir, and Marechal Foch.

Awards: Awards aplenty, with Domaine Reserve oft-cited.

Picnic Area: On the elegant tree-shaded grounds.

Retail Shop: Wines, gift items.

Credit Cards: MasterCard, Visa.

Access for Disabled: Yes, but limited parking.

Foreign Languages: French, German.

Getting There: From Madison: Go west to Middletown on Rtes. 14/151, then take U.S. 12 North. Just before Sauk City, turn north (right) on Hwy. 188. Winery is on the right, two miles from Hwy. 12.

Special Wine & Other Events: Second Sun. in Oct.: Annual Harvest Festival; first Sun. in March: Open House.

&a. Wollersheim, Wisconsin's most important winery, occupies a delightful location in a tree-shaded valley and a major place in wine history. In this peaceful hillside setting overlooking the Wisconsin River, the Hungarian political refugee Agoston Haraszthy, later credited with founding California's commercial wine industry, first tried winemaking here in the 1840s. Haraszthy planted vineyards of European grapes, carved a wine cellar in the hillside, and built a village across the river, which is now Sauk City. After years of disappointment, he hit the road to California's gold rush and supposedly fathered the California wine industry—an accomplishment doubted by today's wine historians.

German immigrant Peter Kehl purchased Haraszthy's property around 1856. He and his wife and four children lived in the old wine cellar while building an elegant home in the style of those along the Rhine; the similarly styled stone winery was completed ten years later. The buildings are now listed on the National Register of Historic Places.

With vineyards planted to labruscas, Kehl prospered by making wine to please local palates. When his son Jacob took over, Kehl's widely popular wines were enjoyed in Milwaukee and Chicago and as far away as Maine. Then Jacob died in 1899 and winemaking was also laid to rest for seventy-five years while the family farmed corn and oats and other crops.

The Wollersheims' purchase of the property in 1972 revitalized the farm winery; they planted vineyards to French-American hybrids, renovated the cellars, and started producing, with first wines in 1975.

TO SEE & DO

Water sports and fishing get top billing in the Lake Wisconsin area, but playing second banana is sight-seeing. A famous attraction is Circus World Museum at Baraboo, where you can step right up and see Ringling's winter headquarters (open daily, mid-May to mid-Sept.; 426 Water Street; tel: 608-356-8341). Scenic riverboat trips are the best way to enjoy the red-cliffed Dells. The MacKenzie Environmental Education Center (Poynette, Wisconsin 53955; tel: 608-635-4498) houses the state's many birds, animals, and trees, and tours can be arranged to see them. The spring walleye run is a major event.

ACCOMMODATIONS

For those who wish to tarry longer, write the Lake Wisconsin Chamber of Commerce, Poynette, Wisconsin 53955, for a list of light housekeeping cottages.

The Barrister's House
226 9th Avenue (Box 166)
Baraboo, Wisconsin 53913
Tel: 608-356-3344
A carefully tended Colonial, once home to a well-known attorney. Evocative names give clues to furnishings in the rooms—the Garden Room is done up in wicker and wrought iron; the Colonial Room has eighteenth-century antiques; the Barrister's Room has a big canopy bed.

The House of Seven Gables
215 Sixth Street
Baraboo, Wisconsin 53913
Tel: 608-356-8387
Restored Gothic Revival home, circa 1860, is furnished throughout in Civil War–period pieces.

Bennett House
825 Oak Street
Wisconsin Dells, Wisconsin 53965
Tel: 608-254-2500
Colonial house with white picket fence, listed on the National Register of Historic Places. Comfortable and convenient to river trips, shops, and restaurants.

Blackhawk Ridge
Highway 78 (P.O. Box 516)
Sauk City, Wisconsin 53578
Tel: 608-643-3775
A 600-acre family-owned wilderness preserve above the Wisconsin River; choose an antique-filled room in the comfortable Barn House Inn, a sheepherder's wagon or cabin, or a tent under the stars. The preserve is dedicated to the enjoyment of canoeing, swimming, hiking, cross-country skiing, and relaxing. Restaurant features homemade muffins, breads and pastries, and Wollersheim wines.

Jamieson House
407 North Franklin Street
Poynette, Wisconsin 53955
Tel: 608-635-4100
Built in the 1800s and furnished with Victorian antiques, this inn has also been modernized with such luxury touches as whirlpools in some rooms. Continental cuisine. (See "Restaurants.")

RESTAURANTS

Barn House Inn
(Located at the Blackhawk Ridge wilderness preserve. See "Accommodations" above for more information.)

Firehouse Restaurant
Water Street
Prairie Du Sac, Wisconsin 53578
Tel: 608-643-2480
Lovely location on the Wisconsin River, downtown in Prairie Du Sac. Reservations suggested in season.

Jamieson House
(See under "Accommodations" for address, telephone.)
Continental dishes and extravagant desserts in a Victorian setting that includes a fabulous Tiffany bar.

Quincy's Grove
Nesbitt Road
Madison, Wisconsin 53711
In a former grand mansion and stable. Try turtle pie and other local dishes. Wine cellar and baking done on site.

Uplands (Southwestern Wisconsin)

Spurgeon Vineyards & Winery

County Highway Q
(P.O. Box 201, R.R. 1)
Highland, Wisconsin 53543
TEL: 608-929-7629
OWNERS: Glen and Mary Spurgeon
FOUNDED: 1981

AT A GLANCE

Tours & Tastings: Apr.–Oct., Mon.–Sun. 10–5; Nov.–March, weekends only, 10–5. Thirty-minute guided tours ($2, adults; 50 cents, children) give a behind-the-scenes look at winemaking and a tasting with cheese; self-guided vineyard tours—directions given at winery.
Closed: Thanksgiving, Christmas, New Year's, and Easter.
Vineyards: Sixteen acres planted to French-American hybrids and labruscas.
Wines: Aurora, Marechal Foch, Concord, proprietary reds and whites.
Awards: Best of Class, bronze—blue-ribboned Concord in both Midwestern and Eastern Wine Competitions.
Picnic Area: Scenic rural setting on family farm.
Retail Shop: Wines sold on-site.
Credit Cards: MasterCard, Visa.
Access for Disabled: None.
Foreign Languages: None.
Getting There: From Prairie Du Sac, Lodi (Wollersheim Winery, Bountiful Harvest Winery): Take Hwy. 60 to Spring Green, turn south on Hwy. 23 to County Hwy. C, then County Hwy. I to Highland. From Main St.: Turn west on County Hwy. Q and follow signs to winery. From Muscoda: Take County Hwy. G South for five miles, then left on County Hwy. Q for seven miles and follow sign.
Special Wine & Other Events: The Uplands buzzes May–Dec. with everything from arts fairs to theater under the stars, plus bed races, barbecues, and corn cob boils.

  Having grown up on a dairy farm in Missouri wine country, Glen Spurgeon feels right at home with a winery on his wife's family dairy farm. Their small winery ferments wines only from grapes grown in their vineyard, which a nearby ridgetop wears like a wavy green crown. To see the vines for yourself means a brisk hike up a hill—so be sure to bring your boots, and don't forget to stop first at the winery for directions.

TO SEE & DO

History and outdoor activities make a delicious combination for tourists to the Uplands in southwestern Wisconsin. The Swiss, Germans, Norwegians, English, and Welsh all were settlers in this area, and their signatures can be seen today in the architecture, museums, crafts, foods, and celebrations. Frank Lloyd Wright lived here as well, and his imprint is evident in and about Spring Green. Wright drew inspiration for his functional structures from rugged stone outcrops and bluffs, as has local resident Alex Jordan for his fanciful creation—the House on the Rock. One of Wisconsin's most popular attractions, it sits jauntily on a chimney-shaped stone, 450 feet high, and is filled with eclectic collections of artifacts in an intricate series of rooms recalling days gone by.

  New Glarus is a place for excellent cheeses—raw milk white cheddar, full-cream Swiss, and smoked Gouda among them. Indeed, some claim early Swiss settlers chose this area because it was so similar to Switzerland that they knew the cows would produce milk good enough to replicate cheeses from their homeland. Today's farmers are mainly second-

and third-generation Swiss who use old family recipes to make their cheeses.

Bikes, boats, and hikes help you explore the many Uplands attractions and the acres of parks dotted with lakes. For more information, write the Uplands Inc., P.O. Box 4, Dodgeville, Wisconsin 53533. Send $1 for "The Uplands" booklet.

ACCOMMODATIONS
Hotel Boscobel
1005 Wisconsin Avenue
Boscobel, Wisconsin 53805
Tel: 608-375-4111
Restored 1865 vintage hotel with gleaming walnut and maple floors, vaulted ceilings, stained glass, and marble fireplaces. Incidentally, this was the birthplace of the Gideon Society, the group that places Bibles in hotel rooms.

The Round Barn
P.O. Box 297
Spring Green, Wisconsin 53588
Tel: 608-588-2568
Historic barn structure with pool and sauna.

Wisconsin House—Stagecoach Inn
2105 East Main Street
Hazel Green, Wisconsin 53811
Tel: 608-854-2233
Neat clapboard house from the 1840s; rooms are named after important inn guests of yesteryear such as Ulysses S. Grant, who spent much time here. Old-fashioned breakfast.

The Duke House
618 Maiden Street
Mineral Point, Wisconsin 53565
Tel: 608-987-2821
Bright and sunny Colonial house furnished with period pieces. Wine and cheese in the afternoon; homemade baked goods for breakfast.

Chalet Landhaus
Highway 69
New Glarus, Wisconsin 53574
Tel: 608-527-5234

Swiss chalet–style motel with cozy atmosphere—wood-beamed lobby, fireplace. Some rooms with whirlpools.

Located downtown, under the same ownership as the Chalet Landhaus above:

New Glarus Hotel
New Glarus, Wisconsin 53574
Tel: 608-527-5244
In addition to having comfortable accommodations, this is said to be the only place this side of the Alps that serves authentic Swiss cuisine.

RESTAURANTS
Restaurants in the Hotel Boscobel and the Wisconsin House—Stagecoach Inn serve local wines (see their listings under "Accommodations" above for more information). Also try:

Dutch Kitchen
127 East Jefferson Street
Spring Green, Wisconsin 53588
Tel: 608-588-2595
A hotel in 1858, it is now a stylish restaurant serving duckling, veal, and seafood dishes. Wine list, garden dining.

The Spring Green
State Highway 23 and County Trunk C
Spring Green, Wisconsin 53588
Tel: 608-588-2571
Overlooking the Wisconsin River and across from Frank Lloyd Wright's Taliesin. This is the only Wright-designed restaurant. Open all year; reservations advised. Steak, seafood on the menu.

Red's Supper Club
Highway 80
Highland, Wisconsin 53543
Tel: 608-929-7511
Serves dinner only Wed.–Sun., but lunch and breakfast every day. More important, will pack picnic for you to take to a winery or elsewhere. At the bottom of Main Street.

Southwestern Wisconsin

Christina Wine Cellars

109 Vine Street
La Crosse, Wisconsin 54601
TEL: 608-785-2215
OWNERS: The Lawlor family (for other Lawlor wineries, see Galena, Illinois, McGregor, Iowa, and Dubuque, Iowa)
FOUNDED: 1979

AT A GLANCE

Tours & Tastings: Mon.–Sat. 10–9, Sun. 12–5. Daily tours cover historic site, winery, tasting (call for tour times).
Vineyards: Prairie Du Chien, Galena, planted to French-American hybrids; additional grapes/fruits purchased.
Wines: Chablis, Burgundy, Marechal Foch, Seyval, Catawba Oktoberfest; Door County cherry, cranberry-apple, to name some.
Awards: (see Ealena Cellars, Illinois)
Picnic Area: On the grounds.
Restaurant: In adjacent old Freight House; awarded seventh best in Wisconsin; serves steaks, seafood specialties.
Retail Shop: Wines, gifts.
Credit Cards: American Express, MasterCard, Visa.
Access for Disabled: Wheelchair access.
Foreign Languages: None.
Getting There: On Mississippi River. From downtown La Crosse: Take 3rd St. north in the direction of Hwy. 53 and 35 to Vine St. Turn west on Vine toward the river; winery is on your right.
Special Wine & Other Events: Memorial Day weekend: May Wine Festival; Fourth of July: Riverfest; first weekend in October: Oktoberfest.

• Christina Wine Cellars, next to pretty Riverside Park in history-rich downtown La Crosse, started out as a nineteenth-century railway freight depot. Today old boxcars serve as boutiques.

The focal point of the redone depot is the antique-filled tasting room, with its handsome turn-of-the-century handcrafted bar. Like other Lawlor wineries in Iowa and Illinois, this one is listed on the National Register of Historic Places. Tours include the winery, where wines are fermented and aged; a tasting; and the extra fillip of a visit to a 1904 vintage Pullman car.

TO SEE & DO

Much of La Crosse's history is tied to the Mississippi River, and can be seen in animation at the unusual Riverside USA (Memorial Dr.; tel: 608-782-2366; open Memorial Day–Labor Day, 10–5), a museum of river history and folklore. River cruises on paddlewheelers offer cool and breezy sight-seeing excursions from around mid-Apr. to mid-Oct., shoving off from the Riverside Park boat dock and also the Holiday Inn dock. The best view of the area is from Granddad Bluff (east on Main Street), 500 feet above the town; looking back is possible at the Swarthout Museum (112 South 9th Street; tel: 608-782-1980; open all year, Tues.–Fri. 10–5, Sat.–Sun. 1–5) and the Italianate Hixon House (429 North 7th Street; tel: 608-784-9500; open June–Labor Day, daily 1–5). For more scenic rewards, take the Wisconsin snippet of the 3,000-mile Canada-to-Mexico Great River Road (Hwy. 35) through miles of classic countryside, with charming country towns tucked into the folds of valleys, sweeping views, and craggy bluffs.

ACCOMMODATIONS

Bed & Breakfast Guest-Homes
Route 2
Algoma, Wisconsin 54201
Tel: 414-743-9742
For reservations statewide.

Radisson
200 Harbor View Plaza
La Crosse, Wisconsin 54601
Tel: 608-784-6680
With a view of the Mississippi, this pleasant hotel offers all modern comforts and conveniences, including an exercise room.

Trillium
Route 2, Box 121
La Farge, Wisconsin 54639
Tel: 414-625-4492
Live on a working farm in Amish country and enjoy home-baked bread and cheese and jams with a full breakfast. The comfortable rooms are in a little cottage on the tree-shaded grounds. La Crosse is forty miles northeast of La Farge.

Eastern Wisconsin/Door County

Stone Mill Winery

N70 W6340 Bridge Road
Cedarburg, Wisconsin 53012
OWNER: James Pape
FOUNDED: 1972

AT A GLANCE
Tours & Tastings: Mon.–Sat. 10–5, Sun. 12–5. Guided forty-five-minute tour includes a short history of 1864 winery site, cellar, tasting of at least six wines.
Closed: Thanksgiving, Christmas, New Year's, Easter.
Vineyards: Grapes and fruits purchased from Wisconsin, Michigan.
Wines: Seyval, Vidal, Niagara and Baco Noir; strawberry, cherry, cranberry-apple.
Awards: Niagara, Strawberry Sweet Cherry.
Retail Shop: Wines sold on-site.
Credit Cards: All major credit cards.
Access for Disabled: Wine shop and tasting room.
Foreign Languages: None.
Getting There: From Milwaukee: Take I-43 North to Cedarburg exit and turn west on Hwy. C (Pioneer Rd.) three miles to Hwy. 57; north on Hwy. 57 to downtown Cedarburg. Winery is in historic Woolen Mill to your right. Your wine route from here to Door County can continue to retrace history. In the 1850s, travelers rested at one of Cedarburg's famous inns (see "Accommodations") and then took the lake route (now I-43) north. The upstate wineries are far more recent additions to the scene.
Special Wine & Other Events: Third weekend in Sept.: Wine & Harvest Festival—grape stomping, home winemaking, arts & crafts fair; Oct. 17–19: Folk Art Fair; first weekend in Dec.: Christmas crafts boutique; first weekend in Feb.: Winter Festival—art sculpting parade, bed races, ice skating, dance; late June: Strawberry Festival—strawberry wine, desserts, contests, music.

&. Only twenty minutes north of Milwaukee you can step back more than one hundred years at the Cedar Creek Settlement. The Stone Mill housing the winery was built in 1864 and is listed on the National Register of Historic Places. Used for processing wool into blankets until 1969, the mill's limestone-walled cellar maintains an even temperature year-round, making it ideal for wines. Today visitors get their history lessons with wine education on both the tour and the visit to the winery's museum.

TO SEE & DO
Poke around historical Cedar Creek Settlement, a village of shops, with cafés for meals and snacks. To be seen are antiques and handcrafted decorative and useful items in iron (blacksmith in atten-

dance); pottery and wood; unique jewelry; vintage and contemporary fashions; fine photography; cheeses; and more (open 10–5 Mon.–Sat., 12–5 Sun.). Travel a short distance north for further nineteenth-century explorations at the Ozaukee County Pioneer Village, a restoration of authentic houses, barns, shops, and public buildings, plus what is believed to be the last covered bridge in Wisconsin. Everything was built mainly in the mid-1800s during the county's settlement and moved from various locations to this site. Open Sun. from the first Sun. in June to the second Sun. in Oct., 12–5; also Wed., June–Labor Day. Tours conducted by costumed guides.

ACCOMMODATIONS

Bed and Breakfasts & Inns
Stagecoach Inn
W61 N520 Washington Avenue
Cedarburg, Wisconsin 53012
Tel: 414-375-0208
Weary travelers of the 1850s found all of life's amenities at this inn, and so it goes even now, thanks to careful restoration and attentive service. Nine cozy guest rooms with antique furnishings, and a breakfast of hot muffins and coffee and herbal teas. An appealing pub, open daily 4–10, has a handsome pressed tin ceiling.

Washington House Inn
W62 N573 Washington Avenue
Cedarburg, Wisconsin 53012
Tel: 414-375-3550
Collectors' Victorian antiques highlight this inn, and whirlpool baths bring it up to date. Home-baked muffins and breads from turn-of-the-century recipes turn up at breakfast today. The inn is located in the historic Washington Avenue district. Just three blocks from Cedar Creek Settlement, at the corner of Washington (Highway 57) and Center.

RESTAURANTS
Barth's at the Bridge
N58 W6194 Columbia Road (Highway 57)

Cedarburg, Wisconsin 53012
Tel: 414-377-0660
Antiques and local artworks decorate this restaurant, where you can eat soups, salads, and sandwiches—and more hearty dishes.

The Cedarburg Woolen Mill Restaurant
W63 N706 Washington Avenue
Cedarburg, Wisconsin 53012
Tel: 414-377-7111
Antique setting; homemade soups, specialty sandwiches, salads for lunch, and roast duck, fresh fish, and BBQ ribs among the dinner entrées. Delectable deserts. Open daily. Sunday brunch.

Cream & Crepe Cafe
N70 W6340 Washington Avenue
Cedarburg, Wisconsin 53012
Tel: 414-377-0900
Rustic setting overlooking Cedar Creek in the center of Cedar Creek Settlement. Light meals, crêpes a specialty.

Tomaso's Italian American Restaurant
W63 N688 Washington Avenue
Cedarburg, Wisconsin 53012
Tel: 414-377-7630
Famous for pizza. Serves wines.

🐎 🐎 🐎

The Door Peninsula Winery

5806 Highway 42 North
Sturgeon Bay, Wisconsin 54235
TEL: 414-743-7431
OWNERS: Mark Feld and Tom Alberts
FOUNDED: 1974

AT A GLANCE
Tours & Tastings: Continuous twenty-five-minute guided tours, May–Oct. 9–5; July–Aug. 9–6; off-season, call for appointments. Tours include slide-taped presentation on winemaking and tasting, cheese sampling.
Closed: Major holidays.

Vineyards/Orchards: All fruits purchased from nearby orchards.
Wines: Fourteen dry and sweet fruit wines, include dry and sweet cherry, apple, plum, pear; semi-sweet cranberry, cranberry-apple, among others.
Awards: Dry cherry, Midwestern Competition.
Picnic Area: On neatly landscaped grounds.
Retail Shop: Wines, wine-flavored cheese, and jams.
Credit Cards: American Express, MasterCard, Visa.
Access for Disabled: Limited.
Foreign Languages: None.
Getting There: Winery is nine miles north of Sturgeon Bay on Hwy. 42.

🐌 Visitors get their educations about fruit wines in a schoolhouse built in 1868, but not at pint-size desks or from chalky boards. When the winery owners renovated the building they tossed out all that kid stuff, but they managed to keep the country school charm. Lessons in fruit wine tasting are well taught by pinafored hostesses or the owners themselves, and follow the tour.

TO SEE & DO
Next to the winery is the Door County Cherry Expo, a display and slide show illustrating the history and development of the fruit-growing industry in Door County, the fruit basket of the state. Exploring Door County is rewarding when it comes to arts and crafts and colorful country fishing villages. The area boasts of no less than five state parks, including Cave Point County Park, where Lake Michigan's waves have carved caves into high cliffs. Be sure to try some of the Swedish food specialties and go to a fish boil, a traditional Door County feast. (For further information contact Door County Chamber of Commerce, P.O. Box 346, Station A, Green Bay Road,

Sturgeon Bay, Wisconsin 54235; tel: 414-743-4456.)

ACCOMMODATIONS

Bed and Breakfasts & Inns
Inn at Cedar Crossing
336 Louisiana Street
Sturgeon Bay, Wisconsin 54235
Tel: 414-743-4200
This stately nineteenth-century structure with mountain-high ceilings and a dramatic staircase is listed on the National Register of Historic Places. Canopied beds, country antiques, rag rugs, and knotty pine paneling are a cozy and comfortable combination for the visitor. A local delicacy, Moravian sugar cake bread, is served with Continental breakfast in the morning; good location for walking to the shops and waterfront.

White Lace Inn—A Victorian Guest House
15 North Fifth Avenue
Sturgeon Bay, Wisconsin 54235
Tel: 414-743-1105
An attractive and well-decorated Victorian home with lovely appointments, brass beds, down pillows, antiques—and indeed lace curtains. Continental breakfast included.

White Gull Inn
4225 Main Street (P.O. Box 159)
Fish Creek, Wisconsin 54212
Tel: 414-868-3517
The buildings date from 1896, but were moved to Fish Creek across the frozen lake from Marinette; a turn-of-the-century instant resort. Rooms are decorated in period furnishings, but the inn is best known for its outstanding fish boils; reservations are essential.

Commodore Inn & Marina
1640 Memorial Drive
Sturgeon Bay, Wisconsin 54236
Tel: 414-743-5555

Cottages with rooms and suites on a yacht basin. Heated pool. Tennis. Box lunches packed for outings. Restaurant. (See below.)

RESTAURANTS
Commodore Inn & Marina
(See above for address, telephone.)
Features freshwater fish. Popular for Sun. brunch.

White Gull Inn
(See under "Accommodations.")

&. &. &.

Von Stiehl Winery

115 Navarino Street
Algoma, Wisconsin 54201
TEL: 414-487-5208
OWNER: William Schmiling
FOUNDED: 1964

AT A GLANCE
Tours & Tastings: Guided tours, on the hour and half hour, Mon.–Sun. 9–5, May 1–Oct. 30; July–Aug., open evenings; Nov.–Dec. 24, 11–5; off-season, call for appointment. Tours cover fermentation, cellar and bottling areas.
Closed: Dec. 25 through Apr.
Vineyards/Orchards: Cherries, apples; grown here and purchased from Door County growers.
Wines: Dry and sweet cherry and apple; cherry cooler.
Awards: Dry and semi-dry cherry.
Retail Shop: Wines; Gift Haus with wine cheeses and jellies.
Credit Cards: MasterCard, Visa.
Access for Disabled: None.

Foreign Languages: None.
Getting There: From Sturgeon Bay: Take Hwy. 42 South directly to Navarino Street in Algoma. From Green Bay: Take Hwy. 54 East thirty miles to Algoma and proceed to Hwy. 42 to Navarino.

&. Set in a picturesque little fishing town, this tiny German-inspired winery is in a one-time brewery built in the 1800s, and produces wines from old family recipes. As you can see on the tour, the wines are cellared in the temperature-perfect limestone rathskeller. In the tasting room visitors sip wines while surrounded by antique portraits.

ACCOMMODATION
(See also information following the Door Pensinula Winery.)

River Hills Motel
820 West North Water Street
Algoma, Wisconsin 54201
Tel: 414-487-3451
Thirty rooms and a boat dock. Café nearby.

RESTAURANTS
Captain's Table
133 North Water Street
Algoma, Wisconsin 54201
Tel: 414-487-5304
In a nautical setting, enjoy freshly caught fish.

Port of Call
310 North Milwaukee Street
Kewaunee, Wisconsin 54216
Tel: 414-388-3369
Overlooks harbor. Fish and seafood dishes. Outdoor dining in warm weather.

7
The Southwest/ West

Val Verde Winery, Del Rio, Texas

᠘**A**rizona, Colorado, New Mexico, Oklahoma, and Texas, devoid of fine wines until a decade or so ago, now are among America's burgeoning wine regions. Until 1975, the only area winery to survive Prohibition was Val Verde in Texas. A little more than a decade later, about fifty wineries region-wide are making European-style wines, with more entering the field all the time. Indeed, both Texas and Arizona growers are fond of pointing out that their soil and climatic conditions are similar to some of the best wine-growing regions of France, but each state has its own winemaking story, history, and future.

᠘ ARIZONA

Current grape growing in Arizona was the outgrowth of favorable research in the 1970s by the University of Arizona. Only four wineries now have their welcome mats out for travelers, but Arizona's wine industry has ambitious expansion plans. Particularly promising is the southeastern part of the state, which many experts foresee as eventually becoming a leading international wine producer. Recognition of its distinct grape-growing regions came in 1984,

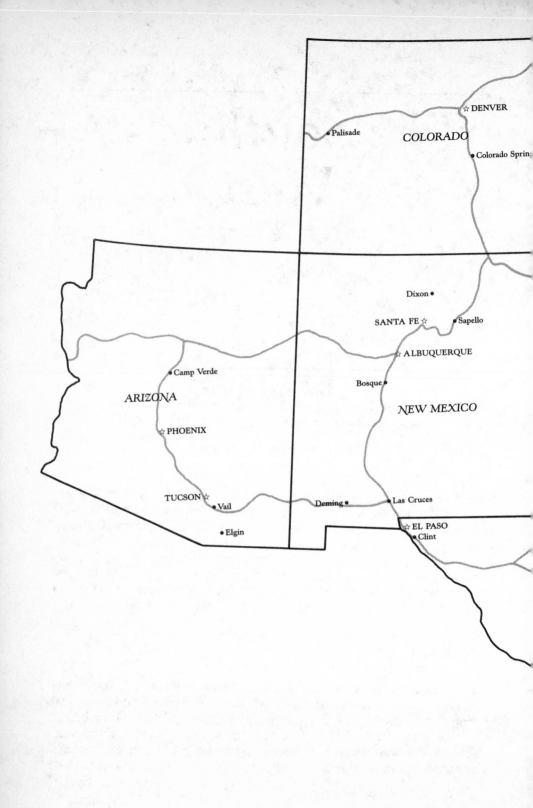

THE SOUTHWEST/WEST

OKLAHOMA

☆ TULSA

☆ OKLAHOMA CITY

Caney •

• Ivanhoe

• Lubbock

• Springtown
☆ DALLAS

TEXAS

• Ballinger

• Tow

• Bryan

• Fort Stockton

• Round Mountain

Fredericksburg •
• Driftwood

☆ HOUSTON

• New Braunfels

☆ SAN ANTONIO

• Del Rio

CORPUS CHRISTI ☆

when Sonoita became Arizona's first federally designated viticultural area. If the future looks bright for grape vines, the here and now is delightful for visitors, who can be among the first to experience a new wine region and enjoy traveling through the lonely beauty of the desert to the lush coolness of a mountain valley and a host of historic sites along the way.

꒰ ꒱ ꒱

R. W. Webb Winery

13605 East Benson Highway
Vail, Arizona 85641
TEL: 602-629-9991
PRESIDENT/WINEMAKER: R. W. Webb
FOUNDED: 1980

AT A GLANCE

Tours & Tastings: Mon.–Sat. 10–5, Sun. 12–5. Guided tours take one hour and cover all aspects of winemaking, with wines tasted as you go to illustrate your lesson.
Closed: Major holidays.
Vineyards: Twenty acres at Willcox planted to vinifera varieties; additional grapes purchased from southwestern Arizona growers.
Wines: Chenin Blanc, French Colombard, Johannisberg Riesling, Cabernet Sauvignon, Petit Sirah, Sauvignon Blanc. Also makes rosé, Blanc de Blanc, dry apple wine.
Awards: 1982 Petit Sirah, bronze; dry apple wine, silver in 1986; among others.
Picnic Area: In an inviting courtyard with fountain.
Retail Shop: Wines, gifts, and deli.
Credit Cards: MasterCard, Visa.
Access for Disabled: Yes
Foreign Languages: Spanish.
Getting There: Vail is seventeen miles east of Tucson. Take I-10 to Vail exit, then go one mile east on Frontage Rd.
Special Wine & Other Events: Participates in Sonoita Wine Festival, held first weekend in Aug.

꒰ Retired naval officer R. W. Webb built a handsome Spanish mission–style building to house Arizona's first bonded winery since Prohibition, and planted his vineyard in the lush lands near Willcox. Webb, a wine hobbyist for years before turning commercial, had long instructed amateur winemakers in southern Arizona. To prepare for his commercial debut, Webb took enology courses at the University of California at Davis.

TO SEE & DO

Pack a picnic and take off on some day trips from Tucson. To be sampled farther to the east is Colossal Cave (six miles north of Vail on Colossal Cave Rd; tel: 602-791-7677). Continuing east to the vineyards in Willcox, the desert dissolves into grass and woodlands and eventually climbs up the Chiricahua Mountains to Chiricahua National Monument. This 12,000-acre park has strangely shaped rocks and good trails for hiking through them (thirty-seven miles southeast of Willcox on Rtes. 186 and 181; tel: 602-824-3560). Nearby Fort Bowie recalls the conflicts between the Apaches and the early settlers approximately twenty-five miles south of Willcox, off Rte. 186; tel: 602-847-2500). Further southeast, and best seen when visiting Sonoita Vineyard Winery (see page 292) is ghost town territory. Tombstone, the town too tough to die and home to Wyatt Earp, is most famous—restored and a national historic landmark—but don't miss the more ramshackle Gleeson and the revitalized Bisbee, an old mining center with good art galleries. At Patagonia, the Stradling Museum of the Horse has Remington paintings (tel: 602-394-2264). Further south is Nogales, Mexico, more a giant curio shop than a town; some genuine bargains can be found in pottery and glassware. West of Tucson, Saguaro National Monument and the Arizona-Sonora Desert Museum combine an outdoor zoological park for local species, a botanical garden, and the Earth Science Center (tel: 602-883-1380). For more details, contact the Tucson Convention and Visitors Bureau, 450 West Paseo Redondo, Tucson, Arizona 85701; tel: 602-624-1817.

ACCOMMODATIONS
Tucson has a wide range of accommodations and makes a good touring base. Check on off-season rates if visiting from the end of May through summer.

Bed and Breakfasts
Barbara's Bed & Breakfast
P.O. Box 13603
Tucson, Arizona 85732
Tel: 602-790-2399
Reservation service; coordinators will take your personal interests into consideration when matching you with hosts.

Myers Blue Corn House
4215 East Kilmer
Tucson, Arizona 85711
Tel: 602-327-4663
On a quiet residential street, this house has a family room filled with arts and crafts. You can use the kitchen for snacks or the barbecue. A full breakfast comes with the rates.

Hotels/Resorts
The Sheraton Tucson El Conquistador
10000 North Oracle Road
Tucson, Arizona 85704
Tel: 602-742-7000; 800-325-3535
About half an hour from town, with splendid mountain view. Tennis, golf, swimming.

The Westward Look
245 East Ina Road
Tucson, Arizona 85704
Tel: 602-297-1151

Also in the foothills, has nice horseback rides and miles of fitness trails.

The Lodge on the Desert
306 North Alvernon Way (P.O. Box 42500)
Tucson, Arizona 85733
Tel: 602-325-3366
Combines in-town convenience with attractive landscaped grounds, charming casitas. Popular restaurant; owned by the same family for decades.

Tanque Verde
14301 East Speedway
(Route 8, Box 66)
Tucson, Arizona 85748
Tel: 602-296-6275
A well-known ranch resort, about twelve miles east of town, offering nearly all possible activities.

Arizona Inn
2200 East Elm Street
Tucson, Arizona 85719
Tel: 602-325-1541; 800-421-1093
Luxurious inn set on fourteen landscaped acres, near downtown and the University of Arizona. For fifty years has provided a cosmopolitan ambience to guests. Eighty-five individually decorated rooms, many with patios.

RESTAURANTS

In Tucson:
Arizona Inn
2200 East Elm Street
Tel: 602-325-1541
Elegant dining; lamb and fish are specialties. Serves Sonoita wines.

Cafe Terra Cotta
5310 North Campbell
St. Phillips Place Plaza
Tel: 602-577-8100
Unusual, delicious dishes such as garlic custard topped with toasted nuts and served warm with vinaigrette salsa; poblano chiles stuffed with corn, cheese, and chicken. Serves Sonoita wines.

Jerome's
6958 East Tanque Verde
Tel: 602-221-0311
Seafood, creole dishes are specialties.

Mi Casa Painted Desert
6335 East Tanque Verde Road
Tel: 602-885-5310
Sophisticated southwestern dishes such as blue corn tortillas with smoked chicken and cheese, roast lamb with Pinot Noir sauce accented with ancho chiles. Lots of California wines.

Rancho Del Rio Tack Room
2800 North Sabino Canyon Road
Tel: 602-722-2800
Elegant Spanish setting with fireplaces and lovely views; Continental menu, with duckling, veal, and fish dishes. Serves Webb Winery's dry apple wine; California selections.

In Vail:
Vail Steakhouse
13000 East Benson Highway
Vail, Arizona 85641
Tel: 602-622-2101
Steak specialty, as name implies.

ે▲ ે▲ ે▲

Sonoita Vineyards

Canelo Road (P.O. Box 33)
Elgin, Arizona 85611
TEL: 602-455-5893
PRESIDENT: Adrian Bosman
WINEMAKER: Gordon R. Dutt
FOUNDED: 1983

AT A GLANCE
Tours & Tastings: Guided tours (daily 12–4 and by appointment) include short walk through vineyards with talk about growing, planting, soil; followed by tour of winery and a tasting.
Vineyards: Thirty acres owned and forty leased, planted to vinifera varieties: three white—Chenin Blanc, Sauvignon Blanc, Sémillon—and two reds—Cabernet Sauvignon, Pinot Noir, with other varieties in experimental acreage.
Wines: Fumé Blanc, Chenin Blanc, Cochise County Colombard, Cabernet Sauvignon.
Awards: Gold medal and Best of Show, 1986, to Cochise County Colombard.
Retail Shop: Wines sold on-site.
Credit Cards: None.
Getting There: Elgin is eighty miles south of Tucson, twenty miles northwest of Sierra Vista. Take I-10 to the Sonoita-Patagonia exit. Take Hwy. 83 through Sonoita. Five miles past Sonoita turn left at the Elgin sign and go on another five miles to the town of Elgin. From Elgin, the winery is four miles on Canelo Rd. Turn right entering vineyards and follow signs to winery.
Special Wine & Other Events: Sonoita Wine Festival, first weekend in Aug. Spring and early summer weekends: hot-air balloon clubs take off from vineyards.

ે▲ Sonoita Vineyards' winery was established jointly in 1983 by three vineyards—Vina Sonoita, Jan Hugo, Viva la Vista—and turns out small amounts of wines from a few vinifera varieties grown in the 300-square-mile Sonoita basin. This viticultural area is characterized by high desert grasslands at elevations up to 5,000 feet. Cool nights and warm sunny days produce good sugar and acid levels in premium grapes. Winery and vineyard manager Richard Dutt, who often instructs visitors in the tasting room, has impressive educational credentials in soil and water sciences and has studied at the University of California at Davis.

ે▲ ે▲ ે▲

Another winery to visit, south of Sonoita, east of Nogales:

Arizona Vineyards

2301 Patagonia Highway
Call 602-287-5026 or 7972 for tour and
tasting times. Tino Ocheltree welcomes
visitors to this rural winery seven days a
week to taste his natural wines.

TO SEE & DO
(See Information following Webb
Winery.)

ACCOMMODATIONS
Stage Stop Hotel
McKeoun Avenue
Patagonia, Arizona 85624
Tel: 602-394-2211
Forty-three rooms, with restaurant and
heated pool; Old West ambience. Sun-
deck. Moderately priced.

Ramada Inn
2047 South AZ-92
Sierra Vista, Arizona 85635
Tel: 602-459-5900
One hundred forty eight rooms, heated
pool, health club, shopping arcade.

RESTAURANTS
See Tucson listings also for restaurants
serving Sonoita wines.

🐚 🐚 🐚

Another winery to visit, this one near
Phoenix.

San Dominique Winery

Camp Verde, Arizona 86322
TEL: 602-945-8583
Tours and tastings May 15–Sept. 15, Fri.
and Sat.; in winter, by appointment only.
William Staltari, fifth generation of winemaker in his family, welcomes visitors to
his winery and vineyard 4,600 feet up in
the hills south of the Verde Valley. From
Phoenix, take I-17 to the Cherry Road
exit, seventy-five miles north of Phoenix.

TO SEE & DO
The state capital, Phoenix has more than
its share of museums, from art to science

and technology, and more sights than
space permits listing here. Among the
most interesting excursions are Heritage
Square, 7th and Monroe (tel: 602-
262-5071), a historical park with restored
turn-of-the-century homes, craft gallery
(Wed.–Sun.; tours every thirty minutes);
and the Pueblo Grande Museum, 4619
East Washington Street (tel: 602-275-
3452), a Hohokam archeological ruin
thought to date from B.C. 250–A.D.
1450, with permanent and changing exhibits (open daily; closed major holidays). In the northern part of the city is
Phoenix Mountain Preserve, 7,500 acres
of desert lands offering superb recreational activities as well as delightful picnic places and unbeatable city views and
other scenic vistas (tel: 602-262-6861).
For current events in and about the city, a
good resource is *Phoenix Magazine*,
found on newsstands.

ACCOMMODATIONS
A wide variety of places to stay and eat
are available in Phoenix. The Phoenix
and Valley of the Sun Convention and
Visitors Bureau (505 North 2nd Street,
Suite 300, Phoenix, Arizona 85004; tel:
602-264-4754) can help with more suggestions. Or contact the state tourism authorities listed in the back of this book.

Arizona Biltmore
24th Street and Missouri Avenue
Phoenix, Arizona 85016
Tel: 602-955-6600; 800-528-0428
Elegant resort, architecturally in tune
with natural environment, surrounded by
250 acres of gorgeous gardens. Three
pools, patios on some rooms, other resort amenities.

The Pointe at Squaw Peak
7677 North 16th Street
Phoenix, Arizona 85020
Tel: 602-997-2626; 800-528-0428
Southwestern ambience with tiled court-
yards and fountains; nicely appointed

rooms have balconies. Seven pools, lighted tennis, among many amenities. Rates are lowered June–Dec.

The Pointe at Tapatio Cliffs
11111 North 7th Street
Phoenix, Arizona 85020
Tel: 602-866-7500; 800-528-0428
Lighted tennis, five pools, and other resort activities. Comfortably furnished rooms with balconies.

RESTAURANTS
California wines well represented on lists, with some Washington State offerings, with nary a local wine found at press time.

Etienne's Different Point of View
The Pointe at Tapatio Cliffs
Tel: 602-866-7500

Elegant dining at top-of-mountain location, splendid views. Outdoor service. French menu with extensive wine list. Dinner 6–10; bar opens at 4:30; brunch Sun.

Point in Tyme
The Pointe at Tapatio Cliffs
Tel: 602-866-7500
Dishes from well-known American restaurants are served in a turn-of-the-century setting. Outdoor service; piano bar. Hours: 7 A.M.–1 A.M.

Orangerie
Arizona Biltmore Resort
Tel: 602-955-6600
Sophisticated menu, featuring fresh seafood and game in quiet setting with pianist. Open 11:30–2, 6–11; bar, 11–1; Sun. from noon.

Ꮨ COLORADO

In the late 1970s, Colorado began to produce the wines that are now gaining a name for themselves around the country. For scenery, both spectacular and Old West historic, Colorado wine routes are in a class by themselves.

Ꮨ Ꮨ Ꮨ

Vintage Colorado Cellars

3553 E Road
Palisade, Colorado 81526
TEL: 303-464-7921
PRESIDENT: Thomas Husband
WINEMAKER: James Seewald
FOUNDED: 1988

AT A GLANCE
Tours & Tastings: Tours by appointment; tastings, sales: June–Aug., Tues.–Sat. 12–4; Sept.–May, Fri.–Sat. 12–4.

Closed: Sun., Mon., major holidays.
Vineyards: Vinifera, French-American hybrid varieties, and fruits from nearby Grand Valley vineyards and orchards.
Wines: White Riesling, Chardonnay, Gewürztraminer, Merlot, Montmorency cherry, peach.
Awards: New label not yet entered in competitions.
Access for Disabled: Easy to enter.
Retail Shop: Wines and wine accessories for sale.
Credit Cards: MasterCard, Visa.

Getting There: The winery is located in western Colorado, ten miles east of downtown Grand Junction and south of Palisade on East Orchard Mesa; off I-70 B, just south of the intersection of E and 35½ Road (maps are available in many Palisade shops). A second tasting room will open in 1989 at exit 42 on I-70.

❧ The label Vintage Colorado Cellars dates from summer 1988. The winery itself goes back further, having been founded in 1978 as Colorado Mountain Vineyards. Winemaker Seewald stayed on when the company was reorganized and plans no changes in the wines. A wise decision—in the past, his White Reisling, Cabernet Sauvignon, and Chardonnay have won high awards in regional and national competitions.

One of the nation's tiniest wineries, Vintage Colorado Cellars is fitted into a hillside for natural temperature control and is filled with up-to-date winemaking equipment. Atop the winery, the southwestern-style tasting room is aglow in soft wood tones and offers a prizewinning view of the famous fruit orchard mesa and Grand Valley.

TO SEE & DO
The area is a fine place to spend a few days enjoying a number of diversions, not the least of which is the great outdoors. At the top of every visitor's list are two main scenic attractions: Grand Mesa, 10,000 feet high and the largest flattop mountain in the world; and Colorado National Monument, with miles of marvelous rock formations. For a truly bird's-eye view of all this majesty, take a flightseeing tour; call Monarch Aviation (tel: 303-243-7500) or Western Aviation (tel: 303-242-8146).

Grand Junction, fourteen miles west of Palisade, has a distinctive historic district along 7th Street, enjoyably covered on a self-guided walking tour. Pick up a guidebook at the Chamber of Commerce Visitors Information Centers, at Grand Avenue or Horizon Drive. Nearby, Main Street has Colorado's largest display of outdoor sculpture, as well as art galleries and antique shops, plus notable museums documenting the history of western Colorado and dinosaurs. For more information, write or phone the Chamber of Commerce, 360 Grand Avenue, Grand Junction, Colorado 81501 (tel: 303-242-3214).

ACCOMMODATIONS
Motels and hotels—thirty-four right in Grand Junction—include the familiar chains such as Best Western, Holiday Inn, Howard Johnson's, Hilton, plus many that are locally owned, but for a decided change of pace try one of the mountain lodges at Grand Mesa, 10,000 feet high and less than one hour's drive east of Grand Junction. This forested paradise offers sparkling trout-filled mountain lakes for fishing, boating, and water skiing, and some of the most spectacular views anywhere on earth.

Grand Mesa Lodge
Grand Mesa
Cedaredge, Colorado 81413
Tel: 303-856-3211

Mesa Lakes Resorts
Grand Mesa, Colorado 81643
Tel: 303-268-5467

RESTAURANTS
The Winery Restaurant
642 Main Street
Grand Junction, Colorado 81501
Tel: 303-242-4100
Steak and salad in a one-hundred-year-old building. Wine list.

❧ ❧ ❧

Pikes Peak Vineyards

3901 Janitell Road
Colorado Springs, Colorado 80906
TEL: 719-576-0075
OWNERS: Taffy McLaughlin, David M.
  Gray, Michael Sinton, John W. Gray
  and Theron D. Barber
WINEMAKER: Theron D. Barber
FOUNDED: 1984

AT A GLANCE

Tours & Tastings: Daily, 11–5. Nothing
formal here. Interested visitors are taken
around and given an explanation of the
winemaking process, and a tasting; vineyard included except during spraying.
Closed: Sun., major holidays.
Vineyards: Twenty acres; began, in 1978,
accenting French-American hybrids, but
recently vinifera varieties have been em-
phasized. Additional fruits purchased
from Colorado growers.
Wines: Cabernet Sauvignon, Riesling,
Chardonnay, Gamay, Sauvignon Blanc,
among others.
Picnic Area: Bucolic atmosphere with
nearby nineteenth-century house.
Retail Shop: Sells wines.
Credit Cards: None.
Access for Disabled: None.
Foreign Languages: Portuguese, Spanish.
Getting There: Take I-25 South to Circle
Dr., exit 138. On Circle Dr., go east to
Janitell Rd., turn right on Janitell and
follow signs to vineyards, half a mile
south on frontage road.
Special Wine & Other Events: Vintage
Wine Harvest Festival, mid-Sept., 10:30–
7. Crushing and pressing, food, music,
entertainment, vineyard tours in old-
fashioned horse-drawn vehicles, tasting.
$5 for adults; children free.

&. Named for neighboring Pikes Peak,
and near the famous mountain's base, the
twenty-acre Pikes Peak Vineyards and its
winery are nearly 6,000 feet above sea
level. The pastoral setting makes it hard
to believe you're only two miles from
downtown.

TO SEE & DO

Colorado Springs is a major tourist destination as well as an important business
center and the home of the United States
Air Force Academy. The following are
attempts to describe only a few of the
many things to do, places to stay and eat.
Excellent pamphlets and maps are available free through the Colorado Springs
Convention and Visitors Bureau, 104
South Cascade, Suite 104, Colorado
Springs, Colorado 80903 (tel: 719-
635-7506; 800-821-0022 out-of-state;
800-331-6520 in-state).

Notable sights include the Garden of
the Gods, Cave of the Winds, Manitou
Cliff Dwellers Museum of prehistoric artifacts, and, of course, Pikes Peak and
the famous Cog Railway—the world's
highest. Other thrills are provided by the
Royal Gorge Bridge—world's highest
suspension bridge—and the Mt. Manitou
Incline, the world's largest scenic cable
railway. Sports include white-water rafting, riding, and skiing.

ACCOMMODATIONS

Bed & Breakfast—Rocky Mountains
P.O. Box 804
Colorado Springs, Colorado 80901
Tel: 719-630-3433
Send $3 for a descriptive directory of
more than one hundred private homes
and small inns in Colorado Springs and a
five-state area.

Broadmoor Hotel
1 Lake Avenue
Colorado Springs, Colorado 80906
Tel: 719-643-7711; 800-634-7711 (out-of-
  state)
Famous lake-view resort, two miles from
downtown, with three pools, tennis, golf.

Antlers Hotel
4 South Cascade Avenue
Colorado Springs, Colorado 80903
Tel: 719-473-5600; 800-232-8886
Luxury hotel in town under same management as posh Broadmoor resort.

Hearthstone Inn
506 North Cascade Avenue
Colorado Springs, Colorado 80903
Tel: 303-473-4413
Restored Victorian mansion with antique furniture, fireplaces, and private porches.

Imperial House of Cripple Creek
123 North Third
Cripple Creek, Colorado 80813
Tel: 719-689-2922
Old mining town above Colorado Springs; furnished in antiques and site of the Summer Melodrama Theater.

RESTAURANTS
Hatch Cover
252 East Cheyenne Mountain Boulevard
Colorado Springs, Colorado 80906
Tel: 719-576-5223
Seafood and aged beef; noted for wine list.

La Petite Maison
1015 West Colorado Avenue
Colorado Springs, Colorado 80904
Tel: 719-632-4887

In restored old house, intimate; contemporary cuisine with French accent.

The London Grill in the Antlers Hotel
Chase Stone Center
4 South Cascade Avenue
Colorado Springs, Colorado 80903
Tel: 719-473-5600
Elegant with harp music background while you eat. Serves Pikes Peak and California Wines. Continental foods and fresh trout from "backyard" stream.

Penrose Room in Broadmoor Hotel
1 Lake Avenue
Colorado Springs, Colorado 80906
Tel: 719-634-7711
Edwardian decor. Mediterranean-accented foods; California wines on list. Located atop Broadmoor South Building, with panoramic view of city and mountains. Tie and coat required; dinner dancing. Reservations recommended.

Historic Briarhurst Manor Inn
404 Manitou Avenue
Manitou Springs, Colorado 80829
Tel: 719-685-5828
A manor that is more than a century old, with veal among the Continental specialties. Wine cellar. Fresh herbs and vegetables from restaurant's garden. Short drive from the Springs.

≈ NEW MEXICO

New Mexico is enjoying a rebirth of a wine industry that first flourished in the seventeenth century when Spanish missionaries brought grape vines to the Rio Grande Valley. In the 1800s, New Mexico ranked fifth among the wine producers of the country; local wineries were producing more than 900,000 gallons of wine from 3,100 acres of vineyards and production was steadily increasing. Like many others, New Mexico's wine industry was wiped out during Prohibition.

Today, in New Mexico, there are eighteen wineries in northern and southern areas, most of them with welcome mats out for visitors. (Not all are in this chapter.) Varied wine routes to them make the journey interesting: they take visitors through the countryside outside of Albuquerque to the rugged vistas of the Sangre de Cristo Mountains and the lush and lovely valleys along the lazy Rio Grande. Fall visitors will find that the wine routes around Las Vegas and Taos have turned into Aspencades, because many motorists are drawn to the sight of these gorgeous trees in golden splendor.

New Mexico USA, a New Mexico State Tourism and Travel Division publication, lists more wineries than space permitted here and is included with other tourism information, sent upon request. See listings at back of book for address.

A special time to visit is during the New Mexico Wine Festival in Bernalillo, first held in 1988 and planned as an annual event each Labor Day weekend. At El Zocalo, 2000 Camino del Pueblo in Bernalillo, eighteen miles north of Albuquerque, the festival, held 12–9, salutes the state's wine industry and the arts with colorful arts and crafts displays, dancing, and live music. For information, call the Vine and Wine Society (tel: 505-294-6217) or the town of Bernalillo (tel: 505-867-3311). Tickets at Ticket Master outlets in Albuquerque and Santa Fe.

Northern New Mexico

Anderson Valley Vineyards

4920 Rio Grande Boulevard, Northwest
Albuquerque, New Mexico 87107
TEL: 505-345-7744
OWNER: Patty G. Anderson
WINEMAKER: Mark Matheson
FOUNDED: 1984

AT A GLANCE
Tours & Tastings: Twenty-minute guided tours, customized to visitors' interests, Tues.–Fri. 12–5:30; Sat. 9–5:30; tastings included. Phone for Sun. appointments.
Closed: Christmas, New Year's days.
Vineyards: Fifteen acres owned, one hundred leased in southern New Mexico, planted mainly to vinifera varieties.
Wines: Johannisberg Riesling, Chenin Blanc, Chardonnay, Sauvignon Blanc, Muscat Canelli, white Zinfandel. Generic Burgundy is among their best known.
Awards: Burgundy is oft-awarded in re-

gional and international competitions; other awarded wines—Chenin Blanc, Muscat Canelli, and white Zinfandel.
Picnic Area: On winery patio or in nearby nature preserve.
Access for Disabled: Yes.
Retail Shop: Wines, local crafts.
Credit Cards: MasterCard, Visa.
Foreign Languages: Spanish.
Getting There: From Albuquerque: Take I-25 West exit; on Montano to Rio Grande Blvd. and continue north to vineyard. Or take I-40 and exit north on Rio Grande, continuing to vineyard. Tourist trams call at various Albuquerque hotels and take visitors to top attractions, including vineyards.

る This winery was founded by the world-record-holding balloonist the late Maxie Anderson and his wife, Patty. The grape-decked balloon logo pays tribute to this past history. Today, son Kris carries on two traditions—he's the vice president of the winery and another world-record-holding balloonist. The tiled tasting room is an agreeable place to learn about rich wines made from New Mexican grapes. The winery shares the site with the Andersons' Arabian horse farm.

Another winery to visit in Albuquerque:

る る る

Sandia Shadows Vineyard & Winery

11704 Coronado Northeast
Albuquerque, New Mexico 87122
TEL: 505-298-8826
Near the Sandia Mountains; produces Chardonnay, Sauvignon Blanc, Seyval Blanc, and Chancellor wines. Grape arbor for picnics. Tours and tastings by appointment.

TO SEE & DO
Albuquerque, New Mexico's largest city, is a particularly interesting base, with a Spanish-flavored Old Town and even older Isleta Pueblo, thirteen miles away. You can ski at Sandia in the nearby mountains, or tour museums devoted to local history and science—past, present, and future—at the National Atomic Museum. Leading events are the Arts and Crafts Fair, held in the last weekend in June; the Albuquerque Festival for local performers, also in June; the state fair in Sept.; and, in Oct., the Hot-Air Balloon Fiesta. In addition, the racetrack operates Jan–Apr. In summer and fall, farmers' markets offer a wide variety of fresh-grown fruits and vegetables for picnics with wine, snacking, or packing for later on.

For more information on what to do in Albuquerque, check with the Albuquerque Convention and Visitors Bureau at 625 Silver Street SW, Suite 210 Alberquerque, NM 26886 (tel: 505-243-3696; 800-284-2282).

ACCOMMODATIONS

Bed & Breakfast
The Corner House
9121 James Place Northeast
Albuquerque, New Mexico 87111
Tel: 505-298-5800
Comfortable southwestern-style house, where a bottle of wine is a gift to visitors. Decor includes collectibles and antiques. Near the Sandia Mountains. Full breakfast with homemade muffins.

Other Accommodations
Clarion Four Seasons
2500 Carlisle Boulevard Northeast
Albuquerque, New Mexico 87110
Tel: 505-888-3311; 800-828-1188
Luxury accommodations.

La Posada da Albuquerque
Copper and Second Northwest
Albuquerque, New Mexico 87102
Tel: 505-242-9090; 800-621-7231
Atmospheric, in restored historic building.

Doubletree Albuquerque
201 Marquette Street Northwest
Albuquerque, New Mexico 87102
Tel: 505-247-3344; 800-545-4444
Thoughtfully done, southwestern decor.

Sheraton Old Town
800 Rio Grande Boulevard
Albuquerque, New Mexico 87104
Tel: 505-843-6300; 800-237-2133
Good location near historic part of town.

RESTAURANTS
Al Monte's
1306 Rio Grande Boulevard
Albuquerque, New Mexico 87104
Tel: 505-243-3709
Elegant decor; seafood, veal, pasta are specialties. Wine list.

Chardonnay's
Ramada Hotel Classic
6815 Menaul Boulevard Northeast
Albuquerque, New Mexico 87110
Tel: 505-881-0000
Quiet setting for Continental dishes and a good wine list.

Lil's
2910 North Yale Boulevard SE
Albuquerque, New Mexico 87106
Tel: 505-843-7000
Small, intimate; in Amtac Hotel. Dinner only. Prime beef and seafood; Victorian decor.

Mayfair Restaurant at the Albuquerque Doubletree
201 Marquette Street North West
Albuquerque, New Mexico 87102
Tel: 505-247-3344, ext. 1605
Elegant, excellent wine list; southwestern decor. Continental menu with southwest accent; specialties are chicken Veracruz, made with green chile; Sandia shrimp, with a spicy sauce; chocolate inferno dessert combines mousse and cake.

🐸 🐸 🐸

Rio Valley Cellars

Highway 116 (P.O. Box 100)
Bosque, New Mexico 87006
TEL: 505-864-4561
PRESIDENT: Don J. Spiers
FOUNDED: 1982

AT A GLANCE
Tours & Tastings: Thurs.–Sun. 12–4:30; individuals anytime; groups by appointment.
Vineyards: Planted to French-American hybrids, primarily Chancellor and Vidal Blanc.
Wines: Chancellor and Vidal Blanc, various blends.
Retail Shop: Wines sold on-site.
Credit Cards: None.
Access for Disabled: None.
Foreign Languages: Spanish.
Getting There: Take I-25 to the exit between Belen and Bernado, approximately forty miles south of Albuquerque, to New Mexico Hwy. 116. Winery is easy to see from I-25.

🐸 Located on a hill overlooking the Rio Grande Valley, Rio Valley Cellars produces two types of Vidal Blanc and Chancellor wines as well as blends—all from locally grown French hybrids from vineyards immediately north of the winery. The goal of co-founders Don Spiers and John L. Sichler is to produce premium wines compatible with foods of the Southwest.

ACCOMMODATIONS
(See listings for Albuquerque, starting on page 299.)

RESTAURANTS
The Luna Mansion
West Main Street (Highway 6 and Highway 85)
Las Lunas, New Mexico 87031
Tel: 505-865-7333
Fresh fish, veal. National historic land-

mark adobe mansion. Approximately twenty miles north toward Albuquerque.

ટ્ટ ટ્ટ ટ્ટ

Sangre de Cristo Wines

Route 2, Box 20-A
Sapello, New Mexico 87745
TEL: 505-425-5077
OWNER/WINEMAKER: Richard Jones
FOUNDED: 1983

AT A GLANCE
Tours & Tastings: Telephone for appointment.
Vineyard: One-quarter of an acre, experimental French hybrid vineyard at 7,250 feet; most grapes purchased from growers in surrounding area.
Wines: Whites—Aurora, Seyval Blanc, Vidal Blanc demi-sec and VB semisweet; Reds—Baco Noir, Foch, De Chaunac, rare Lucie Kuhlmann hybrid.
Awards: 1985 Baco Noir, New Mexico State Fair, first out of thirty entries; at Albuquerque Living Panel, Baco Noir and Vidal Blanc demi-sec were both in top ten of fifty-two. Other awards to 1984 De Chaunac, New Mexico State Fair.
Picnic Area: Rural area ideal for picnicking, hiking, camping.
Retail Shop: No formal shop, but wines sold.
Credit Cards: None.
Access for Disabled: None.
Foreign Languages: "Pretty poor French, abominable Spanish."
Getting There: From Las Vegas: Take Hwy. 3 North for twelve miles to Sapello, then go west for about four miles on Hwy. 94, then left for some three miles on San Miguel County Rte. A4A to mailbox; turn left at driveway for another quarter mile—an impassable road in inclement weather.

ટ્ટ A vintage adventure in the foothills of the mighty Sangre de Cristo Mountains at what may be America's smallest winery—200 feet behind Richard Jones's garage—plus a tiny vineyard. Jones claims this is the only place where you can sample and buy the wine from a rare Lucie Kuhlmann hybrid. He produces only five to six cases a year of this wine, which he compares to a fine European Merlot or Cabernet Sauvignon. Jones, a wine columnist for *Wine World* and the *Albuquerque Journal*, says, "Wine isn't about making money, it's about enjoying a glass with friends."

TO SEE & DO
In Las Vegas, formerly a historic stop on the Old Santa Fe Trail, see the Fort Union National Monument, ruins of an old adobe fort that protected travelers on the Santa Fe Trail (20 miles northeast of Las Vegas; take Ft. Union exit off I-25; tel: 505-425-8025); explore the Las Vegas National Wildlife Refuge (six miles via Hwys. 104 and 281; tel: 505-425-3581). Today, Las Vegas is the site of the New Mexico Highlands University and is also known for the Armand Hammer United College of the American West, located in an old resort castle/hotel.

Special events: Sapello offers the Rough Riders Rodeo in summer, and Las Vegas specialties include the Kiwanis Ice Carnival, second week in Jan.; Rails and Trails, June 7–9, honoring the Santa Fe Trail and Railroad; Fiesta, July 4–6; County Fair, Aug. 8–10; and the People's Fair of Arts and Crafts, Aug. 31. For more information contact the Convention and Visitors Bureau, P.O. Box 148, Las Vegas, New Mexico 87701; tel: 505-425-8631.

ACCOMMODATIONS
Carriage House, Bed & Breakfast
925 6th Street
Las Vegas, New Mexico 87701
Tel: 505-454-1784

Plaza Hotel
230 Old Town Plaza
Las Vegas, New Mexico 87701
Tel: 505-425-3591
Listed on the National Register of Historic Places.

ₔ ₔ ₔ

La Chiripada Winery

Box 191
Dixon, New Mexico 87527
OWNERS: Michael and Patrick Johnson
FOUNDED: 1981

AT A GLANCE
Tours & Tastings: Self- or owner-guided, Mon.–Sat. 10–5 year-round.
Closed: Sun., Christmas, New Year's.
Vineyards: Ten acres owned and ten leased, planted to vinifera and French hybrids; apples. Some grapes purchased from New Mexican growers.
Wines: Johannisberg Riesling, Vidal Blanc, Baco Noir, Pinot Noir, Marechal Foch, Rojo Grande (red blend), and Primavera (white blend). Apple wine and naturally fermented cider.
Awards: Too many to list; Southwestern and New Mexico State Fair.
Retail Shop: La Chiripada wines and stoneware pottery made by the Johnson family.
Credit Cards: MasterCard, Visa.
Foreign Languages: Spanish.
Getting There: In Rio Ariba County; Dixon is fifty scenic miles north of Santa Fe, twenty-three miles north of Espanola, and twenty-five miles south of Taos. Take Hwy. 68 from either Espanola or Taos and turn off on Hwy. 75 for three miles to winery. Memorable, scenic drives from either Espanola or Taos. If you drive Hwy. 85 from Albuquerque to Santa Fe, take a break for a picnic at Cibola National Forest and make sight-seeing stops at San Felipe and Santo Domingo Indian reservations along the way.

Special Wine & Other Events: Memorial Day and Labor Day wine tastings.

ₔ Tiny La Chiripada, one of New Mexico's most highly regarded wineries, is run by brothers Michael and Patrick Johnson, former Californians. They specialize in French hybrids because the winter-hardy vines can withstand the freezing winter temperatures in the 6,100-foot-high Rio Embudo Valley. Some Johannisberg Riesling also comes out of their cellar. The Johnsons' maximum production is 2,000 cases, which are sold primarily to visitors to their white adobe winery. They have no plans to grow beyond their current production but prefer to concentrate now on producing premium wines that go well with New Mexican cuisine.

TO SEE & DO
Espanola: Puye Cliff Dwellings, west of the city; Black Mesa, to the south, was home to Pueblo Indians at one time, and in the area is Bandeller Monument, important Pueblo Indian ruins that once housed the Santa Clara Indians.

Peaceful Pueblo Indians settled this area 700 years ago and remain to this day an important part of the valley's residents along with Anglos and Spanish. These three cultures also interact in events: San Juan Pueblo Feast Day (June 24 at the San Juan Pueblo); Eight Northern Pueblos Artists and Craftsmen (San Idelfonzo, July 19–20); Santa Clara Pueblo Feast Day (Santa Clara Pueblo, Aug. 12); and the annual Espanola Tri-Cultural Arts Festival (Oct. 4–5).

Taos: Pueblo, north of the city; Ranchos de Taos, with a beautiful church renowned throughout the Southwest; and the Kit Carson Museum, State Park, and National Forest. For arts and crafts, visit the Stables Gallery and Millicent Rogers Museum. Outside of town, Rio Grande Gorge Bridge, the second highest expansion bridge in the United States, offers scenic views and picnic areas.

Events accent Taos's importance as an artists' and writers' center, with the Spring Arts Celebration (May 25–June 21), for visual, performing, and literary arts; Arts Festival (Oct. 1–7), a full-scale celebration of all arts that includes lectures and dancing and crafts; and "Meet the Artists" (twice weekly, Oct. 15–Dec. 15), when tourists and locals meet nationally known Taos artists and share their ideas and inspirations through studio tours and visual aides. Also notable is the Taos School of Music Chamber Music Festival (June 15–Aug. 2).

ACCOMMODATIONS
La Puebla House
Route 1, Box 172A
Espanola, New Mexico 87532
Tel: 505-753-3981
Nice southwestern hospitality in a B&B in a picturesque location. Continental breakfast; snacks also.

American Artists Gallery-House
Frontier Road (P.O. Box 584)
Taos, New Mexico 87571
Tel: 505-758-0311
Gallery owners' charming adobe hacienda, decorated with local artworks. Comfortable bedroom has terrific mountain view. Continental breakfast, snacks in the evening.

Mountain Light Bed & Breakfast
P.O. Box 241
Taos, New Mexico 87571
Tel: 505-776-8474
Traditional adobe home, perched on a mesa with a sweeping view; owner is a professional photographer, and this is her home, studio, and gallery. You may have seen her photographs in national magazines. Continental breakfast.

Chamisa Inn
920 North Riverside Drive
Espanola, New Mexico 87532
Tel: 505-753-7291
Fifty-one rooms in above-average budget motel.

The Taos Inn
North Pueblo Road (P.O. Drawer N)
Taos, New Mexico 87571
Tel. 505-758-2233; 800-TAOS-INN
Listed in both State and National Registers of Historic Places, and the place to stay in Taos. Evocative southwestern ambience; award-winning wine list; gathering place for local artists; location of "Meet the Artists" series, mentioned above. Half a mile north of Plaza.

RESTAURANTS
El Paragua
603 Santa Cruz Road
Espanola, New Mexico 87532
Tel: 505-753-3211
Mexican and American dishes in old adobe setting. Wine list.

La Casa Sena
125 West Palace Avenue
Santa Fe, New Mexico 87501
Tel: 505-988-9232
Highly recommended for local wines; nouvelle southwestern cuisine in an adobe casa dating from the 1860s. Twenty-five miles south of Espanola.

Doc Martin's
(See listing for The Taos Inn under "Accommodations" for address and telephone number.)
  New Mexican, American specialties. Prizewinning wine list; Elegant desserts.

Apple Tree Restaurant
26th and Bent Street
Taos, New Mexico 87571
Tel: 505-758-1900
New Mexican and Continental wines. Patio dining in summer, fireplaces indoors in winter.

  Alternatively, Santa Fe, fifty miles south of Dixon and Chimayo, offers many superb places to stay and eat in and things to do in colorful and interesting surroundings.

Southern New Mexico

Binns Vineyards & Winery

3910 West Picacho Avenue
Las Cruces, New Mexico 88005
TEL: 505-526-6738
OWNERS: Eddie and Glen Binns
WINEMAKER: Glen Binns
FOUNDED: 1982

AT A GLANCE
Tours & Tastings: Open Mon.–Fri. 1–5;
tours and tastings by appointment only.
Closed: Sat., Sun., some holidays.
Vineyards: Twenty-six acres planted to
vinifera varieties; some additional grapes
purchased from Mesilla Valley growers.
Wines: Chenin Blanc, French Colom-
bard, Zinfandel, Johannisberg Riesling,
Chardonnay.
Awards: Numerous local and statewide.
Picnic Area: Parklike setting for picnick-
ing.
Retail Shop: Wines, gifts.
Credit Cards: None.
Access for Disabled: None.
Foreign Languages: None.
Getting There: From Las Cruces: Take
Scenic Hwy. 70 to winery.
Special Wine & Other Events: (See the
section following St. Clair Vineyards.)

இ Eddie Binn and son Glen run this
small vineyard/winery located in the fertile Mesilla Valley, just across the Rio
Grande. They are quickly earning a name
for themselves as producers of attractive
wines; among these the Riesling has
been most well received.

இ இ இ

St. Clair Vineyards

P.O. Box 112
Deming, New Mexico 88031
TEL: 505-546-6585

PRESIDENT: Vincent Vuignier
WINEMAKER: Noel Vuignier (degree in
enology, École Superieme
d'Oenologie, Switzerland)
FOUNDED: 1983

AT A GLANCE
Tours & Tastings: Mon.–Sat. 9-5, or by
appointment.
Closed: Sun., Christmas.
Vineyards: 600 acres (355 of them leased)
planted to vinifera varieties.
Wines: Chardonnay, Sauvignon Blanc,
Muscat Canelli, Cabernet Sauvignon,
Merlot, Pinot Noir, Zinfandel, Barbera.
Awards: St. Clair 1984 Blanc Reserve,
gold medal, 1986 Le Monde (Selection
L'Institue International pour les selec-
tions de la qualitié).
Access for Disabled: None.
Retail Shop: St. Clair wines sold on the
premises.
Credit Cards: None.
Foreign Languages: French, Italian, Ger-
man.
Getting There: In Luna County, take
Hwy. I-10 West from Las Cruces for fifty
scenic miles to Hwy. 549, three miles
southeast of Deming.

இ Classic European wines come from
brothers Vincent and Noel Vuignier, who
trace their heritage back 200 years to fine
European winemakers. Swiss-trained
winemaker Noel blends traditional methods with modern technology to produce
prizewinning, estate-bottled wines from
vineyards at 4,320 feet planted to classic
vinifera varieties.

TO SEE & DO
In Deming, visit the Deming/Luna/Mim-
bres Museum for local frontier history
(301 South Silver; tel: 505-546-2382). It's
open 9–11:30, 1:30–5, Mon.–Sat; 1:30–
4, Sun. Most sight-seeing is around the

Las Cruces area, where subtle harmonies of ochre and green cotton and chile fields blend with jagged peaks of the Organ Mountains. Sites that recall the past are the Historic Village at Mesilla (two miles southwest); the Gadsden Museum (three miles southwest via I-10, Mesilla exit), with displays of Indian and Civil War artifacts, and paintings; the Fort Seiden State Monument (twelve miles north on I-25); and the museum at New Mexico State University, also the site of an art gallery and eighteen-hole golf course.

Events: From Sept. to Nov., Las Cruces is alive with annual events; exact dates, times, and places can be checked by contacting the Las Cruces Convention and Visitors Bureau, 311 Downtown Mall, Las Cruces, New Mexico 88001; tel: 505-524-9521. Notable among these are: the Whole Enchilada Fiesta Hot-Air Balloon Rally (Sept.; tel: 505-524-1968); the Whole Enchilada Fiesta (Oct.; tel: 505-524-1968), a street fair featuring the cooking of the world's largest enchilada; Annual Rodders Day (Oct.; tel: 505-382-5742), a parade and show of antique cars from New Mexico and surrounding areas; the Southern New Mexico State Fair (Oct.; tel: 505-589-1131); and the Dona Ana Arts Council Renaissance Arts & Craftfair, featuring works of southwestern artists in a downtown mall (Nov.; tel: 505-524-8521).

ACCOMMODATIONS
Holiday Budget Inn
I-10 East, Exit 85 (P.O. Box 1280)
Deming, New Mexico 88030
Tel: 505-546-2661
Above-average 99-room motel.

The Elms
1110 Carver Road (P.O. Box 1176)
Mesilla Park, New Mexico 88047
Tel: 505-524-1513
A large stucco-and-redwood B&B house set amid old elm trees. Three guest rooms have antique furnishings and Oriental carpeting. Continental breakfast with homemade bread and preserves. Fifty-nine miles east of Deming.

Meson de Mesilla
P.O. Box 1212
Mesilla, New Mexico 88046
Tel: 505-525-9212
Peaceful and picturesque setting. Inn has bikes, or you can stroll to see the town's old plaza.

Quality Inn-Mesilla Real
790 Avenida de Mesilla
I-10 at Mesilla Exit
Mesilla, New Mexico 88005
Tel: 505-524-0331; 800-228-5151
Half a mile from Old Mesilla. One hundred rooms, heated pool.

RESTAURANTS
Double Eagle
Three miles Southwest of Mesilla
Tel: 505-523-6700
Antiques and a Victorian setting form the backdrop for steak, seafood. Good wine list.

❧ OKLAHOMA

Oklahoma's first and only vineyard and commercial winery offers a wine route through the state's serene southeastern hills. Once thought to be suitable only for farming and grazing, the sandy soil and fairly dry climate also offer top conditions for quality grape growing.

❧ ❧ ❧

Cimarron Cellars

Route 1, Box 79
Caney, Oklahoma 74533
TEL: 405-869-6312
OWNERS: Dwayne and Linda Pool
WINEMAKER: Dwayne Pool
FOUNDED: 1983

AT A GLANCE
Tours & Tastings: By appointment.
Vineyards: Forty acres, planted to twenty varieties: vinifera, French hybrids, and native American.
Wines: Marechal Foch, French Colombard, Seyval Blanc, Aurora, Rougeon, Pink Catawba, generic red and white.
Retail Shop: Wines sold on-site.
Credit Cards: None.
Access for Disabled: None.
Foreign Languages: None.
Getting There: Located 120 miles north of Dallas and 150 miles south of Tulsa. Take U.S. 75 from Dallas north to Oklahoma, where it becomes U.S. 69/75, to Cimarron Cellars, south of Caney. There's a travelers information center on U.S. 69/75, two miles north of the Oklahoma border near Colbert.

❧ Dwayne and Linda Pool dreamed of making wine when they lived in the expensive Napa Valley. Their dreams came true when they bought a vineyard in Oklahoma, and they were soon making quite a name for themselves. Their first vintage 1983 Marechal Foch was added to the wine list at the prestigious Mark Hopkins Hotel and was praised by wine dean Leon Adams. Since then, the Pools have built a new winery and increased storage to 32,000 gallons to prepare for a time when Cimarron Cellars is working to full capacity.

TO SEE & DO
Stop by the Three Valley Museum in the Choctaw National Headquarters Building for a look at Indian art and turn-of-the-century artifacts (16th and Locust; tel: 405-920-1907). Drive out to Lake Texoma for a look at the ruins of Fort Washita, originally built to protect the Five Civilized Tribes from the Plains Indians, and to visit the Chickasaw Council House for more information on Indian history (fifteen miles northwest of Durant via Routes 78 and 199). Lake Texoma, named because it forms part of the Oklahoma/Texas border, offers swimming, fishing, boating, tennis, riding, and golf among its outdoor pleasures (tel: 214-465-4990).

ACCOMMODATIONS
The nearest place to stay is in Durant, twenty miles south.

Best Western Markita Inn
2401 West Main Street (U.S. 70)
Durant, Oklahoma 74701
Tel: 405-924-7676; 800-528-1234
Sixty rooms, pool, hot tub. Twenty-four-hour café.

Holiday House
2121 West Main Street (U.S. 69, 70, 75
Bypass)
Durant, Oklahoma 74701

Tel: 405-924-5432
A former Holiday Inn, with eighty-two rooms, pool, café.

Bryan Hotel
101 West Main Street
Durant, Oklahoma 74701
Tel: 405-924-3796
Renovated famous 1929 hotel, opposite the bus depot. Café.

Lake Texoma Lodge
Lake Texoma State Park
U.S. 70 (P.O. Box 248)
Kingston, Oklahoma 73439
Tel: 405-564-2311; 800-654-8240 (nearby states); 800-522-8565 (in-state)
Family resort with 170 rooms and cottages; restaurant, children's programs; full sports facilities—swimming pool, golf, tennis, fishing, and more.

?◆ TEXAS

Texas has twenty-three wineries and 4,500 acres under cultivation. Contrast that with 1975, when there was one winery and 25 vine-covered acres. Wine production was 50,000 gallons in 1982, the first year data was tabulated; more recently it had skyrocketed to 650,000 gallons.

More accurately, winemaking is not new, but newly reborn, in this state: Texans brag that Franciscan missionaries near El Paso were making sacramental wine in 1662, more than a century before they did in California.

In the late 1800s, a Texan and noted viticulturalist, T. V. Munson, from Denison, helped save the French wine industry. He sent to France rootstocks he developed that could resist diseases inadvertently imported to Europe from the United States. For his achievements, Munson received the Legion of Honor from the French government.

Although there were twenty-five wineries in Texas in 1900, all but one, Val Verde, went under during Prohibition. It remained the lone winery in the Lone Star State until the 1970s. But when the University of Texas's research proved that premium grape-growing conditions existed in various parts of the state, the rush to crush was on.

Widely varied wine routes in Texas lead through the piney woods, meadows of spring wildflowers, and abundant orchards of Texas Hill Country, as well as the forests of north-central Texas. Cowboys, cattle, and cotton farms greet the eye in the great western plains. And, virtually everywhere your wine route takes you in Texas, you will be in bird-watching territory, so keep a pair of binoculars handy.

Visitors will find one peculiarity about the Texas wine industry: statewide legislation permits the making of wines in dry counties, but local precincts vote on whether or not wines can be sold. Thus wines made in dry counties where visitors can see the vineyards and production may be tasted and sold only in a visitors' center a few miles away in the next county. One winery also shows an audio-visual presentation on winemaking to those who come to taste and buy wines at the visitors' center.

Special Texas Wine Events
The International Wine Expo, February; the Lone Star State Wine Competition, Texas State Fair, Oct. Both events are held in Dallas. A call to any of the wineries or query to the Convention and Visitors Bureau in Dallas (Information Department 1507 Pacific Avenue, Dallas, TX 75201; tel: 214-954-1111) should produce the exact dates, times and details for planning purposes.

Texas Hill Country

Six wineries are located in the Hill Country of central Texas. This wine route extends roughly eighty miles west of Austin and eighty miles north of San Antonio, through verdant grasslands and groves of hardy cypress and oak trees. Here are lazy creeks and little towns that look as if they have been dozing for the last one hundred years or more when they were home to German and English settlers.

ও ও ও

Guadalupe Valley Winery

1720 Hunter Road
New Braunfels, Texas 78130
TEL: 512-629-2551
OWNERS: Larry and Donna Lehr
WINEMAKER: Larry Lehr (Napa Valley School of Cellaring)
FOUNDED: 1974

AT A GLANCE
Tours & Tastings: Tours Sat. 10–5, Sun. 12–5, July–Aug.; at other times by appointment. 50 cents per person. Tasting room open Mon.–Fri. 10–5; Sat. and Sun. same as tour hours.

Closed: Thanksgiving, Christmas, New Year's.
Vineyards: All fruits purchased from Texas growers.
Wines: Lenoir, Villard Blanc, Chenin Blanc, Riesling, Zinfandel.
Retail Shop: Wines sold on-site.
Credit Cards: None.
Access for Disabled: Wheelchair ramp.
Foreign Languages: None.
Getting There: Located in Gruene, four miles north of New Braunfels. Take I-35 from Austin to New Braunfels; en route are beautiful McKinney Falls State Park right in Austin and Aquarena Mineral Springs near San Marcos. From I-35: Take Exit for FM Road 306 (Canyon Lake Rd). Drive west on FM 306 about two miles to the yellow flashing light, and turn on Hunter Road, going about one-quarter mile to winery.
Special Wine & Other Events: Late July–Sept.: public is invited to witness crushes of freshly picked grapes; New Baunfels's famous Wurstfest is held in fall.

ও Guadalupe Valley Winery, in the historic community of Gruene (pronounced Green), turns out wines in an old warehouse. The building in front of the winery was one of Texas's first electric-powered cotton gins—a registered landmark and now the winery restaurant. In addition to its other historic charms, the restaurant has striking stained-glass windows that form portraits of the original gin owner's daughter and the winery's art deco logo.

TO SEE & DO

Gruene's heyday lasted from the 1840s until 1927, when boll weevil and then the Depression turned it into a ghost town. Rediscovered in 1974 by new investors, Gruene has been revitalized and restored. Walking is the best way to see its varied historic homes: the earliest, dating from the 1850s, was once occupied by town founder Henry Gruene and is now a hotel; the old cotton gins and Texas's oldest dance hall dating from the 1880s; and the latest, built in the 1920s, also in the Gruene family. A number of stores in historic buildings feature the pottery, furniture, and fashions produced by local artisans. Outdoors fans will find good river rafting on the Comal and Guadalupe rivers.

ACCOMMODATIONS

(Rates go up during Wurstfest.)

Gruene Mansion Inn

Gruene Road
New Braunfels, Texas 78130
Tel: 512-629-2641
Victorian charm in the original home of the town's founder, H. D. Gruene, with cottages that have a romantic river view.

Gruene House

Hunter Road
New Braunfels, Texas 78130
Tel: 512-629-2641
More Gruenes—this time Max and Olga's restored Victorian house—for a delightful overnight stay.

Guadalupe Outpost

1273 Gruene Terrace
New Braunfels, Texas 78130
Tel: 512-625-7772
A resort motel.

Prince Solms Inn

295 East San Antonia Street
New Braunfels, Texas 78130
Tel: 512-625-9169
Built in 1898, and decorated with Victorian antiques. Restaurant, Wolfgang's Keller, features German specialties accompanied by owner Bill Knight on the piano.

RESTAURANTS

(All in Gruene or New Braunfels.)

The Old Gruene Gin Restaurant

1724 Hunter Road
Tel: 512-629-0684
As mentioned, adjoins winery and is run by the Lehrs; showcase for their Guadalupe Valley wines. Southern, creole, and Italian foods.

The Grist Mill

1287 Gruene Road
Tel: 512-625-0684
In the ruins of a hundred-year-old cotton gin on the banks of the Guadalupe River.

Wolfgang's Keller

Prince Solms Inn
Tel: 512-625-9169
(See listing above under "Accommodations.")

Guadalupe Smoked Meat Co.

Gruene Road
Tel: 512-625-6121
Smoked green hickory barbecue, Texas wines, and all the trimmings.

≈ ≈ ≈

Moyer Texas Champagne Co.

I-35 East
New Braunfels, Texas 78130
TEL: 512-625-5181
OWNERS: Ken and Mary Moyer
OPENED: 1980

AT A GLANCE
Tours & Tastings: Guided tours, Mon.–Sat. 10–5; free tasting (small charge for large groups).
Closed: Sun.
Vineyards: Various Texas growers.
Wines: *Methode champenoise* champagne.
Awards: Bronze to this bubbly in the *Dallas Morning News* Competition.
Retail Shop: Wine sold on-site.
Credit Cards: None.
Access for Disabled: Yes.
Foreign Languages: None.
Getting There: Take I-35 either south from Austin or north from San Antonio to New Braunfels.

🦃 This Texas sparkler made by the French *methode champenoise* is the one and only star of this modern winery in the old German-settled town of New Braunfels. The wine is bottle-aged for eighteen months to two years before it is sold. Ken Moyer studied champagne-making at the University of California at Davis. The Moyers' main winery is in Manchester, Ohio (see the Ohio section for details).

TO SEE & DO
To Guadalupe River attractions, add the Natural Bridge Caverns (thirteen miles northeast of exit 175, I-35; tel: 512-651-6101) and Cascade Caverns (twenty miles northwest of San Antonio off I-10; tel: 512-755-9285), with a waterfall as sheer as Salome's last veil.

ACCOMMODATIONS
(Remember, rates go up during Wurstfest.)

The White House
217 Mittman Circle
New Braunfels, Texas 78130
Tel: 512-629-9354
Spanish-style home set amid cedars and oak trees with nice-size fish pond on the grounds. Big rooms, comfortably furnished. Tempting pastries and tea upon arrival. Full breakfast.

Quality Inn
375 Texas 46S
New Braunfels, Texas 78130
Tel: 512-626-6282; 800-228-5151
Ninety-two rooms, pool, wading pool, and café.

🦃 🦃 🦃

Oberhellmann Vineyards

Highway 16
(Llano Route, Box 22)
Fredericksburg, Texas 78624
TEL: 512-685-3297
OWNER/WINEMAKER: Robert Oberhelman
FOUNDED: 1976

AT A GLANCE
Tours & Tastings: Sat. only, May–mid-Dec., 10–4. Twenty-minute guided tours every thirty minutes, and tastings.
Closed: Jan.–Easter Sat.
Vineyards: Forty acres planted to vinifera varieties.
Wines: Vintage-dated, estate-bottled varietals—Chardonnay, Johannisberg Riesling, Fumé Blanc, Sémillon, Gewürztraminer, Cabernet Sauvignon, Pinot Noir.
Retail Shop: Wine, wine accessories, books.
Credit Cards: MasterCard, Visa.
Access for Disabled: None.
Foreign Languages: German.
Getting There: From Austin: Take I-35 South to S-290 turnoff; go west to Fred-

ericksburg. From Fredericksburg: Take S-16 for fourteen miles north to vineyards, one-half mile east of the highway.

🐾 On pine-covered Bell Mountain, Oberhellmann's forty-acre all-vinifera vineyards adjoins a château-style winery, producing European-style wines, and especially well regarded whites. Oberhelman spells his name with one *l* and one *n,* but puts two of each on his label to pay tribute to his German ancestry. He is a member of the American Society of Enologists and Viticulturalists; Technical Director Fritz Meier has studied at Geisenheim.

TO SEE & DO
Pack a picnic before you take off; this park-studded route has superb settings for al fresco meals. Select spots from a buffet of choice sites include Pedernales Falls State Park, up in the wooded hills (tel: 512-868-7304), or, on your wine route, U.S. 290, LBJ State Park on the Pedernales River (tel: 512-544-2252). Adajacent LBJ National Historic Park in Johnson City is a trip back to life as lived at the turn of the century (tel: 512-868-7128). In Fredericksburg, the town nearest the winery, is Admiral Nimitz State Historical Park, an outdoor museum honoring Admiral Chester Nimitz, U.S. Naval Commander during World War II (340 East Main Street; tel: 512-997-4379). To the north, more picnic and hiking territory in pink-granite-topped Enchanted Rock State Park (twenty miles north of Fredericksburg off RM 965; tel: 512-247-3903).

ACCOMMODATIONS
Y. O. Ranch Hilton
2033 Sidney Baker
Kerrville, Texas 78029
Tel: 512-257-4440; 800-531-2800
A luxury resort on the famous Schreiner Ranch, still a working spread now covering eighty square miles. Furnishings

combine first-class hotel decor with distinctive Texas touches. Restaurant serves wild game, Continental cuisine, and ranch-style cooking. Located about twenty-five miles southwest of Fredericksburg.

Bed and Breakfast
Southard House
908 Blanco
Austin, Texas 78703
Tel: 512-474-4371
Downtown Austin is the location of this 1900 manor house done with antiques and lace. A big breakfast on weekends and Continental during the week. Eighty miles east of Fredericksburg.

Hotels

The Driskill
604 Brazon Street at 6th
Austin, Texas 78701
Tel: 512-474-5911; 800-252-9367
First hotel southwest of St. Louis with electricity, built over one hundred years ago. Combines historical ambience with all modern conveniences; set in the heart of old Austin.

Four Seasons
96 San Jacinto Boulevard
Austin, Texas 78710
Tel: 512-478-4500; 800-828-1188
Luxury hotel connected to San Jacinto Center Town Lake office with shops and entertainment also. Heated outdoor pool, health club. Overlooks Town Lake.

RESTAURANTS
Gallery Restaurant
Main Street
Fredericksburg, Texas 78624
Tel: 512-997-5157
Seafood, veal, and daily specials; serves Oberhellmann wines, as do some other restaurants in town.

🐾 🐾 🐾

Wimberly Valley Winery

Route 1, Box 65
Driftwood, Texas 78619
TEL: 512-847-2592
OWNER: Wimberly Valley Wines
WINEMAKER: Dean Valentine
FOUNDED: 1983

AT A GLANCE

Tours & Tastings: Winery in dry Hays County, not open to public. Tasting room, near San Marcos, open Sat. 10–5, Sun. 12–5, some holidays and other days (call winery at 512-847-2592 to check). Winery staff also serve at tasting room and describe winemaking to visitors.
Vineyards: Grapes purchased from West Texas growers.
Wines: Vineyard-designated varietals such as Johannisberg Riesling, Chenin Blanc, Cabernet Sauvignon, and Texas Cabernet (a blend of Ruby Cabernet Sauvignon grapes).
Awards: Much beribboned: Chenin Blanc; other winners: Cabernet Sauvignon, Cabernet Blanc, Nouveau Cabernet.
Retail Shop: At tasting room; wines, accessories, books. Other Texas wines.
Credit Cards: MasterCard, Visa.
Access for Disabled: All on one level.
Foreign Languages: None.
Getting There: Take I-35 South from Austin or north from San Antonio to San Marcos, turn onto R.R. 12 and go west ten miles to tasting room on left (or south side of road). It's marked with a big barrel and the only building of any consequence in the vicinity.

• The thirty-acre Wimberly Valley Winery produces award-winning wines from a building with ten-foot-thick walls, handcrafted by winemaker Dean Valentine. Wines are made from expensive premium grapes purchased from West Texas growers—an investment that paid dividends from the start. Wimberly's first release—a 1983 Chenin Blanc—won a silver medal in the Lone Star Wine Competition, and awards keep coming in. The classy gold-accented labels by San Antonio artist Michelle Freisenhahn show Wimberly between two area landmarks, Lone Man and Lone Woman peaks.

TO SEE & DO

Wimberly is another of those Hill Country historic towns that retain much of their 150-year-old flavor. Attractions include Pioneer Town, a reproduction of an 1880s town (tel: 512-847-2517); a yearly gospel festival; and many interesting shops and restaurants. An enchanting way to see the sights is via a stagecoach ride offered around town. North of Wimberly off FM 12 is Wimberly label model Lone Man Mountain, offering a commanding view at 1,450 feet. At San Marcos, Aquarena Springs features a live underwater magic show, and the Republic of Texas Chilympiad turns up the heat here every September. For more information, contact the Chamber of Commerce, PO Box 12, Wimberly, Texas 78676; Tel: 512-847-2201.

Nearby are the city-sights of San Antonio, where South Texas begins. Here is the Alamo, the state's most well known shrine; delightful sidewalk cafés and cabarets line the Paseo del Rio (River Walk) and can be surveyed from a barge or on a stroll under spreading trees, aglow at night with twinkling lights. The past is also commemorated by the Mission Trail, a walk to five historic eighteenth-century missions. Mid-April is fiesta time here.

For more information, contact the Convention and Visitors Bureau, Box 2277, San Antonio, Texas 78298; Tel: 512-224-6163.

Two other Hill Country wineries near Austin conduct tours and tastings and should be contacted directly for details.

Routes to these wineries are most beautiful in the spring at budbreak, when meadows are carpeted with wildflowers, from late March to mid-April.

ঌ ঌ ঌ

Cypress Valley Winery

Ranch Road 962
Round Mountain, Texas 78663
TEL: 512-825-3333
OWNERS: Dale and Penny Bettis

AT A GLANCE
Tours & Tastings: Sat. afternoons and by appointment.
Closed: Jan.–Feb., except by appointment.
Vineyards: Surrounding house, planted to vinifera varieties.
Wines: Chenin Blanc, Sauvignon Blanc, White Riesling, Cabernet Sauvignon.
Getting There: From Austin: Take R.R. 3238 two miles to Cypress Hill stop sign (the road has become R.R. 962). Make a right turn at stop sign and continue another mile before turning right again. The winery is a short distance ahead on the right.

ঌ The Bettises' historic home in a pastoral setting northwest of Austin is surrounded by vinifera vineyards, as seen on their label. The simpler tasting room and winery are nearby. Budbreak in late March and April wildflowers are especially pretty times to visit.

ঌ ঌ ঌ

Fall Creek Vineyards

Tow, Texas 78672
TEL: 915-476-4477
OWNERS: Ed and Susan Auler

AT A GLANCE
Tours & Tastings: Last Sat. of the month, Jan.–Oct. 1–5.
Closed: Mon.–Fri., Sun., Jan.–Oct.; Oct.–Jan.
Vineyards: Sixty acres planted to vinifera.
Wines: Sauvignon Blanc, Chenin Blanc, Emerald Riesling, Chardonnay; Cabernet Sauvignon, Carnelian, and Zinfandel.
Awards: Oft-awarded: Emerald Riesling, among others.
Getting There: From Austin: Take U.S. 183 West to Hwy. 29 at Liberty Hill, continue to Hwy. 261 near Buchanan Dam. Follow Hwy. 261 northwest to Hwy. 2241 and turn north to Tow (rhymes with *cow*). Fall Creek is 2.2 miles northeast of Tow post office.

ঌ This winery is named for the steep falls nearby and is set on the shores of Buchanan Lake. From its sixty-acre vineyard come nationally acclaimed wines. The Aulers first became interested in wines during a visit to France in 1973; they experimented widely with grape varieties to decide which would flourish on their soil. Prizes soon followed the release of their first wines and have continued, as has expansion of the vineyard over the years.

ACCOMMODATIONS
Either New Braunfels or San Antonio can be bases for Wimberly:

Bed & Breakfast Hosts of San Antonio
166 Rockhill
San Antonio, Texas 78209
Tel: 512-824-8036
Recommendations for San Antonio–area bed and breakfasts.

Cardinal Cliff
3806 Highcliff
San Antonio, Texas 78218
Tel: 512-655-2939
Comfortable home, twenty minutes by

car from downtown. Full breakfast with homemade preserves and breads.

International House
4910 Newcombe Drive
San Antonio, Texas 78229
Tel: 512-647-3547
A contemporary home with an Oriental-accented decor. Enjoy Chinese tea on arrival, and choose between Continental or Oriental breakfasts.

Other Accommodations
Four Seasons Hotel
550 South Alamo Street
San Antonio, Texas 78205
Tel: 512-229-1000; 800-268-6282

Next to La Villita Historic District on six landcaped acres, with Spanish-American feeling. Luxury in the heart of downtown. Pool and outdoor arbor and terrace for drinks; excellent restaurant.

St. Anthony Intercontinental
300 East Travis
San Antonio, Texas
Tel: 512-227-4392; 800-327-0200

North-Central Texas

La Buena Vida Vineyards

Highway 199 (WSR Box-3)
Tasting Room: Highway 199 ten miles
   northwest of Fort Worth
Springtown, Texas 76082
TEL: 817-237-9463 (Tasting Room)
OWNER: Dr. Bobby Smith
WINEMAKER: Steve Smith (UC-Davis–
   trained, as is owner)
FOUNDED: 1978

AT A GLANCE
Tours & Tastings: 11–5 Mon.–Sat. 12–5 Sun., by appointment (Call Tasting Room; 817-237-9463); guided vineyard/winery tours (in dry precinct) give in-depth look at winemaking from vine to bottling; tastings and sales 11–5 at comfortably appointed tasting room a few miles away, where there's an audio-visual presentation on winemaking.
Closed: Thanksgiving, Christmas, Easter, Mother's Day.
Vineyards: Twelve acres planted to French-American hybrids; experimental viniferas. Production: 20,000 gallons.
Wines: Rayon D'Or; Vidal Blanc; proprietary reds, whites, rosés; three *methode champenoise* sparkling wines (nonvintage-dated Blanc de Blanc, Blanc de Noir, vintage-dated Tres Jolie); Walnut Creek Cellars Port. Some private vintages at tasting room only.
Awards: Many awards, including golds for Vintage Port, Rayon D'Or, and Vidal Blanc; awards also to Mist Blush and Blanc de Blanc sparkling wine.
Retail Shop: At visitors center—wines, locally crafted gift items including T-shirts, aprons, totes, jewelry, baskets, and grapevine wreaths for the holidays.
Credit Cards: MasterCard, Visa.
Access for Disabled: None.
Foreign Languages: None.
Getting There: Take Hwy. 199 from Fort Worth northwest for twenty-five miles to the vineyards/winery near Springtown. The visitors center/tasting room, a few miles south of winery and about ten

miles northwest of downtown Fort Worth, is two miles northwest of the Lake Worth Bridge, also on Hwy. 199 at the FM 1886 cutoff.

Special Wine & Other Events: Texas Wine Country Chili Cookoff, second weekend of May. Chili cooks from throughout the nation compete for title of world's champion. Entrants lavishly wined, dined, and entertained by winery staff. Proceeds from event go to local police department. All-Texas Grape Stompin' Contest in September.

&. A number of wine greats figure in Smith's success. Consultant André Tchelistcheff advised on the vineyard's location ("wherever peaches and native grapes thrive") in the peach bowl of Texas, while noted Californians Mike Mondavi and John Parducci, and Philip Wagner of Maryland's Boordy Vineyards, counseled Smith on growing and making wines. To top it off, he studied sparkling wine production in the famous champagne cellars at Epernay, France, as well as at the University of California at Davis—the latter also attended by his winemaker son, Steve. Located in a metal barn, the winery is anything but lavish. It's clear here that all the money goes into the best equipment and grapes needed to make great wines.

TO SEE & DO

Winery is located in Veal's Station, one of the oldest communities in Texas; near the winery is a tree from which four women were hung for suspected Union Army connections during the Civil War. Springtown was named for the artesian springs that once flowed from the ground. Weatherford, fifteen miles to the south, is actress Mary Martin's home, and the birthplace of both son Larry Hagman (TV's "Dallas") and his brother, who practices law there today.

&. &. &.

High Plains

Llano Estacado Winery

FM 1585 (P.O. Box 3487)
Lubbock, Texas 79452
TEL: 806-745-2258
OWNER: Llano Estacado, Inc.
PRESIDENT: John Lowey
WINEMAKER: Don M. Brady (trained at both Napa Valley School of Cellaring and UC-Davis)
FOUNDED: 1976

AT A GLANCE

Tours & Tastings: Mon.–Sat. 10–4, Sun. 12–4. Guided tours give comprehensive look at winemaking and conclude with tasting.
Closed: Thanksgiving, Christmas.
Vineyards: Six acres planted to *Vitis vi-* *nifera;* additional grapes purchased from Lubbock growers.
Wines: Most important vintage-dated, vineyard-designated varietals are Chardonnay, Chenin Blanc, Johannisberg Riesling, Cabernet Sauvignon, Gewürztraminer, Fumé Blanc, Sauvignon Blanc, Rosé of Cabernet.
Awards: Double gold to 1984 Chardonnay at 1986 San Francisco Fair Exposition and Wine Competition; gold to 1983 Cabernet Sauvignon; silver to 1984 Johannisberg Riesling; Star of Texas Grand Award to 1983 Gewürztraminer.
Retail Shop: Wines sold on-site.
Credit Cards: MasterCard, Visa.
Access for Disabled: One level, no stairs.
Foreign Languages: Spanish.
Getting There: Take U.S. 87 South to

FM1585; turn east for 3.2 miles to winery on this road.

Special Wine & Other Events: Participates in Lubbock International Wine Festival in Sept.

&. While sixteenth-century explorer Francisco Vásquez de Coronado never found lost cities of gold in these plains, Llano Estacado struck gold twice—in San Francisco with a double gold medal for its 1984 Chardonnay at the 1986 Fair Exposition and Wine Competition. This was the first major national award won by a Texas winery and one of eleven double golds given in a field of 1,955 at the fair. And to think how people laughed when they heard there was a wine grower in Lubbock, the cotton-producing capital of Texas!

Llano Estacado was the first new Texas winery bonded after repeal of Prohibition, and its first wines were made in the basement by Texas Tech professors Bob Reed and C. M. MacPherson while experimenting with "patio grapes." Now, as one of the state's largest wineries, and often cited as among the most promising, its spacious tasting room is built so visitors can see both the winery at work and the vineyards. But it's far more educational to go on the tour; among other things, you learn that *Llano Estacado* is Spanish for "staked plains" and refers to Coronado's practice of driving wooden stakes along his route as he conducted his fruitless search for golden cities.

&. &. &.

Pheasant Ridge Winery

1505 Elkart Avenue (Route 3, Box 191)
Lubbock, Texas 79401
TEL: 806-746-6033
OWNERS: Bobby and Jennifer Cox
WINEMAKER: Bobby Cox
FOUNDED: 1978

AT A GLANCE

Tours & Tastings: By appointment only.
Vineyards: Forty acres planted to vinifera varieties.
Wines: Important wines are Cabernet Sauvignon, Chardonnay, Chenin Blanc, Barbera, Sauvignon Blanc.
Awards: Oft-awarded Cabernet Sauvignon received a gold to a 1983 release at the 1986 San Francisco Fair Exposition and Wine Competition. All other wines above have snapped up medals. Multi-award winners are Chenin Blanc, Chardonnay, Sauvignon Blanc; Barbera has received a silver.
Picnic Area: Near grape arbor.
Retail Shop: No wines sold here. Try the package stores.
Credit Cards: None.
Access for Disabled: None.
Foreign Languages: Spanish.
Getting There: Take U.S. 87 North to blinking yellow light in New Deal at FM 1729; on Farm Road head east for two miles and south one mile.
Special Wine & Other Events: Participates in Lubbock International Wine Festival in Sept.

&. This family-run vineyard/winery takes its name from the many ring-necked pheasants that roam and roost hereabouts. Originally an amateur winemaker, Bobby Cox turned commercial in 1982 after several seasons of selling grapes to other winemakers. To hone his craft, Cox has taken courses at the University of California at Davis.

TO SEE & DO
Famous sights include the art exhibits at the Tech Museum, where a typical old plains windmill is the focal point of the rotunda (4th Street and Indiana Avenue; tel: 806-742-2136). On adjoining land is the Ranching Heritage Center, the world's most complete collection of authentic ranch structures, from pioneer days on (tel: 806-742-2498). MacKenzie

State Park is another Lubbock attraction, with everything from swimming to golf to camping to a prairie dog town (four miles east on Broadway to Park Road 18; tel: 806-762-6411).

ACCOMMODATIONS

Holiday Inn—Civic Center
801 Avenue Q
Lubbock, Texas 79401
Tel: 806-763-1200; 800-HOLIDAY
Two-hundred-ninety-five-room hotel with pool, exercise room, and all amenities.

Lubbock Inn
Nineteenth Street
Lubbock, Texas 79401
Tel: 806-792-5181
Better-than-average. One hundred forty-seven rooms and heated pool.

RESTAURANTS
All in Lubbock.

Depot Restaurant and Bar
19th and Avenue G
Tel: 806-747-1646
Victorian decor in an old train depot. Hearty dishes.

Giorgio's
1901 University Avenue
Tel: 806-747-2583
On the top floor of the Texas Bank Building, with views of the city.

Jeremiah's
3838 50th Street
Tel: 806-793-1919
Continental menu with prime rib and fresh fish as specialties.

West Texas

Bluebonnet Hill Winery

Highway 67 South
Ballinger, Texas 76821
TEL: 915-365-3507
OWNER: Dr. Antoine Robert Albert
WINEMAKER: Helmut Schmitt
FOUNDED: 1985

AT A GLANCE
Tours & Tastings: Mon.–Fri. 7–5.
Vineyards: Twenty acres owned and seventy leased, all vinifera.
Wines: White Riesling, Gewürztraminer, Chardonnay, Cabernet Sauvignon, Sauvignon Blanc, Merlot; proprietary blends.
Awards: Riesling and Texas White—first releases—won silver and bronze respectively at Houston Club Show.
Retail Shop: None.
Credit Cards: None.
Access for Disabled: Everything on one level.

Foreign Languages: French, German when winemaker is present.
Getting There: Bluebonnet Hill is thirty-five miles east of San Angelo and fifty-five miles south of Abilene. On east side of Hwy. 67S, 2 miles west of Ballinger on frontage road; 3.4 miles west of courthouse. Easy to see from road.
Special Wine & Other Events: Annual Wine Festival, mid-May; monthly seminars in association with leased vineyards.

&. Before the turn of the century, the California Company grew many kinds of fruit where Bluebonnet Hill now stands, but no one is able to say if grapes were among them. Today, family practitioner Dr. Antoine Albert, a transplanted French Canadian, considers himself a pioneer grapegrower in this part of Texas.

Dr. Albert and his wife, Danielle, visited vineyards in Europe and California before putting in their vines. Their

German-trained winemaker, Helmut Schmitt, has made Riesling among Bluebonnet Hill's most well regarded wines. The winery is named for the ubiquitous bluebonnets that cover the fields each spring.

TO SEE & DO
The notable landmark hereabouts is historic Fort Concho, thirty-five miles west of Ballinger in San Angelo, the base of MacKenzie's Raiders years ago (213 East Avenue D; tel: 915-657-4441)

ACCOMMODATION
Kiva Inn
5403 South First Street
Abilene, Texas 79605
Tel: 915-695-2150
Two hundred and one rooms, pool, restaurant, putting green.

RESTAURANTS

In Abilene
The Library at Kiva Inn
5403 South First Street
Located in the Kiva Inn

Another West Texas winery:

≈ ≈ ≈

Ste. Genevieve Vineyards

Fort Stockton, Texas 79735
Office: 7312 South I-35
        Austin, Texas 78745
TEL: 915-417-9555
OWNERS: Sanchez, Gil, Richter, Cordier, Ltd. (a French company)
The state's largest winery, on 1,018 acres in the mesas of West Texas, has storage for 1.4 million gallons. Tours for groups by appointment. Call to see if visitors can join a scheduled group if you're traveling west on I-10 near Fort Stockton. Nearest big city is Midland, and the prettiest time to visit is during budbreak in April and May.

East Texas

Messina Hof

Route 7, Box 905
Bryan, Texas 77802
TEL: 409-778-9463
OWNERS: Paul and Merrill Bonarrigo
WINEMAKER: Paul Bonarrigo
FOUNDED: 1983

AT A GLANCE
Tours & Tastings: One-hour guided tours, first and third Sat. of each month, reservation required (maximum twenty-five people, so phone early). Includes a tasting of five wines in your own "Taste of Texas" gift glass; video cassette showing harvest (special harvest tours are also available); visit to vineyard; as well as lesson in how wine is made, stored, and

appreciated. Tastings only, Mon.–Fri. 8–4:30; weekends by appointment.
Closed: First week of Jan.
Vineyards: Thirty acres planted primarily to vinifera varieties; some American Lenoir.
Wines: Chardonnay, Chenin Blanc, Cabernet Blush, Muscat Canelli, Johannisberg Riesling, Sauvignon Blanc, White Zinfandel; vintage port, proprietary blends in red, rosé, white. Blush is a best-seller.
Awards: Total of forty in state and international competitions; examples include gold-medal-winning Chardonnay, and a rich port judged "Best of the Southwest." Oft-awarded: Texas Cabernet, Chenin Blanc, Zinfandel.

Picnic Area: Idyllic, borders two-acre lake.

Retail Shop: Wines, gift items.

Credit Cards: MasterCard, Visa.

Access for Disabled: Ramps to front door, winery, and tasting room.

Foreign Languages: None.

Getting There: From Houston (ninety miles northwest): Take U.S. 6 North to exit at Hwy. 21, travel east two miles to Wallis Rd. and follow signs to winery. En route stop at Washington-on-the-Brazos State Historical Park for a leg-stretcher. The winery is also ninety miles northeast of Austin; and 150 miles away from either Dallas or San Antonio. Accessible by taxi from Bryan. Bike rental in Bryan; small airport adjacent estate.

Special Wine & Other Events: From Aug.–June, Messina Hof hosts many events to celebrate harvest, vintage days, Christmas, and more, from classy black-tie dinners to down-home grape-stompin' meets. Call or write for calendar of events.

  Messina Hof, Texas's fifth largest wine producer, is named for the Sicilian and Bavarian towns from which the ancestors of the owners Merrill and Paul Bonarrigo came. The couple made 2,500 cases from their first crush and now produce 10,000 to 12,000 cases a year. At a typical Messina Hof tasting/tour, visitors are invited into the Bonarrigos' handsome home, constructed of river rock, with antique furnishings and flowing fountain, and get lessons in how to make, store, taste, and serve wines.

Messina Hof also has a six-room bed and breakfast in a Victorian manor house the Bonarrigos dismantled and moved from Bryan. They expect it to be open for guests by Christmas 1989.

TO SEE & DO

In Bryan and College Station make a beeline for the antique stores—the directory is widely available at shops in both towns. Local artists' works can be seen in downtown Bryan and in College Station art galleries. For a pleasant stroll, Bryan's historic home district is west of 25th Street and south of Main Street. The garden district is north of Bryan.

College Station is the site of Texas A & M University (Highway 60 at Texas Avenue); information on touring the campus is available at Rudder Center. College Station is also famous for the Texas World Speedway (Highway 6, south of College Station), rated the fastest in the world.

Prime picnic spots? In Bryan, Country Club Lake and Picnic Pavillion, South College Avenue and Rountree; in College Station, Central Park at west side frontage road of East Bypass 6 and Krenek Tap. For more information, contact the Chamber of Commerce Visitors Bureau, 715 University Drive East, College Station, Texas 77840 (tel: 409-260-9898).

ACCOMMODATIONS

For bed and breakfast recommendations, contact:

The Bed & Breakfast Society of Texas
921 Heights Boulevard
Houston, Texas 77008
Tel: 713-868-4654
Covers entire state.

In Bryan/College Station—hotels, motels, inns. If heading here during any of the big college weekends, book well in advance.

Hilton
801 University Drive East
Tel: 409-693-7500; 800-HILTONS
College Station, Texas 77840
Serves Messina Hof wines in the Sandpiper Restaurant. All Hiltonesque conveniences and a conference center.

La Quinta
607 South Texas Avenue
College Station, Texas 77840
Tel: 409-696-7777
One hundred seventy-six rooms, pool, and above-average restaurant.

Ramada Inn
410 South Texas Avenue
College Station, Texas 77840
Tel: 409-696-4242; 800-2-RAMADA
Three-hundred-room motor hotel.
Also serves Messina Hof wines in the restaurant.

RESTAURANTS
Check with winery for latest names of restaurants serving Messina Hof wines. They are too numerous to list here.

Southwestern Texas

Val Verde Winery

139 Hudson Drive
Del Rio, Texas 78840
TEL: 512-775-9714
FOUNDED: 1883
OWNER/WINEMAKER: Thomas M. Qualia

AT A GLANCE
Tours & Tastings: Mon.–Sat. 9–5; tours upon request from tasting room staff, include tasting and history of winery.
Closed: Sun., holidays.
Vineyards: Total of thirty acres, includes twelve behind the winery and the remainder thirty miles south of town; all planted to Herbemont and Lenoir. Small experimental patch near winery planted to vinifera. Other grapes purchased from West Texas growers.
Wines: Herbemont, Lenoir, Chardonnay, Chenin Blanc, Johannisberg Riesling, Cabernet Sauvignon, Cabernet Blanc, Cabernet and Lenoir rosés; Tawny Port.
Awards: Tawny Port, Lenoir, Rosé of Lenoir, Johannisberg Riesling, Cabernet Sauvignon.
Retail Shop: Wines, gifts.
Credit Cards: None.
Access for Disabled: No. "But there's always someone to help."
Foreign Languages: Spanish.
Getting There: Del Rio is in southwestern Texas, on the Rio Grande. From downtown Del Rio: Take Pecan Street for a pleasant walk south to winery at 139 Hudson Dr. Historical Walking Tour of downtown Del Rio includes winery.

❧ Founded in 1883 by a Milanese, Frank Qualia, Val Verde is the oldest winery in Texas and is now owned and operated by Tommy Qualia, the third generation to carry on the tradition. He describes the historic winery, with eighteen-inch-thick adobe walls, surrounded by pecans and palms, as an "oasis in old Del Rio." For visitors, the old building is fascinating for its display of both antique and modern winemaking equipment. With the help of Italian-trained winemaker Dr. Enrique Ferro, Val Verde has moved into European-style wines—with good results. The first vinifera wine, a Johannisberg Riesling, released to honor the winery's centennial, is an award-winner.

TO SEE & DO
Head thirty miles northwest along U.S. 90 to see the Seminole Canyon Caves, with ancient pictographs dating back 9,000 years; continue another sixty miles to Langtry, site of the Judge Roy Bean Saloon and Museum. Just ten miles away via U.S. 90 is International Lake Amistad, which spreads over some seventy miles, splashing into Mexico and offering some great fishing and water sports. South of Del Rio is the Mexican border town of Ciudad Acuna.

ACCOMMODATIONS
Amistad Lodge
Box 29, HCR3
Del Rio, Texas 78840
Tel: 512-775-8591

On Amistad Lake; pool, café, bar; entertainment on weekends. Free airport transportation.

Ramada Inn
2101 Avenue F
Del Rio, Texas 78840
Tel: 512-775-1511; 800-2-RAMADA
Ninety-seven rooms. Pool, café, bar, dancing. Free airport, bus, railway station transportation. Two and one-half miles north on U.S. 90W.

RESTAURANTS
Applegate's Landing
2211 Avenue F
Del Rio, Texas 78840
Tel: 512-774-3645
Mesquite-grilled entrées, Mexican and Cajun specialties.

8
California
🐦

Jordan Vineyards and Winery, Healdsburg, California

🐦*B*ecause Spanish padres spread grapes along with the gospel, winemaking in this state goes back nearly two centuries. In 1798, ten out of thirteen missions already had vineyards. Thirty years later, Mission San Gabriel alone boasted an annual production of 400 barrels. When the Mexican general Mariano Vallejo secularized the missions, commercial vintners replaced the holy fathers at the wine press, and output increased dramatically. By 1860, thirsty gold miners helped boost California to third place among the country's wine-producing states.

The gold rush duly faded, but the wine crush has endured to this day. It's impossible to discuss American vintages without mentioning the Eureka State. Of 101 federally designated viticultural areas, 57 are located here, with another 4 applications pending. All in all, more than three-quarters of the nation's wine is produced in this one state.

California can be divided into nine distinct wine regions: the Central Valley, Lake and Mendocino counties, Napa County, the North-Central Coast, San Francisco Bay, the Sierra Foothills, Sonoma County, the South-Central Coast, and Southern California. Each region contains at least a few microclimates, so

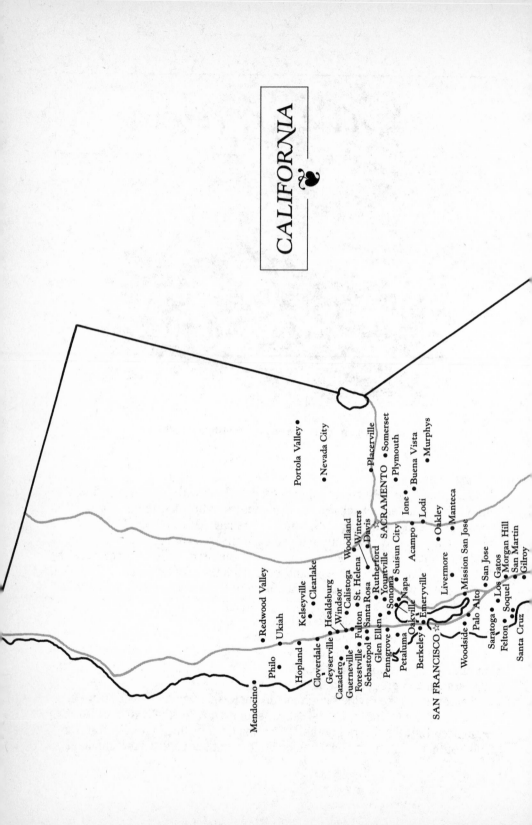

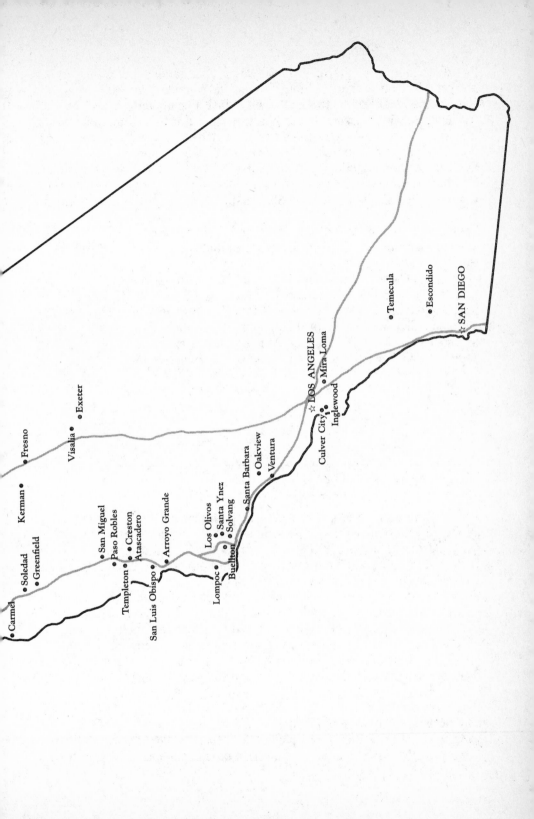

that all of Europe's great winemaking districts have parallels here. This fact has not been lost on formerly snooty Continental vintners, who are paying the state's wineries the ultimate compliment of investing in them.

Wherever you're headed, there is a wide selection of bed and breakfasts, from rustic farmhouses to restored Victorian mansions. In general, two restrictions apply: most California B&Bs ban smoking and children under twelve. Different regions celebrate wine with fairs, festivals, and auctions; some of the best-known events include:

Central Valley: Lodi Spring Wine Show (April), Lodi Grape Festival (September).

Lake County: Lake County Wine and Food Festival (June).

Mendocino County: Mendocino County Fair and Apple Show (September).

Napa County: Napa County Wine Auction (June).

Sierra Foothills: Shenandoah Valley Grape Festival (September).

Sonoma County: Sonoma County Wine Auction (August), Russian River Wine Road Barrel Tasting (March), Russian River Wine Road Wine Festival (May), Sonoma Valley Vintage Festival (September).

South-Central Coast: Paso Robles Wine Festival (May).

Southern California: Temecula Balloon and Wine Festival (May).

❧ CENTRAL VALLEY

This area sprawls more than half the length of inland California, from Sacramento down to the Tehachapi Mountains. Were the Central Valley an independent nation, its 550,000 acres of plantings would make it the world's thirteenth largest grape grower. Some of those grapes are dried rather than crushed; Fresno is to raisins what Newcastle is to coal.

Overshadowed by its northerly neighbors Napa and Sonoma, this region has its own proud history. Stockton boasted several thriving wineries by the mid-1800s; a century later, Lodi was famed for sherry production. Today, the wineries here range from tiny family operations to the enormous Modesto plant of Ernest and Julio Gallo, which is not open to the public (and is therefore not listed in this book). Lodi and Madera are among the localities bearing federal designation as viticultural areas.

This region is warm, even by California standards. In some places, harvest may begin as early as June; blistering midsummer temperatures force some winegrowers to schedule grape picking for evenings. Predictably, Mediterranean varietals thrive here. So plan a spring or fall visit, and toast your travels with wines like Zinfandel, Carignane, and French Colombard.

ૐ ૐ ૐ

Anderson Wine Cellars

20147 Avenue 306
Exeter, California 93221
TEL: 209-592-4682
OWNERS: Don and Cathy Anderson
FOUNDED: 1980

AT A GLANCE
Tours & Tastings: Summer, open daily
10:30–5; winter, weekends only.
Vineyards: Twenty acres planted to
Colombard, Ruby Cabernet. Table
grapes also grown here.
Wines: Colombard, Ruby Cabernet,
Ruby Cabernet Blush.
Retail Shop: Wines, natural juices sold
on-site.
Credit Cards: MasterCard, Visa.
Access for Disabled: None.
Foreign Languages: Spanish.
Getting There: Winery is eleven miles
east of Visalia on Hwy. 198.

ૐ "Anderson is the only small winery
in Tulare County."

ૐ ૐ ૐ

Bianchi Vineyards

5806 North Modoc Avenue
Kerman, California 93630
TEL: 209-846-7356
MANAGING GENERAL PARTNER: Joseph
  Bianchi
FOUNDED: 1974

AT A GLANCE
Tours & Tastings: Mon.–Fri. 8:30–3. No
tours.
Closed: Weekends, holidays.
Vineyards: 358 acres planted to
Thompson, Chenin Blanc, Zinfandel,
French Colombard.
Wines: French Colombard, Chenin
Blanc, Chardonnay, Grenache Rosé,

Chablis, Burgundy, White Zinfandel, Red
Zinfandel, Sauvignon Blanc.
Retail Shop: Wines, as well as red, white,
citrus, and de-alcoholized coolers sold
on-site.
Credit Cards: None.
Access for Disabled: Entrance ramp to
office.
Getting There: Winery is sixteen miles
west of Fresno, along the San Joaquin
River. Take Hwy. 180 to Kerman and
bear right on Modoc Ave. Winery is on
the right, after Shaw Ave.

ૐ "We are miles away from any city,
in the tiny hamlet of Vinland. Kerman is
our mailing address." The 400-foot
Gothic tower at the center of this winery
has become a distinctive trademark, and
it also affords a spectacular view of the
countryside. Grape vineyards stretch
across the valley in every direction, as far
as the eye can see. To sample Bianchi
wines in a maritime setting, visit the tasting room aboard the *Queen Mary*, per-
manently docked in Long Beach.

ૐ ૐ ૐ

Chateau De Leu

1635 West Mason Road
Suisun, California 94585
TEL: 707-823-2488
PRESIDENT: Keith W. Lamb
WINEMAKER: Scott Devitt
FOUNDED: 1981

AT A GLANCE
Tours & Tastings: Open daily 10–4:30.
"Informal tours anytime."
Vineyards: Forty acres planted to Pinot
Noir, French Colombard, Chardonnay,
Sauvignon Blanc, Chenin Blanc.
Wines: Chardonnay, Sauvignon Blanc,
Chenin Blanc, French Colombard, White
Pinot Noir.
Awards: Golds, silvers, and bronzes for
Chardonnays, Fumé Blanc, and French
Colombard in state competitions.

Retail Shop: Wines sold on-site.
Credit Cards: MasterCard, Visa.
Access for Disabled: To main floor only; tasting room is upstairs.
Getting There: Winery is forty-six miles northeast of San Francisco, off I-80. Call for directions.

&. Chateau De Leu enjoys a panoramic view of the aptly named Green Valley. This choice site has been steadily cultivated by grape growers since 1882; the present vineyards were planted in the 1950s.

&. &. &.

Cribari Winery

3223 East Church Avenue
Fresno, California 93725
TEL: 209-485-3080
PRESIDENT: Gerry Pasterick
FOUNDED: 1904

AT A GLANCE
Tours & Tastings: Open daily 10–5. Guided tours at 10, 11, 1, 2, and 3 show how wine and brandy are made.
Closed: Easter, Thanksgiving, Christmas.
Vineyards: None. Grapes purchased from local growers.
Wines: Cabernet Sauvignon, Chardonnay, Zinfandel, White Zinfandel, White Gamay, White Cabernet, Chenin Blanc, Chablis, Blush Chablis, Burgundy, Chianti; champagne; port, white port, Marsala, Madeira, sherry.
Awards: Recent medals include two silvers to extra-dry champagne; silver, bronze to brandy; silver to 1984 White Zinfandel; bronze to 1984 Chenin Blanc.
Retail Shop: All wines—including brandy, port, sherry—sold on-site.
Credit Cards: MasterCard, Visa.
Access for Disabled: All winery areas accommodate wheelchairs.
Getting There: Winery is in Fresno. From Hwy. 99: Take Ventura St. exit to Golden State Blvd. and turn left at Church Ave.

&. Ten years after Italian immigrant Beniamino Cribari began making his own table wine, he found himself at the helm of a booming family enterprise, his vintages served at fine San Francisco restaurants. Today a third generation of Cribaris carries on the traditions established by their grandfather.

&. &. &.

Delicato Vineyards

12001 South Highway 99
Manteca, California 95336
TEL: 209-239-1215, 982-0679
PRESIDENT: Anthony Indelicato
FOUNDED: 1935

AT A GLANCE
Tours & Tastings: Open 9–5:30 daily. Tours take place on Fri. at 10, 2, and 4; minitours are given during crush season.
Closed: New Year's Day, Washington's Birthday, Easter, Memorial Day, July 4th, Labor Day, Thanksgiving, Christmas.
Vineyards: 365 acres planted to Cabernet Sauvignon, Chardonnay, Green Hungarian, Petite Sirah, Zinfandel, Chenin Blanc. Olives and prunes also grown here. Additional grapes purchased from growers within a 100-mile radius of winery.
Wines: Chablis, White Zinfandel, Green Hungarian, Cabernet Sauvignon Rosé, Zinfandel, Barberone, Cabernet Sauvignon, Sweet Marie, Chardonnay, Sauvignon Blanc, Chenin Blanc, white Cabernet, Moselle, Petite Sirah, Burgundy, Sauterne; sherry, cream sherry, port, Zinfandel port; Sangria.
Awards: Most Delicato wines have won medals in recent California judgings.
Picnic Area: Nearby sites at Carter's Trout Farm, 10583 South Airport Way, and Oakwood Lake, 874 East Woodward, both in Manteca.
Retail Shop: Wines, grape juices, and gifts sold on-site.

Credit Cards: American Express, Diner's Club, MasterCard, Visa.
Access for Disabled: Parking lot and rest rooms wheelchair accessible; ramp leads to front door.
Foreign Languages: Italian, Spanish.
Getting There: Winery is ninety miles east of San Francisco and sixty miles south of Sacramento. From I-5: Take French Camp exit and proceed east, toward Hwy. 99.
Special Wine & Other Events: Annual Labor Day Weekend Grape Stomp benefits local charities, as competitors see who can generate the most grape juice in ninety seconds.

&. In 1924, Gaspare Indelicato—father of the three current owners—and his brother-in-law planted a vineyard, selling the harvest to home winemakers. When Prohibition ended, the two men bought a used crusher and set up a winery, with assorted small vats purchased from their neighbors. A half century later, the Indelicatos are still in business.

&. &. &.

Heritage Cellars

2310 South Railroad Avenue
Fresno, California 93721
TEL: 209-442-8452
PRESIDENT: Marvin Riding
FOUNDED: 1983

AT A GLANCE
Tours & Tastings: Open daily 10–5. Tours given on request. Cheese trays can be ordered to accompany complimentary wine tasting.
Closed: Thanksgiving, Christmas.
Vineyards: None. All grapes purchased from California growers.
Wines: Cabernet Sauvignon, Chardonnay, White Zinfandel, Zinfandel, Sauvignon Blanc, French Colombard; California brandy.

Restaurant: Luncheon served in winery restaurant Mon.–Fri. 11–2; moderately priced menu includes homemade breads and soups. Special dinners by appointment only.
Retail Shop: Wines, brandy, deli supplies, and gifts sold on-site.
Credit Cards: American Express, MasterCard, Visa.
Access for Disabled: None.
Getting There: Winery is near downtown Fresno. From Hwy. 99: Take Ventura St. exit to Golden State Blvd. Make a left on Church St., left again on Railroad Ave.

&. Marvin Riding supplied winemakers with crushing and bottling machinery for twenty years before buying and renovating Heritage Cellars, a Mediterranean-style winery originally established in 1921.

&. &. &.

Lost Hills Winery

3125 East Orange Street (P.O. Box C)
Acampo, California 95220
TEL: 209-369-2746
PRESIDENT: Herbert R. Benham, Jr.
WINEMAKER: Neal Overboe (B.S., UC-Davis)
FOUNDED: 1981

AT A GLANCE
Tours & Tastings: Open daily 9–5. No tours.
Closed: Easter, Thanksgiving, Christmas.
Vineyards: None. Grapes purchased from all over California.
Wines: White Zinfandel, Blanc de Blanc, Chardonnay, Grey Riesling, Chenin Blanc, Sauvignon Blanc, Johannisberg Riesling, Beaujolais Blanc, Cabernet Blanc, Blanc de Noir, Cabernet Sauvignon, Burgundy, Zinfandel, Chablis. Also May wine, spiced wine, My Zin (sparkling white Zinfandel), Cremapri.

Awards: Numerous awards taken at state and county fairs every year.
Picnic Area: With barbecue facilities.
Retail Shop: Wines sold on-site.
Credit Cards: MasterCard, Visa.
Access for Disabled: Tasting room accommodates wheelchairs.
Foreign Languages: Some Spanish and Italian.
Getting There: Winery is thirty-five miles south of Sacramento and two miles north of Lodi. From Hwy. 99: Take Acampo Rd. exit and travel west about one mile. Immediately after crossing railroad tracks, turn right.

&ea; You can't get disoriented en route to Lost Hills—the winery's brandy tower, which houses an old-fashioned, inactive distillery, can be seen for miles around. Tall palm trees line the road that leads to the tasting room door.

&ea; &ea; &ea;

The Lucas Winery

18196 North Davis Road
Lodi, California 95240
TEL: 209-368-2006
OWNERS: David and Tamara Lucas
FOUNDED: 1978

AT A GLANCE
Tours & Tastings: Open, by appointment.
Vineyards: Thirty acres planted to Zinfandel.
Wines: Zinfandel, White Zinfandel.
Retail Shop: Wine sold on-site.
Credit Cards: None.
Access for Disabled: Limited wheelchair access.
Getting There: Winery is in Lodi, 2½ hours from Lake Tahoe. From Hwy. 99: Take Turner Rd. west to Davis Rd. and bear right. From I-5: Take Hwy. 12 East to Davis Rd. and bear left.
Special Wine & Other Events: New releases debut at the Lodi Spring Wine

Show in Apr.; the harvest is celebrated at the Lodi Grape Festival in Sept.

&ea; "At the Lucas Winery we make wines from just one varietal, Zinfandel; our vines were planted more than sixty years ago," explains Tamara Lucas. "Each year, we produce fewer than 900 cases. We enjoy showing people our winery, and a tour can be arranged by appointment. Call and visit us soon."

&ea; &ea; &ea;

The R. H. Phillips Winery

1230-A Churchill Downs (P.O. Box 2468)
Woodland, California 95695
TEL: 916-661-6115, 662-3215
OWNERS: John, Karl, and Chris
    Giguiere; Clark Smith
WINEMAKER: Clark Smith (B.S. in
    fermentation science from UC-Davis,
    working on master's thesis in
    enology)
FOUNDED: 1983

AT A GLANCE
Tours & Tastings: Open by appointment.
Vineyards: 250 acres planted to Sémillon, Sauvignon Blanc, Chardonnnay, Zinfandel, Chenin Blanc, French Colombard.
Wines: Sémillon, Sauvignon Blanc, Chardonnay, Zinfandel, Chenin Blanc.
Awards: Recent medals include gold, silver, two bronzes to 1985 Chardonnay; silver, bronze to 1985 White Zinfandel; silver, bronze to 1983 Cabernet Sauvignon; and silver, two bronzes to 1984 Sémillon.
Retail Shop: Wines sold on-site.
Credit Cards: None.
Access for Disabled: No stairs or other obstructions.
Getting There: Phillips is near Sacramento. From I-80: Take Hwy 505 North thirty miles to County Rd. 14 and turn left. Continue three miles to stop sign.

Bear right on County Rd. 87 and go to end of road.

&. John and Karl Giguiere established this winery on the family ranch where their grandfather, the eponymous R. H. Phillips, once farmed wheat. To beat the September heat and keep pulp temperatures low, the Giguieres hit on a novel solution: hand-harvesting grapes at night. The result is dry, delicate wines without any hint of bitterness.

&. &. &.

Quady Winery

13181 Road 24
Madera, California 93637
TEL: 209-673-8068
PRESIDENT: Andrew K. Quady (M.S. in food science with an enology specialization, UC-Davis)
FOUNDED: 1977

AT A GLANCE
Tours & Tastings: Open Mon.–Fri. 8–5; weekends by appointment.
Closed: Legal holidays.
Vineyards: None. Grapes purchased from Amador County growers.
Wines: California dessert wines—Essensia (Orange Muscat), Elysium (black Muscat), port.
Awards: 1985 Essensia: gold; 1985 Elysium: gold; 1982 Vintage Port: gold.
Retail Shop: Wines sold on-site.
Credit Cards: Visa.
Access for Disabled: First floor and bathrooms accommodate wheelchairs.
Getting There: Winery is in San Joaquin Valley, twenty miles north of Fresno. From Hwy. 99 in Madera: Take Rd. 23 offramp to Ave. 14 and turn left. In one mile, turn right on Rd. 24.

&. Andrew Quady's winery is as distinctive as his award-winning wines: His new plant, a dramatic barnlike building with rose-colored stucco walls and a blue enameled-metal roof, has been written up in *Architectural Record*.

&. &. &.

Satiety

1027 Maple Lane
Davis, California 95616
TEL: 916-757-2699, 661-0680
OWNER: Sterling Chaykin
FOUNDED: 1981

AT A GLANCE
Tours & Tastings: Open daily 1–5. Informal tours of vineyard, winery, and tasting room. Winemaker conducts tours on weekends.
Vineyards: Twenty-nine owned and twenty-one leased acres planted to Cabernet Sauvignon, French Colombard, Chenin Blanc, Orange Muscat. Table grapes also grown here.
Wines: Red, white, and rosé table wines.
Awards: 1984 white: gold; 1984 red: bronze; 1985 red: bronze.
Retail Shop: Wines and wine vinegar sold on site.
Credit Cards: None.
Access for Disabled: Ground-level entry, fully outfitted for wheelchairs.
Getting There: Winery is ten miles north of Davis and twenty miles west of Sacramento. From I-80 in Davis: take Hwy. 113 to Rd. 25A and bear right.

&. Vineyardists Sterling and Elaine Chaykin sold their first harvest of table grapes at the Davis Farmers' Market in 1980; the following year they began manufacturing wine vinegar. Table wine production commenced in 1983 in a winery the couple constructed themselves. "At Satiety, everything is done with great care and attention, from the growing of the grapes to the actual bottling of the wine. This is all possible because the entire process is under the Chaykins' personal control."

ન્જી ન્જી ન્જી

Schumacher Cellars

721 Barcelona
Davis, California 95616
TEL: 916-758-1052
PROPRIETOR: John C. Schumacher
  (degree in fermentation science, UC-
  Davis)
FOUNDED: 1983

AT A GLANCE
Tours & Tastings: Open Mon.–Sat. 10–4.
"Quick tour by winemaker plus barrel
samples of fine wines to come."
Closed: Sun., holidays.
Vineyards: None. All grapes bought from
California growers. "Our contracted
vineyards are in selected northern California locations that enhance the specific varietal's characteristics."
Wines: Sauvignon Blanc, Chardonnay,
Cabernet Sauvignon, Pinot Noir, Zinfandel.
Awards: 1984 Doe Mill Zinfandel:
bronze.
Retail Shop: Wines, T-shirts, and aprons
sold on-site.
Credit Cards: None.
Access for Disabled: None.
Getting There: Winery is in the northern
part of Davis. From Hwy. 113: take
Covell Blvd. exit and drive ¼ mile east.

ન્જી Schumacher began making wine at
home when he was in high school, then
decided to turn his hobby into a vocation. After attending UC-Davis, he
gained additional experience at wineries
in Napa Valley and the Santa Cruz
Mountains. This is a small winery devoted to producing vineyard-designated
wines.

ન્જી ન્જી ન્જી

Winters Winery

15 Main Street
Winters, California 95694
TEL: 916-795-3201
PRESIDENT: David R. Storm
FOUNDED: 1980

AT A GLANCE
Tours & Tastings: Open daily 10–5. Tours
by appointment only.
Closed: Easter, July 4th, Labor Day,
Thanksgiving, Christmas.
Vineyards: 7½ leased acres planted to Petite Sirah, Sauvignon Blanc, Sémillon.
Zinfandel grapes bought from Shenandoah Valley growers; Pinot Noir grapes
from Napa Valley.
Wines: Petite Sirah, Sauvignon Blanc, Pinot Noir, Zinfandel.
Awards: 1980 Zinfandel (Bin A): two silvers; 1980 Zinfandel (Bin B): bronze;
1981 Petite Sirah: bronze.
Retail Shop: Wines sold on-site.
Credit Cards: MasterCard, Visa.
Access for Disabled: Yes, except to the
cellar/aging room.
Getting There: Winery is eighty-five miles
northeast of San Francisco and forty
miles west of Sacramento. Take I-80 to
I-505 and head north twelve miles to
Winters.

ન્જી The winery, a brick masonry building, was constructed in 1876; the cool
underground cellars protect and nurture
the wines aging in French and American
oak. Because of the careful attention
given to each vintage, production is limited to 5,000 cases per year.

TO SEE & DO
Fresno is one of California's fastest growing cities, with several theaters, a
resident ballet company, and a symphony orchestra that gives weekend performances from October through April.
The animals are the stars at Fresno Zoo,
inside Roeding Park. During spring and
summer months, visit the flamingo

colony and watch fluffy baby birds emerge from their eggs. The Fresno Metropolitan Museum (1555 Van Ness Avenue) explores local traditions, while the Fresno Arts Center (2233 North First Street) exhibits area artists and craftspeople. Does an antiquarian shopping mall sound like a contradiction in terms? In the historic Tower District, Fulton's Folly (920 East Olive Avenue; tel: 209-268-3856) contains more than one hundred shops under its roof; the goods range from furniture and quilts to mason jars and knickknacks. While you're dwelling on the past, visit the Kearney Mansion Museum on Kearney Boulevard, the elegant estate built for—and named after—a turn-of-the-century Fresno raisin baron (for tour information, call 209-441-0862). In Lodi, to the north, the attractions include two municipal parks. Swim and boat at Lodi Lake, or stroll and picnic at Micke Grove Park. The latter also contains gardens and a small museum. Overshadowed by larger California cities, Sacramento, the state capital, is well worth visiting. Start with a free tour of the recently restored State Capitol (tel: 916-445-5200), its rotunda modeled after that of the U.S. Capitol in Washington, D.C. Nearby is Sutter's Fort State Historic Park (2701 L Street; tel: 916-445-4209), a replica of the settlement established in 1839 by Sacramento's founder, the German-born pioneer John Sutter. The park also incorporates the California State Indian Museum (2618 K Street). If you're loco over locomotives, make a stop at the California State Historic Railroad Museum (125 I Street; tel: 916-445-4209), where antique train cars await inspection; the Central Pacific Passenger Station, a nineteenth-century train terminal, has been reconstructed next door. For information about other historic buildings in the immediate area, contact the Visitor's Center, 1027–1031 Second Street (tel: 916-446-4314). Of special interest is nearby Davis, alma mater

of many American winemakers. The campus library and bookstore have excellent enology departments, so browse until you're sated.

ACCOMMODATIONS

Davis
The Partridge Inn
521 First Street
Davis, California 95616
Tel: 916-753-1211

Fresno
Fresno Hilton Hotel
1055 Van Ness Avenue
Fresno, California 93721
Tel: 209-485-9000; 800-HILTONS
Convenient downtown location. 194 rooms, with a pool and a coffee shop.

Picadilly Inn Shaw
2305 West Shaw Avenue
Fresno, California 93726
Tel: 209-226-3850
Spacious grounds in a quiet location. There are 203 units, many with refrigerators, all with air-conditioning and color TV. Pool and whirlpool, too.

Sheraton Smuggler's Inn
3737 North Blackstone Avenue
Fresno, California 93726
Tel: 209-226-2200, 800-325-3535
Deluxe accommodation with heated pool and exercise room.

Lodi
Lodi Motor Inn
1140 South Cherokee Lane
Lodi, California 95240
Tel: 209-334-6422
Sixty units, with TV and air-conditioning, plus a sauna, whirlpool, and small swimming pool.

Madera
Best Western Madera Valley Inn
317 North G Street
Madera, California 93637
Tel: 209-673-5164

Large rooms and all the usual motel comforts: air-conditioning, cable TV, swimming pool, coffee shop.

Stockton

Holiday Inn and Holidome
221 North Center
Stockton, California 95202
Tel: 209-466-3993
This Holiday Inn has a pleasant surprise—an indoor/outdoor pool, in addition to the anticipated comforts.

Stockton Hilton
2323 Grand Canal Boulevard
Stockton, California 95207
Tel: 209-957-9090, 800-HILTONS
A newly remodeled Hilton with a health club and shopping arcade.

Best Western Stockton Inn
4219 East Waterloo Road
Stockton, California 95205
Tel: 209-931-3131
Complete with restaurant, putting green, and pools for all types—wading, whirlpool, and swimming.

RESTAURANTS

Davis

Colette
802 Second Street
Davis, California 95616
Tel: 916-758-3377
A different menu every week.

Fresno and vicinity

Erna's Elderberry House
Victoria Lane
Oakhurst, California 93644
Tel: 209-683-6800
Savor French and European specialties in an elegant atmosphere. The tables are draped in damask linen and set with silver and crystal that sparkle in the candlelight. More casual, peasant-style suppers are served (Wed.–Fri.) in the wine cellar bar (which stocks local and imported vintages).

Harris Ranch
State Route 198 at I-5
Coalinga, California 93210
Tel: 209-935-0717; 800-942-2333
Ranch-fed beef and home-grown vegetables for first-rate steaks and salads. Tempting desserts, wine cellar, outdoor dining. Nice place to stay, too.

John Pardini's Greenhouse Restaurant
1440 East Shaw Avenue
Fresno, California 93726
Tel: 209-225-1041
Breakfast, lunch, and dinner. At $9.95 for four courses, the early evening supper is an excellent value. A harpist performs on Mon. and Tues. nights, and during Sun. brunch.

John Q's
Centre Plaza Holiday Inn
2233 Ventura Street
Fresno, California 93721
Tel: 209-268-1000
Continental cuisine, with an extensive list of California wines.

Lodi

Cask 'n' Cleaver
1230 West Kettleman Lane
Lodi, California 95240
Tel: 209-333-1554
The Cask pours local and other California wines.

Madera

The Vineyard Restaurant
605 South I Street
Madera, California 93637
Tel: 209-674-0923
Steaks and fish grilled to perfection over aromatic grapewood.

Ripon

Barnwood Restaurant and Deli
338 East Main Street
Ripon, California 95366
Tel: 209-599-4234

Stockton
Joe & Rick's Le Bistro
3121 West Benjamin Holt Drive
Marina Shopping Center
Stockton, California 95207

Tel: 209-951-8885
French-accented fish dishes, superb desserts.

&. LAKE AND MENDOCINO COUNTIES

California's northernmost wine region has been bearing fruit for more than a hundred years. By the 1850s, commercial grape growers were well entrenched in Mendocino's Ukiah Valley; less than two decades later, Lake County's first vineyards were planted. At the turn of the century, some 8,000 acres of grapes were under cultivation, and locally produced wines were winning international prizes. One of the most enthusiastic vineyardists was actress Lillie Langtry, who imported a Bordeaux vintner to make wine on her 4,200-acre Guenoc Valley ranch. (She'd be pleased to learn that Guenoc Valley is California's sixth oldest viticultural area.)

Although the wine was reliable, business was not. Falling prices and rising transportation costs had already crippled the Mendocino and Lake County wine industry when Prohibition destroyed it entirely. The rare visionary, like Adolph Parducci, bided his time (see below under Parducci Wine Cellars), but other winemakers turned their vineyards into fruit and nut orchards.

The late 1960s saw the rebirth of this historic winemaking region. With poetic justice, grape vines began displacing pear trees. Vintners have discovered distinct microclimates in each mountain, valley, and ridge. Many of these sites have attained v.a. status; in addition to Guenoc Valley, local viticultural areas include McDowell Valley, Clear Lake, and Mendocino. Share in this renaissance: sample the woods, the waterfront, and the wines they inspire.

&. &. &.

Blanc Vineyards

10200 West Road
Redwood Valley, California 95470
TEL: 707-485-7352
OWNERS: Robert and Marlys Blanc
FOUNDED: 1983

AT A GLANCE
Tours & Tastings: Open by appointment only.
Vineyards: 140 acres planted to Johannisberg Riesling, Zinfandel, Pinot Noir, Chardonnay, Cabernet Sauvignon, Sauvignon Blanc, Chenin Blanc, Gewürztraminer.

Wines: Cabernet Sauvignon, Cabernet Blanc, Sauvignon Blanc.
Awards: 1982 Cabernet Sauvignon: four bronzes; 1985 Cabernet Blanc: bronze.
Picnic Area: Yes.
Retail Shop: Wines sold on-site.
Credit Cards: None.
Access for Disabled: None.
Foreign Languages: Some Spanish.
Getting There: Winery is in Mendocino County, 100 miles north of San Francisco. From Ukiah: Go north on Hwy. 101 to School Way and turn right. After ⅓ mile, bear left on West Rd.
Special Wine & Other Events: Weibel Art and Wine Show in July, Weibel Harvest Party in Sept.

&❧ Plans call for future expansion, but for the time being, this family-owned winery produces about 2,000 cases of estate-bottled wines each year. Most of Blanc's harvest is sold to other local operations.

❧ ❧ ❧

Greenwood Ridge Vineyards

24555 Greenwood Road
Philo, California 95466
TEL: 707-877-3262, 895-2002
OWNER: Allan Green
FOUNDED: 1980

AT A GLANCE
Tours & Tastings: Open daily 10–6. Tours only by prior arrangement.
Closed: Christmas.
Vineyards: Eight acres planted to White Riesling, Merlot, Cabernet Sauvignon. Apples also grown here.
Wines: White Riesling, Merlot, Cabernet Sauvignon.
Awards: 1985 White Riesling: gold; 1984 White Riesling: two silvers, bronze; 1982 Cabernet Sauvignon: two silvers, five bronzes.

Picnic Area: Yes.
Retail Shop: Wines sold on-site.
Credit Cards: MasterCard, Visa.
Access for Disabled: Ramps and rest rooms accommodate wheelchairs.
Getting There: Winery is in Anderson Valley in Mendocino County, thirty miles southeast of the city of Mendocino. From Hwy. 101; Take Hwy. 128 through Boonville to Philo. Three miles past Philo turn left on Greenwood Rd., also known as Hwy. 132. Winery is in approximately seven miles.
Special Wine & Other Events: Greenwood Ridge sponsors the California Wine Tasting Championships the last weekend of July. Contestants vie in identifying California wines by varietal; novices, amateurs, and professionals try their palates in separate categories.

&❧ Greenwood Ridge Vineyards deliberately limits production to 2,000 cases a year, but every drop counts—the Rieslings have been winning awards since the very first release.

❧ ❧ ❧

Handley Cellars

3151 Highway 128 (P.O. Box 66)
Philo, California 95466
TEL: 707-895-3876
GENERAL PARTNER/WINEMAKER: Milla Handley (enology degree from UC-Davis)
FOUNDED: 1982

AT A GLANCE
Tours & Tastings: Open daily 10–5. Tours by appointment only.
Closed: Easter, Thanksgiving, Christmas, New Year's Day.
Vineyards: Ten acres planted to Pinot Noir, Chardonnay. Additional grapes purchased from growers in Mendocino and Sonoma counties.

Wines: Chardonnay, *methode champenoise* sparkling wines.
Awards: 1982 Chardonnay: gold, bronze; 1984 Chardonnay: silver.
Retail Shop: Wines sold on-site.
Credit Cards: MasterCard, Visa.
Access for Disabled: Tasting room and winery accommodate wheelchairs.
Getting There: Winery is in Anderson Valley in Mendocino County, between the towns of Philo and Navarro on Hwy. 128.

 ✿ Milla Handley spent seven years working at other California wineries before establishing her own in an old homestead.

✿ ✿ ✿

Hidden Cellars Winery

1500 Cunningham Road
Ukiah, California 95482
TEL: 707-462-0301
PRESIDENT: Dennis Patton
FOUNDED: 1981

AT A GLANCE
Tours & Tastings: Open 11–4 daily May–Oct.; 11–4 Mon.–Fri. Nov.–Apr. During these hours, personal tours are given to any interested visitors.
Closed: Weekends, Nov.–Apr.
Vineyards: None. All grapes purchased within Mendocino County.
Wines: Johannisberg Riesling, Late Harvest Johannisberg Riesling, Sauvignon Blanc, Sémillon–Sauvignon Blanc Late Harvest, Gewürztraminer, Chardonnay, Petite Sirah, Zinfandel, Cabernet Sauvignon.
Awards: 1984 Johannisberg Riesling: three silvers, two bronzes; 1984 Late Harvest Johannisberg Riesling; platinum, double gold, two golds, four silvers, bronze; 1984 Chardonnay: two silvers, bronze.

Retail Shop: Wines sold on-site.
Credit Cards: None.
Access for Disabled: Yes.
Getting There: Winery is in Ukiah Valley in Mendocino County, two hours north of San Francisco. From Hwy. 101, take Talmage exit east, then turn south on Cunningham Rd.

 ✿ Dennis Patton comes from an old Santa Clara Valley farming family. He learned about wine under the tutelage of friends in the industry, and honed his skills with enology coursework at UC-Davis. With his first commercial vintage, he produced a gold-medal wine.

✿ ✿ ✿

Husch

4400 Highway 128
Philo, California 95466
TEL: 707-895-3216
OWNERS: The H. A. Oswald family
FOUNDED: 1971

AT A GLANCE
Tours & Tastings: Open daily. Summer hours: 10–6; winter hours: 10–5. Tours conducted by tasting room personnel when time allows; visitors are encouraged to take a stroll through vineyards. Call ahead to arrange group tours.
Vineyards: 200 acres planted to Chardonnay, Sauvignon Blanc, Gewürztraminer, Chenin Blanc, Pinot Noir, Cabernet Sauvignon.
Wines: Chardonnay, Sauvignon Blanc, Gewürztraminer, Chenin Blanc, Pinot Noir, Cabernet Sauvignon, and a blended white.
Picnic Area: Tables always available.
Retail Shop: Wines sold on-site.
Credit Cards: None.
Access for Disabled: Tasting room accommodates wheelchairs.

Getting There: Winery is in Mendocino County, 100 miles north of San Francisco. Drive 5 miles northwest of Philo on Hwy. 128.

❧ Overgrown, rambling roses give Husch's tasting room a quaint, rustic appeal. The winery's atmosphere is rural, with a friendly, unhurried pace. "Our staff has time to give you individual attention."

❧ ❧ ❧

Jepson Vineyards

10400 South Highway 101
Ukiah, California 95482
TEL: 707-468-8936
OWNER: Robert S. Jepson
WINEMAKER: Kurt Lorenzi (M.S. in enology, UC-Davis)
FOUNDED: 1985

AT A GLANCE
Tours & Tastings: By appointment only.
Vineyards: 108 acres planted to Chardonnay, Sauvignon Blanc.
Wines: Chardonnay, sparkling wine, Cognac-style brandy.
Retail Shop: Wines sold on-site.
Credit Cards: None.
Access for Disabled: Ramp leading to public rest rooms.
Getting There: Winery is in Mendocino County, three miles north of Hopland on Hwy. 101.

❧ Jepson, one of Mendocino County's newest wineries, has its headquarters in a beautifully restored nineteenth-century farmhouse.

❧ ❧ ❧

Konocti Winery

Highway 29 at Thomas Drive (P.O. Box 890)
Kelseyville, California 95451
TEL: 707-279-8861
OWNERS: A partnership of Lake County grape growers
FOUNDED: 1974

AT A GLANCE
Tours & Tastings: Open Mon.–Sat. 10–5, Sun. 11–5. Tours of the entire facility by appointment. Visitors see all aspects of the winery operation, then end up in the tasting room for sampling.
Closed: Easter, Christmas.
Vineyards: About 350 acres planted to Sauvignon Blanc, Cabernet Sauvignon, White Riesling.
Wines: Fumé Blanc, White Cabernet, White Riesling, Cabernet Sauvignon, Alegre.
Awards: 1985 Fumé Blanc: two golds, three bronzes; 1985 White Riesling: two golds, four silvers, bronze; 1982 Cabernet Sauvignon: two silvers, bronze.
Picnic Area: In walnut orchard.
Retail Shop: Wines, wine-related gifts, and picnic food sold on-site.
Credit Cards: MasterCard, Visa.
Access for Disabled: Level parking area with walkway into tasting room.
Getting There: Winery is in Lake County, 125 miles north of San Francisco. Head northwest on Hwy. 29; Konocti is midway between Kelseyville and Lakeport.
Special Wine & Other Events: Lake County Wine and Food Festival in June, Konocti Winery Harvest Festival the second weekend in October. Live music on Sun. afternoons in the summer.

❧ Konocti, named after an inactive volcano looming nearby, is one of only four Lake County wineries open to the public.

❧ ❧ ❧

Lazy Creek Vineyards

4610 Highway 128
Philo, California 95466
TEL: 707-895-3623

OWNER: Johann Kobler
FOUNDED: 1973

AT A GLANCE
Tours & Tastings: Open by appointment only.
Vineyards: Twenty acres planted to Pinot Noir, Gewürztraminer, Chardonnay.
Wines: Chardonnay, Pinot Noir, Gewürztraminer.
Awards: Pinot Noir: gold, silver.
Retail Shop: Wines sold on-site.
Credit Cards: None.
Access for Disabled: None
Foreign Languages: French, German.
Getting There: Winery is in Mendocino County, 4½ miles from Philo on Hwy. 128.

🐌 Lazy Creek is a small, family-run winery, producing only 2,000 cases of estate-bottled wine each year.

🐌 🐌 🐌

McDowell Valley Vineyards

3811 Highway 175 (P.O. Box 449)
Hopland, California 95449
TEL: 707-744-1053
PROPRIETORS: Richard and Karen Keehn
WINEMAKER: John Buechsenstein (B.S. and graduate studies in enology and fermentation science, UC-Davis)
FOUNDED: 1978

AT A GLANCE
Tours & Tastings: Open daily 10–5. Tours of winery and vineyard by appointment only. Tastings poured in a hand-carved redwood room that commands a sweeping view of the vineyards below.
Closed: Easter, Thanksgiving, Christmas, New Year's Day.
Vineyards: 360 acres planted to Chardonnay, Sauvignon Blanc, Sémillon, French Colombard, Chenin Blanc, Sylvaner Riesling, Grenache, Cabernet Franc, Syrah.
Wines: Chardonnay, Fumé Blanc, Grenache, Zinfandel Blanc, Cabernet Sauvignon, Sirah, red and white blends.
Awards: 1985 Zinfandel Blanc: two golds, silver; 1984 Fumé Blanc: two silvers, bronze; 1981 Sirah: silver, bronze; 1981 Cabernet: silver, three bronzes; 1984 Chardonnay: gold.
Picnic Area: Use either winery's second-story deck or winery lawn.
Retail Shop: Wines sold on-site. Picnic baskets—fruit, cheese, herb bread baked by winery's chef—and wine sorbets available during summer.
Credit Cards: American Express, MasterCard, Visa.
Access for Disabled: None.
Foreign Languages: Some Spanish, French, German.
Getting There: Winery is located in Mendocino County, four miles east of Hopland on Hwy. 175.
Special Wine & Other Events: McDowell's two annual cooking classes feature American regional chefs, and its several vertical tastings show how the fruit of the vine becomes finished wine; each session concludes with a five-course dinner. In the summer, the joint jumps with the Moonlight and Jazz series. Other concerts, as well as art shows, held each year.

🐌 With some vineyards dating to the nineteenth century and a solar-powered winery anticipating the twenty-first, McDowell Valley is right in step with the times. Both food and drink are celebrated here, preferably together; proprietors Richard and Karen Keehn are nationally recognized cooking authorities who publish their own recipes in the winery's newsletter. Be sure to ask about scheduled events, because the on-site activities are endless. This is one of those fascinating places where the winemakers are musicians and the tasting room doubles as a gallery.

🐌 🐌 🐌

Milano Winery

14594 South Highway 101
Hopland, California 95449
TEL: 707-744-1396
PRESIDENT: James A. Milone
FOUNDED: 1977

AT A GLANCE
Tours & Tastings: Open daily 10–5. Tours by appointment.
Closed: Easter, July 4th, Thanksgiving, Christmas.
Vineyards: Sixty-four acres planted to Cabernet Sauvignon, Chardonnay, Zinfandel. Pears also grown on-site.
Wines: Chardonnay, Cabernet Sauvignon, White Zinfandel, Sauvignon Blanc, dessert wines.
Awards: 1982 Late Harvest Riesling: two golds, three silvers, bronze; 1982 Gewürztraminer: two golds, silver, bronze; 1982 Chardonnay (Mendocino/ San Luis Obispo): gold, two silvers; many other medals.
Retail Shop: Wines sold on-site.
Credit Cards: American Express, MasterCard, Visa.
Access for Disabled: None.
Getting There: In Mendocino County, one hundred miles north of San Francisco—and one mile south of Hopland—on Hwy. 101.

&. James A. Milone is a self-taught winemaker and third-generation grape grower. At the ripe (but hardly old) age of twenty-one, he founded this winery in the hop kiln (for drying hops, used in the brewing of beer) built by his grandfather and father in the early 1900s.

&. &. &.

Mountain House Winery

38999 Highway 128
Cloverdale, California 95425
TEL: 707-894-3074

GENERAL MANAGER/WINEMAKER:
Ronald F. Lipp (graduate studies in viticulture and enology, UC-Davis)
FOUNDED: 1980

AT A GLANCE
Tours & Tastings: Open Fri.–Sun. March–Nov. 10–5; at other times by appointment. A very small working winery. At harvest, visitors can see grapes being crushed, and can even help if they want. Mountain House was the site of a stagecoach stop built in the 1860s, and some of the original buildings remain intact.
Vineyards: Five acres planted to Chardonnay. Additional grapes purchased from growers in Sonoma and Amador counties.
Wines: Chardonnay, Cabernet Sauvignon, Zinfandel, Chenin Blanc, Pinot Noir.
Retail Shop: Wines sold on-site.
Credit Cards: None.
Access for Disabled: None.
Getting There: In Mendocino County, on the west side of Hwy. 128, 7.2 miles north of Cloverdale.
Special Wine & Other Events: Invitational Grape Crush in the fall, a working weekend at the winery.

&. Ron Lipp, a Chicago-based antitrust lawyer, became intrigued with the California wine country in the early 1970s. To dispel any illusions about the romance of winery life, he worked the 1974 harvest at Mayacamas Vineyards in Napa. When he was still intrigued after picking Cabernet on 105-degree days, he exchanged his briefcase for a pair of cellar boots.

&. &. &.

Navarro Vineyards

5601 Highway 128, Box 47
Philo, California 95466
TEL: 707-895-3686

GENERAL MANAGER: Deborah Cahn
WINEMAKER: Edward Bennett
FOUNDED: 1974

AT A GLANCE

Tours & Tastings: Open daily 10–5. Tours by appointment only. Vineyard tour covers trellising experiments and different varietals; winery tour includes barrel sampling.
Vineyards: Fifty acres planted to Gewürztraminer, Chardonnay, Pinot Noir. Additional grapes grown under long-term contract by neighboring vineyards.
Wines: Gewürztraminer, Dry Riesling, Late Harvest Riesling, Pinot Noir, Chardonnay.
Awards: 1984 Gewürztraminer (Anderson Valley): gold, three silvers, seven bronzes; 1984 Premium Reserve Chardonnay: gold, silver, two bronzes; 1982 Pinot Noir: two bronzes; many other medals.
Picnic Area: On deck adjacent to tasting room.
Retail Shop: Wines and grape juices sold on-site.
Credit Cards: MasterCard, Visa.
Access for Disabled: Level entrance, wide doors.
Foreign Languages: Spanish, some French and German.
Getting There: In Mendocino County, one hundred miles north of San Francisco on Hwy. 128.
Special Wine & Other Events: Special events for members of prerelease tasting program. For information, write to winery.

 🥄 Ted Bennett and Deborah Cahn chose this 900-acre sheep ranch as the right place to raise both their children and their grapes. "Since we love dry Alsatian wines, we selected soil that would produce something similar," Bennett reports. The cool, humid climate fosters the noble mold, *Botrytis cineria,* culminating in a sweet harvest wine.

🥄 🥄 🥄

Olson Vineyards

3620 Road B
Redwood Valley, California 95470
TEL: 707-485-7523
OWNER: Donald R. Olson
WINEMAKER: Roger Matson (B.S. with honors in fermentation science and viticulture, UC-Davis)
FOUNDED: 1982

AT A GLANCE

Tours & Tastings: Open daily 10–5. Informal tours given when time allows. Call ahead to arrange group tours.
Closed: Thanksgiving, Christmas.
Vineyards: Thirty-four owned and twelve leased acres planted to Cabernet Sauvignon, Napa Gamay, French Colombard, Sauvignon Blanc, Zinfandel, Petite Sirah. Cherries, raspberries, apricots, mulberries grown on property.
Wines: Chardonnay, Sauvignon (Fumé) Blanc, Zinfandel, Petite Sirah, Cabernet, Napa Gamay Blanc (blush wine).
Awards: 1984 Petite Sirah: gold; 1983 Chardonnay: silver; 1982 Special Reserve Zinfandel: silver.
Picnic Area: In shade of oak trees, with views of Lake Mendocino and Redwood Valley.
Retail Shop: Wines, chutney, preserves, vinegar, and pickles sold on-site.
Credit Cards: MasterCard, Visa.
Access for Disabled: All ground level.
Foreign Languages: Spanish.
Getting There: In Mendocino County. Take Hwy. 101 to Hwy. 20 East. Go 1½ miles to Rd. A, turn left, then turn right on Rd. B and follow signs.

 🥄 Succumbing to a long-suppressed urge to make wine, Los Angeles–area native Donald Olson brought his family north in the 1970s. Neither pesticides nor herbicides are used in the vineyards, which have been accredited by the California Certified Organic Farmers group. In addition to their winery and commercial kitchen, the Olsons operate a small bed and breakfast on the property. Call several months in advance for reservations.

❧ ❧ ❧

Parducci Wine Cellars

501 Parducci Road
Ukiah, California 95482
TEL: 707-462-9463
CHIEF EXECUTIVE OFFICER: Robert
  Fitzpatrick
FOUNDED: 1932

AT A GLANCE
Tours & Tastings: Open daily. Summer hours: 9–6; winter: 9–5. Tours leave on the hour from 10–4, and twenty-five wines can be sampled in tasting room.
Closed: Easter, Thanksgiving, Christmas, New Year's Day.
Vineyards: 500 acres planted to Cabernet Sauvignon, Petite Sirah, Pinot Noir, Zinfandel, Gamay Beaujolais, Chardonnay, Chenin Blanc, Sauvignon Blanc, French Colombard, Mendocino Riesling, Gewürztraminer, Merlot, Flora, and other varietals.
Wines: Cabernet Sauvignon, Petite Sirah, Pinot Noir, Zinfandel, Gamay Beaujolais, Chardonnay, Chenin Blanc, Sauvignon Blanc, French Colombard, Mendocino Riesling, Gewürztraminer, red and white blends.
Awards: More than a thousand awards from various competitions. Recent medals include a gold to 1985 French Colombard; silver to 1981 Petite Sirah; silver to 1983 Pinot Noir; silver to 1983 Merlot; and bronze to 1985 Gewürztraminer.
Picnic Area: Yes.
Restaurant: Sun. champagne brunch served 10–2 either in fireside dining room

overlooking vineyard or under umbrellas on cobblestone patio.
Retail Shop: Wines, crystal, china, cookware, and jewelry sold on-site.
Credit Cards: American Express, MasterCard, Visa.
Access for Disabled: Yes.
Getting There: In Mendocino County, 100 miles north of San Francisco and 138 miles west of Sacramento. From Hwy. 101: Take the Lake Mendocino turnoff immediately north of Ukiah. Head west at the bottom of ramp, and follow signs.

❧ Convinced that Prohibition was a temporary aberration, winemaker Adolph Parducci spent the 1920s acquiring land and equipment. Thus he was able to begin full-scale production as soon as it was legal. By 1944, his bottlings were included on the U.S. Embassy wine list, a sign that California wines had arrived. Today, Parducci Wine Cellars is managed by the founder's sons, and the third generation is rising in the ranks. It's a huge operation: at harvest time, three Mendocino County vineyards keep the presses rolling in grapes.

❧ ❧ ❧

Scharffenberger Cellars

Visitor Center
7000 Highway 128
Philo, California 95466
TEL: 707-895-2065
PRESIDENT: John Scharffenberger
WINEMAKER: Rob McNeill (B.S. in
  fermentation science with emphasis
  on enology, UC-Davis)
FOUNDED: 1981

AT A GLANCE
Tours & Tastings: Open Thurs.–Tues. 10–6. No tours.
Closed: Major holidays.
Vineyards: None. Grapes for sparkling wines purchased from Mendocino

County growers; grapes for still wines come from Scharffenberger ranch in the Mayacamas Mountains.

Wines: Brut, Blanc de Blancs, Brut Rosé *methode champenoise* sparkling wines; Chardonnay, Sauvignon Blanc.
Awards: 1982 Brut: gold, silver, bronze; 1982 Blanc de Blancs: gold, silver.
Retail Shop: Wines sold on-site.
Credit Cards: MasterCard, Visa.
Access for Disabled: Yes.
Foreign Languages: German.
Getting There: Scharffenberger's Visitor Center is in southern Mendocino County, about 115 miles north of San Francisco. From Cloverdale: take Hwy. 128; Visitor Center is 1½ miles north of Philo.

🐚 John Scharffenberger's quest to make some of America's finest sparkling wines led him to Anderson Valley in Mendocino County, where the climate and soil conditions resemble those of France's celebrated Champagne district. Judging by his medal collection, that quest has not been in vain.

🐚 🐚 🐚

Whaler Vineyard

6200 Eastside Road
Ukiah, California 95482
TEL: 707-462-6355
OWNERS: Ann and Ross Nyborg
FOUNDER: 1981

AT A GLANCE
Tours & Tastings: By appointment only.
Vineyards: Twenty-four acres planted to Zinfandel.
Wines: Zinfandel, White Zinfandel.
Awards: 1981 Zinfandel: silver; 1983 Zinfandel: gold, silver; 1984 White Zinfandel: gold; 1985 White Zinfandel: bronze.
Picnic Area: A pool area with six picnic tables and redwood trees—a nice setting for tastings, picnics, swimming, etc.

Retail Shop: Wines sold on-site.
Credit Cards: None.
Access for Disabled: None.
Getting There: In Mendocino County, five miles south of Talmage and ten miles north of Hopland. Take Hwy. 101 to Eastside Rd. and go north ten miles.

🐚 "This is a small winery and vineyard overlooking the Russian River and Ukiah Valley," notes Ann Nyborg. She and her husband used to work aboard charter sailing vessels in the South Pacific; now he is a pilot who guides ships into San Francisco Bay. They both like to share knowledge about wineries and other places of interest with visitors.

TO SEE & DO
Together, these two counties contain several million acres of public beaches and parkland, and that spells outdoor adventure. Local Indian tribes invented legends about Mount Konocti; today this multiple volcano is extinct, but you won't need fireworks to enjoy the view from 4,200 feet. Learn more about Indian lore at the Lake County Historical Museum on Main Street in Lakeport (tel: 707-263-4555). You can swim at either Clear Lake State Park (Kelseyville; tel: 707-279-4293) or Lake Mendocino Recreation Area (Ukiah; tel: 707-462-7582). Other options include hiking, boating, fishing, and waterskiing. From June through September, Lake Mendocino's Interpretive Cultural Center presents exhibits and demonstrations by both the Pomo (the area's indigenous native Americans) and the U.S. Army Corps of Engineers (who created Lake Mendocino in 1958 by damming the Russian River). Rent a bike or a horse and tour MacKerricher State Park (on Highway 1 in Fort Bragg). During winter and spring, watch for Moby Dick as migrating gray whales sport in MacKerricher's coastal waters. At Van Damme State Park (in Little River), the scenery ranges from

towering redwoods to the Pygmy Forest's naturally dwarfed cypresses. Another way to survey the spectacular Mendocino landscape is from the Skunk Train's open observation cars. A nineteenth-century gas-powered logging railroad once so malodorous it could be smelled before it was seen, the Skunk now runs between Fort Bragg and Willits on comparatively inoffensive diesel fuel. For information and reservations, contact California Western Railroad, P.O. Box 907, Fort Bragg, California 95437 (tel: 707-964-6371). Fort Bragg's past as a logging town is commemorated at the Guest House Museum, a three-story lodge built at 343 Main Street in 1892 by a local lumber company. Willits is the site of the Mendocino County Museum (400 East Commercial Street; tel: 707-459-2736), where the collection embraces native American crafts, pioneer artifacts, and county archives. History comes to life in Boonville every September, at Mendocino County's old-fashioned Fair and Apple Show. Partake of local produce, then toast the fair's rodeo winners with local wines.

ACCOMMODATIONS

Agate Cove Inn
11201 North Lansing Street (Box 1150)
Mendocino, California 95460
Tel: 707-937-0551
A country-style bed and breakfast, cozy cottages equipped with fireplaces, unsurpassed ocean views, and ample breakfasts.

Bed & Breakfast Exchange
1458 Lincoln Avenue
Calistoga, California 94515
Tel: 707-963-7756
Historic, elegant, homey—take your choice.

Elk Cove Inn
6300 South Highway 1, Box 367
Elk, California 95432
Tel: 707-877-3321

Enjoy ocean views from this cliffside bed and breakfast. Weekend dinners feature local wines.

The Grey Whale Inn
615 North Main Street
Fort Bragg, California 95437
Tel: 707-964-0640; 800-382-7244
A charming bed and breakfast in a converted nineteenth-century hospital, just a few blocks from the Skunk Train.

Harbor House
5600 South Highway 1 (Box 369V)
Elk, California 95432
Tel: 707-877-3203
A seventy-year-old inn on bluffs overlooking the ocean. Excellent breakfasts and dinners.

Hill House Inn
10701 Palette Drive (Box 625)
Mendocino, California 95460
Tel: 707-937-0554; 937-0557
A scenic, tranquil retreat with lush gardens and spectacular ocean views. Lunch, dinner, and weekend brunch served.

MacCallam House Inn
45020 Albion Street (Box 206)
Mendocino, California 95460
Tel: 707-937-0289
A lovingly preserved landmark. Twenty-room inn has porch and gables trimmed with gingerbread. Restaurant and bar on the premises.

Mendocino Hotel
45080 Main Street (Box 587)
Mendocino, California 95460
Tel: 707-937-0511; 800-352-6686
A hotel established in 1878, suitably furnished with four-poster beds and antiques. Garden cottages also available.

Palace Hotel
Ukiah, California 95482
This ninety-nine-room hotel, built in 1891

and recently restored, is listed on the National Register of Historic Places.

RESTAURANTS

Albion River Inn
Highway 1 (Box 100)
Albion, California 95410
Tel: 707-937-1919
At the mouth of the Albion River, overlooking the ocean. Continental specialties.

Floodgate Cafe
Highway 128
Navarro, California 95463
Tel: 707-895-2422
Innovative new American cuisine served at breakfast, lunch, and dinner.

Cafe Beaujolais
Albion, California 95410
Tel: 707-937-5614
Fresh salmon, local wines. Espresso and rich cakes. Victorian decor.

The Lido
228 East Perkins
Ukiah, California 95482
Tel: 707-463-1443

Main Street Wine & Cheese
101 South Main Street
Ukiah, California 95482
Tel: 707-462-0417
Salads, sandwiches, light entrees, wines.

Mendocino Hotel Restaurant
45080 Main Street (Box 587)
Mendocino, California 95460
Tel: 707-937-0511
Seatings in two different settings—choose either the garden or the formal dining room for light California cuisine. Delicious deep-dish berry pies. Victorian decor.

❧ NAPA COUNTY

Napa Valley was under Mexican control when frontiersman George C. Yount settled here in the late 1820s. To win a land grant—the present site of Yountville—he was required to convert to Catholicism and adopt the middle name Concepcion. He consoled himself by planting cuttings from the Sonoma vineyards of General Mariano Vallejo. Records show that Yount made 200 gallons in 1844, a fair amount of consolation for one man.

While other settlers also cultivated vinifera grapes, the region's first commercial winery wasn't established until 1861. Several more, including Beringer and Inglenook, were opened in the next decade. By 1880, Napa Valley was drowning in 3 million gallons of wine, a surplus that depressed prices. Then the phylloxera louse infested the vineyards, a blow that was swiftly followed by Prohibition.

With Repeal, wineries started to revive, bolstered by European immigrants from winemaking families. The real explosion came in the 1970s. As local vintners left their mark in international competitions, demand increased and vineyard acreage doubled. Today, Napa is an enophile's Nirvana, with nearly 29,000 acres under cultivation by some of the industry's most honored names.

Napa Valley was California's first—and America's second—official viticultural area (for the record, Augusta, Missouri, was the nation's first v.a.). So far, three other Napa County locations enjoy designation: Howell Mountain, which is contained within the Napa Valley v.a., and Los Carneros and Wild Horse Valley, both of which straddle Napa and Sonoma counties. The Stag's Leap District and Mt. Veeder have petitioned for designation.

Two parallel north-south wine routes span the length of Napa—St. Helena Highway (Highway 29) in the east, and the Silverado Trail in the west. Given the county's enological acclaim, these roads are very heavily traveled on summer and fall weekends. To avoid traffic on the road, and long lines at the wineries, schedule a midweek or off-season excursion. All along the way, you'll see historic towns and resorts tucked in between unspoiled mountains where deer still tread.

꙳ ꙳ ꙳ ꙳ ꙳ ꙳

Arroyo Winery

2361 Greenwood Avenue
Calistoga, California 94515
TEL: 707-942-6995
OWNER: Vincent Arroyo
WINEMAKER: Calvin Chase
FOUNDED: 1983

AT A GLANCE
Tours & Tastings: Open by appointment only.
Vineyards: Fifty-five acres planted to Cabernet Sauvignon, Petite Sirah, Chenin Blanc, Chardonnay, Napa Gamay, Pinot Noir.
Wines: Cabernet Sauvignon, Petite Sirah, Gamay Noir.
Picnic Area: Creekside setting.
Retail Shop: Wines sold on-site.
Credit Cards: None. Cash and personal checks only.
Access for Disabled: None.
Getting There: Winery is twenty-five miles north of Napa and sixty miles north of San Francisco. Take Hwy. 29 North; two miles outside Calistoga, bear left on Greenwood Ave. Arroyo entrance is the third driveway on the right.

꙳ Arroyo Winery is housed in a renovated redwood horsebarn built more than one hundred years ago.

Beringer Vineyards

2000 Main Street
St. Helena, California 94574
TEL: 707-963-7115
PRESIDENT: E. M. Moone
WINEMASTER: Edward Sbragia (third-generation winemaker; B.S. in chemistry, UC-Davis; M.S. in enology, Fresno State University)
FOUNDED: 1876

AT A GLANCE
Tours & Tastings: Open daily. Summer hours: 10–6; winter hours: 9–5. Regularly scheduled tours of nineteenth-century wine-storage tunnels conclude with brief wine tasting in Rhine House, a glorious seventeen-room mansion modeled after the Beringer family's German estate. Last tour leaves half an hour before closing. Finer wines may be sampled in second tasting room upstairs, where visitors pay by the glass.
Closed: Major holidays.
Vineyards: Six primary Napa Valley vineyards planted to Chardonnay, Cabernet Sauvignon, Sauvignon Blanc, Riesling.
Wines: Cabernet Sauvignon, Chardonnay, Sauvignon Blanc, Riesling; Cabernet Sauvignon Port.
Awards: Recent medals include multiple

golds and silvers won by 1982 Knights Valley Cabernet Sauvignon, 1981 Private Reserve Cabernet Sauvignon, and 1983 Private Reserve Chardonnay.
Retail Shop: Wines sold on-site.
Credit Cards: American Express, MasterCard, Visa.
Access for Disabled: Ramps to all tour areas and Rhine House, but no wheelchair access to second floor of Rhine House.
Foreign Languages: Spanish, German.
Getting There: Winery is seventy miles from San Francisco, just off Hwy. 29 in St. Helena.
Special Wine & Other Events: "Beringer Celebrates American Food and Wine" is a program featuring guest chefs.

&. After deciding that Napa Valley soil would support a vineyard, German immigrants Jacob and Frederick Beringer directed their attention underground, where they charted a network of storage tunnels. Chinese laborers completed the actual excavation, boring through stone by hand. A century later, their achievement—a wine cellar with naturally cool, even temperatures—is still utilized by Beringer Vineyards. The surface structures here are no less impressive: Rhine House is listed on the National Register of Historic Places as a superior example of 1880s architecture, with one of California's largest collections of stained-glass windows.

&. &. &.

Bouchaine Vineyards

1075 Buchli Station Road
Napa, California 94558
TEL: 707-252-9065
MANAGING DIRECTOR: Eugenia Keegan
FOUNDED: 1980

AT A GLANCE
Tours & Tastings: Open by appointment only, Mon.–Sat. 10–4. Tour lasts 1½

hours and covers crushing, pressing, and bottling operations. Visitors will sample all of the current releases.
Closed: Sun., holidays.
Vineyards: Thirty-one acres planted to Chardonnay. Additional grapes purchased from Napa Valley growers.
Wines: Chardonnay, Pinot Noir.
Awards: 1982 Alexander Valley Chardonnay: two golds: 1983 Napa Valley Chardonnay: double gold, bronze; 1982 Los Carneros Pinot Noir: two silvers; 1984 Los Carneros Chardonnay: silver, two bronzes.
Retail Shop: Wines sold on-site.
Credit Cards: MasterCard, Visa.
Access for Disabled: None.
Getting There: Winery is ten miles southwest of Napa, off Hwy. 121/12. Request directions when making appointment.

&. Established in 1899 as the Garetto Winery, this property changed hands and underwent extensive renovation during the early 1980s. Today Bouchaine continues to draw upon the past. Temperature-controlled stainless steel tanks for white wine fermentation sit next to the original open-top concrete fermentors still used for red wines. French oak barrels are located where 20,000-gallon redwood tanks once stood. Additional improvements include a computer-programmed tank press, a fully automated bottling line, and an elegantly furnished visitors' center.

&. &. &.

Burgess Cellars

1108 Deer Park Road (P.O. Box 282)
St. Helena, California 94574
TEL: 707-963-4766
PRESIDENT: Tom Burgess
WINEMAKER: Bill Sorenson (enology degree, UC-Fresno)
FOUNDED: Circa 1880

AT A GLANCE

Tours & Tastings: Open daily 9–5. Vineyard and winery tours at 10:30 and 2:30 by reservation.
Closed: Major holidays.
Vineyards: Forty-seven owned and twenty-five leased acres planted to Cabernet Sauvignon, Cabernet Franc, Chardonnay.
Wines: Chardonnay, Cabernet Sauvignon, Zinfandel.
Awards: Numerous.
Retail Shop: Wines sold on-site.
Credit Cards: Visa.
Access for Disabled: None.
Getting There: Winery is 4.4 miles northeast of St. Helena. Take the Silverado Trail to Deer Park Rd.

ð Burgess Cellars is a stone-and-redwood mountaintop winery perched precipitously on the eastern rim of Napa Valley. Its adjacent, nearly vertical vineyards were planted by Swiss homesteaders in the 1880s.

ðª ðª ðª

Calafia Cellars

4411 Redwood Road
Napa, California 94558
TEL: 707-963-0114
OWNER: Randle Johnson (M.S. in
   viticulture, UC-Davis)
FOUNDED: 1979

AT A GLANCE

Tours & Tastings: Open by appointment only. Tours of premises—a remodeled stone winery erected in 1860—given on request. Small groups taste barrel samples; large groups taste bottled wine.
Vineyards: One acre planted to Chardonnay. Most grapes purchased from growers in California's Mt. Veeder District.
Wines: Cabernet Sauvignon, Merlot, Sauvignon Blanc, Zinfandel, Chardonnay.

Awards: 1981 Cabernet Reserve: gold; 1982 Cabernet Reserve: gold.
Retail Shop: Wines sold on-site.
Credit Cards: None.
Access for Disabled: Limited.
Foreign Languages: Spanish, some French.
Getting There: Winery is about six miles west of Napa. Take Hwy. 29 north to city of Napa, where freeway portion of highway ends at Redwood Rd. Turn left on Redwood and continue six miles.

ð "All Calafia red wines are made from grapes grown on Mt. Veeder, a rather vast mass located in the Mayacamas Mountains between the southern Napa Valley and Sonoma's Valley of the Moon," reports Randle Johnson. "It is testimony to the wildness of the place that there are mountain lions, coyotes, and bears lurking there still. Grapes grown there have a remarkable intensity—a 1977 Merlot I made from young Mt. Veeder vines convinced me to make wines for a living."

ðª ðª ðª

Carneros Creek Winery

1285 Dealy Lane
Napa, California 94558
TEL: 707-253-9463
OWNER/WINEMAKER: Francis Mahoney
FOUNDED: 1972

AT A GLANCE

Tours & Tastings: Anytime, by appointment only. Complete tour leads visitors from vineyard through production and bottling facilities.
Closed: Major holidays.
Vineyards: Twenty-five acres planted to Pinot Noir. All other grapes purchased within Napa Valley's Carneros District.
Wines: Chardonnay, Pinot Noir, Merlot, Cabernet Sauvignon.
Awards: Recent medals include gold to

Pinot Noir; silver to Cabernet Sauvignon; silver to Merlot.
Picnic Area: In vineyard.
Retail Shop: Wines sold on-site.
Credit Cards: None.
Access for Disabled: Winery has no stairs; bathrooms accommodate wheelchairs.
Foreign Languages: Some French, Spanish, Italian.
Getting There: Winery is fifty miles north of San Francisco and five miles west of Napa. Take Hwy. 29 to Old Sonoma Rd. and bear right on Dealy Ln.

ঽ San Francisco native Francis Mahoney became interested in wine while vacationing in Europe. Before planting his own vineyard, he worked at Mayacamas Winery. Now Mahoney's wines are doing the traveling: Carneros Creek Pinot Noirs have been poured at White House state dinners.

ঽ ঽ ঽ

Casa Nuestra

3473 Silverado Trail
St. Helena, California 94574
TEL: 707-963-4684, 944-8444
OWNERS: the Kirkham family
FOUNDED: 1980

AT A GLANCE
Tours & Tastings: Open weekends, 10–5; other times by appointment. Impromptu tours.
Vineyards: Fourteen owned and three leased acres planted to Chenin Blanc, Cabernet Franc.
Wines: Chenin Blanc, Tinto.
Awards: Too numerous to list.
Picnic Area: Yes.
Retail Shop: Wines sold on-site.
Credit Cards: MasterCard, Visa.
Access for Disabled: None.
Foreign Languages: French.
Getting There: Winery is located between St. Helena and Calistoga on the

Silverado Trail, approximately one mile north of Deer Park Rd. (the main road to Angwin). Look for purple sign on west side of Silverado Trail.

ঽ "At the Casa we believe that wine is a healthful beverage which has a place on every table" proclaim the Kirkhams.

ঽ ঽ ঽ

Cassayre-Forni

1271 Manley Lane
Rutherford, California 94573
TEL: 707-944-2165, 255-0909
PRESIDENT: James L. Cassayre
WINEMAKER: Mike Forni
FOUNDED: 1976

AT A GLANCE
Tours & Tastings: Open daily 10–4:30; appointments preferred.
Closed: Easter, Christmas.
Vineyards: None. Grapes purchased from Napa and Sonoma County growers.
Wines: Cabernet Sauvignon, Chardonnay, Chenin Blanc, Zinfandel.
Awards: 1980 Cabernet Sauvignon: silver, bronze; 1982 Zinfandel: silver, bronze; 1981 Cabernet Sauvignon: bronze.
Retail Shop: Wines sold on-site.
Credit Cards: None.
Access for Disabled: Wheelchair accessible.
Getting There: From Napa, head fourteen miles north on Hwy. 29, then turn left on Manley Ln.

ঽ After designing several California wineries, engineers Mike Forni, James Cassayre, and Paul Cassayre decided to collaborate on their own. This is truly a family operation; during the crush, several generations of Fornis and Cassayres lend their energies (and their names) to the effort.

ঽ ঽ ঽ

Chateau Chevre Winery

2030 Hoffman Lane
Yountville, California 94599
TEL: 707-944-2184
PARTNERS: Gerry P. Hazen and Robert
  Mueller
FOUNDED: 1979

AT A GLANCE
Tours & Tastings: Open by appointment
only.
Vineyards: 17½ acres planted to Merlot,
Sauvignon Blanc, Cabernet Sauvignon,
Cabernet Franc.
Wines: Merlot, Sauvignon Blanc.
Awards: Numerous.
Retail Shop: Wines sold on-site.
Credit Cards: None. Checks accepted.
Access for the Disabled: None.
Getting There: From Napa: Take Hwy. 29
North eight miles to Hoffman Ln. and
bear left. Winery is on the right.

🐐 Retired airline cargo pilot Gerry
Hazen established this small winery in a
converted goat dairy—hence the name
Chateau Chevre. But Chateau Merlot
would now be equally appropriate; most
of the 2,500 cases produced here annually contain this rich red varietal.

🐐 🐐 🐐

The Christian Brothers

P.O. Box 391
St. Helena, California 94574
TEL: 707-963-4480
OWNERS: the Christian Brothers
FOUNDED: 1882

AT A GLANCE
Tours & Tastings: Tours by appointment
only, Mon.–Fri. at 10:30 and 2:30. Visitors walk through crushing and fermenting areas and barrel-aging cellars, then
taste selected wines.
Closed: Weekends, all holidays.
Vineyards: 1,200 acres planted to Char-

donnay, Chenin Blanc, Zinfandel, Cabernet Sauvignon, and other varietals.
Wines: Chardonnay, Chenin Blanc, Fumé
Blanc, Cabernet Sauvignon, Zinfandel;
sparkling wines; brandy; ports.
Awards: Recent medals include three
golds, two silvers, two bronzes to 1985
Chenin Blanc; gold, two silvers, bronze
to 1985 White Zinfandel; two silvers,
bronze to Brut sparkling wine.
Retail Shop: No retail sales.
Access for Disabled: None.
Getting There: Winery is approximately
sixty miles north of San Francisco and
eighteen miles north of city of Napa, on
Hwy. 29.

🐐 Since 1882, this enormous winery
has been owned and operated by the
Christian Brothers, an order of the
Catholic Church. In keeping with monas-
tic tradition, wine sales support the
order's educational work.

🐐 🐐 🐐

Clos Du Val

5330 Silverado Trail
Napa, California 94558
TEL: 707-252-6711
OWNER: John Goelet
WINEMAKER: Bernard M. Portet
  (graduate of France's Montpellier
  School of Agronomy in enology/
  viticulture)
FOUNDED: 1972

AT A GLANCE
Tours & Tastings: Open daily 10–4.
Tours, by appointment only, cover Clos
Du Val's history and methods and con-
clude with an annotated tasting session.
Special group tours can be arranged for
more knowledgeable guests interested in
particular varietals or techniques.
Closed: Easter, Christmas, New Year's
Day.
Vineyards: 120 acres planted to Cabernet

Sauvignon, Merlot, Zinfandel; additional 150 acres under development, planted to Pinot Noir and Chardonnay.
Wines: Cabernet Sauvignon, Merlot, Zinfandel, Pinot Noir, Chardonnay, Sauvignon Blanc.
Awards: Clos Du Val has won more than one hundred medals in regional, national, and international competitions.
Picnic Area: Redwood tables under shade tree near vineyard.
Retail Shop: Wines sold on-site.
Credit Cards: MasterCard, Visa.
Access for Disabled: Wheelchair accessible.
Foreign Languages: French.
Getting There: Winery is five miles north of Napa, on Silverado Trail.

&. John Goelet, scion of Bordeaux wine merchants, established Clos Du Val—French for "Small Vineyard Estate of the Valley"—after conducting a world-wide search for ideal vineyard properties. (He also owns Taltarni Vineyards in Australia.) In another nod to Europe, this winery follows the Continental practice of marking each grape vine row with roses; any mildew affecting the fruit will surface first in the flowers.

&. &. &.

Conn Creek

8711 Silverado Trail
St. Helena, California 94574
TEL: 707-963-9100
OWNER: Stimson Lane Wine & Spirits
WINEMAKER: Daryl Eklund
FOUNDED: 1973

AT A GLANCE
Tours & Tastings: Open daily for retail sales 11–4. Cellar tour and tastings by appointment; unblended and unbottled wines are tasted to illustrate various aspects of winemaking.
Closed: Major holidays.

Vineyards: Less than five acres planted to Cabernet Sauvignon. Most grapes purchased from Napa and Sonoma County growers.
Wines: Cabernet Sauvignon, Chardonnay, Zinfandel, Sauvignon Blanc, Merlot.
Awards: 1980 Cabernet Sauvignon: gold; 1982 Cabernet Sauvignon: silver; 1979 Zinfandel: gold, silver; 1981 Chardonnay: silver; 1982 Chardonnay: bronze.
Retail Shop: Wines sold on-site.
Credit Cards: American Express, MasterCard, Visa.
Access for Disabled: None.
Getting There: Winery is seven miles southeast of St. Helena. From Napa: Take Hwy. 29 North about twelve miles. In Oakville, turn right onto Oakville Crossroads and at end of road turn left onto Silverado Trail. Three miles to winery on left.

&. Following barrel aging, all Conn Creek wines are given an extra year in the bottle before release. The result is wines that can be enjoyed at purchase, although many of the Cabernets reward additional cellaring.

&. &. &.

Domaine Chandon

California Drive
Yountville, California 94599
TEL: 707-944-2280
OWNER: Moet-Hennessy
FOUNDED: 1973

AT A GLANCE
Tours & Tastings: Open Nov.–Apr. Wed.–Sun. 11–6; May–Oct. daily 11–6. Tours, offered from 11–5:30, start in demonstration vineyard and continue through winery with a detailed explanation of the *methode champenoise*. Wines may be purchased by either the glass or the bottle in salon, where complimentary hors d'oeuvres are served.

Closed: Mon.–Tues. Nov.–Apr.
Vineyards: 1,250 acres planted to Pinot Noir, Chardonnay, Pinot Blanc.
Wines: Sparkling wines; Panache (an aperitif resembling the Ratafia made in Champagne).
Restaurant: French restaurant in visitors' center emphasizes the regional specialties of Champagne. Lunch served 11:30–2:30; dinner seatings begin at 6. Reservations advised; call 707-944-2892 between 10 and 5.
Retail Shop: Wines sold on-site.
Credit Cards: American Express, Diner's Club, MasterCard, Visa.
Access for Disabled: None.
Getting There: Winery is approximately sixty miles from San Francisco. In the Napa Valley, exit Hwy. 29 at Yountville–Veterans' Home sign and head west, toward Veterans' Home. Cross railroad tracks and turn right.

ᕕ Domaine Chandon's stone walls and wood-beamed ceilings are vintage California, but the sparkling wines produced within meet strict French standards. In other words, this Moet & Chandon outpost is a proper Champagne winery transplanted to the Napa Valley. Plan ahead: stock up on a magnum and store the bottle on its side until New Year's Eve. Sated diners bubble with enthusiasm over the fabulous restaurant, but be forewarned: prices are high.

ᕕ ᕕ ᕕ

Ehlers Lane Winery

3222 Ehlers Lane
St. Helena, California 94574
TEL: 707-963-0144
GENERAL MANAGER/WINEMAKER:
  Robert H. Moeckly (B.S. in fermentation science, UC-Davis; former director of quality control for Robert Mondavi Winery)
FOUNDED: 1983

AT A GLANCE
Tours & Tastings: By appointment only. Tours cover Ehlers's history and present winemaking techniques, concluding in a tasting of premium wines.
Vineyards: Fifteen acres planted to Cabernet Sauvignon, Cabernet Franc, Merlot, Petite Verdot.
Wines: Sauvignon Blanc, Chardonnay, Cabernet Sauvignon.
Awards: 1983 Sauvignon Blanc: two golds; 1983 Chardonnay: silver, bronze; 1983 Cabernet Sauvignon: gold, two silvers.
Picnic Area: In olive grove.
Retail Shop: Wines sold on-site daily, 10–4:30.
Credit Cards: American Express.
Access for Disabled: None.
Getting There: Ehlers Lane is midway between St. Helena and Calistoga, off Hwy. 29, slightly north of Freemark Abbey.

ᕕ Ehlers Lane is a new venture in an old site—the sandstone-and-basalt winery built by Bernard Ehlers in 1886. Robert Moeckly installed state-of-the-art equipment for efficient, but gentle, grape processing. Skillfully blending individual lots, he creates his wines.

ᕕ ᕕ ᕕ

Franciscan Vineyards

1178 Galleron Road (P.O. Box 407)
Rutherford, California 94573
TEL: 707-963-7111
PRESIDENT: Agustin Hunees
FOUNDED: 1973

AT A GLANCE
Tours & Tastings: Daily public tastings 10–5. Reservations suggested for sensory wine-evaluation sessions.
Closed: Easter, Thanksgiving, Christmas, New Year's Day.
Vineyards: 420 acres planted to Sauvi-

gnon Blanc, Chardonnay, Riesling, Merlot, Zinfandel, Cabernet Sauvignon.

Wines: Sauvignon Blanc, Chardonnay, Riesling, Merlot, Cabernet Sauvignon.

Awards: 1982 Alexander Valley Vintner Grown Chardonnay: three golds; 1978 Napa Valley Private Reserve Cabernet Sauvignon: two golds; 1982 Napa Valley Select Late Harvest Johannisberg Riesling: gold, three bronzes.

Retail Shop: Wines and related gifts sold on-site.

Credit Cards: American Express, MasterCard, Visa.

Access for Disabled: Winery accommodates wheelchairs.

Getting There: Winery is in bay area of Napa County, forty-seven miles north of San Francisco. Galleron Rd. is just off Hwy. 29, between Rutherford and St. Helena.

 In addition to tastings, Franciscan Vineyards offers sensory wine-evaluation sessions every afternoon at 2. These miniseminars explore three or four varietals in greater depth, showing participants what to look for in a wine, from its appearance and bouquet to its taste and texture. The collection of viticultural antiques can be admired at any time.

Freemark Abbey Winery

3022 St. Helena Highway North
St. Helena, California 94574
TEL: 707-963-9694
MANAGING PARTNER: Charles Carpy
FOUNDED: 1886

AT A GLANCE

Tours & Tastings: Open daily 10–4:30. Winery tours each day at 2 trace the grapes from the time they arrive at the winery until wine is ready for sale. Includes crushing, pressing, fermenting, barrel aging, filtering, bottling, and stor-

age. The hospitality room is furnished with antiques, Oriental rugs, and a concert grand piano.

Closed: Easter, July 4th, Thanksgiving, Christmas, New Year's Day.

Vineyards: 129 acres planted to Cabernet Sauvignon, Chardonnay, Johannisberg Riesling, Merlot.

Wines: Chardonnay, Cabernet Sauvignon, Johannisberg Riesling, Cabernet Bosche, Edelwein.

Awards: Recent medal winners include: 1981 Cabernet Sauvignon—gold, silver, bronze; 1982 Cabernet Bosche—two golds; 1983 Chardonnay—two silvers, two bronzes; 1985 Johannisberg Riesling—two silvers, bronze.

Retail Shop: Wines sold on-site.

Credit Cards: MasterCard, Visa.

Access for Disabled: None.

Getting There: In Napa County, sixty miles from San Francisco, Berkeley, and Sacramento. Winery is on Hwy. 29, roughly midway between St. Helena and Calistoga.

 Freemark Abbey was established by Josephine Tychson, probably the first woman to build a winery in California. Several proprietors and ten decades later, Freemark wines were poured at the Williamsburg summit conferences conducted by Ronald Reagan.

Girard Winery

7717 Silverado Trail, Box 105
Oakville, California 94562
TEL: 707-944-8577
PRESIDENT: Stephen A. Girard
WINEMAKER: Fred Payne
FOUNDED: 1980

AT A GLANCE

Tours & Tastings: During summer, open daily 12–5; weekends in winter. Tours by appointment only.

Closed: Winter weekdays.
Vineyards: Eighty-five acres planted to Chardonnay, Cabernet Sauvignon, Chenin Blanc.
Wines: Chardonnay, Cabernet Sauvignon, Chenin Blanc.
Awards: 1983 Chardonnay: silver, three bronzes; 1982 Cabernet Sauvignon: three bronzes; 1983 Napa Valley Cabernet Sauvignon: silver.
Retail Shop: Wines sold on-site.
Credit Cards: MasterCard, Visa.
Access for Disabled: Parking and ramp accommodate wheelchairs.
Getting There: Winery is ten miles north of Napa, at the corner of Silverado Trail and Oakville Crossroad.

🍂 After supplying grapes for Robert Mondavi's reserve bottlings, the Girards constructed their own winery in an oak grove overlooking the vineyard. In recent years, Girard wines have been served at the White House by President Reagan.

🍂 🍂 🍂

Grgich Hills Cellar

1829 St. Helena Highway (P.O. Box 450)
Rutherford, California 94573
TEL: 707-963-2784
PRESIDENT: Miljenko Grgich
FOUNDED: 1977

AT A GLANCE
Tours & Tastings: Open daily 9:30–4:30. Winemaker or his assistant conducts daily tours at 11; appointments required.
Closed: Major holidays.
Vineyards: 210 acres planted to Johannisberg Riesling, Sauvignon Blanc, Chardonnay, Cabernet Sauvignon. Additional grapes purchased from growers in Alexander Valley.
Wines: Chardonnay, Fumé Blanc, Johannisberg Riesling, Late Harvest Johannisberg Riesling, Zinfandel, Cabernet Sauvignon.

Awards: Johannisberg Riesling: gold; Cabernet Sauvignon: gold; Chardonnay: silver.
Retail Shop: Wines sold on-site.
Credit Cards: None.
Access for Disabled: None.
Foreign Languages: Croatian.
Getting There: Winery is north of San Francisco, on Hwy. 29 in Rutherford.
Special Wine & Other Events: Prerelease Wine Festival on July 4th for members of prerelease club.

🍂 As the son of a Croatian vineyardist, Miljenko Grgich was stomping grapes as soon as he could walk. He studied enology and viticulture at the University of Zagreb before emigrating to the United States. In 1976, a Chardonnay he made for another Napa Valley winery defeated some of France's finest white Burgundies in a Parisian competition; the next year, Grgich began putting his own consonant-dense name on the labels. His secret? To let the wines develop as naturally as possible. "I am a wine sitter, not a wine maker," he tells his myriad admirers.

🍂 🍂 🍂

Groth Vineyards & Winery

P.O. Box 412
Oakville, California 94562
TEL: 707-255-7466
OWNERS: Dennis and Judy Groth
WINEMAKER: Nils Venge (completed viticulture and enology program at UC-Davis)
FOUNDED: 1982

AT A GLANCE
Tours & Tastings: Tastings by appointment, Mon.–Fri. 9–5. No tours.
Closed: National holidays, weekends.
Vineyards: 165 acres planted to Sauvignon Blanc, Chardonnay, Merlot, Cabernet Sauvignon.

Wines: Sauvignon Blanc, Chardonnay, Cabernet Sauvignon.
Awards: 1982 Cabernet Sauvignon: two golds, named "King of Cabernets" at Chicago's California Cabernet competition; 1982 Chardonnay: double gold; 1983 Cabernet Sauvignon: gold; 1983 Chardonnay: two silvers, bronze.
Retail Shop: Wines sold on-site.
Credit Cards: MasterCard, Visa.
Access for Disabled: None.
Getting There: Call for directions.

&. "We are committed to producing the best possible wine a vintage can give us, and spare no expense to achieve that goal," proclaims Dennis Groth, formerly an executive with the Atari electronics firm. This winery strives for consistent quality and value. The entire Groth family is in on the act, writing press releases and tying vines.

&. &. &.

Heitz Wine Cellars

TASTING ROOM:
  436 St. Helena Highway South
  St. Helena, California 94574
  Tel: 707-963-3542
WINERY:
  500 Taplin Road
  St. Helena, California 95474
PRESIDENT: J. E. Heitz (B.S. and M.S. in enology, UC-Davis)
FOUNDED: 1961

AT A GLANCE
Tours & Tastings: Tasting room open daily, 11–4:30. Winery tours by appointment only, weekdays at 2.
Closed: Major holidays.
Vineyards: 150 acres planted to Grignolino, Zinfandel, Chardonnay. Additional grapes bought from Napa Valley growers.
Wines: Grignolino, Grignolino Rosé,

Cabernet Sauvignon, Chardonnay, Zinfandel; sherry, port.
Retail Shop: Wines sold on-site.
Credit Cards: None.
Access for Disabled: Yes.
Getting There: Tasting room is 2½ miles south of St. Helena on Hwy. 29.

&. While moonlighting at a winery near Fresno, where he was stationed during World War II, Joe Heitz discovered both his palate and his calling. He studied enology, worked with local vintners, and then established his own operation. Soon, the celebrated winemaker Andre Tchelistcheff was praising Heitz as an extraordinarily gifted innovator. In addition to being the only Napa winery to crush Grignolino, Heitz Cellars is noted for its Cabernet Sauvignon and Chardonnay; a reserve release policy ensures that several vintages are available simultaneously.

&. &. &.

William Hill Winery

P.O. Box 3989
Napa, California 94558
TEL: 707-224-6565
PRESIDENT/WINEMAKER: William Hill
FOUNDED: 1976

AT A GLANCE
Tours & Tastings: Open by appointment Mon.–Fri. 9–4.
Closed: Major holidays.
Vineyards: 385 acres planted to Cabernet Sauvignon, Chardonnay.
Wines: Cabernet Sauvignon, Chardonnay.
Retail Shop: Wines sold on-site.
Credit Cards: None.
Access for the Disabled: Yes.
Getting There: Winery is fifty miles north of San Francisco. Take Hwy. 29 North to Napa, then turn onto Lincoln Ave. East exit.

🖎 William Hill chose vineyard sites with rocky soils likely to deprive vines of water toward the end of the growing season. Under these conditions, harvests tend to be smaller, but the resulting wines are bigger.

🖎 🖎 🖎

Inglenook–Napa Valley

1991 St. Helena Highway (P.O. Box 402)
Rutherford, California 94573
TEL: 707-963-9411
OWNER: Heublein, Inc.
GENERAL MANAGER: Dennis Fife
FOUNDED: 1879

AT A GLANCE

Tours & Tastings: Open daily 10–5. Guides conduct visitors through the winery's original stone aging cellar, which still houses magnificent German oak casks. The next stop is Gustave Niebaum's tasting room, a replica of the captain's cabin on his ship, with carved oak paneling and stained-glass windows. Also featured: a museum of artifacts illustrating Inglenook's history from 1879 to the present. Tour concludes with tastings of award-winning wines.
Closed: Good Friday, Easter, Thanksgiving, Christmas, New Year's Day.
Vineyards: Extensive owned and leased acreage planted to Zinfandel, Muscat Blanc, Cabernet Franc, Petite Sirah, Pinot Noir, Chenin Blanc, Johannisberg Riesling, Gewürztraminer, Chardonnay, Sauvignon Blanc, Sémillon, Cabernet Sauvignon, Charbono, Merlot.
Wines: Chardonnay, Sauvignon Blanc, Sémillon, Gewürztraminer, Late Harvest Gewürztraminer, Chein Blanc, Muscat Blanc, Johannisberg Riesling, White Cabernet, Pinot Noir, Zinfandel, Charbono, Merlot, Cabernet Sauvignon, Cabernet Franc, Petite Sirah; also Napa Valley White and Napa Valley Red (blends).

Awards: Recent medal winners include: 1983 Reserve Merlot—gold, silver, bronze; 1984 Reserve Chardonnay—silver, bronze; 1985 white Cabernet—gold; 1982 Cabernet Sauvignon—two bronzes; 1982 Zinfandel—silver.
Retail Shop: Wines sold on-site.
Credit Cards: American Express, MasterCard, Visa.
Access for Disabled: Parking spaces and rest rooms accommodate wheelchairs.
Foreign Languages: Spanish, German, French.
Getting There: Winery is sixty miles north of San Francisco, on Hwy. 29.
Special Wine & Other Events: Wine-and-food seminars held during year. Catered luncheons and dinners for large groups by advance reservations (tel: 707-963-2616).

🖎 During his years before the mast, Gustave Niebaum must have learned a few foreign languages. Why else would a retired Finnish sea captain with a distinctly German name christen his American winery with a Scottish word meaning "cozy corner"? But at Inglenook, Niebaum abandoned etymology for enology: he wanted his wines to rival the finest European vintages. A century later, other winemakers are at Inglenook's helm, yet their aspirations remain the same.

🖎 🖎 🖎

Louis M. Martini Winery

254 South St. Helena Highway (P.O. Box 112)
St. Helena, California 94574
TEL: 707-963-2736
PRESIDENT: Carolyn Martini
WINEMAKER: Michael Martini (B.S. in fermentation science, UC-Davis)
FOUNDED: 1933

AT A GLANCE

Tours & Tastings: Open daily 10–4:30. Tours, conducted hourly from 10:30 to 4:30, cover wine production from fermentation through wood aging and bottling. Twelve wines poured daily in tasting room.

Closed: Easter, Thanksgiving, Christmas Eve, Christmas, New Year's Day.

Vineyards: 1,000 acres planted to Cabernet Sauvignon, Zinfandel, Pinot Noir, Merlot, Gamay Beaujolais, Napa Gamay, Barbera, Petite Sirah, Pinot St. George, Chardonnay, Chenin Blanc, Gewürztraminer, Johannisberg Riesling, Folle Blanche, Sémillon, Sylvaner. Walnuts grown on ranch. Additional grapes purchased from Napa and Sonoma County growers.

Wines: Folle Blanche, dry Chenin Blanc, Sauvignon Blanc/Sémillon, Chardonnay, Gewürztraminer, Johannisberg Riesling, White Zinfandel, Gamay Beaujolais, Pinot Noir, Merlot, Cabernet Sauvignon, Zinfandel, Barbera, Petite Sirah; also Moscato Amabile (a dessert wine), sherry.

Awards: Recent medal winners include: 1982 Pinot Noir—three bronzes; 1983 Merlot—silver, bronze; 1985 White Zinfandel—silver, bronze; 1982 Petite Sirah—bronze.

Retail Shop: Wines, related gifts sold on-site.

Credit Cards: MasterCard, Visa.

Access for Disabled: Doorways and halls accommodate wheelchairs; the only stairs are on an optional part of the tour.

Foreign Languages: French, Spanish.

Getting There: Winery is just south of St. Helena on Hwy. 29.

❧ This family-owned winery, built at the end of Prohibition, contains a fascinating mixture of old and contemporary equipment. Large redwood "racking" tanks from the 1930s are still used today. Alongside the modern stainless steel fermenting tanks, there are a few open cement fermentors from the early 1950s. Oak oval casks—which date back to the late 1800s—are utilized for wood aging, as are an assortment of new French oak barrels and American oak tanks.

❧ ❧ ❧

Mayacamas Vineyards

1155 Lokoya Road
Napa, California 94559
TEL: 707-224-4030
OWNER/PRESIDENT: Robert B. Travers
FOUNDED: 1889

AT A GLANCE

Tours & Tastings: Tours by appointment Mon. and Wed. at 10, Fri. at 2. Visitors see wine cellars, fermenting and bottling rooms, and any winemaking activity going on at the time. No tastings.

Closed: All major holidays.

Vineyards: Fifty acres planted to Cabernet Sauvignon, Chardonnay, Sauvignon Blanc, Pinot Noir. Additional grapes bought from local growers.

Wines: Cabernet Sauvignon, Chardonnay, Sauvignon Blanc, Zinfandel, Late Harvest Zinfandel, Pinot Noir.

Retail Shop: Wines sold on-site.

Credit Cards: None.

Access for the Disabled: Building, bathrooms wheelchair accessible.

Foreign Languages: Spanish.

Getting There: Winery is fifty miles north of San Francisco. Take Hwy. 29 to Redwood Rd. Bear right on Mt. Veeder Rd. and left on Lokoya Rd.

❧ In a rare case of vinegar leading to wine, a nineteenth-century pickle merchant built this winery to produce bulk reds and whites. Under its current ownership, Mayacamas Vineyards specializes in Chardonnay and Cabernet Sauvignon.

ᵛᵃ ᵛᵃ ᵛᵃ

Louis K. Mihaly Vineyard

3103 Silverado Trail (P.O. Box 2840)
Napa, California 94558
TEL: 707-253-9306
PRESIDENT: Louis K. Mihaly
GENERAL MANAGER/WINEMAKER: John
D. Nemeth (Ph.D. in enology)
FOUNDED: 1979

AT A GLANCE
Tours & Tastings: Open by appointment
Mon.–Fri. 10–4:30; weekends by special
arrangement. A short tour of the tank
room, bottling room, and the bottle-
aging warehouse is combined with barrel
tasting from various types of oak. No
more than six guests per tour. Vertical
tastings are offered in an elegant tasting
room illuminated by a brass chandelier.
These tastings feature six vintages, ac-
companied by cheese and delicacies, de-
pending upon the occasion.
Closed: National holidays.
Vineyards: Thirty-four acres planted to
Chardonnay, Sauvignon Blanc, Pinot
Noir.
Wines: Chardonnay, Sauvignon Blanc,
Pinot Noir.
Retail Shop: Wines sold on-site.
Credit Cards: American Express.
Access for Disabled: Wheelchair accessi-
ble.
Foreign Languages: German, Italian,
Hungarian.
Getting There: Winery is 1½ miles north
of the city of Napa on the Silverado Trail.

ᵛᵃ Because Louis K. Mihaly's family
had been growing grapes in Hungary for
more than 700 years, friends wondered
when and where he would follow suit. In
1977 he settled in the Napa Valley, and
the answers to those questions became
clear. Mihaly has done well by his Tran-
sylvanian ancestors. His estate-bottled,
vintage-dated varietals are keenly sought
by a select group of restaurants and private clubs; these wines cannot be bought
at retail stores.

ᵛᵃ ᵛᵃ ᵛᵃ

Robert Mondavi Winery

7801 South St. Helena Highway (P.O.
Box 106)
Oakville, California 94562
TEL: 707-963-9611
OWNERS: the Robert Mondavi family
FOUNDED: 1966

AT A GLANCE
Tours & Tastings: Open daily; May–Oct.
9–5, Nov.–Apr. 10–4. Regular tours
leave every fifteen minutes. These include a viticultural narrative, a visit to
crushing and winemaking facilities, a
visit to the barrel room, and a tasting
accompanied by discussion of the sensory appreciation of wine. Longer, in-
depth tours of vineyard and winery, with
tasting of barrel samples and finished
wines, offered by appointment, Mon.,
Wed., Fri. at 10.
Closed: Good Friday, Easter, Thanksgiving, Christmas, New Year's Day.
Vineyards: 1,000 acres planted to Cabernet Sauvignon, Pinot Noir, Chardon-
nay, Johannisberg Riesling, Merlot,
Sauvignon Blanc, Fumé Blanc. Addi-
tional grapes supplied on contract by
Napa Valley growers.
Wines: Cabernet Sauvignon, Pinot Noir,
Chardonnay, Fumé Blanc, Johannisberg
Riesling, Chenin Blanc, Moscata d'Oro.
Awards: Too many to mention.
Retail Shop: Wines sold on-site.
Credit Cards: American Express, Mas-
terCard, Visa.
Access for Disabled: Winery accommo-
dates wheelchairs.
Foreign Languages: French, German,
Italian.
Getting There: Winery is fifteen miles
north of the city of Napa, on Hwy. 29

Special Wine & Other Events: Monthly art exhibits, summer jazz concerts, and programs featuring great French and American chefs.

ᨘ This name is known way beyond Napa County limits. Over the years, the Mondavis have established themselves as industry innovators. In their winery, an IBM computer monitors fermentation temperatures, as aromatic grape skins swirl in the gently rotating tanks. But this state-of-the-art technology is happily compatible with the arts of the state: the Mondavis also sponsor concerts, cooking schools, and an on-site gallery.

ᨘ ᨘ ᨘ

Monticello Cellars

4242 Big Ranch Road
Napa, California 94558
TEL: 707-253-2802, 253-2187
OWNER: Jay Corley
WINEMAKER: Alan Phillips (B.S. in
    fermentation science, UC-Davis)
FOUNDED: 1970

AT A GLANCE
Tours & Tastings: Open daily 10–4:30. Complete tours of winery at 10:30, 12:30, and 2:30; appointments appreciated.
Closed: Easter, Thanksgiving, Christmas, New Year's Day.
Vineyards: 225 acres planted to Sémillon, Pinot Noir, Chardonnay, Sauvignon Blanc, Gewürztraminer.
Wines: Chardonnay, Sauvignon Blanc, Gewürztraminer, Cabernet Sauvignon, Pinot Noir, Chevrier Blanc.
Retail Shop: Wines sold on-site.
Credit Cards: MasterCard, Visa.
Access for Disabled: No steps from parking area to tasting room.
Getting There: From city of Napa: Take Silverado Trail to Trancas St. Turn left onto Trancas, right on Big Ranch Rd.
Special Wine & Other Events: Cooking

classes, vineyard tours, and wine seminars held throughout the year.

ᨘ With architecture inspired by that of its Virginia namesake, Monticello Cellars is a living monument to Thomas Jefferson, one of America's first vineyardists. "Jefferson once wrote that good wine is a necessity of life," says Jay Corley, an ardent student of the founding father's life and works. "Those are words to live by here."

ᨘ ᨘ ᨘ

Napa Creek Winery

1001 Silverado Trail
St. Helena, California 94574
TEL: 707-963-9456
PRESIDENT: Jack Schulze
FOUNDED: 1980

AT A GLANCE
Tours & Tastings: Open daily 10–5. This small winery gives personal tours. Visitors welcome at crush time.
Closed: Easter, Thanksgiving, Christmas.
Vineyards: None. All grapes purchased from Napa Valley growers.
Wines: Chardonnay, Johannisberg Riesling, Gewürztraminer, White Zinfandel, Cabernet Sauvignon, Merlot.
Awards: All the wines have won awards in past years.
Retail Shop: Wines sold on-site.
Credit Cards: MasterCard, Visa.
Access for Disabled: Ramps into winery.
Getting There: Winery is two miles east of St. Helena on Silverado Trail.

ᨘ Jack Schulze spent twenty-five years marketing wine before he began making it. His premium varietals are literally fit for a queen—Napa Creek wines were served to Queen Elizabeth aboard the royal yacht *Britannia*.

ᨘ ᨘ ᨘ

Napa Valley Port Works

736 California Boulevard
Napa, California 94559
TEL: 707-257-7777
PRESIDENT: Shawn Denkler (B.S. in
enology from California State
University at Fresno)
FOUNDED: 1984

AT A GLANCE
Tours & Tastings: Open by appointment
Mon. 6–9, Fri.–Sat. 10–5; additional
times may be arranged.
Vineyards: Grapes bought from Napa
and Sonoma County growers.
Wines: Vintage Port, Ruby Port.
Retail Shop: California and Portuguese
ports, other wines sold on-site.
Credit Cards: American Express, Mas-
terCard, Visa.
Access for Disabled: None.
Getting There: Port Works is one mile
west of downtown Napa, near the Third
St. exit from Hwy. 29.
Special Wine & Other Events: Many tast-
ings of fine Portuguese ports held Nov.–
Apr.

&a An alumnus of both California
State University and the University of
California at Davis, Shawn Denkler con-
ducts wine tastings around the country.
In his spare time, he writes about his
favorite subject: port.

&a &a &a

Robert Pecota

3299 Bennett Lane, (Box 303)
Calistoga, California 94515
TEL: 707-942-6625
OWNER: Robert Pecota
WINEMAKER: Kathy Joseph (M.S. in
enology, UC-Davis)
FOUNDED: 1978

AT A GLANCE
Tours & Tastings: Open by appointment,
Mon.–Fri. 9–5.
Closed: Weekends, all major holidays.

Vineyards: Forty-five acres planted to
Cabernet Sauvignon, Sauvignon Blanc,
Muscat Blanc.
Wines: Cabernet Sauvignon, Sauvignon
Blanc, Muscat Blanc.
Awards: Numerous.
Retail Shop: Wines sold on-site.
Credit Cards: None. Cash, checks ac-
cepted.
Access for Disabled: Winery accommo-
dates wheelchairs.
Getting There: Winery is fifty miles north
of San Francisco. Take either Hwy. 128
or Hwy. 29 north past Calistoga to Tubbs
Ln., then turn onto Bennett Ln.

&a "I simply enjoy a life which is tied
to the seasons," says winemaker Robert
Pecota, whose other pleasures range
from writing poetry to playing handball.
He publishes both his verses and game
results in an irregularly released winery
newsletter.

&a &a &a

Peju Province Winery

8466 St. Helena Highway (P.O. Box 478)
Rutherford, California 94573
TEL: 707-963-3600
OWNER: Anthony Peju
FOUNDED: 1983

AT A GLANCE
Tours & Tastings: Open daily 11–6;
winter hours: 11–5. No tours until
winery building is completed.
Vineyards: Thirty acres planted to Cab-
ernet Sauvignon and French Colombard.
Walnuts and strawberries also grown
here.
Wines: Cabernet Sauvignon, Chardon-
nay, Sauvignon Blanc, Colombard.
Awards: Chardonnay: silver, two
bronzes; Sauvignon Blanc: silver.
Retail Shop: Wines, strawberry and
blackberry jam sold on-site.
Credit Cards: MasterCard, Visa.
Access for Disabled: None.
Foreign Languages: Spanish, German.

Getting There: Winery is ten miles north of the city of Napa on Hwy. 29.

❧ The Pejus uprooted themselves from Los Angeles in order to create this small boutique winery, which has already gleaned several medals. Visitors interested in horticulture as well as viticulture should ask to see the owners' extensive flower-and-vegetable gardens.

❧ ❧ ❧

Joseph Phelps Vineyards

200 Taplin Road (P.O. Box 1031)
St. Helena, California 94574
TEL: 707-963-2745
PRESIDENT/OWNER: Joseph Phelps
WINEMAKER: Craig Williams (degree in fermentation science from UC-Davis)
FOUNDED: 1973

AT A GLANCE
Tours & Tastings: Tours by appointment, Mon.–Fri. 11, 2:30; Sat. 10, 11:30, 1, 2:30. Forty-five-minute tour covers the winemaking process—fermentation, aging, fining, cold stabilization, bottling—and links wine with appropriate foods. A fifteen-to-twenty-minute tasting follows.
Vineyards: 800 owned and 7½ leased acres planted to Cabernet Sauvignon, Merlot, Cabernet Franc, French Syrah, and other vinifera varieties.
Wines: Chardonnay, Sauvignon Blanc, Gewürztraminer, Johannisberg Riesling, Scheurebe, Sémillon, Syrah, Cabernet Sauvignon, Zinfandel, Cabernet France.
Awards: Recent medal winners include: 1983 Special Select Late Harvest Johannisberg Riesling—gold, two silvers; 1985 Late Harvest Scheurebe—two golds; 1984 Napa Zinfandel—gold; 1981 Cabernet Sauvignon—silver, bronze.
Retail Shop: Wines sold on-site.
Credit Cards: MasterCard, Visa.
Access for Disabled: None.
Getting There: Winery is seventy-five miles north of San Francisco. Taplin Rd.

is off the Silverado Trail, slightly south of St. Helena.

❧ Colorado native Joseph Phelps made his first wine from a kit set up in his Denver fallout shelter. A few years later he graduated to the Napa Valley and built this striking redwood winery, with its two pavillions joined by a closed bridge. To fuel his other consuming passion—food—Phelps purchased the local Oakland Grocery, a sleepy general store, and transformed it into a gourmet emporium.

❧ ❧ ❧

Plam Vineyards

6200 St. Helena Highway
Napa, California 94558
TEL: 707-944-1102
OWNER: Kenneth H. Plam
WINEMAKER: Nikolaus Koengeter
FOUNDED: 1984

AT A GLANCE
Tours & Tastings: Retail sales daily 10–4. Tours and tastings by appointment.
Vineyards: Six acres planted to Chardonnay. Additional grapes purchased from growers in Carneros and Oak Knoll regions of Napa County.
Wines: Chardonnay, Sauvignon Blanc, Cabernet Sauvignon, Merlot.
Awards: 1984 Chardonnay: gold; 1985 Sauvignon Blanc: four bronzes.
Retail Shop: Wines sold on-site.
Credit Cards: None.
Access for Disabled: Wheelchair accessible.
Foreign Languages: German.
Getting There: Winery is one mile south of Yountville on Hwy. 29.

❧ "Plam produces 7,500 cases a year from top-quality grapes," notes assistant manager Connie Koengeter. "The winery is a picturesque stone building perched on a sheltered green bend of Hopper Creek, with towering California oaks in back and our vineyards in front. It's close enough to Highway 29 to be convenient, yet far enough away to be quiet."

?&. ?&. ?&.

Quail Ridge Cellars & Vineyards

1055 Atlas Peak Road
Napa, California 94558
TEL: 707-996-7459, 257-1712
OWNERS/WINEMAKERS: Elaine Wellesley
and Leon Santoro
FOUNDED: 1978

AT A GLANCE
Tours & Tastings: Open weekends Apr.– Nov. 10–4. Weekdays, winter months, by appointment.
Vineyards: Seventeen acres planted to Chardonnay; other grapes purchased.
Wines: Chardonnay, French Colombard, Cabernet Sauvignon, Merlot.
Retail Shop: Wines sold on-site.
Credit Cards: MasterCard, Visa.
Access for Disabled: None.
Getting There: From the city of Napa: take Silverado Trail north to Trancas St., bear right on Monticello Rd. and left on Atlas Peak Rd. (Winery is ¼ mile south of the Silverado Country Club.)

?&. Elaine Wellesley and Leon Santoro believe in the good old ways. This is a winery in the classic château tradition, right down to the historic hand-hewn storage caves Quail Ridge inherited when it moved here in 1981. In keeping with nineteenth-century practice, all Chardonnays and French Colombards are fermented in the barrel.

?&. ?&. ?&.

Raymond Vineyard & Cellar

849 Zinfandel Lane
St. Helena, California 94574
TEL: 707-963-3141, 963-8511
OWNER/PRESIDENT: Roy Raymond, Sr.
FOUNDED: 1974

AT A GLANCE
Tours & Tastings: Open daily for tastings 10–4. Tours by appointment only.
Vineyards: Eighty acres planted to Cabernet Sauvignon, Chardonnay.
Wines: Cabernet Sauvignon, Chardonnay, Sauvignon Blanc, Johannisberg Riesling, vintage select white and red.
Awards: Recent medal winners include: 1984 Napa Chardonnay: two golds, two silvers, four bronzes; 1981 Private Reserve Cabernet Sauvignon: gold, silver, bronze; 1984 Johannisberg Riesling: silver, bronze.
Retail Shop: Wines sold on-site.
Credit Cards: MasterCard, Visa.
Access for Disabled: Entrance ramp, bathrooms wheelchair accessible.
Foreign Languages: French.
Getting There: Winery is sixty miles north of San Francisco. Take Hwy. 29 to E. Zinfandel Ln. in St. Helena; proceed to the corner of Zinfandel and Wheeler Way.

?&. To visit this winery is to meet an enological dynasty with Cabernet coursing through its veins. Roy Raymond, Sr., former winemaker at Beringer Vineyards, married the founder's granddaughter. When Beringer was sold, Raymond struck out on his own, ably assisted by sons Roy Jr. and Walter. Now the former tends the vines, the latter makes the wines. You'll find grandson Craig working in the cellar.

?&. ?&. ?&.

Rustridge Vineyard & Winery

2910 Lower Chiles Valley Road
St. Helena, California 94574
TEL: 707-965-2871
OWNER: Stanton J. Meyer
FOUNDED: 1985

AT A GLANCE

Tours & Tastings: Open daily for retail sales 10–5. Tastings and tours by appointment. Tours geared to individual interests.

Vineyards: Fifty-five acres planted to Johannisberg Riesling, Chardonnay, Zinfandel.

Wines: Johannisberg Riesling, Chardonnay, Riesling, white blend.

Awards: 1984 Johannsiberg Riesling: silver; 1985 Johannisberg Riesling: bronze.

Picnic Area: Lush grassy area shaded by oak trees.

Retail Shop: Wines sold on-site.

Credit Cards: MasterCard, Visa.

Access for Disabled: Ramps, bathrooms accommodate wheelchairs.

Getting There: Winery is sixty-nine miles north of San Francisco and twenty-nine miles northeast of Napa. Take either Silverado Trail or Hwy. 29 north to Hwy. 128 and travel east, winding around Lake Hennessy. Bear left on Chiles Pope Valley Rd.; several miles later, turn right onto Lower Chiles Valley Rd.

Special Wine & Other Events: Grape Stomp during the first week of Sept.; concerts year-round.

&. After converting this cattle and race horse ranch into a vineyard, the Meyers restored the Thoroughbred breeding facilities; the resident stud is named Napa Valley. Hopes are high that some of the recently released foals will make it to the winner's circle, matching the track record of Rustridge's one- and two-year-old Rieslings.

&. &. &.

Rutherford Hill Winery

200 Rutherford Hill Road
Rutherford, California 94573
TEL: 707-963-9694, 963-7175
MANAGING PARTNER: William Jaeger, Jr.

WINEMAKER: Jerry Luper
FOUNDED: 1976

AT A GLANCE

Tours & Tastings: Open daily 10:30–4:30. Tours at 11:30 and 2:30 visit working wine cellar, caves, and pressing and fermentation area, while guide explains basics of winemaking. Then guests proceed to tasting room to sample a variety of current and past releases.

Closed: Easter, Thanksgiving, Christmas, New Year's Day.

Vineyards: 830 acres planted to vinifera varieties. Additional grapes purchased from Napa Valley growers.

Wines: Cabernet Sauvignon, Merlot, Chardonnay, Gewürztraminer, Sauvignon Blanc.

Awards: 1981 Chardonnay Reserve: gold, silver; 1982 Cabernet Sauvignon: silver, bronze; 1984 Gewürztraminer: silver, bronze; 1982 Merlot: gold, silver, bronze.

Picnic Area: On hillside, shaded by oak and olive trees.

Retail Shop: Wines sold on-site.

Credit Cards: MasterCard, Visa.

Access for Disabled: Ramp into winery.

Getting There: From Napa: Drive north on Silverado Trail about twelve miles to Rutherford Hill Rd., just north of intersection with Hwy. 128.

&. Extending for more than half a mile, Rutherford Hill's network of wine caves is among the largest ever tunneled in America for the aging of wine. The caves, completed in 1986, took thirteen months to construct. Good wines require more than twice as much time, from grape to bottle. "The red varietal Merlot is special to us," report the proprietors. "It is particularly rewarding to achieve success with this wine, and see it become appreciated."

&. &. &.

Saddleback Cellars

7802 Money Road (P.O. Box 141)
Oakville, California 94562
TEL: 707-963-4982
PARTNERS: Robert A. Call and Nils
  Venge
WINEMAKER: Nils Venge (viticulture
  and enology degree, UC-Davis)
FOUNDED: 1983

AT A GLANCE
Tours & Tastings: Open by appointment
only.
Vineyards: Seventeen acres planted to
Cabernet Sauvignon, Chardonnay, Pinot
Blanc.
Wines: Cabernet Sauvignon, Chardon-
nay, Pinot Blanc, Cabernet Rosé, Cab-
ernet Blanc.
Awards: Cabernet Blanc: bronze.
Retail Shop: Wines sold on-site.
Credit Cards: None.
Access for Disabled: None.
Foreign Languages: Danish.
Getting There: From Hwy. 29 in Oakville:
Head 1½ miles east off Oakville Cross
Rd., then go north on Money Rd.

&. Nils Venge conducts tastings because, he notes, "I drink fine wine"—
presumably including his own vintages.
His other qualifications are noted above.

&. &. &.

St. Clement Vineyards

2867 St. Helena Highway (P.O. Box 261)
St. Helena, California 94574
TEL: 707-963-7221
OWNER: William J. Casey
WINEMAKER: Dennis Johns
FOUNDED: 1975

AT A GLANCE
Tours & Tastings: Open by appointment
only. Tours by appointment show entire
winery, including the wine cellar beneath
the Caseys' century-old Victorian home.
Vineyards: 3½ acres planted to Cabernet

Sauvignon. "We purchase additional
grapes from a number of growers all over
the Napa Valley."
Wines: Sauvignon Blanc, Cabernet
Sauvignon, Chardonnay.
Awards: 1983 Chardonnay: silver; 1985
Sauvignon Blanc: silver.
Retail Shop: Wines sold on-site.
Credit Cards: None.
Access for Disabled: Wheelchair accessi-
ble.
Getting There: Winery is on Hwy. 29 in
St. Helena.

&. Native Marylander William Casey,
an eye surgeon, named his winery after
his family's East Coast estate. "In our
early years here, we made a few hundred
cases, using the stone cellars under the
house," he recalls. "Encouraged by the
reception our first wines received, we
built a spacious modern winery that harmonizes with our handsome old mansion. With all this additional storage
room, annual production has reached ten
thousand cases."

&. &. &.

Sequoia Grove Vineyards

8338 St. Helena Highway
Napa, California 94558
TEL: 707-944-2945
PRESIDENT: James Allen
FOUNDED: 1980

AT A GLANCE
Tours & Tastings: Open daily 11–5. Brief
winery tours include tasting.
CLOSED: Good Friday, Easter, Thanksgiv-
ing, Christmas, New Year's Day.
Vineyards: 24 owned and 110 managed
acres planted to Chardonnay, Cabernet
Sauvignon, Cabernet Franc, Merlot, Pe-
tite Verdot.
Wines: Cabernet Sauvignon, Chardon-
nay.
Awards: 1981 Alexander Valley Cabernet
Sauvignon: platinum; 1982 Napa/Alex-

ander Valley Cabernet Sauvignon: gold, silver; 1983 Napa Valley/Estate-Bottled Chardonnay: two golds.
Retail Shop: Wines sold on-site.
Credit Cards: American Express, MasterCard, Visa.
Access for Disabled: Winery accommodates wheelchairs.
Foreign Languages: German.
Getting There: Winery is sixty miles north of San Francisco on Hwy. 29, midway between Oakville and Rutherford.

❧ Sequoia Grove takes its name from the grove of giant redwoods towering over the century-old winery building. The grove is one of the last of its kind in the Napa Valley.

❧ ❧ ❧

Shadow Brook Winery

360 Zinfandel Lane
St. Helena, California 94574
TEL: 707-963-2000
OWNER/PRESIDENT: Emil Hoffman
FOUNDED: 1984

AT A GLANCE
Tours & Tastings: Tours only, by appointment.
Vineyards: Sixty acres planted to Chardonnay, Pinot Noir.
Wines: Chardonnay, Cabernet, Merlot.
Retail Shop: Wines sold during special tastings.
Credit Cards: None.
Access for Disabled: Winery accommodates wheelchairs.
Foreign Languages: German, a little Spanish and French.
Getting There: Winery is two miles south and half a mile east of St. Helena. Take either Hwy. 29 or the Silverado Trail to Zinfandel Ln.

❧ Restaurateur Emil Hoffman has turned an old barn into a small, family-owned premium winery.

❧ ❧ ❧

Shafer Vineyards

6154 Silverado Trail
Napa, California 94558
TEL: 707-944-2877
PRESIDENT: John R. Shafer
WINEMAKER: Doug Shafer (B.S. in viticulture, UC-Davis)
FOUNDED: 1979

AT A GLANCE
Tours & Tastings: By appointment only, Tues.–Fri. at 11. "Whether we're bottling or crushing grapes, visitors have a part of the action—sipping just-bottled wine or nibbling Chardonnay grapes."
Vineyards: Sixty-five acres planted to Cabernet Sauvignon, Chardonnay, Merlot, Cabernet Franc.
Wines: Cabernet Sauvignon, Chardonnay, Merlot.
Awards: Shafer Chardonnay has won golds for every vintage, 1983 to 1986. Other medal winners include: Cabernet Sauvignon: double gold; Merlot: gold.
Retail Shop: Wines sold on-site.
Credit Cards: None.
Access for Disabled: None.
Getting There: Winery is on the Silverado Trail, 7 miles north of Trancas St. in Napa, and ¾ mile south of the Yountville Crossroad.

❧ The Shafers gave up social and financial security in Chicago to take over a neglected Napa Valley vineyard. "With a little ingenuity and the grace of our more experienced neighbors, we learned the business of viticulture," John Shafer observes. "We're located on the quiet, less commercial side of the valley; visitors have a chance to see the actual operation up close." The views are another story. "Slipping around the blind curve just off the Silverado Trail, you drive east through Shafer's vineyards toward the magnificent Stags Leap palisades. On the winery deck, you can take pictures of vineyards, mountains, and the Napa Valley."

 za za za

Charles F. Shaw Vineyard & Winery

1010 Big Tree Road
St. Helena, California 94574
TEL: 707-963-5459
GENERAL PARTNER: Charles F. Shaw
WINEMAKER: Ric Forman (B.S. and
  M.S. in food science, UC-Davis)
FOUNDED: 1979

AT A GLANCE
Tours & Tastings: Open daily 11–5. Tours by appointment.
Vineyards: Forty-seven acres planted to Chardonnay, Sauvignon Blanc, Gamay.
Wines: Chardonnay, Fumé Blanc, Gamay Nouveau, Napa Valley Gamay, Gamay Blanc.
Awards: 1985 Napa Valley Gamay: three golds, two silvers; 1983 Chardonnay: gold, three silvers, four bronzes; 1984 Fumé Blanc: two silvers, two bronzes.
Retail Shop: Wines sold on-site.
Credit Cards: American Express, MasterCard, Visa.
Access for Disabled: None.
Foreign Languages: French.
Getting There: Winery is in Napa Valley, four miles north of St. Helena, off Hwy. 29.

za A West Point graduate turned international banker, Charles Shaw cultivated his love of wine on assignment in Paris. Why the emphasis on Gamay varietals? "I want to be the 'light red guy' of the Napa Valley," he explains. "You can drink Gamay with anything."

za za za

Silverado Vineyards

6121 Silverado Trail
Napa, California 94558
TEL: 707-257-1770

OWNERS: Lillian Disney, Diane Disney Miller, Ronald W. Miller
WINEMAKER: John Stuart (graduate studies in viticulture and enology, UC-Davis)
FOUNDED: 1981

AT A GLANCE
Tours & Tastings: Open daily 11–4. No tours.
Closed: Major holidays.
Vineyards: 180 acres planted to Sauvignon Blanc, Chardonnay, Merlot, Cabernet Sauvignon.
Wines: Sauvignon Blanc, Chardonnay, Merlot, Cabernet Sauvignon.
Awards: 1984 Chardonnay: two golds, three silvers, bronze; 1983 Merlot: gold, four bronzes; 1984 Sauvignon Blanc: two silvers, bronze; 1982 Cabernet Sauvignon: three silvers.
Picnic Area: Umbrella-topped tables outside winery.
Retail Shop: Wines sold on-site.
Credit Cards: MasterCard, Visa.
Access for Disabled: Rest rooms wheelchair accessible.
Foreign Languages: French.
Getting There: Winery is in the city of Napa, approximately sixty miles northeast of San Francisco, on the Silverado Trail.

za When grapes from their vineyards produced award-winning vintages for other wineries, the Disneys yielded to the inevitable temptation to harvest grapes—and medals—for themselves. The winery's stone architecture is traditional, but the equipment within is modern.

za za za

Smith-Madrone

4022 Spring Mountain Road
St. Helena, California 94574
TEL: 707-963-2283
OWNERS/WINEMAKERS: Charles and
  Stuart Smith
FOUNDED: 1972

AT A GLANCE

Tours & Tastings: Open by appointment only. Casual, intimate tours, given by the winemakers themselves, address enology and local history.
Vineyards: Thirty-eight acres planted to Cabernet Sauvignon, Pinot Noir, Chardonnay, Riesling.
Wines: Cabernet Sauvignon, Pinot Noir, Chardonnay, Riesling.
Retail Shop: Wines sold on-site.
Credit Cards: None.
Access for Disabled: None.
Getting There: Winery is in Napa County, 5½ miles west of St. Helena. Take Hwy. 29 to Madrona Ave. and bear right on Spring Mountain Rd.

🐌 Stuart Smith taught viticulture and enology at local junior colleges for twelve years. His students must have been fortunate, indeed: Smith-Madrone's first crush—1977's Riesling—took first place at the Gault-Millau Wine Olympiad. The problem is, there's so little to go around; annual production hovers at only 6,500 cases.

🐌 🐌 🐌

Spring Mountain Vineyards

2805 Spring Mountain Road
St. Helena, California 94574
TEL: 707-963-5233
PRESIDENT: Michael Robbins
FOUNDED: 1968

AT A GLANCE

Tours & Tastings: Open daily 10–5. Grounds tours, departing every thirty minutes, circumnavigate the Spring Mountain house, a splendid nineteenth-century estate designed by the same architect who created the Beringers' Rhine House. Winery tours by appointment only, Mon.–Fri. 10:30 and 2:30; weekends at 10:30. This tour explains the winemaking process as visitors walk through the facilities.
Closed: Christmas.

Vineyards: 145 acres planted to Chardonnay, Sauvignon Blanc, Cabernet Sauvignon.
Wines: Chardonnay, Cabernet Sauvignon, Sauvignon Blanc.
Retail Shop: Wines sold on-site.
Credit Cards: American Express, MasterCard, Visa.
Access for Disabled: Winery accommodates wheelchairs.
Foreign Languages: German.
Getting There: Winery is approximately sixty miles from San Francisco. From Hwy. 29 in St. Helena, at the only stop light, turn left on Madrona Ave. Three blocks later, turn right onto Spring Mountain Rd. Winery is one mile ahead, on the left side.

🐌 "Falcon Crest" fans will recognize this palatial mansion, built in 1885, as the setting of the hit TV series. But beneath the show business wrapping lurks a serious enological endeavor. The winery itself occupies a compatible Victorian-style building of late 1970s vintage; wines are aged in the reinforced cave dug for the mansion's original inhabitants, who produced a few commercial bottlings.

🐌 🐌 🐌

Stag's Leap Wine Cellars

5766 Silverado Trail
Napa, California 94558
TEL: 707-944-2020
OWNERS: Warren and Barbara Winiarski
WINEMAKER: Warren Winiarski
FOUNDED: 1972

AT A GLANCE

Tours & Tastings: Open daily 10–4. Tours by appointment only, for fifteen people or less; format varies depending on group's specific interest.
Closed: Thanksgiving, Christmas, New Year's Day.
Vineyards: 134 acres planted to Cabernet Sauvignon, Merlot. Additional grapes

purchased from growers in northern California.

Wines: Cabernet Sauvignon, Merlot, Chardonnay, Sauvignon Blanc, White Riesling, Gamay Beaujolais under Stag's Leap and Hawk Crest labels.

Awards: Two years in a row, Warren Winiarski won the Harry Waugh trophy for the best California red entered in the International Wine & Spirit Competition in London. Recent medal winners include: 1977 Cask #23 Cabernet Sauvignon: gold; 1978 Cabernet Sauvignon: double gold.

Retail Shop: House wines and imported Portuguese port sold on-site.

Credit Cards: MasterCard, Visa.

Access for Disabled: None.

Foreign Languages: Some Japanese— Ask for Ann Catania.

Getting There: Winery is on Silverado Trail, about seven miles north of Trancas St.

🍇 After toiling in the groves of academe, University of Chicago teachers Warren and Barbara Winiarski decided they would rather labor in the vineyard. It was a good trade. They have been making international history since a 1976 Paris tasting, when their first Cabernet Sauvignon beat Bordeaux's best by more than a nose. In 1983, Queen Elizabeth toasted Ronald and Nancy Reagan's thirty-first anniversary with Stag's Leap wines; two years later, at the Geneva Summit Conference, the Reagans poured Stag's Leap for their dinner guest, Soviet premier Mikhail Gorbachev. On occasion, the Winiarskis appeal to even higher authorities: a local priest blesses their vines twice a year.

🍇 🍇 🍇

Steltzner Vineyards

5998 Silverado Trail
Napa, California 94558
TEL: 707-252-7272, 252-0335

OWNER/PRESIDENT: Richard Steltzner
FOUNDED: 1983

AT A GLANCE

Tours & Tastings: Open by appointment only.

Vineyards: 120 acres planted to Cabernet Sauvignon, Merlot. Kiwi fruit and mandarin oranges are also grown here.

Wines: Cabernet Sauvignon.

Retail Shop: Wines sold on-site.

Credit Cards: None.

Access for Disabled: None.

Getting There: Winery is seven miles north of Napa on the Silverado Trail.

🍇 At this modestly sized winery, traditional methods and modern equipment are used to produce a fine food wine that gets even better with additional aging.

🍇 🍇 🍇

Sterling Vineyards

1111 Dunaweal Lane
Calistoga, California 94515
TEL: 707-942-5151
OWNER: Seagram Classics Wine Co.
WINEMAKER: Bill Dyer (M.S. in enology, UC-Davis)
FOUNDED: 1969

AT A GLANCE

Tours & Tastings: Open Apr.–Dec. daily 10:30–4:30; Jan.–March Wed.–Sun. Self-guided tours.

Closed: Mon., Tues., Jan–March.

Vineyards: 1,080 acres planted to Cabernet Sauvignon, Chardonnay, Merlot, Sauvignon Blanc.

Wines: Cabernet Sauvignon, Chardonnay, Merlot, Sauvignon Blanc, Cabernet Blanc.

Picnic Area: Yes.

Retail Shop: Wines sold on-site.

Credit Cards: American Express, MasterCard, Visa.

Access for Disabled: Tasting room can

accommodate wheelchairs, winery cannot.

Getting There: Winery is two miles south of Calistoga. Take Silverado Trail to Dunaweal Ln.

ₑ For a bird's-eye view of the winery and vineyards, take a ride on Sterling's aerial tramway.

ₑ ₑ ₑ

Sullivan Vineyards Winery

1090 Galleron Road
Rutherford, California 94573
TEL: 707-963-9646
PRESIDENT: James O. Sullivan
FOUNDED: 1979

AT A GLANCE

Tours & Tastings: Open by appointment only.
Vineyards: Thirty acres planted to Cabernet Sauvignon, Merlot, Zinfandel, Chardonnay, Chenin Blanc. Sauvignon Blanc purchased from Knights Valley growers.
Wines: Cabernet Sauvignon, Merlot, Zinfandel, Chardonnay, Chenin Blanc, Sauvignon Blanc.
Awards: National recognition from several wine publications.
Retail Shop: Wines sold on-site.
Credit Cards: None.
Access for Disabled: None.
Foreign Languages: French, Italian, Flemish.
Getting There: Winery is seventy-two miles northeast of San Francisco. Take Hwy. 29 north; one mile past Rutherford Sq., turn right on Galleron Rd.

ₑ This is a small, family-operated winery that makes estate-bottled, 100 percent varietal wines.

ₑ ₑ ₑ

Sutter Home Winery

277 St. Helena Highway South (P.O. Box 248)
St. Helena, California 94574
TEL: 707-963-3104
PRESIDENT: Louis "Bob" Trinchero
FOUNDED: 1874

AT A GLANCE

Tours & Tastings: Open daily 10–4:30. No tours.
Closed: Easter, Thanksgiving, New Year's Day.
Vineyards: 1,000 owned, 750 leased acres planted to Zinfandel, Chardonnay, Sauvignon Blanc, Chenin Blanc, Cabernet Sauvignon.
Wines: White Zinfandel, Amador Zinfandel, California Zinfandel, Sauvignon Blanc, Chardonnay, Chenin Blanc, Cabernet Sauvignon, Sparkler (sparkling White Zinfandel).
Awards: Does not participate in competitive tastings.
Retail Shop: Wines sold on-site.
Credit Cards: MasterCard, Visa.
Access for Disabled: Wheelchair accessible.
Foreign Languages: French, Italian, German.
Getting There: Winery is about sixty miles from San Francisco and two miles south of St. Helena, on the west side of Hwy. 29.

ₑ Sutter Home Winery, the oldest wooden winery in Napa Valley, may well be the region's oldest standing building still used in the manufacture and bottling of wine. The Trinchero family has owned and operated Sutter since 1947.

ₑ ₑ ₑ

Villa Helena Winery

1455 Inglewood Avenue
St. Helena, California 94574
TEL: 707-963-4334

OWNER/WINEMAKER: Donald W.
  McGrath
FOUNDED: 1984

AT A GLANCE
Tours & Tastings: Open by appointment
only. Tours by appointment.
Vineyards: Four acres planted to Char-
donnay. Additional grapes bought from
other Napa Valley growers.
Wines: Chardonnay, Sauvignon Blanc,
Pinot Noir.
Awards: 1984 Chardonnay: bronze.
Retail Shop: Wines sold on-site.
Credit Cards: None.
Access for the Disabled: None.
Foreign Languages: Spanish, Catalan.
Getting There: Winery is two miles south
of St. Helena, and 400 feet west of Hwy.
29 on Inglewood Ave.

ᘍ Don McGrath, a metallurgical engineer, spent fourteen years as an amateur vintner before launching Villa
Helena. Production presently hovers at
2,000 cases.

ᘍ ᘍ ᘍ

Villa Mt. Eden

620 Oakville Crossroads (P.O. Box 147)
St. Helena, California 94562
TEL: 707-944-2414
OWNER: Stimson Lane Wine & Spirits
WINEMAKER: Michael McGrath (B.S. in
  fermentation science, UC-Davis)
FOUNDED: 1881

AT A GLANCE
Tours & Tastings: Open daily 10–4. Tours
by appointment only. Cellar tours provide a closeup view of the operations of a
small family winery.
Closed: Major holidays.
Vineyards: Eighty-seven acres planted to
Chardonnay, Cabernet Sauvignon, Merlot, Cabernet Franc.
Wines: Chardonnay, Cabernet Sauvignon.

Picnic Area: Yes.
Retail Shop: Wines sold on-site.
Credit Cards: MasterCard, Visa.
Access for Disabled: None.
Getting There: Winery is three miles
southeast of St. Helena. Take Hwy. 29 to
Oakville Crossroads and turn right.

ᘍ Early plantings of Zinfandel and
Riesling have been replaced with other
varietals, but the original winery, framed
in 1886, remains in use today.

ᘍ ᘍ ᘍ

Vose Vineyards

4035 Mt. Veeder Road
Napa, California 94558
TEL: 707-944-2254
PRESIDENT: Hamilton Vose III
WINEMAKER: Celia Welch (B.S. in
  fermentation science, UC-Davis)
FOUNDED: 1970

AT A GLANCE
Tours & Tastings: Open May–Oct. 10–4.
No tours.
Closed: Nov.–Apr.
Vineyards: Twenty-one acres planted to
Zinfandel, Chardonnay, Cabernet Sauvi-
gnon.
Wines: Zinfandel, Chardonnay, Caber-
net Sauvignon, Gewürztraminer, Fumé
Blanc, White Zinfandel.
Awards: 1982 Sweet Harvest Zinfandel:
gold, bronze; 1984 Zinblanca: gold, two
bronzes; 1982 Fumé Blanc: bronze.
Picnic Area: Redwood deck, gazebo, bar-
becues.
Retail Shop: Wines sold on-site.
Credit Cards: MasterCard, Visa.
Access for Disabled: Retail area, tasting
room, and picnic grounds all accommo-
date wheelchairs.
Foreign Languages: Spanish.
Getting There: Take Hwy. 29 to Oakville.
Turn west on Oakville Grade, go 3¾
miles to Mt. Veeder Rd. and bear left.

Poised on the slopes of Mt. Veeder, Vose Vineyards surveys Napa Valley from an elevation of 2,000 feet. Deer range here, and the irrigation ponds are stocked with bass and catfish. Sharp-eyed visitors may search the property for obsidian arrowheads left by generations of Indian hunters. There are on-site accommodations for overnight guests; call the winery number for reservations.

Wermuth Winery

3942 Silverado Trail
Calistoga, California 94515
TEL: 707-942-5924
OWNER/WINEMAKER: Ralph Wermuth
FOUNDED: 1982

AT A GLANCE
Tours & Tastings: Open by appointment Tues.–Sat. Scheduled one-hour tours; six people in a group preferred.
Vineyards: Two acres planted to Napa Valley Gamay, Sauvignon Blanc, and Colombard. "One fig tree shares space with our Sauvignon Blanc." Additional grapes purchased from local growers.
Wines: Colombard, Sauvignon Blanc, Cabernet Sauvignon, Napa Valley Gamay, Cabernet Franc.
Retail Shop: Wines sold on-site.
Credit Cards: None.
Access for the Disabled: None.
Foreign Languages: Some French.
Getting There: Winery is on the Silverado Trail, between the Bale Rd. and Larkmead Ln. crossroads.
Special Wine & Other Events: Swim Club in July, Sip and Sample in Oct.

"I have lived in the valley for over ten years," says Ralph Wermuth. "I started making wines with friends as a fun thing to do. Somehow I got the wild idea to run a small operation from my home. If there is such a thing as past

lives, I feel I must have done this before, maybe in France."

Whitehall Lane Winery

1563 St. Helena Highway
St. Helena, California 94574
TEL: 707-963-9454
PRESIDENT: Alan M. Steen
WINEMAKER: Arthur Finkelstein
FOUNDED: 1980

AT A GLANCE
Tours & Tastings: Open daily 11–5. Tours of the contemporary redwood-and-glass winery by appointment.
Closed: Easter, Christmas.
Vineyards: Twenty-six acres planted to Sauvignon Blanc, Chenin Blanc, Chardonnay, Cabernet Sauvignon, Merlot. Additional grapes purchased from Napa and Sonoma County growers.
Wines: Cabernet Sauvignon, Merlot, Pinot Noir, Chardonnay, Sauvignon Blanc, Blanc de Pinot Noir, Late Harvest Johannisberg Riesling, Chenin Blanc.
Awards: Recent medal winners include: 1984 Pinot Noir—gold, bronze; 1983 Cabernet Sauvignon—double gold, two silvers, bronze; 1982 Merlot—three golds; 1984 Chenin Blanc—two bronzes.
Retail Shop: Wines sold on-site.
Credit Cards: MasterCard, Visa.
Access for the Disabled: Yes.
Foreign Languages: Spanish, French, German.
Getting There: Winery is eighteen miles north of the city of Napa, on Hwy. 29.

At Whitehall Lane Winery, brothers Art Finkelstein, an architect, and Alan Steen, a plastic surgeon, turned their winemaking hobby into an award-winning commercial venture. The former designed the winery, the latter manages the vineyards. "Pruning is just a natural extension of my profession," jokes

Steen. Living side by side in homes right on the property, all of the Finkelsteins and Steens contribute to the operation of the winery and vineyard. Their myriad activities are faithfully documented in Whitehall's newsletter, "Le Grand Crew."

TO SEE & DO

Napa Valley is California in microcosm, where trendy stores spring up amid nineteenth-century landmarks; the myriad diversions range from hot springs to hot-air balloons. Well-heeled enophiles may bid on rare vintages at the Napa Valley Wine Auction, an annual June fund-raiser benefiting hospitals and clinics. For details, consult the auction director (P.O. Box 141, St. Helena 95474; tel: 707-963-5246). Three-day seminars at the Napa Valley Wine Library will be of special interest. Contact the course director (P.O. Box 421, St. Helena 95474; tel: 707-963-1170) for class schedule and fees. A good place to start—or end—your wine tour is Vintner's Village (on Hwy. 29 north of St. Helena; tel: 707-963-4082), where twelve wineries maintain tasting rooms. Depend on Calistoga's Old Faithful Geyser (1299 Tubbs Lane; tel: 707-942-6463) to erupt every forty minutes or so, sending 4,000 gallons of superheated steam spurting into the air. Some claim these sulfur-laced waters have salutary effects; if you're in the mood, try the hot springs and mud baths at one of Calistoga's many mineral spas. Get recommendations from the Calistoga Chamber of Commerce (1458 Lincoln Avenue, Calistoga 94515; tel: 707-942-6333). Another town attraction is the California Petrified Forest (4100 Petrified Forest Road; tel: 707-942-6667), where redwoods were turned to stone after Mount St. Helena's explosion six million years ago. In nearby St. Helena, the Silverado Museum (1490 Library Lane; tel. 707-963-3757) commemorates the life and work of writer Robert Louis Stevenson, who based *The Silverado Squatters* on his brief local sojourn. He spent his honeymoon close to the summit of Mount St. Helena (not to be confused with Mount St. Helens in Washington), at what is now Robert Louis Stevenson State Park. Native American artifacts and animal dioramas are on display in the city of Napa at the Carolyn Parr Nature Museum (3107 Brown's Valley Road; tel: 707-255-6465). Bicyclists of all endurance levels can ride with the Napa Family Bike Club; many trips go through wine country, and out-of-towners are welcome. For information and schedules, call Chris Burditt at 707-255-4840, or Bob and Mary Hillhouse at 707-226-7066. If you would rather ride horses, visit the Wild Horse Valley Ranch (Wild Horse Valley Road in Napa; tel: 707-224-0727), where the U.S. Equestrian Team trained for the 1984 Olympics. Or book a berth on an iron horse; the Napa Valley Wine Train makes round trips between Napa and St. Helena, discharging passengers at any of six stops en route. Oh yes, about those balloon rides. Balloon Aviation of Napa Valley (tel: 707-252-7067) and Once in a Lifetime Balloon Company (tel: 707-942-6541) are just two of the companies that will send you aloft for a one-hour flight with enough champagne to keep you floating even as you land.

ACCOMMODATIONS

The Ambrose Bierce House
1515 Main Street
St. Helena, California 94574
Tel: 707-963-3003
Bierce's last residence has been turned into a lavish bed and breakfast. The morning meal of pastries, fruit, juice, and coffee will revive you, although it won't bring back the author, who disappeared in Mexico in 1913.

Auberge du Soleil
180 Rutherford Hills Road
Rutherford, California 94573
Tel: 707-963-1211

Napa County • 373

An elegant, luxurious, and expensive thirty-six-room resort inspired by the French Mediterranean. Tennis courts, a Jacuzzi, and an Olympic-size pool lure guests out of spacious suites that overlook Napa Valley. Well known for its outstanding cuisine (see "Restaurant" listings that follow).

Bale Mill Inn
3431 North St. Helena Highway
St. Helena, California 94574
Tel: 707-963-4545
Five charming rooms above an antique shop of the same name. Continental breakfast.

Beazley House Bed and Breakfast
1910 First Street
Napa, California 94558
Tel: 707-257-1649
The Beazley family welcomes you to this 1902 landmark, furnished in period style, which was the first bed and breakfast founded in the city. Continental breakfast.

Burgundy House
6711 Washington Street (P.O. Box 2766)
Yountville, California 94599
Tel: 707-944-2855
An eight-unit guest house in a converted brandy distillery built in 1874. Continental breakfast.

Calistoga Inn
1250 Lincoln Avenue
Calistoga, California 94515
Tel: 707-942-4101
A gracious, turn-of-the-century landmark with fine dining. Continental breakfast.

The Chateau Hotel
4195 Solano Avenue
Napa, California 94558
Tel: 707-253-9300
A classic hotel that coddles guests in the fashion of a European country inn.

Continental breakfast, complimentary newspapers, heated pool, and spa. Who wants to go home?

Embassy Suites Hotel
1075 California Boulevard
Napa, California 94558
Tel: 707-253-9540
For starters, each unit has two rooms, two telephones, two televisions, and one bar. Swimming pool, sauna, spa.

Hotel St. Helena
1309 Main Street
St. Helena, California 94574
Tel: 707-963-4388
A restored hundred-year-old hotel in the center of town.

Meadowood Resort Hotel
900 Meadowood Lane
St. Helena, California 94574
Tel: 707-963-3646
A secluded 256-acre luxury retreat, with golf course, tennis courts, par course, and swimming pool, so you can graze at all three restaurants without guilt.

Miramonte Country Inn
1327 Railroad Avenue
St. Helena, California 94574
Tel: 707-963-3970
Two suites, with a restaurant on the premises.

Mount View Hotel
1457 Lincoln Avenue
Calistoga, California 94515
Tel: 707-942-6877
A thirty-four-unit hotel done in high art deco with superb restaurant.

Rancho Caymus Inn
1140 Rutherford Road (P.O. Box 78)
Rutherford, California 94573
Tel: 707-963-1777
A Spanish-style inn that captures the rustic spirit of early California.

Silverado Country Club Resort
1600 Atlas Peak Road
Napa, California 94558
Tel: 707-257-0200
As luxurious as it is lovely. All resort amenities and then some: 8 swimming pools, golf, and tennis.

Sutter Home Inn
225 St. Helena Highway
St. Helena, California 94574
Tel: 707-963-4423
Just down the road from Sutter Home Winery.

Vintage Inn
6451 Washington Street
Yountville, California 94599
Tel: 707-944-1112
The vintage is recent and so are the amenities—wine bars, whirlpool baths, and cable TV in many rooms. Continental champagne breakfast.

Wine Country Inn
1152 Lodi Lane
St. Helena, California 94574
Tel: 707-963-7077
Twenty-five units snugly furnished with antiques and hand-sewn quilts.

RESTAURANTS
All Seasons Market & Cafe
1400 Lincoln Avenue
Calistoga, California 94515
Tel: 707-942-9111
Lighter fare, reasonably priced. Extensive wine list.

Auberge du Soleil
180 Rutherford Hill Road
Rutherford, California 94573
Tel: 707-963-1211
Classic and nouvelle French cuisine elegantly served. In resort of same name. Outstanding views of valley, vineyards.

La Belle Helene Restaurant
1345 Railroad Avenue
St. Helena, California 94574

Tel: 707-963-1234
Sophisticated dining accompanied by fine local wines. Come back often; the menu changes daily.

Bosko's Ristorante
1403 Lincoln Avenue
Calistoga, California 94515
Tel: 707-942-9088
Sawdust on the floors, exposed brick walls, and hanging ferns. Fresh pasta prepared daily, but save room for the pastries at the espresso bar.

Silverado Restaurant and Tavern
1374 Lincoln Avenue
Calistoga, California 94515
Tel: 707-942-6725
Mesquite-grilled foods are best bets here, as are the pastas and the rich, delicious ice cream. Well-stocked wine cellar.

Mount View Hotel
1457 Lincoln Avenue
Calistoga, California 94515
Superb restaurant with excellent wine list, pianist. Fish, fresh wild game, rich desserts.

Mustards Grill
7399 St. Helena Highway
Yountville, California 94599
Tel: 707-944-2424
Casual atmosphere; home-smoked meats and home-baked treats.

The Royal Oak
Napa, California 94558
At Silverado Country Club (see "Accommodations" for address, phone). Surf and turf.

St. George Restaurant
1050 Charter Oak
St. Helena, California 94574
Tel: 707-963-7938
Italian and Mediterranean entrées in a handsome restaurant where the woodwork glows and the brass fixtures gleam.

The Swan Court
Napa, California 94558
at Embassy Suites Hotel (see "Accommodations" for address, phone).

Washington Street Restaurant
6539 Washington Street
Yountville, California 94599
Tel: 707-944-2406
California cuisine at reasonable prices; the restaurant is housed in a stately nineteenth-century mansion.

Zebedees
587 South St. Helena Highway
St. Helena, California 94574
Tel: 707-963-2844
A hamburger joint that's a shrine to the 1950s, with James Dean photos on the walls and Elvis records on the jukebox. Put on your saddle shoes.

Anestis' Grill
6518 Washington Street
Yountville, California 94599
Tel: 707-944-1500

Greek specialties, from red caviar pâté to roast suckling pig; Napa Valley wines by the glass or bottle.

Domaine Chandon
California Drive
Yountville, California 94599
Tel: 707-944-2892
Reservations suggested for this fine French restaurant on winery grounds.

The French Laundry
6640 Washington Street
Yountville, California 94599
Tel: 707-944-2380
Complete dinner at a fixed price; reservations required for single sitting. Inventive menu, extensive wine list.

Mama Nina's
6722 Washington Street
Yountville, California 94599
Tel: 707-944-2112
Northern Italian cuisine prepared from the freshest possible ingredients.

❧ NORTH-CENTRAL COAST

Santa Clara County, the heart of this region, showed its enological promise early. Seventeenth-century Spanish explorers stumbled upon, and presumably stomped, grapes (*uvas*) growing wild in a Santa Cruz Mountain glen they promptly named Uvas Valley. Nonetheless, the man most responsible for bringing vinifera grapes to other parts of the state—Agoston Haraszthy, the "father of California viticulture"—suffered defeat here. In 1854, heavy summer fogs choked his young vines, and he fled to Sonoma, where his luck clearly improved.

Despite Haraszthy's unfortunate local example, other vineyardists flocked to the north-central coast. By the 1920s, Santa Clara County rivaled Napa and Sonoma in total acreage under cultivation. Some grape growers survived Prohibition by shipping fruit to home winemakers in the East, but this market withered after Repeal. Now the local wine industry is booming once again, with wineries liberally scattered over both Santa Clara and Santa Cruz counties. Santa Clara Valley has applied for v.a. designation, a status the Santa Cruz Mountains already enjoy.

A slightly different scenario was played out in southern Monterey County. Franciscan padres planted a vineyard at their Soledad mission in the mid-1700s, but few settlers emulated the friars. For the next two centuries, the lush Salinas Valley was known for vegetables rather than fruit. Then University of California at Davis experts designated this area as Region I and II—the same classifications given to Burgundy and Bordeaux. Suddenly viticulturists discovered what some self-trained monks had realized long ago. Today vineyards stretch across 35,000 acres of Monterey County, a viticultural area since 1984.

Highway 101 is the main artery of this region, running inland from Greenfield to Morgan Hill and beyond. When you get to Gilroy, consider a westward detour along Highway 152; wineries cluster along this route, variously known as Hecker Pass and Pacheco Pass (the latter is also the name of a local v.a.). Then it's north to Santa Cruz or south to Monterey. Wherever you go, you'll be near gleaming white beaches; between the fruit of the sea and the fruit of the land, there is much to savor here.

ða ða ða

Bargetto Winery

3535 North Main Street
Soquel, California 95073
TEL: 408-475-2258
Also visit:
Bargetto's Cannery Row Tasting Room
700 Cannery Row
Monterey, California 93940
TEL: 408-373-4053
PRESIDENT: Beverly Bargetto
FOUNDED: 1933

AT A GLANCE
Tours & Tastings: Open daily 10–5:30; informal tours Mon.–Fri. at 11 and 2. Tastings are offered in a rustic creekside room decorated with winemaking equipment of bygone eras. During the summer, wines are also served in the courtyard, where visitors may enjoy the work of local artists. (The Monterey tasting room is open daily 11–6.)
Closed: Easter, Thanksgiving, Christmas, New Year's Day.
Vineyards: None. Grapes and other fruit bought from growers in Napa, Sonoma, Santa Barbara, and the Santa Cruz Mountains.
Wines: Chardonnay, Cabernet Sauvignon, White Riesling, Gewürztraminer, White Zinfandel; raspberry wine, olallieberry wine, apricot wine, pomegranate wine; Chaucer's Mead.
Awards: White Zinfandel: gold; Late Harvest White Riesling: gold; olallieberry wine: gold/best of class.
Retail Shop: Wines, stemmed glassware, and other wine-related items sold on-site.
Credit Cards: MasterCard, Visa.
Access for Disabled: Tasting room entrance wheelchair accessible.
Foreign Languages: Italian.
Getting There: Winery is four miles south of Santa Cruz. From Hwy. 1 in Soquel: Take Bay Ave. exit to North Main St.
Special Wine & Other Events: Bargetto sponsors art shows.

ða Brothers Philip and John Bargetto founded this winery upon emigrating from Italy's Piedmonte region. John's sons, Lawrence and Ralph, duly picked up the family trade, introducing modern techniques. Today the winery is operated by the third-generation Bargettos, who share their forefathers' ambition: to produce wines of superior quality.

≈ ≈ ≈

Bonny Doon Vineyard

10 Pine Flat Road
Santa Cruz, California 95060
TEL: 408-425-3625
GENERAL MANAGER: Randall Grahm
  (B.S. in viticulture, UC-Davis)
FOUNDED: 1983

AT A GLANCE
Tours & Tastings: Open weekends 12–5:30; summer hours: Tues.–Sun. 12–5:30. Tours by arrangement. Tasting room was formerly the Lost Weekend Saloon, a classic roadhouse bar.
Vineyards: Twenty-eight owned and forty leased acres planted to Sirah, Marsanne, Roussane, Viognier, Pinot Noir, Chardonnay, Cabernet Sauvignon, Merlot, Malbec, Cabernet Franc, Petit Verdot. Fraises du bois (wild strawberries) also grown here. Additional grapes bought from other California growers.
Wines: Vin Gris (Mourvedre), Chardonnay, Sirah, Le Cigare Volant, Muscat Canelli.
Awards: 1983 Anderson Valley Cabernet Sauvignon: gold; 1985 California Pinot Blanc: bronze; 1984 Le Cigare Volant: silver.
Picnic Area: Choice of grassy lawn or redwood grove along Mill Creek.
Retail Shop: Wines sold on-site.
Credit Cards: MasterCard, Visa.
Access for Disabled: None.
Foreign Languages: French.
Getting There: Winery is about sixty-three miles south of San Francisco and twelve miles north of Santa Cruz. "If you drive up Hwy. 1, eight miles north of Santa Cruz, you will come to the Bonny Doon Rd. turnoff, a first-rate meandering country road that will take you up

through apple orchards and a redwood forest and deposit you at Pine Flat Rd."

≈ "As a terminal Rhonephiliac, I am dedicated to exploring the possibilities of Rhone varietals in California," vows Randall Grahm. "To this end, I utilize grapes never before grown here, as well as old vineyards planted to traditional varietals."

≈ ≈ ≈

David Bruce Winery

21439 Bear Creek Road
Los Gatos, California 95030
TEL:408-354-4214
PRESIDENT: David Bruce
WINEMAKER: Keith D. Hohlfeldt
  (degrees in microbiology and biochemistry, former microbiologist at Paul Masson)
FOUNDED: 1964

AT A GLANCE
Tours & Tastings: Open Sat. 11–4; other times by appointment. Tours, by appointment only, include a brief history of the vineyard and winery, followed by an explanation of unique vinification techniques and barrel aging; the last stop is the bottling line. If winemaker is giving the tour, a quick barrel sample may be tasted. Bottles are only opened for groups of more than seven.
Vineyards: Twenty-five acres planted to Chardonnay and Pinot Noir. Additional grapes bought from other vineyards in Santa Cruz and Sonoma.
Wines: Chardonnay, Pinot Noir, Cabernet Sauvignon.
Awards: 1982 Estate Chardonnay: gold; Estate Pinot Noir: gold.
Retail Shop: Wines sold on-site.
Credit Cards: American Express, MasterCard, Visa.
Access for Disabled: Limited wheelchair access.

Getting There: Winery is eight miles southwest of Los Gatos and twenty miles north of Santa Cruz. From Los Gatos: Take Hwy. 17 South three miles to Bear Creek Rd.
Special Wine & Other Events: Dinners and "Meet the Winemaker" evenings at the winery.

Former dermatologist David Bruce planted this vineyard while practicing medicine part-time. By trial and error, he discovered what varietals thrived here. "We have proved beyond a doubt that this region can, indeed, produce great Pinot Noir—making the Santa Cruz Mountains one of the few geographical areas in the world that can foster this fickle grape."

Carrousel Cellars

2825 Day Road
Gilroy, California 95020
TEL: 408-847-2060
OWNERS: John and Carol De Santis
FOUNDED: 1981

AT A GLANCE
Tours & Tastings: Open by appointment only. Tours by appointment. Group tastings for up to ten people can be arranged.
Vineyards: Two acres planted to Cabernet Sauvignon.
Wines: Chardonnay, Cabernet Sauvignon, Zinfandel.
Awards: Cabernet Sauvignon: double bronze; Zinfandel: bronze.
Retail Shop: Wines sold on-site.
Credit Cards: None.
Access for Disabled: None.
Getting There: Winery is thirty miles south of San Jose. Take the business branch of Hwy. 101 to Watsonville Rd., turn left on Day Rd.

Few wineries are smaller than Carrousel; its 3,500-gallon cellar is housed in a three-car garage. John and Carol De Santis produce only 500 cases a year, but every drop counts. Their first release, a 1981 estate-bottled Cabernet Sauvignon, took a double bronze in regional competition.

Casa de Fruta

6680 Pacheco Pass Highway
Hollister, California 95023
TEL: 408-842-9316, ext. 145
FOUNDED: 1972

AT A GLANCE
Tours & Tastings: Open daily; winter hours: 9–6, summer hours: 8–8. Tasting room's full-service deli sells cheese and sausage.
Closed: Christmas.
Vineyards: Nineteen acres planted to Gewürztraminer, Johannisberg Riesling, Zinfandel, Chenin Blanc, Muscat Hamberg. Cherries and apricots also grown on-site. Other fruit purchased from local growers.
Wines: Gewürztraminer, Johannisberg Riesling, Soft Johannisberg Riesling, Chenin Blanc, Soft Chenin Blanc, Zinfandel Rosé, White Zinfandel, Black Muscat Blush; apricot, blackberry, pomegranate, raspberry, cherry wines.
Awards: Most wines have won many awards.
Picnic Area: Casa de Fruta's Country Park offers eight acres of tree-shaded lawn and three baseball diamonds. Bring your own lunch or buy it here; sandwiches, catered barbecue meals prepared on the premises.
Restaurant: Twenty-four-hour restaurant on-site.
Retail Shop: Wines and related gifts sold on-site. Other stores sell fresh fruit, candy and baked goods, and souvenirs.
Credit Cards: MasterCard, Visa.
Access for Disabled: Yes.
Getting There: Winery is thirteen miles

east of Gilroy. Take I-5 to Hwy. 152 (known here as Pacheco Pass) and drive twenty-eight miles west.

Special Wine & Other Events: Cherry Jubilee in June dishes out food and fun for everyone; the menu includes pit-spitting and tree-chopping contests, entertainment. During the summer, visitors can dance to live music at Sat. night and Sun. afternoon barbecues.

🐌 While gold panners were sifting creek bottoms, Casa de Fruta's founders hit pay dirt by a more reliable method— they nurtured sweet fresh fruit in the fertile soil of the Pacheco Pass. Those original orchards eventually blossomed into a full-scale edibles complex, with a burger stand, fruit stand, and sweet shop, in addition to the twenty-four-hour coffee shop. A variety of on-site accommodations is available (tel: 408-842-9316). The Casa de Fruta Motel has fourteen garden rooms, each equipped with a small refrigerator; the Casa de Fruta Travel Park has 300 RV hookups and fifty tent spaces, with rest rooms, showers, and laundry facilities.

🐌 🐌 🐌

Chateau Julian Winery

8940 Carmel Valley Road (P.O. Box 221775)
Carmel, California 93922
TEL: 408-624-2600
PRESIDENT: Robert Brower
WINEMAKER: William Anderson (former consultant to Kathryn Kennedy Winery)
FOUNDED: 1982

AT A GLANCE
Tours & Tastings: Open Mon.–Fri. 8:30– 5, weekends 1–4. One-hour tours, departing at 10:30 and 2:30, include tasting of four or five wines. Special T.G.I.F. tour on Fri. at 2:30.

Closed: Easter, Memorial Day, Labor Day, Christmas, New Year's Day.
Vineyards: None. Grapes purchased from Salinas Valley growers.
Wines: Chardonnay, Merlot, Johannisberg Riesling, Sauvignon Blanc; cream sherry.
Awards: Recent medal winners include: 1982 Private Reserve Chardonnay—four golds, two silvers, bronze; 1983 Paraiso Springs Chardonnay—gold, silver, two bronzes; 1983 Merlot—silver, three bronzes; Carmel Cream Sherry—silver, two bronzes.
Retail Shop: Wines sold on-site.
Credit Cards: American Express, MasterCard, Visa.
Access for Disabled: Winery accommodates wheelchairs.
Foreign Languages: Spanish.
Getting There: Winery is five miles outside Carmel, eight miles outside Monterey. The winery is exactly five miles east of Hwy. 1 on Carmel Valley Rd.

🐌 A large French villa on the banks of the Carmel River, Chateau Julien is decorated with antiques and handwoven embroidered carpets.

🐌 🐌 🐌

A. Conrotto Winery

1690 Hecker Pass Highway
Gilroy, California 95020
TEL: 408-842-3053
PRESIDENT: Jim Burr
FOUNDED: 1926

AT A GLANCE
Tours & Tastings: Open weekends. Winter hours: 11–5, summer hours: 11– 6. Rustic tasting room resembles a log cabin.
Closed: Easter, Christmas, New Year's Day.
Vineyards: Fifteen acres planted to vinifera. Additional grapes and other fruit

purchased from growers in the Santa Clara Valley.

Wines: Symphony (a Muscat Alexander/Grenache hybrid), Chardonnay, Barbera, Petite Sirah, Cabernet Sauvignon, Claret, Carignane; apricot wine, plum wine; cream sherry.

Awards: Cream sherry: double gold; plum wine: silver; Chardonnay: bronze.

Picnic Area: Yes.

Retail Shop: Wines sold on-site.

Credit Cards: MasterCard, Visa.

Access for Disabled: None.

Getting There: West end of Gilroy's First St. becomes Hecker Pass Hwy. (also known as Hwy. 152). Take Hecker Pass to the Santa Teresa Blvd. intersection and turn left.

Special Wine & Other Events: Winery sponsors the Spring Festival, and the Fall Wine and Pasta Festival.

&. Anselmo Conrotto left his small northern Italian village to establish this winery; his son Chinto assumed the day-to-day operations in 1957. Today Chinto's children and grandchildren continue a proud family tradition by welcoming you to their tasting room.

&. &. &.

Crescini Wines

2621 Old San Jose Road (P.O. Box 216)
Soquel, California 95073
TEL: 408-462-1466
OWNERS/WINEMAKERS: Richard and
  Paule Crescini
FOUNDED: 1980

AT A GLANCE

Tours & Tastings: Open by appointment on weekends 10–5. Tours for groups of two to twenty. Customized tours with lots of personal attention; barrel tastings.

Closed: Weekdays.

Vineyards: None. Grapes purchased from Napa Valley growers.

Wines: Cabernet Sauvignon, Merlot, Chenin Blanc.

Awards: 1981 Cabernet Sauvignon: gold; 1982 Cabernet Sauvignon: gold.

Retail Shop: Wines sold on-site.

Credit Cards: None.

Access for Disabled: Ramp to one door.

Getting There: From Hwy. 1: Take Soquel/Capitola exit to Porter St. and go north on Old San Jose Rd. After almost 2½ miles, turn left at signpost with number 2621. Winery is on the right, past the third driveway (which is marked 2621).

&. "Just small and personal," is Richard Crescini's description of his winery.

&. &. &.

Devlin Wine Cellars

TASTING ROOM:
  2815 Porter Street
  Soquel, California 95073
TEL: 408-476-7288
OWNERS: Charles and Cheryl Devlin
WINEMAKER: Charles Devlin (degree in
  fermentation science, UC-Davis)
FOUNDED: 1978

AT A GLANCE

Tours & Tastings: Tasting room open daily 12–5. (The winery is somewhat inaccessible and not open for public tours.)

Closed: Thanksgiving, Christmas, New Year's Day.

Vineyards: None. Grapes bought from growers in California's central coast.

Wines: Chardonnay, Sauvignon Blanc, Muscat Canelli, Zinfandel, Pinot Noir, Cabernet Sauvignon, Merlot, White Zinfandel, White Riesling.

Awards: 1981, 1982, 1983 Central Coast Merlots all won golds. 1981 Sonoma Cabernet Sauvignon: gold; 1982, 1983 vintages of the same wine: silvers.

Picnic Area: Yes.

Retail Shop: Wines sold on-site.
Credit Cards: MasterCard, Visa.
Access for Disabled: None.
Getting There: Tasting room is 2½ blocks off Hwy. 1. Take Capitola/Soquel exit to Porter St.
Special Wine & Other Events: Tasting room is also a gallery for local artists; exhibits change montly.

🐌 Charles Devlin caught the wine bug as a high school student employed by the Bargettos, and he hasn't recovered yet. His award-winning wines sell for very reasonable prices; many cost less than $10. When not working his artistry with grapes, he takes the time to design a few of his own labels.

🐌 🐌 🐌

Felton-Empire Vineyards

379 Felton-Empire Road
Felton, California 95018
TEL: 408-335-3939
PRESIDENT/WINEMAKER: Leo P. McCloskey (Ph.D. in microbiology, UC-Santa Cruz)
FOUNDED: 1976

AT A GLANCE
Tours & Tastings: Weekends 12–5. Self-guided tour; winery equipment is located outdoors, adjacent to vineyard.
Closed: Weekdays.
Vineyards: Twelve acres planted to White Riesling. Additional grapes purchased from growers in Sonoma, Santa Barbara, Mendocino, Monterey, and Santa Cruz.
Wines: Chardonnay, Pinot Noir, White Riesling, Gewürztraminer, Cabernet Sauvignon.
Awards: 1985 Santa Barbara Chardonnay: silver; 1984 Santa Cruz Mountains White Riesling: gold; 1984 Gewürztraminer: gold.
Picnic Area: Scenic hillside lawn, redwood deck.

Retail Shop: Wines, sparkling and still varietal grape juices sold on-site.
Credit Cards: MasterCard, Visa.
Access for Disabled: Yes.
Getting There: Felton-Empire Vineyards is located fifteen minutes from downtown Santa Cruz. Take Hwy. 17 turnoff from either Hwy. 101 or Hwy. 280. Proceed on Hwy. 17 through Scotts Valley to the Mt. Hermon/Glenn Canyon off-ramp, and turn right onto Mt. Hermon Rd. Continue for three miles to Graham Hill Rd. Yielding right, proceed across the bridge; Felton-Empire Rd. begins at the signal.
Special Wine & Other Events: Spring release weekend in May celebrates new wines, while Indian Summer Festival in Oct. celebrates newly harvested grapes. Bottling parties, barbecues, concerts in oak-shaded amphitheater throughout summer.

🐌 Maverick vintner Chaffee Hall established Hallcrest Vineyards in 1946, sparing neither expense nor effort in his quest to produce wines of European quality. Thirty years later Leo McCloskey took over the site and followed in Hall's footsteps: Felton-Empire's first crush, an Estate Riesling, garnered a gold medal. Don't overlook the alcohol-free varietal juices, sold under the Empire Vineyards Juice Company brand. These vintage-dated, winelike products—made from Gewürztraminer, White Riesling, Cabernet Sauvignon, and Gamay Beaujolais grapes—are so distinguished they were poured at a White House reception.

🐌 🐌 🐌

Hecker Pass Winery

4605 Hecker Pass Highway
Gilroy, California 95020
TEL: 408-842-8755
OWNER/WINEMAKER: Mario Fortino
FOUNDED: 1972

AT A GLANCE

Tours & Tastings: Open daily 10–5. Tours, by appointment, show crushing area, winery, and warehouse. Rustic tasting room has a twenty-foot redwood bar.

Closed: Major holidays.

Vineyards: Fourteen acres planted to Zinfandel, Ruby Cabernet, Grenache, Petite Sirah, Carignane.

Wines: French Colombard, Chablis, Grenache Rosé, Carignane Rosé, Zinfandel Ruby, Grenache, Petite Sirah, Zinfandel, Carignane; sherry, cream sherry, port.

Awards: Recent medal winners include Zinfandel—gold; Carignane—silver; Petite Sirah—bronze.

Picnic Area: Yes.

Retail Shop: Wines sold on-site.

Credit Cards: MasterCard, Visa.

Access for Disabled: None.

Foreign Languages: Italian.

Getting There: Winery is thirty-five miles south of San Jose. From Hwy. 101: Take Hwy. 152 (Hecker Pass Hwy.) west, past Watsonville Rd.

Special Wine & Other Events: Spring Wine Festival, last Sat. in Apr.; Harvest Wine Festival, first Sat. in Oct.

ᕦ Third-generation vintner Mario Fortino learned his art in Cosenza, Italy, then gained additional experience in a decade of working for various Santa Clara Valley wineries. His old-world traditions are reflected in Hecker Pass's smooth Italian-style wines.

ᕦ ᕦ ᕦ

Jekel Vineyard

40155 Walnut Avenue
Greenfield, California 93927
TEL: 408-674-5522, 674-5525
PRESIDENT: William D. Jekel
WINEMAKER: Rick Jekel (B.S. in enology, UC-Davis)
FOUNDED: 1978

AT A GLANCE

Tours & Tastings: Open daily 10–5. Tours by appointment only include a view and discussion of the entire winemaking process. Wines are bottled from March to Aug.; because of the cool climate, grapes are harvested from Sept. to Nov. Cabernet Sauvignon grapes have been picked as late as Dec. 7.

Closed: Easter, Thanksgiving, Christmas, New Year's Day.

Vineyards: 330 acres planted to Johannisberg Riesling, Chardonnay, Cabernet Sauvignon, Pinot Blanc.

Wines: Johannisberg Riesling, Chardonnay, Cabernet Sauvignon, Pinot Blanc, Pinot Noir, Muscat Canelli, Late Harvest Riesling.

Awards: Recent medal winners include: Cabernet Sauvignon—gold; Johannisberg Riesling—gold; Chardonnay—gold.

Picnic Area: Yes.

Retail Shop: Wines sold on-site.

Credit Cards: MasterCard, Visa.

Access for Disabled: Ramp into tasting room; rest rooms specially equipped.

Getting There: Greenfield is approximately fifty miles southeast of Carmel and Monterey. From Hwy. 101: Take Walnut Ave. off-ramp and drive west one mile.

ᕦ Right down to the windmill, Jekel Vineyard's winery was designed to resemble the redwood dairy barns that dot the Salinas Valley. Vineyards surround the buildings, which include a conference room, a commercial kitchen, and a large banquet room.

ᕦ ᕦ ᕦ

Kirigin Cellars

11550 Watsonville Road
Gilroy, California 95020
TEL: 408-847-8827
OWNER: Nikola Kirigin Chargin (enology degree, University of Zagreb)
FOUNDED: 1976

AT A GLANCE
Tours & Tastings: Open daily 9–6. Tours by appointment.
Vineyards: Forty acres planted to premium white and red varietals.
Wines: Sauvignon Blanc, Chardonnay, Sauvignon Vert, Gewürztraminer, Blanc de Noir, Malvasia, Pinot Noir, Cabernet Sauvignon, Zinfandel: champagne; Vino de Mocca (a proprietary dessert wine).
Awards: Does not enter contests.
Picnic Area: Yes.
Retail Shop: Wines sold on-site.
Credit Cards: MasterCard, Visa.
Access for Disabled: None.
Foreign Languages: Croatian, Italian, French.
Getting There: Take Business Hwy. 101 (also known as the Monterey Hwy.) north of Hwy. 152 turnoff to Watsonville Rd.
Special Wine & Other Events: Annual barbecue and concert in mid-June.

&. Croatian-born Nikola Kirigin Chargin began his career in the vineyard his family had cultivated for generations. Stints at New York and California wineries were followed by his acquisition of this nineteenth-century homestead in a region and climate reminiscent of his homeland on the Adriatic Coast.

&. &. &.

Morgan Winery

526 Brunken Avenue
Salinas, California 93902
TEL: 408-455-1382, 758-1377
PRESIDENT: Daniel Morgan Lee (M.S. in microbiology, UC-Davis; formerly winemaker at Jekel Vineyard)
FOUNDED: 1982

AT A GLANCE
Tours & Tastings: Open by appointment only. Tours by appointment.
Vineyards: None. Chardonnay grapes come from Napa Valley; Sauvignon

Blanc grapes come from Alexander Valley.
Wines: Chardonnay (Morgan label), Sauvignon Blanc (St. Vrain label).
Awards: Both wines have won gold medals in recent competitions.
Retail Shop: Wines sold on-site.
Credit Cards: MasterCard, Visa.
Access for Disabled: Yes.
Foreign Languages: French, Spanish.
Getting There: Winery is twenty miles from Carmel and Monterey, off Hwy. 68. Call for directions.
Special Wine & Other Events: Open House in early Nov.

&. As a pre-med student, Daniel Lee took an enology elective that eventually caused him to rethink his career. Medicine's loss was the wine world's gain. Lee relies on traditional European techniques, such as barrel fermentation, a fact emphasized by the Morgan label—a French coat of arms.

&. &. &.

Pedrizzetti Winery

1645 San Pedro Avenue
Morgan Hill, California 95037
TEL: 408-779-7389
OWNERS: Ed and Phyllis Pedrizzetti
FOUNDED: 1913

AT A GLANCE
Tours & Tastings: Open daily 10–6. Tours by appointment. Only two people run this 50,000-case winery, so advance reservations are necessary for tours, which explain winemaking. Visitors see crushing facility, aging cellar, and bottling facility. The tour concludes with a tasting of any wines of the visitors' choice.
Closed: Easter, Thanksgiving, Christmas, New Year's Day.
Vineyards: None. "All our grapes purchased from the California regions that best produce a particular varietal." All grapes and other fruits grown nearby, in

San Luis Obispo, Monterey, Santa Barbara, and Contra Costa counties.

Wines: Chardonnay, Chenin Blanc, White Zinfandel, Riesling, Zinfandel Rosé, Gewürztraminer, Barbera, Cabernet Sauvignon, Zinfandel, Petite Sirah; apricot wine, strawberry wine, blackberry wine, plum wine; cream sherry, golden sherry; sweet and dry vermouths.

Awards: Barbera: gold; Petite Sirah: double gold; White Zinfandel: two bronzes; Zinfandel Rosé: silver; Cabernet Sauvignon: two bronzes.

Picnic Area: With barbecue.

Retail Shop: Wines sold on-site.

Credit Cards: MasterCard, Visa.

Access for Disabled: Not to the winery itself, although tasting room entrance accommodates wheelchairs.

Getting There: Winery is twenty-five miles south of San Jose. From Hwy. 101 in Morgan Hill: Take Tennant Ave. exit east to Murphy Ave. and turn left. Then make a right onto San Pedro Ave.

Special Wine & Other Events: Wine Festival, last Sat. in Apr.; Grape Stomp and Harvest Festival, first Sat. in Oct.

🍂 In 1945, John Pedrizzetti bought this winery from its founder, a fellow immigrant from Italy's Piedmont wine district. Today the second generation of Pedrizzettis holds court in a winery that has been renovated and enlarged. "We welcome the chance to talk shop at any time," says Phyllis Pedrizzetti, who judges other vintners' wines when she isn't making or bottling her own.

🍂 🍂 🍂

Rapazzini Winery

4350 Monterey Highway (P.O. Box 247)
Gilroy, California 95020
TEL: 408-842-5649
Also visit tasting room at:

The Garlic Shoppe
Highways 101 and 25 (P.O. Box 247)
Gilroy, California 95020
TEL: 408-848-3646
OWNER/PRESIDENT: Jon P. Rapazzini
FOUNDED: 1962

AT A GLANCE

Tours & Tastings: Open daily; winter hours: 9–5, summer hours: 9–6. Tours of winery during bottling, by appointment. (Garlic Shoppe tasting room open daily 10–7.)

Closed: Easter, Thanksgiving, Christmas, New Year's Day.

Vineyards: None. All grapes and other fruits are California-grown, mostly in San Luis Obispo and Sonoma.

Wines: Sauvignon Blanc, Chardonnay, Johannisberg Riesling, Gewürztraminer, Muscat Canelli, White Zinfandel, Gewürztraminer Rosé, Merlot, Cabernet Sauvignon, Petite Sirah, Burgundy; Garlic Dinner Wine; May wine; Apribella (apricot/white wine blend); Ambrosia (citrus fruit/white blend); other fruit wines; honey wine; Crema Marsala, cream sherry.

Awards: Recent medal winners include: Muscat Canelli—bronze; Apribella—silver; Crema Marsala—gold; Chardonnay—silver.

Picnic Area: Yes.

Retail Shop: Rapazzini wines, imported Italian wines, garlic cooking wines, and garlic jelly sold in winery. More garlic items, gourmet food, crystal, and tinware sold at Garlic Shoppe.

Credit Cards: MasterCard, Visa.

Access for Disabled: Wheelchair accessible; rest rooms equipped for disabled.

Foreign Languages: Italian.

Getting There: Winery is three miles south of Gilroy on Hwy. 101, near intersection with Hwy. 25. Garlic Shoppe is around the corner.

Special Wine & Other Events: The biggest event in the area is Gilroy's Garlic Festival, usually scheduled for the last weekend in July.

ক Their twenty years of steady expansion were halted in 1980 by a devastating fire, but the Rapazzinis steadfastly rebuilt their winery and their business. Then they introduced a novelty, Garlic Dinner Wine, as a salute to the pungent herb grown in Gilroy. This blend of dry white wine and fresh local garlic boasts a rich, buttery, garlicky aroma, yet has a subtle taste that enhances scampi, lamb, and pastas.

ক ক ক

Roudon-Smith Vineyards

2364 Bean Creek Road
Santa Cruz, California 95066
TEL: 408-438-1244
Also visit:
Roudon-Smith Tasting Room
2571 Main Street
Soquel, California 95073
OWNERS: Robert Roudon, James Smith
WINEMAKER: Robert Roudon
FOUNDED: 1972

AT A GLANCE
Tours & Tastings: Winery open Sat. by appointment. Informal thirty-minute tours given on request. Tours show winemaking and bottling equipment, with a description of these processes. (Tasting room open Wed.–Sun. 12–6.)
Closed: Christmas.
Vineyards: Small vineyard planted to Chardonnay. Additional grapes purchased from California growers.
Wines: Chardonnay, Cabernet Sauvignon, Zinfandel, Pinot Noir, Pinot Blanc, Petite Sirah, White Zinfandel, Riesling.
Awards: 1984 Mendocino Chardonnay: silver; 1983 Petite Sirah: silver; Santa Cruz Mountains Cabernet Sauvignon: silver.

Picnic Area: Small. One group at a time may picnic, adults only.
Retail Shop: Wines sold on-site.
Credit Cards: MasterCard, Visa.
Access for Disabled: Ramp at winery; tasting room has entry level with parking area.
Foreign Languages: Limited French.
Getting There: Winery is thirty miles south of San Jose and fifty miles north of Monterey. Take Scotts Valley Dr. exit from Hwy. 17. (For tasting room, take Capitola/Soquel exit off Hwy. 1.)

ক Bob Roudon and Jim Smith met while working as engineers in Silicon Valley. The former, an ardent home winemaker, persuaded the latter, an uprooted Wisconsin farmboy, to give up the frenzy of corporate life and start a winery. "Our area was often used by movie companies when they needed country locations," explains co-owner June Smith. "It is rumored that the first *Rebecca of Sunnybrook Farm* was filmed on this property. This story has not been authenticated."

ক ক ক

San Martin Winery

13000 Depot Street (P.O. Box 53)
San Martin, California 95046
TEL: 408-683-4000
GENERAL MANAGER: Ronald S. Niino
 (B.S. in food science and technology, UC-Davis)
FOUNDED: 1906

AT A GLANCE
Tours & Tastings: Open daily 10–5:30. No tours.
Closed: Easter, Thanksgiving, Christmas, New Year's Day.
Vineyards: Eight acres planted to vinifera varieties. Additional grapes purchased from growers in Monterey, San Luis

Obispo, Santa Barbara, and Amador counties.

Wines: Cabernet Sauvignon, Chardonnay, Sauvignon Blanc, Zinfandel, White Zinfandel, Johannisberg Riesling, Late Harvest Johannisberg Riesling, Chenin Blanc, Gamay Beaujolais.

Awards: Recent medal winners include: 1985 White Zinfandel—gold, two bronzes; 1981 Cabernet Sauvignon—gold; 1983 Johannisberg Riesling—gold; 1984 Chardonnay—three bronzes; 1985 Chenin Blanc—silver.

Picnic Area: Yes.

Retail Shop: Wines sold on-site.

Credit Cards: MasterCard, Visa.

Access for Disabled: Ramps.

Foreign Languages: Spanish.

Getting There: Winery is 70 miles south of San Francisco. From Hwy. 101: Take San Martin Ave. exit; go west 1 mile to traffic light and turn left on Monterey Hwy. Tasting room is ¼ mile from light on the left.

Special Wine & Other Events: Harvest Wine Festival and Pasta Festival in the fall.

🐌 San Martin has come a long way from its beginnings as a local vineyardists' cooperative. Extensive restoration and renovation has given this winery state-of-the-art equipment—not to mention a storage capacity of three million gallons. Four lines of wines are produced: vintage-dated varietals, "soft" low-alcohol varietals, nonvintage varietals, and blended California wines.

🐌 🐌 🐌

Sarah's Vineyard

4005 Hecker Pass Highway
Gilroy, California 95020
TEL: 408-842-4278
OWNERS: John and Marilyn Otteman, Craig and Debbie McMonigal, Steve and Donna Hicks
FOUNDED: 1978

AT A GLANCE

Tours & Tastings: Open by appointment only.

Vineyards: Ten acres planted to Chardonnay. Riesling grapes purchased from Mendocino County growers.

Wines: Chardonnay, Riesling.

Picnic Area: Yes.

Retail Shop: Wines sold on-site.

Credit Cards: None.

Access for Disabled: None.

Getting There: Winery is on Hwy. 152 (Hecker Pass Hwy.) in Gilroy.

🐌 This is a small winery nestled at the base of the Santa Cruz Mountains. Production is deliberately limited: "Our focus is on quality rather than quantity."

🐌 🐌 🐌

Smith & Hook Winery

37700 Foothill Road
Soledad, California 93960
TEL: 408-678-2132
PRESIDENT: Nicky Hahn
WINEMAKER: Duane DeBoer
FOUNDED: 1980

AT A GLANCE

Tours & Tastings: Open Mon.–Fri. 10–4, summer weekends by appointment. Tours are given on request at any time between 10 and 4. There is a good chance your guide will be either winemaker Duane DeBoer or viticulturist Steve McIntyre. Tastings and tours during harvest, crush, and bottling.

Closed: Winter weekends.

Vineyards: 250 acres planted to Cabernet Sauvignon, Merlot, Cabernet Franc.

Wines: Cabernet Sauvignon.

Awards: 1983 Cabernet Sauvignon: two golds, silver; 1982 Cabernet Sauvignon: gold, four silvers, three bronzes.

Picnic Area: Yes.

Retail Shop: Wines sold on-site.

Credit Cards: MasterCard, Visa.

Access for Disabled: None.

Foreign Languages: Some Spanish.
Getting There: Winery is fifty miles from Monterey Peninsula. Driving south on Hwy. 101, take the Arroyo Seco exit past Soledad. Turn right on Fort Romie Rd., left on Colony Rd., right on Foothill Rd. Bear left on the dirt drive across from the Mission School and continue for two miles.
Special Wine & Other Events: Three major tastings annually: spring tasting in April; annual release in July; and a holiday sale near Thanksgiving.

&. Smith & Hook perches on former ranchland in the Santa Lucia Mountains, overlooking Salinas Valley. The old stable houses the winery; the tack room contains the lab. With seven slopes planted to Cabernet Sauvignon, as well as small amounts of Merlot and Cabernet Franc for blending, critics feel that Smith & Hook produces a Cabernet Sauvignon that demonstrates unusual complexity and quality.

&. &. &.

Villa Paradiso

1830 West Edmundson Avenue
Morgan Hill, California 95037
TEL: 408-778-1555
OWNER: Hank Bogardus
FOUNDED: 1981

AT A GLANCE
Tours & Tastings: Open weekends 11–5. No tours.
Closed: Weekdays.
Vineyards: None. Grapes purchased from California vineyards.
Wines: Merlot, Zinfandel, Petite Sirah.
Retail Shop: Wines sold on-site.
Credit Cards: None.
Access for Disabled: None.
Getting There: Winery is twenty-five miles south of San Jose. From Hwy. 101: Take the Tennant Ave. off-ramp in Morgan Hill and continue toward the city.

Upon reaching Monterey Hwy. (Business Hwy. 101), turn right and immediately turn left onto Edmundson Ave. Continue west for about two miles.

&. Villa Paradiso is a small family operation; the winery itself is the original home of the Paradise Valley Wine Company, founded in the late 1920s. With its high reinforced-concrete walls and louvered windows, this building stays cool on hot days without any air-conditioning. The winery is a continuing improvement project, with plans for a deck, landscaping, and a home vineyard.

&. &. &.

Walker Wines

11266 Oceanview (P.O. Box F1)
Felton, California 95018
TEL: 408-335-2591
OWNER: Russ Walker
FOUNDED: 1979

AT A GLANCE
Tours & Tastings: Open all year by appointment only. Self-guided tour.
Closed: Major holidays.
Vineyards: Grapes purchased from growers in Monterey, Amador, Santa Cruz, and San Luis Obispo counties.
Wines: Chardonnay, Cabernet Sauvignon, Sauvignon Blanc, Pinot Noir, Petite Sirah, Zinfandel, Barbera.
Awards: Petite Sirah: bronze; Barbera: silver, bronze.
Retail Shop: Wines sold on-site.
Credit Cards: None.
Access for Disabled: None.
Getting There: Winery is four miles from the center of Felton, in Santa Cruz County. Call for directions.

&. The winery is located atop a mountain ridge, with a great view of Monterey Bay.

TO SEE & DO

If all the world's a stage, a disproportionate number of the players must live in Santa Cruz. Between the Louden Nelson Center (tel: 408-429-9600), the Santa Cruz County Actors Theater (1001 Center Street; tel: 408-425-PLAY), and the Performing Arts Complex at the University of California–Santa Cruz (tel: 408-429-4168), the offerings range from Shakespeare to dramatized fairy tales. Rock and jazz fans should drop in at some of the city's clubs, such as O. T. Price's Music Hall, Kuumbwa Jazz Center (320-2 Cedar Street; tel: 408-427-2227), and Catalyst (1011 Pacific Avenue; tel: 408-423-1388). To patronize an art form you can bring home with you, visit the Santa Cruz Potter's Coop (1642 Mission Street), which sells functional stoneware and porcelain hand-thrown by local craftspeople. Down the coast in Monterey the waterfront supplies many diversions. Monterey Bay Aquarium is among the finest in the world, harboring more than 5,500 creatures of the deep; when you're through studying the wolf eels and sharks, stroll along Cannery Row—considerably gentrified since John Steinbeck's time—to Fisherman's Wharf. Nearby is the Presidio of Monterey, home of the U.S. Army Defense Language Institute, the military equivalent of Berlitz. During spring and summer, almost every town has a food fair. Morgan Hill observes Mushroom Mardi Gras in April, Los Gatos sponsors the Strawberry Festival in June (tel: 408-358-1971), and Gilroy holds its Garlic Festival in late July. Other communities celebrate broccoli, artichokes, and calamari. Several summer music programs provide food for the soul. The oldest, the Carmel Bach Festival, has been in business for more than fifty years (tel: 408-624-1521). The younger Cabrillo Music Festival enlivens Santa Cruz with starlight and symphonies under the baton of conductor Dennis Russell Davies (tel: 408-476-9064). In September, the Monterey Jazz Festival helps summer mellow into fall. If you've had enough culture, the Watsonville Racetrack can offer a change of pace. Car races alternate with an occasional test of old-fashioned horsepower, as in the Coors Belgian Draft Horse events. And the annual World Championship Rodeo at the Salinas Fairgrounds presents a medley of mounted sports.

ACCOMMODATIONS

Aptos

Apple Lane Inn
6265 Soquel Drive
Aptos, California 95003
Tel: 408-475-6868
B&B in a restored Victorian farmhouse.

Mangel's House
570 Aptos Creek Road
Aptos, California 95001
Tel: 408-688-7982
B&B in a gracious, southern-style mansion.

Carmel

Carmel is a beautiful place, with dozens of delightful inns and hotels; a sampling is noted here.

The Cobblestone Inn
Junipero Street
Carmel, California 93921
Tel: 408-625-5222
Ample country breakfast in the morning, complimentary snacks in the afternoon. Very popular, so book ahead.

Happy Landing Inn
Monte Verde Street
Carmel, California 93921
Tel: 408-624-7917
B&B with antique-filled rooms overlooking a central garden.

Highlands Inn
Highway 1
Carmel, California 93921
Tel: 408-624-3801
An oceanside resort, just outside of town, with all amenities and facilities.

La Playa Hotel
Eighth & Camino Real
Carmel, California 93921
Tel: 408-624-6476
A classic small hotel, exquisitely restored.

The Quail Lodge
Carmel Valley Road
Carmel, California 93923
Tel: 408-624-1581
A five-star resort with tennis courts, golf course, and several restaurants. Magnificent setting; all amenities.

Sandpiper Inn
2408 Bay View Avenue
Carmel, California 93921
Tel: 408-624-6433
Clean, comfortable, welcoming B&B inn; many rooms with fireplaces.

Davenport
New Davenport Cash Store
31 Davenport Avenue
Davenport, California 95017
Tel: 408-425-1818
A friendly B&B, pottery store and bakery, with many beautiful beaches nearby.

Gilroy
Best Western Motel
360 Leavesley Road
Gilroy, California 95020
Tel: 408-848-1467; 800-528-1234

TraveLodge
8292 Murray Avenue
Gilroy, California 95020
Tel: 408-848-3500; 800-255-3050

Santa Cruz
Babbling Brook Inn
1025 Laurel Street
Santa Cruz, California 95060
Tel: 408-427-2437
Each guest room has a deck and a private bath at this 12-room inn. Full breakfast.

Cliff Crest
407 Cliff Street
Santa Cruz, California 95060
Tel: 408-427-2609
A bed and breakfast in a nineteenth-century mansion with lovely gardens. Wake up to muffins right from the oven.

Darling House
314 West Cliff Drive
Santa Cruz, California 95060
Tel: 408-458-1958
A 1910 mansion with gorgeous ocean views and home-baked goodies. Beach across street.

Dream Inn
175 West Cliff Drive
Santa Cruz, California 95060
Tel: 408-426-4330; 800-662-3838
A 160-room hotel right on the beach. Savor an all-you-can-eat breakfast buffet every day, champagne brunch on Sundays.

RESTAURANTS

Aptos
Arthur's
Aptos, California 95003
Tel: 408-688-0457
Italian cuisine.

Chez Renee
9051 Soquel Drive
Aptos, California 95003
Tel: 408-688-5566
Classic European menu.

Deerpark Tavern
783 Rio Del Mar Boulevard
Aptos, California 95003
Tel: 408-688-5800
American cuisine in a rustic but attractive setting.

Capitola
Shadowbrook Restaurant
1750 Wharf Road
Capitola, California 95010
Tel: 408-475-1511; 475-1222
Cable cars conduct you to this charming restaurant overlooking a creek. Fresh fish, exceptional desserts, good wine list.

Carmel
Casanova Restaurant
Fifth Avenue and Mission
Carmel, California 93923
Tel: 408-625-0501
Italian and French cuisine; local seafood, outdoor dining.

The Covey
Carmel Valley Road
Carmel, California 93923
Tel: 408-624-1581
California interpretations of Continental classics. Located in the Quail Lodge. Extensive local wine list.

Giuliano's
Mission & Fifth Avenue
Carmel, California 93923
Tel: 408-625-5231
Northern Italian cooking with homemade pasta.

Pacific's Edge
Carmel, California 93921
Located at the Highlands Inn (see "Accommodations" for address and phone). Free range chicken, Creole dishes. Dramatic ocean views.

Davenport
New Davenport Cash Store
Davenport, California 95017
(See "Accommodations" for address and phone.) Home-style American cooking that's easy on the wallet.

Monterey
Fresh Cream
100 Pacific
Monterey, California 93940
Tel: 408-375-9798
Classic French cuisine; wine cellar.

The Point
99 Heritage Harbor
Monterey, California 93940
Tel: 408-373-1644
A relaxed spot for mesquite-broiled fish and meat; salad bar.

The Sardine Factory
701 Wave Street
Monterey, California 93940
Tel: 408-373-3775
Despite the name, lamb and veal are served in elegant surroundings. Admirable wine list. Try the prawns and splurge on dessert.

Santa Cruz
Casablanca Restaurant
Santa Cruz, California 95060
(See "Accommodations" for address and phone.) Roast duckling, rack of lamb, fresh seafood specials, and premium wines by the glass. Entertainment on Friday and Saturday nights.

Santa Cruz Hotel
Cedar & Locust Streets
Santa Cruz, California 95060
Tel: 408-475-1511
A local landmark, renowned for Italian and seafood dishes.

The Swan/Heavenly Goose
1538 Pacific Garden Mall
Santa Cruz, California 95060
Tel: 408-425-8988
Inventive Szechuan cuisine, accompanied by local vintages. Wine menu available in braille.

Saratoga
The Plumed Horse
14555 Big Basin Way
Saratoga, California 95070
Tel: 408-867-4711
Continental and French cuisine; wine cellar. Charming Victorian setting; jackets required.

Persimmon House
3010 North Main Street
Soquel, California 95073
Tel: 408-475-4855
The wine list is drawn from local vintners.

₰ SAN FRANCISCO BAY AREA

This region attained international renown in 1889, when a sauterne made by Livermore Valley vintner Charles Wetmore became the first California wine to win a gold medal at the Paris Exposition. Today wineries radiate outward in all directions from San Francisco Bay. Some of these establishments—Almaden, Paul Masson, Mirassou—date back to the 1850s, marking them as some of the oldest in the state.

The largest winery clusters lie to the east, in the Livermore Valley viticultural area, and south, in the mountains overlooking Saratoga. This is one region where it's easy to blend urban adventures and wine touring. Several wineries are just a short drive from San Francisco. Both Rosenblum Cellars and St. George Spirits are ten miles away, in Emeryville; Montali, in Berkeley, is even closer.

₰ ₰ ₰

Almaden Vineyards

1530 Blossom Hill Road
San Jose, California 95118
TEL: 408-269-1312
Also visit:
Almaden Tasting Gardens
8090 Pacheco Pass Highway
Hollister, California 95023
TEL: 408-637-7554
GENERAL MANAGER: Ronald J. Siletto
WINEMASTER: Klaus P. Mathes (degree in enology and viticulture from Enginner School of Viticulture, Bad Kreuznach, Germany)
FOUNDED: 1852

AT A GLANCE
Tours & Tastings: Open daily; Nov.–Feb. 9–3, March–Oct. 10–4. Tours, departing every thirty minutes (except between 12 and 1), encompass original wine cellars, barrel rooms, and historic grounds. At tour's conclusion, an innovative wine-tasting session encourages visitors to discover and pursue their own preferences, based on their responses to an introductory blind tasting. Groups of fifteen or more should make prior arrangements. (The Hollister location is open daily for tasting and sales.)
Closed: Easter, Thanksgiving, Christmas, New Year's Day.
Vineyards: 1,500 owned and 1,884 leased acres planted to Cabernet Sauvignon,

Chardonnay, Sauvignon Blanc, Zinfandel, Gewürztraminer, Johannisberg Riesling, French Colombard.

Wines: Cabernet Sauvignon, Chardonnay, Gewürztraminer, White Zinfandel, White Cabernet, Chablis, Burgundy; champagnes; port, sherry, brandy.

Awards: Recent medal winners include: 1984 San Benito County Select Harvest Gewürztraminer—gold, three silvers, two bronzes; 1981 Monterey County Cabernet Sauvignon — gold, silver, bronze; 1982 Monterey County Late Harvest Sauvignon Blanc—two silvers.

Picnic Area: Patio and gardens for informal meals, outdoor kitchen and lawn tables for catered events.

Retail Shop: Almaden wines and imported vintages sold on-site.

Credit Cards: MasterCard, Visa.

Access for Disabled: Ramp at wine store, elevator and especially equipped bathrooms in headquarters.

Foreign Languages: German, Spanish, French, and Italian.

Getting There: Winery is about six miles south of downtown San Jose and sixty miles south of San Francisco. From I-280: Take Almaden Rd./Expressway south to Blossom Hill Rd. and turn right.

Special Wine & Other Events: "We hold special multicourse haute cuisine dinners accompanied by select top-quality wines."

ن One of California's oldest and largest wineries, Almaden still produces wine on the same land where its two French founders, Charles Lefranc and his father-in-law, Etienne Thee, planted their first vineyard more than one hundred years ago. Both men were lured here by the promise of gold, only to find greater satisfaction and profit in wine. Lefranc adapted to his new environment quickly; one of his many innovations was to make storage tanks out of redwood.

ن ن ن

Cline Cellars

Sellers Avenue (Route 2, Box 175C)
Oakley, California 94561
TEL: 415-625-2175
GENERAL PARTNER: Frederic T. Cline
(degree in agricultural science and management, UC-Davis)
FOUNDED: 1933

AT A GLANCE

Tours & Tastings: Open daily; Oct.–Apr. 9–5, May–Sept. 9–6. Small winery out in the country with a relaxed atmosphere. Informal tours on request. Visitors are shown the vineyards, processing equipment, lab, bottled storage and barrel storage areas, and are given a brief outline of winemaking procedures, with detailed explanations of subjects of particular interest.

Closed: Easter, Thanksgiving, Christmas.

Vineyards: Thirty leased acres planted to Muscat of Alexandria, Zinfandel, Sémillon, Sauvignon Blanc. Additional grapes purchased from growers in Napa and Contra Costa counties.

Wines: Sauvignon Blanc, White Zinfandel, Cabernet Sauvignon, Zinfandel, Muscat of Alexandria, Late Harvest Zinfandel.

Awards: 1984 Temecula Sauvignon Blanc won recommendation from the *Wine and Spirits Buying Guide* and the *Wine Register*.

Picnic Area: Tasting room deck with tables and umbrellas.

Retail Shop: Wines, wine accessories, varietal grape juice, books, nuts, and dried fruit sold on-site.

Credit Cards: MasterCard, Visa.

Access for Disabled: Wheelchair accessible; handrail in rest room.

Foreign Languages: Italian, Spanish.

Getting There: Winery is about eighty miles east of San Francisco. Take Hwy. 4 east of Oakley and turn left on Delta Rd.; then bear left on Sellers.

Special Wine & Other Events: The annual Wine and Jazz Festival, held the weekend after Labor Day, features food, fun, dancing, and grape stomping.

⮞ "This winery is more than fifty years old," reports Fred Cline. "Our antique barrels traveled around the tip of the Horn before the Panama Canal existed, and ancient wine-processing equipment can be found all over the premises." Cline's family is involved with water as well as wine—he's the grandson of vintner Valeriano Jacuzzi, whose other descendants make pumps and whirlpool baths.

⮞ ⮞ ⮞

Congress Springs Vineyards

23600 Congress Springs Road
Saratoga, California 95070
TEL: 408-867-1409
PARTNERS: Victor Erickson and Daniel Gehrs
WINEMAKER: Daniel Gehrs
FOUNDED: 1976

AT A GLANCE
Tours & Tastings: Fri. 1–5, Sat.–Sun. 11–5. Tours by appointment.
Closed: Mon.–Thurs.
Vineyards: Twelve owned acres planted to Chardonnay and Zinfandel. More than one hundred leased acres planted to Chenin Blanc, Cabernet Sauvignon, Pinot Blanc, Sémillon, Cabernet Franc, Pinot Noir, and other varietals.
Wines: Chardonnay, Sémillon, Pinot Blanc, Cabernet Sauvignon, Zinfandel, Pinot Noir, Cabernet Franc.
Awards: Recent medal winners include: 1985 Chardonnay—three golds, three silvers, bronze; 1985 Johannisberg Riesling—two silvers, two bronzes; 1983 Estate-Bottled Zinfandel—gold, two silvers, two bronzes.
Picnic Area: On lawn. Visitors welcome to explore estate's trails and roads.
Retail Shop: Wines sold on-site.

Credit Cards: MasterCard, Visa.
Access for Disabled: None.
Foreign Languages: Some Spanish.
Getting There: Winery is 3½ miles from Saratoga Village. From Hwy. 280: Take Saratoga Ave. to Congress Springs Rd., also known as Hwy. 9.
Special Wine & Other Events: Mustard Festival in Feb., Memorial Festival in May, Meet-the-Winemakers Aug.–Sept., Library Reserve Sale Nov.–Dec. Also, an annual summer picnic for members of winery's Premier Tasting Club.

⮞ Congress Springs dates to 1892, when a young Frenchman, Pierre Pourroy, cleared land and rooted vines where redwoods had towered. After a lapse of some twenty-six years, this winery was revived by the Erickson and Gehrs families, who produce château-style premium wines from locally grown grapes.

⮞ ⮞ ⮞

Cronin Vineyards

11 Old La Honda Road
Woodside, California 94062
TEL: 415-851-1452
PROPRIETOR: Duane Mansell Cronin
FOUNDED: 1980

AT A GLANCE
Tours & Tastings: Open by appointment only. Tours are small, friendly, and short. Tasting of a wine or two follows the tour.
Vineyards: One owned and two leased acres planted to Chardonnay, Cabernet Sauvignon. Additional grapes purchased from growers in Napa and Alexander Valleys and the city of Monterey.
Wines: Chardonnay, Cabernet Sauvignon/Merlot blends, Pinot Noir.
Awards: Does not enter contests.
Retail Shop: Wines sold on-site.
Credit Cards: None.
Access for Disabled: None.
Getting There: Winery is thirty-five miles south of San Francisco, five miles west of

Palo Alto, off Hwy. 84. Call for directions.

Special Wine & Other Events: Two open houses a year: one in the spring, one in the fall.

🍂 Computer professional Duane Cronin established this winery, which overlooks San Francisco Bay and Portola Valley. "I have found that computer work and winemaking complement each other beautifully," he observes.

🍂 🍂 🍂

Thomas Fogarty Winery

19501 Skyline Boulevard
Portola Valley, California 94025
TEL: 415-851-1946
OWNER: Thomas J. Fogarty
WINEMAKER: Michael Martella (B.S. in enology from Fresno State)
FOUNDED: 1981

AT A GLANCE
Tours & Tastings: Open first Sat. of each month, 1–4. Call ahead; tours by appointment.
Closed: All other days.
Vineyards: Twenty acres planted to Chardonnay, Pinot Noir. Additional grapes purchased from growers in the Santa Cruz Mountains, Edna Valley, and the Carneros District of Napa Valley.
Wines: Chardonnay, Pinot Noir, Gewürztraminer, Cabernet Sauvignon.
Awards: An assortment of awards at fairs and other competitions too numerous to list here.
Retail Shop: Wines sold on-site.
Credit Cards: MasterCard, Visa.
Access for Disabled: None.
Getting There: Winery is thirty-five miles south of San Francisco, 5 miles west of Palo Alto. Take either Hwy. 101 or I-280 to Woodside Rd., also known as Hwy. 84. Then take Woodside Rd. to Skyline Blvd. (also known as Hwy. 35) and drive south for 4½ miles.

🍂 After purchasing land in the Portola Valley, cardiovascular surgeon and inventor Thomas Fogarty took up home winemaking. His hobby and his vineyards kept growing, so he built a winery. Today his production is up to 6,500 cases a year.

🍂 🍂 🍂

Kathryn Kennedy Winery

13180 Pierce Road
Saratoga, California 95070
TEL: 408-867-4170
OWNER: Kathryn Kennedy
WINEMAKER: Marty Mathis
FOUNDED: 1979

AT A GLANCE
Tours & Tastings: Sample current release and rare older vintages at Open House on Presidents' Weekend in Feb. No tasting during the rest of the year; tours and sales by appointment only. Visitors tour a very small winery building, walk through vineyards, and discuss viticulture and enology with the winemaker.
Vineyards: Eight acres planted to Cabernet Sauvignon.
Wines: Vintage-dated, estate-bottled, 100 percent varietal Cabernet Sauvignon with the Santa Cruz Mountains Appellation.
Awards: 1982 Cabernet Sauvignon: gold, silver.
Retail Shop: Wines sold on-site.
Credit Cards: None.
Access for Disabled: Yes.
Getting There: Winery is on the eastern edge of the Santa Cruz Mountains, fifty miles south of San Francisco. From I-280: Travel south on Hwy. 85 (also called Saratoga-Sunnyvale Rd.) into Saratoga city limits. Turn right on Pierce Rd.

🍂 Kathryn Kennedy is the founder and sole owner of this small wine estate. Personalized care distinguishes this establishment—Kennedy and her son, Marty Mathis, are the only people permitted to prune the vineyard. With only one varietal to watch, harvest takes place at just the right time to capture the best quality grape possible.

🙞 🙞 🙞

Livermore Valley Cellars

1508 Wetmore Road
Livermore, California 94550
TEL: 415-447-1751
OWNER/WINEMAKER: Chris Lagiss
FOUNDED: 1978

AT A GLANCE
Tours & Tastings: Open daily 11–5. Tours by request.
Closed: During vacation—dates vary.
Vineyards: Thirty-three acres planted to white French varietals.
Wines: Chardonnay, Grey Riesling, Fumé Blanc, French Colombard, Golden Seco, Blanc de Blanc.
Awards: 1982 Grey Riesling: two bronzes; 1982 Golden Seco: bronze; 1982 Blanc de Blanc: bronze.
Retail Shop: Wines sold on-site.
Credit Cards: MasterCard, Visa.
Access for Disabled: None.
Foreign Languages: Greek.
Getting There: Winery is on Livermore's southern city limits. From I-580: Take Hwy. 84 South to Arroyo Rd. Continue driving south on Arroyo to Wetmore Rd.
Special Wine & Other Events: Wine Festival during Labor Day weekend.

🙞 The vineyard is pruned to produce no more than two tons per acre. This low yield, especially for white grapes, creates fruit flavor of unusual intensity and depth, qualities that permit the barrel and bottle aging associated with only the greatest white wines. Further bottle aging will allow the grape and oak to develop even more complexity.

🙞 🙞 🙞

J. Lohr Winery

1000 Lenzen Avenue
San Jose, California 94126
TEL: 408-288-5057
GENERAL PARTNER: Jerry Lohr
WINEMAKER: Barry Gnekow (M.S. in enology, UC-Davis; former research analyst at Paul Masson)
FOUNDED: 1974

AT A GLANCE
Tours & Tastings: Open daily 10–5. Winery tours at 11 and 2 on weekends. No vineyard tours.
Closed: Easter, Christmas, New Year's Day.
Vineyards: 500 acres planted to Sauvignon Blanc, Pinot Blanc, Chardonnay, Chenin Blanc, Johannisberg Riesling, Gamay, Cabernet Sauvignon, Petite Sirah.
Wines: Sauvignon Blanc, Pinot Blanc, Chardonnay, Chenin Blanc, Johannisberg Riesling, Gamay, Cabernet Sauvignon, Petite Sirah, White Zinfandel.
Awards: Recent medal winners include: 1985 Greenfield Vineyards Johannisberg Riesling—two golds, bronze; 1985 Pheasant's Call Vineyard Chenin Blanc—two golds, two silvers; 1985 White Zinfandel—three silvers, three bronzes.
Retail Shop: Wines sold on-site.
Credit Cards: MasterCard, Visa.
Access for Disabled: Tasting room and tours equipped for disabled.
Foreign Languages: Spanish, French.
Getting There: Winery is in San Jose, off I-680.
Special Wine & Other Events: Catered dinners, wine classes, holiday festivals.

🙞 For Jerry Lohr, a South Dakota–born farm boy turned entrepreneur, viticulture was a natural outlet, combining his love of the land and his love of wine. His winery is a mixture of new and traditional equipment; Chardonnay, Pinot Blanc, and Sauvignon Blanc are fermented in French oak, while other varietals are fermented in temperature-controlled, stainless steel tanks.

ᴈ& ᴈ& ᴈ&

Paul Masson Vineyards

14831 Pierce Road
Saratoga, California 95070
TEL: 408-741-5182
OWNER: Joseph E. Seagram and Sons, Inc.
FOUNDED: 1852

AT A GLANCE
Tours & Tastings: Open year-round by advance reservation. Half-hour tours, scheduled at 10, 12, 2, and 4 by appointment, cover historic mountain winery, Paul Masson's original house, and the winery grounds, with their exotic plants.
Closed: Easter, Christmas, New Year's Day.
Vineyards: Twenty acres planted to vinifera varieties. Additional grapes bought from growers in Sonoma, Monterey, and San Joaquin valleys.
Wines: Chardonnay, Chenin Blanc, Fumé Blanc, Johannisberg Riesling, White Zinfandel, French Colombard, Chablis, Burgundy, Grenache Rosé, Gamay Beaujolais, Cabernet Sauvignon, Pinot Noir, Gewürztraminer; Emerald Dry and Rhinecastle (proprietary blends); Sparkling White Zinfandel, brut and extra-dry champagnes; Seagram Wine Coolers; brandy; vermouth.
Awards: Hundreds.
Retail Shop: Wines sold on-site.
Credit Cards: MasterCard, Visa.
Access for Disabled: Full access.
Foreign Languages: Spanish.
Getting There: Winery is just west of San Jose, fifty miles south of San Francisco. Take I-280 to Saratoga Ave. west; in six miles, turn right on Pierce Rd.

Special Wine & Other Events: Special events occur each winter, but most activities take place June through September, when the winery hosts the Paul Masson Summer Series. Programs range from theater and classical music to jazz and blues sessions; past guests have included Metropolitan Opera diva Elena Nikolaidi and the late King of Swing, Benny Goodman.

ᴈ& A registered historic landmark, the Paul Masson Winery is a cultural landmark as well. This is where its namesake, a French-born vintner, gourmet, and bon vivant, entertained the young Charlie Chaplin and the less-youthful Ziegfeld star Anna Held (she reputedly bathed in champagne). Nothing has ever prevented the wines from flowing. Under special government dispensation, the presses operated during Prohibition, and the cellar's sandstone walls have withstood earthquake and fire.

ᴈ& ᴈ& ᴈ&

Mirassou

3000 Aborn Road
San Jose, California 95135
TEL: 408-274-4000
PRESIDENT: Daniel Mirassou
WINEMAKER: Tom Stutz (M.S. in viticulture, UC-Davis; has taught viticulture at Napa Junior College)
FOUNDED: 1854

AT A GLANCE
Tours & Tastings: Open Mon.–Sat. 10–5, Sun. 12–4. Tours scheduled Mon.–Sat. 10:30, 12, 2, 3:30; Sun. 12:30, 2:30.
Closed: Easter, Thanksgiving, Christmas, New Year's Eve, New Year's Day.
Vineyards: 1,200 acres planted to vinifera varieties.
Wines: Chardonnay, White Burgundy, Johannisberg Riesling, Late Harvest Johannisberg Riesling, Gewürztraminer,

Chenin Blanc, Monterey Riesling, White Zinfandel, White Cabernet Sauvignon, Gamay Beaujolais, Zinfandel, Cabernet Sauvignon, Petite Sirah, Chablis, Burgundy, Petite Rosé; Pastel (low-alcohol proprietary blend); champagnes.

Awards: Recent medal winners include: 1985 White Cabernet Sauvignon—gold, bronze; 1982 Brut Champagne—gold, two silvers, three bronzes; 1984 Gamay Beaujolais—silver, bronze; 1983 Cabernet Sauvignon—silver.

Retail Shop: Wines sold on-site.

Credit Cards: American Express, MasterCard, Visa.

Access for Disabled: Winery accommodates wheelchairs.

Foreign Languages: French, Spanish.

Getting There: Winery is fifty miles south of San Francisco. Take Hwy. 101 south of San Jose to Capitol Expwy., east off-ramp. Continue on Capitol Expwy. to Aborn Rd. and turn right.

Special Wine & Other Events: Cask & Candlelight Festival—May; Sunday brunches, sunset dinners—summer; Vintage Festival—Aug. or Sept.; Holiday Festival—Nov. or Dec.; concerts, candelight dinners, and cooking classes held intermittently.

ᴥ Pierre Pellier came to California in search of gold, but the varietal cuttings he brought from France proved just as valuable once he established a vineyard in the Santa Clara Valley. His daughter's marriage to Pierre Mirassou, another French émigré vintner, expanded the enterprise and gave it a name. Today Mirassou is operated by Pellier's great-great-grandchildren.

ᴥ ᴥ ᴥ

Montali Winery

600 Addison Street
Berkeley, California 94710
TEL: 415-540-5551

PRESIDENT: Hubertus Von Wolffen
FOUNDED: 1982

AT A GLANCE

Tours & Tastings: Open daily; winter hours: 12–5, summer hours: 12–6. Tours, by appointment, view winery and aging cellars.

Closed: Thanksgiving, Christmas, New Year's Day.

Vineyards: Grapes purchased from Sonoma Valley growers.

Wines: Chardonnay, Pinot Noir.

Awards: Chardonnay: bronze.

Retail Shop: Wine sold on-site.

Access for Disabled: Ramps.

Getting There: Winery is ten miles from San Francisco. Take University Ave. exit from I-80 and drive up University to the first stoplight. Turn right at Sixth St. and proceed one block. Turn right at Addison St., go three blocks, cross the railroad tracks, and Montali is on your left.

ᴥ Establishing a modern winery in an urban area is not typical of California vintners. But this site was selected for many good reasons. The cooling summer breezes flowing through the Golden Gate to the Berkeley shore keep the temperature ideal for winemaking, and the central location puts Montali reasonably close to the state's major viticultural regions.

ᴥ ᴥ ᴥ

Mount Eden Vineyards

22020 Mount Eden Road
Saratoga, California 95070
TEL: 408-867-5932
OWNER: MEV Corporation
WINEMAKER/GENERAL MANAGER:
    Jeffrey Patterson
FOUNDED: 1972

AT A GLANCE

Tours & Tastings: Open by appointment only, five-day notice required.

Vineyards: Thirty-six acres planted to Chardonnay, Pinot Noir, Cabernet Sauvignon. Additional grapes purchased from Monterey County growers.
Wines: Chardonnay, Pinot Noir, Cabernet Sauvignon.
Retail Shop: Wines sold on-site.
Credit Cards: MasterCard, Visa.
Access for Disabled: None.
Getting There: Winery is fifty miles south of San Francisco, off Hwy. 9 in Saratoga. Call for directions.

❧ Mount Eden Vineyards is a small wine estate situated 2,000 feet above the Santa Clara Valley. The late Martin Ray planted the vineyards in the early 1940s under the guidance of his close friend Paul Masson.

❧ ❧ ❧

Rosenblum Cellars

1401 Stanford Avenue
Emeryville, California 94608
TEL: 415-653-2355
WINEMAKER: Kent M. Rosenblum
FOUNDED: 1978

AT A GLANCE
Tours & Tastings: Open by appointment only. Tour covers crush, fermentation, and barrel storage areas. Discussion of winemaking theory and barrel tasting are included.
Vineyards: Grapes purchased from growers in Napa and Sonoma counties.
Wines: Zinfandel, Cabernet Sauvignon, Petite Sirah, Sauvignon Blanc, Chardonnay, Sparkling Gewürztraminer.
Awards: Napa Zinfandel: gold; Sonoma Cabernet Sauvignon: gold. More than sixty medals in six years.
Retail Shop: Wines sold on-site.
Credit Cards: MasterCard, Visa.
Access for Disabled: None.
Foreign Languages: Some Spanish.
Getting There: Winery is four miles from San Francisco. Take I-80 to Powell St. exit. Drive east on Powell to Hollis St., then right on Hollis for one block, just across the railroad tracks parallel to Stanford Ave.
Special Wine & Other Events: Three open houses a year, by invitation.

❧ A veterinarian doubling as a vintner, Kent Rosenblum bottles 3,500 cases of wine annually. "Our production is small by industry standards—microscopic, in fact—and availability of our wines is limited. We frequently find ourselves sold out shortly after the latest vintages are released."

❧ ❧ ❧

St. George Spirits

1401 Stanford Avenue
Emeryville, California 94608
TEL: 415-655-3055, 658-7934
OWNER: Jorg Rupf
FOUNDED: 1983

AT A GLANCE
Tours & Tastings: Open by appointment only, no tastings.
Vineyards: All fruit purchased from California and Washington growers.
Wines: A wide range of distilled spirits. Raspberry, Williams pear, kiwi, and quince eaux-de-vie (fruit brandies); liqueurs from the same fruits; Muscat and Gewürztraminer Marc brandies; Chardonnay Royale (a fortified wine).
Awards: Williams Pear: gold.
Retail Shop: Wines sold on-site.
Credit Cards: None.
Access for Disabled: None.
Foreign Languages: German, French.
Getting There: Winery is four miles from San Francisco. Take I-80 to Powell St. exit. Drive east on Powell to Hollis St., then right on Hollis for one block, just across the railroad tracks parallel to Stanford Ave.

&. Jorg Rupf left a promising legal career in Germany to settle in California with his American wife. Rather than attend law school all over again, he opened a tiny distillery reminiscent of the one his mother's family operated in the Black Forest.

&. &. &.

Sherrill Cellars

1185 Skyline Boulevard (P.O. Box 1608)
Palo Alto, California 94302
TEL: 415-851-1932
OWNERS: Nat and Jan Sherrill
FOUNDED: 1973

AT A GLANCE
Tours & Tastings: Open May–Aug. Sat. 1–5. "A small winery; you can stand in one place and see it all. We prefer to sit with a glass of wine and talk—about grapes, wine, winemaking, or whatever." Very informal tours.
Closed: Sept.–Nov.
Vineyards: All grapes purchased from Central Coast growers.
Wines: Chardonnay, Cabernet, Zinfandel, Petite Sirah, Gamay, Gamay Blanc.
Awards: Does not enter competitions.
Retail Shop: Wines sold on-site.
Credit Cards: MasterCard, Visa.
Access for Disabled: First floor of winery is wheelchair accessible.
Getting There: Winery is about fifty miles south of San Francisco, on Hwy. 35 (also known as Skyline Blvd.).

&. "We have been enjoying wines— ours and other vintners'—for more than twenty-five years," affirms Jan Sherrill. "Our winery looks much like many others, not old or historic, just a building. The people and the philosophy are what make one winery truly different from another."

&. &. &.

Weibel Vineyards

1250 Stanford Avenue
Mission San Jose, California 94539
TEL: 415-656-2340
Also visit:
Weibel's Mendocino Winery and Tasting Room
7051 North State Street
Redwood Valley, California 95470
TEL: 707-485-0321
PRESIDENT: Fred E. Weibel, Sr.
WINEMAKER: Richard T. Casqueiro (chemistry degree from California State University–Hayward)
FOUNDED: 1869

AT A GLANCE
Tours & Tastings: Open daily 10–5. Informal tours, conducted Mon.–Fri. 10–3, include winery history and bottling. Tastings served in attractive, roughhewn Weibel Hacienda. (The Mendocino Winery is open daily 10–5.)
Closed: Major holidays.
Vineyards: More than 600 acres planted to vinifera varietals. Additional grapes purchased from Mendocino County growers.
Wines: Chardonnay, Sauvignon Blanc, Riesling, Chenin Blanc, White Zinfandel, White Cabernet Sauvignon, White Pinot Noir, Zinfandel, Pinot Noir, Cabernet Sauvignon, Petite Sirah, Refosco (a light, fruity red); sparkling wines; May wine, sherry, port, brandy, Tangor (orange-flavored aperitif), dry and sweet vermouths.
Awards: Recent medal winners include: 1984 Proprietor's Reserve Sauvignon Blanc—gold, three bronzes; 1985 Mendocino County Chenin Blanc—two golds, bronze; 1985 Mendocino County White Pinot Noir—two silvers, two bronzes; Sparkling White Zinfandel— four silvers, ten bronzes.
Picnic Area: In arbored patios. (Mendocino Winery has its own park.)
Retail Shop: Wines sold on-site.

Credit Cards: MasterCard, Visa.
Access for Disabled: None.
Getting There: Mission San Jose winery is at the southern end of San Francisco Bay. From I-680: Take Mission Blvd, to Stanford Ave. (Mendocino Winery is about 110 miles north of San Francisco, near the intersection of Hwys. 101 and 20.)
Special Wine & Other Events: Brunches, dinners, concerts, art and wine festivals; advance reservations usually needed. To get schedule, call for a copy of the winery's newsletter, "The Weibel Grapevine."

℘ Fred Weibel and his family have been producing premium wines for three generations, first in their native Switzerland and, for nearly five decades, in California. Since 1945 the Weibels have made their home in the historic winery Governor Leland Stanford founded in 1869. This state landmark is one of the few wineries remaining in the East Bay area.

℘ ℘ ℘

Wente Brothers

5565 Tesla Road
Livermore, California 94550
TEL: 415-447-3603
Also visit:
    **Wente Brothers Sparkling Wine
    Cellars**
    5050 Arroyo Road
    Livermore, California 94550
    TEL: 415-447-3023
PRESIDENT: Eric Wente
FOUNDED: 1883

AT A GLANCE
Tours & Tastings: Open Mon.–Sat. 9–4:30, Sun. 11–4:30. Extensive tours of winery leave hourly, Mon.–Sat. 10–3, Sun. 1–3. (Sparkling Wine Cellars, over on Arroyo Road, open daily 11–6:30,

with tours leaving hourly 11–6. Visitors walk through vineyards, winery, caves, and bottling room as guides explain *methode champenoise*.
Closed: Easter, Christmas.
Vineyards: 2,200 acres planted to Chardonnay, Cabernet, Zinfandel, Gamay Beaujolais, Grey Riesling, White Riesling, Ugni Blanc, Chenin Blanc, Sémillon, Pinot Noir, Pinot Blanc, Sauvignon Blanc, Petite Sirah, Sylvaner, Gewürztraminer. Walnuts are also grown on-site.
Wines: Chardonnay, Chablis, Grey Riesling, Gamay Beaujolais, Gamay Beaujolais Blanc, Blanc de Blancs, Johannisberg Riesling, Sémillon, Sauvignon Blanc, Zinfandel, Cabernet, Petite Sirah, Chateau Wente (a Sauvignon Blanc/Sémillon blend), Arroyo Seco Riesling (a dessert wine), brut sparkling wine.
Awards: Recent medal winners include: 1983 Estate-Bottled Sémillon—gold, silver, bronze; 1982 Vintner-Grown Arroyo Seco Brut—two golds, silver, three bronzes; 1984 Vintner-Grown Arroyo Seco Chardonnay Reserve—two golds, silver, four bronzes.
Restaurant: Lunch and dinner served at Sparkling Wine Cellars' restaurant. Elegant country menu draws on regional American specialties and classic French cuisine. Reservations recommended (tel: 415-447-3696).
Retail Shop: Wines, related accessories, books, posters, and T-shirts sold at both locations.
Credit Cards: American Express, MasterCard, Visa.
Access for Disabled: Tesla Rd. location is accessible with a specially equipped rest room.
Foreign Languages: Spanish, French, German.
Getting There: From I-580: Take either Livermore Ave. or S. Vasco Rd. to Tesla Rd. (For Wente's Sparkling Wine Cellars, exit from I-580 via Portola Ave. Follow signs for Veterans' Administration Hospital. Turn right on North L St. and con-

tinue five miles—L St. becomes Arroyo Rd.)

Special Wine & Other Events: Art in the Vineyard, first Sun. in June. Three-day Harvest Wine Festival during Labor Day weekend, including the ten-kilometer Cellar-to-Cellar Run that Sun.

&. Upon discovering that his older brother would inherit the family farm, German-born Carl H. Wente struck out for America. The Tesla Road winery stands on the site of the fifty-acre vineyard he bought in 1883. Reluctant to leave his younger sons and daughters penniless, he divided his estate equally among all seven children, two of whom— Ernest and Herman—formed Wente Brothers. The second generation was so devoted to winemaking that during Prohibition they turned to cattle ranching and used the profits to maintain the vineyards and winery. Today, the fourth-generation Wentes run their enterprise with similar dedication.

TO SEE & DO
San Francisco is the main attraction here; start with a walking tour of some of the city's distinctive neighborhoods. In Chinatown, the Chinese Culture Centre (750 Kearny Street, third floor; tel: 415-986-1822) sponsors both a heritage walk and a culinary walk; the latter is followed by lunch. City Guide Walks (tel: 415-558-3770) will lead you around the Civic Center, City Hall, Market Street, and North Beach. Stroll up luxurious Nob Hill and over two blocks for a stop at the Cable Car Museum (Washington and Mason Streets; tel: 415-474-1887), where a short film explains the workings of San Francisco's famous mode of transportation. Alcatraz Island (tel: 415-546-2805) is no less historic, if somewhat grimmer; ferries begin departing Pier 1 at 8:45 in the morning for this former

federal penitentiary. You name the subject, San Francisco has a museum devoted to it, from the graphs and computer games at the World of Economics (101 Market Street; tel: 415-974-3252) to the antique water pumps and hoses at the San Francisco Fire Department Pioneer Memorial Museum (Presidio at Pine; tel: 415-861-8000, ext. 210). Golden Gate Park alone has three world-class institutions: the Asian Art Museum of San Francisco (tel: 415-558-2993), the M. H. de Young Memorial Museum (tel: 415-221-4811), and the California Academy of Sciences Natural History Museum and Aquarium (tel: 415-221-5100). Animals can be seen at the San Francisco Zoo (Zoo Rd. and Skyline Blvd.; tel: 415-661-4844). And with numerous resident performing groups, the city's stages are seldom dark; call the Performing Arts Center (tel: 415-522-8000) for details about plays and concerts. For a different kind of spectacle, cheer on the teams at Candlestick Park, home to football's 49ers (tel: 415-468-2249) and baseball's Giants (tel: 415-467-8000). For more information, contact the San Francisco Convention and Visitors Bureau, P.O. Box 6977, San Francisco, California 94101 (tel: 415-974-6900).

ACCOMMODATIONS & RESTAURANTS
Most enticing places are in San Francisco itself, not in the winery areas. Because the city offers so many choices, space does not permit a full listing here. The San Francisco Convention and Visitors Bureau can provide information on where to stay and eat either by mail (P.O. Box 6977, San Francisco, California 94101, Tel: 415-391-2000; charges postage and handling fee) or on-the-spot at the Visitor Information Center, Swig Pavilion, Hallidie Plaza, Powell and Market Streets, lower level.

San Francisco
Archbishop's Mansion
1000 Fulton Street
San Francisco, California 94117
Tel: 415-563-7872
Built in 1904 as the residence of San Francisco's archbishop, this is a spectacular place, with crystal chandeliers suspended from hand-painted ceilings, Oriental rugs, and canopy beds.

The Bed & Breakfast Inn
4 Charlton Court
San Francisco, California 94123
Tel: 415-921-9784
Two adjoining buildings, with a library and garden, make this a comfortable inn. Convenient downtown location, with a public garage nearby. Continental breakfast.

Four Seasons Clift Hotel
495 Geary Street
San Francisco, California 94102
Tel: 415-775-4700, 800-268-6282
Incomparable elegance and personal service; fine dining too.

Hotel Vintage Court
650 Bush Street
San Francisco, California 94108
Tel: 415-392-4666
A European-style hotel with 106 units, and each one has a stocked service bar. Complimentary wine tastings; wine tours arranged for guests.

The Petite Auberge
863 Bush Street
San Francisco, California 94108
Tel: 415-928-6000
Done in the style of a French country inn, with charming decorator touches—sprightly wallpaper patterns, quilted bedspreads, and plump, hand-sewn pillows. Generous breakfasts, wine and refreshments in the afternoon. A few doors away is its sister establishment, White Swan Inn (845 Bush Street; Tel: 415-775-1755) offering an equally delightful experience in an English environment.

❧ SIERRA FOOTHILLS

Some call it the Mother Lode, others say Gold Country. By any name, this is where the action was in 1848, after James Marshall found that first nugget at Sutter's Mill. Ironically enough, mill owner John Sutter profited little by the gold rush; for the next eighteen years, he derived much of his income from the small vineyard on his 600-acre farm.

Sutter had the right idea. After a hard day panning for ore, frustrated forty-niners needed to quench their thirst, and vineyards sprang up everywhere. By 1870 the Sierra Foothills—including Amador, El Dorado, Calaveras, and part of Tuolomne counties—had more wineries than better-known Napa. As the gold rush grew sluggish, mines closed and drinkers headed elsewhere. Then the sequential scourges of phylloxera and Prohibition caused most of the remaining vineyards to wither.

Zinfandel growers belatedly rediscovered Amador County in the 1960s. At about the same time, University of California enologists used experimental El

Dorado plots to demonstrate what miners had realized a century earlier: the entire region was suitable for vinifera cultivation. In Calaveras County alone, wineries increased from two to more than thirty in the last decade (a leap rivaling that of Mark Twain's fabled frog).

Today, the Sierra Foothills, Fiddletown, and El Dorado are all designated viticultural areas. For winemakers, there's still lots of gold in these hills.

ᏍᎭ ᏍᎭ ᏍᎭ

Amador Foothill Winery

12500 Steiner Road
Plymouth, California 95669
TEL: 209-245-6307
OWNERS: Ben Zeitman
WINEMAKERS: Katie Quinn (M.S. in enology, UC-Davis) and Ben Zeitman
FOUNDED: 1980

AT A GLANCE
Tours & Tastings: Open weekends and holidays 12–5 and by appointment. No formal tours given, but entire winery operation can be seen from the tasting room.
Closed: Thanksgiving, Christmas.
Vineyards: Ten acres planted to Sauvignon Blanc, Cabernet Sauvignon, Sémillon. Zinfandel grapes purchased from neighboring vineyards.
Wines: White Zinfandel, Fumé Blanc, Zinfandel, Cabernet Sauvignon.
Awards: 1985 Fumé Blanc: gold; 1985 White Zinfandel: gold; 1982 Fiddletown Zinfandel (Eschen Vineyard): gold. Plus numerous silver and bronze medals for these and other varieties.
Picnic Area: Yes.
Retail Shop: Wines sold on-site.
Credit Cards: None. Personal checks gladly accepted.
Access for Disabled: Limited wheelchair access.
Getting There: Winery is in the Shenandoah Valley in Amador County, about an hour's drive east of Sacramento. Take Hwy. 49 to Plymouth, then go five miles on E-16 (Shenandoah Rd.) toward River

Pines. Turn left onto Steiner Rd. and watch for winery on your right.
Special Wine & Other Events: Sample wine, cheese, and live music at Open House, the last weekend in Apr.

ᏍᎭ Six years after NASA chemist and amateur vintner Ben Zeitman built this winery, he married the UC-Davis–trained enologist Katie Quinn. Today they share winemaking and vineyard responsibilities at Amador Foothill.

ᏍᎭ ᏍᎭ ᏍᎭ

Boeger Winery

1709 Carson Road
Placerville, California 95667
TEL: 916-622-8094
OWNERS: Greg and Susan Boeger, Dr. and Mrs. George Babbin
WINEMAKER: Greg Boeger (M.S. in agricultural economics with a viticulture minor, UC-Davis)
FOUNDED: 1973

AT A GLANCE
Tours & Tastings: Open Wed.–Sun. 10–5. Tastings poured in century-old stone wine cellar listed on the National Register of Historic Places. Self-guided tours.
Vineyards: Thirty-five owned and twenty leased acres planted to Cabernet Sauvignon, Merlot, Zinfandel, Chardonnay, Sauvignon Blanc, Sémillon, Johannisberg Riesling, and experimental blocks of Flora, Muscat Canelli, Symphony, Cabernet Franc, Petite Verdot.
Wines: Chenin Blanc, Chardonnay, Sauvignon Blanc, White Zinfandel, Merlot, Cabernet Sauvignon, Zinfandel; Si-

erra Blanc, Hangtown Gold, Hangtown Red (proprietary blends).

Awards: More than one hundred medals since 1980. Recent medal winners include: 1983 Merlot—three golds; 1984 Sémillon—gold, silver, bronze; 1985 Sauvignon Blanc—silver; 1981 Cabernet Sauvignon—bronze.

Picnic Area: In fig grove near an old dam.

Retail Shop: Wines sold on-site.

Credit Cards: MasterCard, Visa.

Access for Disabled: None.

Getting There: From Hwy. 50 in Placerville: Take Schnell School Rd. off-ramp to Carson Rd. and head east.

᠊᠊ᴥ The first modern-day winery to locate in El Dorado, Boeger is also the largest, producing 10,000 cases annually. Greg Boeger is the grandson of Anton Nichelini, a Swiss-Italian who founded a Napa County winery that is still operated by his descendants nearly one hundred years later.

ᴥ ᴥ ᴥ

Granite Springs Winery

6060 Granite Springs Road
Somerset, California 95684
TEL: 209-245-6395
OWNERS: Lester S. and Lynne D.
  Russell
FOUNDED: 1981

AT A GLANCE

Tours & Tastings: Open weekends and most holidays 11–5; by appointment on weekdays. Informal winery tours upon request.

Vineyards: Twenty-three acres planted to Zinfandel, Cabernet Sauvignon, Sauvignon Blanc, Petite Sirah.

Wines: Sauvignon Blanc, White Zinfandel, Chenin Blanc, Zinfandel, Cabernet Sauvignon, Petite Sirah; Zinfandel Port, Petite Sirah Port.

Awards: 1985 White Zinfandel: two golds, three silvers, two bronzes; 1985 Chenin Blanc: gold, three silvers, two bronzes; 1983 Zinfandel: gold, silver, bronze; 1983 Petite Sirah: gold, silver, two bronzes.

Picnic Area: By pond or under oak trees on property.

Retail Shop: Wines, T-shirts, and posters sold on-site.

Credit Cards: MasterCard, Visa.

Access for Disabled: No barriers to sales/tasting room, which has concrete floors and no steps; portable rest room facilities cannot accommodate wheelchairs.

Getting There: Winery is 55 miles east of Sacramento and 16 miles southeast of Placerville. From Mt. Aukum Rd.: Take Fairplay Rd. 1.7 miles to gravel road on left. Then drive through double gates on the right, about 500 ft. ahead.

Special Wine & Other Events: Open house during Fairplay Festival, the first weekend in June—sample wine, cheese, and locally produced music and crafts.

᠊᠊ᴥ Lester and Lynne Russell carved their winery out of the Sierra Foothills. The granitic soil that provides such good drainage for the vineyards posed an excavational challenge. "We had to blast away rock to achieve the proper depth for the foundation," notes Lynne Russell. The site's advantages include natural air-conditioning: cooling tubes buried in the hillside bring crisp subterranean air into the storage area.

ᴥ ᴥ ᴥ

Greenstone Winery

Highway 88 at Jackson Valley Road
  (P.O. Box 1164)
Ione, California 95640
TEL: 209-274-2238
OWNERS:Stan and Karen Van Spanje,
  Durward and Jane Fowler
FOUNDED: 1980

AT A GLANCE
Tours & Tastings: Open Sept.–June weekends 10-4; July–Aug. Wed.–Sun. 10–4. Winemaker Stan Van Spanje and viticulturalist Durward Fowler are former educators, so complete, informative tours are the standard.
Closed: All major holidays, including Thanksgiving weekend.
Vineyards: Twenty-three acres planted to French Colombard, Zinfandel, Chenin Blanc, Palamino, and other premium varietals.
Wines: Fumé Blanc, Sauvignon Blanc, Chardonnay, French Colombard, Chenin Blanc, White Zinfandel, California Colombard, Zinfandel Rosé, Cabernet Sauvignon, Barbera, Zinfandel; Zinfandel Port, cream sherry.
Awards: French Colombard: golds; California Colombard: golds; Cabernet Sauvignon: silver, bronze; White Zinfandel: silvers, bronzes.
Picnic Area: Picnic sites, ponds, and wildlife.
Retail Shop: Wines sold on-site.
Credit Cards: American Express, MasterCard, Visa.
Access for Disabled: None.
Foreign Languages: French, German, Spanish, Dutch, Danish.
Getting There: Winery is forty-five miles southeast of Sacramento and one hundred miles west of Lake Tahoe. On Hwy. 88, eleven miles west of the historic gold-mining town of Jackson.

꙾ The Van Spanjes and the Fowlers are college chums who toasted twenty years of friendship by establishing a winery they named for California's state mineral. Fittingly, the main building and tasting room are faced with greenstone, and a natural greenstone outcropping enhances the picnic area.

꙾ ꙾ ꙾

Karly

11076 Bell Road (P.O. Box 729)
Plymouth, California 95669
TEL: 209-245-3922
GENERAL PARTNER: L. L. "Buck" Cobb
FOUNDED: 1979

AT A GLANCE
Tours & Tastings: Open weekends 12–4 and by appointment.
Closed: Non-summer holidays.
Vineyards: Eighteen acres planted to Sauvignon Blanc, Zinfandel, Barbera, Petite Sirah. Chardonnay comes from Tepusquet Vineyards, on the central California coast; other grapes purchased from Amador County vineyards.
Wines: Sauvignon Blanc, Zinfandel, White Zinfandel, Chardonnay, Petite Sirah, Barbera.
Awards: Too numerous to list.
Retail Shop: Wines sold on-site.
Credit Cards: None.
Access for Disabled: None.
Foreign Languages: French and German by prior arrangement.
Getting There: Winery is forty miles east of Sacramento, just off E16. From Plymouth Post Office: Take Shenandoah Valley Dr. 4½ miles east to Bell Rd. and bear left. Follow signs.

꙾ Planted in the Sierra Nevada Range, Karly's vineyards suffer harsh extremes of rainfall and drought—conditions that add character to grapes and grape growers alike. A self-taught vintner, nuclear engineer Buck Cobb invites serious enophiles to try his award-winning vintages.

꙾ ꙾ ꙾

Kenworthy Vineyards

10120 Shenandoah Road
Plymouth, California 95669
TEL: 209-245-3198
PROPRIETORS: John and Pat Kenworthy
FOUNDED: 1979

AT A GLANCE
Tours & Tastings: Open weekends 11–5, other times by appointment. Tours conducted by request.
Vineyards: Eight acres planted to Zinfandel, Cabernet Sauvignon, Muscat Canelli.
Wines: Zinfandel, Cabernet Sauvignon, Chardonnay, Muscat Canelli.
Awards: 1979 Zinfandel: gold; 1982 Zinfandel: silver.
Retail Shop: Wines sold on-site.
Credit Cards: MasterCard, Visa.
Access for Disabled: None.
Getting There: Winery is forty miles southeast of Sacramento. Take Shenandoah Rd. (E-16) half a mile north of its junction with Fiddletown Rd.

🍂 The Kenworthys established their operation on the grounds of an old farm. "The winery and tasting room occupy the much rejuvenated barn," reports John Kenworthy. "We also run a bed and breakfast—suitable for one or two couples—in what used to be a granary building."

🍂 🍂 🍂

Nevada City Winery

321 Spring Street
Nevada City, California 95959
TEL: 916-265-9463
PRESIDENT: Allan S. Halley
WINEMAKER: Tony Norskog (graduate of UC-Davis)
FOUNDED: 1980

AT A GLANCE
Tours & Tastings: Open daily 12–5. Staff explains winemaking process, which can be observed from the tasting room.
Closed: Easter, Christmas.
Vineyards: 200 acres planted to White Riesling, Gewürztraminer, Chardonnay, Sauvignon Blanc, Zinfandel, Charbono, Petite Sirah, Pinot Noir, Cabernet Sauvi-

gnon. Additional grapes purchased from growers in the Sierra Foothills.
Wines: White Riesling, Chardonnay, Sauvignon Blanc, Gewürztraminer, Zinfandel, Douce Noir (from Charbono grapes), Petite Sirah, Pinot Noir, Cabernet Sauvignon, White Zinfandel, champagne.
Awards: Too numerous to list.
Retail Shop: Wines sold on-site.
Credit Cards: MasterCard, Visa.
Access for Disabled: Yes.
Getting There: Take Broad St. exit from Hwy. 49 and turn left. Go one block to North Pine St. and turn left again. After one block, turn right onto Spring St.

🍂 Back in 1913, Nevada City's Chamber of Commerce applauded as crates of locally grown grapes were shipped off to Napa. Now there is a market closer to home. The Nevada City Winery, set up just a few blocks away from the site of its nineteenth-century namesake, purchases all the grapes produced by Nevada County vines. "We stress high-elevation fruit," says winemaker Tony Norskog, who prizes the lively flavor of grapes cultivated above 2,000 feet.

🍂 🍂 🍂

Shenandoah Vineyards

12300 Steiner Road
Plymouth, California 95669
TEL: 209-245-3698
OWNERS: Lee and Shirley Sobon
FOUNDED: 1977

AT A GLANCE
Tours & Tastings: Open daily 11–5. Tours by appointment only.
Vineyards: Twenty-five acres planted to Sauvignon Blanc, Cabernet Sauvignon, Cabernet Franc, French Sirah, Orange Muscat. Zinfandel and Carmine purchased from Shenandoah Valley and Amador County growers; Muscat Ham-

burg purchased from Amador County growers.

Wines: Sauvignon Blanc, White Zinfandel, Zinfandel, Cabernet Sauvignon, Late Harvest Zinfandel, Late Harvest Riesling; Black Muscat, Orange Muscat; Vintage Port, Zinfandel Port.

Awards: Recent medal winners include: 1985 White Zinfandel—two golds; 1985 Sauvignon Blanc—gold, two silvers; 1982 Cabernet Sauvignon—silver, two bronzes; 1984 Black Muscat—gold, five silvers, three bronzes.

Retail Shop: Wines sold on-site.

Credit Cards: MasterCard, Visa.

Access for Disabled: Winery accommodates wheelchairs.

Getting There: Winery is forty miles east of Sacramento. From I-80: Take Power Inn Rd. to Hwy. 16 (Shenandoah Rd.) and travel east. Bear left on Steiner Rd.

Special Wine & Other Events: New exhibits in barrel room art gallery every two months. Shenandoah Valley Grape Festival in Sept.

&. After several years of making wine in their Los Altos basement, the Sobons staked out a claim to a former gold mine, where they founded Shenandoah Vineyards. While they have yet to strike it rich, their venture is paying off in fame, if not in fortune. "After tasting our products, you'll agree that fortune is sure to follow," they promise.

&. &. &.

Stevenot Winery

2690 San Domingo Road (P.O. Box 548)
Murphys, California 95247
TEL: 209-728-3436
OWNER: Barden E. Stevenot
WINEMAKER: Steve Millier (graduate of Fresno State, seven years experience at David Bruce Winery in Los Gatos, California)
FOUNDED: 1978

AT A GLANCE

Tours & Tastings: Open daily 10–5. The winery is a restored hay barn; the tasting room is a sod-roofed cabin. Casual, personal tours on demand as time allows. In this relatively small winery, visitors can see all aspects of winemaking and vineyard work in a twenty-minute tour. Also explored is the historical background of Murphys, a gold rush town.

Closed: Thanksgiving, Christmas.

Vineyards: Twenty-seven acres planted to Cabernet Sauvignon, Chardonnay, Zinfandel. Purchases Zinfandel from Amador County, Muscat from San Luis Obispo, and Chenin Blanc and Fumé Blanc from Calaveras County.

Wines: Cabernet Sauvignon, Chardonnay, Chenin Blanc, Muscat Canelli, Fumé Blanc, Zinfandel, White Zinfandel; apple wine.

Awards: Recent medal winners include: 1984 Muscat Canelli—two golds, two silvers, bronze; 1984 Zinfandel Blanc—gold, two bronzes; 1983 Zinfandel—gold, two silvers.

Picnic Area: Yes.

Retail Shop: Wines sold on-site.

Credit Cards: MasterCard, Visa.

Access for Disabled: None.

Getting There: From Hwy. 4 in Murphys, take Sheepranch Rd. to San Domingo Rd.

&. The great-great-grandson of a forty-niner, Barden Stevenot takes pride in his family's history. His winery is a living museum, with gold-mining and winemaking artifacts prominently displayed at every turn. Although winemaking is a subject near to Stevenot's heart, gold is still in his blood; he's part-owner of the recently reopened Carson Hill Mine, from which a 195-pound nugget—the largest ever discovered in North America—was extracted in 1854.

&. &. &.

Story Vineyard

10525 Bell Road
Plymouth, California 95669
TEL: 209-245-6208, 245-6827
OWNER: Ann Story Ousley
FOUNDED: 1973

AT A GLANCE
Tours & Tastings: Open weekends 11-5, other times by appointment.
Vineyards: Forty acres planted to Zinfandel, Chenin Blanc, Mission. Walnuts are also grown here.
Wines: Zinfandel, Chenin Blanc, Sauvignon Blanc, White Zinfandel.
Awards: 1985 White Zinfandel: gold; 1982 Zinfandel: gold; 1980 Zinfandel: two golds.
Picnic Area: Oak-shaed land overlooking the Cosumnes River Canyon.
Retail Shop: Wines sold on-site.
Credit Cards: None. Checks accepted.
Access for Disabled: Ramp at entrance.
Getting There: Winery is six miles from Plymouth. Take Shenandoah Rd. to Bell Rd. and drive north two miles.

❧ The late Eugene Story and his wife, Ann, were among the serious home winemakers who fell in love with Amador County and its rich, intense Zinfandel. They purchased a 240-acre ranch and expanded its small, intact vineyard, which has been producing prizewinning crushes ever since.

❧ ❧ ❧

Winterbrook Vineyards

4851 Lancha Plana/Buena Vista Road
Buena Vista/Ione, California 95640
TEL: 209-274-2466
OWNERS: Bob and Jan Roberts
WINEMAKER: Christina Benz (M.S. in enology, UC-Davis)
FOUNDED: 1980

AT A GLANCE
Tours & Tastings: Open weekends 11–5, other times by appointment. Informal tours of winery, a restored barn built in 1860.
Vineyards: Sixty acres planted to Chardonnay, Chenin Blanc, and Portuguese Port varieties. Other grapes purchased from local vineyards.
Wines: Chardonnay, Chenin Blanc, White Zinfandel, Zinfandel, Sauvignon Blanc, Johannisberg Riesling, Late Harvest Riesling; Vintage Port.
Awards: 1984 White Zinfandel: gold, four bronzes; 1985 Select Late Harvest Riesling: gold, silver; 1983 Chenin Blanc: gold; 1980 Vintage Port: two silvers.
Picnic Area: 100-acre estate for picnicking and hiking.
Retail Shop: Wines sold on-site.
Credit Cards: MasterCard, Visa.
Foreign languages: French.
Getting There: Winery is in Jackson Valley, 1.7 miles southeast of Buena Vista. From Hwy. 88: Drive south on Lancha Plana/Buena Vista Rd.

❧ A prehistoric lake bed, Jackson Valley traps and holds cool night air, evidently providing an ideal environment for white varietals and port wines. The proof? Winterbrook's first Chenin Blanc and earliest Vintage Port have been collecting medals since their release.

TO SEE & DO
You are unlikely to find any gold, but you can still get a genuine rush from visiting old mine sites, starting with the Marshall Gold Discovery Park and Museum in Coloma (tel: 916-622-3470). Then give panning a try at Roaring Camp Mining Co. (Tabeau Road off Highway 88 East, P.O. Box 278, Pine Grove, California 95665; tel: 916-296-4100). Daytime and evening tours are available. Pine Acres Resort, at the same location, offers overnight accommodation, RV hookups, and camping areas. Columbia is an old gold

rush town that retains much of its nine-teenth-century glitter, thanks to extensive restoration. Tours take in the most important buildings in about one and a half hours with a free walking guide from the Department of Parks and Recreation (tel: 209-532-4301). During summers, a troupe from the University of the Pacific presents plays at Columbia's Fallon House Theater, on Washington Street (tel: 209-946-2311). Nevada City and Grass Valley are also interesting old mining towns. Prospectors for hand-sewn quilts, folk art, and Early American furniture will not be disappointed. Antique stores line Highway 49 in Amador City and Main Street in Sutter Creek. Amador County holds a fair every summer at the fairgrounds in Plymouth; the festivities include a wine competition. For details, contact the Amador County Chamber of Commerce, 30 South Highway 49, P.O. Box 596, Jackson, California 95642 (tel: 209-223-0350).

ACCOMMODATIONS

Amador City
The Mine House Inn
Highway 49 (P.O. Box 226)
Amador City, California 95601
Tel: 209-267-5900
Hosts Peter Daubenspeck III and Ann Marie Joseph preside over a bed and breakfast in the former headquarters of the Keystone Mining Company. Each room has a private bath; in the morning, coffee and orange juice are delivered to your door. Swimming pool in the summer.

Ione
The Heirloom
214 Shakeley Lane (P.O. Box 322)
Ione, California 95640
Tel: 209-274-4468
Magnolias and wisteria shade the verandas of this Colonial mansion, built in 1863. Bed and breakfast guests may lounge in hammocks, play croquet, even play piano. Breakfast fare includes quiches and soufflés.

Jackson
Gate House Inn
1330 Jackson Gate Road
Jackson, California 95642
Tel: 209-223-3500
Hosts Frank and Ursel Walker run this bed and breakfast in a stately Victorian mansion with marble fireplaces, oak parquet floors, crystal chandeliers, and a vast antique clock collection.

Murphys
Dunbar House
271 Jones Street (P.O. Box 1375)
Murphys, California 95247
Tel: 209-728-2897
You'll find fresh flowers and electric blankets in each bedroom of this restored 1880 home. Continental breakfast in the garden or by a crackling fire.

Murphys Hotel
457 Main Street (P.O. Box 329)
Murphys, California 95247
Tel: 209-728-3444
A national historic landmark, dating back to the great fire of 1859. Choose either an atmospheric room in the old hotel or modern motel comfort.

Nevada City
Grandmere's Inn
449 Broad Street
Nevada City, California 95959
Tel: 916-265-4660
Colonial Revival home, filled with antiques, surrounded by gardens.

The National Hotel
211 Broad Street
Nevada City, California 95959
Tel: 916-265-4551
Arrive any time—there's twenty-four-hour registration.

Sutter Creek
The Foxes of Sutter Creek
77 Main Street (P.O. Box 159)
Sutter Creek, California 95685
Tel: 209-267-5882
A mid-nineteenth-century home furnished by hosts Min and Pete Fox in period style. Each suite has a private bath, and guests enjoy complimentary local wine and bountiful breakfasts.

Sutter Creek Inn
75 Main Street
Sutter Creek, California 95685
Tel: 209-267-5606
Fireplaces in some rooms, electric blankets and air-conditioning in all. Private baths, too. Large gardens with furniture and hammocks that invite you to linger.

RESTAURANTS

Coloma
The Vineyard House
Highway 49 at Cold Springs Road
Coloma, California 95613
Tel: 916-622-2217
Enjoy fine food and wine, served with country elegance.

Columbia
City Hotel Restaurant
Columbia State Historic Park
Columbia, California 95310
Tel: 209-532-1479
An outstanding French restaurant with a first-rate wine list.

Jackson
Teresa's Place
1235 Jackson Gate Road
Jackson, California 95642
Tel: 209-223-1786

Authentic Italian food, accompanied by local wines. Open for both lunch and dinner.

Victorian Dining Room
Nevada City, California 95959
Located in the National Hotel (see listing under "Accommodations" for address and telephone number). Reasonable prices, Victorian decor in an 1852 building.

Sutter Creek
Harrower's Sutter Creek Cafe
Amelia and Highway 49 (P.O. Box 984)
Sutter Creek, California 95685
Tel: 209-267-5114
The menu changes daily, but homemade breads and pies are always available. Breakfast buffet on Sundays, 10–2:30.

Pelargonium Restaurant
1 Hanford
Sutter Creek, California 95685
Tel: 209-267-5008
Fresh fish, good beef, delicious baked goods. Old West decor.

Sutter Creek Palace
76 Main Street (Box 338)
Sutter Creek, California 95685
Tel: 209-267-9852
Both lunch and dinner are served at this charming restaurant in a turn-of-the-century hotel. Continental cuisine, Pioneer Saloon.

Other area favorites include Michael's Garden, Seleya's, Culinos, Holbrook.

❧ SONOMA COUNTY

California's first governor, General Mariano Vallejo, became Sonoma's first commercial winegrower in 1834 when he secularized the local Franciscan mission and kept the vineyards for himself. But some thirty years later, the Hungarian-born viticulturist Agoston Haraszthy won the title "Father of California's Premium Wine Industry" without firing a shot. With the promise of state support, Haraszthy sailed over to Europe and brought back thousands of cuttings. (He rooted them, ironically enough, in a Sonoma vineyard purchased from Vallejo's brother.)

The state failed to pay Haraszthy, who went bankrupt and disappeared in Nicaragua a few years later. But the winery he established, Buena Vista, has been back in business since the 1950s. Other Sonoma vintners fared better, especially after railroads linked San Francisco to the rest of the state.

By 1875 the county was producing almost four million gallons of wine a year; the Alexander, Dry Creek, Russian River, and Sonoma valleys had already achieved recognition as distinct wine regions. Today, these valleys are designated viticultural areas. Prohibition closed up most wineries, although the Sonoma County Wine Growers' Association notes that "there was a surprising amount of medicinal wine prescribed during this time."

Now Sonoma has a serious crush on grapes that is unlikely to end. Total acreage greatly exceeds that of Napa, its eastern neighbor across the Mayacamas Mountains. Geography has no respect for county rivalries; two important viticultural areas—Los Carneros and Wild Horse Valley—straddle the Sonoma/Napa county line.

Of course, there's no need for the freewheeling enophile to leave Sonoma. Above Windsor, Highway 101 is densely planted with wineries as it parallels the Russian River. Turn off on Alexander Valley Road to explore the v.a. of the same name, while Dry Creek and West Dry Creek roads are the main wine routes in Dry Creek Valley. The southern part of Sonoma County is less developed; most of the Sonoma Valley v.a. wineries are on small, winding roads branching off Highway 12.

As in Napa, wine touring is something of a local religion here, and the faithful tend to make pilgrimages on weekends, especially in summer and early fall. For a more private audience with the winemakers that interest you, schedule a mid-week or off-season visit, if possible.

❧ ❧ ❧

Adler Fels

5325 Corrick Lane
Santa Rosa, California 95405
TEL: 707-539-3123
OWNER/PRESIDENT: David F. Coleman
FOUNDED: 1980

AT A GLANCE
Tours & Tastings: Open by appointment only. Visitors see the crusher, adjustable top tanks, barrels, champagne cellar, and bottling-and-labeling line. Tour concludes with a personal chat with the owners/winemakers.

Vineyards: Grapes purchased from Sonoma County growers.

Wines: Chardonnay, Sauvignon Blanc, Pinot Noir, Cabernet Sauvignon, Gewürztraminer, Johannisberg Riesling, Mélange à Deux (50 percent Gewürztraminer, 50 percent Johannisberg Riesling *methode champenoise* sparkling wine).

Awards: Recent medal winners include: 1984 Fumé Blanc—three golds, three silvers; 1983 Nelson Chardonnay—gold, three silvers, bronze; 1980 Cabernet Sauvignon—gold, two silvers; 1983 Mélange à Deux—bronze.

Retail Shop: Wines sold on-site.

Credit Cards: None.

Access for Disabled: First floor of winery accommodates wheelchairs, but rest rooms don't.

Getting There: Winery is in Santa Rosa. Take Hwy. 12 to Los Alamos Rd. Call for exact directions.

 ❦ Graphic artist David Coleman entered the wine business as a label designer. "I invented the ten-cent wine label," he remembers. "Back in the early 1970s, no one spent more than a penny for a label; now if you don't have gold foil and embossing or lots of color, people don't think you're a serious winery." After a few years of decorating bottles, Coleman decided to fill them as well. His winery is perched in the Mayacamas Mountains, in the shadow of a craggy overhang known as Eagle Rock. At its 1,500-foot elevation, Adler Fels—German for "Eagle Rock"—is an enological aerie, with an enviable view of the Sonoma Valley from San Francisco Bay to the Sonoma County coast.

Alderbrook

2306 Magnolia Drive
Healdsburg, California 95448
TEL: 707-433-9154
PARTNERS: John Grace, Mark Rafanelli, Philip Staley
WINEMAKER: Philip Staley
FOUNDED: 1981

AT A GLANCE

Tours & Tastings: Open daily 11–5. Tours by appointment only. Winery is a converted, seventy-year-old redwood barn.

Closed: Easter, Thanksgiving, Christmas.

Vineyards: Fifty-five acres planted to Chardonnay, Sauvignon Blanc, Sémillon. Additional grapes purchased from other Dry Creek Valley growers.

Wines: Chardonnay, Sauvignon Blanc, Sémillon.

Awards: 1984 Chardonnay: gold; 1984 Sauvignon Blanc: gold, four silvers; 1984 Sémillon: two golds, two silvers, bronze; 1985 Sémillon: gold.

Picnic Area: Yes.

Retail Shop: Wines sold on-site.

Credit Cards: MasterCard, Visa.

Access for Disabled: Wheelchair accessible.

Getting There: Winery is in Sonoma County, sixty-five miles north of San Francisco. From Hwy. 101 in Healdsburg: Take Westside Rd. exit. Turn left onto Kinley Dr., then right onto Magnolia Dr.

 ❦ Upon purchasing a sixty-three-acre ranch in Dry Creek Valley, Mark Rafanelli teamed up with John Grace and Philip Staley to form Alderbrook. Because this site is influenced by both the Russian River and the Pacific Ocean, coastal fog and cool afternoon breezes alleviate the long, hot summer days. Grapes mature slowly, to yield complex varietal wines.

❦ ❦ ❦

Alexander Valley Vineyards

8644 Highway 128
Healdsburg, California 95448
TEL: 707-433-7209
LIMITED PARTNERS: Harry H. Wetzel,
Jr.; Harry H. Wetzel, III; Dale R.
Goode
WINEMAKER: Harry H. Wetzel, III (B.S.
in enology, UC-Davis)
FOUNDED: 1975

AT A GLANCE
Tours & Tastings: Open daily 10–5. Half-hour tours of crushing area and cellar by appointment, includes historical and winemaking information.
Closed: Easter, July 4th, Thanksgiving, Christmas, New Year's Day.
Vineyards: 240 acres planted to Chardonnay, Cabernet Sauvignon, Johannisberg Riesling, Chenin Blanc, Zinfandel, Gewürztraminer, Pinot Noir, Merlot.
Wines: Chardonnay, Cabernet Sauvignon, Johannisberg Riesling, Chenin Blanc, Zinfandel, Gewürztraminer, Pinot Noir, Merlot.
Awards: Recent medal winners include: 1983 Chardonnay—three silvers, three bronzes; 1982 Chardonnay—gold, two bronzes; 1982 Cabernet Sauvignon—two silvers; 1984 Johannisberg Riesling—silver, three bronzes.
Retail Shop: Wines sold on-site.
Credit Cards: American Express, MasterCard, Visa.
Access for Disabled: Only tasting room and rest rooms accommodate wheelchairs.
Getting There: Winery is seven miles outside Healdsburg in Alexander Valley, on Hwy. 128.

&. Alexander Valley Vineyards stands on land settled by its namesake, Cyrus Alexander, in 1841. This pioneer built the area's first gristmill, brick kiln, church, and school. (Ironically enough, his name is now associated with a famous Sonoma wine region, even though he never constructed a winery.) The Wetzels bought the ramshackle property from Alexander's descendants and restored much of the estate, including the residence, gardens, schoolhouse, and cemetery.

&. &. &.

Balverne Winery and Vineyards

10810 Hillview Road (P.O. Box 70)
Windsor, California 95492
TEL: 707-433-6913
OWNER: Balverne Cellars Inc.
WINEMAKER: Mitch Firestone-Gillis
FOUNDED: 1976

AT A GLANCE
Tours & Tastings: Open by appointment only. Tours primarily for the wine trade.
Vineyards: 250 acres planted to vinifera varieties, including Cabernet Sauvignon, Merlot, and the rare Scheurebe (a Sylvaner-Riesling hybrid developed in Germany by botanist George Scheu).
Wines: Chardonnay, Sauvignon Blanc, Riesling, Gewürztraminer, Scheurebe, Cabernet Sauvignon, Zinfandel.
Awards: Silvers and bronzes for Zinfandel, Gewürztraminer, Chardonnay.
Picnic Area: Several sites on estate, with hiking trails.
Retail Shop: Wines sold on-site.
Credit Cards: MasterCard, Visa.
Access for Disabled: None.
Foreign Language: Spanish.
Getting There: Winery is in Sonoma County, fifty-seven miles north of the Golden Gate Bridge, twelve miles north of Santa Rosa, and three miles south of Healdsburg. From Hwy. 101: Take Windsor exit and cross old Redwood Hwy. Proceed one mile on Brooks Rd., then turn left onto Arata Ln. Turn right on Hillview Rd.

&. This impressive 710-acre property was originally part of Rancho Sotoyome, a Spanish land grant issued to relatives to General Mariano Vallejo. Stone moats and bridges—the legacy of an early water system—still mark the site, named for a Scottish village. European vintners took over the acreage at the turn of the century, cultivating grapes, apples, prunes, and pears. Devastated by Prohibition, the estate lay fallow until Balverne planted the present vineyards.

&ca; &ca; &ca;

Bandiera Winery

155 Cherry Creek Road
Cloverdale, California 95425
TEL: 707-894-4295
PRESIDENT: John B. Merritt, Jr.
FOUNDED: 1937

AT A GLANCE
Tours & Tastings: Open daily 10–5. Tours by appointment only.
Vineyards: Grapes purchased from growers in Mendocino, Sonoma, and Napa counties.
Wines: Chardonnay, White Zinfandel, Zinfandel, Cabernet Sauvignon, Fumé Blanc, Johannisberg Riesling, Chenin Blanc.
Retail Shop: Wines sold on-site.
Credit Cards: MasterCard, Visa.
Access for Disabled: None.
Foreign Languages: French.
Getting There: Winery is in the northernmost section of Sonoma County. Directions provided when appointment is scheduled.

&ca; A recent renovation has equipped this winery to continue making quality wines at reasonable prices. Bandiera is also well known for its engaging wine labels, which carry illustrations of California wildflowers.

&ca; &ca; &ca;

Bellerose Vineyard

435 West Dry Creek Road
Healdsburg, California 95448
TEL: 707-433-1637
OWNERS: Charles and Nancy Gibbs Richard
WINEMAKER: Charles Richard
FOUNDED: 1978

AT A GLANCE
Tours & Tastings: Open by appointment only.
Closed: Major holidays.
Vineyards: Thirty-five acres planted to Cabernet Sauvignon, Malbec, Petit Verdot, Merlot, Sauvignon Blanc, Sémillon.
Wines: Cabernet Sauvigon, Sauvignon Blanc, Merlot.
Retail Shop: Wines sold on-site.
Credit Cards: None.
Access for Disabled: None.
Foreign Languages: Some French.
Getting There: Winery is 70 miles north of San Francisco, 1¼ miles west of Healdsburg. From Hwy. 101: Take the Healdsburg exit. Turn left on Mill St., right on West Dry Creek Rd.

&ca; Bellerose Vineyard is one of the oldest working farms in the Healdsburg area, with a barn dating to 1875. In keeping with this tradition, Charles Richard relies on old-fashioned techniques and natural resources—it's not unusual to find him out in the vineyards behind the team of Belgian draft horses that inspired his proprietary blend, Workhorse Red. "I try to think of those who will follow me on this land," says Richard, who pursued a career as a classical guitarist before turning to winemaking. "Agriculture is the heart and soul of Sonoma County, and the horses symbolize those values."

&ca; &ca; &ca;

Belvedere Winery

4035 Westside Road
Healdsburg, California 95448-9990
TEL: 707-433-8236
PARTNERS: Peter S. Friedman and
   William R. Hambrecht
WINEMAKER: Don Frazer
FOUNDED: 1980

AT A GLANCE
Tours & Tastings: Open daily 10–4:30.
Closed: Major holidays.
Vineyards: Grapes purchased from
growers in Napa and Sonoma counties.
Wines: Cabernet Sauvignon, Sauvignon
Blanc, Pinot Noir, White Zinfandel,
Chardonnay, Gewürztraminer, Merlot,
vintage white and red table wines.
Awards: 1982 Bacigalupi Chardonnay:
Best of Show; 1981 Winery Lake Pinot
Noir: Best of Show, gold; 1979
Bacigalupi Pinot Noir: gold, two silvers.
Retail Shop: Wines sold on-site.
Credit Cards: MasterCard, Visa.
Access for Disabled: None.
Getting There: Winery is in Healdsburg.
From Hwy. 101: Take Westside Rd. exit.

&ล Like many vintners, Peter Friedman produces vineyard-designated wines
using grapes from a few select growers.
But he's also taken a cue from French
negociants: he buys limited quantities of
unbottled wine from other wineries, then
bottles and releases these vintages under
the Belvedere "Discovery Series" label.
This innovative program offers some fine
wines at substantial savings.

ล ล ล

Buena Vista Winery

18000 Old Winery Road (P.O. Box 182)
Sonoma, California 95476
TEL: 707-938-1266
PRESIDENT: Marcus Moller-Racke (B.S.
   in agronomic sciences, University of
Kiel; M.S. in forest sciences, with
   specialization in viticulture,
   University of Bonn)
WINEMAKER: Jill Davis (B.S. in
   fermentation science, UC-Davis;
   formerly enologist at Beringer
   Vineyards)
FOUNDED: 1857

AT A GLANCE
Tours & Tastings: Open daily 10–5. Self-
guided tour; reservations for large
groups. Visitors are welcome to explore
the limestone cellars and sample wines in
the Press House Tasting Room. The
mezzanine of the Press House, where the
original crusher and press previously
stood, is now an art gallery with new
shows every four or five weeks. The cellar houses the "Knights of the Vine"
wine museum, which displays robes and
insignia from the world's famous wine
fraternities. (Buena Vista also serves as
headquarters for the U.S.-based Brotherhood of the Knights of the Vine.)
Closed: Christmas, New Year's Day.
Vineyards: About 900 acres planted to
Chardonnay, Gewürztraminer, Johannisberg Riesling, Pinot Noir, Zinfandel,
Cabernet Sauvignon, Gamay Beaujolais.
Sauvignon Blanc grapes come from
either Lake County or Sonoma County's
Alexander Valley.
Wines: Chardonnay, Fumé Blanc, vari-
etals from above grapes; also Spiceling (a
Gewürztraminer/Johannisberg Riesling
blend), Late Harvest Johannisberg Ries-
ling, Steelhead Run (Blanc de Pinot
Noir). Pinot Jolie (early harvest Pinot
Noir), Pinot Noir, Gamay Beaujolais,
Zinfandel, Cabernet Sauvignon, Sauvi-
gnon Blanc; dry and cream sherries.
Awards: Recent medal winners include:
1984 Fumé Blanc—24 Karat Gold; 1985
Lake County Sauvignon Blanc—three
golds, three silvers, bronze; 1985 Steelhead Run—silver, bronze; 1984
Jeanette's Vineyard Chardonnay—gold,

bronze; nonvintage cream sherry—gold, silver.

Picnic Area: In tree-shaded Fountain Courtyard.

Retail Shop: Wines, nonalcoholic Johannisberg Riesling, imported French Champagnes, and German sekts (white sparkling wine) sold on-site.

Credit Cards: American Express, MasterCard, Visa.

Access for Disabled: Yes; special parking area close to the winery.

Getting There: Winery is in Sonoma, forty-five miles north of San Francisco. Take Hwy. 12 to Napa St. and drive east. Cross railroad tracks; turn left on Old Winery Rd.

Special Wine & Other Events: Midsummer Mozart Festival in July and Aug.; Shakespearean plays in Sept.; Federweiss Harvest Festival in Oct.; art shows and winemaker dinners throughout the year.

ૐ Welcome to the oldest premium winery in the state, the veritable cradle of California wine. For personally introducing European varietals to the West Coast—he crossed the Atlantic with 100,000 cuttings of more than 300 varietals—the Hungarian-born enological pioneer Agoston Haraszthy became known as the father of California's premium wine industry. Ten years after he founded Buena Vista, the winery began winning international medals; the ensuing years have proven rewarding to vintner and enophile alike. With a lineage like this, it's only natural that Buena Vista vintages have graced some very important tables. The 1981 Private Reserve Pinot Noir was served at President Ronald Reagan's State Dinner for the president of Mexico, and the 1979 Zinfandel was poured at the international economic summit at Williamsburg.

ૐ ૐ ૐ

Cambiaso Winery

1141 Grant Avenue (P.O. Box 548)
Healdsburg, California 95448
TEL: 707-433-5508
DIRECTOR/GENERAL MANAGER: Somchai Likitprakong
WINEMAKER: Robert Fredson (B.S. in enology, Fresno State University)
FOUNDED: 1934

AT A GLANCE

Tours & Tastings: Open Mon.–Sat. 10–4. No tasting; retail sales only.

Closed: Sun., holidays.

Vineyards: Fifty-two acres planted to Cabernet Sauvignon, Zinfandel, Merlot, French Colombard.

Wines: Chardonnay, Chenin Blanc, Cabernet Sauvignon, Zinfandel, White Zinfandel, white and red table wines.

Retail Shop: Wines sold on-site.

Credit Cards: None.

Access for Disabled: None.

Getting There: Winery is in Healdsburg, fifty-seven miles north of San Francisco. Take Old Redwood Hwy. to Grant Ave. and travel east.

ૐ Cambiaso Winery is perched in the rolling hills of Sonoma County on a site overlooking the Russian River. Nearby, nestled among the trees, is the fine old country house (built in 1852) that became the Cambiaso residence. The family began by producing handcrafted Burgundy and Chablis for their neighbors; today, in keeping with this tradition, Cambiaso offers these wines under their 1852 House label. Premium vineyard-designated varietals are released under the Domaine St. George label.

ૐ ૐ ૐ

Caswell Vineyards

13207 Dupont Road
Sebastopol, California 95472
TEL: 707-874-2517

OWNER: Dwight Caswell
WINEMAKER: Dwight Caswell, Jr.
FOUNDED: 1982

AT A GLANCE

Tours & Tastings: Open weekends 10–5, other times by appointment. Tours of winery and vineyards on request.
Vineyards: Sixteen acres planted to Chardonnay, Zinfandel, Pinot Noir. Additional grapes purchased from growers in Sonoma and Dry Creek valleys and along the Russian River. Apples and pears are also grown on-site.
Wines: Gewürztraminer, Sauvignon Blanc, Chardonnay, Zinfandel, Pinot Noir, claret (a Bordeaux-style blend).
Picnic Area: Yes.
Retail Shop: Wines, hard cider, apple juice, jams, and jellies sold on-site.
Credit Cards: MasterCard, Visa.
Access for Disabled: Planned.
Getting There: Despite the address, this winery is closer to Occidental than Sebastopol, and is 70 miles north of San Francisco. Take Hwy. 116, 3 miles north of Sebastopol; then go west on Graton Rd. almost 5 miles to Tanuda Rd. Turn right on Tanuda and make a second right onto Harrison Grade. In ¼ mile, Harrison Grade turns left; instead, go straight onto Dupont Rd. and watch for sign 500 yards ahead on the right.
Special Wine & Other Events: New Releases Party, last Sat. in June; Harvest Party, second Sat. in Oct.

🐛 In 1981, the Caswell family purchased Winter Creek Farm, the site of a winery that had thrived until Prohibition. "Suddenly tractors tilled the soil where horses had done the work," Dwight Caswell reports. "Modern drainage systems and drip irrigation changed the old pattern of dry farming. Nonetheless, our wines are made with traditional techniques and an old-fashioned attention to detail. The whole family participates in the various winery activities, from operating the basket press to hand-bottling the finished wines."

🐛 🐛 🐛

Chateau Diana

6195 Dry Creek Road
Healdsburg, California 95448
TEL: 707-433-6992
OWNER: Thomas Manning
FOUNDED: 1979

AT A GLANCE

Tours & Tastings: Open Mon.–Sat. 10:30–4. No tours.
Closed: Sun., holidays.
Vineyards: Grapes purchased throughout California.
Wines: Chardonnay, Cabernet Sauvignon, Cabernet Blanc, White Zinfandel, Chenin Blanc, Sauvignon Blanc, Petite Sirah; port.
Awards: 1965 port: gold; 1985 Monterey Chardonnay: silver; 1983 Napa Cabernet Sauvignon: silver.
Picnic Area: Overlooking Dry Creek Valley.
Retail Shop: Wines sold on-site.
Credit Card: American Express, MasterCard, Visa.
Access for Disabled: Limited access.
Getting There: Winery is 60 miles north of San Francisco and 32 miles north of Santa Rosa. Take Hwy. 101 to the Dry Creek Rd. exit in Healdsburg, make a left on Dry Creek Rd. Continue for about 6½ miles; winery is on the right.

🐛 Thomas and Diana Manning got their enological initiation while working as San Francisco area wine brokers. Their next move was to establish a small Healdsburg bottling plant; a few years later they opened this winery. The estate is particularly lovely, with a bird terrarium and a fish pond.

🐛 🐛 🐛

Chateau Souverain

Independence Lane (P.O. Box 528)
Geyserville, California 95441
TEL: 707-433-8281
OWNER: Wine World, Inc.
FOUNDED: 1973

AT A GLANCE
Tours & Tastings: Open daily 10–5.
Guided tours along overhead bridge give
details on winemaking.
Closed: Christmas.
Vineyards: None. All grapes purchased
from Sonoma County growers.
Wines: Chardonnay, Sauvignon Blanc,
Zinfandel, White Zinfandel, Merlot, Cab-
ernet Sauvignon.
Awards: 1986 Reserve Chardonnay: four
golds; 1986 Zinfandel: gold, bronze; 1984
Merlot: silver, two bronzes.
Restaurant: Lunches served daily; din-
ners served Thur.–Sat. Stunning valley
view, innovative cuisine.
Retail Shop: Wines sold on-site.
Credit Cards: American Express, Mas-
terCard, Visa.
Access for Disabled: Ramps at entrance,
specially equipped bathrooms.
Foreign Languages: Spanish, French.
Getting There: Winery is twenty miles
north of Santa Rosa. Take Hwy. 101 to
Independence Ln. exit and drive west,
under overpass.
Special Wine & Other Events: Holly Ber-
ry Fair during Thanksgiving weekend.

🐚 Chateau Souverain's architecture is
as distinguished as its vintage varietals.
The rustic winery and restaurant complex, with its dramatic view of the Alexander Valley, was inspired by the hops
kilns that used to be a common sight in
Sonoma County.

🐚 🐚 🐚

Clos du Bois

5 Fitch Street
Healdsburg, California 95448
TEL: 707-433-5576
PRESIDENT: Frank M. Woods
FOUNDED: 1974

AT A GLANCE
Tours & Tastings: Open daily 10–5. Ten
wines poured at tastings every day. Tours
by appointment only; show visitors the
bottling line, barrel room, crushing pad,
and storage areas.
Vineyards: 750 acres planted to Sauvi-
gnon Blanc, Chardonnay, Johannisberg
Riesling, Gewürztraminer, Pinot Noir,
Merlot, Cabernet Sauvignon, Cabernet
Franc, Malbec.
Wines: Sauvignon Blanc, Chardonnay,
Early Harvest Johannisberg Riesling,
Early Harvest Gewürztraminer, Pinot
Noir, Merlot, Cabernet Sauvignon.
Awards: Recent medal winners include:
1984 Calcaire Chardonnay—two golds,
three silvers, bronze; 1984 Early Harvest
Johannisberg Riesling—14 Karat Gold;
1984 Flintwood Chardonnay—double
gold, three silvers.
Retail Shop: Wines sold on-site.
Credit Cards: American Express, Carte
Blanche, Diner's Club, MasterCard,
Visa.
Access for Disabled: Winery accommo-
dates wheelchairs.
Foreign Languages: Some Spanish.
Getting There: Winery is in Sonoma
County, seventy miles north of San Fran-
cisco. Take Hwy. 101 to the downtown
Healdsburg exit, then travel north on
Healdsburg Ave. Cross railroad tracks.
At the Plaza, bear right on Mathison;
after several blocks, make a second right
onto Fitch St.
Special Wine & Other Events: Open
houses in the spring and fall.

🐚 Clos du Bois is a no-frills winery
that releases a steady stream of award-

winning wines. Two labels are produced, Clos du Bois and the less-prestigious River Oaks. "If I'm serving a wine I know," says proprietor Frank M. Woods, a former advertising executive, "I like to anticipate what it will taste like. If the wine is new to me, it's an unopened present for which I have high hopes."

≈ ≈ ≈

B. R. Cohn

P.O. Box 1673
Sonoma, California 95476
TEL: 707-938-1212
PRESIDENT: Bruce R. Cohn
WINEMAKER: Helen M. Turley
(experience at Robert Mondavi and Gundlach-Bundschu)
FOUNDED: 1984

AT A GLANCE
Tours & Tastings: Open by appointment only.
Vineyards: Forty-five owned and eight leased acres planted to Chardonnay, Cabernet Sauvignon, Pinot Noir. Olives are also grown on-site.
Wines: Chardonnay, Cabernet Sauvignon, Pinot Noir, Cabernet Blanc; sparkling Blanc de Noirs.
Retail Shop: Wines sold on-site.
Credit Cards: None.
Access for Disabled: None.
Getting There: The winery itself is in Glen Ellen, eight miles north of Sonoma on Hwy. 12.
Special Wine & Other Events: At the annual springtime B. R. Cohn Invitational Golf Tournament, the rock world meets the wine world on the links. In the fall, these two worlds have another close encounter at the B. R. Cohn BBQ Extravaganza, held at the vineyard. Both events benefit a local youth center.

≈ Back in 1974, Bruce Cohn—a rock and roll manager who helped the Doobie Brothers sell eighty million albums—purchased Olive Hill Vineyard. Evidently, he handled grapes with the same skill he had devoted to records; at harvest, eager buyers included Sebastiani and Gundlach-Bundschu. (Ronald Reagan brought Gundlach-Bundschu's 1980 Olive Hill Cabernet Sauvignon to China as a state gift.) Given this success, it was inevitable that Cohn would start a winery of his own.

≈ ≈ ≈

Davis Bynum Winery

8075 Westside Road
Healdsburg, California 95448
TEL: 707-433-5852
PRESIDENT: Davis Bynum
FOUNDED: 1965

AT A GLANCE
Tours & Tastings: Open daily 10–5. Tours by appointment. Winery housed in the last hops kiln built in Sonoma County before an insect blight destroyed the crops in 1953.
Closed: Thanksgiving, Christmas, New Year's Day.
Vineyards: Six acres planted to Merlot, Cabernet Sauvignon. Additional grapes purchased from vineyards in Sonoma Mountain and Russian River, Dry Creek, and Alexander valleys.
Wines: Chardonnay, Fumé Blanc, Gewürztraminer, Pinot Noir, Cabernet Sauvignon, Merlot, red and white table wines.
Awards: Recent medal winners include: 1984 Gewürztraminer — gold, three bronzes; 1982 Pinot Noir—gold, two silvers, two bronzes; 1981 Zinfandel—gold, silver, three bronzes.
Picnic Area: Yes.
Retail Shop: Wines sold on-site.
Credit Cards: American Express, MasterCard, Visa.

Access for Disabled: Tasting room and bathrooms wheelchair accessible.
Foreign Languages: Spanish.
Getting There: Winery is in Healdsburg, 50 miles north of San Francisco. Take Hwy. 101 north 4 miles past Santa Rosa. Turn west on River Rd. and proceed 7 miles to Wohler, which leads to Westside Rd. Turn right on Westside; winery is ahead 1½ miles.

🍂 Newspaper reporter Davis Bynum's first crush was an unremarkable Petite Sirah, vintage 1951. "It wasn't a great wine," he recalls. "But then we drank it all before it was six months old." When his next efforts proved more palatable, Bynum became an avid amateur vintner. He launched this winery in Albany, California, and moved to the present location in 1973. Bynum's wife, Dorothy, oversees the landscaping; their son coordinates sales and marketing.

🍂 🍂 🍂

De Loach Vineyards

1791 Olivet Road
Santa Rosa, California 95401
TEL: 707-526-9111
OWNER/PRESIDENT: Cecil O. De Loach, Jr.
FOUNDED: 1975

AT A GLANCE
Tours & Tastings: Open daily 10–4:30. Tours by appointment.
Closed: Major holidays.
Vineyards: 175 acres planted to Chardonnay, Gewürztraminer, Pinot Noir, Zinfandel, Merlot.
Wines: Chardonnay, Fumé Blanc, Sauvignon Blanc, Gewürztraminer, White Zinfandel, Pinot Noir, Cabernet Sauvignon, Zinfandel.
Awards: Medal winners include: 1983 Russian River Valley White Zinfandel— three golds, silver; 1981 Russian River Valley Chardonnay—double gold, gold,

bronze; 1981 Cabernet Sauvignon—gold; 1981 Estate-Bottled Pinot Noir—gold, two silvers.
Picnic Area: Tables adjacent to vineyard.
Retail Shop: Wines sold on-site.
Credit Cards: American Express, MasterCard, Visa.
Access for Disabled: Ramp to tasting room; rest rooms accommodate wheelchairs.
Foreign Languages: Italian, French, Spanish.
Getting There: Winery is sixty miles north of San Francisco and six miles west of Santa Rosa. From Hwy. 101: Take Steele Ln./Guerneville Rd. exit and head west five miles; then turn right onto Olivet Rd.
Special Wine & Other Events: Barrel tasting, first weekend in March.

🍂 "There were vineyards here when we started, great old Zinfandel vines from 1905 and 1927," explain the De Loaches, a family of vineyardists turned winemakers. "We still make wine from them and will as long as they're producing. There were four wineries here in the immediate area up until Prohibition, so even with our fairly new winemaking operation, we think we're building on a solid Sonoma County legacy."

🍂 🍂 🍂

Domaine Laurier Winery and Vineyards

8075 Martinelli Road (P.O. Box 550)
Forestville, California 95436
TEL: 707-887-2176
PRESIDENT: Jacob Shilo
WINEMAKER: Steve Test (alumnus of enology master's program, UC-Davis)
FOUNDED: 1978

AT A GLANCE
Tours & Tastings: Open by appointment only. Brief tours, unless someone is available to give an extensive tour.

Vineyards: Thirty acres planted to Chardonnay, Sauvignon Blanc, Pinot Noir, Cabernet Sauvignon. Additional grapes purchased from growers in the Russian River Valley.

Wines: Chardonnay, Sauvignon Blanc, Pinot Noir, Cabernet Sauvignon.

Awards: 1982 Cabernet Sauvignon: two golds, silver; 1979 Pinot Noir: gold; 1982 Chardonnay: two golds, three silvers, bronze; 1982 Sauvignon Blanc: gold.

Retail Shop: Wines sold on-site.

Credit Cards: None.

Access for Disabled: None.

Foreign Languages: Limited Spanish.

Getting There: Winery is approximately seventy miles north of San Francisco. In Cotati, take Hwy. 116 West through Sebastopol and past Forestville to the second intersection, Martinelli Rd. Turn right.

&- Domaine Laurier—named for the 150-year-old laurel standing sentry on the estate—uses a traditional, labor-intensive approach to winemaking: for example, during fermentation, the red grape caps are punched manually to extract more color and flavor. All wines are aged in toasted French barrels.

&- &- &-

Dry Creek Vineyard

3770 Lambert Bridge Road
Healdsburg, California 95448
TEL: 707-433-1000
OWNER/PRESIDENT: David S. Stare
WINEMAKER: Larry Levin (B.S. in fermentation science, UC-Davis)
FOUNDED: 1972

AT A GLANCE

Tours & Tastings: Open daily 10:30–4:30. Tours—by appointment only—include tastings and a complete survey of the grounds, from the bottling line and barrel storage areas to the picnic area.

Closed: Easter, July 4th, Thanksgiving, Christmas Eve, Christmas Day, New Year's Eve, New Year's Day.

Vineyards: Fifty-five owned and thirty leased acres planted to Sauvignon Blanc, Chardonnay, Cabernet Sauvignon. Additional grapes purchased from Dry Creek and Alexander valleys.

Wines: Fumé Blanc, Chenin Blanc, Chardonnay, Gewürztraminer, Cabernet Sauvignon, Zinfandel, Petite Sirah, Merlot.

Awards: Recent medal winners include: 1984 Chardonnay—gold, two silvers, bronze; 1985 Fumé Blanc—three golds, three silvers, bronze; 1983 Zinfandel—silver, bronze.

Picnic Area: Shaded lawn in front of winery.

Retail Shop: Wines, Dry Creek Fumé Blanc mustard sold on-site.

Credit Cards: MasterCard, Visa.

Access for Disabled: Winery and bathrooms are wheelchair accessible.

Foreign Languages: French.

Getting There: Winery is seventy miles north of San Francisco and three miles northwest of Healdsburg. From Hwy. 101: Take Dry Creek exit in Healdsburg and head west through the Dry Creek Valley. Winery is on the corner of Lambert Bridge Rd. and Dry Creek Rd.

Special Wine & Other Events: Annual open house the first weekend of May.

&- Inspired by his trip to France in 1970, native Bostonian David Stare transplanted himself to the West to study enology at the University of California at Davis. The next year he bought a parcel of land in Dry Creek Valley that he christened, appropriately, Dry Creek Vineyard. Stare's dream is to make wines rivaling those of Bordeaux and Burgundy. Even his ivory-covered gray-stone winery is reminiscent of the country wine châteaus of France.

&- &- &-

Eagle Ridge Winery of Penngrove

111 Goodwin Avenue
Penngrove, California 94951
TEL: 707-664-WINE
GENERAL PARTNER: Barry C. Lawrence
FOUNDED: 1986

AT A GLANCE

Tours & Tastings: Open daily 11–4, other times by appointment. Tours for large groups only. The winery, located in a nineteenth-century building registered as Sonoma County Landmark Number 133, was the first commercial creamery in Sonoma and Marin counties.
Closed: Major holidays.
Vineyards: 3½ owned and 10 leased acres planted to Ehrenfelser and Sauvignon Blanc. Additional grapes bought from Alexander Valley growers.
Wines: Ehrenfelser (a Riesling-Sylvaner cross), Sauvignon Blanc, Zinfandel, extra-dry champagne.
Picnic Areas: Tables and barbecue area on lawn, amid antique farm implements.
Retail Shop: Wines sold on-site.
Credit Cards: None. Checks accepted.
Access for Disabled: Winery accommodates wheelchairs.
Getting There: Winery is just outside Petaluma, thirty-seven miles north of the Golden Gate Bridge. From Hwy. 101: take Penngrove exit half a mile to Goodwin Ave. and turn left.

&. The private aerie of pilots Barry C. Lawrence and Bernice Heath, Eagle Ridge is a small family operation on a landmark estate. "We have an old farmyard setting, with a wooden silo and one of the largest barns in the area," notes Lawrence. "The restored Victorian and Greek Revival homes nearby help recreate the pastoral atmosphere of a bygone era." Eagle Ridge is the first commercial vineyard in California to plant the German varietal Ehrenfelser.

&. &. &.

Gloria Ferrer Champagne Caves

23555 Highway 121 (P.O. Box 1427)
Sonoma, California 95476
TEL: 707-996-7256
PRESIDENT: Jose Ferrer
WINEMAKER: Eileen Crane (M.S. in nutrition, University of Connecticut; graduate work in enology, UC-Davis; formerly assistant to the winemaker at Domaine Chandon)
FOUNDED: 1982

AT A GLANCE

Tours & Tastings: Open daily 10:30–5:30. Guided tours of winery and wine caves leave hourly; last group departs at 4:30. Half-hour tours take in this Spanish-style winery devoted to making premium sparkling wines by the *methode champenoise*. Visitors get an overview of the primary fermentation tanks and tirage, disgorgement, and labeling areas. Then the tour descends into two man-made caves to see the aging and riddling process. Complimentary *tapas* (appetizers) served with wines in tasting room.
Closed: Thanksgiving, Christmas, New Year's Day.
Vineyards: Fifty acres planted to Pinot Noir and Chardonnay. Additional grapes purchased from growers in Alexander Valley, Russian River, and the Carneros region of Sonoma County.
Wines: Sparkling wines.
Awards: Gloria Ferrer Brut: eight golds.
Retail Shop: Wines sold on-site.
Credit Cards: MasterCard, Visa.
Access for Disabled: Ramp at entrance, elevator service for three floors; rest rooms accommodate wheelchairs.
Foreign Languages: Spanish.
Getting There: Winery is in Sonoma, less than an hour's drive from San Francisco. Take Hwy. 37 to Sears Point, then head north on Hwy. 121 about five miles.
Special Wine and Other Events: Winemaker's Dinner.

&. As scion of a winemaking family whose enological heritage stretches back to fourteenth-century Barcelona, actor Jose Ferrer may find that his most memorable role may be the one he was born to play: president of Freixenet, the Spanish sparkling wine house. This winery, Freixenet's only American outpost, was named after Ferrer's wife. Critical reception has been, well, glorious. The first release, 1983's Gloria Ferrer Brut, immediately collected five gold medals.

≈ ≈ ≈

Fisher Vineyards

6200 St. Helena Road
Santa Rosa, California 95404
TEL: 707-539-7511
OWNER: Fred J. Fisher, II
WINEMAKER: Henryk Gasiewicz
FOUNDED: 1973

AT A GLANCE
Tours & Tastings: Open by appointment only. The elegantly understated winery, constructed from redwoods and Douglas firs grown on the estate, was commended for its design by the California division of the American Institute of Architects.
Vineyards: Sixty-five owned and ten leased acres planted to Chardonnay, Cabernet Sauvignon.
Wines: Chardonnay, Cabernet Sauvignon.
Awards: Numerous.
Retail Shop: Wines sold on-site.
Credit Cards: None.
Access for Disabled: None.
Getting There: Winery and vineyards are located in the mountains, halfway between Santa Rosa, in the Sonoma Valley, and St. Helena, in the Napa Valley. From Santa Rosa: take Hwy. 12 northeast 5 miles and bear left on Calistoga Rd. After 3½ miles, turn right onto St. Helena Rd.

≈ A grandson of one of the automotive industry's Fisher brothers, Fred J. Fisher abandoned a career in financial planning to work with his hands as well

as his head. He bought land, built his own house, and cleared acreage for a vineyard. In Detroit, the Fishers were known for superb craftsmanship, a tradition their heir maintains in Santa Rosa; he brought his family's exacting standards west from the assembly line to the bottling line.

≈ ≈ ≈

Louis J. Foppiano Winery

12707 Old Redwood Highway (P.O. Box 606)
Healdsburg, California 95448
TEL: 707-433-7272
PRESIDENT: Louis J. Foppiano
WINEMAKER: Bill Regan (B.S. in fermentation science, UC-Davis)
FOUNDED: 1896

AT A GLANCE
Tours & Tastings: Open daily 10–4:30. Tours by appointment only. The fermenting room is part of the original winery, built in 1896.
Closed: Easter, Thanksgiving, Christmas, New Year's Day.
Vineyards: 200 acres planted to Sauvignon Blanc, Chardonnay, Cabernet Sauvignon, Merlot, Cabernet Franc, Gamay, Petite Sirah. Additional grapes purchased from local growers.
Wines: Chardonnay, Sauvignon Blanc, Cabernet Sauvignon, Petite Sirah, Chenin Blanc, Colombard Blanc, Fumé Blanc, Zinfandel, White Zinfandel; red, white, and rosé table wines.
Awards: 1984 White Zinfandel (Riverside Farm): gold, silver, bronze; 1982 Zinfandel (Riverside Farm): gold, silver; 1981 Cabernet Sauvignon (Louis J. Foppiano): gold, two bronzes; 1980 Petite Sirah (Louis J. Foppiano): six silvers, seven bronzes.
Picnic Area: Along the Russian River.
Retail Shop: Wines sold on-site.
Credit Cards: MasterCard, Visa.
Access for Disabled: Entrance ramp into tasting room.

Getting There: Winery is just south of Healdsburg, 12 miles north of Santa Rosa and 75 miles north of San Francisco. From Hwy. 101: Take Old Redwood Hwy. exit and go straight ¼ mile.
Special Wine & Other Events: Wine seminars.

🍷 "We've blazed the way into the nation's markets twice," says Louis M. Foppiano, great-grandson of the Genoese immigrant who launched this family business in 1896. "Right after Prohibition ended, my dad rebuilt the winery and started bottling for eastern distribution. For many years we were the second largest bottling winery in Sonoma County." Long associated with generic blends sold under the Riverside Farm label, the winery also produces the Louis J. Foppiano line of vintage-related varietals. For the most discriminating palates, Foppiano releases Fox Mountain premium reserve wines—"the best of the best"—in small quantity.

🍷 🍷 🍷

Geyser Peak Winery

22281 Chianti Road
Geyserville, California 95441
TEL: 707-433-6585
OWNER: Henry Trione
FOUNDED: 1880

AT A GLANCE
Tours & Tastings: Open daily 10–5. Tours by appointment only.
Closed: Easter, Thanksgiving, Christmas, New Year's Day.
Vineyards: 1,050 acres planted to Pinot Noir, Chardonnay, Johannisberg Riesling, Sauvignon Blanc, Zinfandel, Cabernet Sauvignon.
Wines: Chardonnay, Fumé Blanc, Chenin Blanc, Soft Johannisberg Riesling, Gewürztraminer, Cabernet Sauvignon, Pinot Noir, White Zinfandel, Pinot Noir Blanc, Cabernet Blanc, Rosé of Cab-

ernet; Brut Champagne, Blanc de Noirs; Opulence (a dessert wine).
Picnic Area: Yes.
Retail Shop: Wines sold on-site.
Credit Cards: None.
Access for Disabled: Winery accommodates wheelchairs.
Getting There: Winery is twenty-two miles north of Santa Rosa and eighty-five miles north of San Francisco. From Hwy. 101: Take the Canyon Rd. exit (one mile beyond the Geyserville exit). Turn right onto Chianti Rd.

🍷 In 1982, businessman and philanthropist Henry Trione took over Geyser Peak, the first winery established in Geyserville. With his sons, he is maintaining many of the traditions of this cherished local landmark. New structures were built to complement the impressive fieldstone-and-redwood buildings erected more than a century earlier. Vineyards in prime Sonoma grape-growing regions—Alexander Valley, Los Carneros, Russian River Valley—enable Geyser Peak to estate-bottle limited amounts of wine and use specific appellations of origin.

🍷 🍷 🍷

Glen Ellen Winery

1883 London Ranch Road
Glen Ellen, California 95442
TEL: 707-996-1066
OWNERS: Bruno, Mike, Bob, Joey and Jerry Benziger, Tim Wallace, and Mark Stornetta
FOUNDED: 1980

AT A GLANCE
Tours & Tastings: Open daily 10–4:30. Tours lead from vineyard to crushing and aging facilities, concluding in the tasting room where all available wines are open for tasting. Public tastings are on weekends only, every half-hour between 11 and 3:30.

Closed: Thanksgiving, Christmas, New Year's Day.

Vineyards: 100 acres planted to Cabernet, Cabernet Franc, Merlot, Malbec, Petite Verdot, Semillon, Sauvignon Blanc. Additional grapes purchased from major California wine regions.

Wines: Chardonnay, Cabernet, Sauvignon Blanc, Merlot, Semillon, Muscat Canelli, Pinot Blanc, Fume Blanc, Zinfandel; red and white blends; sparkling wine.

Awards: 1987 Sonoma Valley Muscat Canelli—two golds, silver, two bronzes; 1986 Sonoma County Fume Blanc—gold, two silvers, bronze; 1985 Imagery Zinfandel—three golds, two silvers.

Picnic Area: In redwood grove.

Retail Shop: Wines sold on site.

Credit Cards: MasterCard, Visa.

Access for Disabled: Main house and buildings accessible, but difficult entry to tasting room; grounds have steep terrain.

Foreign Languages: Spanish.

Getting There: Winery is in Sonoma Valley, 60 miles north of San Francisco. From Hwy. 12: Take Madrone Rd. west to Arnold Dr. and turn right. Make a left onto London Ranch Rd.

Special Wine and Other Events: Enjoy art exhibitions, pantomimes, plays and musical productions on the premises.

🐾 Mike Benziger wanted to make wine as well as market it. More than a century after his forebears opened Parke Benziger—a wine import business in New York—he found an ideal vineyard site in Sonoma County. In a matter of weeks, Benziger, his parents, and most of his siblings severed their east coast roots and planted themselves on this ranch cut into the side of Sonoma Mountain. Their sudden move paid off. With its earliest releases, Glen Ellen won gold medals, media attention, and consumer loyalty. While it produces its share of premium vintages, this winery is best-known for its "fighting varietals"—good

quality wines that sell for $4 to $6 a bottle.

🐾 🐾 🐾

Gundlach-Bundschu Winery

2000 Denmark Street, Box 1
Vineburg, California 95487
TEL: 707-938-5277
PRESIDENT: Jim Bundschu
FOUNDED: 1858

AT A GLANCE

Tours & Tastings: Open daily 11–4:30. Self-guided tours. The stone winery, standing on its original 1858 site, remains a winery to this day.

Closed: Easter, Thanksgiving, Christmas, New Year's Day.

Vineyards: 385 acres planted to Cabernet Sauvignon, Chardonnay, Merlot, Riesling, Gewürztraminer, Zinfandel, Pinot Noir, Kleinberger.

Wines: Cabernet Sauvignon, Chardonnay, Merlot, Riesling, Gewürztraminer, Zinfandel, Pinot Noir, Kleinberger.

Awards: Dozens.

Picnic Area: Picnic tables dot the hill overlooking the vineyard, with a view of the mountains and San Pablo Bay.

Retail Shop: Wines sold on-site.

Credit Cards: MasterCard, Visa.

Access for Disabled: Yes.

Getting There: "We are one hour north of the Golden Gate Bridge." Take Hwy. 12 to Sonoma Plaza, in the town of Sonoma. Go east on Napa St. Turn right on 8th St. East, then turn left on Denmark St. Follow the road through the vineyard as marked.

🐾 In the 130-plus years since immigrant Bavarian vintners Jacob Gundlach and Charles Bundschu established this award-winning partnership, five generations of their descendants have followed the family trade. There were devastating setbacks along the way, notably the San Francisco earthquake and fire—which ruined the winery warehouse—and the equally destructive Temperance Movement. By supplying fruit to the "juice grape" market, the Bundschus survived Prohibition; with Repeal, they resumed selling grapes to premium wineries. Finally, in the late 1960s, Jim Bundschu (the founder's great-great-grandson) and his brothers-in-law resumed the proud tradition of making Gundlach-Bundschu wines. The medals have been pouring in ever since.

 va va va

Hacienda Winery

1000 Vineyard Lane (P.O. Box 416)
Sonoma, California 95476
TEL: 707-938-3220
PRESIDENT/OWNER: Crawford Cooley
FOUNDED: 1973

AT A GLANCE
Tours & tastings: Open daily 10–5. Tours by appointment only.
Closed: Easter, Thanksgiving, Christmas, New Year's Day.
Vineyards: 110 acres planted to Chardonnay, Sauvignon Blanc, Sémillon, Chenin Blanc, Gewürztraminer, Pinot Noir, Zinfandel, Cabernet Sauvignon, Merlot.
Wines: Chardonnay, Sauvignon Blanc, Chenin Blanc, Gewürztraminer, Pinot Noir, Zinfandel, Cabernet Sauvignon.
Picnic Area: Oak-shaded tables overlooking vineyard.
Retail Shop: Wines sold on-site.
Credit Cards: MasterCard, Visa.
Access for Disabled: None.
Getting There: Winery is forty-six miles north of San Francisco. Take Hwy. 121 to the Sonoma town square. Turn right on East Napa St. and go one mile; at 7th St. East, turn left and follow the signs on Castle Rd.

va Hacienda is situated on the land where the Hungarian nobleman Agoston Haraszthy previously planted European viniferas. Venture capitalist Crawford Cooley purchased Hacienda in 1977, but his wine roots are extremely deep. A fifth-generation Californian, his ancestors—members of the second overland party to reach the state—planted grapes near Cloverdale in 1860.

va va va

Haywood Winery

18701 Gehricke Road
Sonoma, California 95476
TEL: 707-996-4298
OWNERS: Peter Haywood and Rudy Tulipani
WINEMAKER: Charles Tolbert (formerly employed at Buena Vista and other California wineries)
FOUNDED: 1980

AT A GLANCE
Tours & Tastings: Open daily 11–5. Self-guided tours.
Closed: Easter, Thanksgiving, Christmas, New Year's Day.
Vineyards: 100 acres planted to Chardonnay, Cabernet Sauvignon, Zinfandel, White Riesling.
Wines: From varietals noted above.
Awards: 1984 White Riesling: gold, three silvers, five bronzes; 1983 Zinfandel: two golds, three bronzes; 1984 Sonoma Valley Chardonnay: bronze; 1981 Cabernet Sauvignon: gold, silver, bronze.
Picnic Area: Overlooking vineyard.
Retail Shop: Wines sold on-site.
Credit Cards: MasterCard, Visa.
Access for Disabled: Tasting room, bathrooms accommodate wheelchairs.
Getting There: Winery is forty miles north of San Francisco. Take Hwy. 12 to Sonoma Plaza in the town of Sonoma. Drive east on Napa St. and make a left onto East 4th St. Turn right on Lovall Valley Rd., then left on Gehricke Rd.
Special Wine & Other Events: Sonoma County Wine Auction in Aug., Sonoma Valley Vintage Festival in Sept.

This winery is tucked into a steep, rugged valley by the Mayacamas Mountains, which separate Sonoma and Napa counties. "The land tells us what it can do," avers Peter Haywood, a former marine turned vineyardist. "We simply help it along." Haywood speaks with the confidence of a man who has learned from his mistakes. He has yet to serve his earliest crush, a 1977 Gewürztraminer that he squeezed by hand through a stainless steel screen. Most of the vintage exploded because it had been bottled improperly. The sole surviving bottle was decanted, filtered, rebottled, and consigned to the Haywood wine library. Many later awards attest to his more positive experiences.

Hop Kiln Winery

6050 Westside Road
Healdsburg, California 95448
TEL: 707-433-6491
OWNER: L. Martin Griffin
WINEMAKER: Steve Strobl
FOUNDED: 1975

AT A GLANCE
Tours & Tastings: Open daily 10–5. Tours by appointment only. The rustic winery occupies a restored hops barn that has state landmark status.
Closed: Easter, Christmas, New Year's Day.
Vineyards: 200 acres planted to Petite Sirah, French Colombard, Gewürztraminer, Chardonnay, Johannisberg Riesling, Zinfandel.
Wines: From grapes noted above, also, A Thousand Flowers (a blended white), Marty Griffin's Big Red (a blended red).
Awards: Recent medal winners include: 1983 Zinfandel—gold, bronze; 1984 Late Harvest Zinfandel—gold; 1983 Petite Sirah—two silvers; Marty Griffin's Big Red—gold, three bronzes.
Picnic Area: Overlooks vineyards.

Retail Shop: Wines sold on-site.
Credit Cards: MasterCard, Visa.
Access for Disabled: None.
Getting There: Winery is eighty miles north of San Francisco. Take Hwy. 101 to the Westside-Guerneville exit and travel six miles south on Westside Rd.

Doctor, conservationist, public health officer, vintner—Marty Griffith is a man who wears many hats. He became a vineyardist when the ranch he bought as a retirement property proved to be good grape land; bonding his winery was the next logical step.

Jordan Vineyards and Winery

1474 Alexander Valley Road (P.O. Box 878)
Healdsburg, California 95448
TEL: 707-433-6955
OWNER: Thomas N. Jordan, Jr.
WINEMAKER: Rob Davis (degree in fermentation science, UC-Davis)
FOUNDED: 1972

AT A GLANCE
Tours & Tastings: No public tastings. Tours by appointment only, Mon.–Fri.
Closed: Dec. 25–Jan. 2, other major holidays.
Vineyards: 250 acres planted to Cabernet Sauvignon, Merlot, Chardonnay.
Wines: Cabernet Sauvignon, Chardonnay.
Awards: Does not enter competitions.
Retail Shop: Wines sold on-site; old vintages unavailable.
Credit Cards: None.
Access for Disabled: "Limited."
Foreign Languages: French, Spanish, Italian.
Getting There: Winery is seventy-five miles north of San Francisco. Call for directions.
Special Wine & Other Events: Sonoma County Wine Auction in Aug.

⁊ Jordan is a fully integrated vineyard and winery complex organized in the manner of a Bordeaux château. The sunny yellow buildings, with their red shutters and rooftops, bring a bit of nineteenth-century France into twentieth-century California.

⁊ ⁊ ⁊

Korbel Champagne Cellars

13250 River Road
Guerneville, California 95446-9538
TEL: 707-887-2294
PRESIDENT: Gary B. Heck
CHAMPAGNE MASTER: Robert M.
Stashak (B.S. in fermentation science, UC-Davis)
FOUNDED: 1882

AT A GLANCE
Tours & Tastings: Open Oct. 1–Apr. 30, 9–4:30; May 1–Sept. 30, 9–5. In the winter, tours depart hourly, 10–3. In the summer, tours depart every forty-five minutes, 9:45–3:45. Visitors look at a photo exhibit detailing Korbel's history, then progress to the original cellars, where they see an antique wine press, large century-old casks, and automatic champagne riddling racks. Along the way, guides offer a step-by-step narrative on the *methode champenoise*.
Closed: Easter, Thanksgiving, Christmas, New Year's Day.
Vineyards: 400 acres planted to Pinot Noir and Chardonnay. Additional grapes purchased from other California vineyards.
Wines: California champagne, California brandy.
Awards: Numerous.
Picnic Area: Yes.
Retail Shop: Wines sold on-site.
Credit Cards: American Express, MasterCard, Visa.
Access for Disabled: Ramps.
Getting There: Winery is sixty miles northwest of San Francisco. From Hwy.

101, take River Rd. (Guerneville) exit and cross back over the freeway, heading west.
Special Wine & Other Events: Sonoma County Harvest Fair at the Santa Rosa Fairgrounds, in Oct.

⁊ Upon arriving in San Francisco, Bohemian-born brothers Francis, Anton, and Joseph Korbel built a redwood enterprise; they established a lumber mill, a fleet of schooners to transport that lumber, and a factory to turn redwood planks into cigar boxes. After clearing acres of forest land, the Korbels planted grapevines among the tree stumps. Soon they were stomping grapes instead of chopping wood. Korbel Champagne Cellars stayed in the family until 1954, when Adolf Heck—father of the current company president—mortgaged his house in order to purchase the winery. Regardless of ownership, Korbel bubbles tickle important palates. The first case of post-Repeal champagne was shipped to President Franklin D. Roosevelt; half a century later, Korbel Brut was chosen as the official champagne of the 1985 presidential inaugural.

⁊ ⁊ ⁊

Lambert Bridge

4085 West Dry Creek Road
Healdsburg, California 95448
TEL: 707-433-5855
OWNER: Gerard Lambert
WINEMAKER: Ed Killian (enology degree, UC-Davis)
FOUNDED: 1975

AT A GLANCE
Tours & Tastings: Open daily 10–4. Tours given on an informal basis.
Vineyards: Seventy-eight acres planted to Cabernet Sauvignon, Chardonnay, Merlot, Pinot Noir, Johannisberg Riesling.
Wines: Chardonnay, Cabernet Sauvignon, Merlot.

Retail Shop: Wines sold on-site.
Credit Cards: MasterCard, Visa.
Access for Disabled: None.
Foreign Languages: Spanish.
Getting There: Winery is seventy-five miles north of San Francisco. From Hwy. 101: Take Dry Creek Rd. exit and drive west four miles. Turn left at Lambert Bridge Rd., left again on West Dry Creek Rd.

ᔮ Lambert Bridge is a family-operated winery exclusively producing estate-bottled varietals. In a happy coincidence, this establishment takes its name from the Dry Creek bridge built in the last century by one C. L. Lambert, no known relation to winery owners Gerard and Babbie Lambert.

ᔮ ᔮ ᔮ

Landmark Vineyards

9150 Los Amigos Road
Windsor, California 95492
TEL: 707-838-9466
PRESIDENT/WINEMAKER: William R.
   Mabry, III
FOUNDED: 1974

AT A GLANCE
Tours & Tastings: Open Thurs.–Mon. 10–5:30. Winery tours by appointment.
Vineyards: 154 acres planted to Chardonnay.
Wines: Chardonnay.
Awards: 1983 Sonoma County Chardonnay: platinum, four golds, three silvers; 1983 Alexander Valley Chardonnay: silver; 1984 Sonoma County Chardonnay: two silvers.
Picnic Area: Tables near winery.
Retail Shop: Wines sold on-site.
Credit Cards: None.
Access for Disabled: None.
Getting There: Winery is in Windsor, seven miles north of Santa Rosa. From Hwy. 101: Take Windsor exit and go straight at the four-way stop. Turn left at

Brooks Rd., make a second left onto Los Amigos Rd.

ᔮ This Chardonnay estate was named for the unusual landmarks dignifying the home ranch property. These include the majestic century-old cypresses that line the winery driveway, and the office building itself—a Spanish hacienda that is one of the oldest houses in Sonoma County. Winemaker William Mabry has been fascinated by enology since he was a fourth-grader, when his father crushed and vinified some Concord grapes.

ᔮ ᔮ ᔮ

Lytton Springs Winery

650 Lytton Springs Road
Healdsburg, California 95448
TEL: 707-433-7721
PRESIDENT: Richard N. Sherwin
FOUNDED: 1977

AT A GLANCE
Tours & Tastings: Open daily 10–4. Winery tours on request.
Closed: Major holidays.
Vineyards: Fifty acres planted to Zinfandel. Additional grapes purchased from other older vineyards in the area.
Wines: Zinfandel, Chardonnay, Sauvignon Blanc.
Awards: Lytton Spring Zinfandels have won medals every year since the first release.
Picnic Area: Seating for ten at outdoor tables.
Retail Shop: Wines sold on-site.
Credit Cards: MasterCard, Visa.
Access for Disabled: Ground-level building, bathrooms accommodate wheelchairs.
Getting There: Winery is in Healdsburg, seventy-five miles north of San Francisco. From Hwy. 101: Take Lytton Springs Rd. exit and drive half a mile west to Chiquita Rd. Winery is at the

corner of Lytton Springs and Chiquita Rds.

• Lytton Springs stands on the property of Valley Vista Vineyards, which was planted to Zinfandel at the turn of the century. Until the early 1970s, other vintners crushed Valley Vista fruit to considerable acclaim; with the completion of his own winery, Richard Sherwin began keeping his grapes to himself. Lately, he has begun experimenting with white wines, with promising results: in its only competition, the first Lytton Springs Sauvignon Blanc won a gold medal.

• • •

Mark West Vineyards

7000 Trenton-Healdsburg Road
Forestville, California 95436
TEL: 707-544-4813
PRESIDENT/WINEMAKER: Joan C. Ellis
FOUNDED: 1976

AT A GLANCE
Tours & Tastings: Open daily 10–5. Handsome tile-and-redwood hospitality center has both a fireplace and a solar greenhouse. Catered luncheons can be arranged. Casual tours for small groups as time permits; call ahead for special attention.
Closed: Thanksgiving, Christmas, New Year's Day.
Vineyards: Sixty acres planted to Chardonnay, Gewürztraminer, Johannisberg Riesling, Pinot Noir. Zinfandel grapes purchased from vineyards in the Santa Rosa Plain.
Wines: Chardonnay, Gewürztraminer, Johannisberg Riesling, Pinot Noir, Pinot Noir Blanc, Zinfandel; sparkling wines; Angelique (a Pinot Noir aperitif).
Awards: Recent medal winners include: 1984 Gewürztraminer Late Harvest Reserve—double gold, two silvers; 1983 Zinfandel—two golds, silver, two bronzes; 1983 Johannisberg Riesling

Late Harvest—gold, bronze; Angelique—bronze.
Picnic Area: Tables under redwood trees, with a magnificent view of Russian River Valley and Santa Rosa Plain.
Retail Shop: Wines sold on-site.
Credit Cards: MasterCard, Visa.
Access for Disabled: Wheelchair accessible.
Foreign Languages: Spanish.
Getting There: Winery is 65 miles north of San Francisco, along the Russian River. From Hwy. 101: Take River Rd. exit (3 miles north of Santa Rosa). Travel west on River Rd. 5½ miles; turn right on Healdsburg-Trenton Rd.
Special Wine & Other Events: Ongoing art exhibits, featuring Sonoma County and Bay Area artists.

• Mark West is a small family winery, where owners Bob and Joan Ellis personally guide each wine from vineyard to bottle. She makes the wines, while he oversees the vineyards. For the record, winery namesake Mark West was an early Sonoma County pioneer who gave his name to the meandering creek that borders this 116-acre ranch.

• • •

Matanzas Creek Winery

6097 Bennett Valley Road
Santa Rosa, California 95404
TEL: 707-528-6464
PRESIDENT: Sandra P. MacIver
WINEMAKER: David Ramey (M.S. in enology, UC-Davis; formerly assistant winemaker at Simi)
FOUNDED: 1977

AT A GLANCE
Tours & Tastings: Open Mon.–Sat. 8–5. Tours by appointment only.
Closed: Sun., holidays.
Vineyards: Forty-five acres planted to Chardonnay, Merlot, Cabernet Sauvignon.

Wines: Chardonnay, Merlot, Sauvignon Blanc.
Awards: 1979 Chardonnay: gold; 1981 Chardonnay: double gold; 1984 Chardonnay: gold.
Retail Shop: Wines sold on-site.
Credit Cards: None.
Access for Disabled: Ramp at entrance.
Foreign Languages: Spanish, French.
Getting There: Winery is four miles outside Santa Rosa, fifty-five miles north of San Francisco.
Special Wine & Other Events: The winery's cooking school, Hot Chefs and Rising Stars, offers two to four sessions annually. Other events include art shows, concerts, and the New Release Celebration.

&. Eager to raise her children in a rural environment, Sandra P. MacIver purchased a 212-acre tract cluttered with the barns, chicken coops, and sheds of a former dairy farm. Unencumbered by her lack of experience, she planted a vineyard and converted a barn into a rudimentary winery. Her persistence paid off. Within ten years, Matanzas Creek had won both a gold medal and a sterling reputation. The label's popularity led to construction of a state-of-the-art winery where fermentation temperatures are electronically controlled. The old winery has been converted once again—into a wine library.

&. &. &.

The Merry Vintners

3339 Hartman Road
Santa Rosa, California 95401
TEL: 707-526-4441
PARTNERS: Merry Edwards, Charles M. Edwards, Bill Miller, D. J. Edwards
WINEMAKER: Merry Edwards (M.S. in enology, UC-Davis)
FOUNDED: 1984

AT A GLANCE
Tours & Tastings: Open by appointment only. Tour consists of a visit to the wine cellar, with an explanation of the process involved in making two different styles of Chardonnay.
Vineyards: All grapes bought within Sonoma County.
Wines: Chardonnay.
Awards: 1984 Sonoma County Chardonnay: gold; 1985 Sonoma County Chardonnay: silver.
Retail Shop: Wines sold on-site.
Credit Cards: None.
Access for Disabled: Limited wheelchair access.
Foreign Languages: Limited Spanish.
Getting There: Winery is 2 miles outside the Santa Rosa city limits. From Hwy. 101: Take Piner Rd. exit west and continue 1½ miles beyond the intersection with Fulton Rd. Turn right onto Hartman Rd. and proceeed ¼ mile to the end of the road.
Special Wine & Other Events: Annual release party, usually in May or June. Invitations are extended to those on mailing list; if interested, write the winery.

&. "Our premise is that using varied Chardonnay clones from divergent regions creates more complexity than using grapes from a single vineyard," explain the Merry Vintners. "Throughout the year, we work closely with each grower to achieve the ultimate in grape quality." This winery also works closely with label designers. In releasing the 1984 Sonoma County Reserve Chardonnay—which was labeled with a magnified photograph of wine yeasts undergoing cell division—the Merry Vintners launched a series of educational wine labels to illustrate that scientific aspects of winemaking can function as an art form.

&. &. &.

Michtom Vineyards/Jimark Winery

602 Limerick Lane
Healdsburg, California 95448
TEL: 707-433-3118
OWNERS: Mark Michtom and Jim
Wolner
FOUNDED: 1983

AT A GLANCE
Tours & Tastings: Open Wed.–Sun. 10–4.
Vineyard tours by appointment only; no
formal winery tours.
Vineyards: 130 acres planted to Chardonnay, Cabernet Sauvignon, Chenin Blanc,
French Colombard.
Wines: Chardonnay, Cabernet Sauvignon.
Awards: 1983 Chardonnay: bronze; 1984
Chardonnay: bronze; 1981 Cabernet
Sauvignon: silver; 1978 Cabernet Sauvignon: gold.
Retail Shop: Wines sold on-site.
Credit Cards: None.
Access for Disabled: None.
Foreign Languages: Spanish.
Getting There: Winery is in Alexander
Valley, sixty miles north of San Francisco. From Hwy. 101: Take Healdsburg
Ave. exit and turn left. Go one mile to
Limerick Ln. and turn left again.

&. Mark Michtom's grandparents designed the original teddy bear; his father
manufactured the Shirley Temple doll,
building the Ideal Toy and Novelty Company into a multimillion-dollar business.
When his family sold Ideal, Michtom, a
third-generation executive in the firm,
bought this vineyard. After watching
other vintners enjoy the fruit of his investment, he joined forces with winemaker Jim Wolner to form Jimark—as in
Jim and Mark—Winery.

&. &. &.

Mill Creek Vineyards

1401 Westside Road (P.O. Box 758)
Healdsburg, California 95448
TEL: 707-433-5098
OWNERS: the Kreck family
FOUNDED: 1976

AT A GLANCE
Tours & Tastings: Open daily 10–4:30.
Mill Creek's headquarters is a new redwood building constructed of trees felled
on the property. A waterwheel churns the
millpond next to the winery, giving the
property a nineteenth-century appearance.
Closed: July Fourth, Thanksgiving,
Christmas, New Year's Day.
Vineyards: Eighty acres planted to Sauvignon Blanc, Chardonnay, Pinot Noir,
Gamay Beaujolais, Cabernet Sauvignon,
Merlot.
Wines: From varietals noted above; also
Gewürztraminer, Merlot, Pinot Noir,
Gamay Beaujolais, Cabernet Blush.
Awards: Recent medal winners include:
1980 Cabernet Sauvignon—gold, silver,
bronze; 1982 Felta Springs Cabernet
Sauvignon—gold, bronze; 1984 Chardonnay—two silvers, bronze; 1985 Cabernet Blush—silver, three bronzes.
Picnic Area: On deck overlooking vineyards.
Retail Shop: Wines sold on-site.
Credit Cards: MasterCard, Visa.
Access for Disabled: Yes—ramp.
Getting There: Winery is in the Dry
Creek region, one mile west of Healdsburg. From Hwy. 101: Take Westside Rd.
exit and drive west.

&. Mill Creek's beginnings date to
1965, when Charles and Vera Kreck
planted their first small lot of Cabernet
Sauvignon. Four years later the Krecks
expanded their operation, rooting sixty-five acres of vinifera in a former prune
orchard. "The advantage at Mill Creek is
that we have strict control over all phases

of the winery enterprise," note the Krecks. "There is a feeling of continuity and shared goals. Our family has set a production limit of 15,000 cases per year to keep the winery small enough to produce only wines of optimum quality."

&. &. &.

J. W. Morris Winery

101 Grant Avenue (P.O. Box 921)
Healdsburg, California 95448
TEL: 707-431-7015
FOUNDED: 1975
OWNERS: Ken and Tricia Toth
WINEMAKER: Rick Mafit (B.S. in
    fermentation science, UC-Davis)
FOUNDED: 1975

AT A GLANCE
Tours & Tastings: Open Thurs.–Mon. 10–4. Tours by appointment only, offer a detailed description of the cellar operation, bottling line, and laboratory procedures. Vineyard tour includes an explanation of varietals grown and the specific microclimates.
Closed: Tues., Wed.
Vineyards: 115 acres planted to Sauvignon Blanc, Chardonnay, Cabernet Sauvignon, Petite Sirah, Zinfandel.
Wines: Sauvignon Blanc, Cabernet Sauvignon, Chardonnay, Zinfandel; port.
Awards: 1985 Sauvignon Blanc: silver; 1983 Cabernet Sauvignon: bronze; 1983 Vintage Port: silver.
Retail Shop: Wines sold on-site.
Credit Cards: MasterCard, Visa.
Access for Disabled: Sloping entrance to front door, special handles in bathroom.
Foreign Languages: Spanish.
Getting There: Winery is fifty miles north of San Francisco, seventeen miles north of Santa Rosa. Take the Healdsburg Ave. exit off Hwy. 101. Turn right on the first street, Grant Ave.—look for Giorgio's Restaurant.
Special Wine & Other Events: Barrel

Tasting in Apr., with the participation of other local wineries; Russian River Wine Festival in Healdsburg, in May.

&. J. W. Morris launched his enterprise by making California port from vines planted in the early 1900s. Soon he began making premium table wines, too. In 1983 Morris sold his winery to Ken and Tricia Toth, owners of Black Mountain Vineyards, a century-old estate in Alexander Valley. The Toths continue to release port and wine under the J. W. Morris name, reserving the Black Mountain label for a few select bottlings produced in limited quantities.

&. &. &.

Pat Paulsen Vineyards

25510 River Road (P.O. Box 565)
Cloverdale, California 95425
TEL: 707-894-3197
    Tasting Room:
    Asti Road
    Asti, California 95413
    TEL: 707-894-2969
OWNERS: Betty Jane and Patrick L.
    Paulsen
WINEMAKER: Jamie Meves (enology
    degree, UC-Davis)
FOUNDED: 1980

AT A GLANCE
Tours & Tastings: Winery not open to public. Tasting room open daily 10–6.
Closed: Thanksgiving, Christmas.
Vineyards: Seventeen owned and seventeen leased acres planted to Chardonnay, Sauvignon Blanc, Cabernet Sauvignon.
Wines: Chardonnay, Sauvignon Blanc, Cabernet Sauvignon, Muscat Canelli, Refrigerator White (Gewürztraminer–Chardonnay–Sauvignon Blanc blend).
Awards: Recent medal winners include: 1983 Cabernet Sauvignon—two golds, three silvers, bronze; 1983 Sauvignon Blanc—gold, silver, bronze; 1984 Sauvi-

gnon Blanc—gold, silver, bronze; 1984 Refrigerator White—gold, silver.

Picnic Area: Tree-shaded site outside tasting room.

Retail Shop: Wines sold at tasting room.

Credit Cards: American Express, Discover, MasterCard, Visa.

Access for Disabled: Wheelchair accessible; bathroom facilities.

Getting There: Tasting room is ninety miles north of San Francisco. Leave Hwy. 101 by Asti exit and turn right onto Asti Rd.

&ain "My wine has been served in the White House, although I haven't," comments humorist and perennial presidential candidate Pat Paulsen. The medals amassed by this winery's products demonstrate that critics vote for Paulsen regularly, even if the electorate doesn't. Refrigerator White has received its share of awards as well, proving that wit and wine can constitute a winning ticket.

&ain &ain &ain

J. Pedroncelli Winery

1220 Canyon Road
Geyserville, California 95441
TEL: 707-857-3531
OWNERS: Jim and John Pedroncelli, Jr.
FOUNDED: 1927

AT A GLANCE

Tours & Tastings: Open daily 10–5. Tours by appointment only, begin at the weigh station and crusher and end up in the tasting room, where all the wines produced are available for sampling.

Closed: Easter, Thanksgiving, Christmas, New Year's Day.

Vineyards: 130 acres planted to Chardonnay, Cabernet Sauvignon, Pinot Noir, Zinfandel, Gewürztraminer, Johannisberg Riesling. Sixty percent of grapes from growers in Sonoma County's Dry Creek and Alexander valleys. Only

Sonoma County grapes are selected for premium varietals.

Wines: Chardonnay, Sauvignon Blanc, Johannisberg Riesling, Gewürztraminer, White Zinfandel, Zinfandel Rosé, Gamay Beaujolais, Pinot Noir, Zinfandel, Cabernet Sauvignon, Sonoma White, Sonoma Red, Sonoma Blush.

Awards: Recent medal winners include: 1985 White Riesling—gold; 1985 White Zinfandel—gold; 1985 Gewürztraminer—gold.

Retail Shop: Wines sold on-site.

Credit Cards: American Express, MasterCard, Visa.

Access for Disabled: Ramps into tasting room and rest rooms.

Getting There: Winery is 60 miles north of San Francisco and twenty minutes north of Santa Rosa. From Hwy. 101: Take Canyon Rd. exit. Turn west and continue for 1¼ miles.

Special Wine & Other Events: Barrel Tasting by the Russian River Wine Road, the first weekend of March; Russian River Wine Road Wine Festival, mid-May.

&ain Bonded in 1904 by a wholesale grocer, this winery and vineyard were purchased by the Italian-born John Pedroncelli, Sr., in 1927. Through Prohibition, Pedroncelli sold grapes to home winemakers; after Repeal, he utilized his vineyards to produce wine in bulk for other wineries, who bottled it under their own labels. "We started bottling our own vintages in 1949 because my father thought it was a shame to blend them away for bulk wines," says Jim Pedroncelli, who shares winery ownership with his brother, John, Jr.

&ain &ain &ain

Piper Sonoma Cellars

11447 Old Redwood Highway
Healdsburg, California 95448
TEL: 707-433-8843

OWNER: Piper-Heidsieck
WINEMASTER: Rodney Strong
FOUNDED: 1982

AT A GLANCE
Tours & Tastings: Open daily 10–5. Cellar tours depart every half hour until 4:30. Tastings served in Cafe du Chai or on terrace overlooking vineyards.
Closed: Major holidays.
Vineyards: Forty acres planted to Pinot Noir and Chardonnay.
Wines: Brut, Blanc de Noirs, and Tete de Cuvee *methode champenoise* sparkling wines.
Awards: 1981 Blanc de Noirs: three golds.
Restaurant: Light lunches served in Cafe du Chai.
Retail Shop: Wines sold on-site.
Credit Cards: American Express, Carte Blanche, Diner's Club, MasterCard, Visa.
Access for Disabled: Wheelchair accessible.
Foreign Languages: French.
Getting There: Winery is sixty miles north of San Francisco. Take Hwy. 101 to Healdsburg Ave. exit and go south one mile on Old Redwood Hwy.
Special Wine & Other Events: Art shows and theatrical productions throughout the year.

&❧ Although she lost her head over cake, Marie Antoinette was equally fond of the bubbly; Florens-Louis Heidsieck's champagne so pleased the queen that she ordered it served at Versailles. Nearly two centuries later, Piper-Heidsieck established this ultramodern California outpost, with its eight-ton champagne press and computer-operated gyropalettes (machines that reproduce the hand-riddling process). This winery produces three sparkling styles under the direction of Rodney Strong in collaboration with Piper-Heidsieck *chef du caves* Michel LaCroix. Strong also makes award-winning still wines at the Healds-

burg winery bearing his name. (See page 442).

❧ ❧ ❧

Preston Vineyards and Winery

9282 West Dry Creek Road
Healdsburg, California 95448
TEL: 707-433-3372
OWNERS: Lou and Susan Preston
WINEMAKER: Tom Farella
FOUNDED: 1973

AT A GLANCE
Tours & Tastings: Open weekdays 10–4 by appointment. Tours by appointment.
Vineyards: 120 acres planted to thirteen varietals, including Sauvignon Blanc, Zinfandel, Cabernet Sauvignon, Sémillon, Chenin Blanc, Petite Sirah, Gamay Beaujolais, Barbera.
Wines: Sauvignon Blanc, Cuvee de Fumé (a blend of Sauvignon Blanc, Chenin Blanc, and Sémillon), Zinfandel, Cabernet Sauvignon, Dry Chenin Blanc, Sirah-Sirah (a blend of Petite Sirah and French Sirah), Gamay Beaujolais.
Picnic Area: Yes.
Retail Shop: Wines sold on-site.
Credit Cards: None.
Access for Disabled: Limited.
Foreign Languages: Spanish.
Getting There: Winery is seventy-five miles north of San Francisco. From Hwy. 101: Take Canyon Rd. exit and travel west to Dry Creek Rd. Continue west on Yoakim Bridge Rd., then turn right onto West Dry Creek Rd.

❧ Lou Preston has made creative blending his hallmark, challenged by the myriad flavors, spices, and textures of his Dry Creek Valley grapes. The Cuvee de Fumé and Sirah-Syrah are obvious examples of his art; the extensive clonal blending behind the production of his Zinfandels is less obvious, but equally important. Preston's own background is an interesting mixture: upon earning an MBA from Stanford, he promptly enrolled himself in several enology classes at the University of California–Davis, then uprooted pear and prune orchards to plant grape stocks.

ɜ ɜ ɜ

Rabbit Ridge Vineyards

3291 Westside Road
Healdsburg, California 95448
TEL: 707-431-7128
OWNERS: Erich and Catherine Russell
FOUNDED: 1985

AT A GLANCE
Tours & Tastings: Open by appointment only. Private vineyard and winery tours with the winemaker.
Vineyards: Forty-five acres planted to Cabernet Franc, Sauvignon Blanc, Chardonnay, Cabernet Sauvignon, Zinfandel.
Wines: Chardonnay, Cabernet Sauvignon, Zinfandel.
Awards: 1982 Zinfandel: bronze.
Retail Shop: Wines sold on-site.
Credit Cards: None.
Access for Disabled: None.
Foreign Languages: Spanish.
Getting There: Winery is three miles south of Healdsburg. From Hwy. 101: Take Westside Rd. exit and travel southwest.

ɜ Erich and Catherine Russell specialize in "handmade wines from vine to bottle." When the Russells acquired the property in 1979, their steep hillside vineyard consisted of one acre of old Zinfandel. They planted all the other vinifera with tight vine spacing, in the European fashion.

ɜ ɜ ɜ

A. Rafanelli Winery

4685 West Dry Creek Road
Healdsburg, California 95448
TEL: 707-433-1385
OWNER/WINEMAKER: Americo Rafanelli
FOUNDED: 1974

AT A GLANCE
Tours & Tastings: Open daily, by appointment, 10–4:30. Winemaker conducts all tours, by appointment only.
Closed: Major holidays.
Vineyards: Thirty-five acres planted to Zinfandel. Merlot, Cabernet Sauvignon, Gamay Beaujolais, Chardonnay.
Wines: Zinfandel, Cabernet Sauvignon, Gamay Beaujolais.
Awards: Zinfandel won gold medals at most major California judgings.
Retail Shop: Wines sold on-site.
Credit Cards: None.
Access for Disabled: None.
Foreign Languages: Italian, Spanish.
Getting There: Winery is in Healdsburg, sixty-five miles north of San Francisco. From Hwy. 101: Take Dry Creek Rd. exit and go west four miles. Turn left at Lambert Bridge Rd., right on West Dry Creek Rd.
Special Wine & Other Events: Barrel Tasting in the spring.

ɜ This family-owned operation produces red wines in a traditional manner; after small lot fermentation in open fermentors, wines are aged in oak. "I have grown wine grapes and made wine all my life," comments Americo Rafanelli. He runs this winery almost single-handedly, and is usually available to answer questions.

ɜ ɜ ɜ

J. Rochioli Vineyards and Winery

6192 Westside Road
Healdsburg, California 95448
TEL: 707-433-2305
OWNERS: Tom and Joe Rochioli
FOUNDED: 1983

AT A GLANCE
Tours & Tastings: Open daily 10–5. Redwood tasting room doubles as a gallery featuring the work of local artists. Winery tours by appointment.
Closed: Easter, Thanksgiving, Christmas.

Vineyards: Eighty acres planted to Cabernet Sauvignon, Zinfandel, Sauvignon Blanc, Chardonnay, Pinot Noir.
Wines: Varietals from the above.
Awards: 1982 Pinot Noir: two 18 Karat Golds, gold, two silvers, three bronzes; 1984 Sauvignon Blanc: two golds, silver, bronze; 1985 Sauvignon Blanc: double gold, gold, two bronzes.
Picnic Area: Patio, surrounded by roses, overlooks Russian River Valley.
Retail Shop: Wines sold on-site.
Credit Cards: American Express, MasterCard, Visa.
Access for Disabled: Wheelchair accessible.
Getting There: Winery is six miles southwest of Healdsburg, in Sonoma County's Russian River Valley. Take Hwy. 101 to the Westside-Guerneville exit and travel south on Westside Rd.

&. While the Rochioli family has owned these vineyards since the 1930s, the winery itself is of more recent vintage. The father-and-son team of Joe and Tom Rochioli launched this venture less than a week after the latter married a fellow Sacramento State alum. (The new bride was promptly installed as tasting room manager.) Rochioli produces estate-bottled varietals in small lots; production currently hovers at 3,000 cases.

&. &. &.

Sausal Winery

7370 Highway 128
Healdsburg, California 95448
TEL: 707-433-2285
CO-OWNERS: David, Ed, and Roselee Demostene, and Lucinda Nelson
WINEMAKER: David Demostene
FOUNDED: 1973

AT A GLANCE
Tours & Tastings: Open daily 10–4. No tours.
Vineyards: 115 acres planted to Zinfandel, Chardonnay, Cabernet Sauvignon, French Colombard.
Wines: Varietals from the above plus Zinfandel, Chardonnay, Cabernet Sauvignon, White Zinfandel, Sausal Blanc (blend).
Awards: 1982 Zinfandel: gold; 1980 Private Reserve Zinfandel: silver.
Retail Shop: Wines sold on-site.
Credit Cards: MasterCard, Visa.
Access for Disabled: None.
Getting There: Located in Alexander Valley, seventy miles north of San Francisco. From Hwy. 101 in Healdsburg: Take Dry Creek Rd. exit. Go east to Healdsburg Ave., turn left, then turn off Healdsburg Ave. and onto Alexander Valley Rd. Continue seven miles out to Hwy. 128, following signs for Calistoga. (Winery is approximately two miles from junction of Alexander Valley Rd. and Hwy. 128).

&. When Leo Demostene purchased this ranch in 1956, its acreage was planted to prunes and apples, as well as grapes. A would-be vintner, he hoped to convert the prune dehydrator to a winery. After Demostene's death, his four children realized his dream. David shoulders the winemaking responsibilities, Ed manages the vineyards, Roselee serves as winery chemist, and Lucinda takes care of the paperwork.

&. &. &.

Sea Ridge Winery

P.O. Box 287
Cazadero, California 95421
TEL: 707-847-3469
Also visit:
Sea Ridge Tasting Room
935 Highway 1
Bodega Bay, California
TEL: 707-875-3329
PARTNERS: Tim Schmidt and Dan Wickham
FOUNDED: 1980

AT A GLANCE

Tours & Tastings: Winery open by appointment only. Tasting room open daily 12–7. Winery principals are on hand to discuss enological topics. The tasting room incorporates a small marine museum, aquarium, and gallery.

Vineyards: Ten acres planted to Pinot Noir. Other grapes purchased from coastal vineyards in Sonoma County.

Wines: Chardonnay, Pinot Noir, Zinfandel, Sauvignon Blanc.

Awards: 1981 Pinot Noir: gold; 1982 Pinot Noir: two silvers.

Retail Shop: Wines sold on site.

Credit Cards: American Express, MasterCard, Visa.

Access for Disabled: Ramp and toilet facilities at tasting room.

Getting There: The tasting room is twenty miles west of Santa Rosa. Take Hwy. 12 West to the Bodega Hwy.; continue west to Hwy. 1.

   🐌 Marine biologists Tim Schmidt and Dan Wickham met in Bodega Bay, where both were conducting research. They decided to conduct an enological experiment—Would grapes grown in the limestone soil of this maritime climate result in memorable vintages? The answer is resoundingly affirmative. "The cool, extended growing season and limestone-based soils have allowed us to achieve remarkable early success, and we will continue to be innovators."

🐌 🐌 🐌

Sebastiani Vineyards

389 Fourth Street East (P.O. Box AA)
Sonoma, California 95476
TEL: 707-938-5532
OWNERS: The Sebastiani family
WINEMAKER: Mary Sullivan
FOUNDED: 1904

AT A GLANCE

Tours & Tastings: Open daily 10–5. Twenty-to-thirty-minute tours include slide viewings and a visit to the redwood cellar, with carved oak casks. Visitors then go to the tasting room to sample wines. Tours begin shortly after 10; the last departs at 4:20. Another attraction is Sebastiani's Indian Artifact Museum, which displays several thousand ancient relics made by the indigenous Pomo and Wappo tribes—arrowheads, beadwork, pottery, and basketry.

Closed: Good Friday, Easter, Thanksgiving, Christmas, New Year's Day.

Vineyards: 700 acres planted to all major vinifera varietals. (There is also a thirty-seven-acre experimental vineyard.) Additional grapes purchased from growers in Sonoma, Mendocino, and Napa counties.

Wines: French Colombard, Cabernet Sauvignon, Barbera, Burgundy, Chardonnay, Pinot Noir, Zinfandel, Gewürztraminer, Johannisberg Riesling, Green Hungarian, Merlot, Sauvignon Blanc, Chablis, Chenin Blanc, Gamay Beaujolais, Pinot Noir Blanc, White Zinfandel, *methode champenoise* sparkling wine.

Awards: Recent medal winners include: 1983 Gewürztraminer—three golds, two silvers, bronze; 1984 Nouveau Gamay Beaujolais—gold, two silvers; 1983 Late Harvest Johannisberg Riesling—gold; 1980 Proprietor's Reserve Cabernet Sauvignon—gold, silver, two bronzes.

Picnic Area: Tables on the lawn.

Retail Shop: Wines, mustards, cookbooks, and gifts sold on-site.

Credit Cards: American Express, MasterCard, Visa.

Access for Disabled: Tasting room and tour area accommodate wheelchairs.

Foreign Languages: "Spanish, Italian, French (with advance notice)."

Getting There: Winery is in the city of Sonoma, forty-four miles north of San Francisco. Take Hwy. 12 to Sonoma's City Hall, on E. Napa St. Bear right on E. Napa St., then left on First St. East. At East Spain St. turn right and continue to Fourth St. East.

Special Wine & Other Events: Vintage

Festival, late Sept.; Nouveau Celebration, mid-Nov.

🐌 Sebastiani, a state landmark, is a must-see for enological pilgrims. In 1825, on this very site, Franciscan padres planted Sonoma Valley's first vineyard. The mission was secularized ten years later, and General Mariano Vallejo was among the winemakers who crushed the laicized grapes. Samuele Sebastiani purchased this property in 1904; the winery he established has remained in his family ever since. (Ironically enough, he learned winemaking from monks.) Sebastiani's son August garnered international acclaim for his vintages: the Pinot Noir Blanc he dubbed Eye of the Swan helped popularize blush wines. Today, third-generation vintners are working in the cellars, blending old-world traditions with new-world technology. The staff of eight enologists, with their combined 106 years of experience, is fully committed to the production of world-class wines.

🐌 🐌 🐌

Sellards Winery

6400 Sequoia Circle
Sebastopol, California 95472
TEL: 707-823-8293
PROPRIETOR: Tom Sellards
FOUNDED: 1980

AT A GLANCE
Tours & Tastings: Open by appointment only.
Vineyards: Grapes purchased from growers in Sonoma County's Alexander and Dry Creek valleys.
Wines: Chardonnay, Cabernet Sauvignon, Sauvignon Blanc, Zinfandel. Small lots of other varietals are occasionally produced.
Retail Shop: Wines sold on-site.
Credit Cards: None.
Access for Disabled: Special parking; winery accommodates wheelchairs.

Getting There: Winery is nine miles west of Coddingtown. Call for directions.

🐌 No detail is too small to escape Tom Sellards's attention; lacking vineyards of his own, he works closely with the same growers year after year. His primary goal is to harvest each lot of grapes over a two-day period at precisely the desired sugar, acid, and temperature levels. Since cool temperatures retain fruit, he picks at first light. Grapes are typically picked, crushed, pressed, and in the fermentor by noon, rarely having risen above 62 degrees Fahrenheit.

🐌 🐌 🐌

Simi

16275 Healdsburg Avenue (P.O. Box 698)
Healdsburg, California 95448
TEL: 707-433-6981
OWNER: Moet-Hennessy
WINEMAKER: Zelma R. Long (formerly head enologist at Robert Mondavi Winery)
FOUNDED: 1876

AT A GLANCE
Tours & Tastings: Open daily 10–4:30. Guided tours of hand-cut stone winery at 11, 1, and 3.
Closed: Major holidays.
Vineyards: 175 acres planted to Cabernet Sauvignon, Sauvignon Blanc, Cabernet Franc, Petite Verdot, Chardonnay. Additional grapes purchased from growers in Sonoma and Mendocino counties.
Wines: Cabernet Sauvignon, Chardonnay, Sauvignon Blanc, Chenin Blanc, Rosé of Cabernet Sauvignon, Pinot Noir.
Awards: Almost every Simi wine has won a gold medal.
Picnic Area: Yes.
Retail Shop: Wines sold on-site.
Credit Cards: MasterCard, Visa.
Access for Disabled: Visitor Center is wheelchair accessible.

Foreign Languages: French, German, Italian, Spanish, and American Sign Language.
Getting There: Winery is in Healdsburg. From Hwy. 101: Take Dry Creek Rd. exit and drive north on Healdsburg Ave.
Special Wine & Other Events: Throughout year, "Food and Wine Pairings" match gourmet hors d'oeuvres with appropriate varietals.

&. Founded by the Italian-born brothers Giuseppe and Pietro Simi, this winery is something of a feminist monument: upon Giuseppe's death, his daughter Isabelle took over the operation, remaining in charge until 1970. Two years later, under new ownership, Simi made history as well as wine by hiring vintner Mary Ann Graf—the first woman to receive an enology degree from the University of California–Davis. Graf's successor, Zelma Long, also studied at UC–Davis; she left before graduating to work at Mondavi.

&. &. &.

Sonoma-Cutrer

4401 Slusser Road
Windsor, California 95492
TEL: 707-528-1181
OWNER: Brice Jones
WINEMAKER: Bill Bonetti (graduate of the School of Viticulture and Enology, Conegliano, Italy; experience at several California wineries, including E. & J. Gallo and Cresta Blanca)
FOUNDED: 1981

AT A GLANCE
Tours & Tastings: By appointment only.
Vineyards: 800 acres planted to Chardonnay, Pinot Noir, Sauvignon Blanc, White Riesling, Zinfandel, Gewürztraminer.
Wines: Chardonnay.
Awards: Does not enter competitions.
Retail Shop: Wines sold on-site.
Credit Cards: MasterCard, Visa.

Access for Disabled: Ramps at entrance, specially equipped bathrooms.
Foreign Languages: French, Spanish.
Getting There: Take Hwy. 101 North to River Rd. exit and head west four miles. Slusser Rd. is on right.
Special Wine & Other Events: The World Croquet Championships and other croquet competitions are held on the premises.

&. Air force fighter pilot Brice Jones used to fly to London whenever possible to attend Christie's wine auctions. Finally he resigned his commission—no casual gesture from the son and grandson of West Point graduates—and entered Harvard Business School. His ultimate objective: to produce Chardonnays equal to any in the world. Harvard MBA in hand, Jones assembled the funds for a vineyard company; soon he was selling grapes to many premium California wineries. He built his own facility nine years later. Sonoma-Cutrer may be the only winery in the country with two regulation croquet courts—Jones is passionate about the game.

&. &. &.

Sonoma Hills Winery

4850 Peracca Road
Santa Rosa, California 95404
TEL: 707-523-3415
OWNER/WINEMAKER: Teresa Votruba
FOUNDED: 1983

AT A GLANCE
Tours & Tastings: Open by appointment only, Oct.–Feb.
Closed: Dec. 24–Jan. 2.
Vineyards: Eight acres planted to Chardonnay. Additional grapes bought from Sonoma Mountain growers.
Wines: Chardonnay.
Retail Shop: Wines sold on-site.
Credit Cards: None.
Access for Disabled: None.

Getting There: Winery is located in Bennett Valley, between Glen Ellen and Santa Rosa, sixty minutes from the Golden Gate Bridge. From Hwy. 101: Take Penngrove exit to Petaluma Hill Rd. After five miles, turn right on Crane Canyon Rd. Go uphill to Grange Rd., make a right onto Peracca Rd.

Special Wine & Other Events: Special prerelease/crush party and sale in Oct., for mailing list customers and the trade.

🐝 "We are the smallest bonded winery in California, producing just 600 cases annually," reports Teresa Votruba, a former schoolteacher. An amateur vintner since 1977, she turned pro after a trip to France and a year's worth of enological study.

🐝 🐝 🐝

Sotoyome Winery

641 Limerick Lane
Healdsburg, California 95448
TEL: 707-433-2001
PRESIDENT/WINEMAKER: William
  Chaikin
FOUNDED: 1973

AT A GLANCE

Tours & Tastings: Open Fri.–Sun. 11–4:30, other times by appointment. Vineyard and winery tours by appointment year-round.

Vineyards: Eleven acres planted to Petite Sirah and Shiraz.

Wines: Petite Sirah, Pale Shiraz, Shiraz.

Awards: Many awards for Petite Sirah at state fairs.

Picnic Area: Overlooks the distant, gently rolling hills.

Retail Shop: Wines sold on-site.

Credit Cards: None. Personal checks accepted.

Access for Disabled: Level ground-floor entrance to winery; bathroom accommodates wheelchairs.

Foreign Languages: French.

Getting There: Winery is 63 miles from San Francisco. Take Hwy. 101 to Healdsburg Ave. off-ramp. Then go ¾ mile south on Old Redwood Hwy.; at Limerick Ln. turn left.

🐝 Sotoyome, named for a local Indian tribe, is one of Sonoma County's smaller wineries. At age sixty, after a career in government and business, William Chaikin decided to become a vintner. He says, "The winery's charm lies in the informal, cozy ambience of our tasting rooms, and the exceptional quality of our Petite Sirah and Shiraz—varietals rarely offered in this area."

🐝 🐝 🐝

Robert Stemmler Winery

3805 Lambert Bridge Road
Healdsburg, California 95448
TEL: 707-433-6334
OWNERS: Robert Stemmler and
  Trumbull Kelly
WINEMAKER: Robert Stemmler
  (graduate of Bad Kreuznach Wine
  College, Germany; formerly at
  Inglenook and Simi)
FOUNDED: 1977

AT A GLANCE

Tours & Tastings: Open daily 10:30–4:30. On rainy days, warm up in front of the fireplace in the wood-paneled tasting room.

Closed: Easter, Thanksgiving, Christmas, New Year's Day.

Vineyards: All grapes purchased from selected Sonoma County growers.

Wines: Sauvignon Blanc, Chardonnay, Pinot Noir, Cabernet Sauvignon, Late Harvest Sauvignon Blanc.

Awards: 1984 Pinot Noir: two golds, silver, three bronzes; 1982 Cabernet Sauvignon: gold, bronze; 1981 Chardonnay Reserve: silver.

Picnic Area: On redwood deck; call to reserve a table.

Retail Shop: Wines, label posters sold on-site.
Credit Cards: MasterCard, Visa.
Access for Disabled: Ramps, specially equipped bathrooms.
Foreign Languages: German.
Getting There: Winery is in Healdsburg. Take Hwy. 101 to Dry Creek Rd. exit; travel three miles northwest on Dry Creek Rd. to Lambert Bridge Rd. Watch for signs.

ઢ "Good taste, like art, is priceless," runs Robert Stemmler's motto, a reference to both the winemaker's skill and the lovely fourteenth-century Flemish painting that adorns his bottle labels. (A tapestry reproduction of this painting hangs inside the tasting room; the original canvas is in the Cluny Museum in Paris.) Alas, good taste is always in short supply: this winery's capacity is all of 10,000 cases. Stemmler's celebrated Pinot Noir is the first to disappear, and consequently isn't poured in the tasting room. Go ahead, live dangerously—if this varietal is available, buy it unsampled.

ઢ ઢ ઢ

Rodney Strong Vineyards

11455 Old Redwood Highway (P.O. Box 368)
Healdsburg, California 95448
TEL: 707-433-6511
OWNER: Renfield Importers, Ltd.
WINEMASTER: Rodney Strong
FOUNDED: 1959

AT A GLANCE

Tours & Tastings: Open daily 10–5. Dramatic, pyramid-shaped winery building was designed by Craig Roland, a student of Frank Lloyd Wright. Winery tours every hour on the hour explain the wine-making process, leading visitors through production area, crush pad, cellar, etc.

Complimentary tasting takes place at end of tour.
Closed: Easter, Christmas, New Year's Day.
Vineyards: 1,240 owned and 170 leased acres planted to Johannisberg Riesling, Gewürztraminer, Cabernet Sauvignon, Sauvignon Blanc, Pinot Noir, Chardonnay, Zinfandel, Merlot.
Wines: Varietals from grapes above, plus Merlot, Fumé Blanc, Late Harvest Johannisberg Riesling.
Awards: Recent medal winners include: 1985 Claus Vineyards Johannisberg Riesling—bronze; 1984 Charlotte's Home Fumé Blanc—silver; 1980 Alexander's Crown Cabernet Sauvignon—bronze; 1984 LeBaron Johannisberg Riesling—gold.
Picnic Area: Tables on the lawn.
Retail Shop: Wines sold on-site.
Credit Cards: American Express, Carte Blanche, Diner's Club, MasterCard, Visa.
Access for Disabled: None.
Foreign Languages: French, Spanish.
Getting There: Winery is in Windsor, sixty miles north of San Francisco. From Hwy. 101: Take Healdsburg Ave. exit to Old Redwood Hwy. and drive one mile southwest.
Special Wine & Other Events: Sun. concerts June–Aug.

ઢ While performing in Europe, Rodney Strong—a dancer who studied with George Balanchine and Martha Graham—developed a serious interest in wine. Many fine vintages improve with age, but dancers do not; as his first career waned, Strong launched a second—winemaking. Sensing Sonoma County's possibilities, he settled here, turning two floors of a rented Victorian house into a winery. From these humble beginnings he developed a thriving mail-order wine business that remains one of the industry's most successful. Such was his reputation that when the French champagne producer Piper-Heidsieck wanted to set up a California operation, they tapped Strong as a partner. Today he wears two hats; he is winemaster of both Piper Sonoma Cellars (page 434) and Rodney Strong Vineyards.

૨ કરે કરે

Trentadue Winery

19170 Redwood Highway
Geyserville, California 95441
TEL: 707-433-3104
OWNERS: Leo and Evelyn Trentadue
WINEMAKER: Nikko Schoch (who made his first wine at the age of ten under the tutelage of renowned enologist Andre Tchelistcheff)
FOUNDED: 1968

AT A GLANCE
Tours & Tastings: Open daily 10–5. Tours by appointment only.
Closed: Easter, Thanksgiving, Christmas, New Year's Day.
Vineyards: 200 acres planted to Cabernet Sauvignon, Petite Sirah, Carignane, Zinfandel, Gamay, Chardonnay, Chenin Blanc, Sauvignon Blanc, Sémillon, Merlot, French Colombard, Aleatico, Nebbiolo, Malbec, Petite Verdot, Fresia.
Wines: Wines from grapes above, plus Old Patch Red (a proprietary blend).
Awards: Recent medal winners include: 1983 Merlot—four-star gold; 1984 Petite Sirah—four-star gold, gold; 1985 Chenin Blanc—gold; 1984 Cabernet Sauvignon—silver.
Picnic Area: Tables in arbor and on lawn. Box lunches can be ordered in advance.
Retail Shop: Wines, crystal, cookbooks, jams, jellies, and soaps sold on-site.
Credit Cards: American Express, Diner's Club, MasterCard, Visa.
Access for Disabled: None.
Foreign Languages: Spanish.
Getting There: Winery is in Geyserville,

approximately seventy-three miles north of San Francisco. Take Hwy. 101 to the Independence Ln. exit (north of Healdsburg). Turn east onto frontage road. Follow signs to winery, one hundred yards away.
Special Wine & Other Events: "Stage a Picnic," May–Oct.

૨ Fleeing the subdivisions that were carving up Santa Clara Valley, the Trentadues bought a Geyserville ranch. There, Leo Trentadue pioneered plantings of grapes just being introduced by the University of California at Davis. Additional vineyard purchases brought the family's total acreage to 200, including an experimental lot once used by horticulturalist Luther Burbank. "My original plan," recounts Trentadue, "was to grow grapes for sale to neighboring vintners. But friends encouraged me to produce commercially the wines I was making for my own consumption, so in 1968 I established Trentadue Winery."

૨ કરે કરે

Valley of the Moon Winery

777 Madrone Road
Glen Ellen, California 95442
TEL: 707-996-6941
OWNER: Harry Parducci, Sr.
WINEMAKER: Harry Parducci, Jr.
FOUNDED: 1857

AT A GLANCE
Tours & Tastings: Open daily 10–5. No tours. A giant, 400-year-old bay laurel tree stands in front of the tasting room. "With its laurel-like leaves, the tree's regional significance has been recognized with a listing on the National Register of Historic Places."
Closed: Easter, Thanksgiving, Christmas.
Vineyards: 100 acres planted to Zinfandel, Sémillon, French Colombard, Alicante Bouschet (red wine grape).

Additional grapes purchased from Sonoma County growers.

Wines: Chardonnay, Sauvignon Blanc, Sémillon, White Zinfandel, Zinfandel, Pinot Noir; private stock red, white, and rosé wines.

Picnic Area: Yes.

Retail Shop: Wines sold on-site.

Credit Cards: American Express, MasterCard, Visa.

Access for Disabled: Wheelchair accessible.

Foreign Languages: Italian.

Getting There: Winery is five miles north of the city of Sonoma. Take Hwy. 12 between Sonoma and Glen Ellen, turn west onto Madrone Rd.

Special Wine & Other Events: Coors Bicycle Race, Aug.; Vintage Festival, Sept.; and "many others."

&. The history of this site is California's past in microcosm: Pomo Indian artifacts have been found here, and the winery itself dates to a Spanish land grant. Notable owners, such as the Hearst family and the Civil War general John Hooker, reigned over this fertile Sonoma Valley vineyard until it was put out of business by Prohibition. Valley of the Moon was revived in 1942 by San Francisco Sausage Company founder Enrico Parducci, who wanted to make the kind of wines he drank in his native Italy. Today, his son and grandson carry on the family tradition.

&. &. &.

William Wheeler Winery

130 Plaza Street (P.O. Box 881)
Healdsburg, California 95448
TEL: 707-433-8786
OWNER: William Wheeler
WINEMAKER: Julia Iantosca (B.S. in enology and viticulture, UC-Davis)
FOUNDED: 1981

AT A GLANCE

Tours & Tastings: Open Thurs.–Mon. 10–4, Mon.–Tues. by appointment. No tours.

Closed: Good Friday, Easter, July 4th, Thanksgiving (two days), Christmas through New Year's Day (ten days).

Vineyards: Thirty-two acres planted to Cabernet Sauvignon and Zinfandel. Additional grapes purchased from growers in Russian River, Alexander, and Dry Creek valleys.

Wines: Cabernet Sauvignon, Chardonnay, Sauvignon Blanc, White Zinfandel.

Awards: Numerous golds and silvers for Sonoma Chardonnay, Sauvignon Blanc.

Retail Shop: Wines sold on-site.

Credit Cards: None.

Access for Disabled: Parking and rest room facilities for wheelchair users, although it's one flight up to tasting room.

Foreign Languages: French, Spanish.

Getting There: Winery is 1½ hours north of San Francisco. Driving north on Hwy. 101, take the second Healdsburg exit and bear right on Plaza St. to winery, just off the plaza in downtown Healdsburg.

Special Wine & Other Events: Sonoma County Wine Auction, Aug.

&. With the dream of growing fine wine grapes, William Wheeler, a former Foreign Service officer, and his Norwegian-born wife, Ingrid, purchased this 175-acre ranch nestled in the Dry Creek Valley. Then they went to work in France—as guests at a Bordeaux château, where they participated in the harvest and observed winemaking. Back in the States, the couple planted a vineyard; establishing a winery was the next logical step. "There is an old European expression that you plant a vineyard for your children," William Wheeler remarks. "I am only beginning to understand the accuracy of that saying."

&. &. &.

White Oak Vineyards

208 Haydon Street
Healdsburg, California 95448
TEL: 707-433-8429
OWNERS: Bill Myers
WINEMAKER: Paul Brasset (nearly
twenty years experience with cellars
of California wineries)
FOUNDED: 1981

AT A GLANCE
Tours & Tastings: Open daily 10–5. This
is a small operation; tours last five to ten
minutes.
Vineyards: Six acres planted to Chardon-
nay and Cabernet Sauvignon. Additional
grapes purchased from select vineyards
in the Alexander, Russian River, and Dry
Creek valleys.
Wines: Chardonnay, Sauvignon Blanc,
Chenin Blanc, Johannisberg Riesling,
Cabernet Sauvignon, Zinfandel.
Awards: 1982 Zinfandel: two golds, sil-
ver, bronze; 1983 Chardonnay: two sil-
vers, four bronzes; 1982 Johannisberg
Riesling: gold, bronze; 1982 Sauvignon
Blanc: two silvers, two bronzes.
Retail Shop: Wines sold on-site.
Credit Cards: MasterCard, Visa.
Access for Disabled: None.
Getting There: Winery is fifteen miles
north of Santa Rosa and seventy-five
miles north of San Francisco. Take Hwy.
101 North to the Healdsburg Ave. exit.
Turn right on Mill St., right again on East
St., and left on Haydon.
Special Wine & Other Events: Salmon
feast given by Mr. Bill Myers.

&. What do commercial fishermen do
when they need a break? Bill Myers decided to go winemaking. Before launching his winery, he spent two years testing
fruit from northern Sonoma County vineyards. Myers hasn't given up fishing entirely; he still runs a few salmon boats in
Alaska. After all, he needs something to
eat with White Oak whites.

&. &. &.

Williams Selyem

P.O. Box 195
Fulton, California 95439
TEL: 707-887-7480
OWNERS: Ed Selyem and Burt Williams
FOUNDED: 1981

AT A GLANCE
Tours & Tastings: Open by appointment
only.
Vineyards: None. Grapes purchased from
local growers.
Wines: Pinot Noir, Zinfandel.
Awards: 1982 Pinot Noir: two golds; 1983
Pinot Noir: gold; 1984 Pinot Noir: two
golds; 1982 Zinfandel: gold; 1983 Zin-
fandel: two golds.
Retail Shop: Wines sold on-site.
Credit Cards: None.
Access for Disabled: None.
Getting There: Winery is two miles
northwest of Santa Rosa. Call for direc-
tions.

&. This two-family partnership runs a
very small operation. Co-owners Ed Selyem and Burt Williams report: "We
make two varieties for people who know
and appreciate the very best." As proof,
they cite many gold medals.

Special Wine Events: Every August, just
before harvest time, the Sonoma County
Winegrowers Association sponsors a
three-day showcase and wine auction,
with seminars, dinner dances, and of
course, wine tasting. Proceeds are divided between Santa Rosa Memorial
Hospital and the Sonoma County Wine
Library. For details, write to the Sonoma
County Showcase and Auction, 50 Mark
West Springs Road, Santa Rosa, California 95401. The wineries along Sonoma's
Russian River Wine Road host barrel
tastings in March, and the Wine Fest in
mid-May at the Healdsburg Plaza. The
Sonoma Valley v.a. sponsors its own Vintage Festival in September.

TO SEE & DO

Sonoma, founded by Franciscan padres in 1823, ranks as California's seventh oldest city, and the partially reconstructed Mission San Francisco Solano de Sonoma (Spain and First Street East; tel: 707-938-1578) is its oldest building. Mexican general Mariano Vallejo, who secularized the mission and governed much of California, had two homes in town. Little is left of the mansion, La Casa Grande, on Spain Street, but the two-story wooden house he called *Lachryma Montis* ("mountain tear") is still intact, along with a cottage and a storage house (West Spain Street and First Street East; tel: 707-938-1578). A few miles away, livestock still populate Vallejo's rancho, once the largest in the state (3325 Adobe Road, Petaluma; tel: 707-762-4871). The handsome adobe has been restored and furnished in period style. Winners' Circle (5911 Lakeville Highway, Petaluma; tel: 707-762-1808) is a very different kind of ranch, breeding horses that stand less than three feet tall. Although too small to ride, these miniature equines are strong enough to pull a cart carrying two passengers. Petaluma's other attractions include iron-front commercial buildings and stately Victorian homes; the Chamber of Commerce (314 Western Avenue, Petaluma, California 94952; tel: 707-762-2785) can equip you with a map for a walking tour. The call of the wild may have taken writer Jack London farther north, but he lived—and died—in Glen Ellen. His cottage is open to the public, and there's also a museum and park on the site (Jack London Ranch Road, Glen Ellen; tel: 707-938-5216). Fittingly, there is no admission fee for visitors entering on foot or horseback.

Santa Rosa, the seat of Sonoma County, is better known as the hometown of horticulturist Luther Burbank. His residence has been turned into a museum (Sonoma and Santa Rosa Avenues, Santa Rosa; tel: 707-576-5115); stroll through Burbank's spectacular experimental gardens free of charge. Also worthy of note is the Robert J. Ripley's "Church of One Tree" (492 Sonoma Avenue, Santa Rosa; tel: 707-528-5233). The Russian River takes its name from the fur traders who came here in the early nineteenth century, long before détente. Fort Ross State Historic Park (north of Jenner on Highway 1; tel: 707-847-3286) is their former outpost, with its redwood stockade, barracks, officers' houses, and chapel. The river itself is a fabulous recreational area, with many resort towns and campgrounds.

ACCOMMODATIONS

Many comfortable bed and breakfasts are within easy reach of wineries and vineyards, but some are a bit remote from fine restaurants and other diversions. Space does not permit more than a "tasting" of bed and breakfasts. The reservation service below can supply more extensive listings. Wherever you plan to stay, note that space is scarce during Vintage Festival (last week in Sept.) and Harvest Fair (first week in Oct.), as well as many summer and early fall weekends, so be sure to reserve rooms well in advance.

Bed & Breakfast Exchange
1458 Lincoln Avenue
Calistoga, California 94508
Tel: 707-965-3885
B&B listings in Napa, Sonoma counties, northern California coast, and Gold Rush country.

Cloverdale
Ye Olde' Shelford House
29955 River Road
Cloverdale, California 95425
Tel: 707-894-5956
A restored Victorian house where the stagecoach used to stop. Each room is furnished with family antiques, handsewn quilts, and fresh flowers, plus full breakfast. Tour local wineries aboard Shelford's horse-drawn surrey.

Vintage Towers
302 North Main Street
Cloverdale, California 95425
Tel: 707-894-4535
A bed and breakfast in a lovely turn-of-the-century mansion—and a national historical landmark—one block east of Highway 101. Breakfasts are served in the formal dining room or in the gazebo when weather permits.

Geyserville
Campbell Ranch Inn
1475 Canyon Road
Geyserville, California 95441
Tel: 707-857-3476
Be sure to bring your camera—the spectacular view from this hilltop home is one you will want to remember. Tennis court, Ping-Pong table, swimming pool, and hot tub; full breakfast, and homemade pie as a bedtime snack.

Hope-Bosworth and Hope-Merrill Houses
21238-21253 Geyserville Avenue (P.O. Box 42)
Geyserville, California 95441
Tel: 707-857-3356
Two Victorian homes that have been impeccably restored, from the silk-screened wallpapers to the period furnishings. Enjoy a glass of wine in the gazebo or parlor, relax on the front porch swing, swim in the pool, survey the vineyard and grape arbor.

Glen Ellen
Beltane Ranch
11775 Sonoma Highway (P.O. Box 395)
Glen Ellen, California 95442
Tel: 707-996-6501
Guest rooms have private baths and outside entrances at this bed and breakfast with vineyard views.

Guerneville
Ridenhour Ranch House Inn
12850 River Road
Guerneville, California 95446
Tel: 707-887-1033
Wallpaper, Oriental rugs, and stained glass add to the warmth of this handsome redwood home adjacent to the Korbel Winery. Decanters of sherry are found in each room; guests awake to a meal of cheeses, fruit, nut breads, muffins, and pastries.

Healdsburg
L'Auberge du Sans-Souci
25 West Grant Street
Healdsburg, California 95448
Tel: 707-431-1110
Experience French hospitality in a stately Victorian house nestled under spruce, cedar, and redwood trees. In the morning, host Mme. Ginette serves hot croissants and coffee; after a day of touring, she will introduce you to a few premium varietals you may have overlooked.

Inn on the Plaza
116 Matheson Street (P.O. Box 1196)
Healdsburg, California 95448
Tel: 707-433-6991
Sparkling with antiques and stained glass, this one-time Wells Fargo location also has an enclosed roof garden. Enjoy both a complimentary breakfast and a glass of wine in the afternoon.

The Grape Leaf Inn
539 Johnson Street
Healdsburg, California 95448
Tel: 707-433-8140
Host Kathy Cookson invites you to stay at her Queen Anne Victorian home with many modern conveniences. Complete breakfast; in the afternoon, enjoy local wines in the front parlor or on the veranda.

Madrona Manor
1001 Westside Road
Healdsburg, California 95448
Tel: 707-433-4231
A twenty-room luxury country inn, built in 1880. Air-conditioning, swimming pool. Gorgeous views, gardens, walking trails, and outstanding dinners. Advance reservations essential.

Santa Rosa
Los Robles Lodge
925 Edwards Avenue
Santa Rosa, California 95401
Tel: 707-545-6330; 800-552-1001
Luxury touches include a heated pool and poolside service; well-furnished rooms, some with private patio and balconies.

New Flamingo Resort
2777 4th Street
Santa Rosa, California 95405
Tel: 707-545-8530; 800-848-8300
Set on landscaped grounds, the commodious rooms come with a Continental breakfast; pool and tennis courts are among the diversions.

Sheraton Round Barn
3555 Round Barn Boulevard
Santa Rosa, California 95401
Tel: 707-523-7555; 800-833-9595 (in-state); 800-325-3535 (out-of-state)
Earlier, a winery inhabited these scenic hillsides. The hotel's 247 rooms have all the amenities expected of a top chain, including a pool and jogging path. Golf and tennis nearby.

Fountaingrove Inn
101 Fountaingrove Parkway
Santa Rosa, California 95401
Tel: 707-578-6001; 800-222-6101 (in-state)
A waterfall decorates the lobby of this redwood-accented 85-room hotel. Heated pool, complimentary Continental breakfast. Golf nearby.

Vintners Inn and John Ash & Co.
4350 Barnes Road
Santa Rosa, California 95401
Tel: 707-575-7350; 800-421-2584
John Ash & Co., Tel: 707-527-7687
A comfortable bucolic feeling pervades well-furnished 44-room inn set in a lush vineyard. Nearby are pool, golf and tennis. Unforgettable food is prepared by talented chef, John Ash.

Sonoma
El Dorado Inn
405 First Street West
Sonoma, California 95476
Tel: 707-996-3030
An inn for history buffs: this adobe was the residence of Salvador Vallejo, brother of Sonoma's founder, General Mariano Vallejo. Thirty rooms, restaurant.

RESTAURANTS

Bodega Bay
Bay View Room
Inn at the Tides
800 Highway 1
Bodega Bay, California 94923
Tel: 707-875-2751; 800-541-7788
The menu changes weekly, but fresh seafood and produce are always featured.

Forestville
Russian River Vineyard
5700 Gravenstein Highway
Forestville, California 95436
Tel: 707-887-1652
Winery, vineyard setting, and Continental cuisine with Greek accents. Good wine list.

Geyserville
Christine's Hoffman House
21712 Geyserville Avenue
Geyserville, California 95441
Tel: 707-857-3224
California cuisine, accompanied by California wines.

Glen Ellen
Grist Mill Inn
14301 Arnold Drive
Glen Ellen, California 95442
Tel: 707-996-3077
Savor mesquite-grilled fish, chicken, and beef in a rustic creekside setting. The large waterwheel, built by General Mariano Vallejo, attests to the building's original purpose.

Gualala
St. Orres
36601 Highway 1
Gualala, California 95445
Tel: 707-884-3303
Fabulous food and wine beneath a Russian-style onion-domed roof.

Healdsburg
Jacob Horner
106 Matheson Street
Healdsburg, California 95448
Tel: 707-433-3939
Full bar, with coffee drinks a specialty. Sonoma County wines poured by the glass.

Madrona Manor
(See listing under "Accommodations" for address and phone number.)
Excellent French and California cuisine, extensive local wine list.

Plaza Grill
109A Plaza Street
Healdsburg, California 95448
Tel: 707-431-8305
Fine California cuisine and wines.

Western Boot Steakhouse
9 Mitchell Lane
Healdsburg, California 95448
Tel: 707-433-6362
Steaks, seafood, chicken, and ribs. Sonoma County wines served at the wine bar.

Santa Rosa
La Province
521-525 College Avenue
Santa Rosa, California 95404
Tel: 707-526-6233
Haute cuisine that does not require diners to wear haute couture: casual attire is welcome at this fine French restaurant.

La Gare
208 Wilson Street
Santa Rosa, California 95401
Tel: 707-528-4355
Country French cuisine, first-rate local wines.

Matisse
620 5th Street
Santa Rosa, California 95404
Tel: 707-527-9797
A modern setting with an inspired menu and daily specials. French food with an American accent. Game is a winner and so is the wine list. Luscious desserts.

Sonoma
Au Relais
691 Broadway at Andrieux
Sonoma, California 95478
Tel: 707-996-1031
Excellent wine list complements a Continental menu in a provincial setting. Baked goods made fresh here.

Depot Hotel 1870
241 First Street W
Sonoma, California 95478
Tel: 707-958-2980
Italian dishes in an old hotel. Wine list. Dine outdoors in lovely garden with pool.

Pasta Nostra
139 East Napa Street
Sonoma, California 95476
Tel: 707-938-4166
Fresh pasta and local vintages.

❧ SOUTH-CENTRAL COAST

Eighteenth-century Franciscan priests may have taken vows of chastity and poverty, but they weren't asked to give up wine; indeed, masses couldn't be celebrated without it. Coastal towns tended to grow up around Spanish missions, and most of these missions maintained vineyards. The first commercial wineries in this area started appearing about one hundred years later.

Among the enthusiastic enophiles who settled here was the Polish pianist and politician Ignacy Paderewski, who established a vineyard on the ranch he owned west of Paso Robles. No amateur grape stomper, he had neighboring winemakers vinify his fruit. But Paderewski was proud enough of the finished product to serve it to guests at his Switzerland residence.

With its warmth tempered by ocean breezes, the south-central coast is hospitable to cool climate varietals such as Pinot Noir, Chardonnay, and White Riesling. Consequently, the past decade has brought winemakers here in droves. Many have taken root along Highways 101 and 46 in the Paso Robles viticultural area. Another cluster of wineries lures the wine traveler south to Los Olivos, Solvang, and other towns in the Santa Ynez Valley v.a.

❧ ❧ ❧

Adelaida Cellars/Tonio Conti

2170 Adelaida Road (Adelaida Star
   Route)
Paso Robles, California 93446
TEL: 805-239-0190, 238-5706
OWNER/WINEMAKER: John Munch
FOUNDED: 1983

AT A GLANCE

Tours & Tastings: Open daily 10–5. Tours conducted daily.
Closed: Major holidays.
Vineyards: 200 acres planted to Chardonnay, Cabernet Sauvignon, Pinot Noir, Petite Sirah. Additional grapes purchased locally.
Wines: Cabernet Sauvignon, Chardonnay; sparkling wines under the Tonio Conti label.
Awards: 1981 Cabernet Sauvignon: double gold; 1982 Cabernet Sauvignon: gold; 1983 Chardonnay: silver.
Retail Shop: Wines sold on-site.

Credit Cards: American Express, Diner's Club, MasterCard, Visa.
Access for Disabled: None.
Foreign Languages: French, Spanish.
Getting There: Winery is in Paso Robles, twenty-five miles north of San Luis Obispo. From Paso Robles: Go three miles east on Hwy. 46. Turn left on Jardine Rd., continue for three miles to Ranchita Canyon Rd. Follow Ranchita Canyon Rd. two miles, then bear right on Von Dollen; Adelaida Rd. is two miles ahead.
Special Wine & Other Events: Paso Robles Wine Festival, May.

❧ Self-taught winemaker John Munch entered the business in 1980, leasing space at Estrella Winery while his own facilities were under construction. In addition to still wines, he produces sparkling wines according to the time-consuming process of *methode champenoise*. The first Tonio Conti crush was released four years after harvest. "By that time," muses Munch, "each bottle had been touched by human hands 150 to 200 times."

ᴈ❧ ᴈ❧ ᴈ❧

Babcock Vineyards

5175 West Highway 246
Lompoc, California 93436
TEL: 805-736-1455
OWNERS: the Babcock family
FOUNDED: 1984

AT A GLANCE
Tours & Tastings: Open weekends 11–4:30, weekdays by appointment. A 7,000-case, family-operated winery. Informal tours. Visitors taste barrel, tank, and finished wines.
Vineyards: Forty-five acres planted to Pinot Noir, Gewürztraminer, Chardonnay, Sauvignon Blanc, Johannisberg Riesling. Red Delicious, Golden Delicious, and Granny Smith apples are also grown on property.
Wines: Varietals from above grapes. Apple wine on occasion.
Awards: In Babcock's first year, four wines collected thirteen medals in five competitions.
Retail Shop: Wines sold on-site. Through Sept. and Oct. there is always a good chance to get spectacular Granny Smith apples.
Credit Cards: MasterCard, Visa.
Access for Disabled: None.
Getting There: Winery is 40 miles from Santa Barbara, 30 miles from Santa Maria, and 15 miles from Solvang. From Hwy. 101: Take Hwy. 246 west 9½ miles. Babcock Vineyards is on the right, after passing both endpoints of the semicircular Campbell Rd.
Special Wine & Other Events: Apple harvest, Oct.

ᴈ❧ The Babcocks became fascinated with wine while compiling a wine list for their Seal Beach restaurant, Walt's Wharf. Their research led to an appreciation of—and the desire to produce—fine, premium vintages. The Babcocks purchased old ranch land, and planted forty acres of vineyards in 1979. With the success of their first crush, they decided to make the transition from vineyard grower to vintner.

ᴈ❧ ᴈ❧ ᴈ❧

J. Carey Vineyards and Winery

1711 Alamo Pintado Road
Solvang, California 93463
TEL: 805-688-8554
OWNERS: James Carey, Sr.; James Carey, Jr.; and Joseph Carey
WINEMAKER: Scott Meyer (alumnus of California Culinary Academy, San Francisco)
FOUNDED: 1978

AT A GLANCE
Tours & Tastings: Open Mon.–Fri. 10–4, Sat.–Sun. 10–5. Informal tours given by request; groups of eight or more are asked to call for an appointment. Visitors are guided through the winery; special attention is given to production methods.
Closed: Thanksgiving, Christmas, and when production timing so dictates—that is, harvest in the fall.
Vineyards: Forty-six acres planted to Sauvignon Blanc, Chardonnay, Cabernet Sauvignon, Merlot, Cabernet Franc. Additional grapes purchased from vineyards in Santa Barbara County.
Wines: Varietals from above grapes.
Awards: More than forty medals in the past six years, including eleven golds for our Sauvignon Blancs, Chardonnays, and Cabernet Blancs.
Picnic Area: Tables outside winery and tasting room.
Retail Shop: Wines sold on-site.
Credit Cards: MasterCard, Visa.
Access for Disabled: None.
Foreign Languages: Spanish, French.
Getting There: Winery is actually in the

community of Ballard, halfway between Solvang and Los Olivos, thirty miles north of Santa Barbara. From Hwy. 101: Take Hwy. 246 East. Bear left on Alamo Pintado Rd.

Special Wine & Other Events: Winery Open House, Apr. J. Carey Fun Run, Memorial Day weekend—one- and five-kilometer runs through steep vineyard terrain, followed by barbecue and live jazz to refresh the weary; proceeds benefit local hospital.

🐾 This is a small operation in a lovely, rustic setting; a local paper described it as "the West Coast version of Thoreau's Walden Pond." The winery occupies a converted dairy barn, while the tasting room is next door, in an old yellow farmhouse.

🐾 🐾 🐾

Castoro Cellars

1829 El Camino Real (P.O. Box 1973)
Atascadero, California 93422
TEL: 805-466-0287
OWNER: Berit Udsen
WINEMAKER: Niels Udsen
FOUNDED: 1983

AT A GLANCE
Tours & Tastings: Open by appointment only.
Vineyards: None. All grapes bought from growers in Paso Robles area.
Wines: Chardonnay, Cabernet Sauvignon, Zinfandel, Fumé Blanc, White Zinfandel; *methode champenoise* Blanc de Noir.
Awards: 1982 Cabernet Sauvignon: three golds; 1984 Chardonnay: gold; 1985 White Zinfandel: silver.
Retail Shop: Wines sold on-site.
Credit Cards: MasterCard, Visa.
Access for Disabled: None.
Foreign Languages: Danish, Italian.
Getting There: Winery is twenty miles north of San Luis Obispo, off Hwy. 101. Call for directions.

🐾 Shortly after birth, Niels Udsen became known as "Beaver," the result of his brothers' unsuccessful efforts to say "baby." The nickname followed him to Italy, where he acquired a fondness for good red wine while working in a spaghetti sauce factory. "I used to tell my friends, 'Someday, *il castoro* [Italian for beaver] will have a winery, too,'" Udsen recalls. Thus Castoro Cellars got both its name and its distinctive label, which features a grape-eating beaver.

🐾 🐾 🐾

Chamisal Vineyard

7525 Orcutt Road
San Luis Obispo, California 93401
TEL: 805-544-3576
OWNER: Norman L. Goss
WINEMAKER: Scott Boyd (studied
    enology at UC-Davis)
FOUNDED: 1980

AT A GLANCE
Tours & Tastings: Open Wed.–Sun. 11–5. Tours given on request.
Closed: Christmas.
Vineyards: Fifty-seven acres planted to Chardonnay, Cabernet Sauvignon.
Wines: Chardonnay, Cabernet Sauvignon.
Picnic Area: Overlooks vineyard.
Retail Shop: Wines sold on-site.
Credit Cards: MasterCard, Visa.
Access for Disabled: None.
Foreign Languages: French.
Getting There: Winery is in the Edna Valley, six miles south of San Luis Obispo. From Hwy. 101: Take California Blvd. exit to Johnson Ave. and drive southeast to Orcutt Rd. Continue southeast on Orcutt, past Biddle Ranch Rd.

🐾 Forty years after visiting pianist Ignacy Paderewski in Switzerland and sampling wine from his San Luis Obispo County vineyard, restaurateurs Norman and Carolyn Goss put down some regional roots of their own—30,000 vines, to be exact. With its cool climate, long sloping foothills, rich soil, and abundance of water, the Edna Valley proved to be the perfect spot for planting Chardonnay.

≈ ≈ ≈

Corbett Canyon Vineyards

2195 Corbett Canyon Road (P.O. Box 3159)
San Luis Obispo, California 93403
TEL: 805-544-5800
Also visit:
Corbett Canyon Tasting Room
353 Shell Beach Road
Shell Beach, California 93449
Tel: 805-773-3929
OWNER: Glenmore Distilleries Co.
WINEMAKER: Cary Gott
FOUNDED: 1979

AT A GLANCE
Tours & Tastings: Open Mon.–Sat. 10–5, Sun. 11–5. Tours scheduled Mon.–Fri. at 1 and 3; weekends at 11, 1, and 3; also by appointment. Tour covers the winemaking process, and imparts general information about wines. (Shell Beach tasting room is open daily May–Oct. 11–6, Nov.–Apr. 11–5.)
Vineyards: Grapes purchased from growers in Edna Valley, Santa Maria Valley, and San Luis Obispo County.
Wines: Chardonnay, Sauvignon Blanc, Cabernet Sauvignon, Zinfandel, White Zinfandel, Muscat Canelli, Gewürztraminer; proprietary blends; sparkling wines under Shadow Creek label.
Awards: Recent medal winners include: 1984 San Luis Obispo County Sauvignon Blanc—two golds, two silvers; 1983 Shadow Creek Blanc de Noir—two golds, bronze; 1983 Central Coast Cabernet Sauvignon—silver, three bronzes.
Picnic Area: Overlooks Edna Valley.
Retail Shop: Wines sold on-site.
Credit Cards: American Express, MasterCard, Visa.

Access for Disabled: Yes.
Foreign Languages: French, Arabic, Spanish.
Getting There: Winery is 7.2 miles south of San Luis Obispo. From Hwy. 101: Take Hinds Ave./Price Canyon exit and drive south on Broad St.—also called Hwy. 227—to Corbett Canyon Rd. (For tasting room, take Shell Beach Rd. exit off Hwy. 101.)
Special Wine & Other Events: Local craftspeople hold demonstrations and exhibit and sell their wares at Corbett Canyon's Christmas Festival.

≈ Corbett Canyon's mission-style winery is a healthy bike ride away from San Luis Obispo. A specialty here is the Coastal Classic line of both vintage-dated varietals and generic blends in convenient, one-liter, carafe-size bottles.

≈ ≈ ≈

Creston Manor Vineyards and Winery

17 Mile Post, Highway 58
Creston, California 93432
TEL: 805-238-7398
Also visit:
Creston Manor Tasting Room
Highway 101 and Vineyard Drive
Templeton, California 93465
Tel: 805-434-1399
GENERAL PARTNER: Lawrence Rosenbloom
WINEMAKER: Victor Hugo Roberts (enology degree from UC-Davis)
FOUNDED: 1982

AT A GLANCE
Tours & Tastings: Winery open by appointment only. Tasting room is open daily during spring, summer, and fall, 10–5; during winter, Tues.–Sun. 10–5.
Closed: Mon. in winter.
Vineyards: Ninety-five acres planted to Cabernet Sauvignon, Pinot Noir, Sauvignon Blanc, Chardonnay. Additional

grapes purchased from growers in Edna Valley and Santa Barbara County.

Wines: Chardonnay, Cabernet Sauvignon, Sauvignon Blanc, Pinot Noir.

Awards: Medals from the San Francisco Fair, the Los Angeles County Fair, and the Eastern International Wine Competition.

Retail Shop: Wines sold on-site.

Credit Cards: MasterCard, Visa.

Access for Disabled: Ramps to winery; rest rooms wheelchair accessible.

Getting There: Winery is southeast of Paso Robles, in the La Panza Mountains. Take Hwy. 101 to exit for Hwy. 58, Santa Margarita. Stay on Hwy. 58 through many turns to 17 Mile Post and Creston Manor.

🍂 This winery wasted no time in attracting admirers. The first release, a 1982 Sauvignon Blanc, won a medal after only a few months in the bottle, and winemaker Victor Hugo Roberts has been accumulating awards ever since. In addition to these honors, Creston Manor was one of the thirty wineries selected to participate in the fiftieth American Presidential Inaugural in January 1985.

🍂 🍂 🍂

Eberle Winery

Highway 45 East (P.O. Box 2459)
Paso Robles, California 93446
TEL: 805-238-9607
GENERAL MANAGER/WINEMAKER: W. Gary Eberle (Ph.D. in enology from UC-Davis; co-founded Estrella River Winery (see page 455) with half-brother Cliff Giacobine)
FOUNDED: 1981

AT A GLANCE

Tours & Tastings: Open daily; summer hours: 10–6, winter hours: 10–5. Oak-paneled tasting room has a huge fireplace and viewing bays of cellar floor and crush areas. No tours.

Closed: Thanksgiving, Christmas, New Year's Day.

Vineyards: Fifty-two acres planted to Chardonnay, Muscat, Cabernet Sauvignon.

Wines: Varietals from above grapes.

Awards: 1982 Cabernet Sauvignon: gold; 1983 Chardonnay: gold; 1981 Cabernet Sauvignon: silver.

Picnic Area: Patio adjoining the tasting room.

Retail Shop: Wines sold on-site.

Credit Cards: MasterCard, Visa.

Access for Disabled: None.

Getting There: Winery is in San Luis Obispo County, halfway between San Francisco and Los Angeles.

Special Wine & Other Events: "Dinners at the Winery," multicourse meals prepared by celebrated California chefs and complemented by products drawn from thirty-five wineries. Reservations required.

🍂 A former Penn State football star courted by the Detroit Lions, Gary Eberle was working on a doctorate in cytogenetics when his older half-brother enticed him into the wine trade. After a few years, Eberle struck out on his own. His enthusiasm proved contagious. Now his wife is a wine distributor and their daughter helps out in sales and promotion. "Some winemakers talk about wines as if they were their children," Eberle muses. "But I know that the difference between wine and children is that you can sit down and reason with a bottle of Cabernet."

🍂 🍂 🍂

El Paso de Robles Winery and Vineyard

Highway 46 West at Bethel Road (P.O. Box 548)
Paso Robles, California 93447
TEL: 805-238-6986

PRESIDENT: Joel Wildman
WINEMAKER: Stan Hall
FOUNDED: 1981

AT A GLANCE
Tours & Tastings: Open daily 10–5.
Winery tours by appointment.
Closed: Thanksgiving, Christmas.
Vineyards: Twenty-nine acres planted to
Zinfandel, Cabernet Sauvignon, Chenin
Blanc. Additional grapes purchased from
Paso Robles growers. Walnuts are also
grown on-site.
Wines: Chenin Blanc, Sauvignon Blanc,
White Zinfandel, Pinot Noir, Cabernet
Sauvignon, Merlot, Petite Sirah.
Awards: 1984 Petite Sirah: bronze; 1982
Merlot: gold; 1982 Zinfandel: bronze.
Picnic Area: Tables available.
Retail Shop: Wines, gifts, picnic lunches
sold on-site.
Credit Cards: MasterCard, Visa.
Access for Disabled: Parking area and
walkway wheelchair accessible.
Getting There: Winery is 30 miles west of
San Luis Obispo, 150 miles south of San
Francisco. From Hwy. 101: Take Hwy. 46
West 3 miles toward Hearst Castle.

🍇 This winery stands on the historic
Spanish land grant of its namesake, the
El Paso de Robles Ranch. Grapes have
been grown here since Franciscan fathers
first planted vineyards to produce wine
for the chain of Spanish missions along
the El Camino Real.

🍇 🍇 🍇

Estrella River Winery

Highway 46 East (Shandon Star Route)
Paso Robles, California 93447-0096
TEL: 805-238-6300
GENERAL PARTNER: Clifford R.
   Giacobine
WINEMAKER: Tom Meyers (M.S. in
   enology, UC-Davis)
FOUNDED: 1977

AT A GLANCE
Tours & Tastings: Open daily 10–5. Informal twenty-minute tours given on
request. Tours begin in the vineyard and
proceed to the crush facility; during harvest, visitors can taste the grapes that are
being crushed. Tour continues through
the fermentation area and views the cen-
trifuge to the aging room, where various
oaks are shown and described. The last
stops are the bottling line and the tasting
room.
Closed: Easter, Thanksgiving, Christmas.
Vineyards: 875 acres planted to Chardonnay, Sauvignon Blanc, Chenin Blanc,
Johannisberg Riesling, Cabernet Sauvignon, Zinfandel, French Syrah, Barbera.
Wines: Varietals from grapes above; also
Fumé Blanc, Johannisberg Riesling,
Muscat Canelli, Late Harvest Muscat
Canelli, Zinfandel, White Zinfandel,
Syrah Blanc, Blanc de Blanc sparkling
wine *methode champenoise.*
Awards: Recent medal winners include:
1982 Blanc de Blanc Star Cuvee—gold,
two silvers, five bronzes; 1980 Cabernet
Sauvignon—gold, three silvers; 1985
Muscat Canelli—gold, two silvers,
bronze; 1982 Syrah—three silvers, three
bronzes.
Picnic Area: Canopy-covered facility
overlooking vineyard.
Retail Shop: Wines sold on-site.
Credit Cards: MasterCard, Visa.
Access for Disabled: Yes.
Foreign Languages: Basic Spanish.
Getting There: Winery is seven miles east
of Paso Robles and thirty-five miles north
of San Luis Obispo. From Hwy. 101:
Take Hwy. 46 East seven miles.
Special Wine & Other Events: Estrella 10-
K Harvest Run, first Sun. in Nov.

🍇 Clifford Giacobine began planting
grapes in 1974; since then, his star has
steadily risen. Estrella is one of the district's largest wineries, and its wines consistently harvest a bumper crop of state,
national, and international awards. The

Cabernet Sauvignon is particularly noteworthy; to date, each vintage has won gold and silver medals. "Life is an Estrella Cabernet," enthuses Winemaker Tom Myers, who recommends that visitors buy a vertical selection of this varietal. Another stellar choice is the Syrah Blanc, perhaps the only wine of this type produced anywhere in the world. For a marvellous view, climb the observatory tower.

ð ð ð

Farview Farm Vineyard

Bethel Road (Route 2, Box 40)
Templeton, California 93465
TEL: 805-461-0699, 434-1133
OWNER/WINEMAKER: Ray Krause
  (alumnus of Fresno State University,
  where he majored in enology and
  minored in viticulture)
FOUNDED: 1979

AT A GLANCE
Tours & Tastings: Open daily 10–6. Tours upon request.
Closed: Easter, Christmas, New Year's Day.
Vineyards: Fifty-four acres planted to Chardonnay, Merlot, Zinfandel. Sauvignon Blanc grapes purchased from local growers.
Wines: Chardonnay, Merlot, Zinfandel, White Zinfandel, Savvy (dry Sauvignon Blanc), Eminence (late harvest Sauvignon Blanc).
Awards: 1980 Reserve Zinfandel: gold; 1985 White Zinfandel: silver; 1980 Merlot: silver.
Retail Shop: Wines sold on-site.
Credit Cards: MasterCard, Visa.
Access for Disabled: Ramps.
Getting There: Winery is in Templeton in northern San Luis Obispo County, just south of Paso Robles. Take Hwy. 101 south of Paso Robles to Hwy. 46 and go west for 1½ miles, then bear left on Bethel Rd.

ð Ray Krause began his enological career by working in the tasting room at Mirassou; three years later, he planted vineyards at this lovely, turn-of-the-century farmstead. But the property's rustic beauty wasn't its only selling point. "Every afternoon, sea breezes flowing from Cambria through the Highway 46 pass provide natural air-conditioning for my grapes," he explains. Kraus claims to make the world's driest White Zinfandel; but for dessert, Eminence, his late harvest Sauvignon Blanc, is as sweet as grapes plucked from the vine.

ð ð ð

The Firestone Vineyard

Zaca Station Road (P.O. Box 244)
Los Olivos, California 93441
TEL: 805-688-3940
OWNER: A. Brooks Firestone
WINEMAKER: Alison Green (B.S. in
  enology, UC-Davis)
FOUNDED: 1974

AT A GLANCE
Tours & Tastings: Open Mon.–Sat. 10–4. Tour the entire winery, where all operations take place, from crushing to sales. Tastings served in the spacious, Spanish-tiled reception area.
Closed: Sun., major holidays.
Vineyards: 270 acres planted to Chardonnay, Cabernet Sauvignon, Gewürztraminer, Johannisberg Riesling, Merlot, Pinot Noir, Sauvignon Blanc.
Wines: Varietals from grapes above, plus Cabernet Sauvignon Rosé, White Cabernet Sauvignon, Merlot Rosé, Gewürztraminer.
Awards: Recent medal winners include: 1978 Vintage Reserve Cabernet Sauvignon—gold, bronze; 1984 Johannisberg Riesling—three golds, silver; 1984 Cabernet Sauvignon Rosé—two golds, silver; 1983 Gewürztraminer—gold.
Retail Shop: Wines sold on-site.
Credit Cards: MasterCard, Visa.

Access for Disabled: Wheelchair accessible.

Getting There: Winery is 35 miles north of Santa Barbara, 30 miles south of Santa Maria. Take Hwy. 101 to Zaca Station Rd., 6½ miles north of Buellton, and turn east. Proceed 2½ miles to the winery.

᠘ Breaking with family tradition, Brooks Firestone—grandson of rubber magnate Harvey Firestone—decided he would rather make wine than tires. So he built a winery on land his father had purchased in the Santa Ynez Valley. One planting, the Ambassador Vineyard, commemorates his dad's tenure in Belgium representing the Nixon administration. Lately, Firestone bottlings have assumed a diplomatic role of their own: in London, Prime Minister Margaret Thatcher served a 1980 Chardonnay to Vice President George Bush, and President Ronald Reagan traveled to the People's Republic of China bearing a 1981 Chardonnay for Chairman Deng Xiaoping.

᠘ ᠘ ᠘

The Gainey Vineyard

3950 East Highway 246 (P.O. Box 910)
Santa Ynez, California 93460
TEL: 805-688-0558
OWNER: Daniel J. Gainey
WINEMAKER: Richard Longoria
   (formerly employed by the Firestone
   Vineyard and J. Carey Cellars)
FOUNDED: 1984

AT A GLANCE
Tours & Tastings: Open daily 10–5. Winery is a Spanish-style adobe with the traditional red-tile roof. Tours begin in the "Visitor's Vineyard" and proceed through all winery operations, including crushing and fermentation areas, the laboratory, and barrel and bottle aging cellars.
Closed: Thanksgiving, Christmas.

Vineyards: Fifty-four acres planted to Sauvignon Blanc, Chardonnay, Cabernet Sauvignon, Johannisberg Riesling, Merlot.

Wines: Varietals from the grapes above plus Late Harvest Johannisberg Riesling.

Awards: Recent medal winners include: 1985 Special Select Late Harvest Johannisberg Riesling—three golds, bronze; 1984 Sauvignon Blanc—two golds; 1984 Chardonnay—silver, five bronzes.

Retail Shop: Wines sold on-site.

Credit Cards: MasterCard, Visa.

Access for Disabled: Wheelchair accessible.

Foreign Languages: German.

Getting There: Winery is in Santa Barbara County, three miles east of Solvang on Hwy. 246.

Special Wine & Other Events: Cooking classes, wine-appreciation seminars, art shows, jazz and classical concerts.

᠘ "My personal interest in wines comes from spending more than twenty years in this region," says Daniel Gainey. "I wanted to produce something of significant value from land that holds so much promise. Also, since ancient Greek and Roman days, communities have gathered at vineyards to celebrate festivals of art, music, and drama. The events at Gainey Vineyard are part of that traditional wine experience."

᠘ ᠘ ᠘

Houtz Vineyards

2670 Ontiveros Road
Los Olivos, California 93441
TEL: 805-688-8664
OWNERS: David and Margy Houtz
WINEMAKER: John Kerr
FOUNDED: 1982

AT A GLANCE
Tours & Tastings: Open weekends 10–4, and by appointment. Small groups (fewer than twenty-five) only.

Vineyards: Sixteen acres planted to Chardonnay, Sauvignon Blanc, Cabernet Sauvignon. Chenin Blanc grapes bought from neighboring vineyards. Apples are also grown on-site.
Wines: Varietals from grapes above.
Awards: 1985 Sauvignon Blanc: gold; 1985 Chenin Blanc: silver; 1985 Chardonnay: bronze.
Picnic Area: Limited facilities available near the pond.
Retail Shop: Wines sold on-site.
Credit Cards: None.
Access for Disabled: None.
Getting There: Winery is thirty-five miles north of Santa Barbara. From Hwy. 154: Take Roblar west half a mile to Ontiveros Rd.

🐦 This small, rustic winery, with a capacity of 3,500 cases a year, is housed in a traditional California-style redwood barn. The surrounding farmstead is populated with a cheerful menagerie of ducks, dogs, cats, horses, sheep, goats, and chickens.

🐦 🐦 🐦

Leeward Winery

2784 Johnson Drive
Ventura, California 93003
TEL: 805-656-5054
OWNERS: Chuck Brigham and Chuck Gardner
WINEMAKER: John Albàn
FOUNDED: 1978

AT A GLANCE
Tours & Tastings: Open daily 10–4. Brief tours cover winemaking operation.
Closed: Easter, Thanksgiving, Christmas, New Year's Day.
Vineyards: Grapes purchased from growers in Monterey County and the Santa Maria, Alexander, and Edna valleys.
Wines: Chardonnay, Cabernet Sauvignon, Coral (Pinot Noir–Blanc de Noir blend).

Awards: 1984 Central Coast Chardonnay: two golds, three silvers, bronze; 1984 Edna Valley Chardonnay: vineyard designated "MacGregor Vineyard," gold, silver, two bronzes; 1985 Coral: two bronzes.
Retail Shop: Wines sold on-site.
Credit Cards: MasterCard, Visa.
Access for Disabled: Winery accommodates wheelchairs.
Getting There: Winery is thirty miles south of Santa Barbara. From Hwy. 101 in Ventura: travel north on Johnson Dr.
Special Wine & Other Events: Spring Open House, Memorial Day weekend (May); Harvest Weekend, Columbus Day weekend (Oct.); Fall Open House, Nov. (the weekend before Thanksgiving).

🐦 In 1982 Leeward dropped anchor at its current site, with a temperature-controlled barrel fermentation room especially designed for production of the winery's distinguished Chardonnays. Future releases will include Merlot. "We prefer to specialize in a few varieties and concentrate on making them well," notes president Chuck Brigham.

🐦 🐦 🐦

Maison Deutz Winery

453 Deutz Drive
Arroyo Grande, California 93420
TEL: 805-481-1763
PRESIDENT: Andre Lallier
WINEMAKER/GENERAL MANAGER: Harold A. Osborne (B.S., UC-Davis)
FOUNDED: 1983

AT A GLANCE
Tours & Tastings: Open daily, by appointment, 11–5.
Vineyards: 160 acres planted to Pinot Noir, Chardonnay, Pinot Blanc. Also buys grapes from Santa Maria Valley.
Wines: Sparkling wines only.
Retail Shop: Wines sold on-site.
Credit Cards: MasterCard, Visa.

Access for Disabled: Ramps, special rest rooms.
Foreign Languages: French, Spanish.
Getting There: Winery is 2 miles south of Arroyo Grande on Hwy. 101.

❧ The California arm of France's Deutz Champagne, this winery makes French-style sparkling wines by the time-honored *methode champenoise*—the grapes undergo malolactic fermentation, the bottles are hand riddled. Located just four miles inland, Maison Deutz's vineyards thrive in the damp, cool ocean breezes.

❧ ❧ ❧

Martin Brothers Winery

Buena Vista Drive (P.O. Box 2599)
Paso Robles, California 93447
TEL: 805-238-2520
OWNER: Martin and MacFarlane, Inc.
WINEMAKER: Dominic Martin (B.S. in enology, UC-Davis)
FOUNDED: 1981

AT A GLANCE
Tours & Tastings: Open daily 11–5. Special tours of this very small winery consist of an explanation of the winemaking process and a tasting and discussion of the wines. Sometimes barrel samples or old vintages are offered. The winery used to be a dairy, and tastings are conducted in a modified stucco barn.
Closed: Major holidays—Easter, Thanksgiving, Christmas.
Vineyards: Sixty acres planted to Zinfandel, Nebbiolo (Italian red grape), Sémillon, Chardonnay, Sauvignon Blanc, Chenin Blanc.
Wines: Varietals from grapes above.
Awards: Recent medal winners include: 1984 Dry Chenin Blanc—gold, three silvers; 1983 Sauvignon Blanc—gold, silver, three bronzes; 1983 Zinfandel—gold, two bronzes.
Picnic Area: Overlooking vineyards.

Retail Shop: Wines sold on-site.
Credit Cards: MasterCard, Visa.
Access for Disabled: Entrance and rest rooms wheelchair accessible.
Foreign Languages: German.
Getting There: Winery is 225 miles south of San Francisco, 225 miles north of Los Angeles and 35 miles north of San Luis Obispo. From Hwy. 101: Take Hwy. 46 East to Buena Vista Dr. and go north 1 mile.
Special Wine & Other Events: Mozart Festival, first Sun. in May, salutes Wolfgang Amadeus with wine, food, and music.

❧ The Martins cannot remember a time when they weren't interested in wines; their father was the advertising manager for a southern California winery. After Dominic Martin got winemaking experience at another establishment, he and his brother set up a shop of their own. Despite the winery's fraternal name, the Martin sisters and wives are represented on the sales and marketing staff, as well as on the board of directors.

❧ ❧ ❧

Mastantuono

1555 Willow Creek Road
Paso Robles, California 93446
TEL: 805-238-1078
Also visit:
Mastantuono Tasting Room
Highway 46 West and Vineyard Drive
Paso Robles, California 93446
Tel: 805-238-0676
OWNER/PRESIDENT: Pasquale Mastan
FOUNDED: 1977

AT A GLANCE
Tours & Tastings: Country-style tasting room open daily; winter hours: 10–5, summer hours: 10:30–6. Winery tours by appointment only.
Closed: Christmas.
Vineyards: Fifteen acres planted to

Zinfandel, Orange Muscat. Additional grapes purchased from Paso Robles growers.

Wines: Zinfandel, Muscat Canelli, Cabernet Sauvignon, White Zinfandel, Chardonnay.

Awards: 1984 Muscat Canelli: double gold; 1982 Templeton Zinfandel: two silvers; 1981 Zinfandel: gold.

Picnic Area: Yes.

Retail Shop: Wines, wine-related gifts, picnic items sold in tasting room.

Credit Cards: MasterCard, Visa.

Access for Disabled: Tasting room accommodates wheelchairs.

Getting There: Tasting room is in Paso Robles. From Hwy. 101: Take Hwy. 46 West to Vineyard Dr. "On the way to Hearst Castle."

&. An unabashed Zinfandel fan—his license plate reads "Zinman 1"—Pasquale Mastan learned winemaking from both of his Italian-born grandfathers. He has abbreviated his name, but he takes no shortcuts with his craft; he spent twenty-two years as a home vintner before perfecting the formula that gave him the confidence to turn pro. Then he sold his furniture-manufacturing business, and the airplanes and sports cars it subsidized, to establish a farm and vineyard a healthy distance from his old Los Angeles stomping grounds. Mastan's children also prefer the rural life; one daughter is a park ranger, the other runs her own goat-and-sheep ranch.

&. &. &.

The Ojai Vineyard

P.O. Box 952
Oakview, California 93022
TEL: 805-649-1674
OWNER/WINEMAKER: Adam Tolmach
FOUNDED: 1984

AT A GLANCE

Tours & Tastings: Open by appointment only. The winery is heavily insulated, built into the earth, and completely temperature controlled. With the flick of a switch it can be cooled down to a chilly 38 degrees Fahrenheit.

Vineyards: 5½ acres planted to Sirah, Sauvignon Blanc, Sémillon, Marsanne, Viognier.

Wines: Sirah, Sauvignon Blanc–Sémillon.

Awards: Does not enter competitions.

Retail Shop: Wines sold on-site.

Credit Cards: None.

Access for Disabled: None.

Getting There: Call for directions.

&. Vintner Adam Tolmach, who took viticulture and enology courses while earning a B.A. from the University of California–Davis, is trying to produce fine wines in a rustic style, with complexity and interest.

&. &. &.

Rolling Ridge Winery and Vineyards

Magdelina Drive (P.O. Box 250)
San Miguel, California 93451
TEL: 805-467-3130, 239-1456
GENERAL PARTNER: Alan G. S. West
WINEMAKER: Cliff Hight (enology degree from UC-Davis)
FOUNDED: 1983

AT A GLANCE

Tours & Tastings: Open by appointment only.

Vineyards: Forty acres planted to Cabernet Franc, Chardonnay, Petite Sirah, Zinfandel. Additional grapes purchased from local vineyards. Apple and apricot orchards also on-site.

Wines: Chardonnay, Cabernet Sauvignon, Zinfandel, Petite Sirah.

Awards: 1986 Red Table Wine (100 per-

cent Cabernet Sauvignon): gold; 1986 Red Table Wine (100 percent Petite Syrah): bronze.
Retail Shop: Wines sold on-site.
Credit Cards: None.
Access for Disabled: None.
Foreign Languages: Some Spanish.
Getting There: Winery is in San Luis Obispo County, nine miles north of Paso Robles, across the Salinas River. Take Hwy. 101 to Mission San Miguel, then take North River Rd. south of Magdelina Dr.

In the early 1970s, when he couldn't afford wines that he liked, Cliff Hight decided to produce a few of his own. Within a couple of years, he gave up his career in Santa Clara's booming electronics industry and opened a supply store serving home brewers and vintners while continuing to make his own. A Zinfandel Hight made from Paso Robles grapes proved so successful that he moved here in 1980.

Sanford Winery

7250 Santa Rosa Road
Buellton, California 93427
TEL: 805-688-3300
OWNERS: J. Richard and Thekla B. Sanford
WINEMAKER: Bruno D'Alfonso (enology degree from UC-Davis)
FOUNDED: 1983

AT A GLANCE
Tours & Tastings: Open Mon.–Sat. 11–4. Winery is constructed of adobe bricks manufactured on the property, a restored 738-acre ranch that was part of the original Santa Rosa land grant. No tours.
Closed: Sun., holidays.
Vineyards: 100 acres planted to Pinot Noir, Chardonnay, Sauvignon Blanc. Additional grapes purchased from Santa Barbara County growers.

Wines: Pinot Noir, Chardonnay, Sauvignon Blanc, Pinot Noir–Vin Gris, Merlot.
Awards: Recent medal winners include: 1983 Pinot Noir—platinum, silver, two bronzes; 1985 Sauvignon Blanc—silver; 1984 Pinot Noir–Vin Gris—two bronzes.
Picnic Area: Adjoins tasting room.
Retail Shop: Wines and poster-size label reproductions sold on-site.
Credit Cards: MasterCard, Visa.
Access for Disabled: Wheelchair accessible.
Foreign Languages: Spanish, French.
Getting There: In the Santa Ynez Valley, five miles west of Buellton. From Hwy. 101: Take Santa Rosa Rd. and drive west.

At this winery, enthusiasm for quality extends from the vintages to their packaging. Sanford's stunning labels feature specially commissioned paintings of California wildflowers.

Santa Barbara Winery

202 Anacapa Street
Santa Barbara, California 93101
TEL: 805-963-3633
PRESIDENT: Pierre Lafond
WINEMAKER: Bruce McGuire
FOUNDED: 1962

AT A GLANCE
Tours & Tastings: Open daily 9:30–5. Self-conducted winery tours during business hours; no tours of vineyards, but questions welcomed. Original watercolor label designs are on display.
Closed: Easter, Christmas.
Vineyards: Fifty-five acres planted to Pinot Noir, Riesling, Cabernet Sauvignon, Chardonnay, Chenin Blanc, Zinfandel, Sauvignon Blanc.
Wines: Chardonnay, Sauvignon Blanc, Dry Chenin Blanc, Cabernet Sauvignon, Zinfandel, White Riesling, Johannisberg

Riesling, White Zinfandel, Cabernet Sauvignon Blanc, Nouveau Zinfandel, Pinot Noir.

Awards: Recent medal winners include: 1985 Johannisberg Riesling Late Harvest—three golds; 1985 Cabernet Sauvignon Blanc—gold, silver, bronze; 1985 Zinfandel "Beausejour"—two golds, bronze; 1981 Cabernet Sauvignon Reserve—two bronzes.

Retail Shop: Wines sold on-site.

Credit Cards: American Express, MasterCard, Visa.

Access for Disabled: Wheelchair accessible.

Getting There: Winery is just a shell's throw from the beach in Santa Barbara, ninety miles north of Los Angeles. From Hwy. 101: Take Anacapa St. exit; winery is right there.

Special Wine & Other Events: Santa Barbara County Vintners Festival, Apr.

👄 Now approaching its thirtieth anniversary, this is the oldest winery in Santa Barbara County—and one of the most honored. Since winemaker Bruce McGuire joined the staff in 1981, Santa Barbara Winery has amassed more than fifty medals in state competitions.

👄 👄 👄

Santa Ynez Winery

343 North Refugio Road
Santa Ynez, California 93460
TEL: 805-688-8381
PRESIDENT: Boyd Bettencourt
WINEMAKER: Michael Brown (M.S. in enology, UC-Davis)
FOUNDED: 1976

AT A GLANCE

Tours & Tastings: Open daily 10–4. Tour starts in vineyard and proceeds through crushing and fermentation areas, barrel aging room, bottling room, and tasting room.

Closed: Thanksgiving, Christmas, other holidays.

Vineyards: 110 acres planted to Cabernet Sauvignon, Chardonnay, Gewürztraminer, Sauvignon Blanc, Sémillon, Johannisberg Riesling, and other vinifera varieties.

Wines: Chardonnay, Sauvignon Blanc, Sémillon, Cabernet Sauvignon, Johannisberg Riesling, Gewürztraminer, Muscat, Merlot; Riesling and Gewürztraminer dessert wines; Cabernet port.

Awards: Recent medal winners include: 1984 Sauvignon Blanc—two golds, silver, bronze; 1985 Johannisberg Riesling Reserve—gold, two bronzes; 1983 Chardonnay—gold, Best of Class.

Picnic Area: On redwood deck overlooking vineyards.

Retail Shop: Wines sold on-site.

Credit Cards: MasterCard, Visa.

Access for Disabled: Ramp for wheelchairs.

Getting There: Winery is between the towns of Solvang and Santa Ynez, 30 miles northwest of Santa Barbara. From either Hwy. 101 or Hwy. 154: Take Hwy. 246 to Refugio Rd. and drive ¾ mile south.

Special Wine & Other Events: Open house with music, food, and new and old wines: first Sat. in June; harvest party: last Sat. in Sept.

👄 After running experimental vineyards for the University of California–Davis, Boyd Bettencourt planted vines on his own property, a nineteenth-century college transformed into a dairy ranch by his wife's family. The college's chapel became part of the farmhouse. A few months before Santa Ynez's first crush, milk was the primary beverage bottled here. Some of the original dairy equipment is still used at the winery, along with stainless steel wine tanks, and imported and domestic oak barrels.

👄 👄 👄

Tobias Vineyards

2001 Kiler Canyon Road (P.O. Box 733)
Paso Robles, California 93446
TEL: 805-238-6380
OWNERS: Doug Beckett and Pat Wheeler
WINEMAKER: Pat Wheeler
FOUNDED: 1980

AT A GLANCE
Tours & Tastings: Open by appointment
only.
Vineyards: Grapes purchased from
growers in San Luis Obispo County.
Wines: Zinfandel, Petite Sirah, Cabernet
Sauvignon, Merlot, Chardonnay, Sauvi-
gnon Blanc.
Awards: Zinfandel: gold, silver; Petite
Sirah: silver.
Retail Shop: Wines sold on-site.
Credit Cards: None.
Access for Disabled: None.
Getting There: Winery is in San Luis
Obispo County. In Paso Robles, take
Hwy. 101 to Kiler Canyon Rd. and travel
west.

• Once he had vinified Templeton
grapes, Pat Wheeler wouldn't be satisfied
with anything else. He transplanted himself here from the Los Angeles area and
founded Tobias with partner Doug Beckett. Their winery is the smallest in San
Luis Obispo County, with an annual production of about 2,000 cases, primarily
robust reds. "We make big wines that
make a statement in your mouth," says
Wheeler.

• • •

Vega Vineyards Winery

9496 Santa Rosa Road (P.O. Box 1849)
Buellton, California 93427
TEL: 805-688-2415
PRESIDENT/WINEMAKER: William Mosby
FOUNDED: 1979

AT A GLANCE
Tours & Tastings: Open daily 10–4. Tours
upon request cover basic winery history,
grape growing, and winemaking. A more
specific tour is available with advance
notice. Winery, a Victorian-style carriage
house, is patterned after a local landmark
that was leveled by a 1977 windstorm.
Closed: Thanksgiving, Christmas, New
Year's Day.
Vineyards: Approximately forty acres
planted to White Riesling, Gewürztraminer, Pinot Noir. Chardonnay grapes
purchased from Santa Maria Hills Vineyard.
Wines: Johannisberg Riesling, Late Harvest Johannisberg Riesling, Gewürztraminer, Alsatian (Dry) Gewürztraminer,
Pinot Noir Chardonnay.
Awards: 1984 Johannisberg Riesling:
gold; 1985 Late Harvest Johannisberg
Riesling: bronze; 1985 Gewürztraminer:
bronze.
Retail Shop: Wines sold on-site.
Credit Cards: MasterCard, Visa.
Access for Disabled: Yes, no special fea-
tures.
Getting There: Winery is three miles west
of Solvang in the Santa Ynez Valley of
Santa Barbara County. Take Hwy. 101 to
Santa Rosa Rd. exit.
Special Wine & Other Events: Open
house, either last Sun. in Apr. or first
Sun. in May; Harvest Festival, first Sat.
in Oct.

• A dentist in nearby Lompoc,
William Mosby inherited his winemaking
hobby from his parents; he refines his
skills by attending several seminars each
year at the University of California–
Davis. (His son Gary continues the family tradition as winemaker at a nearby
winery.) Mosby's other interests include
historic preservation. He and his wife
live near the winery in a sprawling adobe
built here in 1853.

• • •

York Mountain Winery

York Mountain Road (Route 2, Box 191)
Templeton, California 93465
TEL: 805-238-3925
OWNER: Max Goldman
WINEMAKER: Steve Goldman
FOUNDED: 1882

AT A GLANCE

Tours & Tastings: Open daily 10–5. No tours. The original nineteenth-century winery, built of hand-formed bricks baked on the premises, still houses winery and tasting room. Cellar is visible from tasting room, which is decorated with wine medals and antique winemaking equipment once used at York Mountain.

Closed: Easter, Christmas, New Year's Day.

Vineyards: Five acres planted to Chardonnay, Pinot Noir, Zinfandel, Cabernet Sauvignon. Additional grapes purchased from local vineyards.

Wines: Chardonnay, Pinot Noir, Cabernet Sauvignon, Zinfandel, Merlot; red, white, and rosé table wines; champagne; port, dry sherry.

Awards: Recent medal winners include: 1982 Pinot Noir—two golds, Best of Class; 1981 Cabernet Sauvignon—silver; 1983 Merlot—silver; 1982 Zinfandel—bronze.

Retail Shop: Wines, wine jelly, herbed wine vinegar, and mustard sold on-site.

Credit Cards: None. Checks accepted.

Access for Disabled: Wheelchair accessible.

Getting There: Winery is in San Luis Obispo County, about thirty miles north of the city of San Luis Obispo. From Hwy. 101: Take Hwy. 46 about seven miles west to York Mt. Rd. York Mt. Rd. makes a loop off Hwy. 46; the winery is located in the middle of the loop.

⚓ This is one of the oldest wineries in the central coast area, with a particularly rich history. "Andrew York founded his winery on land deeded by President Ulysses S. Grant—we have the original deed," notes owner Max Goldman with pride. "In the 1920s, the pianist and vineyardist Ignacy Paderewski brought grapes here for processing from his nearby ranch. The winery remained in the York family until I purchased it in 1970." Goldman's son and daughter-in-law have a hand in the business. The former makes wines; the latter makes wine jelly and vinegar.

TO SEE & DO

Paso Robles sponsors a Wine Festival in May. During the rest of the year, you can sample the wares of many Paso Robles wineries just a short drive south on Highway 101 at Templeton Corner (Sixth and Main streets, Templeton; tel: 805-434-1763). Compare all the local Chardonnays, or concentrate on the products of just one establishment. The deli section will fill your picnic basket with regional delicacies, such as goat cheese cured in olive oil. Don't leave the area without surveying the Country Fair (Fourteenth and Pine Streets, Paso Robles; tel: 805-239-1001), where a host of antique stores share a single roof. Then head further south to San Luis Obispo, one of California's earliest Spanish settlements; masses are still said at the city's namesake, the Mission San Luis Obispo de Tolosa (782 Monterey Street; tel: 805-543-6850). The priests' simple quarters have been turned into a small museum housing Indian and Spanish artifacts. Accommodations were anything but simple at Hearst Castle, in nearby San Simeon (tel: 800-446-7275). Newspaper baron William Randolph Hearst built this overwhelming 100-room mansion as a private retreat, but the doors were opened to the public a few years after his death. Advance reservations for the tours are essential, so be sure to call well ahead. In August, the San Luis Obispo County Mid-State Fair pitches its tent in Paso Robles. Watch cowboys bust broncos, or hear how they break hearts—country western singers such as Dolly Parton and the Judds have made appearances here. For schedules and ticket information, write the General Manager, San Luis Obispo Mid-State Fair, P.O. Box 8, Paso Robles, CA 93446 (tel: 800-238-3565, local 238-3565).

Solvang is another historic Franciscan outpost, and Old Mission Santa Ines (1760 Mission Drive; tel: 805-688-4815) contains wonderful Indian frescoes. But in this century Solvang is better known as a Danish community, and most of the shops and restaurants have a Scandinavian theme, particularly during "Danish Days" in September. To work off the effects of the smorgasbord, visit Zaca Lake in Los Olivos. The aquatic activities include fishing, swimming, and boating; landlubbers can explore the bridle paths and hiking trails.

In the southern part of this region, the lovely beach resort of Santa Barbara boasts an elaborate eighteenth-century mission, with a museum and library (2201 Laguna Street at Los Olivos; tel: 805-682-4149). The Santa Barbara Presidio was founded at about the same time, but for a vastly different purpose: this restored adobe complex was the last Spanish fort built on the California coast. While you're in the neighborhood, stroll through the Santa Barbara County Courthouse (1120 Anacapa Street; tel: 805-962-6464), a handsome Spanish Colonial Revival building justly famed for both its architecture and its murals.

ACCOMMODATIONS

Atascadero:
Atascadero Inn
6505 Morro Road
Atascadero, California 93422
Tel: 805-46-MOTEL
A thirty-unit motel with a whirlpool spa to ease away the strain of all that wine tasting.

Avila Beach
San Luis Bay Inn
Avila Road
Avila Beach, California 93424
Tel: 805-595-2333; 800-592-5928 (in-state)
A luxurious beachside resort near San Luis Obispo with restaurant, tennis, heated pool, and golf. Afternoon tea and hors d'oeuvres.

Buellton
Best Western/Pea Soup Andersen's Inn
51 East Highway 246 (P.O. Box Y)
Buellton, California 93427
Tel: 805-688-3216; 800-528-1234
Pool and putting green, specialty restaurant.

Cambria
The J. Patrick House
2990 Burton Drive
Cambria, California 93428
Tel: 805-927-3812
Traditionally furnished log home, offering home-baked breakfast with fresh fruit and yogurt.

Los Olivos
Los Olivos Grand Hotel
2449 Baseline Avenue (P.O. Box 526)
Los Olivos, California 93441
Tel: 805-688-7788; 800-654-7263 (in-state); 800-626-7249 (out-of-state)
Twenty-one European-style guest rooms, all with fireplaces; fine elegant French cuisine.

Morro Bay
The Inn at Morro Bay
19 Country Club Lane
Morro Bay, California 93442
Tel: 805-772-5651
On the bay, with marina, swimming pool, and bicycles, surrounded by state park and golf course.

Oxnard
Embassy Suites
2101 Mandalay Beach Road
Oxnard, California 93030
Tel: 805-984-2500; 800-362-2779

On the beach, plus tennis and heated pool; 250 one- and two-bedroom suites. Restaurant and free breakfast.

Paso Robles
Black Oak Motor Lodge
1135 Twenty-fourth Street
Paso Robles, California 93446
Tel: 805-238-4740
On-premises dining at western-style restaurant, as well as a coffee shop. Well-equipped rooms, plus full aquatic activities.

Paso Robles Inn
1103 Spring Street
Paso Robles, California 93446
Tel: 805-238-2660
Moderately priced motel and restaurant; attractive grounds near Village Square.

San Luis Obispo
Madonna Inn
100 Madonna Road
San Luis Obispo, California 93401
Tel: 805-543-3000
Imagine over one hundred rooms, each decorated flamboyantly in a different style or period. Gold Rush Dining Room.

Santa Barbara
Brinkerhoff Inn
523 Brinkerhoff Avenue
Santa Barbara, California 93101
Tel: 805-963-7844; 800-BEST-BNB (in-state), 800-824-4845 (out-of-state)
Renovated nineteenth-century mansion located in the historic district. Continental breakfast usually served beneath a hundred-year-old avocado tree.

The Cheshire Cat Inn
36 West Valerio
Santa Barbara, California 93101
Tel: 805-569-1610
Two adjoining houses furnished country-style, with floral fabrics and wallpaper and English antiques. Guests may borrow the bicycles to pedal around town, then unwind in the hot tub. Continental breakfast, afternoon snack of wine and cheese.

El Encanto
1900 Lasuen Road
Santa Barbara, California 93103
Tel: 805-687-5000
A luxurious resort comprising one hundred well-equipped cottages. Excellent restaurant, gorgeous gardens, fountains, tennis courts, and a swimming pool.

Four Seasons Biltmore
1260 Channel Drive
Santa Barbara, California 93108
Tel: 805-969-2261; 800-228-9290
Imposing Spanish-style hotel complex, with ocean or mountain views. Swimming pools, hot tub, tennis courts, putting green, and croquet court. Two restaurants on-site.

Villa Rosa
15 Chapala Street
Santa Barbara, California 93101
Tel: 805-966-0851
A small, elegant Spanish-style inn "84 steps" from the beach. Some rooms with fireplace. Complimentary continental breakfast and afternoon wine and cheese.

Solvang
Ballard Inn
2436 Baseline Avenue
Solvang, California 93463
Tel: 805-688-7770
Fifteen rooms distinctively decorated to commemorate some aspect of Santa Ynez Valley. Continental breakfast and tea.

Danish Country Inn
1455 Mission Drive
Solvang, California 93463
Tel: 805-688-2018
Modern, well-run, and comfortable motel.

Ventura
Clocktower Inn on Mission Park
185 East Santa Clara
Ventura, California 93001
Tel: 805-652-0141
Southwestern decor overlooking the Old Mission.

RESTAURANTS

Buellton
The Hitching Post II
Highway 246
Buellton, California 93427
Tel: 805-688-0676
Oak-grilled beef is the headliner; enjoy it with the owner's wine, well worth sipping.

Pea Soup Anderson's
(See "Accommodations" for address, phone.) Delicious pea soup, tempting pastries.

Cambria
Brambles
4005 Burton Drive
Cambria, California 93428
Tel: 805-927-3305
Oak-grilled fish, prime rib. Victorian setting, wine list.

The Hamlet at Moonstone Gardens
Highway 1
Cambria, California 93428
Tel: 805-927-8649
Oceanview dining; on patio in good weather.

Ian's
2150 Center Street
Cambria, California 93428
Tel: 805-927-8649
California cuisine. Full-service bar with a lengthy wine list.

Sea Chest Oyster Bar
6216 Moonstone Beach Drive
Cambria, California 93428
Tel: 805-927-4514
A seafood house right on the ocean.

Los Olivos
Mattei's Tavern
Highway 154
Los Olivos, California 93441
Tel: 805-688-4820

Remington Restaurant
At the Los Olivos Grand Hotel (See listing under "Accommodations" for address and phone number). A menu inspired by French and California cuisine.

Ojai
The Ranch House
South Lomita Drive
Ojai, California 93023
Tel: 805-646-2360
Popular restaurant with a Continental menu. Outdoor dining plus a wine terrace.

Paso Robles
Chez K
1202 Pine Street
Paso Robles, California 93446
Tel: 805-239-3622
Continental dining in a French country atmosphere; patio seating is available. Extensive local wine list.

Joshua's
512 Thirteenth Street
Paso Robles, California 93446
Tel: 805-238-7515
In a former church, now the services are typical American foods. Local wine list.

Paso Robles Inn
(See listing under "Accommodations" for address and phone number.)
Chicken, ribs, good desserts in a rustic setting.

San Luis Obispo
Cafe Roma
1819 Los Osos
San Luis Obispo, California 93401
Tel: 805-541-6800
Informal Italian restaurant; a local favorite.

Carmel Beach
450 Margh Street
Tel: 805-543-FISH
San Luis Obispo, California 93401
An old home, now a seafood restaurant. Local wine list.

San Simeon
Europa
9240 Castillo Drive
San Simeon, California 93452

Tel: 805-927-3087
American and Continental food prepared with a Hungarian accent. Specialties include fresh seafood and pasta.

Santa Barbara
Andria's Seafood
214 State Street
Santa Barbara, California 93101
Tel: 805-962-8159
Enjoy fresh fish and pasta in a turn-of-the-century fish storehouse.

El Encanto
(See listing under "Accommodations" for address and telephone number.)

Maison Robert
1325 State Street
Santa Barbara, California 93101
Tel: 805-962-1325
French impressionist paintings line the walls, with cuisine to match. Everything fresh; fish a specialty.

Solvang
Ballard Store Restaurant
2449 Baseline Avenue
Solvang, California 93463
Tel: 805-688-5319
Continental cuisine, with lamb and duck specialties. Save room for the vast assortment of desserts. Wine cellar. Renovated country store.

Belle Terrasse
1564 Copenhagen Drive
Solvang, California 93463
Tel: 805-688-2762

The French name is misleading; this is an elegant Italian eatery in a Danish-American neighborhood.

Copenhagen Restaurant
467 Alisal Road
Solvang, California 93463
Tel: 805-688-6622
Continental dishes served Wed.–Mon. from 9 A.M. to 10 P.M.

Danish Inn
1547 Mission Drive
Solvang, California 93463
Tel: 805-688-4813
Something to please every palate: steaks, seafood, and a traditional Danish smorgasbord.

Templeton
Templeton Corners
590 Main Street
Templeton, California 93465
Tel: 805-434-1763

Ventura
Pierpont Inn
550 Sanjon Road
Ventura, California 93001
Tel: 805-643-6144
Gaze at the ocean while enjoying fresh seafood. Nice wine list.

Sportsman
53 South California Street
Ventura, California 93001
Tel: 805-643-2851
Charcoal-broiled specialties, outdoorsy decor.

🐌 SOUTHERN CALIFORNIA

Bounded by Los Angeles in the north and San Diego in the south, this region is the cradle of California's wine industry: the Franciscan monks who founded the San Diego mission in 1769 established the future state's first vineyard shortly thereafter. The padres reserved most of their crush for use at mass or at meals. Still, some bottles were sold to settlers, even if the thirst they suffered was not religious in nature.

During the next century, the wine business gradually fell into the hands of secular vintners. One of the earliest was Bordeaux-born Jean Louis Vignes, who imported European varietals to Los Angeles in the 1830s. A grapeful L.A. named Vignes Street in his honor. Today filmmakers outnumber winemakers, but a few wineries linger in the vicinity of Los Angeles. Visit San Antonio Winery, in the city itself; Ballona Creek Winery, in Culver City; and McLester Winery, in nearby Inglewood.

Urban sprawl has eaten up much of the once-famous Cucamonga wine district, but other parts of southern California are ripe for an enological revival. Vintages from the Temecula v.a. already enjoy an excellent reputation, and Rancho California Road, in Temecula proper, is becoming a small wine route of its own.

🐌 🐌 🐌

The Ballona Creek Winery

11837 Teale Street
Culver City, California 90230
TEL: 213-870-0320
OWNER: Gerard Antoine
FOUNDED: 1986

AT A GLANCE
Tours & Tastings: Open by appointment only.
Vineyards: Grapes purchased from central coast vineyards.
Wines: Chardonnay, Chenin Blanc.
Retail Shop: Wines sold on-site.
Credit Cards: None.
Access for Disabled: None.
Foreign Languages: French, Spanish, Chinese, German.
Getting There: Winery is at the junction of Hwy. 405 and Hwy. 90.
Special Wine & Other Events: St. Gerard Grande Fete.

🐌 Polyglot vintner Gerard Antoine owned vineyards and a château in France; in the United States, he has to content himself with a winery.

🐌 🐌 🐌

Callaway Vineyard and Winery

32720 Rancho California Road
Temecula, California 92390
TEL: 714-676-4001
OWNERS: Hiram Walker & Sons, Inc.
WINEMAKER: Dwayne Helmuth (B.S. in enology, California State University–Fresno)
FOUNDED: 1974

AT A GLANCE
Tours & Tastings: Open daily 10–5. Hourly tours cover vineyard, crush area, cellar, bottling line, and warehouse. An optional lecture-style tasting follows, for a nominal fee.
Closed: Easter, July Fourth, Thanksgiving, Christmas, New Year's Day.

Vineyards: 320 acres planted to Chardonnay, Sauvignon Blanc, Chenin Blanc. Additional grapes purchased from Temecula Valley growers.

Wines: Chardonnay, Chenin Blanc (dry), Pinot Blanc, Sauvignon Blanc, Fumé Blanc, White Riesling, Muscat Canelli, Gewürztraminer, Sweet Nancy (late harvest Chenin Blanc), Late Harvest Chardonnay.

Awards: Recent medal winners include: 1982 Sweet Nancy—gold, two bronzes; 1983 Late Harvest Chardonnay—gold, silver, four bronzes; 1984 Chardonnay—four silvers, three bronzes; 1984 Sauvignon Blanc—two silvers, two bronzes.

Picnic Area: Under a grape arbor, with tables indoors in case of bad weather.

Retail Shop: Wines sold on-site.

Credit Cards: American Express, MasterCard, Visa.

Access for Disabled: Wheelchair accessible; rest rooms are specially equipped.

Getting There: Winery is 60 miles north of San Diego and 90 miles southeast of Los Angeles. From I-15: Take Rancho California Rd. east 4½ miles to winery entrance.

Special Wine & Other Events: Temecula's Balloon and Wine Festival, May. Throughout the year, winery sponsors food and wine seminars, art exhibitions, and holiday events.

🐌 This is one of southern California's largest wineries, annually producing more than 140,000 cases of premium white wine.

🐌 🐌 🐌

Ferrara Winery

1120 West Fifteenth Street
Escondido, California 92025
TEL: 619-745-7632
OWNER: Gasper D. Ferrara
WINEMAKER: George D. Ferrara (B.S. in enology from Fresno State)
FOUNDED: 1932

AT A GLANCE

Tours & Tastings: Open Mon.–Fri. 9–5:30, weekends 10–5:30. Self-guided tours with carefully captioned photos show equipment in use. Small wine museum. Staff-guided tours by advance reservation.

Closed: Easter, Thanksgiving, Christmas, New Year's Day.

Vineyards: Three acres planted to Muscat of Alexandria. Additional grapes purchased from growers in the Pauma Valley of San Diego County, and Rancho California.

Wines: Carignane Blanc (a blush), Zinfandel, Sauvignon Blanc, Johannisberg Riesling; Generations III (a tawny port); cream sherry; Nectar de Luz (Muscat dessert wine); mint, coffee, cocoa, orange, and almond cordials; generics.

Awards: Generations III: silver, bronze; Almond de Luz: silver.

Retail Shop: Wines, nonalcoholic wine coolers, grape juices, wine marinade, books, and souvenirs sold on-site.

Credit Cards: MasterCard, Visa.

Access for Disabled: Ramp into tasting room, special rest rooms, wide gates, and concrete floors.

Foreign Languages: Spanish, Albanian, Italian.

Getting There: Winery is thirty miles north of San Diego, in San Diego County. From I-15: Take Ninth Ave. exit east. Bear right on Upas, right again on Fifteenth St.

🐌 In 1932, on the assurance that Prohibition was almost over, a savvy grape grower named George Ferrara began making wine for commercial distribution. Soon wineries sprouted throughout Escondido. Today Ferrara Winery is a state "Historical Point of Interest," the only winery left in Escondido's city limits. Managed by the founder's grandsons, Ferrara has expanded to a capacity of 100,000 gallons, but the sales policy hasn't changed: you buy only what you like, after you taste it.

ᴥ ᴥ ᴥ

Galleano Winery

4231 Wineville Road
Mira Loma, California 91752
TEL: 714-685-5376
PRESIDENT/OWNER: Donald D. Galleano
FOUNDED: 1933

AT A GLANCE
Tours & Tastings: Open Mon.–Sat. 9–6,
Sun. 10–5. Tours by appointment only.
Closed: Major holidays.
Vineyards: More than 600 leased acres
planted to Emerald Riesling, Burger, Palomino, Golden Chesla, Zinfandel, Sal-
vador-Alacante, Pinot Noir, Mission.
Wines: Zinfandel, Pinot Noir, White Zinfandel, Mission, Rhine wine; sauterne,
Chianti, Pink Chablis, Burgundy; sherry,
cream sherry, Marsala, Tokay, port,
sweet port, muscatel; brandy; champagne; coffee, apricot, anise, and crème
de menthe cordials; strawberry, loganberry, apricot, cherry, apple, raspberry,
red currant, and blackberry fruit wines.
Awards: White Zinfandel: bronze;
Chianti: bronze; sherry: honorable men-
tion.
Picnic Area: Yes. Sandwiches and snacks
may be purchased on-site.
Retail Shop: Wines, grape juices, hard
cider, food products, and gifts sold on-
site.
Credit Cards: None.
Access for Disabled: None.
Foreign Languages: Spanish, Italian.
Getting There: Winery is located in Mira
Loma, midway between Ontario and
Riverside, in the Cucamonga Valley. Take
Freeway 60 to Wineville Rd.
Special Wine & Other Events: Rancho
Cucamonga Wine Festival, date varies.

ᴥ Factories and apartment houses
have displaced many Cucamonga Valley
vineyards, but a few hardy establishments remain. "I will raise my children
in the life-style I grew up in," vows vintner Donald Galleano, whose grandfather
founded this winery. To keep his family's
label on local tables, Galleano tends a
scattered assortment of parcels that have
escaped the eastward spread of Los Angeles.

ᴥ ᴥ ᴥ

McLester Winery

10670-D South La Cienega Boulevard
Inglewood, California 90304
TEL: 213-641-9686
OWNER/WINEMAKER: Cecil McLester
FOUNDED: 1979

AT A GLANCE
Tours & Tastings: Open Sat. 12–5, other
times by appointment. Informal winery
tours and tasting, upon request.
Closed: Sun.–Fri.
Vineyards: All grapes purchased from
San Luis Obispo County growers.
Wines: Cabernet Sauvignon, Zinfandel,
Merlot, Fumé Blanc, Muscat; proprie-
tary blends.
Retail Shop: Wines sold on-site.
Credit Cards: MasterCard, Visa.
Access for Disabled: Yes.
Getting There: Winery is adjacent to Los
Angeles Airport. From Freeway 405:
Take the Imperial Hwy. off-ramp west to
La Cienega Blvd. and drive north.
Special Wine & Other Events: Open
houses every other month with special
discounts on selected wines.

ᴥ If you're flying in to Los Angeles,
you might get an aerial view of McLester
Winery. "We're located directly in the
flight pattern for L.A. Airport," reports
vintner Cecil McLester.

ᴥ ᴥ ᴥ

Mount Palomar Winery

33820 Rancho California Road
Temecula, California 92390
TEL: 714-676-5047

PROPRIETOR: John Poole
PRESIDENT: Peter Poole
WINEMAKER: Joseph Cherpin
FOUNDED: 1975

AT A GLANCE
Tours & Tastings: Open daily 9–5. Comprehensive tours lasting more than an hour depart Mon.–Fri. at 1:30 and 3:30, Sat.–Sun. 11:30, 1:30, and 3:30. Tour begins with vineyard and goes through winery with complete explanation.
Closed: Major holidays.
Vineyards: 101 acres planted to White Riesling, Chardonnay, Sauvignon Blanc, Chenin Blanc, Cabernet Sauvignon, Gamay Beaujolais, Sémillon, Palomino.
Wines: Varietals from above grapes plus cocktail sherry, cream sherry, Cabernet Sauvignon port.
Awards: "Too numerous to list."
Picnic Area: Lovely locations, including a covered pavillion, and a hilltop site overlooking vineyards.
Retail Shop: Wines, wine jellies, red wine vinegar, crystal stemware, books, and gourmet food sold on-site.
Credit Cards: MasterCard, Visa.
Access for Disabled: Tasting room, rest rooms, some picnic tables wheelchair accessible.
Foreign Languages: French, Spanish.
Getting There: Winery is in Riverside County, fifty miles north of San Diego and sixty-five miles south of Los Angeles. From I-15: Take Rancho California Rd. exit and drive five miles east.
Special Wine & Other Events: Temecula's Wine and Balloon Festival, third weekend of May. In mid-Nov., Mount Palomar Winery celebrates release of Gamay Beaujolais Nouveau with an elegant dinner party; by reservation only.

🍂 Locals know John Poole as the founder of radio station KBIG in Catalina Island. Previously he was a tuna fisherman, merchant seaman, shipboard radio operator, U.S. Army officer, and radar instructor. This jack-of-all-trades sold KBIG in 1969 in order to purchase and plant his first vineyard; Mount Palomar began generating liquid assets six years later. In some senses, Poole is still in the broadcasting business: he remains his winery's most animated and entertaining tour guide.

🍂 🍂 🍂

San Antonio Winery

737 Lamar Street
Los Angeles, California 90031
TEL: 213-223-1401
   Additional San Antonio Winery locations:
   86 West Colorado Boulevard
   Pasadena, California 91105
   Tel: 818-449-2648
   1418 South Pacific Coast Highway
   Redondo Beach, California 90277
   Tel: 213-316-4585
   2801 South Milliken
   Ontario/Pomona, California 91761
   Tel: 714-947-3995
   Hi-Time Cellars
   495 East Seventeenth Streeth
   Newport–Costa Mesa, California 92627
   Tel: 714-548-9314
   9411 Reseda Boulevard
   Northridge, California 91324
   Tel: 818-701-0556
   2122 North Tustin Avenue
   Santa Ana–Tustin, California 92701
   Tel: 714-547-8792
PRESIDENT: Steve Riboli
FOUNDED: 1917

AT A GLANCE
Tours & Tastings: Open Mon.–Sat. 10–4, Sun. 11–4. Winery is a charming, tile-roofed pueblo tucked into an industrial zone. Self-guided tours go through wine cellars, where an antique corkscrew collection and other wine-related memorabilia are displayed.

Closed: Holidays.
Vineyards: 300 owned and 600 leased acres planted to vinifera varieties.
Wines: Chardonnay, Cabernet Sauvignon, Johannisberg Riesling, White Zinfandel, White Barbera, Cabernet Blanc, Chenin Blanc, Green Hungarian, French Colombard, Muscat Canelli; champagnes; brandy; sherry, cream sherry, port, sweet vermouth, dry vermouth; Amaretto, coffee, chocolate, fruit liqueurs; ollaliberry, raspberry, pomegranate, apricot, strawberry, plum, blackberry, and Concord grape wines.
Awards: More than 200 national and international awards since 1963.
Picnic Area: In gardens.
Restaurant: Sandwiches and Italian specialties served in cafeteria-style restaurant, which does not accept credit cards (tel: 213-223-2236).
Retail Shop: Wines, wine and herb vinegars, cheeses, and crackers sold on-site. Winery recycles its own bottles and awards rebates on returned empties.
Credit Cards: MasterCard, Visa.
Access for Disabled: Winery accommodates wheelchairs.
Foreign Languages: Spanish, Japanese, Chinese, Italian.
Getting There: Winery is in Los Angeles, near Civic Center. Take I-5 to Main St. exit. On the 1700-1800 block of North Main St., turn south onto Lamar St.
Special Wine & Other Events: Live music on Sun., 12–4. Los Angeles's last producing winery is a cherished local landmark, still owned and supervised by the founder's descendants. San Antonio's methods and quality haven't changed—wines age in wooden casks imported from Europe over a century ago. "It's more a way of life than a business," comments Steve Riboli. This operation is small but hardy, having survived both Prohibition and urban sprawl; in 1966, when a growing public transportation center threatened to engulf San Antonio, the winery was designed a Cultural His-

torical Monument by the Los Angeles Cultural Heritage Board.

TO SEE & DO

Los Angeles beckons fans of the big and small screens. Stroll along Hollywood Boulevard's star-studded Walk of Fame and compare your hand—or foot—to the prints in front of Mann's Chinese Theater (6925 Hollywood Boulevard). Then go behind the scenes on a tour of Universal Studios (100 Universal City Plaza, Universal City; tel: 818-508-9600). Or visit NBC's television studios at 3000 West Alameda Avenue in beautiful downtown Burbank (tel: 818-840-3537). Mickey, Minnie, and Donald reign over Disneyland (1313 Harbor Boulevard, Anaheim; tel: 714-999-4000). If you really want to rub shoulders with celebrities, plan a shopping expedition to Rodeo Drive, the address of L.A.'s most exclusive stores. Equally fascinating creatures live in the Los Angeles Zoo (5333 Zoo Drive; tel: 213-666-4090), inside Griffith Park. Pay your respects to the lions and tigers, then reach for the (real) stars at Griffith Observatory and Planetarium (2800 East Observatory Road; tel: 213-664-1191). Among Griffith Park's many amenities are extensive trails for humans and horses, and concerts in the Greek Theater. The last remains of woolly mammoths, saber-toothed tigers, and other burly Ice Age beasts fill the George C. Page Museum of La Brea Discoveries (5801 Wilshire Boulevard; tel: 213-936-2230). Urban archeologists will prefer El Pueblo de Los Angeles State Historic Park, with its mix of nineteenth-century Spanish and Mexican buildings and twentieth-century shops and restaurants. For additional information, consult the Greater Los Angeles Visitors and Convention Bureau, 5051 South Flower Street, Los Angeles, California 90071 (tel: 213-239-0204).

To the south, San Diego's Balboa Park has something for everyone. Attractions include the Reuben H. Fleet Space Theater and Science Center, the largest planetarium in the United States (tel: 619-238-1168); the San Diego Museum of Art (tel: 619-232-7931); and the San Diego Hall of Champions—a gallery of sports heroes (tel: 619-234-2544). The San Diego Zoo (tel: 619-234-3153) enjoys international fame; Sea World (1720 South Shores Road; tel: 619-226-3901) is also worth a detour. Continue your study of marine biology with a San Diego Harbor Excursion (tel: 619-233-6872). Then board the ships at the Maritime Museum Association (1306 North Harbor Boulevard; tel: 619-234-9153). Upon returning to terra firma, head for Old Town San Diego State Historic Park (2645 San Diego Avenue). This complex of some of the city's earliest buildings comprises both adobes and wood frames. The San Diego Convention and Visitors Bureau (11 Horton Plaza, San Diego, California 92101; tel: 619-263-1212) can supply the details about these and other sights.

ACCOMMODATIONS

For more information on places to stay and eat in the Los Angeles and San Diego area, contact the tourist offices listed above.

La Jolla
The Bed & Breakfast Inn at La Jolla
7753 Draper Avenue
La Jolla, California 92037
Tel: 619-456-2066
In this "Cubist" pink stucco inn designed by architect Irving Gill, each room hs a different feel, from romantic to elegant. Have your Continental breakfast in bed; the china matches your room's decor.

Colonial Inn
910 Prospect Street
La Jolla, California 92037
Tel: 619-454-2181; 800-826-1278 (instate); 800-832-5525 (out-of-state)

A small hotel just a block from the beach, with large, comfortable rooms, lush gardens, and lovely views. Restaurant downstairs. Continental breakfast.

Los Angeles
Hotel Bel-Air
701 Stone Canyon Road
Los Angeles, California 90077
Tel: 213-472-1211; 800-223-6800
Only minutes from Beverly Hills, this luxurious retreat is a world unto itself. The grounds are magnificent, and swans swim in the hotel pond. Many rooms have patios and Jacuzzis. Swimming pool, piano bar, excellent restaurant.

Terrace Manor
1353 Alvarado Terrace
Los Angeles, California 90006
Tel: 213-381-1478
Hosts Sandy and Shirley Spillman welcome you to their richly decorated, turn-of-the-century landmark in downtown Los Angeles. Ample breakfasts, complimentary wine and hors d'oeuvres during afternoon social hour.

North Hollywood
La Maida House
11159 La Maida Street
North Hollywood, California 91601
Tel: 818-769-3857
A sprawling villa, built in the 1920s and lavishly trimmed in marble and mahogany. Owner Megan Timothy has decorated La Maida with her own stained glass; she takes time away from her studio to prepare wonderful meals, using vegetables grown in the inn's gardens.

RESTAURANTS

Limited space does not permit us to do justice to this area's fabulous restaurants. For suggestions, contact the information sources listed above.

9
The Northwest and Beyond
❦

Weston Vineyards, Caldwell, Idaho

❧*T*asting is believing. The rich soil of Idaho, Oregon, and Washington has proven remarkably hospitable to vinifera grapes—and with good reason. Vintners in this burgeoning wine region proudly explain that their vineyards are planted in the same brisk latitudes that define those hallowed French wine districts, Burgundy and Bordeaux. And who are these enterprising new winemakers? Many of them bottled their first vintages in California, then headed north (and east) where land was inexpensive and undeveloped.

Predictably, this region favors grapes that thrive in cold weather. Idaho and Washington remain best known for whites, such as Chardonnay, Gewürztraminer, and Riesling, while Oregon already enjoys international acclaim for the "Burgundy" red, Pinot Noir.

As balmy as the northwest is chilly, Hawaii has a long enological history going back more than a century. But in one respect, this state takes after its northwestern sisters: the only Hawaiian winery producing island-grown wine was founded by former Californians.

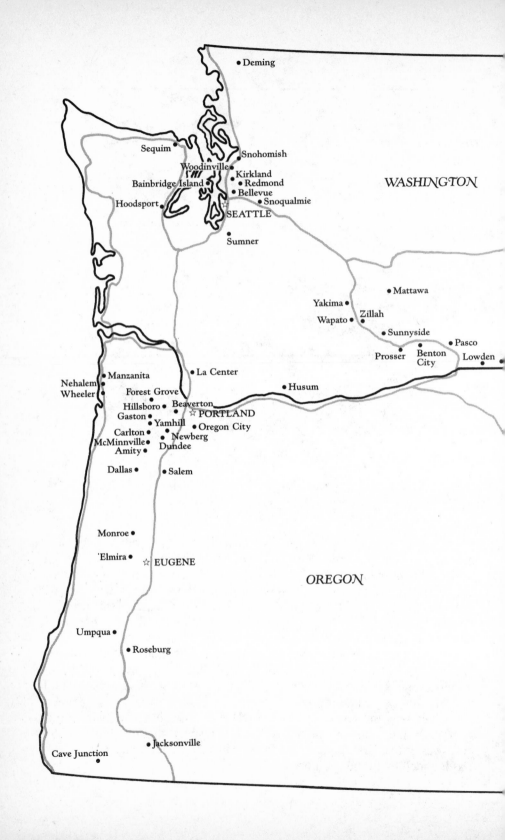

WASHINGTON

Deming

Sequim

Snohomish
Woodinville
Kirkland
Bainbridge Island
Redmond
Hoodsport
Bellevue
Snoqualmie
SEATTLE

Sumner

Mattawa

Yakima
Zillah
Wapato

Sunnyside

Prosser
Benton
City
Pasco
Lowden

Manzanita
La Center

Nehalem
Wheeler
Forest Grove
Husum

Hillsboro
Beaverton
Gaston
PORTLAND
Yamhill
Carlton
Oregon City
Newberg
McMinnville
Dundee
Amity

Dallas
Salem

Monroe

'Elmira
EUGENE

OREGON

Umpqua

Roseburg

Jacksonville

Cave Junction

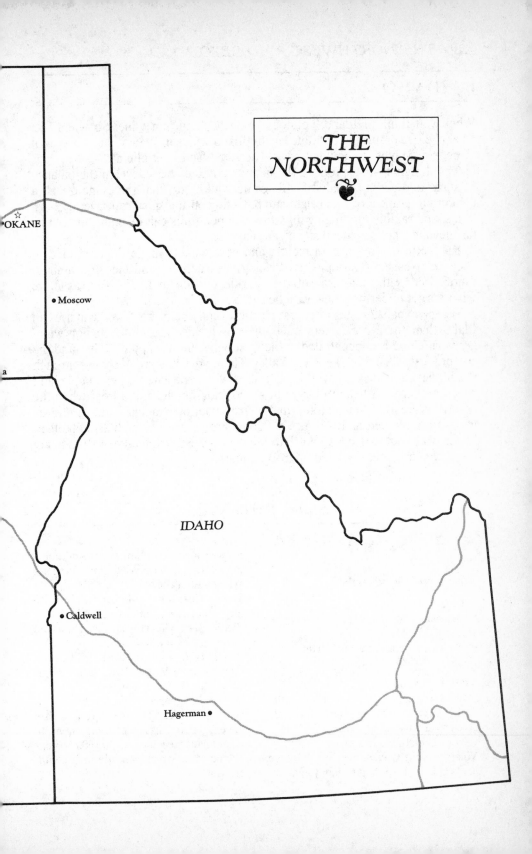

❧ IDAHO

When you think of Idaho, potatoes come to mind, not wine. So when Ste. Chapelle began turning out noteworthy Idaho wines in 1976, it surprised a lot of people. Maybe it shouldn't have. The same factors of climate—warm days and cool nights—that produce the famous potatoes help develop the balance of sugar and acidity needed for first-rate wines. Not that the climate isn't a concern to grape growers: bright sun reflecting off the snow can severely burn vines, and rapidly fluctuating nighttime temperatures can be injurious, but so far they have not produced significant damage.

The warm dry days, cool nights, and cold winters make the area kind to such cold-resistant varieties as Riesling, Chardonnay, and Gewürztraminer. Pinot Noir is the mainstay of the sparklers made in Idaho, and, as more wineries get under way, new varieties are sure to be tested.

Recent expansion has been rather slow, and there are fewer wineries in Idaho than there are fingers on both your hands. The state's major wine-growing region is concentrated in the west between the capital, Boise, and the sumptuously fertile Snake River Valley. There your wine routes wind through small hills and valleys, a fruit basket filled with prize cherry, pear, apple, and peach orchards. A beautiful sight at spring blossoming, and a treat when the ripe fruits are for sale in markets and on pick-your-own ranches. The vineyards to visit are planted at 1,000 feet but some are perched as high as 2,500 feet. These wine routes also lead north to Moscow, where, if you take one too many turns, you might easily wind up in Washington.

Snake River Valley

❧ ❧ ❧

Rose Creek Vineyards

111 West Hagerman Avenue
Hagerman, Idaho 83332
TEL: 208-837-4413
OWNERS: Jamie and Susan Martin
FOUNDED: 1985

AT A GLANCE
Tours & Tastings: Mon.–Sun. 11:30–5:30, or by appointment. Tastings and tours given to anyone interested.
Closed: Christmas, Easter.
Vineyards: Thirty-eight owned and leased acres planted to Chardonnay, Johan-nisberg Riesling, Pinot Noir. Additional Pinot Noir is purchased from Oregon's Willamette Valley.
Wines: Chardonnay, Johannisberg Riesling, Pinot Noir, Cabernet Sauvignon.
Picnic Area: Nearby scenic Thousand Spring outlet for Lost River.
Retail Shop: Wines, cheeses, fruits.
Credit Cards: MasterCard, Visa.
Access for Disabled: None.
Foreign Languages: None.
Getting There: 1½ hours from Boise. Take I-84 to Bliss and follow signs to Hagerman; the winery is on 1000 Springs Scenic Rte., which runs through southern Idaho.

The Martins' small family-run winery at the south end of Hagerman blends dramatic river scenery with a bit of history. The winery is in the cellar of a landmark built in 1887 as the Morris Roberts Store. Three-foot-thick lava walls maintain proper temperatures for making wines and aging them. Rose Creek's elegant label by local artist Pamela Swenson Knox captures the scenic beauty of river canyons and vines tinged with the colors of sunset. Nearby are beautiful hiking trails and river raft rentals.

ᶻᵃ ᶻᵃ ᶻᵃ

Ste. Chapelle

Highway 55 (Lowell Road)
Route 4 (P.O. Box 775)
Caldwell, Idaho 83605
TEL: 208-888-7222
OWNERS: The Symms family
WINEMAKER: Mimi Mook (formerly of
   J. Lohr, San Jose)
FOUNDED: 1976

AT A GLANCE
Tours & Tastings: Summer: Mon.–Sat. 10–6; winter: 10–5, Sun. 12–5. Twenty-five-minute guided tours on the hour show winemaking and cellaring, include tasting.
Closed: Thanksgiving, Christmas, Easter.
Vineyards: 190 acres owned, 200 acres leased, in Idaho and Washington. Planted to Riesling, Chardonnay, Chenin Blanc, Gewürztraminer, Pinot Noir.
Wines: Fifteen wines focus on vintage-dated, white varietals; 25 percent of production is champagnes, including a *methode champenoise* Blanc de Noir. Also Spicewein, a blend of Riesling and Gewürztraminer, and Washington Muscat Canelli, a dessert wine.
Awards: Chardonnay, Johannisberg Riesling are most frequently cited.
Picnic Area: Handsomely landscaped lawns overlook vineyards.

Retail Shop: Wines, wine accessories, some Idaho-produced foods.
Credit Cards: MasterCard, Visa.
Access for Disabled: Ramps to both front and back doors.
Getting There: From Boise: Take I-84 West to Marsing/Karcher Mall exit; then go right 200 yards to Karcher Rd. (Hwy. 55). Turn left and travel thirteen miles to winery signs; turn left at Lowell Rd. for 300 yards to winery on left.
Special Wine & Other Events: June–Aug.: Sunday Jazz Concerts, 1–4:30.

From a winery that began in a farmhouse in 1976, Ste. Chapelle has grown to be one of the largest in the Northwest and one of the industry's greatest success stories. It was Ste. Chapelle's prizewinning Riesling in 1976 that showed the world Idaho could produce critically acclaimed wines.

Today, visitors see a handsome winery styled after the famous Ste. Chapelle church in Paris. They learn about wines in an oak-finished tasting room with huge multipane windows offering gorgeous views of vineyards and orchards.

In all this elegance, nothing but notes in the winery's brochure hints of Ste. Chapelle's modest beginnings. From an initial output of 600 cases, Ste. Chapelle now produces about 110,000 cases annually. Widely distributed, the wines are sold throughout the United States and in some countries abroad.

ᶻᵃ ᶻᵃ ᶻᵃ

Weston

Route 4, Box 759
Caldwell, Idaho 83605
TEL: 208-454-1682
OWNERS: C. H. Weston III and C. H.
   Weston, Jr.
WINEMAKER: C. H. Weston III
FOUNDED: 1982

AT A GLANCE

Tours & Tastings: Mon.–Sun. 11–5. Strictly informal tours and tastings.

Vineyards: Ten acres at Caldwell, 2,700 feet above sea level, and forty acres leased along the Snake River in Treasure Valley, ten minutes to the south. Planted to Riesling, Chardonnay, Gewürztraminer, Sémillon, Pinot Noir, Cabernet Sauvignon, Chenin Blanc.

Wines: Varietals, some vintage-dated, from above grapes.

Awards: White Riesling, Chardonnay; Blanc de Blanc, a blend of Chardonnay and Riesling; at various Northwest competitions.

Retail Shop: Wines sold on-site.

Credit Cards: MasterCard, Visa.

Access for Disabled: Limited.

Foreign Languages: None.

Getting There: Weston is on Hwy. 55 about one mile before Ste. Chapelle. From Boise: Take I-84 to Marsing/Karcher Mall exit 35 at Nampa. Go right approximately 200 yards to Karcher Rd. (Hwy. 55), turn left and travel approximately twelve miles on Hwy. 55 to winery's doorstep.

Special Wine & Other Events: Last Sat. in June: Idaho Home Winemakers Festival—a chance to try a statewide assortment of amateurs' wines. Entire month of Oct.: crush open to public.

🍂 Though winery founder Weston has worked for Ste. Chapelle and Sebastiani, his winery is a simpler place. At 2,700 feet it is said to be the highest vineyard in the Northwest. Everything is family-done at Weston, from tending the vineyard to the handsome hand-painted labels created by son Jeff.

Area Events: Winter carnival in February and dogsled races in March, both at McCall. In and about wine country itself, action starts in late April into May with quarter horse racing at Emmett, a gem and mineral show at Caldwell, and the Apple Blossom Festival at Payette (held from the last week in April through the first weekend in May), with the Queen's Ball, an ice cream social, a pancake breakfast, and many other activities. In August is the Annual River Fun Run on the Snake River.

TO SEE & DO

This area has been nicknamed Idaho's "Treasureland" and is indeed chock full of riches for visitors who enjoy sightseeing and adventuring. Alpine lakes, bone-dry deserts, ghost towns, six state parks, and three skiing areas offer pleasures for visitors. At the hub of it all is the capital, Boise, known as the gateway to Sun Valley—and now also to wine country. Here a tour train takes in the city sights; visitors can also experience all kinds of recreational activities in one of America's largest national forests, covering 2.6 million acres (Boise National Forest, 1750 Front Street, Boise, Idaho 83702; tel: 208-344-1516). Adventure further to find tumbling waterfalls and thrill-a-minute Snake River guided float trips that call on birds of prey in their nesting places. Just about any place in the area is picnic-perfect, but better yet, add a bottle of local wine. A plus for picnickers and travelers in general are the many fruit stands and pick-it-yourself ranches for produce to nibble at once or take along with you. For more information, contact Treasureland, P.O. Box 2106, Boise, Idaho 83701; tel: 800-635-5240 or 208-344-7777.

ACCOMMODATIONS

Boise is a major city well represented by all the major chains: Best Western, Holiday Inn, Nendel's, Red Lion, Rodeway, and Super 8. For information on guest ranches, contact the Idaho Travel Council (see Appendix for address).

Bed and Breakfasts and Inns
Bed and Breakfast of Idaho
P.O. Box 7323
Boise, Idaho 83702
Tel: 208-336-5174

Idaho Heritage Inn
109 West Idaho Street
Boise, Idaho 83702
Tel: 208-342-8066
An inviting B&B in the historic Warm Springs District; rates include Continental breakfast and Idaho wine.

Hotels and Inns
Idanha Hotel
928 Main Street
Boise, Idaho 83702
Tel: 208-342-3611
Downtown, has deluxe historic suites; complimentary Continental breakfast; limo to airport.

Owyhee Plaza
1109 Main Street
Boise, Idaho 83702
Tel: 208-343-4611; 800-821-7500 (in
    state); 800-233-4611 (out-of-state)
Dates from 1910 and now features one hundred rooms and suites, private baths, telephone, TV. Swimming pool.

Elsewhere Near Wineries
Everygreen Bed and Breakfast
Caldwell, Idaho 83605
Tel: 208-726-9502

Van Slyke Home
Tel: 208-459-2631
A B&B neighboring Weston winery.

Greystone Hotel
120 12th Avenue South
Nampa, Idaho 83651
Tel: 208-466-4601
Historic building, recently renovated.

Sundowner Motel
1008 Arthur Street
Caldwell, Idaho 83605
Tel: 208-459-1585
Seventy rooms, Continental breakfast; pool, wheelchair access.

RESTAURANTS
Gamekeeper
Owyhee Plaza Hotel
1109 Main Street
Boise, Idaho 83702
Tel: 208-343-4611
Continental cuisine. Good wine list. (Also see under "Accommodations.")

Jake's
100 South 6th Street
Boise, Idaho 83702
Tel: 208-336-1670
In the old part of town with antique cash registers on display, this restaurant serves good seafood and steaks. Wine list.

Prime Minister Oyster Bar
9 South Orchard
Boise, Idaho 83705
Tel: 208-383-9011
Oysters, as the name implies, are the specialty here, but a prime rib fancier would be pleased as well. Salad bar. Wine list. Closed major holidays. Reservations required.

Sun Valley/Ketchum
Space does not permit mention of more than a few of the choice spots recommended for wine lists as well as foods served.

Christiania
303 Walnut Street
Ketchum, Idaho 83340
Tel: 208-726-3388
Continental dishes, with veal a specialty. Wine list. Decadent desserts. Dine outdoors. Open in spring and fall.

Evergreen
171 First Avenue
Ketchum, Idaho 83340
Tel: 208-726-3888
Old house turned into a delightful restaurant with terrific view of Old Baldy; outdoor dining area, too. Serves Continental menu with duckling among the headliners.

Le Club
716 North Main
Ketchum, Idaho 83340
Tel: 208-726-4386
Chef/owner knows how to dish up delicious trout among other dishes. Does own baking.

Louie's
311 Leadville North
Ketchum, Idaho 83340
Tel: 208-726-7775
In century-old church glowing with stained glass; enjoy pizza and other Italian specialties.

Northern Idaho

Camas Winery

521 Moore
Moscow, Idaho 83843
TEL: 208-882-0214
OWNERS/WINEMAKERS: Stuart and
   Susan Scott
FOUNDED: 1983

AT A GLANCE

Tours & Tastings: By appointment only.
Vineyards: 3,000-ft. elevation gives viniferas slim chance of surviving; all grapes purchased from growers in Columbia Valley, Washington, and Clearwater Valley, Idaho.
Wines: Chardonnay, Cabernet Sauvignon, White Riesling; Hog Heaven Red and White, Blanc de Noir. Newest release is Sarah's Blush.
Awards: Cabernet Sauvignon in Northwest Wine Competition; Blanc de Noir in Spokane Wine Festival.
Retail Shop: Wines, Camas and Hog Heaven logo sweatshirts and T-shirts.
Credit Cards: None.
Access for Disabled: None.
Foreign Languages: None.
Getting There: Take Main St. north to D St., go east on D to Moore, north on Moore to #521.
Special Wine & Other Events: Third weekend in Feb.: Mardi Gras; first weekend in May: Renaissance Faire; July: repertory theater at University of Idaho, musical theater at WSU in Pullman—a mere sampling. With two universities within eight miles, there are always concerts, symphonies, lectures, football and basketball games, and umpteen other things going on around here. No summer visit would be complete without a stop at the Farmers' Market (every Sat. morning on Friendship Square), with an inviting mélange of produce, flowers, crafts, baked goods, and music.

🍂 Taking a cue from Tom Sawyer and his whitewash fence brigade, the Scotts get everyone interested in helping with chores around the basement/backyard winery. They—and visitors who wish to—crush and press grapes, bottle, and foil and label about 1,200 cases of wine each year. Work like this has ample rewards—a close-up look at how wine is made, followed by a tasting guided by the owners themselves.

The winery is named for the Camas lily, a wildflower native to the Palouse that once turned this rolling terrain into an ocean of blue blossoms. And Hog Heaven, now the label of red and white proprietary Camas wines, was the original name of Moscow, christened by early settlers whose pigs, as local lore says, went "hog wild" after snacking on Camas bulbs.

TO SEE & DO

Idaho's great Hell's Canyon, the deepest gorge in the United States, towering at times 9,300 feet above the Snake River, can be a thrilling experience by float or jet boat ride. Or take a trip along the old Lewis and Clark Trail, adjacent to Hwy. 12, beside the turbulent Loscha River, so rugged even today that visitors wonder how the old explorers ever made it.

Gentler excursions are the breakfast bike tours from Moscow on summer Sundays at 8 A.M. (for information and rentals, contact Paradise Creek Bicycles, 605½ Third Street, Moscow; tel: 208-882-0703) to cafés in the countryside—a short ride but with enough calorie burn-off to merit an extra piece of coffee cake. When there is no group ride, rent a bike and pedal through rolling farmland and river routes where secret hollows still sprout Camas flowers. Bike rental stores can help you map your itinerary. Winter visitors head for the hills to ski in the Bitterroot Mountains, about two hours east of Moscow-Pullman.

Travelers interested in western history will want to visit the Appaloosa Horse Museum, with paintings and artifacts relating to Appaloosas, cowboys, and the Nez Percé Indians (Moscow-Pullman Highway; tel: 208-882-5578); and the Nez Percé National Historical Park, headquartered in Spalding, eleven miles south of Lewiston, with a visitors center and a museum explaining the role of this tribe and the westward expansion of the United States (Route 95, P.O. Box 93, Spalding, Idaho 83551; tel: 208-843-2261).

For more information, pick up a copy of *Palouse Summer* or *Palouse Journal* at Book People of Moscow (512 Main Street, Moscow), a small store with the best selection of information on the latest goings on. Some restaurants and other stores also carry the Palouse publications.

ACCOMMODATIONS

Ask about special rates when booking in summer. For bed and breakfasts, see the Bed and Breakfast of Idaho listing following the Snake River section.

Best Western University Inn
1516 Pullman Street
Moscow, Idaho 83843
Tel: 208-882-2500; 800-528-1234
Landscaped courtyard, putting green, indoor pool, twenty-four-hour restaurant, and 122 rooms with all the comforts you need. Gets conventions up to 600 people, though.

Cavanaugh's Motor Inn
645 Pullman Street
Moscow, Idaho 83843
Tel: 208-882-1611
Comfortable rooms, hot tub, restaurant; near shops and entertainment.

Dahmen Guest House
200 Main Street
Lewiston, Idaho 83501
Tel: In U.S., 800-635-1519 (ask for travel dept.); in Idaho, 800-826-2209; 208-799-9020
In historic district, has three luxury sites.

Huckleberry Heaven
Elk River, Idaho 83827
Tel: 208-826-3405
Good for families; private or group rooms, fireplace and lounge; boat rental, four-wheelers, horse rentals; tours to Dworshak Reservoir, Elk Creek Falls, and back country. East of Moscow-Pullman area.

RESTAURANTS

Moscow
Biscuitroot
415 Main Street
Tel: 208-835-6791
Three hundred items on menu.

Cavanaugh's Landing Restaurant
In Cavanaugh's Motor Inn (see listing under "Accommodations" for address and phone number).

Sit n' Soak
316 North Main Street
Tel: 208-882-5228
Hot tubs with food service. A touch of southern California?

❧ OREGON

The pioneers who settled this state enjoyed a glass of good wine or a mug of hard cider, and orchards and vineyards were soon commonplace. By the turn of the century, Oregon wines were winning gold medals at national competitions. This table wine industry thrived for a few decades more, then dried up because of Prohibition.

A second wave of pioneers began resurrecting Oregon's viticultural heritage in the 1960s. The state's cool nights, intermittent rains, and long, moderate growing season have proven particularly suitable for the classic varietals—Pinot Noir, Chardonnay, White Riesling, Gewürztraminer—originally nurtured in Burgundy and Alsace. And the industry is still expanding. The 1987 harvest weighed more than 7,000 tons, almost a 75 percent increase over the previous year. Fruit wines, a local specialty, also remain popular.

Quality has kept pace with quantity: in test after test, Oregon wines have stood up to European competitors. The reds have been singled out for special praise. Recently, a few California wineries have begun buying grapes grown here, particularly the red grape Pinot Noir, which favors cooler weather. Still higher praise has come from the famed Burgundy vintner Robert Drouhin, who has planted his first U.S. vineyard in Oregon.

The state's legislative climate is extremely supportive. Oregon has the nation's strictest wine labeling regulations. No wine produced here may be given a generic name, so a Burgundy is known as Pinot Noir, and a Bordeaux is called Cabernet Sauvignon. If a label bears a vintage date, rest assured that at least 95 percent of the grapes used were harvested that year.

Western Oregon is wine country, most notably developed around northerly Yamhill and Washington counties; nearly all the vineyards and wineries described in this section are west of I-5. The Willamette Valley viticultural area (v.a.) cuts a long swath roughly from Eugene to Washington County, while the Umpqua Valley v.a. lies to the south in Douglas County.

A number of wineries in Washington and Yamhill counties are accessible from Portland, which offers sophisticated city pleasures after wine touring. Some wineries, however, are conveniently seen from more tranquil corners in the countryside and coastal resorts. In the south, wine routes wind through forest preserves of stirring beauty.

Wherever you go in the state, an Oregon winery is typically a small family business; many are run from the home. The person officiating in the tasting room may well be the winemaker, or the winemaker's spouse, and enophiles will receive a warm welcome.

Douglas County

Bjelland Vineyards

Bjelland Vineyards Lane
Roseburg, Oregon 97470
TEL: 503-679-6950
OWNERS: Paul and Mary Bjelland
FOUNDED: 1969

AT A GLANCE
Tours & Tastings: Open daily 11–5.
Closed: Easter, Thanksgiving, Christmas.
Vineyards: Nineteen acres planted to European vinifera. Berries are also grown on the premises.
Wines: Pinot Noir, Chardonnay, Cabernet Sauvignon, Johannisberg Riesling, Sémillon, May wine, Sauvignon Blanc, Gewürztraminer, Sparkling Chardonnay, Sparkling Sémillon. blackberry, boysenberry, raspberry wines.
Awards: Wild Blackberry: Governor's Trophy; Boysenberry: gold; Raspberry: bronze.
Picnic Area: Table next to winery.
Retail Shop: Wines, boysenberry and blackberry jellies, and garlic pickles sold on-site.
Credit Cards: MasterCard, Visa.
Access for Disabled: None.
Getting There: Winery is twelve miles from Winston, twenty-two miles from Roseburg. From Hwy. 42: Take Douglas County Rd. 5 toward Reston. Follow Vineyard Tour Route signs; Bjelland Vineyards Ln. will be on your right.

    The Bjellands' winery is part of the working 200-acre farm this versatile couple established after fleeing Los Angeles in the 1960s. Paul Bjelland tends to the livestock while Mary Bjelland teaches public school. Their limited production of about 4,000 gallons has an impressive range of twenty fruit wines and varietals.

Garden Valley Winery

251 Camino Francisco
Roseburg, Oregon 97470
TEL: 503-673-3010
OWNER: Garden Valley Winery, Inc.
FOUNDED: 1984

AT A GLANCE
Tours & Tastings: Open daily Apr.–Oct., 12:30–5:30; weekends Nov.–March, 12:30–5:30.
Vineyards: Forty acres planted to Chardonnay, Gewürztraminer, Pinot Noir; apples, pears, plums, cherries are grown in fruit orchard. Additional grapes and fruit bought from local growers.
Wines: Chardonnay, Gewürztraminer (dry and late harvest styles), Pinot Noir (German style), White Pinot Noir, White Riesling (late harvest style).
Awards: Gewürztraminer: gold; White Pinot Noir: bronze; and other medals.
Retail Shop: Wines sold on-site.
Credit Cards: MasterCard, Visa.
Access for Disabled: Tasting room can accommodate wheelchairs.
Foreign Languages: German, limited French.
Getting There: Winery is five miles west of Roseburg, seventy miles south of Eugene, and ninety miles north of Medford. Take Garden Valley exit off I-5 to Melrose Rd., cross South Umpqua River, turn right on Busenbark.

The winery is housed in an authentic 1878 building with hand-hewn timbers.

❧ ❧ ❧

Girardet Wine Cellars

895 Reston Road
Roseburg, Oregon 97470
TEL: 503-679-7252
OWNERS: Philippe and Bonnie Girardet
FOUNDED: 1983

AT A GLANCE

Tours & Tastings: Open daily May–Sept. 12–5; Sat. Oct.–Apr. 12–5; and by appointment. Winery tours upon request; no vineyard tours.
Closed: Jan.
Vineyards: Eighteen acres planted to Riesling, Gewürztraminer, Chardonnay, Pinot Noir, Cabernet Sauvignon, Zinfandel, Merlot, and numerous French-American hybrids. Some additional grapes purchased from local Umpqua Valley growers.
Wines: Riesling, Gewürztraminer, Chardonnay, Pinot Noir; Oregon Vin Blanc and Oregon Vin Rouge (blends).
Awards: 1983 Riesling: silver; 1984 Riesling: silver; 1985 Chardonnay: silver; 1983 Vin Rouge: silver; 1984 Vin Rouge: silver; 1985 Vin Blanc: bronze.
Picnic Area: Yes.
Retail Shop: Wines sold on-site.
Credit Cards: MasterCard, Visa.
Access for Disabled: Winery and tasting room on one level.
Foreign Languages: French.
Getting There: Umpqua Valley is eighteen miles southwest of Roseburg. Take exit 119 from I-5, follow Hwy. 99 to Winston. In Winston, take Hwy. 42 toward Coos Bay. Nine miles west of Winston, turn right on Reston Rd. Winery on right after half a mile.
Special Wine & Other Events: Girardet Cellars celebrates its anniversary the first weekend in June with entertainment,

wine tasting, and special discounts. Umpqua Wine Festival is held in Sept.

❧ One of Oregon's newer establishments, Girardet cultivates perhaps the most extensive collection of French hybrids on the West Coast—including Aurora, Baco Noir, Foch, Millot, Rosette, Rougeon, Seyval Blanc, and Verdelet; these disease-resistant grapes may make distinctive varietal wines. Meanwhile, they add complexity to this winery's award-winning red and white blends, inspired by the blended wines Philippe Girardet remembers from his native Switzerland.

❧ ❧ ❧

Henry Winery

1599 Hubbard Creek Road
Umpqua, Oregon 97486
TEL: 503-459-5120
PRESIDENT/WINEMAKER: Scott Henry
FOUNDED: 1978

AT A GLANCE

Tours & Tastings: Open daily 11–5. Tour covers winemaking from harvest to bottling and concludes with tastings.
Closed: Major holidays.
Vineyards: Thirty-one acres planted to Chardonnay, Pinot Noir, Gewürztraminer, White Riesling.
Wines: Chardonnay, Gewürztraminer, Early Harvest Pinot Noir, Pinot Noir, Pinot Rosé.
Awards: 1978 Pinot Noir: gold, silver; 1979 Pinot Noir: gold; 1980 Pinot Noir: gold; 1979 Chardonnay: silver; 1982 Gewürztraminer: bronze; red table wine: silver.
Picnic Area: Yes.
Retail Shop: Wines sold on-site.
Credit Cards: None.
Access for Disabled: Ramp into winery.
Getting There: Winery is in Douglas County, thirteen miles northwest of Roseburg. In Umpqua, take Douglas

County Rd. 9 to Hubbard Creek Rd. Turn left on Hubbard Creek Rd. and right at end of bridge.
Special Wine & Other Events: Umpqua Valley Wine Festival in mid-Sept.

&❧ When aeronautical engineer Scott Henry left California to run his family's Umpqua Valley ranch, he brought along cuttings from his friends' vineyards. Soon he was supplying grapes to local wineries, and a few years later he set up his own plant. Although a computerized weather service helps Henry plan harvests, fall and winter tourists will see weeding done the old-fashioned way—by grazing sheep.

❧ ❧ ❧

Hillcrest Vineyard

240 Vineyard Lane
Roseburg, Oregon 97470
TEL: 503-673-3709
OWNER: Richard H. Sommer
WINEMAKER: Phil Gale
FOUNDED: 1961

AT A GLANCE
Tours & Tastings: Open daily 10–5. Tours of winery and vineyard on request. Explanation of bottling Apr.–June; harvest can be observed Oct.–Nov.
Closed: Major holidays (July 4th, Thanksgiving, Christmas).
Vineyards: Thirty owned and ten leased acres planted to Cabernet Sauvignon, Gewürztraminer, Pinot Noir, and White Riesling.
Wines: White Riesling, Pinot Noir, Cabernet Sauvignon, Gewürztraminer, Malbec, Merlot, Sauvignon Blanc, Sémillon, Zinfandel, sparkling wines.
Awards: 1979 Pinot Noir: silver.
Picnic Area: Indoor and outdoor tables.
Retail Shop: Wines sold on-site.
Credit Cards: None.
Access for Disabled: Yes.
Getting There: Winery is thirteen miles

west of Roseburg in Umpqua Valley Region of Douglas County. From exit 125 on I-5: Travel west on Garden Valley Rd. Cross Umpqua River, turn right on Cleveland Hill Rd. and left on Orchard Ln. Elgarose Rd., on the right, leads into Vineyard Ln.
Special Wine & Other Events: Umpqua Valley Wine Festival in mid-Sept.

❧ Meet the father of the modern Oregon wine industry. More than twenty-five years ago, armed with a viticulture degree from the University of California–Davis, Richard H. Sommer planted this vinifera vineyard. In doing so, he helped revive a state table wine–making tradition that predated Prohibition. He was also reviving a family tradition—his grandparents had grown grapes in the Rogue River Valley. Although many vintners have followed in Sommer's footsteps, Hillcrest remains one of Oregon's leading Riesling producers, annually bottling about 14,000 gallons of this popular white. Given a long season, Sommer holds out for late harvest Riesling; one year ripe grapes that froze on the vine were crushed while still frozen to create a rich, sweet ice wine.

❧ ❧ ❧

Jonicole Vineyard

419 Winery Lane
Roseburg, Oregon 97470
TEL: 503-679-5771
OWNER: Jon Marker
FOUNDED: 1973

AT A GLANCE
Tours & Tastings: Open daily 11:30–6. Tours of vineyard and winery on request.
Vineyards: Five acres planted to Cabernet, Chardonnay.
Wines: Cabernet Rosé, Pinot Noir, White Riesling, white table wine.
Picnic Area: Yes.
Retail Shop: Wines sold on-site.

Credit Cards: MasterCard, Visa.
Access for Disabled: Wheelchair accessible.
Getting There: Winery is five miles from Roseburg. Take I-5 to exit 119, then go west on Hwy. 42. Second possible left is Winery Ln.

🍃 This pleasant, easygoing winery underwent expansion after Jon Marker bought out his original partners.

TO SEE & DO
Douglas County is a haven for hikers, cyclists, swimmers, and other outdoor enthusiasts. For less-active adventures, visit Wildlife Safari in Winston (tel: 503-679-6761), a 250-acre wildlife preserve. There are elephant rides, weather permitting, and a petting zoo lures those who like their animals domesticated. If you're in the market for a surrey (with or without fringe), Carriage Works, in Oakland (tel: 503-459-9100), builds old-fashioned horse-drawn carriages. Learn how the West was tamed at the Douglas County Museum (tel: 503-440-4507), which displays logging equipment, a steam traction engine, and other artifacts of pioneer life. Continue your journey through the past in Roseburg, the site of many historic homes. Among them: Lane House, the home of Oregon's first territorial governor (tel: 503-459-1393). For more details about these and other Douglas County attractions, contact the Roseburg Visitors and Convention Bureau, P.O. Box 1262, 410 S.E. Spruce Street, Roseburg, Idaho 97470 (tel: 503-672-9731).

ACCOMMODATIONS
Pringle House
P.O. Box 578
Oakland, Oregon 97462
Tel: 503-459-5038
A beautifully restored Victorian landmark listed on the National Register of Historic Places. A light breakfast.

Windmill Inn
1450 Northwest Mulholland
Roseburg, Oregon 97470
Tel: 503-673-0901; 800-452-5315 (in-state); 800-547-4747 (out-of-state)
A motel complex with sauna, Jacuzzi, swimming pool, and charming outdoor courtyard. Restaurant. Well-run northwestern chain.

RESTAURANTS
P. B. Clayton's
968 Northeast Stephens
Roseburg, Oregon 97470
Tel: 503-672-1142
A friendly, reasonably priced steak-and-seafood house, casual at lunch and fancier at dinner. Wine list highlights local wineries.

Tolly's
115 Locust Street
Oakland, Oregon 97462
Tel: 503-459-3796
An ice-cream parlor by day that serves heartier fare at night. Some Greek specialties; local wines served.

Eugene Area

Alpine Vineyards

25904 Green Peak Road
Monroe, Oregon 97456
TEL: 503-424-5851
OWNERS: Dan and Christine Jepsen
FOUNDED: 1976
Also visit:
The Wood Gallery (tasting room)
818 Southwest Bay Boulevard
Newport, Oregon 97365
Tel: 503-265-6843

AT A GLANCE
Tours & Tastings: Open daily, June 15–Sept. 15, 12–5; weekends, Sept. 16–Dec. 31 and Feb. 1–June 14, 12–5; and by appointment. Tour covers winery, processing area, and vineyard. (The Wood Gallery tasting room is open daily 12–5.)
Closed: Jan.
Vineyards: Twenty acres planted to Pinot Noir, Chardonnay, Riesling, Cabernet, Gewürztraminer.
Wines: Varietals from above grapes.
Awards: 1986 Chardonnay: gold; 1986 Gewürztraminer: silver; 1986 Riesling: silver; 1984 Pinot Noir Blanc: gold; and other medals.
Picnic Area: Facilities overlook vineyard.
Retail Shop: Wines sold on-site.
Credit Cards: MasterCard, Visa.
Access for Disabled: Limited wheelchair access.
Getting There: Winery is in Benton County in the Willamette Valley, 18 miles south of Corvallis and 30 miles north of Eugene. Take Hwy. 99W to Alpine Rd., Alpine. Green Peak Rd. is on the right about 1½ miles from town.

🐦 Doctor, cellist, vintner—Dan Jepsen is a Renaissance man. Upon completing four years with the Peace Corps, he and his wife settled here and turned their winemaking hobby into a commercial enterprise. Their first wine earned a silver medal, and they've been harvesting awards ever since.

🐦 🐦 🐦

Forgeron Vineyard

89697 Sheffler Road
Elmira, Oregon 97437
TEL: 503-935-1117
OWNER: George L. Smith
FOUNDED: 1972

AT A GLANCE
Tours & Tastings: Open daily, June–Sept., 12–5; weekends, Oct.–Dec. and Feb.–May, 12–5. Tours given daily during summer, upon request during winter; lecture is accompanied by a twelve-minute slide presentation. Small gallery above tasting room features work by local artists.
Closed: Jan.
Vineyards: Twenty-three acres planted to Chardonnay, Pinot Gris, Pinot Noir, Cabernet, Muller-Thurgau, White Riesling.
Wines: Varietals from above grapes.
Awards: Cabernet Sauvignon: gold; Pinot Noir: gold; White Riesling: bronze.
Picnic Area: Indoor and outdoor tables; formal wine garden.
Retail Shop: Wines sold on-site.
Credit Cards: MasterCard, Visa.
Access for Disabled: Yes.
Getting There: Winery is in Lane County, thirteen miles west of Eugene. Take Hwy. 126 toward Elmira, then head north on Territorial Rd. Make a left on Warthen Rd. and a right on Sheffler Rd.
Special Wine & Other Events: Annual Bluegrass Festival: third weekend in July—with tours, tastings, barbecue, and live music. Art in the Vineyard: a charity fund-raiser, held either on the third or last weekend in July.

🐚 With its gracious gardens and spectacular view of the snow-capped Cascade Mountains, this vineyard is as pleasing to the eye as its wines are to the palate. Owners George and Linda Smith enjoy discussing wines with visitors: "People deserve personal attention," says Linda. Energetic visitors can hike the historic Applegate Trail that runs close to Forgeron's property.

TO SEE & DO
Eugene, Oregon's second largest city, is home to the University of Oregon, on Franklin Boulevard between Eleventh and Eighteenth Avenues. There is usually something happening on the campus, from competitive sports to concerts; check the schedule at Hult's Performing Arts Center. Changing exhibits at the Lane County Museum (740 West Thirteenth Avenue) trace local history from pioneer days to the present. Bicycling is almost a religion here, and city parks contain 150 miles of bike paths. Of course, the local urban diversions include shopping: the Fifth Street Market's stalls overflow with farm-fresh fruit and vegetables, while once a week the Saturday Market turns a downtown parking lot into an open-air thrift shop. (The Saturday Market is at Eighth and Oak, Apr.–Dec.) In good weather, you can't go wrong taking a leisurely drive around the countryside, a rich sampler of orchards, pastures, and rivulets spanned by covered bridges. For more information, contact the Eugene Chamber of Commerce, 1401 Willamette Street, P.O. Box 1107, Eugene, Oregon 97440 (tel: 503-484-1314).

ACCOMMODATIONS
Griswold's Bed and Breakfast
552 West Broadway
Eugene, Oregon 97401
Tel: 503-683-6294
Near downtown in a stately part of Eugene. Hearty breakfast of fresh fruit, omelets, homemade breads and jams, and coffee.

The House in the Woods
814 Lorane Highway
Eugene, Oregon 97405
Tel: 503-343-3234
A lovely turn-of-the century home with all the trimmings—hardwood floors, Oriental rugs, antiques, and a grand piano. Enjoy eggs, home-baked breads, and fruit soups for breakfast.

Shelley's Guest House
1546 Charnelton Street
Eugene, Oregon 97401
Tel: 503-683-2062
A 1920s cottage comfortably furnished in period style; the only anachronism is the hot tub in the gazebo. Breakfast on eggs Benedict and strawberry-drenched waffles; light afternoon snacks.

Valley River Inn
1000 Valley River Way (P.O. Box 10088)
Eugene, Oregon 97440
Tel: 503-687-0123; 800-547-8810 (instate); 800-452-8960 (out-of-state)
Fine view of the Willamette River from this well-run 258-room motor hotel. Restaurant, heated pool, health club.

Hilton
66 East 6th Avenue
Eugene, Oregon 97401
Tel: 503-342-2000; 800-HILTONS
Twelve-story Hilton with expected amenities.

RESTAURANTS
Gazebo
3443 Hillyard Street
Eugene, Oregon 97405
Tel: 503-683-6661
Mediterranean and Middle Eastern foods served in attractive plant-filled surroundings; wine list.

Mill Camp
215 Q Street
Springfield, Oregon 97477
Tel: 503-747-8480
Prime rib and other hearty entrées.

Sweetwaters
Valley River Inn
(See "Accommodations" for address, telephone.)
Romantic river view and cozy fireplace,

with fresh fish and fowl dishes, leading a list of Continental specialties. Nice wine selection.

Treehouse
1769 Franklin Boulevard
Eugene, Oregon 97403
Tel: 503-485-3444
Cheerful wicker setting with chef specialties that include salmon and grilled dishes. Wine list.

Mid-Willamette Valley/Salem Area

Bethel Heights Vineyard

6060 Bethel Heights Road Northwest
Salem, Oregon 97304
TEL: 503-581-2262
PRESIDENT: Marilyn Webb
WINEMAKER: Terry Casteel (apprenticed at Sokol Blosser Winery in Dundee, Oregon)
FOUNDED: Vineyard founded in 1977, winery in 1984

AT A GLANCE
Tours & Tastings: Open Tues.–Sun. 11–5. Tours of vineyard and/or winery by appointment.
Closed: Mon.
Vineyards: Fifty-one acres planted to Pinot Noir, Chardonnay, Gewürztraminer, Chenin Blanc, Riesling, Cabernet.
Wines: Varietals from above grapes.
Awards: 1984 Pinot Noir: gold, bronze; 1985 Gewürztraminer: bronze; 1985 Late Harvest Gewürztraminer: bronze.
Picnic Area: Yes.
Retail Shop: Wines sold on-site.
Credit Cards: MasterCard, Visa.
Access for Disabled: Ramp access to second-floor tasting room.
Foreign Languages: French, Spanish by appointment.

Getting There: Winery is in Polk County, 12 miles northwest of Salem. Travel west on Hwy. 221, 6 miles from West Salem bridge. Bear left at Lincoln onto Zena Rd. After 4½ miles turn right at Bethel Heights Rd., then follow signs.
Special Wine & Other Events: Tastevin tour (see To See & Do) of participating Salem area wineries during Memorial Day weekend in May features three days of new releases, food, music.

🐸 Twin brothers Terry and Ted Casteel and their families independently developed a passion for wines, then pooled their resources to buy Bethel Heights Vineyard. The winery stands on the site of an apple orchard planted by nineteenth-century pioneers. The settlers' church and cemetery, located nearby, merit a visit.

🐸 🐸 🐸

Ellendale Vineyards

300 Reuben Boise Road
Dallas, Oregon 97338
TEL: 503-623-5617
PRESIDENT: Robert Hudson
FOUNDED: 1981

AT A GLANCE

Tours & Tastings: Open daily 12–6. Co-owner Ella Mae Hudson gives cheerful, chatty tours on request to all visitors.

Vineyards: Fifteen acres planted to Pinot Noir, White Riesling, Chardonnay, Aurora, Niagara, Cabernet Franc, Gewürztraminer, Cabernet Sauvignon. Fruits purchased from Willamette Valley growers.

Wines: Varietals from above grapes and carbonated wines; mead; loganberry and other fruit wines.

Awards: White Riesling: gold; White Pinot Noir: bronze; Gewürztraminer: bronze.

Picnic Area: In grove beside vineyards.

Retail Shop: Wines sold on-site.

Credit Cards: MasterCard, Visa.

Access for Disabled: Yes.

Getting There: Winery is in Polk County, three miles west of Dallas and twenty miles west of Salem. Take Hwy. 223 to Ellendale Rd. in Dallas. Go a couple of miles west on Ellendale Rd. and bear right on Reuben Boise Rd. Watch for directions on blue highway signs.

Special Wine & Other Events: Oregon Trail Festival: last weekend of July—combines wine tasting with exhibit of Robert Hudson's oil landscapes.

🐌 Ellendale is named after an Oregon community that dates to 1844, and the winery and vineyards are part of the original land grant. One suspects, however, that less-historic considerations inspired the Hudsons to dub their sweet fruit blend "Woolly Booger;" ask what it means when you get there.

🐌 🐌 🐌

Glen Creek Winery

6057 Orchard Heights Road Northwest
Salem, Oregon 97304
TEL: 503-371-9463
OWNERS: Thomas and Sylvia Dumm
FOUNDED: 1982

AT A GLANCE

Tours & Tastings: Open Tues.–Sun. 12–5. Winemaking process explained in detail, from crushing through bottling. Other vineyard talks given on request. Reservations required for large parties.

Closed: Christmas, New Year's Day.

Vineyards: Ten acres planted to Chardonnay and Gewürztraminer.

Wines: Chardonnay, Gewürztraminer, Pinot Noir, Pinot Noir Blush, Sauvignon Blanc, Whole Cluster Fermented Pinot Noir.

Picnic Area: Partially covered area adjacent to vineyard and winery.

Retail Shop: Wines sold on-site.

Credit Cards: MasterCard, Visa.

Access for Disabled: Limited.

Getting There: Winery is an easy ten-minute drive west of Salem. From Hwy. 22: Head north on Oak Grove Rd. about 2½ miles, then bear right on Orchard Heights Rd. N.W.

Special Wine & Other Events: Memorial Day weekend wine festival with food, live music, art exhibit.

🐌 While operating a wine store in Long Beach, California, the Dumms became home winemakers; in 1975 they moved to Oregon to set up their own state-of-the-art boutique vineyard. Whites are the specialty here, although Glen Creek's first red sold out rapidly, so further releases can be expected.

🐌 🐌 🐌

Honeywood Winery

501 Fourteenth Street Southeast
Salem, Oregon 97301
TEL: 503-362-4111
Also visit Honeywood's Tasting Room:
30 Southeast Highway 101
Lincoln City, Oregon 97367
Tel: 503-994-2755
PRESIDENT: Paul L. Gallick

WINEMAKERS: Bill Wrey, Richard Miller (participated in seminars given by Oregon State University and Oregon Winemakers Association)
FOUNDED: 1934

AT A GLANCE
Tours & Tastings: Open Mon.–Fri. 9–5, Sat. 10–5, Sun. 1–5. Brief tours at 10 and 2 cover entire production procedure, from receiving fruit to bottling wine; a tasting session follows. Group tours by appointment. (Lincoln City site is open daily 9–5.)
Closed: Christmas, New Year's Day.
Vineyards: None. Riesling, Chardonnay, Gewürztraminer, Pinot Noir, fruits, and berries grown under contract by Willamette Valley suppliers.
Wines: Enormous range of fruit wines including apricot, apple, blackberry, raspberry, strawberry; mead; kosher wines; Pinot Noir, Pinot Noir Blanc, Chardonnay, Riesling.
Awards: Blackberry: gold; raspberry: silver; apricot: silver.
Retail Shop: Wines, fruit wines, non-alcoholic ciders, wine jellies sold on-site.
Credit Cards: American Express, Diner's Club, MasterCard, Visa.
Access for Disabled: All facilities on ground floor except tasting room.
Getting There: Winery is in Salem, forty-two miles south of Portland. From I-5: Go west on Hwy. 22 to 14th St. SE.
Special Wine & Other Events: Salem Wine Festival: first weekend of Nov.

❧ Established on the day Prohibition ended (Dec. 5, 1933), this is Oregon's oldest producing winery—and one of the largest, with room to ferment and store more than 200,000 gallons. If you can think of a fruit wine, the odds are Honeywood makes it, from blackberry to guava. Vinifera varietals were added in 1982 under the Gallico brand name.

TO SEE & DO
All of these wineries participate in the Memorial Day Weekend Tastevin Tour, named for the shallow tasting cup used by some wine judges. Salem's own Wine Festival takes place in November. Salem is Oregon's capital, so civic-minded tourists may want to visit the state government buildings, starting with the State Capitol at Court and Summer streets. You can see Mt. Hood from the Capitol's tower. Mission Mill Village Museum, a restored wool factory at 1313 Mill Street SE, is one block away from Honeywood Winery. Willamette University is also nearby, at 900 State Street. Founded in 1842, this is the oldest institute of higher learning west of Missouri. Nineteenth-century landmarks—homes, churches, cemeteries—dot the greater Mid-Willamette Valley. Of particular note is the Brunk House, on Hwy. 22 between Salem and Rickreall. Built in 1861 by a pioneer couple, the house has been carefully restored by the Polk County Historical Society; outside Brunk House is a formal rose-and-herb garden. The Oregon Museums Association publishes a guide to the region's historic buildings; for a copy, write the Marion County Historical Society, P.O. Box 847, Salem, Oregon 97308.

If you'll be in Salem during late August or early September, head for the fairgrounds to see the Oregon State Fair. After viewing the wine competition, you can stop at the Farmer's Market to pick up some picnic treats (2330 17th Street NE; 503-378-3247).

ACCOMMODATIONS
(All in Salem. For more listings in the area, see also the Yamhill County section.)

Executive Inn
200 Commercial Street Southeast
Salem, Oregon 97301
Tel: 503-363-4123
Usual amenities plus swimming pool and Jacuzzi. Restaurant.

Best Western Pacific Highway Inn
4526 Portland Road Northeast
Salem, Oregon 97301
Tel: 503-390-3200; 800-528-1234
The usual comforts of a Best Western, with golf privileges, heated pool.

Chumaree Comfortel
3301 Market Street Northeast
Salem, Oregon 97301
Tel: 503-370-7888; 800-248-6273
Motor hotel amenities in a 150-room, four-story structure. Indoor pool. Restaurant.

RESTAURANTS (Both in Salem)
Steamer's
(See Chumaree Comfortel in "Accommodations" for address, telephone.)
As the name implies, steamed clams get top billing here, but there are also a selection of other dishes. Good desserts.

The Terrarium
156 Church Street
Tel: 503-363-1611
Eclectic menu with Polynesian accents, made of the freshest possible ingredients. Local wines served.

Northern Oregon Coast

Nehalem Bay Winery

34965 Highway 53
Nehalem, Oregon 97131
TEL: 503-368-5300
OWNER: Patrick O. McCoy
FOUNDED: 1973

AT A GLANCE
Tours & Tastings: Open daily 10–5. Visitors may take a self-guided tour through the winery, a renovated 1909 cheese factory built in the Tudor style. The attic is a gallery and studio for local artists, some of whom serve as winery staff.
Closed: Thanksgiving, Christmas.
Vineyards: Five acres recently planted to Pinot Noir. Grapes and fruit purchased from Willamette Valley growers.
Wines: Chardonnay, Pinot Noir, Pinot Noir Blanc, Niagara, Riesling; plum, apple, rhubarb, blackberry.
Retail Shop: All wines sold on-site.
Credit Cards: MasterCard, Visa.
Access for Disabled: Wheelchair accessible.
Getting There: Winery is in Tillamook County, twenty-five miles south of Seaside and eighty miles west of Portland.

From Hwy. 101 in Nehalem: Head one mile northeast on Hwy. 53.
Special Wine & Other Events: Ask about the Tillamook County Cheese, Food, and Wine Tour, an informal excursion that starts at this winery and ends at McCoy's Blue Heron Cheese Factory, twenty-six miles to the south on Hwy. 101. (Next door is the Old Trapper Sausage Factory, another real McCoy enterprise.)

ɛ. A dedicated gourmet with an entrepreneurial bent—his ventures include cheese and sausage factories—Patrick McCoy went into winemaking guided only by his palate. Starting with fruit wines, which need little aging, he then branched into vinifera. A sideline is animal husbandry. He hopes that the piglets he deposited on a nearby uninhabited Columbia River island will breed a herd of succulent wild boars.

TO SEE & DO
This rugged, scenic region eighty miles west of Portland is known for the shipping, fishing, and logging industries. Recreational fishers and clam diggers will

have a field day. In the summer the Nehalem Bay Players present "Shakespeare in the Park" in Manzanita, several hundred miles away from a similar and better-known series in Ashland. Coastal resorts here include Lincoln City, with many arts and crafts galleries, and Seaside, a popular getaway since the 1800's.

ACCOMMODATIONS
The Captain's Lady Bed & Breakfast
127 South Miller Street
Rockaway Beach, Oregon 97136
Tel: 503-355-2966
Five spacious bedrooms decorated with Victorian antiques. Full breakfast in the

morning, deli plates and homemade pies at night.

Sunset Surf Hotel
458 Ocean Road
Manzanita, Oregon 97130
Tel: 503-368-5224
A forty-one-unit hotel right on the coast; fireplaces in many rooms.

RESTAURANT
Crab Broiler
Hamlet Route
Seaside, Oregon 97138
Tel: 503-738-5313
Rich chowders, fresh seafood. Good wine list, delicious desserts.

Portland Area

Adams Vineyard Winery

1922 Northwest Pettygrove Street
Portland, Oregon 97209
TEL: 503-294-0606
OWNERS: Peter and Carol Adams
FOUNDED: 1985

AT A GLANCE
Tours & Tastings: By appointment only.
Vineyards: Thirteen acres near Newberg—a forty-minute drive from the winery—planted to Pinot Noir, Chardonnay, Gamay Noir.
Wines: Chardonnay, Pinot Noir.
Awards: Pinot Noir: silver.
Retail Shop: Wines sold on-site.
Credit Cards: MasterCard, Visa.
Access for Disabled: None.
Getting There: Take Rte. 405 to northwest Portland. Winery is on the corner of Northwest 19th and Pettygrove St., near the Freemont Bridge.

   ❧ After a brief stint retailing wines, Peter Adams went into the business of making his own. This tiny urban winery

is the first and to date the only one within Portland's city limits. It's a family affair; Carol Adams, an artist and food columnist, conducts tastings and designs the labels.

❧ ❧ ❧

Henry Endres Winery

13300 South Clackamas River Drive
Oregon City, Oregon 97045
TEL: 503-656-7239
OWNER/WINEMAKER: Henry C. Endres
FOUNDED: 1935

AT A GLANCE
Tours & Tastings: Open Mon.–Sat. 10–7. No tours.
Closed: Sun., holidays.
Vineyards: Five acres planted to Concord, White Niagara, White Riesling. Apples, elderberries, and plums are also grown on the premises; other fruits are bought from local farms.
Wines: Concord, White Niagara; apple,

elderberry, loganberry, plum, rosé; and mead.

Retail Shop: Wines sold on-site.
Credit Cards: None.
Access for Disabled: None.
Getting There: Winery is on south bank of Clackamas River, two miles north of Oregon City and fourteen miles south of Portland. Take U.S. 205 to exit 10, bear right on Clackamas.

ka Henry Endres was founded by the current proprietor's grandfather, whose mother entrusted him with the family recipes she brought from Germany. No pretensions about this place; samples are poured in paper cups and all wines are sold by 1½-liter, screw-top bottles.

TO SEE & DO

In Portland, Oregon's biggest city, Canyon Road (SW) is an avenue of attractions: admire fauna at the Washington Park Zoo (tel: 503-226-1561), then examine flora at the Western Forestry Center (tel: 503-228-1367). The Oregon Museum of Science and Industry is also in this neighborhood (tel: 503-222-2828). For contrast, get a dose of high culture at the Portland Art Museum (1219 Southwest Park Avenue, tel: 503-226-2811). Test your hand-eye coordination—or merely your mettle—on the archery grounds and tennis courts of Washington Park, on Canyon Road. Then take a soothing stroll in the park's formal Japanese garden (tel: 503-228-1367). The Columbia River undulates just north of Portland; it's well worth the detour to trace this mighty river—the fourth largest in North America—west to Columbia Gorge, a thrilling sixty-mile chasm that is one of the wonders of North America. For more information, contact the Greater Portland Convention and Visitors Association, 26 Southwest Salmon Street, Portland, Oregon 97204 (tel: 503-222-2223).

ACCOMMODATIONS & RESTAURANTS

Contact the Convention and Visitor Bureau (address above) for more information on Portland hotels and restaurants.

Corbett House B & B
7533 Southwest Corbett Avenue
Portland, Oregon 97219
Tel: 503-245-2580
A small, elegant inn filled with antiques and contemporary art. Robes and hair dryers; continental breakfast.

Heathman Hotel
Southwest Broadway at Salmon Street
Portland, Oregon 97205
Tel: 503-241-4100; 800-551-0011
A small but elegant luxury hotel perfect for a self-indulgent splurge. Restaurant specializes in northwestern cuisine, local wines.

International Dunes
1900 Clackamette Drive
Oregon City, Oregon 97045
Tel: 503-655-7141
One hundred twenty rooms, with balconies overlooking the river; swimming pool, sauna.

Nendels Inn
9900 Southwest Canyon Road
Portland, Oregon 97225
Tel: 503-297-2551; 800-547-0106
Motel and restaurant with country inn atmosphere.

Portland's White House
1914 Northeast 22nd Avenue
Portland, Oregon 97212
Tel: 503-287-7131
This impressive historic landmark really does look just like its namesake, only you can stay overnight at this lovely B&B without winning a national election. Full breakfast.

RiverPlace Alexis
1510 Southwest Harbor Way
Portland, Oregon 97201
Tel: 503-228-3233; 800-227-1333

Elegant luxury hotel on the RiverPlace Esplanade. Fine restaurant with good wine list.

Southern Oregon

Siskiyou Vineyard

6220 Oregon Caves Highway
Cave Junction, Oregon 97523
TEL: 503-592-3727
OWNER: C. J. David
WINEMAKER: Donna A. Devine (on-the-job experience with Dr. William Nelson, consulting enologist to several Oregon wineries)
FOUNDED: 1978

AT A GLANCE
Tours & Tastings: Open daily 11–5. Individual tours given on request.
Closed: Never.
Vineyards: Twelve acres planted to Cabernet Sauvignon, Merlot, Gamay Beaujolais, Pinot Noir, Gewürztraminer, Chenin Blanc.
Wines: Cabernet Sauvignon, Chardonnay, Early Muscat, Gewürztraminer, Merlot, Muller-Thurgau, Pinot Noir, White Riesling, Bordeaux Blush.
Awards: Cabernet Sauvignon: silver; Early Muscat: bronze; Pinot Noir: bronze.
Picnic Area: Yes.
Retail Shop: Wines sold on-site.
Credit Cards: MasterCard, Visa.
Access for Disabled: Wheelchair accessible.
Foreign Languages: French, German, Spanish.
Getting There: Winery is off Hwy. 199 in Cave Junction, midway between Grants Pass, Oregon, and Crescent City, California.
Special Wine & Other Events: Annual

Wine Festival, second weekend of June, features food and crafts fair.

• This winery takes its name from the nearby Siskiyou National Forest. With hiking trails and a trout lake on the property, few sites are lovelier. History buffs take note: the winery buildings include one of the oldest homesteads in Oregon's Illinois Valley.

Valley View

1000 Applegate Road
Jacksonville, Oregon 97530
TEL: 503-899-8468
   Also visit: **The Tasting Room**
   690 North Fifth Street
   Jacksonville, Oregon 97530
   Tel: 503-899-1001
PRESIDENT: Robert Wisnovsky
WINEMAKER: John Guerrero (degree in fermentation science from UC-Davis)
FOUNDED: 1978

AT A GLANCE
Tours & Tastings: Open daily 11–5. Tours upon request.
Closed: Thanksgiving, Christmas.
Vineyards: Twenty-six acres planted to Cabernet, Chardonnay, Merlot.
Wines: Cabernet, Chardonnay, Merlot, Pinot, Gewürztraminer.
Awards: 1979 Cabernet: four stars; 1980 Cabernet: four stars; 1981 Merlot: silver.
Retail Shop: Wines sold on-site.
Credit Cards: MasterCard, Visa.

Access for the Disabled: Limited.
Getting There: Winery is fifteen miles southwest of Medford. Applegate Rd. is off Hwy. 238 in Ruch.
Special Wine & Other Events: Vintage Jacksonville celebration, Memorial Day weekend.

🍂 The Wisnovskys established themselves here, along with their vineyard, in 1972. Six years later they opened their winery in a renovated, turn-of-the-century hay barn.

TO SEE & DO
One attraction in Southern Oregon is the Oregon Caves National Monument. Guides conduct would-be spelunkers on a one-hour tour through these marble caverns; children under six are not permitted (baby-sitting is provided). Jacksonville, once a pioneer outpost, is now a National Historic Landmark, and the original county courthouse, at 206 North Fifth Street, has been turned into a museum. Other restored nineteenth-century attractions include the Beekman Bank, at California and Third streets, and the Rogue River Railroad Depot, at North Oregon and C streets. From July through September, the Britt Festivals—named for local settler Peter Britt—bring world-class performers to nearby Medford. The musical offerings run the gamut from classical concertos to bluegrass standards. For details, write to P.O. Box 1124-S, Medford, Oregon 97501 (tel: 800-33-BRITT [in-state]; 800-88-BRITT [out-of-state]). The Oregon Shakespearean Festival comes to Ashland from February to September. This acclaimed repertory company presents twelve plays on three stages. Tickets are scarce, so contact the festival ahead of time at P.O. Box 158, Ashland, Oregon 97520 (tel: 503-482-2111). For Shakespeare Festival tour packages, consult the Southern Oregon Reservation Center, Box 1048, Ashland, Oregon 97520 (tel: 503-488-1011).

ACCOMMODATIONS
Romeo Inn
295 Idaho Street
Ashland, Oregon 27520
Tel: 503-488-0884
Cape Cod-style B&B in the pines. Sumptuous breakfasts.

Junction Inn Motel
Redwood Highway at Oregon Caves
   Highway
Cave Junction, Oregon 97523
Tel: 503-592-3106
Sixty units just a short drive from the Oregon Caves, with playground and heated pool.

Oregon Caves Chateau
Caves Highway
Oregon Caves, Oregon 97523
Tel: 503-592-3400
Reasonably priced six-story lodge open only in the summer.

Jacksonville Inn
175 East California Street
Jacksonville, Oregon 97530
Tel: 503-899-1900
Dates from the 1800s and has eight comfortably furnished rooms. Restaurant. Better known for delicious food and wine list.

Livingston Mansion Inn
4132 Livingston Road (P.O. Box 1476)
Tel: 503-899-7107
This small inn dates from the 1900s. Swimming pool, hot tub, patio on property, and near Rouge River for water sports.

McCully House
240 East California Street
Jacksonville, Oregon 97530
Tel: 503-899-1942

A charming inn in one of the first homes to be built in Jacksonville. Restaurant.

RESTAURANTS
Chateaulin
50 East Main Street
Ashland, Oregon 97520
Tel: 503-482-2264
Classic French cuisine just a block away from the Shakespeare Festival.

Jacksonville Inn
(See "Accommodations" for address, phone.)
Well-prepared fresh fish and veal dishes. Good wine list.

Winchester Inn
35 South Second Street
Ashland, Oregon 97520
Tel: 503-488-1113
Continental cuisine, good wine list.

Woodland Echoes
7901 Oregon Caves Highway
Cave Junction, Oregon 97523
Tel: 503-592-3406
Italian specialties, with an emphasis on homemade lasagna, ravioli, and other pasta dishes.

Washington County

Oak Knoll Winery

Route 6, Box 184
Burkhalter Road
Hillsboro, Oregon 97123
TEL: 503-648-8198
 Also visit:
 Shipwreck Cellars
 3521 Southwest Highway 101
 Lincoln City, Oregon 97367
 Tel: 503-996-3221
OWNER/WINEMAKER: Ron Vuylsteke
FOUNDED: 1970

AT A GLANCE
Tours & Tastings: Open Wed.–Sun. 12–5, Sat. 11–5, Mon.–Tues. by appointment only. Self-guided tours. (Shipwreck Cellars open daily 11–5.)
Vineyards: None. Grapes and fruit are purchased from Willamette Valley growers.
Wines: Chardonnay, Pinot Noir, White Riesling, Pinot Noir Blanc, Gewürztraminer, raspberry, loganberry.
Awards: Both Pinot Noir and raspberry have won Governor's Trophies. Numerous gold medals in international competitions.
Picnic Area: Ten tables.
Retail Shop: Wines, winemaking and beer-making supplies, related gift items sold on-site.
Credit Cards: MasterCard, Visa.
Access for Disabled: Limited wheelchair access.
Getting There: Winery is twenty miles west of Portland. Burkhalter Rd. is four miles south of Hillsboro off Hwy. 219.
Special Wine & Other Events: Bacchus Goes Bluegrass Wine Festival, third weekend of May, honors the god of the grape with music, arts and crafts, food, and of course, wine.

➔ One summer, stuck with more blackberries than he could eat, electronics engineer Ron Vuylsteke decided to drink them instead. When his amateur winery sprawled across the entire garage, dispossessing his car, he decided to move here and turn pro. Three large silos punctuate the grounds, testifying to Oak

Knoll's previous existence as a dairy farm. While Vuylsteke continues to make fruit wines, vinifera varietals now constitute three-quarters of his substantial, 50,000-gallon production, and for good reason: his Pinot Noir has been hailed by noted wine consultant Andre Tchelistcheff.

🍂 🍂 🍂

Ponzi Vineyards

Route 1, Box 842
Beaverton, Oregon 97007
TEL: 503-628-1227
OWNERS: Richard and Nancy Ponzi
FOUNDED: 1970

AT A GLANCE
Tours & Tastings: Open Sat.–Sun. 12–5, on other days by appointment only.
Closed: All holidays.
Vineyards: Twelve owned and thirty-five leased acres planted to Pinot Gris, Pinot Noir, Chardonnay, Riesling.
Wines: Pinot Gris, Pinot Noir, Chardonnay, Riesling.
Awards: More than one hundred regional, national, and international awards won since 1975.
Picnic Area: On the lawn.
Retail Shop: Wines sold on-site.
Credit Cards: MasterCard, Visa.
Access for Disabled: Yes.
Foreign Languages: Italian, Spanish.
Getting There: Winery is in Washington County, 5 miles from Washington Square shopping district and 15 miles southwest of Portland. From Washington Square: Take Hwy. 210 toward Scholls for 4½ miles. Bear left on Vandermost; Ponzi is off this street.
Special Wine & Other Events: Early Summer Wine Festival: Memorial Day weekend, with live jazz, food, new wines. Vineyard Jazz presents the best northwestern combos the last Sun. of each summer month. Annual Valley Wine Tour: Thanksgiving weekend.

🍂 In 1904, Tualatin Valley wines earned gold medals at the St. Louis World's Fair, but this region's vineyards were plowed under during Prohibition. Ironically enough, three decades later, Oregon Department of Agriculture officals told the Ponzis not to plant vinifera here—advice these award-winning vintners wisely ignored. Extensive European travels have helped these self-taught vintners refine their methods.

🍂 🍂 🍂

Shafer Vineyard Cellars

Star Route, Box 269
Forest Grove, Oregon 97116
TEL: 503-357-6604
OWNERS: Harvey and Sofia Shafer
FOUNDED: 1981

AT A GLANCE
Tours & Tastings: Sat.–Sun. 12–5. Group tours only.
Closed: Jan.
Vineyards: Twenty acres planted to vinifera varieties.
Wines: Chardonnay, Pinot Noir, Pinot Noir Blanc, Riesling, Sauvignon Blanc, Gewürztraminer.
Awards: Local and national medals, including golds for the Chardonnay.
Picnic Area: Six tables in a shaded grove.
Retail Shop: Wines sold on-site.
Credit Cards: MasterCard, Visa.
Access for Disabled: None.
Getting There: Shafer Vineyard is on Hwy. 8 in Gales Creek Valley, 4½ miles west of Forest Grove and 30 miles west of Portland.
Special Wine & Other Events: Sunday Jazz concerts during summer months.

🍂 Convinced that "the wines are made on the vine," Harvey Shafer saved some grapes for himself after six years of selling his entire harvest to wineries. Thus another vintner was born. Demand has led to a fivefold increase in production over the first commercial crush of 3,000 gallons.

ᴥ ᴥ ᴥ

Tualatin Vineyards

Route 1, Box 339
Forest Grove, Oregon 97116
TEL: 503-357-5005
PRESIDENT: William Malkmus
WINEMAKER: William Fuller (bachelor's in chemistry from San Francisco State; master's in enology from UC-Davis; former director of the American Society of Enologists)
FOUNDED: 1973

AT A GLANCE
Tours & Tastings: Open Mon.–Fri. 9–3, Sat.–Sun. 1–5. Tours by appointment include winemaking from harvest to bottle; vineyard operations.
Closed: Jan., holidays.
Vineyards: Eighty-three acres planted to Pinot Noir, Chardonnay, White Riesling, Gewürztraminer, Early Muscat, Muller-Thurgau, Flora.
Wines: Varietals from grapes above.
Awards: 1981 Chardonnay: Robert Mondavi Trophy, gold, bronze; 1980 Pinot Noir: John Sutcliffe Trophy, three golds, silver; 1984 Gewürztraminer: silver; 1984 White Riesling: bronze; 1985 Pinot Noir Blanc: bronze; 1983 Pinot Noir: bronze; and other medals.
Picnic Area: Picturesque picnic site overlooks vineyard and Willamette Valley.
Retail Shop: Wines sold on-site.
Credit Cards: MasterCard, Visa.
Access for Disabled: Ramp at entrance.
Getting There: Tualatin is twenty-six miles west of Portland, between Forest Grove and Banks. Take U.S. 26 to Hwy. 6 and then head south on Hwy. 47. Bear right at intersection with Greenville Rd. and continue to Clapshaw Hill Rd.; bear right again on Seavy Rd.
Special Wine & Other Events: July 4th Barrel Tasting; annual sale, Aug.; art show, Thanksgiving weekend.

ᴥ William Fuller has been in the wine business since 1958. Before moving here, he spent nine years as chief chemist at Napa Valley's Louis M. Martini Winery. Fuller's methods at Tualatin synthesize the old and the new: small traditional French oak barrels, modern stainless steel tanks, presses, and filters. Production, presently about 40,000 gallons of premium estate-bottled wine, will increase slightly as the younger plantings mature.

TO SEE & DO
Handsome Victorian homes line the streets of Forest Grove, so a walking tour is definitely in order. Maps are available from the Chamber of Commerce, 2417 Pacific Avenue. Add Pacific University to your itinerary; this private school, founded in 1849, stands in the center of town, on College Way. The Old College Hall, built in 1850, houses a museum of pioneer artifacts. Fittingly, two of Forest Grove's annual events celebrate the past. February is brightened by the Gay Nineties Festival and its highlight, the popular Barber Shop Quartet Competition. In August, the Concourse d'Elegance—an antique auto show—pulls into town. More vehicular rarities can be seen at the Trolley Park on Gales Creek in Glenwood (tel: 503-357-3574). The intact, working specimens include an English double-decker.

ACCOMMODATIONS
Holiday Motel
3224 Pacific Avenue
Forest Grove, Oregon 97116
Tel: 503-357-7411
A stone's throw from Pacific University.

Nyberg Inn
7125 Southwest Nyberg Road
Tualatin, Oregon 97062
Tel: 503-692-5800

RESTAURANTS

(All in Forest Grove, except where noted.)

Anthony's Old-Fashioned Eatery
3018 Pacific Highway
Forest Grove, Oregon 97116
Tel: 503-357-6989
And:
640 Southeast Tenth Avenue
Hillsboro, Oregon 97123
Tel: 503-640-2024
Burgers, sandwiches, omelets, and local wine.

Creative Kitchen
Ballad Town Square
2834-D Pacific Avenue
Tel: 503-357-6366
It's a store, it's a wine shop, it's a deli—it's all three. Local products are emphasized.

Jan's Food Mill
1819 Nineteenth Avenue
Tel: 503-357-6623
Steaks, seafood, and Oregon wines served in a historic granary.

Yamhill County

Adelsheim Vineyard

22150 Northeast Quarter Mile Lane
Newberg, Oregon 97132
TEL: 503-538-3652
OWNERS: David and Virginia Adelsheim
FOUNDED: 1971

AT A GLANCE
Tours & Tastings: Open during Rain Revels (second weekend in June), Sat.–Sun. 2–5; Thanksgiving weekend, Fri.–Sun. 11–5. At other times open "grudgingly" by appointment.
Vineyards: Eighteen acres planted to vinifera varieties.
Wines: Pinot Noir, Chardonnay, White Riesling, Merlot, Pinot Gris, Sauvignon Blanc, Sémillon, Gamay Noir.
Awards: Does not enter competitions.
Retail Shop: Wines sold on-site.
Credit Cards: MasterCard, Visa.
Access for Disabled: None.
Foreign Languages: French, German.
Getting There: Winery is five miles northwest of Newberg, twenty-five miles southwest of Portland. Take Hwy. 99W toward Newberg, then pick up Rte. 240. Bear right on Tangen Rd., then left on North Valley Rd. One mile later turn right on Hillside Dr., which leads into Quarter Mile Lane.

🐦 To enhance his wine's flavor, David Adelsheim will take apart his barrels and toast the interiors over an oak fire—a technique he learned while conducting research at European test stations and France's Lycee Viticole. His perfectionism encompasses ecology as well as enology. To keep birds from eating his grapes, Adelsheim covers ripening vines with rigid nylon netting. While chemical spraying would be cheaper, he explains: "The robins were there first." Such attention to detail makes this one of Oregon's most respected wineries. Craft goes into the bottle as well as its contents. Artist Virginia Adelsheim thanks helpful friends and relatives by working their portraits into her graceful wine labels, available in poster form. But don't bother looking for lists of recent medals. After amassing a minor mint in a few years, the Adelsheims withdrew from competitions; now they would rather be judged by the public.

🐦 🐦 🐦

Amity Vineyards

18150 Amity Vineyards Road
Amity, Oregon 97101
TEL: 503-835-2362
PRESIDENT: Myron Redford
FOUNDED: 1976

AT A GLANCE
Tours & Tastings: Open June–Oct. daily 12–5; Oct.–May, weekends 12–5; and by appointment.
Closed: Dec. 24–Jan. 31.
Vineyards: Seventeen acres planted to Pinot Noir, White Riesling, Chardonnay, Gewürztraminer, Muscat. Additional grapes purchased from other Oregon wineries, primarily Sunnyside Vineyards in Salem.
Wines: Pinot Noir, Pinot Noir Nouveau, Oregon Blush, White Riesling, Gewürztraminer.
Awards: 1983 Pinot Noir: gold, silver, three bronzes; 1982 Pinot Noir: gold, two silvers, two bronzes; 1983 Chardonnay: bronze.
Picnic Area: Yes, with one of Oregon's most spectacular views, a panorama of the Willamette Valley and the coast range.
Retail Shop: Wines sold on-site.
Credit Cards: MasterCard, Visa.
Access for Disabled: Limited wheelchair access.
Foreign Languages: Limited French, Turkish.
Getting There: Winery is twenty-two miles northwest of Salem, forty-five miles southwest of Portland. In the town of Amity, turn onto Rice Ln., which runs perpendicular to Hwy. 99W. Amity Vineyards Rd. SE branches left off Rice Ln.
Special Wine & Other Events: Summer Solstice Wine Festival, on the weekend nearest June 21, offers music, food, and wine tours. Pinot Noir release is celebrated the third weekend of Sept. Oregon Winter Winetasting is held in the Lawrence Gallery, second weekend in Dec.

ॐ Shortly after he earned a bachelor's degree in political science, Myron Redford invited himself to Associated Vintners (now known as Columbia Winery) in Seattle, Washington's oldest premium winery; he worked there for several years, literally learning the business from the ground up. His wines seem to win awards wherever they are entered, and fans include the columnists Roy Andries De Groot and Terry Robards. Not one to rest on his grape leaves, Redford prides himself on being the first U.S. vintner to make a Nouveau Pinot Noir.

ॐ ॐ ॐ

Chateau Benoit

6580 Northeast Mineral Springs Road
Carlton, Oregon 97111
TEL: 503-864-2991, 864-3666
OWNERS: Fred and Mary Benoit
WINEMAKER: Gerard Rottiers (formerly of Domaine Gerard Rottier, a Grand Cru vineyard in Chablis, France)
FOUNDED: 1979

AT A GLANCE
Tours & Tastings: Open Mon.–Fri. 11–5, Sat.–Sun. 12–5. Informal tours, time permiting.
Closed: Christmas.
Vineyards: Forty-five acres planted to vinifera varieties.
Wines: Pinot Noir, Chardonnay, Riesling, Pinot Noir Nouveau. Best known for Sauvignon Blanc, Muller-Thurgau, sparkling wine.
Awards: 1985 Sauvignon Blanc: gold, two silvers, bronze; 1985 Muller-Thurgau: gold, three silvers; 1984 White Riesling: silver; Brut: silver, bronze.
Picnic Area: Yes, with great view.
Retail Shop: Wines sold on-site.
Credit Cards: MasterCard, Visa.
Access for Disabled: Limited.
Foreign Languages: French.
Getting There: Winery is 35 miles south-

west of Portland. From Hwy. 99W at Lafayette: travel 1½ miles up Mineral Springs Rd. to winery.
Special Wine & Other Events: Red, white, and blue sale on July 4th. Bastille Day Celebration on weekend nearest July 14. Wine Country Thanksgiving for the three days following Thanksgiving. Open houses.

🐸 Fred Benoit, the fourth generation of his family in Yakima Valley, cultivates grapes where his ancestors raised fodder; Mary Benoit, similarly, is descended from Washington pioneers. But their winery is steeped in the traditions of the Continent—all their winemakers have had professional European training. Sparkling wines are hand-riddled and disgorged in the traditional manner.

🐸 🐸 🐸

Elk Cove Vineyards

27751 Northwest Olson Road
Gaston, Oregon 97119
TEL: 503-985-7760
OWNERS/WINEMAKERS: Joe and Patricia
  Campbell
FOUNDED: 1977

AT A GLANCE
Tours & Tastings: Tastings daily 12–5. Tours by appointment only.
Closed: Thanksgiving, Christmas.
Vineyards: Twenty-seven acres planted to Pinot Noir, Chardonnay, Riesling, Gewürztraminer. Additional grapes supplied by Dundee Hills and Wind Hill Vineyards.
Wines: Gewürztraminer, Pinot Noir, White Pinot Noir, Chardonnay, Riesling, Late Harvest Riesling, Late Harvest Gewürztraminer, Cabernet Sauvignon.
Picnic Area: Yes.
Retail Shop: Wines sold on-site.
Credit Cards: MasterCard, Visa.
Access for Disabled: Ramp to tasting room.

Foreign Languages: French, German.
Getting There: Gaston is 30 miles southwest of Portland. From Hwy. 47 in Gaston: Turn onto Olston Rd.; Elk Cove is ahead 2.8 miles.
Special Wine & Other Events: Riesling Festival, Memorial Day weekend, features Alsatian food and Bavarian music. Pinot Noir Picnic, Labor Day weekend, serves up food and live music.

🐸 The Campbells' undergraduate degrees—his in biology and chemistry, hers in French and German—proved surprisingly useful when they took up winemaking. With an annual production of 20,000 gallons, their resident viticultural crew of five children comes in handy, too. Spring visitors might see the Roosevelt elk herd that inspired the winery's name.

🐸 🐸 🐸

Eyrie Vineyards

935 East Tenth Avenue
McMinnville, Oregon 97128
TEL: 503-472-6315
OWNERS: David and Diana Lett
WINEMAKER: David Lett (degree in
  viticulture from UC-Davis)
FOUNDED: 1970

AT A GLANCE
Tours & Tastings: Open Thanksgiving weekend and by appointment. Brief, self-guided tours.
Vineyards: Twenty-six acres in Dundee planted to Pinot Noir, Chardonnay, Pinot Gris, Muscat Ottonel, Pinot Meunier.
Wines: Pinot Noir, Chardonnay, Pinot Gris, Muscat Ottonel, Pinot Meunier.
Awards: Too numerous to list.
Retail Shop: Wines sold on-site.
Credit Cards: MasterCard, Visa.
Access for Disabled: Yes.
Getting There: Winery is in Yamhill County, thirty-six miles southwest of Portland. From Hwy. 99W in McMinn-

ville: head south on Lafayette Ave., then make a right onto E. Tenth St.

🍎 Like latter-day Johnny Appleseeds of the vine, David and Diana Lett brought Pinot Noir cuttings to the Willamette Valley and pioneered the region's premium wine industry. His European research and Napa Valley training led him to choose this area as the next best to Burgundy itself. Scarcely a decade later, Lett's judgment was confirmed: in two unrelated French competitions held in 1979 and 1980, Eyrie's 1975 Pinot Noir ranked with the top Gallic entries— the first American Pinot Noir to do so. Today $150 couldn't buy a bottle of that wine, but recent vintages are appreciably cheaper. "Our only competition," says Lett with pride, "comes from Burgundy."

🍎 🍎 🍎

Hidden Springs Winery

9360 Southeast Eola Hills Road
Amity, Oregon 97101
TEL: 503-835-2782, 363-1295
OWNERS: Donald R. Byard and Alvin
  Alexanderson
FOUNDED: 1980

AT A GLANCE
Tours & Tastings: Open June–Aug. Wed.–Tues. 12–5; weekends March–May and Sept.–Nov. 12–5; and by appointment. Winery once housed a prune dryer, while the vineyard was a plum orchard. Tasting room displays artwork from the Schubert Gallery in Albany, Oregon.
Closed: Dec.–Feb.
Vineyards: Twenty-five acres planted to Pinot Noir, Chardonnay, Riesling.
Wines: Pinot Noir, Chardonnay, Riesling, Pinot Gris, Pacific Sunset (blend).
Awards: 1980 Pinot Noir: gold, two silvers; 1982 Pinot Noir Blanc: bronze; 1981 Pinot Noir Reserve: silver, bronze;

1984 Pinot Noir Blanc: bronze; 1983 Pinot Noir: gold, bronze.
Picnic Area: Tables in orchard and on winery deck. During summer months, the patio is arranged like a French café.
Retail Shop: Wines, Brooks prunes, and English holly grown and sold on-site.
Credit Cards: MasterCard, Visa.
Access for Disabled: Winery and tasting room on ground level.
Foreign Languages: French, German, and Spanish interpreters available.
Getting There: Winery is 18 miles southwest of Salem, 35 miles southwest of Portland. Take 99W to Amity, head east 1 mile on Nursery St. Then go south about ¾ mile to Eola Hills Rd.
Special Wine & Other Events: Tastevin Tour, Memorial Day weekend; Wine Country celebration, Thanksgiving weekend.

🍎 Limited enological training has not hampered Donald Byard, a highway planner, and Alvin Alexanderson, a lawyer; their first commercial crush took a gold medal. Try the Brooks prunes while you still can. In bygone years, prune sales helped subsidize the winery, but with the success of Hidden Springs' Pinot Noir, the plum orchard is yielding way to grapevines.

🍎 🍎 🍎

Knudsen Erath Winery

17000 Northeast Knudsen Lane
Dundee, Oregon 97115
Tel: 503-538-3318
  Also visit:
  Dundee Tasting Room
  110 Southwest Highway 99W
  Dundee, Oregon 97115
  Tel: 503-538-6975
PARTNERS: Richard C. Erath and Cal
  Knudsen
WINEMAKER: Richard C. Erath
FOUNDED: 1972

AT A GLANCE

Tours & Tastings: Open daily 11–5. (The Dundee Tasting Room is open daily 10–6.)

Closed: Easter, Christmas.

Vineyards: 110 acres planted to Pinot Noir, Chardonnay, White Riesling. Additional grapes are purchased from local vineyards.

Wines: Pinot Noir, Chardonnay, White Riesling, sparkling wine, proprietary blends.

Awards: More than fifty regional and national medals. 1980 Select Pinot Noir: American Wine Championship, three golds; 1981 Merlot: gold; 1981 Chardonnay: silver.

Picnic Area: On-site and nearby at Crabtree Park.

Retail Shop: Wines sold on-site.

Credit Cards: MasterCard, Visa.

Access for Disabled: Yes.

Foreign Languages: French, German, Spanish spoken by some staff members.

Getting There: Winery is thirty-five miles southwest of Portland. From 99W in Dundee: Take Ninth St. northwest to Worden Hill Rd., then bear left. Northeast Knudsen Ln. branches left off Worden Hill Rd.

Special Wine & Other Events: Harvest Wine Festival, one of the last weekends in Aug.—with music, food, and wine. Open House, Thanksgiving weekend—all wines available for tasting.

: This celebrated winery has helped put the Willamette Valley on the map. Richard Erath, the son and grandson of Rhineland winemakers, pursued a career in electrical engineering before taking up the family trade. Three years after planting his vineyard, he joined forces with Cal Knudsen, another would-be vintner. There hasn't been a merger this important to Oregon since Lewis met Clark. Among enophiles, Knudsen Erath is a name to conjure with—Knudsen handles the finances, Erath handles the grapes.

Outside of a short course or two, the latter's knowledge has been acquired during repeated pilgrimages to France and Germany. And anyway, blood is thicker than wine.

: : :

Rex Hill Vineyards

30835 North Highway 99W
Newberg, Oregon 97132
TEL: 503-538-0666
OWNER: Paul C. Hart
FOUNDED: 1981

AT A GLANCE

Tours & Tastings: Open Apr.–Dec. daily 11–5; Jan.–March Fri.–Mon. 11–5. Regular weekend tours of winery.

Closed: Tues.–Thurs. Jan.–March.

Vineyards: Ten owned and twenty managed acres planted to Pinot Noir, Chardonnay. Additional grapes are purchased from area vineyards.

Wines: Vineyard-designated Pinot Noir, Chardonnay.

Picnic Area: Yes.

Retail Shop: Wines sold on-site.

Credit Cards: American Express, Visa.

Access for Disabled: Entrance and lavatory wheelchair accessible.

Getting There: Winery is 20 miles west of Portland, at Hwy. 99W and Ladd Hill Rd. about 5½ miles outside Sherwood. Veritas Vineyard is on opposite side of highway.

: The winery is housed in a converted, turn-of-the-century nut dryer that has been lovingly restored.

: : :

Sokol Blosser Winery

5000 Sokol Blosser Lane
Dundee, Oregon 97115
TEL: 503-864-2282
PRESIDENT: William Blosser

WINEMAKER: Robert McRitchie
(biochemist and microbiologist;
formerly chemist at Franciscan
Vineyards in Napa Valley)
FOUNDED: 1977

AT A GLANCE
Tours & Tastings: Open daily 11–5. Dramatic contemporary tasting room was designed by noted Oregon architect John Storrs.
Closed: Thanksgiving, Christmas, New Year's Day.
Vineyards: Forty-five acres planted to Pinot Noir, Chardonnay, White Riesling, Muller-Thurgau. Cherries, apples, and prunes are also grown on the premises.
Wines: Pinot Noir, Chardonnay, White Riesling, Muller-Thurgau, Gewürztraminer, Sauvignon Blanc.
Awards: 1983 Pinot Noir: Governor's Trophy. Numerous regional and international medals.
Picnic Area: Tables with sweeping views of Mt. Hood and Willamette Valley.
Retail Shop: Wines, fruits, souvenirs sold on-site.
Credit Cards: MasterCard, Visa.
Access for Disabled: Yes.
Foreign Languages: French, Spanish.
Getting There: Winery is 30 miles southwest of Portland. Take Hwy. 99W to Dundee, then turn right on Blanchard Ln., about 2½ miles past the Dundee Post Office.

* William and Susan Sokol Blosser founded their vineyard as a hobby, and the hobby gradually took over. They're not complaining, and neither is the public. A few years ago, when winery production exceeded 50,000 gallons, they gleefully quit their 9-to-5 jobs—he was an urban planner, she taught college-level American history. Careful planning, or perhaps good old American ingenuity, enabled them to use their property's rough terrain to singular advantage: because it is deliberately embedded in a rocky knoll, their wine cellar remains at a constant temperature year-round.

* * *

Veritas Vineyard

31190 Northeast Veritas Lane
Newberg, Oregon 97132
TEL: 503-538-1470, 636-0836
OWNERS: John and Diane Howieson
FOUNDED: 1984

AT A GLANCE
Tours & Tastings: Open May–Aug. daily 11–5; Sept.–Apr. weekends 11–5. Tours by appointment only.
Vineyards: Twenty acres planted to Pinot Noir, Chardonnay, White Riesling. Additional grapes are purchased from Willamette Valley vineyards.
Wines: Pinot Noir, Chardonnay, White Riesling.
Picnic Area: Yes.
Retail Shop: Wines sold on-site.
Credit Cards: MasterCard, Visa.
Access for Disabled: Winery and rest rooms wheelchair accessible.
Getting There: Winery is 20 miles west of Portland, at Hwy. 99W and Ladd Hill Rd., about 5½ miles outside Sherwood. Rex Hill Vineyards is on opposite side of highway.
Special Wine & Other Events: Activities scheduled during summer and Thanksgiving weekend.

* Neuroradiologist John Howieson began making wine as a diversion from the pressures of practicing medicine. A dedicated amateur for many years, he finally went commercial for the fun of it, and now enjoys recognition for operating one of the state's newer, most promising wineries.

TO SEE & DO
You can sample local art and wine simultaneously at the Lawrence Gallery in Sheridan (tel: 503-843-3787); Amity

Vineyards' Oregon Winetasting Room occupies the rear of the building, and most Yamhill County wineries are represented. Want to drink in local color as well? Herbert Hoover grew up in the Newberg home of his uncle Henry John Minthorn. Now the Hoover-Minthorn House (113 South River Street) admits the public for a fee; the adjacent Hoover Park is free of charge. More historic buildings, including a French prairie settlement, are on the grounds of Champoeg State Park. Linfield College, a small liberal arts school in nearby McMinnville, presents concerts and lectures in its Little Theater. For a change of pace, try picnicking in Maud Williamson State Park in Hopewell, then take the Wheaton ferry across the Willamette River. You'll disembark in Willamette Mission State Park, where the options include fishing, boating, and bicycling.

ACCOMMODATIONS
(See also listings at the end of the Mid-Willamette Valley and Portland sections.)

Safari Motel
345 North Highway 99W
McMinnville, Oregon 97128
Tel: 503-472-5187

Cozy rooms, a heated swimming pool, and a restaurant serving three meals a day, smack in the middle of wine country.

RESTAURANTS
Augustine's
Highway 18
Sheridan, Oregon 97378
Tel: 503-843-3225
Above the Lawrence Gallery. Elegant light lunches, more substantial surf-and-turf dinners, and a wide choice of Oregon wines.

Nick's Italian Cafe
521 East Third Street
McMinnville, Oregon 97128
Tel: 503-472-7919
Informal *trattoria* where the servings of northern Italian cuisine are generous. A hangout for vintners. Local labels, of course. Reservations are necessary on weekends.

Roger's
2121 East 27th Street
McMinnville, Oregon 97128
Tel: 503-472-0917
Seafood is the star. Attractive wooded setting. Well stocked with Oregon wines.

❧ WASHINGTON

Washington is what wine historian Leon Adams calls "one of the great wine-growing districts of the world." With 11,000 acres under cultivation, it's a rather large district, second only to California in the volume of premium vinifera grapes cultivated: the record 1987 harvest weighed in at a staggering 40,000 tons.

For all its heft, this industry is surprisingly young. The state's first winery, founded on Stretch Island in 1872, crushed a labrusca—or native American grape—called Island Belle. Even after Prohibition's repeal, labrusca bottlings dominated Washington. Protectionist tariffs levied against out-of-state wines meant that local vintners had little incentive to improve their product, since it faced no competition.

Vinifera grapes did not take root here until the late 1960s, when revised tax laws finally put local wines on an equal footing with Californian and European vintages. Suddenly, new vineyards appeared, planted to classic cold-climate viniferas such as Riesling and Chardonnay. The boom continues to this day; between 1980 and 1987 the number of Washington wineries quadrupled.

Some of these wineries were started by Californians who pulled up stakes and headed to the north, and others are purely local enterprises. Most grapes are grown inland, east of the Cascades in the southeastern part of the state, known for hot dry summers and cold, snowy winters. Although Washington vintners are producing more reds each year, this is primarily white wine territory, while fruit wines provide a nice change of pace.

Three of Washington's wine-growing areas are particularly well known: Walla Walla Valley and Yakima Valley, which are designated viticultural areas in the southeastern part of the state, and Columbia Gorge, in the Columbia v.a. just north of Portland. The Tri-Cities region, midway between the Walla Walla and Yakima Valleys, also supports a promising bunch of wineries. More establishments are clustered around Puget Sound North, Puget Sound South, and Seattle. And because there are winemaking outposts in the Olympic Peninsula and Spokane, visitors to this ruggedly beautiful land are never more than an hour's drive from a winery.

Columbia Gorge

Charles Hooper Family Winery

Spring Creek Road (P.O. Box 215)
Husum, Washington 98623
TEL: 509-493-2324
OWNERS: Charles and Beverlee Hooper
FOUNDED: 1985

AT A GLANCE
Tours & Tastings: Open Apr.–Sept. weekends 11–6, and by appointment. Continuous tours of winery and vineyard.
Vineyards: Fifteen acres planted to Riesling. Additional grapes are bought from vineyards within a thirty-mile radius.
Wines: White Riesling, Gewürztraminer, Pinot Noir Blush, Chardonnay.
Picnic Area: Yes.
Retail Shop: Wines sold on-site.
Credit Cards: MasterCard, Visa.
Access for Disabled: Limited.
Getting There: Winery is near Columbia

Gorge in southwest Washington, 9 miles north of White Salmon and 55 miles east of Vancouver. Take Hwy. 141 north toward Husum. Stay on Hwy. 141 until you see the sign reading "Trout Lake—16 miles," then turn left at the next corner, on Spring Creek Rd. When road divides, bear right on gravel road and continue 1½ miles to barn; Hooper sign is 100 yds. ahead on left.
Special Wine & Other Events: May Festival in White Salmon and Bingen, third weekend in May. Huckleberry Festival in the same two towns, mid-Aug.

❧ While working in Europe for the Department of Defense's schools, the Hoopers visited many vineyards, sampling wines and even picking grapes. After twenty-two years abroad, they moved back to the States and turned their home into a winery. Production, currently about 2,000 gallons, will at most triple. "When you get too large," says Charles Hooper, "you lose contact with the grapes."

❧ ❧ ❧

Salishan Vineyards

Route 2, Box 8
La Center, Washington 98629
TEL: 206-263-2713
OWNERS: Joan and Lincoln Wolverton
FOUNDED: Vineyards planted in 1971, winery built in 1982

AT A GLANCE

Tours & Tastings: Open weekends from May through last weekend before Christmas, 1–5; and by appointment. Tours allow visitors to see every stage of wine grape growing and processing.
Closed: Dec. 20–Apr. 30, weekdays, except by appointment.
Vineyards: Twelve acres planted to vinifera varieties.
Wines: Pinot Noir, Riesling, Chardonnay, Chenin Blanc, Cabernet and/or Cabernet-Merlot.
Awards: Recent medal winners include: 1982 Pinot Noir—bronze; 1984 Dry White Riesling—silvers, bronze; 1985 Dry White Riesling—silver, bronze.
Picnic Area: Yes.
Retail Shop: Wines sold on-site.
Credit Cards: None.
Access for the Disabled: Limited.
Foreign Languages: French.
Getting There: Winery is in Clark County, 30 miles north of Portland, Oregon, and 30 miles south of the Washington volcano Mount St. Helens. From I-5: Take exit 16 east 1½ miles to La Center Rd., then north on North Fork Rd. 1 mile.

❧ Joan Wolverton gave up journalism to run Salishan; Lincoln Wolverton, she reports pithily, "works as an economist to pay for it." Their vineyard is the first

modern-day planting of vinifera varietals west of Washington's Cascade Mountain Range. The Wolvertons produce fruity, bone-dry, European-style wines with the invaluable assistance of sons James, a bottling line and vineyard aide, and Thomas, bottle capper and labeling aide.

TO SEE & DO

The lava has cooled and the volcano is slumbering, but Mt. St. Helens remains a must on any tourist's list. The grass and trees are greener along Columbia Gorge's precipitous slopes; the attractions there include fishing, white-water rafting, hiking, and for the hardy, bicycling. For a detailed map of the region's innumerable parks, write or call the Army Corps of Engineers, 319 Southwest Pine, Portland, Oregon 97204; tel: 503-221-6021. To the north, in Mt. Adams's sub-alpine parkland, Bird Creek Meadows burst into riotous bloom from July through October. While in the area, take a self-guided tour through the lava caves near Trout Lake. Another point of interest is Broughton Lumber's nine-mile flume, which sends roughly dressed logs floating down the White Salmon River from the company's sawmill in Willard. Trivia fans take note: This is the longest active American lumber flume. Nearby you'll find Spring Creek Fish Hatchery, the Columbia River's first salmon hatchery.

ACCOMMODATIONS

The Flying L Ranch
Route 2, Box 28
Glenwood, Washington 98619
Tel: 509-364-3488
An appealing cross between a bed and breakfast and a dude ranch, located in the foothills of Mt. Adams. Open Apr.–Oct. Ranch-style breakfasts; art workshops, wilderness seminars.

Columbia Gorge
4000 West Cliff Drive
Hood River, Oregon 97031
Tel: 503-386-5566; 800-346-1921

Just across the Columbia River is this deluxe hotel in renovated 1920s structure; lovely gardens and river view. Atmospheric. Elegant dining with outstanding salmon, duck. Bountiful wine list.

Orchard Hill Inn
Route 2, Box 130
White Salmon, Washington 98672
Tel: 509-493-3024
A secluded bed and breakfast in the scenic White Salmon River Valley. Whirlpool bath, hiking trails, spectacular views.

Shilo Inn
13206 Northeast Highway 99
Hazel Dell, Washington 98665
Tel: 206-573-0511; 800-222-2244

Motel a convenient twelve miles south of Salishan Vineyards.

RESTAURANTS
The Logs
Highway 141
BZ Corner, Underwood, Washington
  98651
Tel: 509-493-1402
A rustic local hangout that has dished out ribs and fried chicken for more than fifty years.

Vancouver (Washington) favorites include The Crossing and Eaton's.

Olympic Peninsula

Bainbridge Island Vineyard and Winery

682 State Highway 305 NE
Winslow, Bainbridge Island, Washington
  98110
TEL: 206-842-WINE, 842-6711
OWNERS: Jo Ann and Gerard Bentryn
FOUNDED: 1982

AT A GLANCE
Tours & Tastings: Open Wed.–Sun. 12–5. No tours. Appointments needed for groups of ten or more. Tasting room houses a small museum of wine-related objects that date to 2000 B.C. Glass pieces, as well as enological curiosities, are sold at Jo Ann Bentryn's on-site antique shop.
Closed: Mon.–Tues.
Vineyards: Two acres planted to French and German vinifera varietals. Additional grapes are bought from other Washington vineyards. Strawberries are grown on Bainbridge Island.
Wines: Muller-Thurgau, Siegerrebe, Chardonnay, White Riesling, Gewürztraminer, Madeleine Sylvaner, Ferryboat White (a blend); strawberry wine.
Awards: 1985 Siegerrebe: seven medals; 1985 Muller-Thurgau: two medals; strawberry wine: gold.
Picnic Area: Yes.
Retail Shop: Wines sold on-site.
Credit Cards: None. Traveler's checks accepted.
Access for Disabled: None.
Foreign Languages: German and Polish.
Getting There: Winery is seven miles west of Seattle. Take thirty-five-minute ferry ride from Seattle. From Winslow Ferry Terminal: Walk or bicycle a quarter mile on Hwy. 305. Or drive to Bainbridge Island on Hwy. 305.
Special Wine & Other Events: The owners conduct wine tastings, wine ap-

preciation seminars, and a three-hour course on cool-climate grape growing.

❧ While living in Nuremberg, the Bentryns grew enamored of both German wine and the environment that fostered it. Deciding to plant a vineyard, they moved here because, Jo Ann Bentryn explains, "It was the closest we could get to Germany's climate." Their entire operation fills the handsome blue barn that Gerard Bentryn built. His next task may be to construct a showcase for medals: in only a few years, Bainbridge's first 24 wines have already collected 21 awards.

❧ ❧ ❧

Hoodsport Winery

N23501 Highway 101
Hoodsport, Washington 98548
TEL: 206-877-9894
OWNER: Hoodsport Winery, Inc.
FOUNDED: 1980

AT A GLANCE
Tours & Tastings: Open daily 10–6. Tours on weekends and at any time by appointment.
Closed: Thanksgiving, Christmas, New Year's Day.
Vineyards: None. All fruit is purchased from Washington and Oregon growers.
Wines: Chardonnay, Johannisberg Riesling, Gewürztraminer, Chenin Blanc, White Cap, Cabernet Rosé, Merlot, Island Belle; rhubarb, loganberry, gooseberry, and raspberry wines.
Awards: Raspberry: three golds; Gewürztraminer: silver; Island Belle: silver, bronze; and others.
Retail Shop: Wines sold on-site.
Credit Cards: MasterCard, Visa.
Access for Disabled: All of winery, except bathroom, wheelchair accessible.
Getting There: Winery is forty miles north of Olympia. From I-5: Take Hwy. 101 toward Shelton.

Special Wine & Other Events: Annual Octoberfest. Visitors may pick Island Belle grapes on Stretch Island in Puget Sound.

❧ Hoodsport's forte is fine fruit wines. Another specialty is Island Belle, made from the grapes of the same name. To sip this labrusca wine is to taste history: Island Belle, one of the country's first commercial grapes, was developed in the nineteenth century.

❧ ❧ ❧

Lost Mountain Winery

730 Lost Mountain Road
Sequim, Washington 98382
TEL: 206-683-5229
OWNER: Romeo J. Conca
FOUNDED: 1981

AT A GLANCE
Tours & Tastings: Open "whenever I am here," says the owner. Tours conducted on demand.
Closed: "Whenever I am not here."
Vineyards: Grapes bought from growers in Washington, Oregon, and California.
Wines: Cabernet Sauvignon, Petite Sirah, Zinfandel, Merlot, Pinot Noir, Muscat, blends.
Retail Shop: Wines sold on-site.
Credit Cards: None.
Access for Disabled: Nearly level entrance to winery. No bathroom facilities.
Foreign Languages: Some Italian, French, and German.
Getting There: Winery is in Clallam County, fifteen miles east of Port Angeles and sixty-five miles northwest of Seattle. Call for directions.

❧ A retired research chemist, Romeo J. Conca now devotes much of his time to analyzing wine. He's equally ardent about food, and makes his own bacon, prosciutto, and sausage. That's part of his heritage; his father was a noted Italian chef. As a result of his third passion—literature—Conca has inaugurated Poetry Series wines: these wines are released in tandem with a local poet's verse, and the bottles bear elegant, limited-edition labels.

ಣ ಣ ಣ

Neuharth Winery

148 Still Road
Sequim, Washington 98382
TEL: 206-683-9652, 683-3706
PRESIDENT: Eugene Neuharth
FOUNDED: 1979

AT A GLANCE

Tours & Tastings: Open May 15–Sept. 30 daily 9:30–5:30; Oct.–May 15 Wed.–Sun. 12–5. Tours by appointment.
Vineyards: Half an acre experimentally planted to thirty-four hybrids. Some of these are added in minute amounts to blended wines. Most of Neuharth's grapes come from eastern Washington.
Wines: Chardonnay, Johannisberg Riesling, Merlot, Cabernet Sauvignon, and three proprietary blends—Dungeness White, Dungeness Rosé, and Dungeness Red.
Awards: Many regional, state, and international medals.
Picnic Area: None at winery; Carrie Blake Park is half a mile away.
Retail Shop: Wines sold on-site.
Credit Cards: MasterCard, Visa.
Access for Disabled: None.
Foreign Languages: Spanish, Portuguese.
Getting There: Winery is on east edge of Sequim, seventy miles north and west of Seattle. From Hwy. 101: Take Still Rd. south a quarter of a mile. Watch for sign.
Special Wine & Other Events: Special holiday sales.

ಣ Eugene Neuharth is a retired Californian vineyardist, and Maria Neuharth is a born saleswoman, so their winery seems preordained. Walk through the tasting room's arched doors and look around; the stuccoed walls, stone floor, and solid oak bar, not to mention the gracious service, will transport you to a bygone era.

TO SEE & DO
In Olympic National Park, 600 miles of trails lead hikers through the forest primeval. Swim in Lake Crescent during the summer, ski Hurricane Ridge during the winter. Details available from the concessionaire at Star Route 1, Port Angeles, Washington 98362 (tel: 206-928-3211). Fishing, bird-watching, and shell collecting are the main activities at Dungeness Spit, a protected seven-mile promontory. Request pamphlets and maps from Nisqually National Wildlife Refuge, Box 1487, Olympia, Washington 98507.

Bainbridge Island offers numerous recreational opportunities: hiking and equestrian trails, tennis courts, golf courses, ball fields, and picnic sites. This small community also serves as a gateway to the rest of the Kitsap Peninsula, where diverse cultures exist side-by-side. The city of Poulsbo celebrates its Nordic heritage with the Viking Fest in May, Skandia Midsommarfest in June, and the Yule Log Festival in November. Port Gamble, by contrast, resembles a classic New England village, with an authentic nineteenth-century general store. Native American customs are perpetuated in Suquamish, Chief Seattle's final resting place; one of this town's main attractions is the Tribal Center and Museum. For additional information, consult the Bremerton/Kitsap County Visitor and Convention Bureau, P.O. Box 836, Bremerton, Washington 98310 (tel: 206-479-3588).

ACCOMMODATIONS
Bombay House
Beck Road
Bainbridge Island, Washington 98110
Tel: 206-842-3926
Antique-filled rooms overlook sloping

lawns. Peace and quiet just 35 minutes by ferry from Seattle. Home-baked breakfast.

The Captain's House
234 Parfitt Way
Bainbridge Island, Washington 98110
Tel: 206-842-3557
A delightful three-room bed and breakfast. Hosts provide a rowboat and bicycles.

Red Ranch Inn
830 West Washington
Sequim, Washington 98382
Tel: 206-683-4195
Motel with western decor.

Tudor Inn
1108 South Oak
Port Angeles, Washington 98362
Tel: 206-452-3138
A beautifully restored English-style inn built in 1910. Wine is served in the library; morning coffee can be delivered to your door before you come down to a generous breakfast.

Lizzie's
731 Pierce Street
Port Townsend, Washington 98368
Tel: 206-385-4168
A delightful century-old B & B, furnished in period style, located in a beautifully restored Victorian seacoast town.

RESTAURANTS
Saltwater Cafe
403 Madison Street
Bainbridge Island, Washington 98110
Tel: 206-842-8839
A wonderful seafood restaurant on the waterfront.

Three Crabs
101 Three Crabs Road
Dungeness, Washington
Tel: 206-683-4264
Steak year-round, fresh cracked Dungeness crab Oct.–March.

Puget Sound—North

Mount Baker Vineyards

4298 Mount Baker Highway (P.O. Box 626)
Deming, Washington 98244
TEL: 206-592-2300
PRESIDENT: Albert Stratton
WINEMAKER: Brent Charnley (degree in viticulture and enology from UC-Davis)
FOUNDED: 1981

AT A GLANCE
Tours & Tastings: Open Jan.–March weekends 11–5, Apr.–Dec. Wed.–Sun. 11–5. Cellar and vineyards open to visitors during tasting room hours.

Vineyards: Twenty-five acres planted to Chardonnay, Gewürztraminer, Madeline Angevine, Muller-Thurgau, Okanogan Riesling, Madeline Sylvaner, Precoce de Malingre. Plums are also grown on-site.
Wines: From viniferas above and Late Harvest Select Cluster Johannisberg Riesling, proprietary blends, plum wine.
Awards: Too numerous to list individually.
Picnic Area: Yes.
Retail Shop: Wines sold on-site.
Credit Cards: MasterCard, Visa.
Access for Disabled: Limited.
Getting There: Winery is in the Nooksack Valley, approximately one hundred

miles north of Seattle. From I-5: Take Sunset Dr., exit 255 east, toward Mt. Baker for about eleven miles. Turn left to the winery on Hilliard Rd. A perfect stop on your way to Vancouver.

Special Wine & Other Events: Annual Grape Stomp and Nooksack Valley Cuisine, last weekend in Sept.

&. Upon his retirement, military surgeon Albert Stratton received a home winemaking kit from his family. Rapidly rising in winemaking ranks, he soon became vintner for the Northwestern Washington Research and Extension Unit of Washington State University. Stratton brought this same experimental spirit to his own enterprise, Washington's northernmost winery. Some of Mt. Baker's most successful varietals are relatively unusual in the United States, such as Madeline Angevine, Madeline Sylvaner, and Precoce de Malingre.

&. &. &.

Quilceda Creek Vintners

5226 Machias Road
Snohomish, Washington 98290
TEL: 206-568-2389
PRESIDENT: Alex P. Golitzin
FOUNDED: 1978

AT A GLANCE

Tours & Tastings: Open by appointment only. No tours.
Vineyards: None. All grapes are purchased from Yakima Valley growers.
Wines: Cabernet Sauvignon.
Awards: 1979 Cabernet Sauvignon: Grand Prize, gold; 1980 Cabernet Sauvignon: gold; 1981 Cabernet Sauvignon: silver; 1982 Cabernet Sauvignon: gold.
Retail Shop: Wines sold on-site.
Credit Cards: None.
Access for Disabled: None.
Foreign Languages: French, Russian.
Getting There: Winery is twenty-five

miles north of Seattle. From I-5: Take Hewitt exit to Hwy. 9 and head south to Bunk Foss Rd. Turn left on Bunk Foss Rd. and left again on Machias Rd. (If you hit New Machias Hwy. you've gone too far.)

&. Dedicated to the proposition that less is more, Alex Golitzin makes scarcely two hundred cases of one varietal, so each year's bottling is superb. If Cabernet Sauvignon is your wine, Quilceda Creek is your destination. How does a chemical engineer turn into an outstanding vintner? It helps to be the French-born son of prominent Russian émigrés—and the nephew of famed winemaker Andre Tchelistcheff. The latter steered Golitzin to the Washington vineyardists who grow Quilceda Creek's grapes. But don't spend any more time reading. Hurry to the winery before the last bottle is sold.

TO SEE & DO

Puget Sound is sprinkled with little islands and towns all the way to Canada. Edmonds is green and pretty, with a municipal fishing pier, and parks wherever you turn. Ferries run regularly to the Kitsap Peninsula. Snohomish is also worth a stroll; after admiring the lovely old homes, visit the stores that crowd Antique Mall, at 821 Second Street. Farther north, near the Canadian border, Bellingham boasts its own museum and handsome turn-of-the-century houses. Western Washington University, on High Street in Bellingham, has outdoor installations of sculptures by such contemporary masters as Isamu Noguchi, Mark di Suvero, and Richard Serra. Rental boats await would-be captains at nearby Lake Whatcom. While you're there, board the Lake Whatcom Railway for a brief scenic ride through the woods (tel: 206-734-6430). Outside Ferndale, Hovandale Homestead's picnic sites overlook the Nooksack River.

ACCOMMODATIONS

(For more information, see Seattle section)

The Castle B & B
1103 15th Street
Bellingham, Washington 98225
A majestic mauve mansion, built in 1890 and furnished entirely with antiques.

Anderson House
2140 Main Street (P.O. Box 1547)
Ferndale, Washington 98248
A Victorian bed and breakfast near Bellingham. Breakfast on fresh fruit, baked goods, and Kona coffee; afternoon tea.

Heather House
1011 B Avenue
Edmonds, Washington 98020
Tel: 206-778-7233 (5–6:30 P.M.)

A bed and breakfast in Harry and Joy Whitcutt's contemporary home boasting a terrific view of Puget Sound and the Olympic Mountains. Breakfast features homemade jams, jellies, and marmalades.

RESTAURANTS

Oyster Creek Inn
240 Chuckanut Drive
Bellingham, Washington 98226
Tel: 206-766-6185
An oyster bar.

Chuckanut Manor
302 Chuckanut Drive
Bow, Washington 98232
Tel: 206-766-6191
Fresh seafood and steak are specialties; view of Samish Bay is another attraction. Near Bellingham.

Puget Sound—South

Manfred Vierthaler Winery

17136 Highway 410 East
Sumner, Washington 98390
TEL: 206-863-1633
PRESIDENT: Manfred J. Vierthaler
FOUNDED: 1976

AT A GLANCE

Tours & Tastings: Open daily 12–6. Tours by appointment.
Closed: Christmas, New Year's Day.
Vineyards: Five owned and five leased acres planted to White Riesling and Muller-Thurgau. Additional grapes are purchased from California growers.
Wines: White Riesling, Muller-Thurgau, Goldener Gutedel, Cabernet Sauvignon, Pinot Noir, Rhine Rosé, Moselle.
Restaurant: Lunch and dinner are served in the winery's Bavarian restaurant. En-

trées range from German standards such as wurst and goulash, to wild boar schnitzel. Separate menu of salads and sandwiches in roof garden.
Retail Shop: Wines sold on-site.
Credit Cards: American Express, MasterCard, Visa.
Access for Disabled: Yes.
Foreign Languages: German.
Getting There: Winery is fifteen miles east of Tacoma and thirty miles south of Seattle. Take Hwy. 410 East toward Sumner.

&. Want to experience Bavaria without leaving the West Coast? Visit the five-story chalet that houses the Manfred Vierthaler Winery, the Manfred Vierthaler restaurants, and the Manfred Vierthaler family. The German-born proprietor has created a formidable tourist attraction, and offers eminently potable wines made from locally grown grapes.

TO SEE & DO

Tacoma offers two sizable attractions: Mt. Rainier National Park to the southeast, and Point Defiance State Park to the north. Every schoolchild knows that Rainier (formerly known as Mt. Tacoma) is the tallest peak in Washington. At Point Defiance (tel: 206-591-3690), visit the zoo, the replica of Fort Nisqually, and endless beaches and forests. Boats and tackle can be rented at the Point Defiance Boathouse (4912 North Waterfront, Tacoma, Washington 98407; tel: 206-591-5325).

ACCOMMODATIONS

(See also Seattle section)

Keenan House
2610 North Warner
Tacoma, Washington 98407
Tel: 206-752-0702
A bed and breakfast in a beautifully furnished eighty-year-old house in Tacoma's historic district. Tea in the afternoons, full breakfast with fruit and croissants in the morning.

Tail Ship Ketch *Krestine*
3311 Harborview Drive
Gig Harbor, Washington 98335
Tel: 206-858-9395
Now hear this: unique shipboard lodging in the captain's cabin, with private bath.

RESTAURANTS

Balsano's Italian Restaurant
127 Fifteenth Street Southeast
Puyallup, Washington 98372
Tel: 206-845-4222
Veal, seafood, and pasta. Fine pastries complete your meal.

Neville's Shoreline Restaurant
8827 North Harborview Drive
Gig Harbor, Washington 98335
Tel: 206-851-9822, 627-1784
Fresh seafood served on the waterfront. Dock space available for sailors.

Seattle Area

Cavatappi

9702 Northeast 120th Place
Kirkland, Washington 98034
TEL: 206-823-6533
PRESIDENT: Peter Dow
FOUNDED: 1984

AT A GLANCE

Tours & Tastings: By appointment only.
Vineyards: None. Grapes purchased from Washington growers.
Wines: Sauvignon Blanc, Merlot, Muscat, Zinfandel, Nebbiolo.
Awards: Merlot: bronze.
Restaurant: Cavatappi is owned and operated by the proprietor of Cafe Juanita, at the same address (tel: 206-823-1505). This sumptuous restaurant serves northern Italian cuisine. Open nightly.
Retail Shop: Wines sold only at Cafe Juanita.
Credit Cards: MasterCard, Visa.
Access for Disabled: Restaurant accommodates wheelchairs.
Foreign Languages: Italian.
Getting There: Ten miles from Seattle. Head north on I-405 and take 116th St. exit. After 1½ miles, turn right on 97th.

🍇 Peter Dow was the Washington sales rep for a Maryland winery before he opened Cafe Juanita; his preoccupation with food only increased his interest in wine.

ᨄ ᨄ ᨄ

Chateau Ste. Michelle

One Stimson Lane (P.O. Box 1876)
Woodinville, Washington 98072
TEL: 206-488-1133
Also visit two other Chateau Ste.
Michelle locations:
205 West Fifth
Grandview, Washington 98930
Tel: 509-882-3928
And:
Route 221 (P.O. Box 231)
Paterson, Washington 99345
Tel: 509-875-2061
OWNER: U.S. Tobacco
DIRECTOR OF WINERY OPERATIONS:
Peter Bachman (graduate of
California Polytechnic State
University; subsequently studied
under expert enologist Richard G.
Peterson and noted consultant Andre
Tchelistcheff)
FOUNDED: 1934

AT A GLANCE

Tours & Tastings: Open daily 10–4:30
(Memorial Day–Labor Day, weekend
hours are 10–6). Guided tours of cellar
area, departing every twenty minutes,
explain winemaking, as it pertains to
Washington and Chateau Ste. Michelle.
Tastings conducted at tour's end cover a
range of wines from dry to sweet.
(Grandview winery open daily 10–5; the
Paterson winery is open daily 10–4:30.)
Closed: Easter, Thanksgiving, Christmas,
New Year's Day.
Vineyards: 3,180 acres planted to eleven
vinifera varieties. Loganberries also
grown on-site.
Wines: Blanc de Noir, Cabernet Sauvi-
gnon, Chardonnay, Chenin Blanc, Fumé
Blanc, Gewürztraminer, Grenache Rosé,
Johannisberg Riesling, Merlot, Muscat
Canelli, Rosé of Cabernet, Sémillon,
Sémillon Blanc, White Riesling, proprie-
tary blends, Loganberry liqueur.

Awards: 1984 Gewürztraminer: two
golds, three bronzes; 1984 Sémillon
Blanc: silver, two bronzes; 1984 Rosé of
Cabernet: silver, bronze; 1981 Cabernet
Sauvignon: gold, bronze; and many
other medals.
Picnic Area: Lush eighty-seven-acre
property with pathways and trout ponds.
Retail Shop: Wines, Whidbey's Loganberry Liqueur, picnic foods, and gifts
sold on-site.
Credit Cards: MasterCard, Visa.
Access for Disabled: Wheelchair lifts into
cellar.
Getting There: Woodinville is fifteen
miles northeast of Seattle. From I-405:
Take exit 23 east (Hwy. 552) to Woodinville exit. Turn right at stop sign and continue to NE 175th St. Turn right and go
over railroad tracks to stop sign. Turn left
and take Hwy. 202 about two miles to
winery.
Special Wine & Other Events: Concerts,
plays, classic auto shows, and sports
events held throughout year. Call for
schedule.

ᨄ Originally, a small company dedicated to fruit wines, Chateau Ste.
Michelle began releasing vinifera varietals in the 1960s. In the two decades
since, this winery has become Washington's largest—and one of its best,
earning scores of medals. Now, Chateau
Ste. Michelle comprises three wineries:
all reds are produced at Granville; fragrant whites, such as Johannisberg Riesling and Gewürztraminer, are produced
at Paterson; and the wood-aged whites,
such as Chardonnay and Sémillon, are
produced here in Woodinville. This site
was the estate of a Seattle lumber baron,
and the antique-filled mansion that
serves as corporate headquarters invites
exploration, as do the carefully landscaped grounds.

ᨄ ᨄ ᨄ

Columbia Winery

1445 120th Avenue Northeast
Bellevue, Washington 98005
TEL: 206-453-1977
PRESIDENT: Dan Baty
WINEMAKER: David Lake (Master of
Wine, the highest professional
designation in the British wine
industry; viticulture and enology
studies at UC-Davis)
FOUNDED: 1962

AT A GLANCE
Tours & Tastings: Open daily 10:30–4:30.
Closed: Major holidays.
Vineyards: Grapes are purchased from
Washington vineyards.
Wines: Sémillon, Chardonnay, Cabernet
Sauvignon, Merlot.
Awards: 1982 Red Willow Vineyard Cabernet Sauvignon: gold, silver, bronze;
1983 Merlot: gold, three silvers; 1984
Sémillon: silver, three bronzes; 1983
Chardonnay: silver; 1983 Pinot Noir: two
bronzes; and many other medals.
Retail Shop: Wines sold on-site.
Credit Cards: MasterCard, Visa.
Access for the Disabled: None.
Getting There: Winery is ten miles east of
Seattle. From I-5: Take Hwy. 520 East to
Bellevue, then take 120th Ave. NE.

๖ If one were to gamble at competitions, Columbia would be a safe bet—its
wines usually stand in the winner's circle. This premium winery, formerly
known as Associated Vintners, sold off
its vineyards a few years ago so employees could focus exclusively on making and marketing wines. Resident
vintner David Lake came here after
working at several noted Oregon establishments, including Eyrie Vineyards and
Amity Vineyards. He is one of the only
British masters of wine working in the
U.S.

๖ ๖ ๖

French Creek Cellars Winery

15372 Northeast 96th Place
Redmond, Washington 98502
TEL: 206-833-0757
OWNERS: Trudi Doerr and Bill Mandy

AT A GLANCE
Tours & Tastings: Open Thurs.–Sat. 12–
5, and by appointment. Tours given anytime tasting room is open or when cellarmaster is present. Children may enjoy
free juice tastings.
Closed: Sun.–Wed.
Vineyards: Grapes bought from vineyards in south-central Washington.
Wines: Dry and off-dry Riesling, Chardonnay, Muscat Canelli, Sémillon, Cabernet Sauvignon, Merlot, Pinot Noir,
Lemberger.
Awards: 1984 Pinot Noir: bronze; 1984
Riesling: bronze; 1984 Chardonnay: one
star; 1980 Riesling: three bronzes; 1985
Muscat Canelli: gold.
Picnic Area: Yes.
Retail Shop: Wines sold on-site.
Credit Cards: MasterCard, Visa.
Access for Disabled: Limited.
Foreign Languages: German, French.
Getting There: Winery is thirty minutes
northeast of Seattle's business district.
From I-405: Take exit 18 (Kirland-Redmond Rd.) east and turn left on Willows
Rd. Bear right on NE 95th St., at Willows
Business Center; then left on 153rd NE.
Special Wine & Other Events: Three
times a year—spring, summer, and after
fall crush—open house weekends feature
wine specials, free food, and tastings of
smoked salmon and chocolate.

๖ Several Seattle-area families founded an amateur winemaking group in
1973, and French Creek was the eventual
result. "Only premium quality wines are
produced under carefully controlled conditions," says co-owner Bill Mundy.
Cyclists are in luck: a bike trail con-

necting the towns of Redmond and Both-ell runs in front of the winery.

ટ ટ ટ

Haviland

1 Manor Lane and Northeast 145th
Woodinville, Washington 98072
TEL: 206-488-0808
OWNERS: Heath Gunn, Pat Ackermann,
and George de Jarnatt
WINEMAKER: George de Jarnatt
FOUNDED: 1980

AT A GLANCE
Tours & Tastings: Open daily, Mon.–Fri. 11–5, weekends 10–5. In-depth tours followed by tastings every thirty minutes or when demand dictates.
Closed: Christmas, New Year's.
Vineyards: More than seventy acres planted to Cabernet Sauvignon, Merlot, Chardonnay. Additional grapes are purchased from Columbia Valley growers.
Wines: Cabernet Sauvignon, Chardonnay, Merlot, Riesling, Fumé Blanc, Chevrier (Sémillon).
Awards: Numerous.
Retail Shop: Wines sold on-site.
Credit Cards: American Express, MasterCard, Visa.
Access for the Disabled: Wheelchair accessible.
Foreign Languages: French, Spanish, German, Italian.
Getting There: Winery is fifteen miles from Seattle, across the street from Chateau Ste. Michelle. From I-405: Take exit 23 east (Hwy. 522) to Woodinville exit. Turn right at stop sign and continue to NE 175th St. Turn right and go over railroad tracks to stop sign. Turn left and take Hwy. 202 about two miles to winery.

ટ When accountant George de Jarnatt bought a twenty-year-old vineyard as a tax shelter, he discovered that the grapes made excellent Cabernet Sauvignon. The state of Washington lost a CPA

and gained a vintner. He's especially proud of moving the Havilland winery to this recently completed Victorian-style building, with its spacious production area. A twenty-mile bike trail runs along the property.

ટ ટ ટ

Snoqualmie Winery

1000 Winery Road
Snoqualmie, Washington 98065
TEL: 206-888-4000; from Seattle
206-392-4000
PRESIDENT/WINEMAKER: Joel Klein
(enology degree from UC-Davis)
FOUNDED: 1983

AT A GLANCE
Tours & Tastings: Open daily 10–4:30. Hours may be extended during ski and summer seasons. Scheduled tours on weekends, tours upon arrival during off-season. Visitors view fermentation tanks, aging barrels, and the modern European bottling line. A tasting session concludes tour.
Closed: Thanksgiving, Christmas, New Year's Day.
Vineyards: Leased vineyard planted to vinifera varieties. Additional grapes are purchased from Yakima Valley growers.
Wines: Johannisberg Riesling, Gewürztraminer, Sémillon, Chenin Blanc, Merlot, Cabernet Sauvignon, Chardonnay, Late Harvest White Riesling.
Picnic Area: Yes. Stunning view of Snoqualmie Valley, Mt. Si, and the Cascade Mountain Range.
Retail Shop: Wines sold on-site.
Credit Cards: MasterCard, Visa.
Access for Disabled: Limited.
Getting There: Winery is twenty-seven miles due east of Seattle. From I-90: Take either exit 27 (eastbound) or exit 31 (westbound) and drive toward Snoqualmie Falls.
Special Wine & Other Events: Snoqualmie Winery holds the Medieval May

Festival, first weekend of May; the Anniversary Celebration in July; and the Holiday Gift Show, first weekend of Dec.

≈ After a few years as a chemical engineer, Joel Klein decided to leave the lab for the vineyard. He studied enology in California, married into a viticulturally inclined family, and worked at a Sonoma County winery. Then he spent eight years at Washington's Chateau Ste. Michelle making wines under the tutelage of Andre Tchelistcheff.

≈ ≈ ≈

Paul Thomas Winery

1717 136th Place Northeast
Bellevue, Washington 98005
TEL: 206-747-1008
OWNER: Paul Thomas
WINEMAKER: Brian Carter (two years in
  master's program at UC-Davis)
FOUNDED: 1979

AT A GLANCE
Tours & Tastings: Open Fri.–Sat. 12–5, and by appointment. Three or four wines are poured per day in antique-filled tasting room.
Closed: Dec. 24–Jan. 2.
Vineyards: None. All fruit is bought from Washington growers; grapes come from Columbia River, rhubarb from Puyallup Valley, raspberries from Bellingham, pears from Naches Valley.
Wines: Crimson (rhubarb), Dry Bartlett (pear), Washington Raspberry, Sauvignon Blanc, Chenin Blanc, Johannisberg Riesling, Muscat Canelli, Cabernet Sauvignon.
Awards: Crimson: silver; Dry Bartlett: silver; Muscat Canelli: gold, silver; Johannisberg Riesling: gold, silver; Cabernet Sauvignon: Governor's Trophy, gold, silver, bronze; and other medals.
Retail Shop: Wines sold on-site.
Credit Cards: None.

Access for Disabled: Wheelchairs accommodated.
Foreign Languages: French.
Getting There: Winery is ten miles east of Seattle. From I-405: Head east on NE Eighth St. Turn left on Bel-Red Rd., sharply left on NE Sixteenth St., and right on 136th Pl. NE.
Special Wine & Other Events: Events throughout year, dates set only a couple of months in advance. Call for details.

≈ Paul Thomas was once a high school teacher. Having left academe, he still tries to educate people, and his subject nowadays is the virtue of dry fruit wine. Thomas contends that Crimson and Dry Bartlett are wonderful table wines—and judging by his soaring sales figures, he has gained a lot of adherents.

TO SEE & DO
Seattle has all the urban advantages—excellent restaurants, numerous museums, a fine symphony orchestra—with few liabilities. If you're not tired of touring, survey five blocks of intact nineteenth-century buildings that were buried underground when the street level was raised ten feet. Bill Speidel's excursions leave from 610 First Avenue (tel: 206-682-4646). From May through October, scenic harbor cruises depart from Pier 55 on Seneca Street (tel: 206-623-1445). Emulate Dr. Doolittle and talk to the animals at Woodland Park Zoo (Phinney Avenue North; tel: 206-789-7919) and the Seattle Aquarium (Pier 59, Waterfront Park; tel: 206-625-4357). Humans can test the waters at the pool in Lincoln Park or at the many Lake Washington beaches. In bad weather, retreat inside; the Seattle Art Museum (14th Avenue East and East Prospect Street) will keep you profitably occupied (tel: 206-443-6740). Pike Place Market (First Avenue and Pike Street) is the country's oldest continuously operating farmers' market. Seattle Center, site of the 1962

World's Fair, remains an exciting stop; the amusement park, 605-foot-tall observation tower, and monorail rides have a timeless appeal. Outside the city limits, attractions include the town of Snoqualmie, with its landmark train station, historical train ride, and celebrated Snoqualmie Falls. For further details, contact the Seattle/King County Visitor & Convention Bureau (1815 7th Avenue, Seattle 98119; tel: 206-447-4200).

ACCOMMODATIONS

Alexis Hotel Seattle
1007 First Avenue
Seattle, Washington 98104
Tel: 206-624-4844; 800-426-7033
Originally an office building designed in 1901, the Alexis is the award-winning result of a total renovation, resulting in a European-style luxury hotel. Fresh flowers and antiques highlight soothing decor. The Cafe Alexis serves American cuisine, with northwestern flair, featuring fresh, locally grown ingredients and a fine wine list.

Beech Tree Manor
1405 Queen Anne Avenue North
Seattle, Washington 98109
Tel: 206-281-7037
A turn-of-the-century B&B just a trolley ride from downtown. All-cotton sheets, fluffy towels, and home-baked Continental breakfast.

Chambered Nautilus
5005 22nd Avenue Northeast
Seattle, Washington 98105
Tel: 206-522-2536
A handsome Georgian Colonial, perched on a hill in the university district and decorated throughout in a seashell theme. Wholesome full breakfast.

Inn at the Market
86 Pine Street
Seattle, Washington 98101
Tel: 206-443-3600; 800-446-4484
A delightful luxury hotel located in the heart of Seattle's wonderful Pike's Place Market. Roof garden has a great view of the market, the ferries, and the sunset.

The Sorrento Hotel
900 Madison Street
Seattle, Washington 98104
Tel: 206-622-6400; 800-426-1265
Behind the Italian-style grand façade lies a handsome luxury hotel. The hotel restaurant, the Hunt Club, prepares innovative northwestern cuisine as well as traditional American. Exceptional salmon, tasty rabbit. Extensive wine list with many Washington and Oregon selections.

Cedarym
1101 240th Avenue Northeast
Redmond, Washington 98053
Tel: 206-868-4159
Bed and breakfast in a colonial-style home with wall stenciling, antique brass beds, and hand-dipped candles. Full breakfast. Twelve miles east of Seattle.

RESTAURANTS

See also listings above for the Alexis Hotel, the Inn at the Market, and the Sorrento Hotel.

Anthony's Homeport
Kirkland, Washington 98033
Tel: 206-822-0225

Cafe Juanita
9702 Northeast 120th Place
Kirkland, Washington 98034
Tel: 206-823-1505
(See "Restaurant" section of Cavatappi winery listing.)

Enoteca
414 Olive Way
Seattle, Washington 98101
Tel: 206-624-9108
Light but innovative cuisine—mesquite-grilled duck salad sprinkled with raspberry vinaigrette—accompanied by a wide

range of regional wines, some of them available by the glass.

Le Tastevin
19 West Harrison Avenue
Seattle, Washington 98119
Tel: 206-283-0991
Classic French cuisine and well-stocked regional wine cellar. Dine outdoors in fair weather.

1904
1904 4th Avenue
Seattle, Washington 98101
Tel: 206-682-4142
Salmon in various guises distinguishes this Art Deco-accented restaurant.

Amply stocked wine cellar as well as by-the-glass selections.

Ray's Boathouse
6040 Seaview Avenue N.W.
Seattle, Washington 98107
Tel: 206-789-3770
Seattle's oldest seafood restaurant perches on a pier jutting into Shishole Bay. Well-rounded wine list.

Simon's
17401 South Center Parkway
Seattle, Washington 98188
Tel: 206-575-3500
Atrium setting for stylish Continental cuisine. Lavish desserts. Wine cellar.

Spokane Area

Arbor Crest Winery

East 4506 Buckeye
Spokane, Washington 99207
Also visit:
Arbor Crest Cliff House
North 4705 Fruithill Road
Spokane, Washington 99207
TEL: 509-927-9463 (for both locations)
OWNERS: David and Harold Mielke
WINEMAKER: Scott Harris (B.S. in fermentation sciences from UC-Davis)
FOUNDED: 1982

AT A GLANCE
Tours & Tastings: Winery open daily 12–5. No organized tours; interested tasters are shown through facility on an informal basis. At Cliff House, a mansion listed on the National Register of Historic Places, tours and tastings are held by appointment only, Mon.–Fri. 12–4.
Closed: Major holidays.
Vineyards: 87 acres in the Columbia Valley planted primarily to white viniferas. Additional grapes are currently pur-

chased from south-central Washington growers.
Wines: Chardonnay, Sauvignon Blanc, Cabernet Sauvignon, Merlot, White Riesling, Johannisberg Riesling, Jardin des Fleurs (blush), Muscat Canelli, Late Harvest Gewürztraminer, Select Late Harvest Johannisberg Riesling.
Awards: Recent award winners include: 1984 Sauvignon Blanc—gold; 1983 Merlot—gold; 1982 Cabernet Sauvignon—gold.
Picnic Area: Yes.
Retail Shop: Wines sold on-site.
Credit Cards: MasterCard, Visa.
Access for Disabled: None.
Getting There: Winery is 5 miles east of downtown Spokane, north of the Spokane River. From I-90: Take exit 283-B. Head north on Freya, cross Mission, and continue north on Greene. Bear right on Upriver Dr.; Buckeye comes up on the left. Cliff House is 12 miles east of downtown Spokane, north of the Spokane River. From I-90: Take Argonne Rd. exit (*not* 283-B). Head 1½ miles north on Ar-

gonne Rd., turn right on Upriver Dr. and continue for 1 mile. Turn left on Fruithill Rd. House is at top of the hill.

&. While pursuing a medical career, Harold Mielke was seeing less and less of his brother David, the family's third-generation orchardist. Growing grapes together seemed like one way to keep from growing apart. Fraternity proved fruitful—Arbor Crest was a success from the beginning, reaping a bumper crop of medals from the very first crush. Now the Mielkes are renovating Cliff House, a sixty-year-old mansion that will eventually become their winery's headquarters. Designed for the tramway mogul Royal N. Riblet, Cliff House was famed for such laborsaving devices as a motorized contraption that brought mail to the house from the mailbox 1,000 feet away.

&. &. &.

Latah Creek Wine Cellars

East 13030 Indiana Avenue
Spokane, Washington 99216
TEL: 509-926-0164
OWNERS: Mike Conway and Mike
  Hogue
WINEMAKER: Mike Conway (formerly a
  microbiologist for Gallo Winery in
  California; winemaking experience at
  Parducci Winery in California and
  Worden's Winery in Washington)
FOUNDED: 1982

AT A GLANCE
Tours & Tastings: Open Mon.–Sat. 10–5, Sun. 12–5. Informal tours throughout the day.
Closed: Christmas, New Year's Day.
Vineyards: Grapes are purchased from growers in Yakima and Columbia Basin.
Wines: Chardonnay, Sémillon, Johannisberg Riesling, Chenin Blanc, Muscat Canelli, Merlot Blush, May wine, Late Harvest Gewürztraminer, Late Harvest (botrytis) White Riesling.

Awards: 1983 Chardonnay: gold; 1983 Chenin Blanc: Best of Show; 1984 Sémillon: gold, five silvers, bronze; 1984 Johannisberg Riesling: gold, bronze.
Picnic Area: Yes.
Retail Shop: Wines sold on-site.
Credit Cards: MasterCard, Visa.
Access for Disabled: Limited.
Getting There: Winery is five miles east of Spokane. From I-90: Take exit 289 and turn north on Pines Rd. Drive north to Indiana, the first street marked by a stoplight, and turn right. Proceed east on Indiana two blocks.
Special Wine & Other Events: June: case buyers' premiere of new vintages; July: winery anniversary; Sept.: craft show.

&. Mike Conway was happily ensconced at another winery when Mike Hogue (see the Hogue Cellars, listed in the Yakima Valley section) helped him launch Latah Creek. This is an easygoing, family enterprise. The gracious, mission-style winery includes an art gallery and a gift shop, and the lovely tiled courtyard encourages visitors to linger over lunch. Latah Creek is serious about wine; four years after the first crush, production had increased more than eightfold, to 35,000 gallons.

&. &. &.

Worden's Washington Winery

7217 West 45th
Spokane, Washington 99218
TEL: 509-455-7835
OWNER: Jack Worden
FOUNDED: 1980

AT A GLANCE
Tours & Tastings: Open Mon.–Sun. 12–4; summer hours: 12–5. Tours of winery, including brief slide show, given on request.
Vineyards: None. Grapes are purchased from southern Washington growers.
Wines: Johannisberg Riesling, Chenin,

Chardonnay, Fumé, Cabernet, Merlot, Blush, Rosé, Gewürztraminer.

Awards: 1985 Gamay Rosé: gold; 1985 Gewürztraminer: silver; 1985 Johannisberg Riesling: silver.

Picnic Area: Yes.

Retail Shop: Wines, hors d'oeuvres sold on-site.

Credit Cards: MasterCard, Visa.

Access for Disabled: None.

Getting There: Winery is five miles from Spokane. From I-90: Take exit 276 and follow signs.

Special Wine & Other Events: Grape Stomp, first Sat. in Oct. A competitive event in which participants stomp grapes for one minute; prizes are awarded to those who make the most juice. Wine barrel races, tastings, tours.

&. The tasting room of Spokane's oldest winery is lodged in an unpretentious log cabin surrounded by pine trees; except for the large picture windows, it's the sort of place where future presidents used to be born. Winemaking actually occurs farther back in the woods, in a shed. Production has grown steadily from the initial crush of 4,200 cases but, promises owner Jack Worner, "It is the firm commitment of this winery never to compromise quality."

TO SEE & DO

Spokane is the heart of the lumber-and-mining territory Washingtonians call the Inland Empire. This is excellent camping country, hot and dry in summer, and fishermen should bring along rods and reels. During the winter, of course, consider packing skis—and long johns. In Spokane itself there is plenty to do. Expo 74 has departed Riverfront Park (Spokane Falls Boulevard and Howard Street; tel: 509-456-5512), but the carousel and skating rink remain. The Cheney Cowles Memorial Museum displays Indian crafts and pioneer relics; next door is the Campbell House, a grand mansion built in 1898. Glorious Manito Park promises

you rose gardens—and Japanese gardens as well. Shoppers can invest in the work of local artisans at two Spokane stores: Homestead Handicrafts (North 1301 Pines Road; tel: 509-928-1986) and Made in Washington (Riverpark Square; tel: 509-838-1517). For more information, contact: Spokane Regional Convention & Visitors Bureau, West 301 Main Street, Spokane, Washington 99201, Tel: 509-624-5055.

ACCOMMODATIONS

(All in Spokane, except where noted.)

Cavanaugh's Inn at the Park
West 303 North River Drive 99201
Tel: 509-326-8000; 800-THE-INNS
Also:
Cavanaugh's River Inn
North 700 Division Street 99202
Tel: 509-326-5577; 800-THE-INNS
Excellent local motel chain.

Fotheringham House
2128 West Second 99201
Tel: 509-838-4363
A bed and breakfast in a turn-of-the-century home with lots of original detail: tinned ceilings, curved window glass in entry. Patsy Clark's Mansion (a restaurant) is next door. Continental breakfast features stuffed homemade croissants.

Red Lion Motor Inn
I-90 and Sullivan Road
Veradale, Washington 99037
Tel: 509-924-9000; 800-547-8010
Patios, balconies, and all the expected features.

RESTAURANTS

(All in Spokane.)

Cavanaugh's
Fine dining at both motel sites. (See listing under "Accommodations" for addresses and telephone numbers.)

Otter Bay Restaurant
South 104 Freya
Tel: 509-534-5329
Comfortable bistro with a large menu.

Patsy Clark's Mansion
2208 West Second
Tel: 509-838-8300

A mining baron's home, painstakingly restored and turned into a stylish restaurant with an impressive wine list. Duck, seafood specialties.

Tri-Cities Area

Bookwalter Winery

2505 Commercial Avenue, Suite A
Pasco, Washington 99301
TEL: 509-547-8571
OWNERS: Jerrold R. and Jean M.
  Bookwalter
FOUNDED: 1984

AT A GLANCE
Tours & Tastings: Open daily 10–5.
Closed: Major holidays.
Vineyards: Grapes are purchased from Columbia Basin growers.
Wines: Chenin Blanc, Chardonnay, Cabernet Sauvignon, Johannisberg Riesling.
Awards: 1984 Johannisberg Riesling: gold, bronze, silver, Best of Festival; 1983 Johannisberg Riesling: silver, bronze; 1983 Chardonnay: gold, silver, two bronzes.
Retail Shop: Wines, gift items sold on-site.
Credit Cards: MasterCard, Visa.
Access for Disabled: None.
Foreign Languages: Spanish.
Getting There: Winery is on the northern edge of Pasco. Commercial Ave. is off Hillsboro Rd., just northeast of the interchange of Hwys. 395 and 12.

🌰 Jerrold R. Bookwalter wants to build on the success of Washington State wines by offering only small lots of very high quality premium wines. His extensive experience as a vineyard manager enables him to choose the best possible grapes.

🌰 🌰 🌰

Gordon Brothers Cellars

531 Levey Road
Pasco, Washington 94301
TEL: 509-547-6224
OWNERS: Jeff and Vicki Gordon; Bill
  Gordon and Kathy Huntley
FOUNDED: 1985

AT A GLANCE
Tours & Tastings: Usually open weekends, May–Aug. 11–5, at other times by appointment. Call ahead to be sure the winery is open. Tours by appointment only.
Vineyards: Eighty-three acres planted to Cabernet Sauvignon, Gewürztraminer, Chardonnay, Chenin Blanc, Merlot, Sauvignon Blanc.
Wines: Chardonnay, Chenin Blanc, Johannisberg Riesling, Sauvignon Blanc, Merlot, Cabernet Sauvignon.
Awards: 1984 Johannisberg Riesling: two silvers, Consumer Choice; 1984 Sauvignon Blanc: gold, bronze; 1983 Chardonnay: three bronzes; 1984 Chenin Blanc: silver.
Picnic Area: Levey Park is near winery.
Retail Shop: Wines sold on-site.
Credit Cards: MasterCard, Visa.
Access for Disabled: None.

Getting There: Winery is ten miles northeast of Pasco. Take I-182 to Kahlotus Hwy. Levey Rd. is on the right, after Ice Harbor Rd.

Special Wine & Other Events: Winter Wine Fair is held in Pasco in March; Prosser hosts a Wine and Food Fair in Aug.

ed In just a few years, Gordon Brothers Cellars has established an enviable record: all of their first releases have won medals in northwestern wine competitions. This small winery also boasts a magnificent view of the Snake River, with the Blue Mountains looming in the background.

ed ed ed

Kiona Vineyards and Winery

Sunset Road
Route 2, Box 2169E
Benton City, Washington 99320
TEL: 509-588-6716
PARTNERS: J. J. Holmes and J. A. Williams
FOUNDED: 1972

AT A GLANCE
Tours & Tastings: Open daily 12–5.
Closed: Thanksgiving, Christmas, New Year's Day.
Vineyards: Thirty acres planted to Cabernet Sauvignon, Chardonnay, Merlot, White Riesling, Chenin Blanc, Lemberger.
Wines: Varietals from above viniferas.
Awards: 1984 Chardonnay: gold, two silvers, four bronzes; 1985 White Riesling: four silvers, bronze; 1984 Dry White Riesling: silver, three bronzes; 1985 Chenin Blanc: three bronzes; 1983 Lemberger: silver, two bronzes; and many other medals.
Picnic Area: Finished patio, tables in vineyards.
Retail Shop: Wines sold on-site.
Credit Cards: MasterCard, Visa.

Access for Disabled: Yes.
Getting There: Winery is 20 miles northwest of Pasco. Take I-84 to Benton City, then head west on Rte. 224 for 1½ miles. Watch for sign on left.

ed Kiona Vineyards is one of the oldest wineries in this region. Yet after more than fifteen years, James Holmes and John Williams still think of themselves as pioneers; they describe their joint venture as "essentially a frontier effort in an open wilderness location, with no other activity in the immediate area." No matter—their award-winning wines provide enough of a draw.

ed ed ed

Franz Wilhelm Langguth Winery

2340 Winery Road
Mattawa, Washington 99344
TEL: 509-932-4943
OWNERS: German Wine Corp. and Wolfgang Langguth
WINEMAKER: Max Zellweger (degree in enology and fruit juice technology from College for Fruit and Wine Technology, Wadenswil, Switzerland; graduated first in class, 1979)
FOUNDED: 1981

AT A GLANCE
Tours & Tastings: Open daily 10–5. Complete tours of winery—including crush area, treatment, tanking, and bottling—available upon request, time permitting; otherwise by appointment. No tours of vineyard.
Closed: Christmas, New Year's Day.
Vineyards: 265 acres planted to Johannisberg Riesling, Chardonnay, Gewürztraminer.
Wines: Specializes in German-style whites. Also some white and red blends.
Awards: 1982 Late Harvest Riesling: three golds; 1982 Select Harvest Special Release Johannisberg Riesling: Grand Prize, golds, bronzes; 1984 Late Harvest

Johannisberg Riesling: gold, silvers, bronzes; 1983 Chardonnay: silver; and many other medals.

Retail Shop: Wines sold on-site.

Credit Cards: MasterCard, Visa.

Access for Disabled: Wheelchair accessible.

Foreign Languages: German.

Getting There: Winery is thirteen miles east of Mattawa, fifty miles north of Richland. From Vernita Bridge: take Hwy. 243 to SW Rd. 24, which leads into Winery Rd.

Special Wine & Other Events: Langguth Weinfest at winery on third weekend of July.

🍂 Nearly two centuries after German vintner Franz Wilhelm Langguth sold his very first bottle, the Moselle-based firm that bears his name established this American outpost. It's an enormous modern winery, with a tank capacity of 550,000 gallons and state-of-the-art equipment—grapes are weighed electronically and crushed by remote control. Langguth's founding father wouldn't recognize anything except the wines, an assortment of Rieslings that taste as though they were made in the old country.

🍂 🍂 🍂

Mercer Ranch Vineyards

HC 74, Box 401
Prosser, Washington 99350
TEL: 509-894-4741, 894-4149
OWNERS: Don and Linda Mercer
WINEMAKER: Stephen Redford
FOUNDED: 1985

AT A GLANCE

Tours & Tastings: Open Mon.–Sat. 9–5, Sun. (May–Oct.) 11–5, and by appointment. Informal tours explain whatever work is underway—pruning, training vines, harvesting, crushing, etc. Visitors are welcome to stroll on their own through flower gardens and adjacent vineyards. The Mercers are third-generation ranchers, descended from sheep ranchers. The colorful life-style of the past is shown in photographs that decorate the tasting room's walls.

Closed: Sun. (Nov.–Apr.), Christmas, New Year's Day.

Vineyards: 132 acres planted to Cabernet Sauvignon, Lemberger, White Riesling, Chardonnay, Muscat de Canelli, Chenin Blanc.

Wines: Cabernet Sauvignon, Lemberger, Sadie Louise (blended blush), Muscat Canelli (sweet), Cabernet Sauvignon–Merlot blend.

Awards: 1984 Lemberger: silver, bronze; Cabernet-Merlot: two silvers, bronze.

Picnic Area: Yes.

Retail Shop: Wines and Lemberger wine jelly sold on-site.

Credit Cards: MasterCard, Visa.

Access for Disabled: Level sidewalk from driveway to winery, rest room and doors wide enough to accommodate wheelchairs.

Getting There: Winery is in eastern Klickitat County, seventeen miles west of Paterson. Technically Mercer Ranch is in Alderdale, but this tiny village (pop. 33) isn't on most maps. Take Hwy. 14 to Alderdale Rd. Head north on Alderdale about five miles.

Special Wine & Other Events: Prosser Wine and Food Fair in Aug.

🍂 With irrigation, the Mercers transformed nearly 10 percent of their arid 27,000-acre ranch into fertile farmland; then, as an experiment, a small plot was planted to Cabernet Sauvignon. The results were splendid. Other vintners made these grapes into wines so good they were vineyard-designated from the very first vintage. Donald Mercer duly took the hint and started making wine himself. He sees great potential in his twelve-acre Lemberger planting, one of the largest in the country. Very few vineyards raise this premium red varietal, but Mercer's earliest crushes are getting a lot of attention. "That grape is an old-world treasure," he reports.

᠊ᢀ ᠊ᢀ ᠊ᢀ

Preston Wine Cellars

502 East Vineyard Drive
Pasco, Washington 99301
TEL: 509-545-1990
OWNERS: S. W. "Bill" and Joann
    Preston
FOUNDED: 1976

AT A GLANCE
Tours & Tastings: Open daily 10–5:30. Self-guided tours. At least four wines available at tasting bar every day.
Closed: Easter, Thanksgiving, Christmas, New Year's Day.
Vineyards: 181 acres planted primarily to white vinifera varieties. Some Royalty (a California-developed hybrid) and Pinot Noir for red wines. Additional grapes are bought from neighboring vineyards.
Wines: Chardonnay, Fumé Blanc, Pinot Noir Blanc, Gewürztraminer, Johannisberg Riesling, Chenin Blanc, Gamay Beaujolais Rosé, Merlot, Cabernet Sauvignon, and the proprietary blends Desert Gold, Desert Blossom, and Desert Red; sparkling wines.
Awards: Recent medal winners include: 1981 Chardonnay: silver, four bronzes; 1982 Fumé Blanc: gold, two silvers, six bronzes; 1981 Gewürztraminer: silver, bronze; 1980 Pinot Noir Blanc: gold; 1984 Johannisberg Riesling: three silvers, two bronzes.
Picnic Area: Winery has its own park with cooking facilities.
Retail Shop: Wines and wine-related gifts sold on-site.
Credit Cards: MasterCard.
Access for Disabled: Wheelchair accessible.
Getting There: Winery is five miles north of Pasco. Take Hwy. 395 north of Pasco, watch for sign on east side of highway.

᠊ᢀ Bill and Joann Preston were far-sighted enough to plant white viniferas when many people couldn't even pronounce the word "Gewürztraminer." Now they lay claim to Washington's largest family-owned and family-operated winery, producing about 130,000 gallons a year. The tasting room is suitably grand, with an elevated deck and veranda that afford a panoramic view of the vineyards.

᠊ᢀ ᠊ᢀ ᠊ᢀ

Quarry Lake Vintners

2505 Commercial Avenue, Suite C
Pasco, Washington 99301
TEL: 509-547-7307
PRESIDENT: Otto Geisert
GENERAL MANAGER: Maury Balcom
    (B.S. in enology and viticulture from
    California State University–Fresno)
FOUNDED: 1985

AT A GLANCE
Tours & Tastings: Open Fri.–Mon. 12–5. Vineyard tours by appointment.
Closed: Tues.–Thurs., major holidays.
Vineyards: 110 acres planted to Johannisberg Riesling, Chenin Blanc, Sauvignon Blanc, Gewürztraminer, Chardonnay, Pinot Noir, Cabernet Sauvignon, Merlot. Apples and cherries are also grown on-site.
Wines: Varietals from grapes above.
Retail Shop: Wines sold on-site.
Credit Cards: MasterCard, Visa.
Access for Disabled: None.
Getting There: Winery is on the northern edge of Pasco. Commercial Ave. is off Hillsboro Rd., just northeast of the interchange of Hwys. 395 and 12.

᠊ᢀ Finally, after more than a decade of selling exceptional grapes to other vintners, Quarry Lake is releasing wines under its own label. This move was long anticipated; Quarry's vineyards, planted in 1971, are among the oldest and finest in the state.

TO SEE & DO

You name the sport, Tri-Cities (Pasco, Kennewick, Richland) probably has it, from minor-league baseball in Richland (tel: 509-943-0622) to quarter horse races in Kennewick (tel: 509-586-9211). At Sacajawea State Park and Interpretive Center (tel: 509-545-2361) visitors can swim, picnic, and learn about both the Lewis and Clark expedition and the local Indian tribes it encountered. Continue surveying the past at the Benton County Historical Museum in Prosser (tel: 509-786-3842), the East Benton County Historical Museum (205 Keewaydin Drive, Kennewick; tel: 509-582-7704), and the Franklin County Historical Museum (305 North Fourth, Pasco; tel: 509-547-3714). If you have energy left, discover how to conserve it through the films and hands-on exhibits at the Hanford Science Center in Richland (tel: 509-376-6374).

The Ice Harbor Lock and Dam in neighboring Pasco is at 103 feet among the world's tallest navigation locks and a dramatic area attraction. There's a visitor center and a tour covering the premises including its powerhouse and a view of a fish ladder; call 509-547-7781 for information.

Wine Festival: The Tri-Cities Northwest Wine Festival comes to Kennewick—the grape center of Washington—in July; tickets are limited, so place orders in advance through the Tri-Cities Visitors and Convention Bureau (tel: 509-735-8486; in Washington, 800-835-0248).

ACCOMMODATIONS

(See also Yakima Valley listings.)

Cavanaugh's Motor Inn
1101 North Columbia Center Boulevard
Kennewick, Washington 99336
Tel: 509-783-0611

An excellent local chain; this site is adjacent to Columbia Shopping Center. Live music and dancing.

Clover Island Inn
435 Clover Island
Kennewick, Washington 99336
Tel: 509-586-0541
Amenities include cable TV, Jacuzzi, sauna, outdoor pool, and boat dock. Comfortably set on an island in the Columbia River.

Hanford House Thunderbird
802 George Washington Way
Richland, Washington 99352
Tel: 509-946-7611
Motel located on the banks of the Columbia River. Tennis courts, jogging path nearby; boat docks, water skiing. Restaurant.

Red Lion Motor Inn
2525 North 20th
Pasco, Washington 99301
Tel: 509-547-0701; 800-547-8010

RESTAURANTS

The Barn Restaurant and Roundup Room
Highway 12
Prosser, Washington 99350
Tel: 509-786-1131
Steaks, seafood, and fine local wine.

Hanford House Thunderbird
(see "Accommodations" above)
Veal, steak, wine and a river view.

Everything's Jake
100 North Morain
Kennewick, Washington 99336
Tel: 509-735-6022
A family-owned specialty deli dishing out the best chili in the Tri-Cities area. Other dishes complement local wines.

Walla Walla Valley

L'Ecole No. 41

41 Lowden School Road
Lowden, Washington 99360
TEL: 509-525-0940
OWNERS: Baker and Jean T. Ferguson
FOUNDED: 1978

AT A GLANCE

Tours & Tastings: Open by appointment only, except mid-Nov. to Dec. 31. Complete tours take about half an hour and conclude with tasting.
Closed: Thanksgiving, Christmas, New Year's Day.
Vineyards: Grapes are purchased from Tri-Cities vineyards.
Wines: Sémillon, Merlot.
Awards: 1983 Merlot: gold, bronze.
Picnic Area: Shady backyard with a barbecue. Swings and seesaws, too.
Restaurant: Small restaurant with seatings in a tasting room; by reservation only.
Retail Shop: Wines sold on-site.
Credit Cards: MasterCard, Visa. Personal checks accepted.
Access for Disabled: Wheelchair accessible.
Foreign Languages: French.
Getting There: Winery is 32 miles east of Tri-Cities and 12½ miles west of Walla Walla. East end of Lowden, just off the north side of Hwy. 12. Woodward Canyon Winery is nearby, to the west.
Special Wine & Other Events: Open house during Walla Walla's Balloon Stampede, first weekend in May. Also open without appointment from two weeks before Thanksgiving to New Year's Day.

❦ About ten years ago the Fergusons purchased District 41 Lowden Schoolhouse, formerly a grade school built in 1915, and turned it into a winery. Vats and barrels replaced desks and chairs, but the building's name, translated into French, underwent only minimal alteration. Even winemaker Jean Ferguson is a retired chemistry teacher. Classrooms have become tasting rooms, and prices are neatly chalked on the careworn blackboard where several generations of schoolmarms wrote out multiplication tables. Fittingly, children's art appears on L'Ecole's wine labels.

❦ ❦ ❦

Woodward Canyon Winery

Route 1, Box 387
Lowden, Washington 99360
TEL: 509-525-4129
OWNERS: Rick and Darcy Small, Ray and Jean Small
FOUNDED: 1981

AT A GLANCE

Tours & Tastings: Mon.–Sat. 10–5, Sun. 12–5 (May–Sept.); Mon.–Sat. 10–4, Sun. 12–4 (Oct.–Apr.). Informal tours.
Closed: Major holidays.
Vineyards: Ten acres planted to Chardonnay. Additional grapes are purchased from other Washington vineyards.
Wines: Cabernet Sauvignon, Merlot, Chardonnay, Estate Chardonnay, Select Cluster Riesling, Sémillon, Riesling.
Awards: 1983 Cabernet Sauvignon: four golds; 1984 Chardonnay: two silvers; 1985 Sémillon: bronze. Many other medals for previous years' releases.
Picnic Area: Yes.
Retail Shop: Wines sold on-site.
Credit Cards: None. Checks accepted.
Access for Disabled: No steps; winery is on ground level.
Getting There: Winery is fifteen miles west of Walla Walla and forty miles east of Tri-Cities. Right on Hwy. 12.
Special Wine & Other Events: Walla Walla Hot-Air Balloon Stampede, ac-

companied by Spring Release, first weekend in May. Fall Release, first weekend after Labor Day.

๛ Rick Small—a descendant of this area's original settlers and an alumnus of District School 41—had no formal winemaking education. He acquired a taste for good wine while traveling in Europe. After returning to Washington, he began making wine at home. Woodward Canyon is small, producing 4,000 gallons per year. Everything is done by hand in a corrugated tin building with a cement floor. A dozen local restaurants serve his wine; ask for details.

TO SEE & DO
Stock up for a Saturday picnic by paying a morning visit to the Farmers' Market in downtown Walla Walla. Then visit historic Whitman College (founded in 1859) in Walla Walla. The Pioneer Village and Indian burial grounds at Fort Walla Walla Museum are noteworthy; guided tours are available (tel: 509-525-7703). A few miles away, Whitman Mission National Historic Site marks the place where medical missionary Marcus Whitman and his family were killed in an 1847 Indian uprising.

ACCOMMODATIONS
(See also listings in the Tri-Cities Area section.)

Best Western/Pony Soldier Motor Inn
325 East Main Street
Walla, Walla, Washington 99362
Tel: 509-529-4360; 800-524-1234
Relax in the outdoor pool, then tune in cable TV. Complimentary Continental breakfast and newspaper.

The Rees Mansion
East Birch and South Palouse
Walla Walla, Washington 99362
Tel: 509-529-7845
Bed and breakfast in a restored Victorian mansion. Excellent restaurant with fine selection of local vintages.

RESTAURANTS
Patit Creek
725 East Dayton Avenue
Dayton, Washington 99328
Tel: 509-382-2625
The entrées are both well prepared and reasonably priced, the wine list is extensive, and it's only a thirty-minute drive from Walla Walla.

Rees Mansion
(See "Accommodations" above.)

Yakima Valley

Blackwood Canyon Vintners

Route 2, Box 2169H
Benton City, Washington 99320
TEL: 509-588-6249
GENERAL PARTNER/WINEMAKER:
   M. Taylor Moore (B.S. in
   fermentation science from UC-Davis)
FOUNDED: 1982

AT A GLANCE
Tours & Tastings: Open weekends 10–6, Mon.–Fri. by appointment. Informal tours are given as time permits; barrel samples frequently included.
Vineyards: Fifty-one acres planted to Chardonnay, Sémillon, Cabernet Sauvignon, Merlot.
Wines: Chardonnay, Sémillon, Cabernet Sauvignon, Late Harvest Riesling.
Awards: 1982 Chardonnay: bronze; 1983 Sémillon: gold, silver, bronze; 1983 Ultra Late Harvest: silver.
Picnic Area: Yes, with a view of the Yakima Valley.

Retail Shop: Wines sold on-site.
Credit Cards: MasterCard, Visa.
Access for Disabled: None.
Foreign Languages: Spanish.
Getting There: Winery is 15 miles west of the Tri-Cities and 15 miles east of Prosser. From I-82: Take Benton City exit and drive 1½ miles east on Hwy. 224. Then go 2 miles north on Sunset Rd.

🐚 All Blackwood Canyon wines are made with traditional European techniques. The dry whites are barrel fermented; stainless steel is not used here.

🐚 🐚 🐚

Chinook Wines

Route 3, Box 3622
Wittkopf Road
Prosser, Washington 99350
TEL: 509-786-2725
OWNERS: Clay Mackey and Kay Simon
FOUNDED: 1985

AT A GLANCE
Tours & Tastings: Open Fri.–Sun. 12–5, and other days by appointment. Tours given by appointment only. Original farm buildings serve as the winery, storage area, and tasting room.
Closed: Christmas, New Year's Day.
Vineyards: Grapes are bought from Washington State growers.
Wines: Chardonnay, Sauvignon Blanc, Sémillon–Sauvignon Blanc blend, Merlot, Sparkling Riesling.
Picnic Area: Yes, under the shade trees.
Retail Shop: Wines sold on-site.
Credit Cards: None.
Access for Disabled: None.
Getting There: Winery is 50 miles southeast of Yakima. From I-82: Take exit 82; go east ⅛ mile to intersection with Wittkopf Rd.

🐚 Clay Mackey and Kay Simon met at the University of California–Davis. He

was studying food science and viticulture, she was studying fermentation science and enology. This winery is one joint venture; their marriage is another.

🐚 🐚 🐚

Covey Run Vintners

Route 2, Box 2287
Zillah, Washington 98953
TEL: 509-829-6235
OWNERS: Partnership of Washington residents
WINEMAKER: Wayne Marcil (degree in fermentation science from UC-Davis)
FOUNDED: 1982

AT A GLANCE
Tours & Tastings: Open Mon.–Sat. 10–5, Sun. 12–5. Guided tours by appointment.
Closed: Easter, Thanksgiving, Christmas, New Year's Day.
Vineyards: 180 leased acres planted to Riesling, Cabernet, Chardonnay, Merlot, Gewürztraminer, Muscat Blanc, Chenin Blanc, Sémillon, Sauvignon Blanc.
Wines: Johannisberg Riesling, White Riesling, Chardonnay, Merlot, Cabernet Sauvignon, Aligote, Morio Muskat, Lemberger, Chenin Blanc, Gewürztraminer.
Awards: Recent medal winners include: 1983 Merlot—gold, bronze; 1984 Lemberger—three silvers, two bronzes; 1982 Johannisberg Riesling—Governor's Award, two golds, two silvers, two bronzes; 1984 Aligote—gold, silver, four bronzes.
Picnic Area: Yes.
Retail Shop: Wines sold on-site. Gift shop and small gallery adjacent provide a showcase for local artists.
Credit Cards: MasterCard, Visa.
Access for Disabled: Limited wheelchair access.
Getting There: Winery is twenty miles southeast of Yakima. Take exit 52 off I-82. Travel north on Fifth St., cross Old Hwy. 12, and continue north on Rosa Dr.

Head east on Highland Dr. and north again on Morris Rd., which leads to winery.

Special Wine & Other Events: Bacchus Celebration, at the beginning of harvest, with the Greek god of wine blessing the ripened grapes, and vineyard tours via horse-drawn wagon. Also, open house in Apr., a winery picnic in July, wreath making in Nov., Christmas concert in Dec.

🐚 Sound advice and careful planning helped make this enterprise the enological equivalent of an overnight success: three years after its vineyards were planted, Quail Run Vintners bottled its first wines, almost all of them award winners. The enthusiastic reception given subsequent releases proved that there was more involved than beginner's luck. Now called Covey Run, this winery is known both for its superb Rieslings and for popularizing the less familiar varietals Aligote, Lemberger, and Morio Muskat.

🐚 🐚 🐚

Hinzerling Vineyards

1520 Sheridan Avenue
Prosser, Washington 99350
OWNER/WINEMAKER: Mike Wallace
(graduate work in enology at UC-
Davis)
TEL: 509-786-2163
FOUNDED: 1976

AT A GLANCE
Tours & Tastings: Open Mon.–Sat. 10–12 and 1–5, Sun. 1–5, Apr.–Dec. 24. Call for appointment. No formal tours, but visitors can often observe winemaking operations directly.
Closed: Dec. 25–March 31, Thanksgiving.
Vineyards: Thirty acres planted to Riesling, Gewürztraminer, Cabernet Sauvignon, Chardonnay, Merlot.

Wines: Riesling, Gewürztraminer, Cabernet Sauvignon, Chardonnay, Merlot.
Awards: Too numerous to list.
Picnic Area: Yes.
Retail Shop: Wines sold on-site.
Credit Cards: MasterCard, Visa.
Access for Disabled: None.
Getting There: Winery is in city of Prosser. Take Hwy. 12 to Prosser. If coming from Yakima, take Gap Rd. exit and follow Old Hwy. 12 to Sheridan Ave. From the Tri-Cities: Take Industrial Park exit to Old Hwy. 12 and go to Sheridan Ave.
Special Wine & Other Events: Prerelease tastings, barrel tastings, and seminars announced in newsletters. To be added to mailing list, write to winery.

🐚 A local newspaper's account of Washington State University's vineyard research so intrigued Mike Wallace that he packed himself off to California for classes in enology. Soon, the former medical technician was tending his own vines in Yakima Valley, and conducting tests at the research station he had read about the previous year. His was the first family-owned winery in this region. Hinzerling was producing estate-grown varietals before most local vineyards bore fruit. The winery building, a cinder block box, used to be a truck garage.

🐚 🐚 🐚

The Hogue Cellars

Route 2, Box 2898
Prosser, Washington 99350
TEL: 509-786-4557
OWNER: Michael Hogue (M.S. in agricultural economics from Cornell University)
WINEMAKER: Rob Griffin (B.S. with honors in enology from UC-Davis)
FOUNDED: 1983

AT A GLANCE
Tours & Tastings: Open daily 10–5. Complimentary tours and tastings.

Closed: Easter, Thanksgiving, Christmas, New Year's Day.

Vineyards: 250 acres planted to White Riesling, Chenin Blanc, Chardonnay, Sauvignon Blanc, Cabernet Sauvignon, Merlot. Additional grapes are purchased from Washington State growers.

Wines: Fumé Blanc, Sémillon, Chardonnay, Chenin Blanc, Johannisberg Riesling, White Riesling, Cabernet Sauvignon, Merlot, sparkling wine.

Awards: 1983 Cabernet Sauvignon: Best of Show, gold; 1984 Fumé Blanc: Highest Honors, gold, two silvers, three bronzes; 1984 White Riesling (Markin Vineyard): Best of Category, gold, two silvers, two bronzes.

Picnic Area: Tables on the lawn.

Retail Shop: Wines and pickled asparagus sold on-site.

Credit Cards: MasterCard, Visa.

Access for Disabled: All doors, hallways, and rest rooms wheelchair accessible.

Getting There: Winery is in Benton County, 200 miles east of Seattle. From I-82: Take exit 82 onto Meade Ave. and drive east to Lee Rd.

Special Wine & Other Events: Hogue Cellars sponsors cooking classes and exhibits by local artists, as well as barrel tastings and a gala anniversary open house.

&. After writing his master's thesis in viticulture, Michael Hogue added a few vineyards to a family farm already renowned for its spearmint, Concord grapes, and hops. His first vintage was all of 5,000 gallons. Now production exceeds 100,000 gallons, and the only way Hogue can survey his numerous ranches is from the controls of a twin-engine plane. Quantity has not been achieved at the expense of quality; in competitions across the country, both reds and whites have struck gold.

&. &. &.

Horizon's Edge Winery

Route 2, Box 2396
Zillah, Washington 98953
TEL: 509-829-6401
OWNER/WINEMAKER: Thomas Campbell (graduate work in viticulture and enology at UC-Davis)
FOUNDED: 1985

AT A GLANCE

Tours & Tastings: Open daily Apr. 1–Dec. 24 11–5. Tours given upon request.

Closed: Dec. 25–March 31.

Vineyards: Eighteen acres planted to Chardonnay, Pinot Noir, Muscat Canelli. Additional grapes are bought from Yakima Valley and Columbia Valley growers.

Wines: Chardonnay, Johannisberg Riesling, Pinot Noir, Cabernet Sauvignon.

Awards: 1984 Chardonnay: gold, silver.

Picnic Area: Yes.

Retail Shop: Wines sold on-site.

Credit Cards: MasterCard, Visa.

Access for the Disabled: None.

Getting There: Winery is 2½ miles east of Zillah. From I-82: Take exit 54 north to East Zillah Dr.

&. Thomas Campbell's résumé reads like a *Who's Who* of northwestern wineries: before founding Horizon's Edge, he worked at Chateau Ste. Michelle, Covey Run, Stewart Vineyards, and other Washington establishments. He is best known for Chardonnays.

&. &. &.

Pontin Del Roza Winery

Route 1, Box 1129
Prosser, Washington 99350
TEL: 509-786-4449; 786-1797
OWNERS: Nesto and Scott Pontin
FOUNDED: 1984

AT A GLANCE

Tours & Tastings: Open daily 10–5.

Vineyards: Fifteen acres planted to White

Riesling. Other grapes purchased from local growers.

Wines: White Riesling, Chenin Blanc, Chardonnay.

Picnic Area: Yes.

Retail Shop: Wines sold on-site.

Credit Cards: MasterCard, Visa.

Access for Disabled: None.

Getting There: Winery is 3½ miles outside Prosser. From I-82: Take exit 80 to Gap Rd. Bear right on Kingtull Rd. and left on Hinzerling Rd.

ఈ "In Italian, our winery's name means 'Pontin family farm on the Roza'—a Yakima Valley site my parents began farming more than thirty years ago," explains Scott Pontin. "This winery has been a family dream since my grandfather came here. In 1975 we traveled to Italy to visit relatives and to see their well-established, high-trellised vineyards. Now we invite you to visit 'the Roza.' "

ఈ ఈ ఈ

Staton Hills Vineyard and Winery

2290 Gangl Road
Wapato, Washington 98951
TEL: 509-877-2112

Also visit:

Staton Hills Winery–Seattle
1910 Post Alley
Seattle, Washington 98101
Tel: 206-443-8084

OWNERS: David and Susanne Staton
WINEMAKER: Rob Stuart (B.S. in enology from UC-Davis)
FOUNDED: 1984

AT A GLANCE

Tours & Tastings: Open Tues.–Sun. 11–5. Tours given by appointment. Elegant tasting room with two-story stone fireplace, cathedral ceiling, oak floors, and Oriental carpets lend an old-world elegance to the New World. (Seattle winery is open Mon.–Sat. 11–6, Sun. [Jun.–Aug.] 11–6. Self-guided tours at this site.)

Closed: Mon.

Vineyards: 20 owned and 450 leased acres planted to vinifera varieties. Apple, cherry, peach, and apricot orchards are also on-site.

Wines: Cabernet Sauvignon, Merlot, Chardonnay, Sémillon, Chenin Blanc, Gewürztraminer, Riesling, port, champagne.

Awards: All wines from the 1984 crush won regional or international medals.

Picnic Area: Terraced lawns, picnic tables, and barbecue pit—at Wapato winery only.

Retail Shop: Wines and gourmet foods sold on-site at both locations.

Credit Cards: MasterCard, Visa.

Access for Disabled: Yes.

Foreign Languages: Spanish.

Getting There: Winery is four miles southeast of Yakima. From I-82: Take exit 40; pass Plath Rd. and Thorp Rd., turn onto Gangl Rd. (The Seattle winery is in Pike Place Market.)

Special Wine & Other Events: Annual spring barrel tasting.

ఈ Although David and Susanne Straton wanted to establish a vineyard, they hedged their bets by becoming commercial fruit growers first. Only then did they plant a vinifera test block near their orchards. Fortunately, the grapes thrived, so the Statons cultivated a larger site and built a lovely country-style winery overlooking Yakima Valley and Mount Adams. Their Seattle branch was founded two years later.

ఈ ఈ ఈ

Stewart Vineyards

Cherry Hill Road
Granger, Washington 98932
TEL: 509-854-1882
OWNER: George D. Stewart

WINEMAKER: Michael Januik (M.S. in enology from UC-Davis)
FOUNDED: 1983

AT A GLANCE
Tours & Tastings: Open Mon.–Sat. 10–5, Sun. 12–5. Informal tours, as requested by guests, include a walk through the winery followed by a tasting session in the upstairs cedar tasting room decorated in traditional Stewart plaid.
Closed: Major holidays.
Vineyards: Fifty acres planted to Cabernet Sauvignon, Chardonnay, White Riesling, Muscat Canelli, Gewürztraminer. Apples and cherries are also grown on-site.
Wines: Cabernet Sauvignon, Chardonnay, Johannisberg Riesling, Select Late Harvest White Riesling, Muscat Canelli, Gewürztraminer, Cherry Hill Blush (blended table wine).
Awards: 1984 Muscat Canelli: two golds, two silvers, three bronzes; 1984 Late Harvest White Riesling: two golds, three silvers, three bronzes; 1984 Chardonnay: two golds, silver, bronze; 1985 Johannisberg Riesling: two golds, silver.
Picnic Area: Tables under cherry trees.
Retail Shop: Wines sold on-site.
Credit Cards: None.
Access for Disabled: Ramp into tasting room.
Getting There: Winery is thirty miles south of Yakima. From I-82: Take exit 58. Head south on Hwy. 223 and turn onto Outlook Rd., a semicircular street leading into Cherry Hill Rd.

&. The Stewart family grows grapes in both Yakima Valley and the Columbia Valley, two distinctly different viticultural areas. To intensify the floral qualities of each varietal, the fruit is deliberately harvested a little earlier than that of some other wineries. All Stewart wines are estate-bottled.

&. &. &.

Tucker Cellars

Highway 12 at Ray Road
Sunnyside, Washington 98944
TEL: 509-837-8701
OWNER: Dean Tucker
FOUNDED: 1981

AT A GLANCE
Tours & Tastings: Open May–Oct. daily 9–6, Nov.–Apr. 9–5. Usually one wine tasting per week.
Closed: Major holidays.
Vineyards: Sixty-five acres planted primarily to white vinifera varieties. Fruits and vegetables are also grown on the farm.
Wines: Chardonnay, Pinot Noir, Cabernet Sauvignon, Riesling, Chenin Blanc, Muscat Canelli, Gewürztraminer.
Awards: Gewürztraminer: two silvers, two bronzes; Johannisberg Riesling: three bronzes; Muscat Canelli: silver, two bronzes; Cabernet Sauvignon: silver.
Picnic Area: Tables in a small vineyard.
Retail Shop: Wines sold on-site. Adjacent produce market sells fresh fruits and vegetables, popcorn, fruit-blossom honey, pickled asparagus, and cider in season.
Credit Cards: MasterCard, Visa.
Access for Disabled: None.
Getting There: Winery is thirty-two miles south of Yakima. From I-82: Take either exit 69 or exit 73 to Hwy. 12.
Special Wine & Other Events: Tucker Open House and Anniversary, June 2.

&. There's very little that isn't grown on this family farm, which has been around for half a century. A small vinifera plot dates to 1933. But most of the vineyards were planted in the late 1970s, after the local sugar beet refinery closed, leaving farmers—Dean Tucker among them—with a suddenly valueless crop. Leery of raising something he could not sell, Tucker decided to have his grapes and crush them, too. Not one to be tied to tradition, he stocks the tasting room with Tucker White Cloud Popcorn.

🐚 🐚 🐚

Yakima River Winery

Route 1, Box 1657
Prosser, Washington 99350
TEL: 509-786-2805
OWNER: John W. Rauner
FOUNDED: 1978

AT A GLANCE

Tours & Tastings: Open daily 10–5. Tours by appointment or chance, include the winery. All but Ice Wines are tasted.
Vineyards: Most grapes are purchased from Yakima Valley growers, a small amount from Columbia Valley growers.
Wines: Fumé Blanc, Chardonnay, Pinot Noir, Cabernet, Merlot, Chenin, Johannisberg Riesling, White Pinot, White Cabernet, Late Harvest White Riesling, Select Cluster White Riesling, Dry Berry White Riesling, Ice Wine.
Awards: Fumé Blanc: silver; Merlot: platinum; Cabernet Sauvignon: silver; and many more.
Picnic Area: Yes.
Retail Shop: Wines sold on-site.
Credit Cards: MasterCard, Visa.
Access for Disabled: None.
Getting There: Prosser is 40 miles east of Yakima. Traveling east on I-82, take exit 80. Turn left on Sixth St. and travel 1½ miles, then turn right on River Rd. and follow winery signs.
Special Wine & Other Events: Barrel tasting and seminar, last weekend in Apr.; Open House, July 4th weekend; a taste of current vintages, Thanksgiving weekend. The Annual Pow Wow Rodeo/Pioneer Fair, at the Toppenish Fairgrounds on the July 4th weekend, offers a wine tasting as well as more traditional fair amusements. The second Saturday in August, local vintages can also be tasted at the Prosser Wine and Food Fair, which also includes a race, the Vinifera Run.

🐚 John Rauner did not really care about wine until he sampled some bottles from a now-defunct Yakima Valley vintner. A few years later, he and his wife left New York to make their home—and their wines—in Washington. Production ranges from dry whites and reds to rich, sweet Ice Wines.

TO SEE & DO

By far the most pleasant and easiest way to see Yakima's sights is aboard the restored vintage tram that shows you both the city and countryside. Board at 4th and Pine (Apr.–Labor Day; Tel: 509-575-1700). Then, make a shopping stop at Yesterday's Village (15 West Yakima Avenue, Yakima, Washington 98902; tel: 509-457-4981), an old-fashioned farmers' market where antiques and crafts are sold alongside fresh produce and baked goods. Go further back into the past with a visit to the Yakima Indian National Cultural Center (P.O. Box 151, Toppenish, Washington 98948; tel: 509-865-2800). The seven-acre complex comprises a museum, a theater, a library, and an authentic winter lodge.

ACCOMMODATIONS

(See also listings in the Tri-Cities Area section.)

The Tudor Guest House
3111 Tieton Drive
Yakima, Washington 98902
Tel: 509-452-8112
Tudor-style mansion, built in 1929 and restored to mint condition with leaded glass windows, marble and tile accents. Continental breakfast.

Holiday Inn Motor Hotel
9th St. & Yakima Avenue
Yakima, Washington 98901
Tel: 509-452-6511; 800-HOLIDAY
One hundred sixty-six rooms, heated pool, hot tub. Restaurant.

Red Lion
1507 North First Street
Yakima, Washington 98901
Tel: 509-248-7850; 800-547-8010
Downtown location with two swimming pools, restaurant.

Whistlin' Jack Lodge
18936 Highway 410
Naches, Washington 98937
Tel: 509-658-2433
A peaceful setting on scenic Chinook Pass.

RESTAURANTS
Birchfield Manor Gourmet Restaurant
Yakima, Washington 98901
Tel: 509-452-1960
An elegant restaurant with good food and wine list. Open only Fri.–Sun.; reservations required.

Cafe Renaissance
Route 1, Wilson Highway, Box 1940
Grandview, Washington 98930
Tel: 509-882-4480

Intimate family-owned restaurant with well-prepared innovative dishes.

Gasperetti's Restaurant
1013 North First Street
Yakima, Washington 98901
Tel: 509-248-0628
Cheerful local hangout with first-rate Italian food.

Greystone Restaurant/The Wine Cellar
5 North Front Street
Yakima, Washington 98901
Tel: 509-248-9801
The menu changes constantly but the quality remains excellent. Continental cuisine with a local accent. Also home to an outstanding wine and cheese shop.

Tillicum Restaurant
Highway 12
Sunnyside, Washington 98944
Tel: 509-837-7222
A prime rib and steak house serving only Yakima Valley wines.

&. HAWAII

Hawaii is perhaps where you least expect to find a vineyard, but is certainly one of the most dramatic places to visit. In the 1800s, a Spanish horticulturalist, don Francisco de Paula Marin, got a land grant from King Kamehameha I to produce wines for the royal family from his Oahu vineyard— thus, you find Vineyard Street in Honolulu today. In the 1900s, a commercial winery was snuffed out by Prohibition, and the Depression put an end to an attempt by the Portuguese to make wine from rootstocks they brought to upcountry Makwao. Today Tedeschi Vineyard, on the southern side of Haleakala, the massive hunk of volcanic mountain dominating east Maui, produces the only island-grown wine and champagne.

Visitors who take this wine route leading 2,000 feet up the mountainside, find wine is just one of the rewards. They also savor one of the most spectacular views in America—all the way down the crumpled slope to the white-gold beaches rimming the blue Pacific below. Visitors range from a handful in summer to busloads in winter months, when the majority of tourists flock to the islands.

ఆ ఆ ఆ

Tedeschi Vineyard

Intersection of Highways 377 and 37
P.O. Box 953
Ulupalakua, Maui, Hawaii 96790
TEL: 808-878-6058
PRESIDENT/WINEMAKER: Emil Tedeschi
FOUNDED: 1977

AT A GLANCE

Tours & Tastings: Mon.–Sun. 9–5; self-guided tours, tastings conducted by Tedeschi himself.
Closed: Major holidays.
Vineyards: Twenty acres at 2,000 feet planted to Carnelian, a Californian hybrid cross between viniferas Cabernet Sauvignon, Grenache, and Carignane varieties.
Wines: *Methode champenoise* Blanc de Noirs champagne; blush and nouveau wines; dry pineapple wine.
Awards: Erdman-Tedeschi Blanc de Noirs champagne: oft-awarded at international wine competitions. Served at President Reagan's 1985 inaugural banquet.
Retail Shop: Wines, wine accessories, Maui products.
Credit Cards: American Express, MasterCard, Visa.
Access for Disabled: None.
Foreign Languages: None.
Getting There: From Kahului: Take Hwy. 37 to Ulupalakua. Tour buses go to winery in season.
Special Wine & Other Events: Tedeschi Vineyard 10-K Run.

ఆ Does a cattle ranch on a dormant volcano sound like a strange place to produce *methode champenoise* champagne? Then how about prizewinning champagne that made it all the way to President Reagan's 1985 inaugural banquet?

Champagne was not initially consid-ered by partners Emil Pardee Erdman, owner of the 20,000-acre Ulupalakua Ranch, and Emil Tedeschi, third-generation winemaker from Napa Valley. The former Californians planted their twenty-acre vineyard to Carnelian—after testing 140 grape varieties—to produce a dry red table wine. They switched to sparkling wine on the advice of Dimitri Tchelistcheff, who, like his father, Andre, is a noted wine consultant. Thus came the champagne that was not only elected to the president's table, but has won consistent critical acclaim even in California tastings since its first release in 1983.

The winery's well-known Maui Blanc, a delicate, dry pineapple wine, was to be phased out once the champagne took off. It is still around, however, and so popular they make it in ever-larger amounts. The Tedeschi winery now produces 2,000 cases of Blanc de Noir champagne and 10,000 of Maui Blanc.

The Ulupalakua Ranch dates back to 1845, with New England–style buildings and the ruins of an old sugar mill. The tasting room is housed in the former jail.

TO SEE & DO

The daring will enjoy Cruiser Bob's Haleakala Downhill (505 Front St., Lahaina; tel. 808-667-7777), an all-day biking adventure coasting down the slopes of the dormant volcanic mountain; all gear and lunch provided. There is also a two-day crater hike or trailride with camping (tel: 808-244-4354). Or fly over the crater with Alexair (tel: 808-871-0792). Must-see sights are Kula Botanical Gardens and Protea Gardens.

ACCOMMODATIONS

Bed & Breakfast "Maui Style"
P.O. Box 886
Kihei, Maui, Hawaii 96753
Tel: 808-879-7865
Recommendations for Maui from old plantation to modern-style.

Kilohana
212 Kawehi Place
Kula, Maui, Hawaii 96790
Tel: 808-879-6086
Updated plantation-style home, with sweeping view of Lanai and Molokai islands. A delicious full breakfast includes fresh fruits and juices, yogurt, homemade pastry, sausage, and tea or coffee.

Viticultural Areas

American Viticultural Areas
(July 1, 1988)

Approved   *Effective Date*

Augusta, MO	07-20-80
Napa Valley, CA	03-31-81
Santa Maria Valley, CA	09-04-81
San Pasqual Valley, CA	09-16-81
Fennville, MI	10-10-81
Guenoc Valley, CA	12-21-81
Sonoma Valley, CA	01-04-82
Santa Cruz Mountains, CA	01-04-82
McDowell Valley, CA	01-04-82
Leelanau Peninsula, MI	04-29-82
Lancaster Valley, PA	06-11-82
Edna Valley, CA	06-11-82
Lime Kiln Valley, CA	07-06-82
Hudson River Region, NY	07-06-82
Chalone, CA	07-14-82
Paicines, CA	09-15-82
Cienega Valley, CA	09-20-82
Isle St. George, OH	09-20-82
Finger Lakes, NY	10-01-82
Livermore Valley, CA	10-01-82
Suisun Valley, CA	12-27-82
Loramie Creek, OH	12-27-82
Carmel Valley, CA	01-13-83
Shenandoah Valley, CA	01-27-83
Shenandoah Valley, VA & WV	01-27-83
Solano County Green Valley, CA	01-28-83
Rocky Knob, VA	02-11-83

Yakima Valley, WA 05-04-83
Cole Ranch, CA 05-16-83
North Fork of Roanoke, VA 05-16-83
Arroyo Seco, CA....................................... 05-16-83
Santa Ynez Valley, CA................................. 05-16-83
Merritt Island, CA 06-16-83
Dry Creek Valley, CA.................................. 09-06-83
Willow Creek, CA...................................... 09-19-83
Los Carneros, CA...................................... 09-19-83
Linganore, MD 09-19-83
Anderson Valley, CA 09-19-83
Hermann, MO 09-19-83
York Mountain, CA 09-23-83
Ohio River Valley, OH, IN, KY, WV 10-07-83
North Coast, CA....................................... 10-21-83
Fiddletown, CA.. 11-03-83
Paso Robles, CA....................................... 11-03-83
Catoctin, MD.. 11-14-83
El Dorado, CA... 11-14-83
Lake Michigan Shore, MI 11-14-83
Potter Valley, CA..................................... 11-14-83
Grand River Valley, OH................................ 11-21-83
Lake Erie, NY, PA, OH................................. 11-21-83
Knights Valley, CA 11-21-83
Chalk Hill, CA.. 11-21-83
Russian River Valley, CA.............................. 11-21-83
Sonoma County Green Valley, CA........................ 12-21-83
Willamette Valley, OR................................. 01-03-84
Howell Mountain, CA 01-30-84
Monticello, VA.. 02-22-84
Walla Walla Valley, WA & OR........................... 02-22-84
Clarksburg, CA 03-07-84
Pacheco Pass, CA 04-11-84
Central Delaware Valley, NJ & PA...................... 04-18-84
Southeastern New England, CT, MA, RI 04-27-84
Umpqua Valley, OR 04-30-84
Clear Lake, CA 06-07-84
Altus, AR 06-29-84
Mendocino, CA 07-16-84
Monterey, CA.. 07-16-84
Mississippi Delta, LA, MS, TN 10-01-84
Temecula, CA 11-23-84
Alexander Valley, CA.................................. 11-23-84
Sonoita, AZ 11-26-84
Columbia Valley, OR & WA 12-13-84

Madera, CA	01-07-85
Martha's Vineyard, MA	02-04-85
Sonoma Mountain, CA	02-22-85
Mesilla Valley, NM & TX	03-18-85
The Hamptons, Long Island, NY.......................	06-17-85
Northern Sonoma, CA.................................	06-17-85
Cumberland Valley, MD & PA	08-26-85
North Yuba, CA	08-30-85
Central Coast, CA....................................	11-25-85
Mimbres Valley, NM..................................	12-23-85
South Coast, CA	12-23-85
Lodi, CA	03-17-86
Kanawha River Valley, WV............................	05-08-86
Ozark Mountain, AR, MO, OK	07-01-86
Arkansas Mountain, AR	10-27-86
Bell Mountain, TX	11-10-86
North Fork of Long Island, NY	11-10-86
San Lucas, CA	03-02-87
Northern Neck/George Washington Birthplace, VA	05-21-87
Old Mission Peninsula, MI	07-08-87
Sonoma Coast, CA	07-13-87
Ozark Highlands, MO	09-30-87
San Benito, CA	11-04-87
Sierra Foothills, CA	12-18-87
Ben Lomond Mountain, CA	01-08-88
Middle Rio Grande Valley, NM	03-03-88
Western Connecticut Highlands, CT....................	03-10-88
Cayuga Lake, NY	04-25-88
Stags Leap District, CA...............................	01-27-89

Petitions in Process For

Arroyo Grande Valley, CA
Eastern Shore of Virginia, VA
Fredericksburg in the Texas Hill Country, TX
Mt. Veeder–Napa Valley, CA
Nooksack Valley, WA
Oakley, CA
Santa Clara Valley, CA
Warren Hills, NJ
Wild Horse Valley, CA

Source: BATF.

Winery Information

&**T**he following are informational resources for wineries. Where inquiries must be written, no telephone numbers are listed.

Most wine-producing states have wine trade associations, but not all of them offer materials helpful to the traveler (they assist the trade only). This is why not all states in this book are listed. In some wine-growing areas in California, chambers of commerce and convention and visitors' bureaus also give out wine information. Where this is the case, addresses are listed below.

Primarily, however, convention and visitors bureaus, local chambers of commerce, and other regional groups can help with tourism information concerning where to stay and eat, and what to see and do, greatly expanding on those sections in this book. Many of these resources have been listed throughout the book where they apply and are not repeated here.

On the pages following this list, state tourism resources are given. They may be contacted for tourism information, including wineries. However, winery information may not always be automatically included in state packets. Nor, oddly enough, are state maps. Be sure to request both when ordering from the agencies.

ARIZONA

Arizona Wine Growers Association
P.O. Box 43301
Tucson, Arizona 85733

CALIFORNIA

El Dorado Winery Association
P.O. Box 1614
Placerville, California 95667
Tel: 916-622-8094

Gilroy Visitors and Convention
  Bureau
7780 Monterey Street
Gilroy, California 95020
Tel: 408-842-6437

Lake County Grape Growers
  Association
65 Soda Bay Road
Lakeport, California 95453
Tel: 707-263-0911

Livermore Valley Winegrowers
  Association
P.O. Box 2052
Livermore, California 94550

Lodi Chamber of Commerce
215 West Oak Street
Lodi, California 95240
Tel: 209-334-4773

Mendocino County Vintners
  Association
P.O. Box 1409
Ukiah, California 95482
Tel: 707-463-1704

Monterey Wine Country Associates
P.O. Box 1793
Monterey, California 93942-1793
Tel: 408-375-9400

Napa Valley Vintners Association
P.O. Box 141
St. Helena, California 95474
Tel: 707-963-0148

The Wineries of Paso Robles
P.O. Box 457
Paso Robles, California 93447
Tel: 805-238-0506

Russian River Wine Road
P.O. Box 127
Geyersville, California 95411
Tel: 707-433-6935

Santa Barbara County Vintners
  Association
P.O. Box WINE
Santa Ynez, California 93460

Santa Clara Winegrowers Association
1480 East Main Street
Morgan Hill, California 95070

Santa Cruz Mountain Vintners
  Association
P.O. Box 2856
Saratoga, California 95070

Santa Ynez Valley Viticultural
  Association
P.O. Box 61
Santa Ynez, California 93460

Sierra Foothills Winery Association
P.O. Box 425
Somerset, California 95684

Sonoma County Winegrowers
  Association
Luther Burbank Center for the Arts
50 Mark West Springs Road
Santa Rosa, California 95401
Tel: 707-527-7701

Sonoma Valley Vintners Association
P.O. Box 238
Sonoma, California 95476

South Coast Vintners Association
P.O. Box 1601
Temecula, CA 92390

Temecula Valley Chamber of
  Commerce
P.O. Box 264
27521 Ynez Road
Temecula, California 92390
Tel: 714-676-5090

INDIANA

Indiana Winegrowers Guild
411 Massachusetts Avenue
Indianapolis, Indiana 46204
Tel: 317-771-4122

MARYLAND

Association of Maryland Wineries
818 Silver Run Valley
Westminster, Maryland 21157

MISSOURI

Missouri Department of Agriculture
Grape and Wine Program
P.O. Box 630
Jefferson City, Missouri 65102
Tel: 314-751-3374; 800-392-WINE (in-
  state)

NEW MEXICO

New Mexico Wine & Vine Society
P.O. Box 27651
Albuquerque, New Mexico 87125

NEW YORK

New York Wine & Grape Foundation
350 Elm Street
Penn Yan, New York 14527
Tel: 315-536-7442

OHIO

Ohio Wine Producers Association
822 North Tate Road
Austinburg, Ohio 44010
Tel: 216-466-4417

OREGON

Oregon Wine Advisory Board
1324 Southwest 21st Avenue
Portland, Oregon 97201
Tel: 503-224-8167

Yamhill County Wineries Association
P.O. Box 871
McMinnville, Oregon 97128
Tel: 503-434-5814

PENNSYLVANIA

Pennsylvania Wine Association
R.D. 3
Stewartstown, Pennsylvania 17363
Tel: 717-993-2431

TEXAS

Texas Department of Agriculture
Marketing Division
P.O. Box 12847
Austin, Texas 78711
Tel: 512-463-7624

VERMONT

New England Wine Council
P.O. Box 11, River Road
Jacksonville, Vermont 05342

VIRGINIA

Wine Marketing Program
Virginia Wine Advisory Board
P.O. Box 1163
Richmond, Virginia 23209
Tel: 804-786-0481

WASHINGTON

Wine Marketing Program
Washington State Department of
    Agriculture
406 General Administration Building
Olympia, Washington 98504
Tel: 206-753-1604

Washington Wine Institute
1932 First Avenue, Room 510
Seattle, Washington 98101
Tel: 206-441-1892

Yakima Chamber of Commerce
P.O. Box 1490
Yakima, Washington 98907
Tel: 509-248-2021

Yakima Valley Winegrowers
    Association
P.O. Box 39
Grandview, Washington 98930

*For both Oregon and Washington, try
also:*

Enological Society of the Pacific
    Northwest
5806 16th Avenue Northwest
Seattle, Washington 98105
Tel: 206-523-4372

State Tourist Offices

&a.*L*isted here are addresses and telephone numbers for the tourist offices of all the United States. When you write or call one of these offices, be sure to request a map of the state and a calendar of events. If you will be visiting a particular city or region, or if you have any special interests, be sure to specify this as well.

Alabama Bureau of Tourism and
  Travel
532 South Perry Street
Montgomery, Alabama 36104
Tel: 205-261-4169; 800-252-2262 (out-
  of-state); 800-392-8096 (in-state)

Alaska Division of Tourism
P.O. Box E
Juneau, Alaska 99811
Tel: 907-465-2010

Arizona Office of Tourism
1100 West Washington Street
Phoenix, Arizona 85077
Tel: 602-255-3618

Arkansas Department of Parks and
  Tourism
1 Capitol Mall
Little Rock, Arkansas 72201
Tel: 501-371-7777; 800-643-8383 (out-
  of-state); 800-482-8999 (in-state)

California Office of Tourism
1121 L Street, Suite 600
Sacramento, California 95814
Tel: 916-322-1396, 322-1397;
  800-862-2543

Colorado Department of Tourism
1625 Broadway, Suite 1700
Denver, Colorado 80202
Tel: 303-592-5410; 800-255-5550

Connecticut Department of Economic
  Development/Vacations
210 Washington Street
Hartford, Connecticut 06106
Tel: 203-566-3948; 800-243-1685 (out-
  of-state); 800-842-7492 (in-state)

Delaware Tourism Office
99 Kings Highway
P.O. Box 140
Dover, Delaware 19903
Tel: 302-736-4271; 800-441-8846 (out-
  of-state); 800-282-8667 (in-state)

Washington, D.C., Convention and
  Visitors' Assoc.
Suite 250
1575 I Street, N.W.
Washington, D.C. 20005
Tel: 202-789-7000

Florida Division of Tourism
Fletcher Building
101 East Gaines Street

Mailing address:
126 Van Buren Street
Tallahassee, Florida 32399-2000
Tel: 904-487-1462

Georgia Tourist Division
Box 1776
Atlanta, Georgia 30301
Tel: 404-656-3590; 800-847-4842

Hawaii Visitors Bureau
Waikiki Business Plaza, Suite 801
2270 Kalakaua Avenue
Honolulu, Hawaii 96815
Tel: 808-923-1811
or: New York Office
441 Lexington Avenue, Room 1407
New York, New York 10017
Tel: 212-986-9203

Idaho Department of Commerce
Capitol Building, Room 108
Boise, Idaho 83720
Tel: 208-334-2470; 800-635-7820

Illinois Office of Tourism
310 South Michigan Avenue, Suite 108
Chicago, Illinois 60604
Tel: 312-793-2094; 800-545-7300 (out-of-state); 800-359-9299 (in-state)

Indiana Tourism Development
 Division
1 North Capitol, Suite 700
Indianapolis, Indiana 46225-2288
Tel: 317-232-8860; 800-2-WANDER

Iowa Tourism Office
200 East Grand Avenue
Des Moines, Iowa 50309-2882
Tel: 515-281-3679; 800-345-4692

Kansas Department of Economic
 Development
Travel and Tourism Division
400 West 8th Street, Suite 500
Topeka, Kansas 66603
Tel: 913-296-2009; 800-252-6727 (in-state)

Kentucky Department of Travel
 Development
Capitol Plaza Tower, 22nd Floor
Frankfort, Kentucky 40601
Tel: 502-564-4930; 800-225-8747 (out-of-state)

Louisiana Office of Tourism
P.O. Box 94291
Baton Rouge, Louisiana 70804-9291
Tel: 504-342-8119; 800-334-8626 (out-of-state)

Maine Publicity Bureau
P.O. Box 23000
97 Winthrop Street
Hallowell, Maine 04347
Tel: 207-289-2423; 800-533-9595

Maryland Office of Tourist
 Development
217 East Redwood Avenue
Baltimore, Maryland 21202
Tel: 301-974-3517; 800-331-1750

Massachusetts Division of Tourism
Department of Commerce and
 Development
100 Cambridge Street, 13th Floor
Boston, Massachusetts 02202
Tel: 617-727-3201; 800-533-6277 (out-of-state)

Michigan Travel Bureau
Department of Commerce
P.O. Box 30226
Lansing, Michigan 48909
Tel: 517-373-1195; 800-543-2-YES

Minnesota Tourist Information Center
375 Jackson Street
Farm Credit Service Building
St. Paul, Minnesota 55101
Tel: 612-296-5029; 800-328-1461 (out-of-state); 800-652-9747 (in-state)

Mississippi Division of Tourism
P.O. Box 22825
Jackson, Mississippi 39205
Tel: 601-359-3414; 800-647-2290

Missouri Division of Tourism
P.O. Box 1055
Jefferson City, Missouri 65102
Tel: 314-751-4133

Montana Promotion Division
1424 9th Avenue
Helena, Montana 59620
Tel: 406-444-2654; 800-541-1447

Nebraska Division of Travel and
Tourism
P.O. Box 94666
Lincoln, Nebraska 68509
Tel: 402-471-3796; 800-228-4307 (out-of-state); 800-742-7595 (in-state)

Nevada Commission on Tourism
Capitol Complex
600 East Williams Street, Suite 207
Carson City, Nevada 89710
Tel: 702-885-4322; 800-237-0774

New Hampshire Office of Vacation
Travel
P.O. Box 856
Concord, New Hampshire 03301
Tel: 603-271-2343, 271-2666;
800-258-3608 (in the Northeast
outside of New Hampshire)

New Jersey Division of Travel and
Tourism
C.N. 826
Trenton, New Jersey 08625
Tel: 609-292-2470; 800-537-7397

New Mexico Travel Division
Joseph Montoya Building
1100 Saint Francis Drive
Santa Fe, New Mexico 87503
Tel: 505-827-0291; 800-545-2040 (out-of-state)

New York State Division of Tourism
1 Commerce Plaza
Albany, New York 12245
Tel: 518-474-4116; 800-225-5697 (in the
Northeast except Maine)

North Carolina Travel and Tourism
Division
430 North Salisbury Street
Raleigh, North Carolina 27611
Tel: 919-733-4171; 800-VISIT-NC
(out-of-state)

North Dakota Tourism Promotion
Liberty Memorial Building
State Capitol Grounds
Bismarck, North Dakota 58505
Tel: 701-224-2525; 800-437-2077 (out-of-state); 800-472-2100 (in-state)

Ohio Office of Tourism
P.O. Box 1001
Columbus, Ohio 43266-0101
Tel: 614-466-8844; 800-BUCKEYE
(out-of-state)

Oklahoma Division of Tourism
500 Will Rogers Building
Oklahoma City, Oklahoma 73105
Tel: 405-521-2409; 800-652-6552 (in
neighboring states); 800-522-8565
(in-state)

Oregon Economic Development
Tourism Division
595 Cottage Street, N.E.
Salem, Oregon 97310
Tel: 503-378-3451; 800-547-7842 (out-of-state); 800-233-3306 (in-state)

Pennsylvania Bureau of Travel
Development
Department of Commerce
439 Forum Building
Harrisburg, Pennsylvania 17120
Tel: 717-787-5453; 800-847-4872

Rhode Island Department of
Economic Development
Tourism and Promotion Division
7 Jackson Walkway
Providence, Rhode Island 02903
Tel: 401-277-2601; 800-556-2484 (East
Coast from Maine to Virginia; also
West Virginia and Ohio)

South Carolina Division of Tourism
1205 Pendleton Street
Columbia, South Carolina 29201
Tel: 803-734-0122

South Dakota Division of Tourism
Capitol Lake Plaza
711 Wells Avenue
Pierre, South Dakota 57501
Tel: 605-773-3301; 800-952-2217 (out-
of-state); 800-843-1930 (in-state)

Tennessee Tourist Development
P.O. Box 23170
Nashville, Tennessee 37202
Tel: 615-741-2158

Texas Tourist Development
P.O. Box 12008
Capitol Station
Austin, Texas 78711
Tel: 512-426-9191; 800-888-8839

Utah Travel Council
Council Hall
Capitol Hill
Salt Lake City, Utah 84114
Tel: 801-538-1030

Vermont Travel Division
134 State Street
Montpelier, Vermont 05602
Tel: 802-828-3236

Virginia Division of Tourism
202 North 9th Street
Suite 500
Richmond, Virginia 23219
Tel: 804-786-4484; 800-847-4882

Washington Department of Trade and
  Economic Development
Tourism Division
101 General Administration Building
Olympia, Washington 98504
Tel: 206-586-2088; 800-544-1800 (out-
  of-state)

Travel West Virginia
West Virginia Department of
  Commerce
State Capitol
Charleston, West Viriginia 25305
Tel: 304-348-2286; 800-CALL-WVA

Wisconsin Division of Tourism
P.O. Box 7970
123 West Washington
Madison, Wisconsin 53707
Tel: 608-266-2161; 800-372-2737
  (within Wisconsin and neighboring
  states); 800-432-8747 (out-of-state)

Wyoming Travel Commission
I-25 and College Drive
Cheyenne, Wyoming 82002
Tel: 307-777-7777; 800-225-5996 (out-
  of-state)

Bibliography

Wine Books

Adams, Leon D. *The Wines of America.* 3d ed. New York: McGraw Hill, 1985.

Henriques, Frank E. *The Signet Encyclopedia of Wine.* Rev. ed. New York: New American Library, 1984.

Kaufman, William I. *Encyclopedia of American Wine.* Boston: Tarcher/Houghton Mifflin, 1984.

Lichine, Alexis. *Alexis Lichine's New Encyclopedia of Wines & Spirits.* 3d ed. New York: Alfred A. Knopf, 1984.

Travel & Lodging Guides (published annually)

Mobil Travel Guides: Northeastern, Northwest and Great Plains States, Great Lakes Area, California & the West, Middle Atlantic, Southeastern, Southwest and South-Central areas. Englewood Cliffs, N.J.: Prentice-Hall.

Rundback, Betty, and Kramer, Nancy. *Bed & Breakfast U.S.A.* New York: E. P. Dutton.

Soule, Sandra W. *America's Wonderful Little Hotels and Inns.* East and West eds. New York: St. Martin's Press.

Index